300 Big & Bold
Barbecue
& Grilling
recipes

Karen Adler and Judith Fertig

Robert
ROSE

For complete cataloguing information, see page 407.

Disclaimer
The recipes in this book have been carefully tested by our kitchen and our tasters. To the best of our knowledge, they are safe and nutritious for ordinary use and users. For those people with food or other allergies, or who have special food requirements or health issues, please read the suggested contents of each recipe carefully and determine whether or not they may create a problem for you. All recipes are used at the risk of the consumer.

We cannot be responsible for any hazards, loss or damage that may occur as a result of any recipe use.

For those with special needs, allergies, requirements or health problems, in the event of any doubt, please contact your medical adviser prior to the use of any recipe.

Design and Production: Daniella Zanchetta/PageWave Graphics Inc.
Editor: Sue Sumeraj
Recipe Editor: Jennifer MacKenzie
Proofreader: Sheila Wawanash
Indexer: Gillian Watts
Photography: Colin Erricson
Food Styling: Kathryn Robertson
Prop Styling: Charlene Erricson

Cover image: Szechuan Tea-Smoked Duck Breasts (see recipe, page 294)

We acknowledge the financial support of the Government of Canada through the Book Publishing Industry Development Program (BPIDP) for our publishing activities.

Published by Robert Rose Inc.
120 Eglinton Avenue East, Suite 800, Toronto, Ontario, Canada M4P 1E2
Tel: (416) 322-6552 Fax: (416) 322-6936

Printed and bound in Canada

1 2 3 4 5 6 7 8 9 TCP 17 16 15 14 13 12 11 10 09

Contents

A World of Flavor 4

Part 1: Mastering the Art of the Barbecue

Signature Grilling 6

Championship Smoking 13

Utensils for Grilling and Smoking 19

Specialty Equipment and Techniques 20

Where Big, Bold Flavor Begins 27

Part 2: Big & Bold Recipes

Rubs and Sauces 30

Fish 71

Shellfish 107

Poultry 137

Pork 177

Beef 217

Lamb 261

Specialty Meats 285

Vegetables 311

Fruit 351

Soups, Salads, Breads and Sandwiches 373

Glossary 401

Index 408

A World of Flavor

FROM THE TIME our ancestors discovered the power of fire, cooking over an open flame has made us appreciate the taste that sizzle and smoke add to any food. Over time, many regions have developed their own unique barbecue methods:

- leaf-wrapping and pit barbecue in tropical climates;
- grilling skewered foods in the Middle and Far East;
- planking on the east and west coasts of North America;
- smoking over hardwood in North America, Europe and Africa;
- grilling over herbs in the Mediterranean;
- grilling on a spit in tribal cultures worldwide.

Since the 1950s, when the development of charcoal briquettes made grilling easier, cooking outdoors has made a cultural comeback all over the world. Today, outdoor rooms are designed around the latest in infrared, stainless steel, high-BTU barbecue equipment. At the same time, the simple charcoal kettle grill has never gone out of style, or out of use.

Whatever type of outdoor barbecue equipment you have, you can produce memorable dishes full of bold flavor from barbecue traditions all over the world.

PART 1

Mastering the Art of the Barbecue

LIKE A GOOD DETECTIVE gathering clues to a crime, the savvy barbecuer works backwards. You start with the "what" of the finished dish, then discover the how, when and where. For example, if you want your rib eye steak to have a charry exterior and a rare interior, that means a good rub on your steak, a hot fire with your steak in close proximity to it and a short cooking time. If you want your steak to have grill marks and a smoky flavor, that means some time over direct heat to get the grill marks, but also some time over indirect heat with lots of hardwood smoke and the grill lid closed, a technique we call "a kiss of smoke." If you want your lamb steak to have the aroma and vivid flavor of fresh rosemary, that means a rosemary rub, an herb grilling technique or a rosemary compound butter to finish — or possibly all three.

Let's get started on our barbecue "how did you do it?" with basic grilling and smoking techniques, then special variations on each.

Signature Grilling

GRILLING IS GENERALLY hot and fast, accomplished over direct heat (350°F to 700°F/180°C to 370°C). Boneless meats, fish fillets and vegetables are all delicious cooked this way. But there are also special ways to grill bone-in meats, whole fish, game, cheese and fruit, involving an indirect fire, a kiss of smoke, leaf-wrapping, planking and other techniques.

Your grill can be your artist's canvas to bring vivid flavors to the fore. And that involves decisions. What type of equipment? How hot a fire? How far away to place the food from the heat? Close the grill lid or keep it open? Smolder wood, herbs, corncobs or leaves for extra flavor? Use an Australian stone or a cast-iron griddle? Grill and baste foods on a spit?

We'll take you through basic grilling to the most common variations and innovations so you can develop your own signature style.

✦ Lighting the Fire ✦

Charcoal Grills

Charcoal fires can be started in any of several safe, ecologically sound ways. We like using hardwood charcoal because it is natural and gives a better wood flavor, but we also use charcoal briquettes or a combination of hardwood charcoal and briquettes. If you like, mix them together, as many of our barbecue competition buddies do. Hardwood charcoal is available at some grocery stores and at hardware, barbecue and home improvement stores. Briquettes are more readily available at grocery stores, convenience shops and hardware and home improvement stores.

A charcoal chimney, an electric fire starter or lighter fluid can be used to light a charcoal fire. The charcoal chimney is an upright cylindrical metal canister, like a large metal coffee can with a handle. Fill the top of the chimney with hardwood lump charcoal and/or briquettes. Place the chimney on a nonflammable surface, such as concrete or the grill rack. Tip the chimney slightly and stuff one or two sheets of crumpled newspaper in the convex bottom. Light the paper with a match. After 5 minutes, check to make sure the fire is still going. If not, stuff with paper and light again. The coals should be red hot and starting to ash over in 15 to 20 minutes. Carefully dump the coals onto the bottom of the grill grate and add more charcoal if needed. You will also use the charcoal chimney to add coals if you're grilling something over a low fire for a longer time.

To use an electric fire starter, place it on the bottom grill grate. Mound the charcoal on top and plug it in. The coals will take about 15 minutes to ignite. Carefully remove the starter and set it in a safe place to cool.

Lighter fluid, a petroleum product, can impart an unpleasant flavor if improperly used. Used correctly, it will not impart any flavor to your food. Douse the charcoal with lighter fluid according to the manufacturer's directions and light with a match. Don't start to grill until the coals have burned down to an ashen coating over glowing embers. That way, any petroleum residue will have burned off.

Gas Grills

Follow your manufacturer's directions for starting your gas grill. This will include attaching the propane tank to the grill, turning on the propane valve, then lighting the burners of the grill. About 40,000 combined BTUs (British thermal units, which measure the maximum heat output of a burner) are optimum. Many grills have thermometers attached to the grill lid, so close the lid and let it heat up to the desired temperature. If you use natural gas as your fuel, there will be a lever or valve that you open before you turn your gas grill burners on. Always have the lid of your grill open before you turn the gas on and ignite your burners.

✦ *Getting Ready to Grill* ✦

The grill should be clean and the grill rack(s) lightly oiled with vegetable oil or Grate Chef Grill Wipes (premoistened towelettes for the grill). Have all of your equipment handy.

The Hand Method for Judging a Grill's Temperature

If your grill does not have a thermometer, hold your hand 5 inches (12.5 cm) above the heat source. If you can only hold it there for about 2 seconds, your fire is hot (500°F/260°C or more) and perfect for grilling; 3 seconds is a medium-hot fire (about 400°F/200°C) for grilling; 4 seconds is a medium fire (about 350°F/180°C) for grilling or higher-heat indirect cooking; and 5 to 6 seconds is a low fire (225°F to 250°F/110°C to 120°C), the ideal temperature for slow smoking.

Adjusting Your Grill's Temperature

On a charcoal grill, you can lower the temperature by slightly closing the side vents or by closing the lid. Don't close the vents and the lid at the same time, or the fire will go out. You can raise the temperature by opening the side vents or by adding more charcoal to the fire.

On a gas grill, you adjust the heat by turning the heat control knobs to the desired level. It's pretty simple!

When ready to grill, place the food over the hot fire. Grill food on one side for half the cooking time, allowing for good searing and grill marks. Turn once and finish cooking.

✦ *Cooking on Charcoal Grills* ✦

Direct Fire

After you have started the fire, wait until the charcoal is red hot and beginning to ash over before putting on the oiled grill grate. Place food on the grill grate, directly over the hot coals. Leave the grill lid open or closed, depending on the recipe. If you need to add more coals, ignite them in the charcoal chimney first. Lift the grill grate and spread the new hot coals on top of the existing ones.

Variations

- *Herb grilling:* Place branches of fresh, woody herbs such as rosemary, thyme, bay or lavender directly on the hot coals. Place the food on the grill grate and close the lid to grill so you capture the aroma in the food. Alternatively, instead of placing branches on the coals, you can place them on the grill grate, then put your food on top of the branches. The herbs will smolder and sizzle, imparting flavor to your food, but your food will not have grill marks. Herb grilling is best with chicken, lamb, fish and shellfish.

- *Kiss of smoke:* Wood chips can be added to a fire for direct grilling, too. Toss a handful of water-soaked wood chips onto a hot charcoal fire. When the chips begin to smoke, it's time to grill. The grilling time will be short, so just a kiss of smoke will penetrate the food, but the lovely aroma in the air is worth it.

- *Hearth grilling:* Use a Tuscan grill — an elevated grill rack inside your fireplace. Make sure you use only hardwood (not pine or processed fire "logs") for this type of grilling, as resins from wood other than hardwoods will not burn as well and will impart off-flavors to your food. Prepare your charcoal or wood fire directly under the grill rack. This simple, high-heat method works best with steaks and chops.

- *Australian hot stone or Italian piastra grilling:* Choose a large, nonporous stone such as granite, marble or terra cotta, or a ceramic pizza stone. (Porous stones such as shale can retain water, which may explode when heated to a high temperature.) Place the stone or stone griddle over direct heat to get very, very hot — so hot that a drop of water sizzles and evaporates almost immediately. Then grill directly on the stone, oiling the food rather than the stone. You will get scorch marks instead of grill marks, but the heat distribution is very even. This technique works well with lamb, fish, steaks and shellfish (with the grill lid down).

- *Grill pan or griddle grilling:* Use a heavy metal or cast-iron skillet, grill pan or griddle over direct heat. As with hot stone grilling, the metal or cast iron needs to get very, very hot, so that it has a grayish cast. Again, you oil the food, not the pan. This method works well with lamb, fish, steaks and shellfish (with the grill lid down).

Indirect Fire

Prepare a direct fire first. Once your hot coals are on the fire grate, push them to the side of the grill. One side of the grill will have hot coals — that is the direct-heat cooking side. The other side is the indirect-heat cooking side. Carefully place a disposable aluminum pan filled with water on the indirect side, next to the hot coals on the bottom of the grill or smoker. (Smoking and indirect grilling are slower, so you need the extra moisture from the water in the water pan.)

Variations

- *Indirect herb grilling:* Place fresh herb branches on top of the coals. Replace the grill grate. To cook this way, you must close the grill lid.

- *Kiss of smoke:* For wood smoke flavoring, place water-soaked wood chunks or chips or dry wood pellets in a foil packet and poke holes in the foil. Place the packet on top of the coals and replace the grill grate. To cook this way, you must close the grill lid.

- **Grill-roasting:** Indirect grilling at 350°F (180°C) or higher. Crank up the heat, place your food on the indirect side, close the lid and use your grill like an oven, only with more flavor!

✦ *Cooking on Gas Grills* ✦

Direct Fire

Turn the burners on and close the lid to preheat the grill for 10 to 15 minutes. Place the food on the grill grate, directly over the hot burners. To cook this way, you can leave the grill lid either up or down. If your grill has less than 40,000 BTUs, closing the lid allows the heat to build up, making a hotter fire.

Variations

- **Herb grilling:** Because you don't want debris from smoldering material to clog the gas jets, you need to put herb branches in a foil packet with holes punched in it or in a metal smoker box. Place the packet or box on the grill grate in a hot spot so the herbs will smolder safely. Close the lid to grill so you capture the aroma in the food. Herb grilling is best with chicken, lamb, fish and shellfish.

- **Kiss of smoke:** Wood chips can be added for direct grilling, too. Place dry wood chips in a foil packet poked with holes or in a metal smoker box and set over the flames, preferably toward the back of the grill. When the chips begin to smoke, it's time to grill. The grilling time will be short, so just a kiss of smoke will penetrate the food, but the lovely aroma in the air is worth it.

- **Infrared grilling:** This gas grill technology adds extra cooking power through infrared rays, so your food cooks even faster. You simply turn on the infrared and carefully watch your food, grilling with the lid up.

- **Australian hot stone or Italian piastra grilling:** Place a large stone or stone griddle over direct heat to get very, very hot — so hot that a drop of water sizzles and evaporates almost immediately. Then grill directly on the stone, oiling the food rather than the stone. You will get scorch marks instead of grill marks, but the heat distribution is very even. This technique works well with lamb, fish, steaks and shellfish (with the grill lid down).

- **Grill pan or griddle grilling:** Use a heavy metal or cast-iron skillet, grill pan or griddle over direct heat. As with hot stone grilling, the metal or cast iron needs to get very, very hot, so that it has a grayish cast. Again, you oil the food, not the pan. This method works well with lamb, fish, steaks and shellfish (with the grill lid down).

Indirect Fire

Light the burners on one half of the grill only. The side without lit burners is the indirect-heat side. Place a disposable aluminum pan filled with water over direct heat. To cook this way, you must close the grill lid.

Variations

- **Indirect herb grilling:** Because you don't want debris from smoldering material to clog the gas jets, you need to put herb branches in a foil packet with holes punched in it or in a metal smoker box. Place the packet or box on the grill grate in a hot spot so the herbs will smolder safely. Close the lid to grill so you capture the aroma in the food. Herb grilling is best with chicken, lamb, fish and shellfish.

- **Kiss of smoke:** Because you don't want debris from smoldering material to clog the gas jets, you need to put dry wood chips or pellets in a foil packet poked with holes or in a metal smoker box. Place the packet or box on the grill grate in a hot spot so the wood will smolder safely. To cook this way, you must close the grill lid.

- **Grill-roasting:** Indirect grilling at 350°F (180°C) or higher. Crank up the heat, place your food on the indirect side, close the lid and use your grill like an oven, only with more flavor!

✦ *Grilling Times* ✦

Estimated grilling times are just that: estimates, not hard and fast "set your watch by it" times. In every recipe, we give you an estimate of how long something will take to grill. We also guide you with a recommended internal temperature and/or a description of the look of a food when it is done. When you cook outdoors, the weather is always a factor. On hot days, food grills faster; on cold days, food grills more slowly.

Don't worry that your food won't get done on the grill. You can always fix that by returning it to the grill, zapping it in the microwave or putting it in the oven. What you can't fix is overcooked food.

✦ Doneness Chart for Grilling ✦

Because foods continue to cook for a few minutes after they're taken off the grill, we recommend pulling them off the heat at the temperatures listed below, such as 150°F (65°C) for pork loin. If you pull a pork loin off at that point, it will go up to 155°F (68°C) on its own. If you leave it on the grill or smoker to reach 155°F (68°C), the meat will end up well done, dry and less appetizing. This applies to larger pieces of meat, such as roasts or whole birds, especially if they are tented with foil, so allow for this extra rise in temperature when you cook. Smaller pieces, such as chicken breasts or pork chops, won't retain as much heat (the cause of carry-over cooking) so they should be cooked to the desired doneness.

Because burgers are made with ground meat, they need to be cooked to well done.

Food	Doneness Indicator
Burgers (beef, pork, veal, lamb)	160°F (71°C) for well done
Burgers (turkey, chicken)	165°F (74°C) for well done
Burgers (fish)	155°F (68°C)
Beef steak or roast	120°F (50°C) for rare, 130°F (54°C) for medium-rare, 140°F (60°C) for medium, 150°F (65°C) for medium-well, 165°F (74°C) for well done
Chicken and turkey	165°F (74°C) for medium-well, 175°F (80°C) for well done
Fish fillets or steaks	Beginning to flake when tested with a fork in thickest part
Shellfish	Opaque and somewhat firm to the touch
Lamb chops or roast	120°F (50°C) for rare, 130°F (54°C) for medium-rare, 140°F (60°C) for medium, 150°F (65°C) for medium-well, 165°F (74°C) for well done
Pork loin, rib chops, or roast	150°F (65°C) for medium, 165°F (74°C) for well done
Pork tenderloin	130°F (54°C) for rare, 145°F to 150°F (63°C to 65°C) for medium, 160°F (71°C) for well done
Veal chops or roast	130°F (54°C) for medium-rare, 140°F (60°C) for medium, 150°F (65°C) for medium-well, 165°F (74°C) for well done
Vegetables	Done to your liking

If you're a grill novice, use an instant-read thermometer to test the doneness of most grilled foods. To get the best reading, insert the thermometer into the thickest part of the meat, making sure you're not touching bone, stuffing or gristle, and read the temperature.

Thin meats, such as chicken paillards, aren't thick enough for a thermometer to give an accurate reading, so the best way to tell whether the food is done is to cut into the thickest part with the tip of a sharp knife and look at the color of the meat. For example, chicken breasts are done when they are no longer pink inside; chicken thighs are done when the juices run clear when the thighs are pricked with a fork.

After some experience, you'll be able to tell the doneness of grilled foods by touch alone. When you hold a pork tenderloin with tongs and it's charred on the outside but still soft and wiggly, that's rare. If the tenderloin offers some resistance, it's medium. When it feels solid, it's well done.

Championship Smoking

MOST GRILLS CAN be set up to function as smokers. However, smokers are usually set up just to smoke, not to grill.

When you slow-smoke food, the temperature is lower (225°F to 250°F/110°C to 120°C) than when grilling (350°F to 700°F/180°C to 370°C). You use hardwoods to smolder and release smoke, so the food is cooked with the lid down. Because the temperature is lower, the cooking process takes longer, so smoking is especially good for tougher cuts of meat that need a long time to tenderize. You'll need to be available to check your smoker every 30 minutes, so relax and enjoy the smoking experience.

Because of the time commitment involved, it's a good idea to slow-smoke more food than you need for one occasion. Barbecue lots of ribs, pork butt, brisket, whole chickens or whatever, then freeze the extra for later use.

✦ Higher-Temperature Smoking ✦

Certain types of equipment — Kamado- or ceramic-style egg-shaped grills like the Big Green Egg — are very efficient users of charcoal. A little goes a long way. In a Big Green Egg, food smokes at a higher temperature (around 350°F/180°C). You can still prepare the recipes in this book, but realize that your food will get done faster.

✦ Cold Smoking ✦

Cold smoking means smoking foods at temperatures below 225°F (110°C). Foods to be cold-smoked are usually cured first with a mixture of salts, spices and sugars to draw moisture out of the meat, as is done with bacon and ham. Because the smoldering wood must be far away from the food, you need specialized equipment for this process. Great Lakes fishermen use reconfigured refrigerators. Others use restaurant-style equipment, such as the Smokin Tex.

✦ Preparing an Indirect Fire for Smoking ✦

Charcoal Grills

Use hardwood charcoal and/or briquettes to start a fire. When the coals have ashed over, use a long grill spatula to push them over to one side of the grill. Place a metal or disposable aluminum pan of water on the bottom of the grill next to the coals (or use a spray bottle of liquid to add moisture to the food periodically while smoking). Place the grill rack over the top of the grill. If your grill has adjustable heights, set the rack about 5 inches (12.5 cm) from the heat. The side with the coals is direct heat; the side with the pan of water is indirect heat.

Gas Grills

Gas grills are not the equipment of choice to smoke anything for longer than 3 hours or so, although you can slow-smoke for that time on the gas grill, then finish the dish in the oven. On a gas grill, you will not get the depth of smoke flavor you can on a charcoal grill or smoker, but they're great for a "kiss of smoke" flavor.

To prepare an indirect fire on a gas grill, you need the type of grill that has at least two separate burners. Turn one burner on and leave the other off. The side with the burner on is direct heat; the side with the burner off is indirect heat. If your grill has more than two burners, you can have the indirect portion of the grill in the middle, with the burners on either side turned to the desired temperature. You can place a water pan in the back of the grill on the direct side (or use a spray bottle of liquid to add moisture to the food periodically while smoking).

Bullet Smokers

A bullet smoker is a space-saving vertical unit that has the heat source on the bottom, a water pan in the middle and one or two racks above for the food. Gas and electric bullet smokers may have only one temperature, or will have a temperature gauge for you to set to the low heat desired (225°F to 250°F/110°C to 120°C). Turn on the gas or plug in the electrical cord, and you're ready to cook. It's like an outdoor slow cooker (Crock-Pot). In an electric unit, the water-soaked chunks of wood are added around the coils. In a gas bullet smoker, the wood needs to be wrapped in foil so that the jets don't get clogged. Most manufacturers recommend using three chunks of wood for the smoking process. Be careful if you choose to add more — you may over-smoke the food.

A charcoal bullet smoker takes more effort, because the fire needs to be tended in order to maintain a steady temperature. Use a charcoal chimney to start the coals and add them to the smoker. Wait until the coals die down and the temperature of the smoker gets to the desired temperature (225°F to 250°F/110°C to 120°C). Every hour or so, add two to three unlit coals to the fire to keep the temperature steady. If the temperature takes a dive due to the outside weather (rain or wind), start several coals in the chimney again to maintain your fire.

Bullet smokers are small, compact and easy to move. If you are smoking on a day with lots of wind or low temperatures, move the smoker out of the wind or under an overhang, being careful to stay a safe distance from any wood structures. (Never grill or smoke in the garage, even if the door is open.)

✦ *How to Add Wood for Wood-Smoke Flavor* ✦

When you're slow-smoking at a low temperature, the flavor comes from smoldering aromatic woods — such as hickory, cherry, oak, mesquite or pecan — which are placed on or near the fire. Depending on the type of smoking equipment you have, there are several types of wood you can use and ways to use them.

- *Fine wood chips:* A little bigger than sawdust, these are used in the stovetop smoker indoors. You use them dry and in small amounts — 1 to 2 tablespoons (15 to 25 mL) — placed in the middle of the bottom of the stovetop smoker. When you place the stovetop smoker over a heat source, these fine chips smolder and burn, giving off aromatic smoke.

- ***Wood chips:*** These can be used dry or moistened. Try them both ways to see how they work best on your grill or in your smoker. They should smolder, not burn up. Use about 1 cup (250 mL) at a time, and replenish every 45 minutes for 2 to 3 hours of wood-smoking. Make a foil packet to enclose the chips (poke holes in the packet) or place in a metal smoker box, and place either on the grill rack over the heat or below on the lava rock (in a gas grill) or around the electric coil (in an electric smoker). Experiment to find what gives the best results for your equipment.

- ***Wood pellets:*** These are pellet-shaped bits of compressed sawdust. The wood-pellet grill uses these for both fuel and wood-smoke flavor. The pellets can also be used with other grills and with smokers. Wood pellets must be used dry; if you moisten them, they turn into mushy sawdust. For smoking, use ⅓ cup (75 mL) at a time. Make a foil packet to enclose the dry pellets (poke holes in the packet) or place in a metal smoker box. Place directly on the coals in a charcoal grill, on the grill rack over the heat in a gas grill or around the electric coil in an electric bullet smoker. Wood pellets must be replenished about once an hour.

- ***Wood chunks:*** Bigger pieces of aromatic wood, chunks are 2 to 3 inches (5 to 7.5 cm) long and wide. Soak them for at least 30 minutes before using them. Wood chunks are most often placed directly on hot coals or around but not touching the electric coil on an electric bullet smoker. We don't recommend using wood chunks with a gas grill; they're not as effective as wood pellets or chips and can clog the gas jets as they smolder and disintegrate.

    On a charcoal fire, begin with two to three water-soaked wood chunks and replenish with two to three more after about 30 minutes. Three wood chunks will last for about 2 hours in an electric smoker and may be all the wood flavor you need.

- ***Wood "sticks" or "logs":*** Even bigger pieces of wood, these are cut to fit the diameter of the firebox on a competition-style rig or a large charcoal grill, and are placed right on the hot coals. You generally use three sticks to start with and replenish as necessary.

✦ A World of Hardwood Flavors for Smoking ✦

Whether you use logs, sticks, chunks, pellets or chips, hardwoods can infuse food with great smoke flavor. Traditional barbecue uses locally available hardwoods, from post oak in southern Texas to sugar maple in Ontario, but you can find all kinds of unique woods, from mulberry to sassafras and black walnut.

Here's a list of the most common hardwoods available for smoking. Mix and match for your own custom smoke blend. If you don't buy them at a grilling store, make sure you buy untreated, food-safe wood.

- **Alder** gives a light, aromatic flavor that's perfect with seafood. Used to smoke fish in Scandinavia, Germany and the Pacific Northwest.

- **Apple** provides a sweeter, aromatic flavor that is good with poultry or pork. Used to smoke and grill in Europe and North America.

- **Cherry** lends a deeper, sweeter note to smoked foods, and is delicious with beef tenderloin, pork, poultry or lamb.

- **Chestnut** gives a medium flavor to foods. Used in France, Italy and Spain.

- **Hickory** gives a stronger, hearty smoke flavor to beef, pork or poultry.

- **Mesquite** provides the strongest, smokiest flavor and is well suited to beef, especially brisket. It's also good with poultry and pork.

- **Oak** provides a medium smoke flavor without being bitter, and pairs well with any food. A favorite in Italy, Spain, Texas and California.

- **Olive wood**, a Mediterranean favorite, lends a medium smoke flavor.

- **Pecan** creates a medium smoke flavor, less pronounced than hickory but more so than oak. Pecan is great to use for grilling with a kiss of smoke.

✦ *Getting Ready to Smoke* ✦

The grill or smoker should be clean and the rack(s) lightly oiled with vegetable oil or premoistened grill towelettes. Have all of your equipment handy. Place the wood of your choice on or near the heat source on your smoker. Have the water pan in place or a spray bottle of liquid (usually water or apple juice) nearby to add moisture to the food. Smoke with the lid closed as much as possible. This will trap the heat, allowing it to circulate. With the lid down, the smoke will be more concentrated and will permeate the food better.

Judging a Smoker's Temperature

Ideally, smoking is done at a temperature (measured on the indirect side) of 225°F to 250°F (110°C to 120°C). If possible, use grill thermometers to monitor the temperature on both sides of the grill. If you don't have grill thermometers, hold your hand 5 inches (12.5 cm) above the indirect side of the grill, or over the rack on a smoker. If you can hold it there for 5 to 6 seconds, then you have a low fire (225°F to 250°F/110°C to 120°C).

Adjusting Your Smoker's Temperature

On a charcoal grill, lower the temperature by slightly closing the side vents. Raise the temperature by opening the side vents or by adding more wood or ashed-over charcoal. Keep the grill lid closed while smoking, for a steady temperature and more smoke.

On a gas grill, adjust the temperature by turning the control knobs to the desired level. For smoking, adjust the heat control on one burner while leaving the other burner off.

On a charcoal bullet smoker, lower the temperature by letting the charcoal die down. Raise the temperature by replenishing the charcoal.

On an electric bullet smoker, the temperature may be a set low heat; if not, there will be a temperature knob you can turn to adjust the heat.

✦ *How to Smoke* ✦

When the smoker is at the proper temperature for your recipe, place the food in a disposable aluminum pan or directly on the grate of the smoker, on the indirect side. Let it cook for 45 to 60 minutes before checking it. The more you open the smoker, the more the temperature will drop and the longer your food will take to get done.

Check periodically — about once every 30 minutes — to make sure the temperature is holding, your water pan has enough liquid and you have enough fuel and wood.

✦ *Smoking Times* ✦

Estimating smoking times is a challenge, because the time required to cook a food varies depending on the heat of the fire, the temperature outdoors and whether the day is windy, sunny, overcast or rainy. The better you can control the heat and the temperature of your smoker, the better barbecue you'll produce. With smoking, it is less crucial to be exact than with grilling, as smoking is a gentler cooking process that takes longer. But smoking food too long with too much smoke will give it a bitter, acrid flavor. We recommend smoking with wood for only the first 2 to 3 hours of the cooking process.

Refer to the suggested cooking times we provide in each recipe, but also watch your food while it's smoking and use an internal meat thermometer or an instant-read thermometer to gauge its doneness. We always recommend allowing extra time — an hour or two, perhaps — as a cushion when smoking any kind of food.

Utensils for Grilling and Smoking

THE RIGHT TOOL can make all the difference when you're grilling and smoking. You can find these tools in kitchen shops, hardware stores or barbecue and grill stores. Because they'll be used outdoors and in contact with heat and smoke, choose utensils that are heavy, of superior quality and very durable. Long handles are preferable on everything, to keep you at a safe distance from the fire. Remember to oil your utensils, grill racks and gadgets on both sides to prevent sticking and make cleanup easier.

✦ The Barbecuer's Toolbox ✦

- A **stiff wire brush** with a scraper makes cleaning the grill a simple job (tackle this while the grill is still warm).

- Two **natural-bristle basting brushes**, one for applying oil to the grill grates and the other for basting food during grilling or smoking, will make these tasks a breeze.

- **Perforated grill racks** are grates placed on top of the grill to accommodate small or delicate items, such as chicken wings, fish fillets, scallops, shrimp and vegetables. Oil them before use.

- **Hinged grill baskets** hold foods in place and make turning an easy process.

- **Heat-resistant oven or grill mitts** offer the best protection for your hands.

- Long-handled **spring-loaded tongs** are easier to use than the scissors type. They are great for turning most food and skewers.

- A **spray bottle** filled with water will douse any flare-ups.

- **Charcoal chimneys or electric fire starters** are terrific for starting charcoal fires.

- A **long-handled offset fish spatula** with a 5- to 6-inch (12.5 to 15 cm) blade makes turning fish fillets easy.

- Two **long-handled spatulas** are also welcome utensils, especially when you're turning a large fish fillet. Position the spatulas at each end of the fillet and roll quickly to turn.

- **Disposable aluminum pans** hold liquid during the smoking process. You can also use the pans as tents to cover thick steaks that need a bit more cooking time on the indirect side of the grill.

- **Instant-read thermometers** give a quick temperature read when you're cooking meat and poultry.

- **Metal smoker boxes** are useful for holding wood chips or pellets. Their perforations allow smoke to escape but keep chips from falling out.

Specialty Equipment and Techniques

WHEN YOU'VE GOT basic grilling and smoking techniques down pat, try venturing into new territory. With the right equipment and grill gadgets, you can skewer, leaf-wrap, stir-grill, plank, rotisserie cook and even use a stovetop smoker to smoke foods.

✦ *Skewers* ✦

The first choice is the basic skewer itself, and you've got lots of options here. The old standby is the inexpensive wooden (bamboo) skewer, which comes in packages at the grocery store. These skewers need to be soaked in cold water for at least 30 minutes before they are threaded with food and grilled. After grilling, just throw the charred skewers away.

Reusable metal skewers (some with prongs on both ends) or the new metal coil skewers can be easily cleaned with soapy water after grilling, then towel-dried so they don't get water spots.

Natural skewers, such as fresh rosemary or lavender branches, bamboo, lemongrass or sugarcane, are all safe for food to touch. You can even use campfire sticks from the yard; however, before branching out into unknown territory, check to make sure the branch you want to use is food-safe. Avoid pine and other resinous woods, as they will give an off-flavor to your food.

We've found that the best way to make sure all food gets done at the same time is to avoid those '50s-style kabobs with meat or chicken and vegetables all on one stick. Put the meat pieces on their own skewers and the vegetables on their own skewers. Leave about a ⅛-inch (0.25 cm) space between each piece of food on a skewer. If the food is squashed together, the place where the pieces touch will not cook as quickly. You don't want chicken sushi on a stick.

To make sure your food doesn't twirl around on the skewers while you're grilling it — so annoying! — you can either use flat metal or bamboo skewers rather than the rounded kind, or run two skewers parallel through the food to keep it more stable.

Kabob baskets are another option. They are great time-savers, as you simply place the cubed food in the basket rather than threading the chunks onto skewers. Spray or brush the baskets with oil before grilling so that the food doesn't stick.

✦ Leaf-Wrapping ✦

Wrapping foods in fresh or frozen and thawed leaves before grilling or smoking is an ancient way of cooking. Although you don't get grill marks, you do get moist, delicious food infused with the gentle, herb-like flavor unique to each type of leaf. The leaves char slightly and make a beautiful, rustic presentation. Make sure you select organic or unsprayed leaves.

✦ Grill Woks or Baskets ✦

To stir-grill, you need a metal grill wok or basket with perforations, which allows for more of the wood and charcoal fire aromas to penetrate the food. Grill woks and baskets can be square, oval or round. They are usually about 12 inches (30 cm) across and can accommodate enough food to feed four. If you are cooking for eight and need to double the recipe, it's better to cook in two batches

✦ Turn Over A New Leaf ✦

Leaf	Use	Flavor
Avocado	Under cabrito or lamb on grill	Anise
Banana	To enclose fish or pork	Artichoke
Basil	To wrap shellfish or veggies	Aromatic basil
Corn husk	To enclose fish or shellfish	Sweet, newly mown hay
Chard	To wrap around foods	Black olive
Wild lime	To wrap shellfish or add to a skewer	Citrus, lime
Grape	To wrap around foods	Black olive
Mint	To wrap shellfish or add to a skewer	Mint
Pandanus	To wrap around foods	Sweet, smoky
Shiso	To wrap shellfish or add to a skewer	Mint
Taro	To enclose fish or pork	Artichoke

or in two woks at the same time (if they fit on your grill together). Although they are harder to find, we prefer a 15-inch (38 cm) grill wok because it has a larger surface area exposed to the fire and can hold food for up to six people without crowding.

The technique is easy: Marinate the food in a sealable plastic bag in the refrigerator. Prepare a hot fire in the grill. Spray both sides of the grill wok with nonstick cooking spray. Then place the prepared wok over the sink and dump the marinated food into the wok. The excess marinade will drain away. Place the wok on a double layer of two baking sheets and take it outside to the grill. Place the wok over direct heat and, using metal grill spatulas or long-handled wooden paddles or spoons, stir-grill the food until done. Place the wok on the clean (bottom) baking sheet to carry it back to the kitchen.

✦ *Planks* ✦

Plank-cooking is easy, too. You can buy untreated hardwood planks at a lumberyard or barbecue shop. The most common plank sizes are 16 by 8 by $\frac{3}{8}$ inch (40 by 20 by 0.75 cm), 12 by 10 by 1 inch (30 by 25 by 2.5 cm) and 15 by 6½ by $\frac{3}{8}$ inch (38 by 16 by 0.75 cm). Use whatever size best fits in your grill. We also use those 2- to 3-inch (5 to 7.5 cm) thick reinforced cedar planks (made for oven use, but also great on the grill), available at kitchen or barbecue and grill shops. Food cooks in about the same time on thin and thick planks, but thicker planks last longer. Planks can be reused until they're either too charred or too brittle to hold food.

Although planking on cedar is the universal favorite because that wood gives the most aromatic flavor, any regional hardwood — such as alder, hickory, maple, oak or pecan — will produce great-tasting planked food too.

To use the plank, submerge it in water for at least an hour. Either a deep sink or a large rectangular plastic container that you can fill with water will work. Use a couple of large cans to weigh down the plank so that it stays under the surface. A water-soaked plank produces maximum smoke flavor and is more resistant to charring on the grill.

Prepare an indirect fire or a dual-heat fire (high or medium-high on one side, low on the other) in a grill. You can make a dual-heat fire in a gas grill with two burners, or in a charcoal grill by massing two-thirds of the hot coals on one side and one-third of the hot coals on the other side.

Food touching the wood takes on more flavor, so don't crowd the food on the plank. Use two planks, if necessary. Place the plank on the indirect, or low-heat, side. Then close the grill lid and cook according to the time specified in the recipe. Stay close by, though, in case of flare-ups. Keep a spray bottle filled with water handy, just in case.

For a rustic restaurant–style effect, serve the food right on the plank, as if it was a platter. After you've cooked and served on the plank, clean it with a little hot, soapy water and a good rinse. Eighty-grit sandpaper may also be used to help clean the plank. Rinse it well after sanding.

✦ Hardwoods for Planking ✦

Before you buy a hardwood plank, gently sniff the wood. If there is no fragrance, there won't be any flavor imparted to your food. The most fragrant and thus flavorful plank is cedar. It's also the most commonly available.

- **Alder** gives a light, aromatic flavor and is great paired with fish.

- **Cedar** is the most aromatic of the woods, lending a deep but gentle woodsy flavor to foods of all kinds.

- **Hickory** lends a stronger, hearty wood flavor to beef, pork or poultry.

- **Maple** smolders to a sweet, milder flavor that pairs well with poultry, vegetables or fish.

- **Oak** gives a medium woodsy aroma without being bitter. It works well with any food.

✦ *Rotisserie* ✦

To spit-roast, or rotisserie-cook, first set up your rotisserie on the grill. Every gas grill has a different way to set up a rotisserie, so this is just an overview. Please refer to your manufacturer's directions for the best way to set up the rotisserie on your grill. The drip pan should contain 2 to 3 inches (5 to 7.5 cm) of liquid — marinade, vinegar, juice, beer, wine or just plain water — whatever you would like for aroma. The liquid will steam up into the food, adding moisture and a wonderful aroma as the food turns and cooks. Replenish with additional liquid as necessary.

Run through your setup first. Do not skewer the food and place it on a lit grill until you are certain that everything is set properly. With the grill off or unlit, measure the food over the drip pan. The pan will prevent flare-ups, so make sure the meat, poultry or fish is not larger than the drip pan you are planning to use. If it is, use either a larger pan or an additional drip pan. For easy cleanup, we prefer disposable aluminum pans.

Trim the meat, poultry or fish, then season it. Slide one of the pronged attachments, or spit forks, onto the rotisserie rod. Position the attachment and clamp to tighten. Slide the rod through the center of the meat, fish or fowl. Slide the second prong attachment so that the tines are touching the food. Holding a prong attachment in each hand, press both attachments into the food so that the food is held firmly in place. Secure and tighten the clamps for the pronged attachments. Use pliers to tighten the thumbscrews on the spit forks to prevent loosening during the rotisserie process.

If you're using the rotisserie basket (which is great for fish or other delicate foods), spray it with nonstick cooking spray, place the food inside the basket and close it firmly.

It's very important to balance the meat on the spit so it can turn easily. If the meat is not balanced, it could shorten the life of your rotisserie. To balance the rod, hold it so each end lies across the palms of your hands; the heavy side of the food will rotate down. Position the food on the rod so that there is no heavy side.

Tie any loose bits to the body of the meat with water-soaked kitchen string to prevent singeing. Insert a meat thermometer in the thickest part of the meat, away from the bone. Make sure the thermometer is positioned so that you can read it, and also so that it will turn freely as the meat turns.

Place the spit on the rotisserie. Start the rotisserie, letting it rotate until you're sure the meat turns easily. Place the drip pan under the food and add 2 to 3 inches (5 to 7.5 cm) of liquid to the pan. (This helps keep the food moist and prevents the drippings from burning.)

Check to make sure the grill's lid will close while the rotisserie is on. Depending on the temperature of your grill, you may want to prop the grill lid open a bit with bricks or metal cans so that it doesn't get too hot.

Heat the grill to medium-high. Close the lid and cook. After 30 minutes, check with a grill thermometer (or using the hand method) to make sure you have achieved a temperature of close to 350°F (180°C). Continue to check the food, the temperature and the drip pan at least once an hour. You may need to add liquid to the drip pan during cooking.

Sometimes the thumbscrews can loosen, or the meat may shrink and the forks may need to be adjusted, so keep a clean pair of pliers handy just in case. When the food is done, lift the rotisserie off the grill. Place it on a baking sheet, then remove the rod and retrieve your food.

✦ *Stovetop Smoker* ✦

Made of stainless steel, the stovetop smoker is designed to trap and smolder tiny wood particles so that the resulting smoke permeates the food but doesn't make your kitchen smoke alarm go crazy. Because you're smoking indoors, you want to choose foods that will cook quickly, such as fish fillets, shrimp, a log of goat cheese, tomatoes or boneless chicken breasts. You can also use foil to cover a spiral-sliced ham (it's too large for the top of the smoker to slide over and close) to double-smoke it in the stovetop smoker. Karen has experimented with beef brisket, getting smoke flavor in the stovetop smoker, then braising the brisket in the oven until tender.

To use the stovetop smoker, place 1 to 2 tablespoons (15 to 25 mL) of very fine wood chips in the center of the base of the smoker. These wood chips are available in many different varieties, from alder and apple to cherry, corncob, hickory, oak, maple, mesquite and pecan. You can also use very fine dried organic lavender buds or dried tea leaves. Make sure the wood chips, buds or leaves are dry when you put them in the smoker, so they smolder effectively.

A metal drip tray fits snugly on top of the wood chips, then a coated, footed wire rack is placed on the tray. Coat or brush the food you're smoking with olive oil, then season with salt and pepper. Arrange the food in a single layer on the rack, so that the most surface area is exposed to the smoke — the same idea as in planking. (If you want to double the recipes, smoke the foods in two separate batches.)

Slide the metal lid almost closed. Extend the handles and place the stovetop smoker over a burner. (Gas or electric coil burners work just fine, but you'll need to increase the cooking time by 20% if your stove has flat ceramic burners.) Turn the burner to medium or medium-high. (Although the instructions enclosed with the stovetop smoker say to keep the heat on medium, you'll get maximum smoke in a shorter time with higher heat.) Start counting the cooking time when you see the first wisp of smoke escaping from the smoker. Then close the lid tightly.

It's easy to tell when your food is done. Fish and shellfish should have a golden-bronze cast and be opaque all the way through. Poultry, beef and pork will also appear golden-bronze, but doneness should be confirmed with an instant-read thermometer. Vegetables and cheeses are done when they have the amount of smoke flavor you desire.

For meats such as pork or beef tenderloin, we prefer to use a grill or an indoor grill pan to get grill marks on the meat first — for taste and aesthetic reasons — then finish the cooking in the stovetop smoker. That way, you get a slight caramelization on the exterior and a smoky, juicy interior. Perfect!

After you're finished smoking, remove the smoker from the heat. Be careful, as it will be very hot. Let it sit for a minute or two before opening the lid so that the smoke can dissipate. Remove the food and let the smoker cool before handling it. When it is cool, discard the ashes by rinsing them with cold water and washing them down the drain or disposing of them safely outdoors. Do not throw them in your wastebasket — they could be a fire hazard. Clean your stovetop smoker by hand with hot, soapy water or put the parts in the dishwasher.

Where Big, Bold Flavor Begins

ONCE YOU KNOW the barbecue methods and techniques involved and you have your equipment, it's time to think about other ways to build flavor.

Basically, any raw food other than a fruit or vegetable starts out bland and slightly sweet. Your aim as a barbecuer is to round out and build bold flavor before, during and after grilling or smoking.

✦ Build Bold Flavor ✦

Sweet	Sour	Salty	Bitter	Umami
Honey	Vinegar	Salt	Paprika	Soy sauce
Sugar	Citrus	Mustard	Beer	Miso
Maple syrup	Wine	Anchovy	Coffee	Fish sauce
Fruit	Fruit juice	Worcestershire	Spice	Dried mushrooms

You're working with the five basic taste components: sweet, sour, salty, bitter and umami (that deep, mysterious flavor experienced when you taste soy sauce or dried mushrooms). You can also add citrus, herbal or spice notes with rubs, marinades and brines before cooking; flavored moisture with bastes and sprays during cooking; and finishing sauces and butters afterwards.

The barbecue process itself adds flavor: caramelization and char from grilling; wood smoke from smoking; aromatic wood flavor from planking. All of these methods add varying amounts of bitterness, with aromatic planking adding the least and heavy char or smoke adding the most.

The barbecuer's quest is to orchestrate all these flavors — and optimum textures — to a culinary crescendo.

PART 2

Big & Bold
Recipes

_____

Rubs and Sauces

All-Purpose Barbecue Rub 34

Blue Ribbon Rub 34

Brisket Rub 35

Cajun Spice Rub 35

Red-Hot Rub 36

Sugar & Spice Rub 36

All-Purpose Lemon Brine 37

Maple Mustard Brine 37

Sour Orange Marinade 38

Sherry Marinade 38

Soy-Ginger Marinade 39

Wasabi Vinaigrette 39

Walnut Vinaigrette 40

Caesar Dressing 40

Work of Art Drizzle 41

Honey Orange Drizzle 41

Aji-li-Mojili 42

Sun-Dried Tomato Pesto 42

Four-Herb Pesto 43

Fresh Herb Paste for Poultry, Pork and Fish 44

Provençal Flavoring Paste 45

Mustard-Mayonnaise Slather 45

Food Processor Aïoli 46

The Doctor Is In Easy Aïoli 47

White Truffle Aïoli 48

Mustard Seed Sauce 49

Creamy Mustard Sauce 49

Lemon Tarragon Cream Sauce 50

Satay Sauce 50

Romesco Sauce 51

Cherry Barbecue Glaze 52

Brandied Cherry Sauce 52

Cilantro Butter 53

Hot Pepper Mint Butter 53

Caesar Butter 54

Lemon Tahini 54

Béarnaise Sauce 55

Mustard-Cornichon Butter Sauce 56

Tzatziki 57

Coconut Chutney 58

Bloody Mary Salsa 59

Pumpkin Seed Salsa 60

Golden Papaya Salsa 61

Pineapple Mandarin Salsa 61

Grilled Guacamole 62

Vinegar Barbecue Sauce 62

Smoked Chile Barbecue Sauce 63

Not-So-Secret Sauce 64

Asian Barbecue Sauce 64

Nectar of the BBQ Gods 65

Mango Chipotle Barbecue Sauce 66

Spicy Raspberry Jalapeño Barbecue Sauce 66

Kentucky-Style Black Barbecue Sauce 67

Alabama White Sauce 68

Carolina Mustard Barbecue Sauce 69

Kansas City–Style Smoky Tomato Barbecue Sauce 70

This chapter concentrates on all-purpose, classic yet contemporary renditions of barbecue flavor builders — before, during and after cooking. These rubs, brines, marinades, slathers, pastes, drizzles, bastes, glazes, compound butters, barbecue sauces, aïolis and finishing sauces work with the food, your barbecue equipment and you as the conductor to orchestrate a symphony of full flavor.

✦ Butter Up ✦

When you add one or more ingredients to softened butter, you have a compound butter. Go mild by adding just a few ingredients or robust by adding ample quantities of herbs, spices and seasonings. Add even bolder flavor by toasting nuts, smoking or grilling vegetables and grilling fruits before combining them with the butter.

Begin with 1 cup (250 mL) unsalted butter. Combine the additional ingredients with the butter until fully incorporated. Spoon the butter into a ramekin and cover with plastic wrap. The butter may also be spooned onto a piece of waxed paper, rolled into a log and covered with plastic wrap. Refrigerated, the butters will keep for about 1 week. Frozen, the butters will keep for about 3 months (wrapped in additional freezer plastic or paper).

Try mixing and matching these ingredients to create your own delicious compound butter:

Herb	Spice	Condiment	Nut/Seeds	Fruit	Vegetable	Protein	Cheese
chives	smoked paprika	mustard	almonds	peach	garlic	bacon	Cheddar
basil	ginger	balsamic vinegar	pine nuts	citrus zest	tomato	pancetta	goat cheese
dill	curry	horseradish	pecans	apple	bell peppers	ham	blue cheese
sage	peppercorns	chili sauce	walnuts	pear	scallions	shrimp	Parmesan
cilantro	wasabi	miso	cashews	plum	fennel	anchovy	feta
thyme	chipotle pepper	capers	pepitas (pumpkin seeds)	fig	truffles	bottarga	pecorino

Flavor Builders

Rub: A dry mixture, usually of sugar, salt and spices, that is sprinkled on food.

Marinade: A wet mixture of an acid (usually vinegar or citrus juice), oil and flavoring agents such as garlic, lime, hot pepper sauce, etc. A marinade imparts flavor and sometimes tenderizes. Do not let delicate fish or shellfish marinate for longer than 30 minutes, as the acid in marinades "cooks" the fish into ceviche. Use marinades on thin meats, poultry, fish, vegetables or fruit, or use a culinary injector to place marinades deep inside roasts or thicker cuts of meat and poultry.

Brine: A salt solution with other flavoring agents such as spices, bourbon, maple syrup, etc. Foods such as whole turkey and chicken, game and pork better retain their juiciness after brining. Make sure you rinse the food in several changes of cold water after brining and before grilling or smoking.

Slather: A smooth, spreadable paste that is brushed on food to be planked or smoked. A slather keeps moisture in, helps a rub adhere to the surface and adds flavor. Slathers are generally based either on mustard or a mustard and mayonnaise mixture.

Flavoring paste: A spreadable mixture thicker than a slather that is spread on food to be grilled, planked, rotisserie-cooked or smoked.

Drizzle: A vinaigrette that can be used as both a marinade and a light finishing sauce.

Baste: A mixture, usually containing a fat such as oil or butter, that is brushed on food on the grill or smoker to add flavor and moisture.

Glaze: A mixture, usually containing sugar, that is brushed on food on the grill or smoker to add flavor and/or give it a sheen.

Compound butter: Softened butter to which herbs, garlic or other flavoring agents have been added. A dollop of compound butter adds a finishing touch to grilled foods.

Barbecue sauce: A sauce meant to accompany grilled or slow-smoked foods. Alabama-style white sauce is mayonnaise-based and goes well with barbecued chicken. Carolina-style sauces are based on vinegar and are meant to accompany rich smoked pork barbecue. Memphis-style sauces are tomato-based and spicy. Kansas City–style sauces are tomato-based, sweet, spicy and sometimes smoky. Texas-style sauces are usually tomato-based and might have added zing from chile peppers. Canadian-style tomato-based sauces are often sweetened with maple syrup, applesauce or other fruits.

Aïoli: A garlic mayonnaise that goes well with grilled fish, shellfish, chicken and vegetables. You can customize an aïoli with other ingredients, such as fresh basil, smoked paprika, smoked garlic or smoked tomato.

Finishing sauce: A sauce, anything from classic béarnaise or bordelaise to mango-lemon or romesco, meant to add the final jolt of flavor to barbecued foods.

All-Purpose Barbecue Rub

**MAKES ABOUT
2 CUPS (500 ML)**

Sprinkle this rub on fish, pork, poultry, beef and vegetables that are going out to the grill or the smoker.

½ cup	granulated sugar	125 mL
¼ cup	granulated garlic	50 mL
¼ cup	onion salt	50 mL
¼ cup	dried celery flakes	50 mL
¼ cup	freshly ground black pepper	50 mL
¼ cup	smoked paprika	50 mL
¼ cup	chili powder	50 mL
1 tbsp	dry mustard	15 mL
1 tsp	dried oregano	5 mL

1. In a glass jar with a tight-fitting lid, combine sugar, garlic, onion salt, celery flakes, pepper, paprika, chili powder, mustard and oregano; cover and shake to blend.
2. Store in a cool, dark place for up to 4 weeks.

Blue Ribbon Rub

**MAKES ABOUT
2 CUPS (500 ML)**

This all-purpose seasoning can be sprinkled over anything you want to slow-smoke; it adds color, flavor and a good crust, or bark, on meats.

✦ TIP ✦

To get brown sugar really dry so it doesn't clump in a dry rub, scatter it over a baking sheet and let it dry in a 100ºF (50ºC) oven for several hours or overnight. Let cool, then use in a dry rub recipe.

½ cup	freshly ground black pepper	125 mL
½ cup	smoked or sweet Hungarian paprika	125 mL
¼ cup	granulated garlic or garlic powder	50 mL
¼ cup	onion salt	50 mL
¼ cup	packed brown sugar (see tip, at left)	50 mL
3 tbsp	dry mustard	45 mL
3 tbsp	celery seeds	45 mL
3 tbsp	chili powder	45 mL

1. In a glass jar with a tight-fitting lid, combine pepper, paprika, garlic, onion salt, brown sugar, mustard, celery seeds and chili powder; cover and shake to blend.
2. Store in a cool, dark place for up to 3 months.

Brisket Rub

**MAKES ABOUT
1½ CUPS (375 ML)**

*This simple mixture
is packed with
flavor and makes
for a luscious, smoky
brisket. Sprinkle it
over the brisket and
refrigerate for at least
2 hours or overnight
before smoking.*

◆ TIP ◆

Think beef with this rub
and sprinkle it on a whole
beef tenderloin or a nice
thick steak.

⅓ cup	smoked paprika	75 mL
⅓ cup	cracked black peppercorns	75 mL
⅓ cup	granulated garlic	75 mL
¼ cup	firmly packed dark brown sugar	50 mL
2 tbsp	coarse kosher salt	25 mL
1 tbsp	dry mustard	15 mL
1 tbsp	cayenne pepper	15 mL

1. In a glass jar with a tight-fitting lid, combine
   paprika, black pepper, garlic, brown sugar, salt,
   mustard and cayenne; cover and shake to blend.
2. Store in a cool, dark place for up to 3 months.

Cajun Spice Rub

**MAKES ABOUT
½ CUP (125 ML)**

*Seventeenth-century
French settlers in New
Brunswick, Nova Scotia
and Prince Edward
Island were deported
in the mid-1700s when
Britain took over.
Many Acadians settled
in Louisiana, where
they became known
as Cajuns. Use this
rub when you want
"mo betta" flavor on
grilled fish, shellfish,
poultry, game or pork.*

4	bay leaves, ground in a spice grinder	4
1 tbsp	filé powder (also known as filé gumbo) or ground anise	15 mL
1 tbsp	dried oregano	15 mL
1 tbsp	chili powder	15 mL
1 tbsp	smoked or sweet Hungarian paprika	15 mL
1 tbsp	freshly ground white pepper	15 mL
1 tbsp	freshly ground black pepper	15 mL
1 tbsp	cayenne pepper	15 mL
2 tsp	celery salt	10 mL

1. In a glass jar with a tight-fitting lid, combine
   bay leaves, filé powder, oregano, chili powder,
   paprika, white pepper, black pepper, cayenne
   and celery salt; cover and shake to blend.
2. Store in a cool, dark place for up to 3 months.

Red-Hot Rub

MAKES ABOUT 1 CUP (250 ML)

This rub has a vibrant flavor and a kick of heat. It's perfect for poultry, fish, pork and game.

½ cup	lemon pepper	125 mL
3 tbsp	chili powder	45 mL
3 tbsp	ground cumin	45 mL
1 tbsp	packed brown sugar	15 mL
1 tsp	celery salt	5 mL
1 tsp	hot pepper flakes (or to taste)	5 mL

1. In a glass jar with a tight-fitting lid, combine lemon pepper, chili powder, cumin, brown sugar, celery salt and hot pepper flakes; cover and shake to blend.
2. Store in a cool, dark place for up to 3 months.

Sugar & Spice Rub

MAKES ABOUT ¾ CUP (175 ML)

This sweet rub is perfect for sprinkling over fruit to be grilled.

½ cup	packed brown sugar	125 mL
2 tbsp	ground cinnamon	25 mL
1 tbsp	ground cloves	15 mL
1 tbsp	ground allspice	15 mL
½ tsp	hot pepper flakes	2 mL
½ tsp	kosher salt	2 mL

1. In a glass jar with a tight-fitting lid, combine brown sugar, cinnamon, cloves, allspice, hot pepper flakes and salt; cover and shake to blend.
2. Store in a cool, dark place for up to 3 months.

All-Purpose Lemon Brine

*The simplest brine for
meat is water and salt.
But many cooks agree
that the addition of
sugar and a flavoring
agent make a brine
that much better. This
is enough brine for
a couple of chickens,
ducks or pheasants.
It will cover a turkey,
roast, brisket or a big
tenderloin or two.
Brine for 12 to 16 hours,
then rinse the meat in
cold water to remove
excess salt before
cooking.*

8 cups	water	2 L
½ cup	kosher salt	125 mL
½ cup	packed dark brown sugar	125 mL
¼ cup	freshly squeezed lemon juice	50 mL
¼ cup	cider vinegar	50 mL

1. In a container big enough to hold the meat you plan to brine, combine water, salt, brown sugar, lemon juice and vinegar, stirring until salt and sugar dissolve.

2. Store in an airtight container in the refrigerator for up to 7 days.

Maple Mustard Brine

*Brining helps meat
and poultry stay juicy
during cooking. Make
sure you rinse the
foods several times
under cold running
water to remove as
much salt as possible
before grilling or
smoking. This brine is
delicious with pork,
poultry or game.*

8 cups	water	2 L
¾ cup	pure maple syrup (Grade B/medium is ideal)	175 mL
½ cup	kosher salt	125 mL
2 tbsp	granulated garlic or garlic powder	25 mL
1 tbsp	cracked black peppercorns	15 mL
2 tsp	English mustard powder	10 mL

1. In a large saucepan, over high heat, bring water, maple syrup, salt, garlic, pepper and mustard powder to a boil, stirring until salt dissolves. Remove from heat and let cool.

2. Store in airtight containers in the refrigerator for up to 7 days.

Sour Orange Marinade

**MAKES ABOUT
1 CUP (250 ML)**

Tangy and savory, this marinade adds big flavor to pork, chicken, fish or shellfish. Sour, or Seville, oranges are usually available only in January or February, but you can create a similar flavor with Valencia oranges and lime juice.

✦ TIP ✦

You'll need about 3 sour oranges to make 1 cup (250 mL) juice. If you can't find sour oranges, use ¼ cup (50 mL) freshly squeezed Valencia orange juice mixed with ¾ cup (175 mL) freshly squeezed lime juice (from 8 to 10 limes).

8	cloves garlic, chopped	8
1 cup	freshly squeezed sour orange juice (see tip, at left)	250 mL
½ cup	olive oil	125 mL
1 tbsp	cracked black peppercorns	15 mL
1 tbsp	kosher salt	15 mL
2 tsp	dried oregano	10 mL

1. In a bowl, combine garlic, orange juice, olive oil, pepper, salt and oregano.
2. Store in an airtight container for up to 3 days.

Sherry Marinade

**MAKES ABOUT
1½ CUPS (375 ML)**

This marinade gives Spanish flair to fish, shellfish, lamb, pork or chicken destined for the grill or smoker.

12	cloves garlic, minced	12
½ cup	olive oil	125 mL
½ cup	dry sherry	125 mL
2 tbsp	dried oregano	25 mL
2 tsp	hot pepper flakes	10 mL
2 tsp	smoked or sweet Hungarian paprika	10 mL
1 tsp	kosher salt	5 mL

1. In a bowl, combine garlic, olive oil, sherry, oregano, hot pepper flakes, paprika and salt.
2. Store in an airtight container in the refrigerator for up to 3 days.

Soy-Ginger Marinade

MAKES ABOUT ¾ CUP (175 ML)

This splendid Asian marinade is great for fish, shellfish, chicken, pork and vegetables.

2	cloves garlic, minced	2
1	1-inch (2.5 cm) piece gingerroot, sliced	1
⅓ cup	soy sauce	75 mL
⅓ cup	rice vinegar	75 mL
3 tbsp	liquid honey	45 mL
1 tsp	toasted sesame oil	5 mL

1. In a glass bowl, combine garlic, ginger, soy sauce, vinegar, honey and sesame oil.
2. Store in an airtight container in the refrigerator for up to 3 days.

Wasabi Vinaigrette

MAKES ABOUT 1 CUP (250 ML)

This can be used as both a marinade and a finishing sauce. It's great with seafood, poultry and vegetables.

✦ TIP ✦

Wasabi is a Japanese horseradish. If you don't normally stock wasabi, you can substitute horseradish. Adjust the amount by how hot you like it.

1 tbsp	wasabi powder	15 mL
1 tbsp	boiling water	15 mL
2	cloves garlic, minced	2
½ cup	peanut oil	125 mL
¼ cup	rice vinegar	50 mL
¼ cup	sake	50 mL
1 tbsp	granulated sugar	15 mL
1 tbsp	chopped onion	15 mL
	Kosher salt	

1. In a small bowl, dissolve wasabi powder in boiling water.
2. In a food processor or blender, combine wasabi mixture, garlic, peanut oil, vinegar, sake, sugar, onion and salt to taste; pulse until blended.
3. Store in an airtight container in the refrigerator for up to 3 days.

Walnut Vinaigrette

**MAKES ABOUT
1 CUP (250 ML)**

*This is delicious
drizzled over grilled
vegetables, chicken,
lamb or pork, and is
especially wonderful
with salads that have
toasted walnuts
and grilled fruit as
ingredients.*

⅓ cup	walnut oil	75 mL
⅓ cup	extra-virgin olive oil	75 mL
⅓ cup	balsamic vinegar	75 mL
1 tbsp	minced onion	15 mL
2 tsp	Dijon mustard	10 mL
1 tsp	granulated sugar	5 mL
½ tsp	kosher salt	2 mL

1. In a glass jar with a tight-fitting lid, combine walnut oil, olive oil, vinegar, onion, mustard, sugar and salt; cover and shake to blend.
2. Store in the refrigerator for up to 2 weeks.

✦ Variation ✦

Substitute flavored oils or vinegars to give this vinaigrette a different spin.

Caesar Dressing

**MAKES ABOUT
¾ CUP (175 ML)**

*This creamy Caesar
dressing packs a bit of
a punch and is great as
a dip with raw, grilled
or smoked vegetables.*

2	cloves garlic, minced	2
½ cup	mayonnaise	125 mL
⅓ cup	freshly grated Parmesan cheese	75 mL
2 tbsp	freshly squeezed lemon juice	25 mL
2 tsp	anchovy paste	10 mL
1 tsp	Dijon mustard	5 mL
¼ tsp	hot pepper flakes	1 mL
	Fine kosher salt and freshly ground black pepper	

1. In a small bowl, whisk together garlic, mayonnaise, cheese, lemon juice, anchovy paste, mustard, hot pepper flakes and salt and black pepper to taste.
2. Store in an airtight container in the refrigerator for up to 2 weeks.

Work of Art Drizzle

MAKES ABOUT
½ CUP (125 ML)

This potent vinaigrette adds a big hit of flavor. Use as a marinade or as a finishing drizzle on grilled vegetables, fish, shellfish or chicken.

1	large clove garlic	1
1 tsp	kosher or sea salt	5 mL
3 tbsp	freshly squeezed lemon juice	45 mL
3 tbsp	extra-virgin olive oil	45 m

1. In a mortar and pestle, mash garlic and salt to a fine paste. Stir in lemon juice and olive oil. Use immediately.

Honey Orange Drizzle

MAKES ABOUT
¾ CUP (175 ML)

This aromatic drizzle is wonderful over grilled fruit, carrots, beets or pork.

2 tbsp	unsalted butter	25 mL
2 tbsp	liquid honey	25 mL
2 tsp	grated orange zest	10 mL
½ cup	freshly squeezed orange juice	125 mL
Pinch	cayenne pepper	Pinch
	Kosher or sea salt	

1. In a small saucepan, melt butter over medium heat. Stir in honey and orange zest until well blended. Stir in orange juice and remove from heat. Stir in cayenne and salt to taste.

Aji-li-Mojili

*Use this Caribbean
blend of garlic, olive
oil and citrus as a
marinade and/or a
finishing sauce for
any grilled food.*

4	cloves garlic, minced	4
1 cup	olive oil	250 mL
¼ cup	freshly squeezed lime juice (from 3 to 4 limes)	50 mL
2 tbsp	white wine vinegar	25 mL
½ tsp	salt	2 mL
¼ tsp	hot pepper flakes	1 mL

1. In a bowl, whisk together garlic, olive oil, lime juice, vinegar, salt and hot pepper flakes.

2. Store in an airtight container in the refrigerator for up to 3 days.

Sun-Dried Tomato Pesto

*This is a little sweeter
than regular basil pesto.
It's nice on fish and
poultry or served in a
ramekin as a spread
for grilled bread.*

✦ TIP ✦

Buy the sun-dried
tomatoes that are
packaged in a bag,
similar to dried fruit.
They are softer and
don't need to be
reconstituted. If buying
them in bulk, you'll
need about 4 cups
(1 L), loosely packed.

12 oz	sun-dried tomatoes (not oil-packed)	375 g
8	cloves garlic, minced	8
½ cup	extra-virgin olive oil	125 mL
4 tsp	balsamic vinegar	20 mL
2 cups	firmly packed fresh basil or flat-leaf (Italian) parsley	500 mL
1 tsp	liquid honey	5 mL
	Freshly ground black pepper	

1. In a food processor, coarsely chop tomatoes and garlic. With the motor running, through the feed tube, gradually add olive oil and vinegar; process for 1 minute. Add basil, honey and pepper to taste; pulse until thoroughly incorporated.

2. Store in an airtight container in the refrigerator for up to 2 weeks or in the freezer for up to 6 months.

Four-Herb Pesto

**MAKES ABOUT
2 CUPS (500 ML)**

This classic pesto recipe uses a combination of herbs. The addition of chives and mint or lemon balm keeps the pesto a brilliant grassy green.

✦ TIPS ✦

To toast nuts, spread them on a baking sheet and toast in a 350°F (180°C) oven until light brown, about 8 minutes.

Pesto turns into a luscious marinade when mixed with several tablespoons of oil and vinegar.

3	cloves garlic	3
½ cup	packed fresh flat-leaf (Italian) parsley	125 mL
½ cup	packed fresh basil	125 mL
½ cup	packed fresh mint or lemon balm	125 mL
½ cup	snipped chives or garlic chives	125 mL
½ cup	extra-virgin olive oil	125 mL
⅓ cup	pine nuts or walnut halves, toasted (see tip, at left)	75 mL
⅓ cup	freshly grated Parmesan or Romano cheese	75 mL
	Kosher salt and freshly ground black pepper	

1. In a food processor, pulse garlic, parsley, basil, mint and chives until finely chopped. With the motor running, through the feed tube, gradually add olive oil. Add nuts and pulse several times to chop. Add cheese and pulse until you have a coarse-grained green pesto. Season to taste with salt and pepper.

2. Store in an airtight container in the refrigerator for up to 2 weeks or in the freezer for up to 6 months.

✦ Variation ✦

For other flavorful pestos, use different mixes of herbs, such as tarragon, mint, oregano and cilantro.

Fresh Herb Paste
for Poultry, Pork and Fish

**MAKES ABOUT
1⅓ CUPS (325 ML)**

This is a delicious lemony herb paste for marinating. Coat food with paste and refrigerate for up to 2 hours, then grill. It is also a great sauce to serve on the side.

1	onion, coarsely chopped	1
⅓ cup	snipped chives	75 mL
⅓ cup	packed fresh parsley	75 mL
¼ cup	packed fresh mint or lemon balm	50 mL
⅓ cup	freshly squeezed lemon juice	75 mL
⅓ cup	olive oil	75 mL
2 tbsp	white wine vinegar	25 mL
1 tbsp	poultry seasoning	15 mL
1 tsp	ground allspice	5 mL
1 tsp	hot pepper flakes	5 mL
1 tsp	freshly ground black pepper	5 mL
½ tsp	kosher salt	2 mL

1. In a blender or food processor, combine onion, chives, parsley, mint, lemon juice, olive oil, vinegar, poultry seasoning, allspice, hot pepper flakes, black pepper and salt; blend to a thick paste.

Provençal Flavoring Paste

**MAKES ABOUT
½ CUP (125 ML)**

Give your grilled and smoked foods a true south-of-France flair when you slather fish, lamb, pork or chicken with this bold mixture.

✦ TIP ✦

If you don't have lavender buds, substitute dried rosemary.

2	cloves garlic, minced	2
¼ cup	Dijon mustard	50 mL
¼ cup	olive oil	50 mL
2 tsp	dried herbes de Provence	10 mL
½ tsp	dried culinary lavender buds (organic or unsprayed)	2 mL
	Kosher or sea salt and freshly ground black pepper	

1. In a bowl, combine garlic, mustard, olive oil, herbes de Provence, lavender and salt and pepper to taste.
2. Store in an airtight container in the refrigerator for up to 3 days.

Mustard-Mayonnaise Slather

**MAKES 1 CUP
(250 ML)**

This is a great slather on salmon or any other fish you plan to plank. It is also a great dipping sauce for grilled asparagus and steamed artichokes.

✦ TIP ✦

Any of the aïoli recipes (pages 46–48) can be used as slathers.

½ cup	mayonnaise	125 mL
½ cup	Dijon mustard	125 mL

1. In a bowl, whisk together mayonnaise and mustard.
2. Store in an airtight container in the refrigerator for up to 1 week.

✦ Variations ✦

Artichoke Slather: Add ½ cup (125 mL) chopped artichoke hearts.

Onion Slather: Add ½ cup (125 mL) finely chopped onion.

Caper Slather: Add ¼ cup (50 mL) chopped drained capers.

Food Processor Aïoli

*The trick to making
light and fluffy aïoli
in a food processor is
using the whole egg
instead of just egg
yolks. Use fresh garlic
mayonnaise on meats,
fish and vegetables and
as a sandwich spread.*

✦ TIP ✦

This recipe contains
raw eggs. If the food
safety of raw eggs is a
concern for you, use
pasteurized eggs in
their shells or 1/2 cup
(125 mL) pasteurized
liquid whole egg.

2	eggs	2
2 to 4	cloves garlic, minced	2 to 4
1 tbsp	freshly squeezed lemon juice	15 mL
1 tbsp	Dijon mustard	15 mL
1 tbsp	olive oil	15 mL
1½ cups	olive oil	375 mL

1. In a food processor, combine eggs, garlic to taste, lemon juice, mustard and the 1 tbsp (15 mL) olive oil; pulse to blend. With the motor running, through the feed tube, gradually add the 1½ cups (375 mL) olive oil; process until thick and creamy.

2. Store in an airtight container in the refrigerator for up to 1 day.

✦ Variations ✦

Smoked Garlic Aïoli: Use 2 to 4 cloves smoked garlic instead. To smoke garlic, leave the cloves whole, with the skin on, brush with olive oil and place in a foil pan. Prepare an indirect fire for smoking in your grill or smoker. Place foil pan on the indirect side of the grill, close the lid and smoke for 2 hours.

For a wonderfully herb-fragrant twist, add 1 to 2 tbsp (15 to 25 mL) of a fresh herb such as basil, chives or tarragon to the aïoli.

The Doctor Is In Easy Aïoli

**MAKES ABOUT
1 CUP (250 ML)**

Shortcut aïoli can be very good when you use a good-quality store-bought mayonnaise. Canola-based mayonnaise is very creamy and makes for a more authentic "doctored" aïoli. However, any good-quality mayonnaise you like will taste fine.

2	cloves garlic, minced	2
1 cup	good-quality mayonnaise	250 mL
	Grated zest and juice of 1 lemon	
	Fine kosher salt	

1. In a bowl, whisk together garlic, mayonnaise, lemon zest, lemon juice and salt to taste.

2. Store in an airtight container in the refrigerator for up to 10 days.

✦ Doctored Up Aïoli ✦

To 1 cup (250 mL) prepared mayonnaise, add:

- 2 tbsp (25 mL) prepared horseradish to make *Horseradish Aïoli* (great on steak or smoked or rotisserie beef sandwiches).

- ½ cup (125 mL) finely chopped roasted red bell peppers to make *Roasted Red Pepper Aïoli*.

- ¼ cup (50 mL) chopped sun-dried tomatoes to make *Sun-Dried Tomato Aïoli*.

- ½ cup (125 mL) finely chopped fresh herbs to make *Fresh Herb Aïoli* (a combination of mint and chives is especially nice with lamb).

- 2 tbsp (25 mL) homemade or prepared pesto to make *Pesto Aïoli*.

White Truffle Aïoli

**MAKES ABOUT
1½ CUPS (375 ML)**

White truffle oil is available at gourmet shops or online. It has an earthy fragrance, and a few drops added to mashed potatoes or risotto is delicious. We love this aïoli with grilled or smoked beef tenderloin, grilled potatoes or grilled seafood, especially tuna.

✦ TIP ✦

This recipe contains raw egg yolks. If the food safety of raw eggs is a concern for you, use pasteurized eggs. Many grocery stores now carry pasteurized eggs in their shells. Alternatively, use ¼ cup (50 mL) pasteurized liquid whole egg; the aïoli won't be quite as rich.

2	egg yolks	2
1	large clove garlic, minced	1
1 tsp	freshly squeezed lemon juice	5 mL
¼ tsp	kosher salt	1 mL
¼ tsp	freshly ground white pepper	1 mL
1 cup	olive oil	250 mL
2 tbsp	white truffle oil (or to taste)	25 mL

1. In a glass bowl, whisk together egg yolks, garlic, lemon juice, salt and white pepper until smooth. Gradually whisk in olive oil and truffle oil until the sauce thickens.

2. Store in an airtight container in the refrigerator for up to 1 day.

Mustard Seed Sauce

This is a delicious sauce to serve with grilled fish, poultry and vegetables.

♦ TIP ♦

This sauce can also be used as a slather for planked fish, pork or chicken.

½ cup	Dijon mustard	125 mL
½ cup	whole-grain mustard	125 mL
½ cup	mayonnaise	125 mL
1 tbsp	freshly squeezed lemon juice	15 mL
1 tsp	dried dillweed	5 mL
1 tsp	Worcestershire sauce	5 mL
½ tsp	freshly ground white pepper	2 mL

1. In a bowl, whisk together Dijon mustard, whole-grain mustard, mayonnaise, lemon juice, dill, Worcestershire sauce and white pepper.

2. Store in an airtight container in the refrigerator for up to 1 week.

Creamy Mustard Sauce

This easy sauce stirs together in a saucepan in minutes, and is delicious with grilled or smoked pork, turkey, chicken or lamb. You can also use it as a slather for planked chicken breasts.

¾ cup	whipping (35%) cream	175 mL
1 tbsp	whole-grain mustard	15 mL
1 tbsp	Dijon mustard	15 mL
1 tbsp	prepared yellow mustard	15 mL
1 tsp	Worcestershire sauce	5 mL
½ tsp	granulated sugar (or to taste)	2 mL
½ tsp	freshly ground white pepper	2 mL

1. In a saucepan, over medium heat, whisk together cream, whole-grain mustard, Dijon mustard, yellow mustard, Worcestershire sauce, sugar and white pepper. Simmer, whisking occasionally, until the sauce has thickened slightly and the flavors have blended, about 3 minutes.

2. Store in an airtight container in the refrigerator for up to 7 days.

Lemon Tarragon Cream Sauce

This luscious sauce tastes wonderful with smoked chicken, turkey or lamb.

1 tbsp	butter	15 mL
2 tbsp	finely chopped shallots	25 mL
2 tbsp	tarragon-flavored vinegar	25 mL
1 tbsp	cracked black peppercorns	15 mL
1 cup	dry white wine	250 mL
1 cup	chicken stock	250 mL
1 cup	whipping (35%) cream	250 mL
	Grated zest and juice of 2 lemons	
1 tsp	chopped fresh tarragon	5 mL
	Kosher salt	

1. In a saucepan, melt butter over medium heat. Sauté shallots, vinegar and pepper until shallots are tender. Add wine and chicken stock; increase heat and bring to a boil. Reduce heat to medium and simmer for 10 minutes, until reduced by about a third. Add cream, lemon zest and lemon juice; simmer, stirring occasionally, for 10 minutes, until slightly thickened. Stir in tarragon and salt to taste.

2. Store in an airtight container in the refrigerator for up to 3 days. Reheat gently.

Satay Sauce

This easy Indonesian sauce tastes wonderful with almost any kind of skewered and grilled food.

1½ cups	coconut milk	375 mL
2 tsp	Thai red curry paste	10 mL
½ cup	chunky peanut butter	125 mL
1 tsp	tamarind paste or freshly squeezed lime juice	5 mL
¼ cup	finely chopped fresh cilantro	50 mL

1. In a saucepan, over medium-low heat, stir coconut milk and curry paste until well blended and warmed through. Stir in peanut butter and tamarind paste; simmer for 10 minutes, until slightly thickened. Stir in cilantro. Serve immediately.

Romesco Sauce

A classic Spanish sauce thickened with ground almonds, romesco tastes wonderful on grilled fish, shellfish, chicken, pork, lamb or vegetables.

✦ TIPS ✦

To toast nuts, spread them on a baking sheet and toast in a 350°F (180°C) oven until light brown, about 8 minutes.

You can use store-bought roasted peppers in a jar or roast your own. To roast peppers, preheat broiler or your grill to high. Broil or grill whole peppers until blackened, blistered and tender. Place peppers in a brown paper bag and close the top. Set aside for about 5 minutes, until cool. Slice peppers open to remove the core and seeds. Rub excess char off the skins. Use immediately or store in an airtight container in the refrigerator for up to 2 days.

½ cup	blanched almonds, toasted (see tip, at left)	125 mL
2	roasted red bell peppers (see tip, at left), roughly chopped	2
2	cloves garlic, minced	2
1	slice white bread, crust removed, toasted and crumbled	1
1 tbsp	roughly chopped fresh flat-leaf (Italian) parsley	15 mL
½ tsp	hot pepper flakes	2 mL
⅓ cup	red wine vinegar	75 mL
⅔ cup	extra-virgin olive oil	150 mL
	Kosher salt and freshly ground black pepper	

1. In a food processor, grind almonds. Add roasted peppers, garlic, bread, parsley and hot pepper flakes; purée to a smooth paste. Add vinegar and pulse to blend. With the motor running, through the feed tube, gradually add olive oil in a steady stream until the mixture thickens like mayonnaise. Season to taste with salt and black pepper.

2. Store in an airtight container in the refrigerator for up to 2 days.

Cherry Barbecue Glaze

MAKES ABOUT 1½ CUPS (375 ML)

For a sweet finish on chicken, turkey, pork or game birds, brush with this glaze during the last minutes of grilling or smoking.

1 cup	cherry preserves or jam	250 mL
¼ cup	cider vinegar	50 mL
¼ cup	barbecue sauce	50 mL

1. In a small saucepan, over medium heat, heat preserves, vinegar and barbecue sauce until preserves melt.

2. Store in an airtight container in the refrigerator for up to 4 weeks.

Brandied Cherry Sauce

MAKES ABOUT 1¾ CUPS (425 ML)

Enjoy this easy sauce with grilled or smoked pork, poultry or game.

1	clove garlic, minced	1
1	jar (12 oz/375 g) good-quality cherry preserves or jam	1
¼ cup	brandy or cognac	50 mL
1 tbsp	Dijon mustard	15 mL
1 tsp	freshly ground white pepper	5 mL

1. In a saucepan, over medium-low heat, combine garlic, preserves, brandy, mustard and white pepper; simmer for 10 minutes. Serve warm.

2. Store in an airtight container in the refrigerator for up to 1 week. Reheat before serving.

✦ Variation ✦

Substitute apricot, peach or blackberry preserves for the cherry.

Cilantro Butter

Serve this butter atop Mexican-style grilled steak or chicken, corn on the cob or vegetables.

1	clove garlic, minced	1
1 cup	unsalted butter, softened	250 mL
½ cup	chopped fresh cilantro	125 mL

1. In a bowl, combine garlic, butter and cilantro. Serve immediately or spoon into a ramekin and cover with plastic wrap. (Or spoon onto a piece of waxed paper, roll into a log and wrap in plastic wrap.)

2. Store in the refrigerator for up to 1 week or wrap in additional freezer plastic or paper and freeze for up to 3 months.

Hot Pepper Mint Butter

On fish and shellfish hot from the grill or smoker, this butter adds a pop of flavor.

1 cup	unsalted butter, softened	250 mL
½ cup	chopped fresh mint	125 mL
½ tsp	hot pepper flakes	2 mL
½ tsp	grated lemon zest	2 mL

1. In a bowl, combine butter, mint, hot pepper flakes and lemon zest. Serve immediately or spoon into a ramekin and cover with plastic wrap. (Or spoon onto a piece of waxed paper, roll into a log and wrap in plastic wrap.)

2. Store in the refrigerator for up to 1 week or wrap in additional freezer plastic or paper and freeze for up to 3 months.

Caesar Butter

**MAKES ABOUT
¾ CUP (175 ML)**

*This makes a great
spread for bruschetta
or topping for grilled
fish and shellfish.*

✦ TIP ✦

Recipes that can be kept
in the freezer, then pulled
out to use in a jiffy, are
truly frozen assets!

1	clove garlic, minced	1
½ cup	unsalted butter, softened	125 mL
2 tbsp	freshly grated Parmesan cheese	25 mL
1 tbsp	anchovy paste	15 mL
1 tsp	Dijon mustard	5 mL
½ tsp	Worcestershire sauce	2 mL
	Grated zest of 1 lemon	

1. In a small bowl, combine garlic, butter, cheese, anchovy paste, mustard, Worcestershire sauce and lemon zest. Serve immediately or spoon into a ramekin and cover with plastic wrap. (Or spoon onto a piece of waxed paper, roll into a log and wrap in plastic wrap.)
2. Store in the refrigerator for up to 2 weeks or wrap in additional freezer plastic or paper and freeze for up to 3 months.

Lemon Tahini

**MAKES ABOUT
1½ CUPS (375 ML)**

*This sauce/dip/spread
goes well with grilled
bread and vegetables,
fish or chicken.*

✦ TIP ✦

Look for tahini, a paste
made of ground sesame
seeds, at health food
stores or the international
section of large
supermarkets.

2	cloves garlic, minced	2
1 cup	tahini (see tip, at left)	250 mL
¼ cup	freshly squeezed lemon juice	50 mL
2 tbsp	plain yogurt	25 mL

1. In a bowl, whisk together garlic, tahini, lemon juice and yogurt.
2. Store in an airtight container in the refrigerator for up to 3 days.

Béarnaise Sauce

This is a bolder version of the classic, understated béarnaise, which makes it perfect for grilled foods, from burgers and steak to chicken, fish and shellfish.

✦ TIP ✦

Emulsion sauces like this one sometimes get cranky and separate — usually if you've left them on the heat too long. If that happens, don't despair. Remove the sauce from the heat and gently whisk in a small ice cube, and all should be well.

⅓ cup	dry white wine	75 mL
¼ cup	tarragon-flavored vinegar	50 mL
1 tbsp	finely chopped shallot	15 mL
1 tsp	dried tarragon	5 mL
¼ tsp	fine kosher or sea salt	1 mL
¾ cup	unsalted butter, cut into pieces	175 mL
3	egg yolks, lightly beaten	3
	Cayenne pepper	
	Additional dried tarragon (optional)	

1. In a small saucepan, bring wine, vinegar, shallot, tarragon and salt to a boil over high heat. Boil until reduced to about 2 tbsp (25 mL), about 8 minutes. Reduce heat to low and whisk in butter, one piece at a time, until melted. Whisk in egg yolks and cook, whisking constantly, for 4 to 5 minutes, or until slightly thickened.

2. Remove from heat and whisk in cayenne to taste. Taste and whisk in more tarragon, if desired.

✦ Variation ✦

Sauce Paloise: Substitute dried mint for the tarragon.

Mustard-Cornichon Butter Sauce

**MAKES ABOUT
1½ CUPS (375 ML)**

Similar in piquant flavor to béarnaise, this beurre blanc is easy to make, and it's a great way to use up that odd jar of cornichons (small, whole pickled cucumbers) left over from the last time you served pâté. We love the sauce on grilled lamb, beef, chicken, fish or vegetables.

◆ TIP ◆

To keep the sauce warm, place the saucepan over a larger saucepan of hot water for up to 30 minutes.

½ cup	unsalted butter, softened	125 mL
⅓ cup	Dijon mustard	75 mL
1	shallot, minced	1
1 cup	dry white wine	250 mL
⅓ cup	tarragon-flavored vinegar	75 mL
12	cornichons, finely chopped (about ½ cup/125 mL)	12
⅓ cup	whipping (35%) cream	75 mL
2 tbsp	minced fresh tarragon (or 2 tsp/10 mL dried)	25 mL
	Kosher salt and finely ground black pepper	

1. In a small bowl, mash butter and mustard until well blended. Cover and refrigerate for 15 minutes.

2. In a small saucepan, bring shallot, wine and vinegar to a boil over high heat. Boil until reduced by about two-thirds, about 10 minutes. Reduce heat to medium and whisk in butter mixture, 1 tbsp (15 mL) at a time, until all the butter has been incorporated and the sauce has thickened slightly.

3. Remove from heat and whisk in cornichons, cream and tarragon. Season to taste with salt and pepper. Serve warm.

Tzatziki

Creamy and cool, this sauce goes with grilled lamb, fish, shellfish, vegetables and flatbread.

1	cucumber, peeled, seeded and finely shredded	1
2 cups	plain yogurt	500 mL
1	clove garlic, minced	1
1 tbsp	olive oil	15 mL
1 tsp	finely chopped fresh dill or oregano	5 mL
½ tsp	grated lemon zest	2 mL
	Kosher salt and finely ground black pepper	

1. Place the cucumber in a strainer set over a bowl. Blot with paper towels and press into the strainer to release some of the moisture. Let drain for 1 hour.

2. Place the yogurt in another strainer set over a bowl and drain for 1 hour.

3. In a bowl, combine cucumber, yogurt, garlic, olive oil, dill and lemon zest; stir well. Season to taste with salt and pepper. Cover and refrigerate for at least 1 hour before serving.

4. Store in an airtight container in the refrigerator for up to 3 days.

Coconut Chutney

MAKES ABOUT 1½ CUPS (375 ML)

Serve this chutney with simple grilled fish, shellfish, flatbread or meats.

✦ TIPS ✦

This is best made and served the same day.

Fresh or frozen curry leaves are available at Indian or Pakistani markets.

1 cup	shredded unsweetened coconut (fresh or frozen and thawed)	250 mL
2	green onions, cut into pieces	125 mL
¼ cup	plain yogurt	50 mL
1 tsp	grated gingerroot	5 mL
1 tsp	finely minced green chile pepper (such as jalapeño, serrano or Thai)	5 mL
2 tbsp	vegetable oil	25 mL
8	curry leaves (or 2 bay leaves)	8
2	small dried red chile peppers	2
1 tsp	mustard seeds	5 mL
1 tsp	black gram (urad dal) (optional)	5 mL
	Freshly squeezed lemon juice	
	Kosher salt	

1. In a food processor, pulse coconut, green onions, yogurt, ginger and chile pepper until very finely chopped. Transfer to a bowl and stir in enough water to make a thick consistency.

2. In a small skillet, heat oil over medium heat. Sauté curry leaves, dried peppers, mustard seeds and black gram until seeds pop and gram turns red. Pour over coconut mixture and stir to blend. Stir in lemon juice and salt to taste.

Bloody Mary Salsa

**MAKES ABOUT
8 CUPS (2 L)**

This medley of fresh vegetables is a zesty taste sensation. Serve it for brunch, lunch or dinner with seafood, poultry, pork or steak.

4	large tomatoes, chopped	4
2	stalks celery, thinly sliced	2
1	red bell pepper, chopped	1
1	small cucumber, peeled, seeded and chopped	1
1	small red onion, chopped	1
1½ tbsp	Worcestershire sauce	22 mL
2 tsp	prepared horseradish	10 mL
1½ tsp	hot pepper sauce	7 mL
½ tsp	celery salt	2 mL
½ tsp	freshly ground black pepper	2 mL
	Zest and juice of 1 lime	

1. In a bowl, combine tomatoes, celery, red pepper, cucumber, red onion, Worcestershire sauce, horseradish, hot pepper sauce, celery salt, black pepper, lime zest and lime juice. Serve immediately or cover and refrigerate for up to 1 day.

Pumpkin Seed Salsa

**MAKES ABOUT
3 CUPS (750 ML)**

*This salsa provides
a lively texture and
color, delicious with
grilled chicken, pork
or fish.*

1 tbsp	olive oil	15 mL
6	cloves garlic	6
1 cup	packed fresh cilantro, stems removed	250 mL
1 cup	pumpkin seeds (pepitas), toasted	250 mL
	Grated zest and juice of 1 lime	
1½ cups	drained canned diced tomatoes with green chiles	375 mL
¼ cup	olive oil	50 mL
¼ tsp	hot pepper flakes (or to taste)	2 mL
	Kosher salt	

1. In a skillet, heat oil over medium-high heat. Sauté garlic for 2 or 3 minutes, or until light golden brown.

2. In a food processor, pulse garlic, cilantro, pumpkin seeds, lime zest and lime juice until a paste forms. Transfer to a bowl and stir in tomatoes with chiles, olive oil and hot pepper flakes. Season to taste with salt.

3. Cover and let stand at room temperature for 1 to 2 hours to let flavors blend. If the salsa is too thick, stir in 1 to 2 tbsp (15 to 25 mL) water.

4. Store in an airtight container in the refrigerator for up to 3 days.

✦ Variation ✦

Pumpkin Seed Pesto: Use half the amount of diced tomatoes with chiles and blend all of the ingredients in a food processor.

Golden Papaya Salsa

**MAKES ABOUT
2 CUPS (500 ML)**

*Fragrant, colorful
and delicious, this
easy salsa is a great
accompaniment to
grilled fish, shellfish,
chicken, lamb or pork.*

2 cups	chopped papaya or mango	500 mL
1 tsp	grated lime zest	5 mL
2 tbsp	freshly squeezed lime juice	25 mL
1 tsp	hot pepper flakes	5 mL

1. In a bowl, combine papaya, lime zest, lime juice and hot pepper flakes. Serve immediately or cover and refrigerate for up to 8 hours.

Pineapple Mandarin Salsa

**MAKES ABOUT
4 CUPS (1 L)**

*This snappy, tangy
salsa goes well with
fish, chicken or pork.*

♦ TIP ♦

Refresh canned
mandarin oranges by
draining the liquid and
placing them in a bowl
of ice-cold water for
5 to 10 minutes. Drain
and use. The metallic
taste from the can will
be gone.

6	fresh mint leaves, julienned	6
1	pineapple, peeled, cored and cubed	1
1 cup	drained canned mandarin oranges	250 mL
1/4 tsp	hot pepper flakes	1 mL
	Grated zest and juice of 1 lime	

1. In a bowl, gently toss together mint, pineapple, oranges, hot pepper flakes, lime zest and lime juice.
2. Store in an airtight container in the refrigerator for up to 2 days.

Grilled Guacamole

**MAKES ABOUT
2 CUPS (500 ML)**

Lightly grilling the avocado first deepens the flavor. Serve this with grilled tortillas or flatbread, fish, chicken, beef or pork.

✦ TIP ✦

Grill the lime halves at the same time for a little bit more char flavor. Plus, you'll get more juice from the warm grilled lime.

4	ripe avocados, halved and pitted	4
2	jalapeño peppers, seeded and finely diced	2
1	small red onion, finely diced	1
¼ cup	chopped fresh cilantro	50 mL
	Juice of 1 lime (or to taste)	

1. Prepare a hot fire in your grill. Grill avocados, cut side down, for 2 to 3 minutes, or until you have good grill marks. Peel and cut into chunks.

2. In a bowl, mash together avocados, jalapeños, red onion, cilantro and lime juice. Serve immediately.

Vinegar Barbecue Sauce

**MAKES ABOUT
2 CUPS (500 ML)**

This quick and easy Southern-style barbecue sauce makes a great baste for ribs and pork butt; apply during the last hour of smoking.

1 cup	ketchup	250 mL
1 cup	cider vinegar	250 mL
3 tbsp	packed dark brown sugar	45 mL
1½ tbsp	prepared yellow mustard	22 mL
1 tbsp	light (fancy) molasses	15 mL
1 tsp	kosher salt	5 mL
½ tsp	hot pepper flakes	2 mL

1. In a bowl, combine ketchup, vinegar, brown sugar, mustard, molasses, salt and hot pepper flakes; stir well to dissolve the sugar.

2. Store in an airtight container in the refrigerator for up to 2 weeks.

Smoked Chile Barbecue Sauce

Bold and brash, this sauce holds up well to the deep, smoky flavor of beef.

✦ TIPS ✦

This sauce will be chunky. If you prefer a thinner sauce, purée it with a hand-held blender, thinning with a little water, if desired.

Look for canned fire-roasted tomatoes (such as Muir Glen or Hunt's) in health food stores or the organic section of well-stocked supermarkets.

3 tbsp	unsalted butter	45 mL
2	onions, chopped	2
3 cups	ketchup	750 mL
1 cup	chopped roasted red bell peppers (see tip, page 51)	250 mL
1 cup	canned fire-roasted diced tomatoes (see tip, at left), with juice	250 mL
½ cup	packed brown sugar	125 mL
½ cup	Worcestershire sauce	125 mL
⅓ cup	steak sauce	75 mL
3 tbsp	red wine vinegar	45 mL
2 tbsp	canned chipotle chile purée	25 mL

1. In a large saucepan, melt butter over medium-high heat. Sauté onions until golden, about 5 minutes. Add ketchup, roasted peppers, tomatoes with juice, brown sugar, Worcestershire sauce, steak sauce, vinegar and chile purée; reduce heat and simmer, stirring occasionally, for about 1 hour, until flavors have blended.

2. Store in an airtight container in the refrigerator for up to 1 month.

Not-So-Secret Sauce

**MAKES ABOUT
16 CUPS (4 L)**

*This tangy, spicy sauce
goes well with pork
barbecue of all kinds,
but especially with
pork steaks, tenderloin
or ribs, or a North
Carolina Pig Pickin'
(page 308).*

1	bottle (28 oz/875 mL) ketchup	1
16 cups	cider vinegar	4 L
2¾ cups	firmly packed light brown sugar	675 mL
½ cup	granulated garlic	125 mL
¼ cup	kosher or sea salt	50 mL
¼ cup	hot pepper flakes	50 mL
1 tbsp	freshly ground black pepper	15 mL
1 tsp	ground allspice	5 mL

1. In a large pot, bring ketchup, vinegar, brown
   sugar, garlic, salt, hot pepper flakes, black pepper
   and allspice to a boil over medium-high heat,
   stirring often. Reduce heat to medium-low and
   simmer, stirring occasionally, for 30 minutes, until
   sauce coats the back of a spoon. Remove from
   heat and let cool.

2. Store in airtight containers in the refrigerator for
   up to 3 months.

Asian Barbecue Sauce

**MAKES ABOUT
2 CUPS (500 ML)**

*On chicken wings, pork
tenderloin, baby back
ribs or pork steaks, this
easy no-cook sauce is
a winner.*

2	cloves garlic, minced	2
2 cups	spicy barbecue sauce	500 mL
¼ cup	soy sauce	50 mL
2 tbsp	toasted sesame oil	25 mL

1. In a bowl, combine garlic, barbecue sauce, soy
   sauce and sesame oil.

2. Store in an airtight container in the refrigerator
   for up to 10 days.

Nectar of the BBQ Gods

Fruity and savory at the same time, this finger-lickin' sauce goes well with pork, game birds, duck or lamb.

✦ TIP ✦

Look for apricot nectar in the juice aisle at the grocery store.

1 cup	chicken stock	250 mL
1 cup	apricot nectar	250 mL
1 cup	apricot syrup (for pancakes or ice cream)	250 mL
1 cup	peach brandy	250 mL
½ cup	grenadine	125 mL
½ cup	vegetable oil	125 mL
½ cup	Worcestershire sauce	125 mL
2 tbsp	ancho chili powder	25 mL
2 tbsp	granulated garlic	25 mL
2 tbsp	onion salt	25 mL
2 tbsp	smoked paprika	25 mL
1 tbsp	celery seeds	15 mL

1. In a large saucepan, bring chicken stock, apricot nectar, apricot syrup, brandy, grenadine, oil, Worcestershire sauce, chili powder, garlic, onion salt, paprika and celery seeds to a boil over medium-high heat, stirring often. Reduce heat to medium-low and simmer, stirring occasionally, for 30 minutes, until sauce coats the back of a spoon. Remove from heat and let cool.

2. Store in airtight containers in the refrigerator for up to 2 months.

Mango Chipotle Barbecue Sauce

MAKES ABOUT 2 CUPS (500 ML)

This sauce is simply delicious with fish, shellfish, chicken, pork, lamb or game birds.

✦ TIPS ✦

This sauce is best used the day it is made.

To make mango purée, pulse mango flesh in a food processor until a thick purée forms.

1½ cups	mango purée (see tip, at left)	375 mL
¼ cup	chipotle hot pepper sauce	50 mL
2 tbsp	freshly squeezed lime juice	25 mL

1. In a bowl, whisk together mango purée, chipotle sauce and lime juice.

Spicy Raspberry Jalapeño Barbecue Sauce

MAKES ABOUT 1½ CUPS (375 ML)

Sweet, spicy, tangy and hot, this barbecue sauce goes well with pork and chicken.

1	jalapeño pepper, seeded and finely diced	1
1 cup	tomato-based barbecue sauce	250 mL
1 cup	seedless raspberry jam	250 mL
¼ cup	cider vinegar	50 mL
½ tsp	hot pepper flakes	2 mL

1. In a small saucepan, warm jalapeño, barbecue sauce, jam, vinegar and hot pepper flakes over medium heat, stirring often, until jam dissolves.

2. Store in an airtight container in the refrigerator for up to 1 week.

Kentucky-Style Black Barbecue Sauce

MAKES ABOUT 1 CUP (250 ML)

With distinctive flavors of Worcestershire sauce and vinegar, this tangy sauce goes well with grilled or smoked lamb or vegetables, and is also yummy as a steak sauce.

2 tsp	vegetable oil	10 mL
¼ cup	finely chopped onion	50 mL
⅓ cup	Worcestershire sauce	75 mL
¼ cup	white vinegar	50 mL
2 tbsp	packed light brown sugar	25 mL
2 tsp	freshly squeezed lemon juice	10 mL
½ tsp	ground allspice	2 mL
½ tsp	hot pepper sauce	2 mL
	Kosher salt and freshly ground black pepper	

1. In a saucepan, heat oil over medium-high heat. Sauté onion until golden, about 5 minutes. Stir in Worcestershire sauce, vinegar, brown sugar, lemon juice, allspice, hot pepper sauce and salt and pepper to taste; bring to a boil. Reduce heat and simmer, stirring often, for 15 minutes, until sauce coats the back of a spoon.

2. Store in an airtight container in the refrigerator for up to 2 months.

Alabama White Sauce

MAKES ABOUT 2½ CUPS (625 ML)

Alabama white sauce is traditionally served with barbecued chicken, but is also great with turkey or pork. It's lightly brushed on the meat during the last few minutes of grilling. It tends to be very mild and is unlike any other regional sauce, most of which use tomato, vinegar or mustard as a key base ingredient. We've spiced this version up just a bit.

✦ TIP ✦

This barbecue sauce is also great as a dipping sauce, so set some aside before you start grilling.

1½ cups	mayonnaise	375 mL
1 cup	cider vinegar	250 mL
2 tbsp	freshly squeezed lemon juice	25 mL
1½ tbsp	freshly ground black pepper	22 mL
1 tbsp	Worcestershire sauce	15 mL
1 tsp	kosher salt	5 mL
¼ tsp	cayenne pepper	1 mL

1. In a bowl, combine mayonnaise, vinegar, lemon juice, black pepper, Worcestershire sauce, salt and cayenne. Cover and refrigerate for at least 8 hours before using.

2. Store in an airtight container in the refrigerator for up to 2 weeks.

Carolina Mustard Barbecue Sauce

South Carolina's signature sauce is a tangy mustard barbecue sauce made with yellow mustard, cider vinegar, brown sugar and spices. It's typically served with pork and chicken, but can be used on game and fish too. Use it as a baste during the last hour of smoking.

1 cup	prepared yellow mustard	250 mL
2/3 cup	cider vinegar	150 mL
1/3 cup	packed dark brown sugar	75 mL
2 tsp	Worcestershire sauce	10 mL
1 tsp	smoked paprika	5 mL
1 tsp	freshly ground white pepper	5 mL
1 tsp	cayenne pepper	5 mL
	Kosher salt and freshly ground black pepper	

1. In a bowl, combine mustard, vinegar, brown sugar, Worcestershire sauce, paprika, white pepper and cayenne; stir well to dissolve sugar. Season to taste with salt and black pepper.

2. Store in an airtight container in the refrigerator for up to 1 month.

Kansas City–Style Smoky Tomato Barbecue Sauce

This recipe has a little more vinegar and kick than the typical sweet tomato barbecue sauces on the grocery store shelves.

✦ TIP ✦

After you empty the ketchup and chili sauce bottles, pour some of the cider vinegar into each empty bottle. Recap the bottles and shake, then pour.

3 cups	ketchup	750 mL
1½ cups	chili sauce	375 mL
¾ cup	cider vinegar	175 mL
½ cup	firmly packed dark brown sugar	125 mL
½ cup	liquid honey	125 mL
½ cup	blackstrap molasses	125 mL
¼ cup	dry mustard	50 mL
¼ cup	water	50 mL
1 tbsp	hot pepper flakes	15 mL
1 tbsp	celery seeds	15 mL
1 tbsp	garlic salt	15 mL
1 tbsp	Worcestershire sauce	15 mL
1 tbsp	liquid smoke	15 mL

1. In a large saucepan, bring ketchup, chili sauce, vinegar, brown sugar, honey, molasses, mustard, water, hot pepper flakes, celery seeds, garlic salt, Worcestershire sauce and liquid smoke to a simmer over medium-low heat. Simmer for 45 to 60 minutes, or until sauce coats the back of a spoon.

2. Store in an airtight container in the refrigerator for up to 3 months.

Fish

Leaf-Wrapped Barramundi on the Barbie 74

Sea Bass Tandoori-Style 75

Stir-Grilled Sea Bass with Orange-Basil Cream Sauce 76

Arctic Char with Grilled Lemon Halves 78

Grenada-Style Grouper with
  Lemon Pomegranate Beurre Blanc 79

Thai-Style Halibut on Lemongrass Skewers 80

Grilled Halibut with Red Pepper Aïoli 81

Grilled Mackerel with Savory Lemon Chutney 82

Macadamia-Buttered Mahi Mahi 83

Grilled Monkfish with Rouille 84

Grill-Roasted Monkfish with Roasted Red Pepper Shatta 85

Grilled Blackened Redfish 86

Char-Grilled Salmon Patties 87

Caipirinha-Glazed Salmon 88

Martini Smoked Salmon 89

Grill-Roasted Northwest King Salmon
  with Honey Soy Glaze 90

Planked and Pepper-Crusted Maple-Glazed Salmon 91

Harissa-Rubbed Snapper Skewers
  with Golden Papaya Salsa 92

Mesquite-Grilled Snapper with Avocado Corn Salsa 93

Grilled Sturgeon with Charred Chile Salsa 94

Grilled Swordfish with Sun-Dried Tomato Relish 96

Grilled Swordfish Steaks with Lemon Truffle Oil 97

Herb-Rubbed Tilapia with Cucumber Relish 98

Wood-Grilled Trout 99

Grill-Smoked Trout with Cilantro Gremolata 100

continued on next page…

Smoked Trout with Lemon Caper Butter. 101

Flame-Kissed Ahi Tuna Steaks with Wasabi Vinaigrette. 102

Grill-Smoked Whitefish with Horseradish Sauce 103

Cedar-Planked Fish with Mustard-Mayo Slather 104

Vietnamese Grilled Fish and Cellophane Noodle Salad 105

Baja Fish Tacos with Napa Slaw and Guacamole 106

Ocean and freshwater fish taste wonderful grilled, planked or smoked. To get the best flavor from barbecued fish, use aromatic herbs and vegetables, compound butters, nuts, citrus and tropical fruits, white wine, rum, soy, ginger, capers and chiles in seasonings, marinades, sauces and drizzles. Mild to medium wood flavors work well with fish, especially alder, maple and fruit woods such as apple, cherry and peach.

The rule of thumb for direct-grilling fish fillets is 10 minutes per inch (2.5 cm) of thickness over a hot fire, turning once. Measure the fish in the thickest part — before grilling! Fish is done when it begins to flake in the thickest part when tested with a fork. Fish like tuna taste best rare or medium-rare, and some people even prefer their salmon medium-rare.

When grilling fish, there's one important rule to keep in mind: if it's undercooked, you can always put it back on the grill, microwave it or finish it in the oven. Overcooked fish can't be rescued.

✦ Fish and Shellfish Substitution Chart ✦

Use this guide to help you select the freshest fish and shellfish at the market. If your fish choice is not available, substitute another fish/shellfish from the same category. If a fish is endangered, substitute one that is abundant and "green." Note that delicate-textured fish may need to be cooked on a griddle, wrapped in foil or placed on a grill rack so that it doesn't fall apart.

	Mild Flavor	Moderate Flavor	Full Flavor
Firm texture	halibut, lobster, monkfish, prawns, sea bass, shrimp, soft-shell crab	cobia, John Dory, salmon, shark, skate, sturgeon, swordfish	cuttlefish, escolar, marlin, ono, oysters, squid, tuna
Medium-firm texture	catfish, grouper, haddock, halibut, ocean perch, pompano, scallops, snapper, striped bass, tilefish, whitefish, wolf fish	arctic char, barracuda, mahi mahi, porgy, salmon fillet, tilapia, trout, walleye pike	amberjack, kingfish, mackerel, mullet, permit, sablefish, yellowtail jack, yellowtail snapper, wahoo
Delicate texture	bass (freshwater), cod, flounder, fluke, hake, pink snapper, red snapper, sand dab, turbot	butterfish, herring, pomfret, shad, smelt/ whitebait	anchovies, bluefish, buffalo fish, sardines

✦ Best Barbecue Methods for Fish ✦

Fish fillet: Grill, stir-grill, skewer, herb-grill, leaf-wrap, plank, smoke

Whole fish: Indirect grill, grill-roast, leaf-wrap, smoke

Leaf-Wrapped Barramundi on the Barbie

Barramundi is a line-caught sporting fish, similar in flavor to red snapper or grouper, from the tropical northern waters of Australia. It's now farm-raised in North America. Barramundi gets the full tropical treatment here: wrapped in a banana leaf and grilled.

✦ TIPS ✦

You'll find fresh banana leaves at Hispanic or Asian markets. Look for frozen banana leaves at larger grocery stores catering to an ethnic population or at www.goya.com.

The seasoning is lemon myrtle, a citrusy Australian herb that you can sometimes find as an herbal tea. If you can't find it, use a combination of lemon pepper and lime zest.

Brush the cut sides of halved lemons and/or limes with oil and grill them, cut side down, to serve with this dish.

1	large banana leaf, fresh or frozen and thawed	1
1	whole baby barramundi (2 to 3 lbs/1 to 1.5 kg), cleaned	1
	Olive oil	
2 tsp	dried lemon myrtle	10 mL
	Kosher or sea salt and freshly ground black pepper	

1. Prepare a hot indirect fire in your grill.

2. For a fresh banana leaf, remove center core and discard. Run the leaf under hot water until pliable. Pat leaf dry with paper towels and cut in half horizontally; overlap the two pieces of leaf so that they will cover the fish. (For a frozen and thawed banana leaf, separate sections of the leaf and overlap them so that they will cover the fish.)

3. Rinse fish and pat dry with paper towels. Score the body of the fish with three slashes on each side. Brush fish with olive oil and sprinkle with lemon myrtle and salt and pepper to taste. Place fish on the banana leaves, fold in the left and right sides and roll up like a burrito, completely covering the fish.

4. Place fish over direct heat, with the lid up. When banana leaves start to smolder, in 4 to 5 minutes, turn fish over and let the other side start to smolder, 4 to 5 minutes. Transfer fish to the indirect side, close the lid and grill for 10 to 15 minutes, or until fish is opaque and flakes easily with a fork. To serve, carefully peel back the top wrapping and serve the fish on a platter.

Sea Bass Tandoori-Style

SERVES 6 TO 8

Cool, refreshing yogurt is a perfect foil for a hot summer day. This meal is fresh, fast and fabulous. Serve with Pistachio Couscous (see page 163), and grill a couple of tomato slices per person for a few minutes while you're grilling the fish. Make a double recipe of the yogurt mixture to dollop on the tomatoes. Your meal is complete.

✦ TIPS ✦

The spiciness of the tandoori sauce is complemented by a cucumber relish or a raita.

Turn fish only once, halfway through the grilling time.

● 13- by 9-inch (3 L) glass casserole dish

Tandoori Sauce

4 to 5	cloves garlic, minced	4 to 5
1	2-inch (5 cm) piece gingerroot, grated	1
1 cup	plain yogurt	250 mL
¼ cup	extra-virgin olive oil	50 mL
2 tsp	ground cumin	10 mL
2 tsp	ground coriander	10 mL
1 tsp	cayenne pepper	5 mL
1 tsp	kosher salt	5 mL
3 lbs	skinless sea bass fillets	1.5 kg

1. *Prepare the tandoori sauce:* In a bowl, combine garlic to taste, ginger, yogurt, olive oil, cumin, coriander, cayenne and salt.

2. Rinse fish and pat dry with paper towels. Place fish in casserole dish and pour in tandoori sauce. Cover and refrigerate for at least 30 minutes and for up to 60 minutes.

3. Meanwhile, prepare a hot fire in your grill. Lift fish out of the sauce, discarding sauce, and place flesh side down on the grill. Grill for 10 minutes per inch (2.5 cm) of thickness, turning once, until fish is opaque and flakes easily with a fork. Serve hot.

Stir-Grilled Sea Bass with Orange-Basil Cream Sauce

This stir-grilled medley of fish and colorful, tasty vegetables puts a new spin on a one-dish dinner. The sea bass holds together nicely and, even if you overcook it a bit, it stays moist.

✦ TIPS ✦

Sea bass is a very moist fish and can forgive a little overcooking.

See page 21 for more information on using a grill wok or basket.

- Grill wok or basket, oiled
- Baking sheet

Orange-Basil Cream Sauce

2 tbsp	unsalted butter	25 mL
3	green onions, thinly sliced	3
1	clove garlic, minced	1
2 cups	dry white wine	500 mL
	Grated zest of 1 orange	
⅔ cup	freshly squeezed orange juice, with pulp	150 mL
1½ cups	whipping (35%) cream	375 mL
	Grated zest and juice of 1 lemon	
	Kosher salt and freshly ground black pepper	
3 tbsp	thinly sliced fresh basil leaves	45 mL
2 lbs	skinless sea bass fillets, cut into 1-inch (2.5 cm) strips	1 kg
12 oz	thin green beans	375 g
1	red onion, slivered	1
2 tbsp	olive oil	25 mL
	Kosher salt and freshly ground black pepper	

1. Prepare a hot fire in your grill.

2. *Prepare the sauce:* In a saucepan, melt butter over medium-high heat. Sauté green onions and garlic for 3 minutes, until softened. Add wine, orange zest and orange juice; cook until liquid is reduced and syrupy. Add cream, reduce heat to medium and simmer, stirring constantly, until reduced by half. Do not let boil. Remove from heat and whisk in lemon zest and juice. Season to taste with salt and pepper. Stir in basil and keep warm.

Add a side dish of rice,
garlic mashed potatoes
or crusty bread to sop
up the sauce.

3. In a bowl, combine sea bass, beans, red onion and olive oil. Toss to coat and season to taste with salt and pepper. Transfer to prepared grill wok. Set wok on baking sheet and carry out to the grill.

4. Place wok on the grill. Grill, tossing several times with long-handled wooden paddles, for 12 to 15 minutes, or until fish is opaque and flakes easily with a fork and vegetables have scorched.

5. Spoon warm sauce on the bottom of each plate. Serve sea bass and vegetables over sauce.

♦ Variation ♦

Use colorful, seasonal vegetables to change this recipe and make it your own.

Arctic Char
with Grilled Lemon Halves

4	skinless arctic char fillets (about 1½ lbs/750 g total)	4
	Olive oil	
	Kosher salt and freshly ground black pepper	
2	lemons, halved	2
1 tbsp	chopped fresh basil leaves	15 mL

1. Prepare a hot fire in your grill.

2. Rinse fish and pat dry with paper towels. Brush fish with olive oil and season to taste with salt and pepper.

3. Place fish flesh side down on the grill. Grill for 10 minutes per inch (2.5 cm) of thickness, turning once, or until fish is opaque and flakes easily with a fork.

4. Meanwhile, lightly brush the cut side of each lemon half with olive oil. Grill cut side down for about 3 minutes, until lightly browned and warmed through.

5. Sprinkle fish with basil and serve with half a grilled lemon on the side.

✦ Variation ✦

Grill lemons, limes and small oranges for a beautiful array of colors.

Grenada-Style Grouper with Lemon Pomegranate Beurre Blanc

Grenada *is the Spanish word for "pomegranate"; hence, the cocktail syrup grenadine, made from pomegranate juice. You'll soon find any excuse to make this pomegranate-flavored beurre blanc, which goes well with grilled fish, shellfish, chicken or pork.*

✦ TIP ✦

Use a wide fish spatula or two grill spatulas to turn the fish.

Lemon Pomegranate Beurre Blanc

1 cup	dry white wine	250 mL
2 tbsp	minced shallots	25 mL
2 tbsp	grenadine or pomegranate syrup	25 mL
1 cup	unsalted butter (2 sticks), cut into cubes	250 mL
	Freshly squeezed lemon juice	
	Kosher or sea salt and freshly ground white pepper	
4	skinless grouper fillets (each about 6 oz/175 g)	4
	Olive oil	
	Kosher or sea salt and freshly ground white pepper	

1. Prepare a hot fire in your grill.

2. *Prepare the beurre blanc:* In a saucepan, bring wine and shallots to a boil over high heat. Boil until reduced by two-thirds, about 8 minutes. Remove from heat and whisk in grenadine. Return to low heat and whisk in butter, one cube at a time. Season to taste with lemon juice, salt and white pepper. Remove from heat and keep warm.

3. Rinse fish and pat dry with paper towels. Brush fish with olive oil and season to taste with salt and pepper.

4. Place fish flesh side down on the grill. Grill for 10 minutes per inch (2.5 cm) of thickness, turning once, until fish is opaque and flakes easily with a fork. Serve each fillet with a dollop of sauce on top.

✦ Variation ✦

Substitute red snapper, halibut, orange roughy or haddock.

Thai-Style Halibut on Lemongrass Skewers

Served on a tropical leaf platter with a bowl of Golden Papaya Salsa, this aromatic appetizer is perfect for hot weather.

✦ TIPS ✦

It's always a good idea to oil the grill rack well before heating the grill, but it's especially important when you're grilling delicate foods like fish, so they don't stick.

Lemongrass can be found with the herbs at Asian markets and some well-stocked supermarkets. For thicker stalks, trim lengthwise into skewers.

Flat bamboo skewers, rather than the round kind, help keep delicate fish pieces anchored.

● Twelve 8-inch (20 cm) fresh lemongrass stalks or flat bamboo skewers, soaked for at least 30 minutes

Green Curry Marinade

1	can (14 oz/400 mL) coconut milk (regular or light)	1
2 tsp	finely grated lime zest	10 mL
2 tbsp	freshly squeezed lime juice	25 mL
1 tbsp	Thai green curry paste	15 mL
2 lb	skinless halibut fillet, cut into 3-inch (7.5 cm) pieces	1 kg
1	recipe Golden Papaya Salsa (page 61)	1

1. *Prepare the marinade:* In a bowl, whisk together coconut milk, lime zest, lime juice and curry paste.

2. Place fish in a large sealable plastic bag and pour in marinade. Seal bag, toss to coat and refrigerate for at least 30 minutes or up to 8 hours, tossing occasionally.

3. Meanwhile, prepare a medium-hot fire in your grill.

4. Remove fish from marinade, discarding marinade, and thread onto lemongrass stalks, leaving space between pieces. Grill for 10 minutes per inch (2.5 cm) of thickness, turning once, until fish is opaque and flakes easily with a fork. Serve with Golden Papaya Salsa.

Grilled Halibut with Red Pepper Aïoli

Red Pepper Aïoli

2	cloves garlic, minced	2
1	roasted red bell pepper (see tip, at left)	1
1½ cups	mayonnaise	375 mL
1 to 2 tbsp	freshly squeezed lemon juice	15 to 25 mL
2 lb	skinless halibut fillet	1 kg
	Olive oil	
	Kosher salt and freshly ground black pepper	
2	lemons, cut into wedges	2
	Chopped fresh flat-leaf (Italian) parsley	

1. *Prepare the aïoli:* In a food processor or blender, purée garlic, roasted pepper and mayonnaise. Transfer to a bowl and stir in lemon juice to taste. Cover and refrigerate until ready to use.

2. Prepare a hot fire in your grill.

3. Rinse fish and pat dry with paper towels. Lightly brush fish with olive oil and season to taste with salt and pepper.

4. Place fish flesh side down on the grill. Grill for 10 minutes per inch (2.5 cm) of thickness, turning once, until fish is opaque and flakes easily with a fork.

5. Place fish on a platter and surround with lemon wedges. Spoon aïoli down the center of the fillet, then sprinkle with parsley.

Grilled Mackerel with Savory Lemon Chutney

The lovely, tart chutney contrasts nicely with the buttery flesh of the grilled mackerel.

✦ TIPS ✦

The chutney can be stored in an airtight container in the refrigerator for up to 4 days.

Turn fish only once, halfway through the grilling time.

You can fillet the cooked fish in the kitchen before serving or serve intact and let diners remove the skin and bones.

Savory Lemon Chutney

2	lemons	2
⅓ cup	water	75 mL
¼ cup	granulated sugar	50 mL
1 tsp	coriander seeds, crushed	5 mL
1 tsp	black peppercorns, crushed	5 mL
2	plum (Roma) tomatoes, seeded and chopped	2
4	whole mackerel (each about 1 lb/500 g), cleaned and heads removed	4
	Kosher salt and freshly ground black pepper	
1	lemon, quartered	1
	Olive oil	

1. *Prepare the chutney:* Thinly slice lemons crosswise, discarding the ends. Quarter the slices, place in a saucepan and add water and sugar. Cook over medium heat, stirring until sugar dissolves. Add coriander and peppercorns; reduce heat and simmer, stirring occasionally, for 20 to 30 minutes, or until liquid is syrupy and lemons are translucent and tender. Remove from heat and stir in tomatoes. Transfer to a serving bowl and set aside to cool.

2. Prepare a hot fire in your grill.

3. Rinse fish and pat dry with paper towels. Make three slashes across the fattest part of each fish on both sides. Season the cavities with salt and pepper to taste and place a quarter lemon in each cavity. Lightly brush the outside of the fish with olive oil and season to taste with salt and pepper.

4. Place flesh side down on the grill. Grill for 10 minutes per inch (2.5 cm) of thickness, turning once, until fish is opaque and flakes easily with a fork. Serve with chutney on the side.

Macadamia-Buttered Mahi Mahi

SERVES 4

Also known as dorado or dolphinfish, mahi mahi is a sweet, white-fleshed fish that is delicious grilled. Serve it with flavored butters, aïoli or fruit salsas.

✦ TIPS ✦

If not serving the macadamia butter immediately, spoon into a ramekin and cover with plastic wrap. (Or spoon onto a piece of waxed paper, roll into a log and wrap in plastic wrap.) Store in the refrigerator for up to 1 week or wrap in additional freezer plastic or paper and freeze for up to 3 months.

Fruit salsas make a light and very refreshing accompaniment to fish dishes. Slice a peach, a nectarine and a papaya, toss together and squeeze lime juice over all. Add 1 tbsp (15 mL) chopped fresh cilantro and you've got a fruit salsa. Add a shake of hot pepper flakes if you want some heat.

Macadamia Butter

½ cup	unsalted butter, softened	125 mL
¼ cup	chopped macadamia nuts	50 mL
¼ cup	chopped fresh flat-leaf (Italian) parsley	50 mL
1 tbsp	freshly squeezed lemon juice	15 mL
4	skinless mahi mahi fillets (each about 6 oz/175 g)	4
	Olive oil	
	Kosher salt and freshly ground black pepper	

1. *Prepare the butter:* In a small bowl, combine butter, nuts, parsley and lemon juice. Set aside.
2. Prepare a hot fire in your grill.
3. Rinse fish and pat dry with paper towels. Brush fish with olive oil and season to taste with salt and pepper.
4. Place fish flesh side down on the grill. Grill for 10 minutes per inch (2.5 cm) of thickness, turning once, until fish is firm. Serve each fillet with a dollop of Macadamia Butter on top.

Grilled Monkfish with Rouille

Thick and meaty, monkfish has been called "poor man's lobster" for good reason: it has a similar texture without being as sweet. Here it's paired with rouille, the classic Mediterranean garlic mayonnaise.

♦ TIP ♦

This recipe contains raw egg yolks. If the food safety of raw eggs is a concern for you, use pasteurized eggs. Many grocery stores now carry pasteurized eggs in their shells. Alternatively, use ¼ cup (50 mL) pasteurized liquid whole egg; the rouille won't be quite as rich.

The rouille can be stored in an airtight container in the refrigerator for up to 4 days.

It's always a good idea to oil the grill rack well before heating the grill, but it's especially important when you're grilling delicate foods like fish, so they don't stick.

Fish fillets are usually about ¾ inch (2 cm) thick in the thickest part. Over a hot fire, that means a fish fillet will need to cook for about 3 to 4 minutes on each side.

Rouille		
4 to 6	cloves garlic	4 to 6
4	egg yolks, at room temperature	4
¼ tsp	saffron threads	1 mL
¼ tsp	kosher or sea salt	1 mL
¼ tsp	cayenne pepper	1 mL
1 cup	extra-virgin olive oil	250 mL
2½ lbs	skinless monkfish fillets	1.25 kg
	Olive oil	
	Kosher or sea salt and freshly ground black pepper	

1. *Prepare the rouille:* In a food processor or blender, combine garlic to taste, egg yolks, saffron, salt and cayenne; process until smooth. With the motor running, through the feed tube, gradually add olive oil in a steady stream until the mixture thickens. Cover and refrigerate until ready to use.

2. Prepare a hot fire in your grill.

3. Rinse fish and pat dry with paper towels. Brush fish with olive oil and season to taste with salt and pepper.

4. Grill fish for 10 minutes per inch (2.5 cm) of thickness, turning once, until fish is firm. Serve each portion with a dollop of rouille.

Grill-Roasted Monkfish with Roasted Red Pepper Shatta

The regions that rim the Mediterranean favor finely chopped vegetable mixtures that function equally well as flavoring pastes, sauces, dips, spreads or condiments. Shatta, from Yemen, is wonderful on grilled bread or pita chips, but also makes a wonderful slather for grill-roasted or planked fish, chicken, lamb or pork. Salmon, halibut or Mediterranean fish such as John Dory would also be delicious this way.

✦ TIPS ✦

The shatta can be stored in an airtight container in the refrigerator for up to 3 days. Bring to room temperature before using.

Be an efficient barbecuer. Grill or smoke garlic cloves, peppers and onions when you're already barbecuing something else. Then wrap and freeze the vegetables for later use in sauces and side dishes.

● **Foil pan or perforated grill rack**

Roasted Red Pepper Shatta

2	cloves garlic, minced	2
1	roasted red bell pepper (see tip, page 81)	1
½ cup	chopped fresh cilantro	125 mL
½ cup	chopped fresh flat-leaf (Italian) parsley	125 mL
½ tsp	ground cumin	2 mL
½ cup	extra-virgin olive oil	125 mL
	Kosher or sea salt and freshly ground black pepper	
1	skinless monkfish fillet (about 2 lbs/1 kg)	1

1. Prepare a hot indirect fire in your grill.
2. *Prepare the shatta:* Using a chef's knife or in a food processor, finely chop garlic, roasted pepper, cilantro, parsley and cumin. Mix in olive oil and season to taste with salt and pepper.
3. Rinse fish and pat dry with paper towels. Place fish in foil pan or on grill rack and slather with shatta.
4. Place pan or grill rack on the indirect side of the grill, close the lid and grill-roast until fish is opaque and flakes easily with a fork, about 30 minutes. Transfer to a platter to serve.

✦ Variations ✦

Plank the fish by soaking a plank in water for at least an hour. Place the fish on the plank and slather with shatta. Place the plank on the indirect side of the grill, close the lid and plank for 30 minutes.

Add a kiss of smoke to the fire.

Grilled Blackened Redfish

SERVES 4

Redfish, while delicious, gets very smoky when cooked indoors. This grilled version lets the fish sizzle outdoors on a grill. Instead of redfish, you could use red snapper or orange roughy.

✦ TIP ✦

Paul Prudhomme created the blackened redfish craze in Louisiana. The redfish is traditionally sprinkled with a hot peppery Cajun seasoning and cooked indoors in a red-hot skillet. It became so popular in the 1980s that redfish was put on the endangered list and couldn't be fished. Luckily, thanks to good game management, the Gulf is once again teeming with redfish.

4	skinless redfish fillets (each about 8 oz/250 g)	4
	Olive oil	
⅓ cup	blackened seasoning or Cajun Spice Rub (see recipe, page 35), divided	75 mL
½ cup	unsalted butter, softened	125 mL

1. Rinse fish and pat dry with paper towels. Brush fish with olive oil and sprinkle each fillet with 1 tbsp (15 mL) of blackened seasoning, coating evenly. Set aside.

2. In a small bowl, combine butter and the remaining blackened seasoning. Set aside.

3. Prepare a hot fire in your grill.

4. Place fish flesh side down on the grill. Grill for 10 minutes per inch (2.5 cm) of thickness, turning once, until fish is opaque and flakes easily with a fork. Serve each fillet with a dollop of seasoned butter.

✦ Variation ✦

Catfish and tilapia are good substitutions for redfish.

Char-Grilled Salmon Patties

Using fresh raw salmon for these patties elevates them from the old-fashioned croquettes made from canned salmon. Serve them as appetizers or as a main course. They make dynamite sandwiches, too.

✦ TIPS ✦

Be sure to carefully remove all small bones from salmon before chopping.

Serve the salmon patties with a sauce such as Lemon Truffle Oil (see recipe, page 97), Ginger-Lime Hollandaise (see recipe, page 242) or White Truffle Aïoli (see recipe, page 48). In a word, they'll become "sublime."

● **Perforated grill rack, oiled**

1½ lb	skinless salmon fillet, roughly chopped	750 g
1	egg, beaten	1
½ cup	fresh sourdough bread crumbs	125 mL
½ cup	finely chopped green onions	125 mL
2 tbsp	Dijon mustard	25 mL
2 tbsp	freshly squeezed lemon juice	25 mL
2 tbsp	anchovy paste	25 mL

1. In a food processor, pulse salmon until the texture resembles raw hamburger. Add egg, bread crumbs, green onions, mustard, lemon juice and anchovy paste; pulse to blend (do not overmix). Lightly mold salmon mixture into four or eight 1-inch (2.5 cm) thick patties. Cover and refrigerate for 30 minutes.

2. Prepare a medium-hot fire in your grill. Set the grill rack directly over the fire.

3. Place patties on the grill rack and grill for 5 minutes per side, turning once, until patties are crisp on the outside and hot in the center. Serve immediately.

Caipirinha-Glazed Salmon

SERVES 6 TO 8

Made with cachaça, a liquor distilled from sugarcane, a caipirinha muddled with fresh lime is a working man's drink in Brazil. Here, it's a zippy glaze for a perfectly grilled salmon fillet. And what to drink with this dish? Hmmmm. The recipe for the drink is the same as for the glaze — just serve it over ice.

◆ TIP ◆

It's always a good idea to oil the grill rack well before heating the grill, but it's especially important when you're grilling delicate foods like fish, so they don't stick.

Caipirinha Glaze

2	limes, each cut into 6 wedges	2
2 tsp	superfine sugar	10 mL
¼ cup	cachaça or white rum	50 mL
1	salmon fillet (about 3 lbs/1.5 kg), skin on or off	1
	Vegetable oil	
	Kosher or sea salt and freshly ground black pepper	

1. *Prepare the glaze:* In a cocktail shaker or bowl, using a pestle or a wooden spoon, muddle lime wedges and sugar. Pour in cachaça and shake or stir until well blended. Strain into a small bowl. Set aside.

2. Prepare a hot fire in your grill.

3. Rinse fish and pat dry with paper towels. Brush fish with oil and season to taste with salt and pepper.

4. Place fish flesh side down on the grill. Grill for 10 minutes per inch (2.5 cm) of thickness, turning once and brushing or drizzling with glaze after turning, until fish is opaque and flakes easily with a fork.

Martini Smoked Salmon

Smoking is the most flavorful way to cook a whole salmon. It gets a nice smokiness and is very moist and tender. Leftovers never go to waste.

✦ TIP ✦

Leftover salmon, flaked and combined with cream cheese and a little lemon juice, makes a great cocktail spread.

- Large foil pan
- **Suggested wood:** oak, apple or alder

Baste

1	clove garlic, minced	1
¼ cup	gin or vodka	50 mL
¼ cup	dry vermouth	50 mL
¼ cup	freshly squeezed lemon juice	50 mL
3 tbsp	unsalted butter, melted	45 mL
2 tbsp	juniper berries	25 mL
1 tbsp	prepared horseradish	15 mL
½ tsp	hot pepper sauce	2 mL
1	whole salmon, cleaned and head removed (3 to 4 lbs/1.5 to 2 kg)	1
3	lemons, sliced, divided	3
8	sprigs fresh dill, divided	8
1 cup	Food Processor Aïoli (page 46)	250 mL

1. Prepare a medium-hot indirect fire with a kiss of smoke in your grill.

2. *Prepare the baste:* In a small saucepan, combine garlic, gin, vermouth, lemon juice, butter, juniper berries, horseradish and hot pepper sauce; bring to a boil. Remove from heat.

3. Rinse fish and pat dry with paper towels. Place fish in foil pan and stuff the cavity with the slices of 1 lemon and 6 sprigs of dill. Pour baste over fish.

4. When you see the first wisp of smoke from the wood, place pan on the indirect side of the grill. Close the lid and grill for 1 hour. Carefully turn fish over, close the lid and grill until fish is opaque and flakes easily with a fork, about 1 hour.

5. Transfer the salmon to a cutting board, discarding pan juices. Bone the salmon and serve the 2 fillets on a platter with the remaining lemon slices surrounding the fish and the aïoli spooned down the center of the fillets. Tuck the remaining 2 sprigs of dill on the platter for garnish.

Grill-Roasted Northwest King Salmon with Honey Soy Glaze

With a kiss of smoke from smoldering alder, wild-caught salmon truly is the king.

- **Perforated grill rack**
- **Suggested wood: alder**

Honey Soy Glaze

2 tbsp	liquid honey	25 mL
2 tbsp	soy sauce	25 mL
1 tbsp	vegetable oil	15 mL
1 tsp	lemon pepper	5 mL
1	salmon fillet (about 3 lbs/1.5 kg), skin on or off	1

1. Prepare a hot indirect fire with a kiss of smoke in your grill.

2. *Prepare the glaze:* In a bowl, whisk together honey, soy sauce, oil and lemon pepper.

3. Rinse fish and pat dry with paper towels. Place fish skin side down on grill rack and brush with glaze.

4. When you see the first wisp of smoke from the wood, place grill rack on the indirect side of the grill. Close the lid and grill-roast until fish is opaque and flakes easily with a fork, about 30 minutes. Transfer fish to a platter to serve.

Planked and Pepper-Crusted Maple-Glazed Salmon

SERVES 6

Planked salmon makes a perfect party appetizer for a crowd. The plank does double duty as the cooking vessel and the serving platter. A large salmon fillet will easily serve 12 as an appetizer.

● Maple, cedar or alder plank, soaked for at least 1 hour

2 lb	skinless salmon fillet	1 kg
¼ cup	pure maple syrup, divided	50 mL
½ tsp	kosher salt	2 mL
1 tsp	coarsely ground black pepper	5 mL

1. Prepare a hot indirect fire in your grill.

2. Rinse fish and pat dry with paper towels. If necessary, trim fish to fit the plank. Place fish skin side down on plank. Brush flesh side with half the maple syrup and sprinkle with salt and pepper.

3. Place plank on the indirect side of the grill. Close the lid and plank for 30 minutes. Drizzle with the remaining maple syrup, close the lid and plank until fish is opaque and flakes easily with a fork, about 15 minutes. Serve from the plank.

Harissa-Rubbed Snapper Skewers with Golden Papaya Salsa

SERVES 6 TO 8
AS AN APPETIZER

Golden Papaya Salsa cools down these fiery appetizers, great with a cold beer. You can find jars of harissa, a Middle Eastern chile pepper condiment, at grocery stores, gourmet shops and Middle Eastern markets — and a little goes a long way.

✦ TIPS ✦

It's always a good idea to oil the grill rack well before heating the grill, but it's especially important when you're grilling delicate foods like fish, so they don't stick.

Flat bamboo skewers, rather than the round kind, help keep delicate fish pieces anchored.

● Twelve 12-inch (30 cm) flat bamboo skewers, soaked for at least 30 minutes

2 lbs	skinless red snapper fillets, cut into 3-inch (7.5 cm) pieces	1 kg
½ cup	prepared harissa	125 mL
1	recipe Golden Papaya Salsa (page 61)	1

1. Prepare a medium-hot fire in your grill.
2. Thread fish onto skewers, leaving space between pieces, and brush with harissa. Grill for 3 to 4 minutes per side, or until fish is opaque and flakes easily with a fork. Serve with Golden Papaya Salsa.

Mesquite-Grilled Snapper with Avocado Corn Salsa

Snapper is a mild-flavored, medium-textured fish that does nicely on the grill. You can spice it up or serve it simply with a squeeze of lemon. The addition of wood to a hot fire imparts a lovely smokiness to the backyard. You'll only get a hint of it on the fish when it is grilled this way, but the odor lingers, and it is part of your sense of taste, so enjoy!

✦ TIP ✦

Metal smoker boxes have small holes all over so that maximum smoke is emitted. Since smoker boxes are made especially for gas grills (so wood chip residue does not fall through the grates and clog the gas jets), give them a try. Place the box filled with dry wood chips over the flame at the back of the grill and close the lid for 10 to 15 minutes; when smoke is coming from the box, start smoking.

● **Suggested wood: mesquite or oak**

Avocado Corn Salsa

2	ripe avocados, chopped	2
2	cloves garlic, minced	2
1 cup	cooked corn kernels (thawed if frozen)	250 mL
1/4 cup	chopped green onion	50 mL
2 tbsp	chopped fresh cilantro	25 mL
1 tsp	hot pepper sauce	5 mL
	Grated zest and juice of 1 lime	
	Kosher salt and freshly ground black pepper	
4	skinless snapper fillets (each 6 to 8 oz/175 to 250 g)	4
	Olive oil	
	Kosher salt and freshly ground black pepper	

1. *Prepare the salsa:* In a bowl, combine avocados, garlic, corn, green onion, cilantro, hot pepper sauce, lime zest and lime juice. Season to taste with salt and pepper. Set aside.

2. Prepare a hot fire in your grill and add a handful of water-soaked wood chips to the fire.

3. Rinse fish and pat dry with paper towels. Brush fish with olive oil and season to taste with salt and pepper.

4. When you see the first wisp of smoke from the wood, place fish flesh side down on the grill. Grill for 10 minutes per inch (2.5 cm) of thickness, turning once, until fish is opaque and flakes easily with a fork. Serve topped with salsa.

Grilled Sturgeon
with Charred Chile Salsa

SERVES 4

Wild sturgeon may be restricted because of its prized roe, but white sturgeon is farmed in California and has a taste and texture similar to those of turkey. Searing the sturgeon over hot coals, then finishing it over an indirect fire creates perfection.

✦ TIP ✦

You can use store-bought roasted peppers in a jar or roast your own. To roast peppers, preheat broiler or your grill to high. Broil or grill whole peppers until blackened, blistered and tender. Place peppers in a brown paper bag and close the top. Set aside for about 5 minutes, until cool. Slice peppers open to remove the core and seeds. Rub excess char off the skins. Use immediately or store in an airtight container in the refrigerator for up to 2 days.

- 13- by 9-inch (3 L) glass casserole dish
- **Suggested wood:** oak, alder or mesquite

Charred Chile Salsa

2	roasted red bell peppers (see tip, at left), chopped	2
1	jalapeño pepper, seeded and diced	1
1	tomato, seeded and chopped	1
1	red onion, chopped	1
	Grated zest and juice of 1 lime	
	Kosher salt and freshly ground black pepper	

Marinade

2	cloves garlic, minced	2
½ cup	chopped green onions	125 mL
½ cup	olive oil	125 mL
½ cup	balsamic vinegar	125 mL
2 tsp	freshly ground black pepper	10 mL
1 tsp	kosher salt	5 mL
1½ lbs	skinless sturgeon fillets	750 g

1. *Prepare the salsa:* In a bowl, combine roasted peppers, jalapeño, tomato, red onion, lime zest and lime juice. Season to taste with salt and pepper. Set aside.

2. *Prepare the marinade:* In a bowl, combine garlic, green onions, olive oil, vinegar, pepper and salt.

3. Rinse fish and pat dry with paper towels. Lay fish skin side down in a casserole dish and drizzle with marinade. Cover and refrigerate for 1 hour.

4. Meanwhile, prepare a hot indirect fire with a kiss of smoke in your grill.

5. Remove fish from marinade, discarding marinade, and sear over direct heat for 1 minute on each side. When you see the first wisp of smoke from the wood, transfer fish skin side down to the indirect side of the grill, close the lid and grill for 10 minutes per inch (2.5 cm) of thickness, turning once, until fish is opaque and flakes easily with a fork. Serve with salsa.

✦ Variation ✦

A traditional dill caper sauce is good with any fish, and certainly with salmon. To make the sauce, combine $\frac{1}{2}$ cup (125 mL) softened unsalted butter, $\frac{1}{4}$ cup (50 mL) finely chopped fresh dill, 3 tbsp (45 mL) crushed capers and the grated zest of 1 lemon. Serve a dollop on each fish fillet.

Grilled Swordfish with Sun-Dried Tomato Relish

SERVES 4 TO 6

Swordfish is usually sold in steaks. For this recipe, a 2-inch (5 cm) thick piece (or pieces) would do nicely.

✦ TIPS ✦

The relish can be stored in an airtight container in the refrigerator for up to 3 days. It's a lovely spread for a fish sandwich and is a great dip for crudités.

Do not overcook; swordfish dries out quickly.

● Foil pan

Sun-Dried Tomato Relish

½ cup	mayonnaise	125 mL
¼ cup	sun-dried tomatoes, chopped	50 mL
2 tbsp	drained capers	25 mL
2 tbsp	anchovy paste	25 mL
	Grated zest and juice of 1 lemon	
	Kosher salt and freshly ground black pepper	
2 lbs	swordfish steaks	1 kg
½ cup	dry white wine	125 mL
2 tbsp	olive oil	25 mL
2	cloves garlic, slivered	2
	Kosher salt and freshly ground black pepper	
	Fresh parsley sprigs	

1. *Prepare the relish:* In a food processor, combine mayonnaise, sun-dried tomatoes, capers, anchovy paste, lemon zest and lemon juice; pulse to blend. Transfer to a bowl and season to taste with salt and pepper. Cover and refrigerate until ready to use.

2. Prepare a hot indirect fire in your grill.

3. Rinse fish and pat dry with paper towels. Place fish in foil pan. Pour wine over fish, drizzle with olive oil and sprinkle garlic over top. Season to taste with salt and pepper.

4. Place pan on the indirect side of the grill. Close the lid and grill-roast for about 45 minutes, basting with juices every 10 to 15 minutes, until a meat thermometer inserted in the thickest part of the fish registers 150°F (65°C).

5. Cut swordfish into portions. Serve hot, garnished with relish and parsley. Or let cool, refrigerate for up to 2 days and serve cold, garnished with relish and parsley.

clockwise from top: Blue Ribbon Rub (page 34), Vinegar Barbecue Sauce (page 62) and Cherry Barbecue Glaze (page 52)

Arctic Char with Grilled Lemon Halves (page 78)

Thai-Style Halibut on Lemongrass Skewers (page 80)

Chilled Grilled Shrimp with Jalapeño Slaw
and Bloody Mary Salsa (page 124)

Wasabi-Grilled Scallops with Japanese Beans (page 115)

Sicilian Grill-Roasted Chicken (page 101)

Smoky Chicken and Poblano Chowder (page 141)

Jamaican Jerk Chicken (page 145)

Grilled Swordfish Steaks with Lemon Truffle Oil

This giant of a fish grows to be 16 feet (5 m) long! Now available all year long, swordfish's mild-flavored, dense flesh is perfect for the grill.

✦ TIPS ✦

Truffle oil is available in gourmet shops. If you can't find it, substitute olive oil for the truffle oil.

Add a fruit salsa to complete the meal. Make a bit more of the lemon truffle oil and use it to dress the seasonal fruit of your choice.

● 13- by 9-inch (3 L) glass casserole dish

3 tbsp	truffle oil	45 mL
3 tbsp	freshly squeezed lemon juice	45 mL
6	swordfish steaks (each 6 to 8 oz/175 to 250 g)	6
	Kosher salt and freshly ground white pepper	
3	lemons, quartered	3

1. Prepare a hot fire in your grill.
2. In a bowl, whisk together truffle oil and lemon juice.
3. Rinse fish and pat dry with paper towels. Place fish in casserole dish and drizzle with half the oil mixture. Reserve the other half as a finishing sauce. Lightly season each fish steak with salt and white pepper. Let stand while the fire is heating.
4. Grill fish for about 9 minutes per inch (2.5 cm) of thickness, turning once, until fish is firm and opaque. Do not overcook; swordfish dries out quickly.
5. Serve drizzled with the remaining lemon truffle oil, with lemon wedges on the side.

Herb-Rubbed Tilapia with Cucumber Relish

Tilapia is a very popular and reasonably priced fish. It's easiest to grill just the meatiest part of the fillet. Do so by removing the very thin strip of fish if it hasn't already been removed. It is so thin it tends to stick to the grill.

◆ TIP ◆

The relish can be stored in an airtight container in the refrigerator for up to 3 days.

Cucumber Relish

4	sprigs fresh dill (or 1 tsp/5 mL dried dillweed)	4
2 cups	chopped seeded peeled cucumber	500 mL
½ cup	sliced green onions	125 mL
½ cup	vegetable oil	125 mL
3 tbsp	freshly squeezed lemon juice	45 mL
½ tsp	kosher salt	2 mL
1 tbsp	dried basil	15 mL
1 tbsp	dried tarragon	15 mL
1 tsp	garlic salt	5 mL
	Freshly ground black pepper	
6	skinless tilapia fillets	6
	Olive oil	

1. *Prepare the relish:* In a blender or food processor, combine dill, cucumber, green onions, oil, lemon juice and salt; process until smooth. Set aside.

2. In a bowl, combine basil, tarragon, garlic salt and pepper to taste.

3. Prepare a medium-hot fire in your grill.

4. Rinse fish and pat dry with paper towels. Lightly brush fish with olive oil and sprinkle with herb mixture.

5. Place fish flesh side down on the grill. Grill for 10 minutes per inch (2.5 cm) of thickness, turning once, until fish is opaque and flakes easily with a fork. Serve with relish.

Wood-Grilled Trout

There are few recipes quite as simple and delicious as this one. Whole trout are filled with butter, lemon and herbs, then grilled over aromatic wood. Packet potatoes — thinly sliced potatoes drizzled with olive oil, seasoned to taste and enclosed in a foil packet — are the classic accompaniment.

✦ TIPS ✦

Use a wide fish spatula or two grill spatulas to turn the fish.

You can fillet the cooked fish in the kitchen before serving or serve intact and let diners remove the skin and bones.

- 2 hinged metal fish baskets, oiled, or 1 perforated grill rack, oiled
- **Suggested wood:** apple, maple or oak

4	whole trout, cleaned (each about 12 oz/375 g)	4
½ cup	unsalted butter, melted	125 mL
2	lemons, thinly sliced	2
1 cup	mixed fresh herbs (such as basil, parsley, dill and chives)	250 mL
	Kosher or sea salt and freshly ground black pepper	

1. Prepare a medium-hot fire with a kiss of smoke in your grill.

2. Rinse fish and pat dry with paper towels. Open each trout like a book and brush with butter. Arrange lemon slices and herbs over top and season to taste with salt and pepper. Close the trout and brush the exterior with butter. Place fish in fish baskets or on grill rack.

3. When you see the first wisp of smoke from the wood, place fish basket or grill rack on the grill. Close the lid and grill for 25 to 30 minutes, turning fish every 5 minutes, until fish is opaque and flakes easily with a fork.

✦ Variation ✦

Omit the butter and wrap each fish in bacon or pancetta, securing the meat with toothpicks.

Grill-Smoked Trout with Cilantro Gremolata

Removing the skin allows the smoke to penetrate the trout more easily. Just about any fish can be smoked this way. You will get about 8 oz (250 g) of fillet from a 1-lb (500 g) whole trout.

✦ TIPS ✦

A Microplane zester makes easy work of zesting. The zest is pungent, so you don't need lots of it. For marinades or bastes, it accentuates the final product.

You can fillet the cooked fish in the kitchen before serving or serve intact and let diners remove the skin and bones.

- Foil pan
- **Suggested wood:** apple, oak, mesquite or pecan

4	whole trout, cleaned (each about 1 lb/500 g)	4
¼ cup	cider vinegar	50 mL
4 tsp	All-Purpose Barbecue Rub (see recipe, page 34)	20 mL

Cilantro Gremolata

1	bunch fresh cilantro (about 1 cup/250 mL packed)	1
1	jalapeño pepper, seeded	1
	Grated zest of 1 lemon	

1. Prepare a hot indirect fire with a kiss of smoke in your grill.

2. Bring a large pot of water to a boil over high heat. Using tongs, dip each trout in boiling water for 20 to 30 seconds, or until skin begins to peel off. Peel skin from trout. Brush each trout with vinegar, sprinkle with rub and place, cut side down and splayed open, in foil pan.

3. When you see the first wisp of smoke from the wood, place the pan on the indirect side of the grill. Close the lid and grill for 1½ to 2 hours, or until fish is opaque and flakes easily with a fork.

4. *Prepare the gremolata:* On a wooden cutting board, using a chef's knife, finely chop cilantro, jalapeño and lemon zest together.

5. Sprinkle gremolata over fish and serve hot. Or let fish cool, refrigerate for up to 2 days and serve cold. Prepare gremolata right before serving and sprinkle it over the fish.

Smoked Trout
with Lemon Caper Butter

Smoke enough for leftovers, then make a delicious smoked trout spread for appetizers and finger sandwiches. Here's how: In a bowl, using a fork, stir together leftover smoked trout, softened butter, grated lemon zest, fresh dill or dried dillweed and salt — all to taste.

The easiest way to smoke fish fillets is to put them on your charcoal grill when the fire is slowly dying after you've already grilled something else. Add a little wood to the dying embers, close the lid and smoke for about 45 minutes, or until fish is opaque and flakes easily with a fork.

You can fillet the cooked fish in the kitchen before serving or serve intact and let diners remove the skin and bones.

- Foil pan
- **Suggested wood:** alder, apple, hickory, oak, peach or pecan

4	whole trout, cleaned (each 14 to 16 oz/400 to 500 g)	4
½ cup	unsalted butter, melted	125 mL
2 to 3 tbsp	Blue Ribbon Rub (see recipe, page 34)	25 to 45 mL

Lemon Caper Butter

½ cup	unsalted butter, softened	125 mL
¼ cup	drained capers, crushed	50 mL
	Grated zest and juice of 1 lemon	

1. Prepare an indirect fire for smoking in your grill or smoker.

2. Bring a large pot of water to a boil over high heat. Using tongs, dip each trout in boiling water for 20 to 30 seconds, or until skin begins to peel off. Peel skin from trout. Brush each trout with melted butter, sprinkle to taste with rub and place, cut side down and splayed open, in foil pan.

3. Place pan on the indirect side of the grill, close the lid and smoke for 1½ to 2 hours, or until fish is opaque and flakes easily with a fork.

4. *Meanwhile, prepare the butter:* In a bowl, whisk together butter, capers, lemon zest and lemon juice. Serve alongside trout.

Flame-Kissed Ahi Tuna Steaks with Wasabi Vinaigrette

SERVES 4

Connoisseurs agree that ahi tuna cooked rare is divine. That being said, if you like to cook your tuna a little more (hopefully not to more than medium-rare or medium), this recipe will still be delicious.

¼ cup	whole pink peppercorns	50 mL
¼ cup	drained whole green peppercorns	50 mL
4	ahi tuna steaks	4
2	lemons, halved	2
2 tbsp	olive oil	25 mL
4 cups	mixed greens	1 L
½ cup	Wasabi Vinaigrette (see recipe, page 39)	125 mL

1. Prepare a hot fire in your grill.

2. With a mortar and pestle or in a clean coffee or spice grinder, crush pink and green peppercorns.

3. Rinse fish and pat dry with paper towels. Coat each fish steak and the cut sides of the lemon halves with olive oil and crushed pepper.

4. Grill fish for about 3 minutes per side for rare. (Note the short cooking time; tuna will toughen if overcooked.) Put lemons onto grill, cut side down, when you turn the tuna.

5. Serve tuna over greens, squeezing lemons over the tuna. Drizzle with vinaigrette.

Grill-Smoked Whitefish with Horseradish Sauce

North America's northern lakes are teeming with whitefish. It's a feisty fish to catch and provides the fisherman and his friends with a delectable result.

✦ TIP ✦

The smoked whitefish and horseradish sauce are especially nice as an appetizer, served with crackers or toast points. It will serve about 12 people.

- 2 foil pans
- **Suggested wood:** maple, hickory or oak

4 cups	unsweetened apple cider, divided	1 L
8	skinless whitefish fillets	8
1 tbsp	lemon pepper	15 mL
1 tbsp	freshly ground white pepper	15 mL

Horseradish Sauce

¾ cup	sour cream	175 mL
3 tbsp	prepared horseradish	45 mL
	Chopped fresh flat-leaf (Italian) parsley	

1. Prepare a hot indirect fire with a kiss of smoke in your grill. Fill one foil pan with 3½ cups (825 mL) of the apple cider and place on the indirect side, next to the hot coals.

2. Rinse fish and pat dry with paper towels. Brush fish with the remaining cider and sprinkle with lemon pepper and white pepper. Place fish skin side down in the other foil pan, overlapping as necessary.

3. When you see the first wisp of smoke from the wood, place pan of fish on the indirect side of the grill. Close the lid and grill for 1½ to 2 hours, or until fish is opaque and flakes easily with a fork.

4. *Prepare the sauce:* In a small bowl, combine sour cream and horseradish.

5. Serve fish with a dollop of horseradish sauce and a sprinkle of parsley.

Cedar-Planked Fish with Mustard-Mayo Slather

Planking gives you the aromatic flavor of wood and is the easiest way to grill fish. Just place the fish fillet on the plank, slather on the flavoring paste and place the plank on the indirect side of the grill. You can also serve the fish from the plank, making cleanup easier.

● Cedar or oak plank, soaked for at least 1 hour

⅔ cup	mayonnaise	150 mL
⅔ cup	Dijon mustard	150 mL
2 tbsp	dried dillweed	25 mL
2 to 3 lbs	skinless fish fillet (salmon, char, halibut, monkfish or sea bass), trimmed to fit the plank	1 to 1.5 kg
4 to 5	sprigs fresh dill or flat-leaf (Italian) parsley	4 to 5

1. In a small bowl, whisk together mayonnaise, mustard and dill.

2. Rinse fish and pat dry with paper towels. Place fish skin side down on plank and slather with mayonnaise mixture. Arrange dill on top. Set aside.

3. Prepare a dual-heat fire, hot on one side and medium-low on the other, in your grill.

4. Place plank on the medium-low side of the grill. Close the lid and plank for 20 to 30 minutes, or until fish is opaque and flakes easily with a fork. Serve from the plank.

Vietnamese Grilled Fish and Cellophane Noodle Salad

This dish is delicious when the fish is hot off the grill, but equally tasty when everything is chilled for a summer meal. The marinade and drizzle are one and the same.

✦ TIPS ✦

The drizzle can be stored in an airtight container in the refrigerator for up to 3 days. Bring to room temperature before using.

Turn fish only once, halfway through the grilling time.

Serve the grilled fish with Carrot and Daikon Relish (see recipe, page 151).

Vietnamese Drizzle

2	cloves garlic, minced	2
2	small red chile peppers, seeded and finely diced	2
2 tbsp	grated gingerroot	25 mL
2 tsp	packed brown sugar	10 mL
2 tbsp	Vietnamese fish sauce, or nam pla	25 mL
2 tbsp	vegetable oil	25 mL
1 tsp	toasted sesame oil	5 mL
	Juice of 1 lime	
1½ lbs	skinless fish fillets (such as haddock, snapper or farm-raised catfish)	750 g
6 oz	cellophane noodles, prepared according to package directions	175 g
4	green onions, sliced on the diagonal	4
1 cup	finely diced seeded peeled cucumber	250 mL

1. *Prepare the drizzle:* In a bowl, whisk together garlic, chiles, ginger, brown sugar, fish sauce, vegetable oil, sesame oil and lime juice.

2. Prepare a hot fire in your grill.

3. Rinse fish and pat dry with paper towels. Remove ¼ cup (50 mL) of the drizzle and brush fish on both sides. Reserve the remaining drizzle for the salad.

4. Place fish flesh side down on the grill. Grill for 10 minutes per inch (2.5 cm) of thickness, turning once, until fish is opaque and flakes easily with a fork.

5. On a platter, combine noodles, green onions and cucumber. Arrange fish on top and dress with the remaining drizzle.

Baja Fish Tacos with Napa Slaw and Guacamole

SERVES 4

Here's the classic fish taco from the coast of Baja California.

✦ TIP ✦

If napa cabbage isn't available, use precut packed slaw mix instead.

Napa Slaw

2 cups	shredded napa cabbage	500 mL
½ cup	chopped green onions	125 mL
¼ cup	tarragon-flavored vinegar	50 mL
¼ cup	sour cream	50 mL
	Juice of 2 lemons	
1½ lbs	skinless halibut or mahi mahi fillets	750 g
	Olive oil	
2 to 3 tbsp	Cajun Spice Rub (see recipe, page 35)	25 to 45 mL
8	flour tortillas, warmed	8
1	recipe Grilled Guacamole (page 62)	1

1. *Prepare the slaw:* Place cabbage and green onion in a large bowl. In a small bowl, combine vinegar, sour cream and lemon juice. Pour dressing over slaw and toss to coat. Set aside.

2. Prepare a hot fire in your grill.

3. Rinse fish and pat dry with paper towels. Brush fish with olive oil and sprinkle to taste with rub.

4. Place fish flesh side down on the grill. Grill for 10 minutes per inch (2.5 cm) of thickness, turning once, until fish is firm and opaque.

5. Cut fish fillets into strips. Lay several strips on each flour tortilla and top with slaw and guacamole. Fold tortillas around filling and serve.

✦ Variation ✦

This recipe is also delicious with grilled chicken.

Shellfish

Grilled Clams with Warm Lime-Gingerroot Vinaigrette 110

Wood-Grilled Clams with Piquillo Pepper Butter 111

Warm Smoked Mussels with Curried Onion Butter 112

Wood-Grilled Oysters with Pancetta and Basil Aïoli 113

Sea Scallops Wrapped in Radicchio and Prosciutto 114

Wasabi Grilled Scallops with Japanese Beans 115

Stir-Grilled Scallops with Snow Peas
and Red Pepper Strips 116

Pistachio-Buttered Scallops on a Plank 117

Scallops alla Piastra with Lemony Prosciutto
Crumb Topping. 118

Smoked Scallops with Smoked Chile Butter Drizzle 119

Grilled Yabbies with Cilantro Lime Sauce 120

Balinese Shrimp Satay on Lemongrass Stalks 121

Orange-Basted Shrimp on the Barbie. 122

Grilled Shrimp and Pasta Soup with
Roasted Red Peppers *123*

Chilled Grilled Shrimp with Jalapeño Slaw
and Bloody Mary Salsa. 124

Stir-Grilled Coconut Shrimp 126

Wok-Grilled Shrimp with Sugar Snap Peas,
Teardrop Tomatoes and Red Onion Slivers 127

Planked Shrimp with Garlic Chive Butter and Ciabatta 128

Corncob-Smoked Shrimp with Classic Cocktail Sauce. 129

Grilled Spot Prawns in Garlic-Wine Marinade
with Zesty Peanut Sauce 130

Wood-Grilled Crab Cakes with Lemon Chive Butter 132

Champagne-Buttered Lobster Tails with Mâche Florets 133

Venetian Grilled Lobster 134

continued on next page…

Aussie Grilled Shellfish Salad with
  Lemon Dill Rémoulade 135
Char-Grilled Squid and Octopus Tapas
  in Peppered Sherry Marinade 136

Rich, sweet and succulent shellfish taste even better straight from the grill, plank or smoker. Shellfish take to contrasting, sharp flavors, such as citrus, spices, herbs, white wine and aromatic wood, and to complementary buttery flavors.

Mild to medium wood smoke flavors are best for shellfish, especially fruitwoods such as apple, cherry and peach, as well as alder, corncob, oak and pecan.

The best shellfish for grilling are squid and octopus, which need a hot, hot fire (if grilled for too long, they get tough); clams, mussels and oysters, which need a hot fire to open their shells; large sea scallops; large shrimp; and lobster.

The best shellfish for smoking are clams, mussels and oysters, which need a hot fire first to open their shells, large sea scallops and shrimp.

When done, shellfish should be opaque and firm, but still moist and tender. Pull them off the grill or smoker shortly before you think they're done, as they'll continue cooking for about 30 seconds longer, and that could mean the difference between done just right and overcooked.

✦ Consider the Oyster ✦

Now that oysters are farm-raised in both warm and cold waters, you don't have to limit them to months containing an "R." Wild oysters spawn in the summer months and can have an "off" flavor at that time. But farm-raised oysters spawn at different times, depending on where they're farmed, so there is usually a good supply all year long.

Beware of any raw oyster that is partially opened or looks or smells less than briny fresh. The best advice is to trust your fishmonger. And choose oysters from Maine, Prince Edward Island, Nova Scotia, British Columbia or northern California during the summer months.

Here are some varieties of North American oysters you can look for throughout the year:

Bras d'Or (Nova Scotia)

Caraquet (New Brunswick)

Cotuit (Massachusetts)

Dungeness (Washington)

Hammersley (Washington)

Kumamoto (California)

Malpeque (Prince Edward Island)

Olympia (Washington)

Royal Miyagi (British Columbia)

Wellfleet (Massachusetts)

✦ Types of Shellfish and Best Barbecue Methods ✦

Clams: Grill, herb-grill, grill pan or griddle, indirect grill, smoke, plank

Lobster: Grill, herb-grill, grill pan or griddle

Mussels: Grill, herb-grill, grill pan or griddle, indirect grill, smoke, plank

Octopus: Grill

Oysters: Grill, herb-grill, grill pan or griddle, indirect grill, smoke, plank

Scallops: Grill, leaf-wrap, skewer, indirect grill, smoke, plank

Shrimp: Grill, leaf-wrap, skewer, indirect grill, smoke, plank

Squid: Grill

Grilled Clams with Warm Lime-Gingerroot Vinaigrette

Shellfish in the shell require a hot fire to really open up. Drizzle the cooked clams with this fabulous vinaigrette, and you're done.

✦ TIPS ✦

Buy fresh clams and mussels and use within a day. Select tightly closed shells or slightly open shells that close when tapped. Discard any mussels with open, broken or chipped shells. Scrub clams and mussels under cold running water with a stiff-bristled brush. Remove the beards by pulling the threads toward the hinged part of the shell. Keep shellfish cool before barbecuing.

The vinaigrette can be stored in an airtight container in the refrigerator for up to 1 week.

● Perforated grill rack or 2 large foil pans

Warm Lime-Gingerroot Vinaigrette

1	clove garlic, minced	1
3 tbsp	grated gingerroot	45 mL
2 tbsp	minced shallots	25 mL
3 tbsp	chicken or vegetable stock	45 mL
3 tbsp	freshly squeezed lime juice	45 mL
2 tbsp	olive oil	25 mL
1 tbsp	liquid honey	15 mL
1 tbsp	soy sauce	15 mL
4 lbs	littleneck or Manila clams, scrubbed and debearded (see tip, at left)	2 kg
	Finely chopped fresh cilantro	

1. Prepare a medium-hot fire in your grill.

2. *Prepare the vinaigrette:* In a bowl, whisk together garlic, ginger, shallots, stock, lime juice, olive oil, honey and soy sauce. Set aside.

3. Arrange clams on grill rack and place over the fire. Close the lid and grill for 3 to 4 minutes. Stir and remove any clams that have opened. Close the lid and grill for 3 to 4 minutes, or until remaining clams open. Discard any clams that have not opened.

4. Place clams in a large serving bowl or on a deep platter, drizzle with vinaigrette and sprinkle with cilantro. Serve hot.

✦ Variations ✦

Grill these clams with a kiss of hickory, mesquite or pecan smoke.

Mussels are also delicious this way.

Wood-Grilled Clams with Piquillo Pepper Butter

SERVES 8 AS AN APPETIZER

With their flavor of the hearth and a little zip in the finishing butter, these clams make a fabulous tapas offering or appetizer. Serve with lots of crusty bread and chilled fino sherry or a cold beer.

✦ TIPS ✦

Piquillo peppers are small red peppers from Spain that have been roasted over an oak fire and pickled. You'll find them in jars at gourmet shops or online. If you can't find them, substitute ½ cup (125 mL) roasted red bell peppers, ½ tsp (2 mL) liquid smoke and ¼ tsp (1 mL) cayenne pepper.

If not serving the Piquillo Pepper Butter immediately, spoon into a ramekin and cover with plastic wrap. Store in the refrigerator for up to 1 week or wrap in additional freezer plastic or paper and freeze for up to 3 months. Let thaw, then slice into rounds while still cold.

Piquillo Pepper Butter is also delicious on grilled fish, pork or beef.

- Perforated grill rack or 2 large foil pans
- **Suggested wood:** oak

Piquillo Pepper Butter

2	piquillo peppers (see tip, at left)	2
1	clove garlic, minced	1
½ cup	unsalted butter, softened	125 mL
2 tbsp	chopped fresh flat-leaf (Italian) parsley	25 mL
4 lbs	littleneck or Manila clams, scrubbed and debearded (see tip, page 110)	2 kg

1. Prepare a medium-hot fire with a kiss of smoke in your grill.

2. *Prepare the butter:* In a food processor, purée piquillo peppers, garlic, butter and parsley until smooth. Scrape into a bowl.

3. When you see the first wisp of smoke from the wood, arrange clams on grill rack and place over the fire. Close the lid and grill for 3 to 4 minutes. Stir and remove any clams that have opened. Close the lid and grill for 3 to 4 minutes, or until remaining clams open. Discard any clams that have not opened.

4. Place clams in a large serving bowl or on a deep platter and dollop with Piquillo Pepper Butter. Serve hot.

✦ Variation ✦

Mussels are also tasty this way.

Warm Smoked Mussels with Curried Onion Butter

The best way to smoke mussels and other shellfish is to steam them first to snap open the shells, then smoke them for 20 to 30 minutes.

◆ TIP ◆

If not serving the Curried Onion Butter immediately, let cool, spoon into a ramekin and cover with plastic wrap. (Or spoon onto a piece of waxed paper, roll into a log and wrap in plastic wrap.) Store in the refrigerator for up to 1 week or wrap in additional freezer plastic or paper and freeze for up to 3 months. Melt in a saucepan over medium-low heat before serving. It also makes a flavorful spread for bread.

- **2 foil pans**
- **Suggested wood:** oak, alder, mesquite or apple

2	cloves garlic, minced	2
1 cup	dry white wine	250 mL
¼ cup	freshly squeezed lemon juice	50 mL
2 tbsp	snipped fresh chives	25 mL
4 lbs	mussels (about 4 dozen), scrubbed and debearded (see tip, page 110)	2 kg

Curried Onion Butter

1 cup	unsalted butter	250 mL
½ cup	finely chopped onion	125 mL
1	clove garlic, minced	1
1 tsp	curry powder (or to taste)	5 mL

1. Prepare an indirect fire for smoking in your grill or smoker.

2. In a large pot, bring garlic, wine, lemon juice and chives to a boil over high heat. Add mussels, cover and steam for 8 to 10 minutes, or until mussels open. Transfer open mussels to foil pans, discarding any that have not opened.

3. Place pans on the indirect side of the grill, close the lid and smoke for 20 to 30 minutes, or until mussels have a smoky aroma.

4. *Meanwhile, prepare the butter:* In a small pan, melt butter over medium-high heat. Sauté onion and garlic for 3 or 4 minutes, or until softened. Whisk in curry powder. Keep warm.

5. Place a dozen smoked mussels on each plate, along with a ramekin of warm butter.

Wood-Grilled Oysters with Pancetta and Basil Aïoli

SERVES 4 TO 6 AS A MAIN COURSE, 12 AS AN APPETIZER

With a crisp white wine, nothing's finer than these wood-grilled oysters.

✦ TIPS ✦

The aïoli recipe contains raw egg yolks. If the food safety of raw eggs is a concern for you, use pasteurized eggs. Many grocery stores now carry pasteurized eggs in their shells. Alternatively, use ¼ cup (50 mL) pasteurized liquid whole egg; the aïoli won't be quite as rich.

The aïoli can be stored in an airtight container in the refrigerator for up to 3 days.

- 2 baking sheets
- **Suggested wood:** alder, apple, hickory, oak, pecan or mesquite

Pancetta and Basil Aïoli

2	egg yolks	2
2	drained canned anchovies, minced	2
2	cloves garlic, minced	2
2 tbsp	chopped fresh basil	25 mL
1 tbsp	freshly squeezed lemon juice	15 mL
½ tsp	Worcestershire sauce	2 mL
½ tsp	red wine vinegar	2 mL
1½ cups	extra-virgin olive oil	375 mL
	Hot pepper sauce	
4	thin slices pancetta or bacon, cooked crisp and crumbled	4
36	fresh oysters on the half shell	36

1. *Prepare the aïoli:* In a food processor or blender, combine egg yolks, anchovies, garlic, basil, lemon juice, Worcestershire sauce and vinegar. With the motor running, through the feed tube, gradually add olive oil in a steady stream until the mixture thickens. (If the aïoli is too thick, thin with a little warm water.) Season to taste with hot pepper sauce. Stir in pancetta.

2. Prepare a hot fire with a kiss of smoke in your grill.

3. Arrange oysters on baking sheets and top each with a teaspoonful (5 mL) of aïoli, reserving the remaining aïoli.

4. When you see the first wisp of smoke from the wood, transfer oysters to the grill, using tongs. Close the lid and grill for 3 to 5 minutes, or until edges of oysters begin to curl. (For very large oysters, allow a few minutes more, but don't overcook.) Serve oysters with the reserved aïoli.

Sea Scallops Wrapped in Radicchio and Prosciutto

● 24 toothpicks, soaked for at least 30 minutes

24	large sea scallops, trimmed of hard side muscles	24
2 tbsp	olive oil	25 mL
	Kosher salt and freshly ground black pepper	
24	radicchio leaves	24
12	slices prosciutto, halved lengthwise	12

1. Prepare a hot fire in your grill.
2. Rinse scallops under cold running water and pat dry. Place in a large bowl. Coat with olive oil and season to taste with salt and pepper. Wrap each scallop in a radicchio leaf and wrap prosciutto around the leaf. Secure each wrap with a toothpick.
3. Grill scallops for about 2 minutes per quarter turn, until scallops are opaque and somewhat firm to the touch and prosciutto is crispy.

✦ Variation ✦

Substitute 24 slices of pancetta for the prosciutto.

Wasabi Grilled Scallops with Japanese Beans

*Clean, fresh flavors —
a hallmark of Japanese
seaside cuisine —
characterize this dish.*

✦ TIP ✦

The sauce can be stored
in an airtight container in
the refrigerator for up to
1 week.

Japanese Beans

1 lb	fresh or frozen Chinese long beans or French thin green beans (haricots verts), trimmed	500 g
2 tbsp	toasted sesame seeds	25 mL
1 tbsp	granulated sugar (or to taste)	15 mL
2 tbsp	soy sauce	25 mL
1 tbsp	yellow miso paste	15 mL
1 tbsp	vegetable oil	15 mL

Wasabi Sauce

2 tbsp	wasabi powder	25 mL
1 tbsp	packed brown sugar	15 mL
2 tbsp	vegetable oil	25 mL
1 tbsp	water	15 mL
1 tbsp	soy sauce	15 mL
	Toasted light or dark sesame seeds	
24	large sea scallops, trimmed of hard side muscles	24

1. *Prepare the beans:* Bring a large pot of salted water to a boil over high heat. Cook beans until tender-crisp, 2 to 3 minutes for fresh beans, 4 to 5 minutes for frozen. Drain and refresh in cold water. Pat dry and place in a large bowl.

2. In a small bowl, whisk together sesame seeds, sugar, soy sauce, miso paste and oil. Pour over beans and toss to coat. Set aside.

3. Prepare the sauce: In a bowl, whisk together wasabi powder, brown sugar, oil, water and soy sauce.

4. Prepare a hot fire in your grill.

5. Rinse scallops under cold running water and pat dry. Brush scallops with sauce.

6. Grill scallops for 2 to 3 minutes per side, turning once, until opaque, somewhat firm to the touch and with good grill marks. Serve scallops atop beans and sprinkle with sesame seeds.

Stir-Grilled Scallops with Snow Peas and Red Pepper Strips

Color is what makes a stir-grilled dish eye-catching and pretty.

✦ TIP ✦

Serve with soba noodles or rice for a complete meal.

● Grill wok or basket, well oiled
● Baking sheet

16	large sea scallops, trimmed of hard side muscles	16
2	red bell peppers, cut into strips	2
8 oz	sugar snap peas, trimmed	250 g

Marinade

1	clove garlic, minced	1
¼ cup	freshly squeezed lemon juice	50 mL
¼ cup	dry vermouth	50 mL
¼ cup	vegetable oil	50 mL
2 tbsp	chopped fresh parsley	25 mL
½ tsp	kosher salt	2 mL

1. Rinse scallops under cold running water and pat dry. Place scallops, red peppers and peas in a large glass bowl.

2. *Prepare the marinade:* In a bowl, whisk together garlic, lemon juice, vermouth, oil, parsley and salt. Pour over scallop mixture, cover and refrigerate for 1 hour.

3. Meanwhile, prepare a hot fire in your grill.

4. Place prepared grill wok over the kitchen sink and pour in scallop mixture, draining the marinade. Set wok on baking sheet and carry out to the grill.

5. Place wok on the grill. Grill, tossing with long-handled wooden spatulas every 3 to 4 minutes, for 12 to 15 minutes, or until scallops are opaque and somewhat firm to the touch.

Pistachio-Buttered Scallops on a Plank

SERVES 4

These scallops look pretty with the flecks of green in the butter. The presentation on the plank is very appealing, and the taste is great.

● Cedar or oak plank, soaked for at least 1 hour

Pistachio Butter

½ cup	unsalted butter, softened	125 mL
½ cup	chopped pistachio nuts	125 mL
	Kosher salt	
16	large sea scallops, trimmed of hard side muscles	16

1. *Prepare the butter:* In a small bowl, combine butter and pistachios. Season to taste with salt.

2. Prepare a hot indirect fire in your grill.

3. Rinse scallops under cold running water and pat dry. Place scallops on plank and spoon about 1 tbsp (15 mL) pistachio butter on top of each scallop.

4. Set plank on the direct-heat side for about 3 minutes, then move to the indirect side. Close the lid and plank until scallops are opaque and somewhat firm to the touch, about 10 minutes. Serve immediately from the plank.

✦ Variation ✦

Top the scallops with any flavored butter or aïoli to change it up.

Scallops alla Piastra with Lemony Prosciutto Crumb Topping

A piastra is an Italian stone griddle used on a grill, but feel free to use a cast-iron skillet, grill pan or griddle for this dish. Getting the piastra really, really hot produces the best sear on the scallops. Serve them with pasta, if you like.

- Piastra, cast-iron skillet, grill pan or griddle

Lemony Prosciutto Crumb Topping

2 oz	prosciutto, diced	60 g
3	green onions, chopped	3
1	small jalapeño pepper, seeded and diced	1
1 cup	panko bread crumbs	250 mL
½ cup	chopped fresh flat-leaf (Italian) parsley	125 mL
2 tbsp	olive oil	25 mL
	Grated zest and juice of 1 lemon and 1 orange	
16	large sea scallops, trimmed of hard side muscles	16
	Olive oil	
	Kosher or sea salt and freshly ground black pepper	

1. Prepare a hot fire in your grill. Place piastra over direct heat for at least 15 minutes to get very hot.

2. *Prepare the crumb topping:* In a bowl, combine prosciutto, green onions, jalapeño, bread crumbs, parsley, olive oil, lemon zest, lemon juice, orange zest and orange juice.

3. Rinse scallops under cold running water and pat dry. Brush scallops with olive oil and season to taste with salt and pepper.

4. Place scallops on piastra and sprinkle with crumb topping. Sear scallops for 3 minutes. Quickly turn scallops and sear on the other side for 2 to 3 minutes, or until scallops are opaque and somewhat firm to the touch.

5. Transfer scallops to a platter, scraping up the crumb topping and scattering it over the scallops.

Smoked Scallops with Smoked Chile Butter Drizzle

**SERVES 4 AS
A MAIN COURSE,
8 AS AN APPETIZER**

These succulent, smoky and spicy scallops are delicious with a glass of chilled, crisp Sauvignon Blanc.

- Foil pan
- **Suggested wood:** apple, cherry, oak, orange or peach

Smoked Chile Butter Drizzle

1	large garlic clove, minced	1
1/2 cup	unsalted butter, melted	125 mL
2 tbsp	freshly squeezed lime juice	25 mL
1 tsp	chipotle pepper powder or ancho chili powder	5 mL
	Kosher or sea salt	
16	jumbo sea scallops, trimmed of hard side muscles	16
	Chopped fresh cilantro	

1. Prepare an indirect fire for smoking in your grill or smoker.

2. *Prepare the drizzle:* In a bowl, whisk together garlic, butter, lime juice, and chipotle pepper. Season to taste with salt.

3. Rinse scallops under cold running water and pat dry. Place scallops in foil pan. Remove half the drizzle and brush scallops on both sides. Reserve the other half as a finishing sauce.

4. Place pan on the indirect side of the grill, close the lid and smoke until scallops are opaque, have a mild smoky aroma and are somewhat firm to the touch, 20 to 60 minutes (depending on the size of the scallops).

5. Portion scallops onto plates, drizzle with the reserved butter and garnish with cilantro.

Grilled Yabbies
with Cilantro Lime Sauce

From Australian waters, yabbies are freshwater crustaceans much like crayfish. If you like, substitute shrimp, spot prawns, langoustines or large crayfish. A large yabbie can weigh up to 3 ounces (90 g); smaller ones weigh 1 to 2 ounces (30 to 60 g).

Cilantro Lime Sauce

2	jalapeño or serrano peppers, seeded and finely chopped	2
½ cup	diced tomato	125 mL
2 tsp	chopped garlic	10 mL
1 tbsp	packed light brown sugar	15 mL
4 tbsp	olive oil, divided	60 mL
¼ cup	chopped fresh cilantro	50 mL
	Juice of 1 lime	
	Kosher or sea salt	
2 lbs	yabbies	1 kg
	Olive oil	
	Kosher or sea salt and freshly ground black pepper	

1. *Prepare the sauce:* In a saucepan, heat jalapeños, tomato, garlic, brown sugar and 1 tbsp (15 mL) of the olive oil over medium heat, stirring, for 2 to 3 minutes, or until sugar dissolves. Remove from heat and stir in cilantro, lime juice and the remaining olive oil. Season to taste with salt. Keep warm.

2. Prepare a medium-hot fire in your grill.

3. Bring a large pot of salted water to a boil. Add yabbies and cook for 5 to 6 minutes, or until they turn red. Using tongs, remove yabbies, run under cold water and transfer to a cutting board. With a large, sharp knife, remove and discard the tail shells. Brush yabbies on all sides with olive oil and season to taste with salt and pepper.

4. Place yabbies on the grill, close the lid and grill for 2 minutes. Turn yabbies, close the lid and grill for 2 minutes. Serve yabbies with sauce.

Balinese Shrimp Satay on Lemongrass Stalks

Asian-style street food translates into North American poolside or party food quite easily. You can find lemongrass stalks at Latin or Asian markets or simply use bamboo skewers instead. The skewers need to be soaked in water before you can place them on the grill, but there's no need to soak fresh lemongrass stalks.

✦ TIP ✦

Lemongrass can be found with the herbs at Asian markets and some well-stocked supermarkets. For thicker stalks, trim lengthwise into skewers.

- Six or twelve 12-inch (30 cm) fresh lemongrass stalks or flat bamboo skewers, soaked for at least 30 minutes

24	large shrimp, peeled and deveined	24
1	recipe Satay Sauce (page 50)	1

1. Prepare a hot fire in your grill.

2. Rinse shrimp under cold running water and pat dry. Thread shrimp onto skewers, leaving space between pieces. Remove half the sauce and brush shrimp liberally on both sides. Reserve the other half as a finishing sauce.

3. Grill skewers for 2 to 4 minutes per side, turning once and basting with sauce after turning, until shrimp are pink and opaque and have good grill marks. Serve skewers drizzled with the reserved sauce.

Orange-Basted Shrimp on the Barbie

SERVES 6 AS A MAIN COURSE, 12 AS AN APPETIZER

"Throw a shrimp on the barbie," said Crocodile Dundee (Paul Hogan) in a famous television ad for Australian tourism. If this dish is as close to Down Under as you get, the trip will be well worth it. Unless you use large spot prawns or langoustines, which can grill on their own without falling through the grill grates, the easiest ways to grill shrimp are on skewers or in a grill wok. Here they're skewered, but feel free to adapt the recipe to stir-grilling.

✦ TIP ✦

Thread shrimp onto the skewers without crowding so they'll grill evenly.

● Six or twelve 12-inch (30 cm) flat bamboo skewers, soaked for at least 30 minutes

Orange-Ginger Baste

2	green onions, finely chopped	2
2 tsp	grated gingerroot	10 mL
1 tsp	grated orange zest	5 mL
1 cup	freshly squeezed orange juice (from about 4 oranges)	250 mL
¼ cup	unsalted butter, melted	50 mL
2 tbsp	freshly squeezed lime juice	25 mL
2 tbsp	dry sherry or rum (white or dark)	25 mL
24	large shrimp, peeled and deveined	24

1. *Prepare the baste:* In a bowl, whisk together green onions, ginger, orange zest, orange juice, butter, lime juice and sherry.

2. Prepare a hot fire in your grill.

3. Rinse shrimp under cold running water and pat dry. Thread shrimp onto skewers, leaving space between pieces. Remove half the baste and brush shrimp liberally on both sides. Reserve the other half as a finishing sauce.

4. Grill skewers for 2 to 4 minutes per side, turning once and basting after turning, until shrimp are pink and opaque and have good grill marks. Serve skewers drizzled with the reserved baste.

Grilled Shrimp and Pasta Soup with Roasted Red Peppers

SERVES 6

This recipe puts leftover roasted red peppers and grilled shrimp to great use!

✦ TIPS ✦

Grill the shrimp as in Orange-Basted Shrimp on the Barbie (opposite), omitting the baste.

Look for canned fire-roasted tomatoes (such as Muir Glen or Hunt's) in health food stores or the organic section of well-stocked supermarkets.

Be an efficient barbecuer. Wrap and freeze leftover grill-roasted red peppers for later use in dishes like this one.

2 tbsp	olive oil	25 mL
3	cloves garlic, minced	3
1	large onion, chopped	1
4 cups	chicken stock	1 L
½ cup	orzo pasta	125 mL
2 cups	canned fire-roasted diced tomatoes (see tip, at left), with juice	500 mL
3	roasted red bell peppers (see tip, page 94), coarsely chopped	3
1 lb	large shrimp, grilled (see tip, at left) and coarsely chopped	500 g
	Grated zest and juice of 1 lime or lemon	
	Kosher salt and freshly ground black pepper	
	Chopped fresh herbs (such as basil, parsley or chives)	

1. In a large pot, heat olive oil over high heat. Sauté garlic and onion for 3 to 4 minutes, or until onion is somewhat translucent. Add chicken stock and bring to a boil. Add orzo and cook for 8 to 10 minutes, until tender to the bite. Add tomatoes with juice and heat until bubbling. Add peppers, shrimp, lime zest and lime juice. Season to taste with salt and pepper. Serve warm, sprinkled with chopped herbs.

Chilled Grilled Shrimp with Jalapeño Slaw and Bloody Mary Salsa

Big flavor is what this recipe is all about. Make up a batch of Bloody Marys or margaritas and kick back and enjoy.

● Large perforated grill rack, oiled

Jalapeño Slaw

2	jalapeño peppers, seeded and finely diced	2
1	package (8 oz/250 g) red cabbage slaw	1
1	package (8 oz/250 g) green cabbage slaw	1
⅔ cup	vegetable oil	150 mL
⅔ cup	cider vinegar	150 mL
1 tbsp	granulated sugar	15 mL
1 tbsp	dry mustard	15 mL
1 tsp	kosher salt	5 mL
½ tsp	celery seeds	2 mL
½ tsp	chipotle pepper powder	2 mL
3 lbs	large shrimp, peeled and deveined	1.5 kg
2 tbsp	olive oil	25 mL
	Kosher salt and freshly ground black pepper	
1	recipe Bloody Mary Salsa (page 59)	1

1. *Prepare the slaw:* In a large bowl, combine jalapeños, red cabbage slaw and green cabbage slaw.

2. In a small bowl, whisk together oil, vinegar, sugar, mustard, salt, celery seeds and chipotle pepper. Pour over slaw and toss to coat. Set aside.

3. Prepare a hot fire in your grill. Set grill rack directly over the fire.

The slaw can be stored in an airtight container in the refrigerator for up to 1 day.

One pound (500 g) of any type of packaged slaw could be used instead of the green and red cabbage for this recipe.

4. Rinse shrimp under cold running water and pat dry. Place shrimp in a large glass bowl, toss with olive oil and lightly season with salt and black pepper.

5. Working in two batches, place shrimp on grill rack and grill for 6 to 8 minutes, turning once, until shrimp are pink and opaque. Keep warm.

6. Spoon slaw onto each plate and arrange shrimp on top. Serve with salsa on the side.

✦ Variation ✦

Instead of placing shrimp on the grill rack, thread onto eight soaked 12-inch (30 cm) flat bamboo skewers. Grill for 2 to 4 minutes per side, turning once, until shrimp are pink and opaque and have good grill marks. Remove from skewers to serve.

Stir-Grilled Coconut Shrimp

**SERVES 8 AS
AN APPETIZER**

*Served over inky
black rice, this dish
makes a startlingly
good appetizer or
first course.*

✦ TIP ✦

If it is a cool, windy day,
the shrimp may need
to grill longer, and you
may want to close the lid
when you're not stirring.

- Grill wok or basket
- Baking sheet

Spicy Coconut Marinade

2	green onions, thinly sliced on the diagonal	2
1½ cups	coconut milk	375 mL
1 tbsp	finely minced jalapeño pepper	15 mL
1 tbsp	finely minced serrano pepper	15 mL
	Grated zest and juice of 1 lime	
1 lb	large shrimp, peeled and deveined	500 g
½ cup	unsweetened shredded coconut	125 mL
1 cup	black or jasmine rice, cooked	250 mL

1. *Prepare the marinade:* In a bowl, whisk together green onions, coconut milk, jalapeño, serrano, lime zest and lime juice.

2. Rinse shrimp under cold running water and pat dry. Place shrimp in a large sealable plastic bag and pour in three-quarters of the marinade. Seal, toss to coat and refrigerate for at least 30 minutes or up to 8 hours, tossing occasionally. Cover and refrigerate the remaining marinade until ready to use.

3. Meanwhile, prepare a medium-hot fire in your grill.

4. Place grill wok over the kitchen sink and pour in shrimp mixture, draining the marinade. Sprinkle shrimp with coconut. Set wok on baking sheet and carry out to the grill.

5. Place wok on the grill. Grill, tossing with long-handled wooden spatulas every 3 to 4 minutes, for 12 to 15 minutes, or until shrimp are pink and opaque.

6. Toss black rice with the reserved marinade and serve with the shrimp.

Wok-Grilled Shrimp with Sugar Snap Peas, Teardrop Tomatoes and Red Onion Slivers

With this recipe, you'll enjoy a colorful, flavorful one-dish meal.

◆ TIP ◆

Grill woks or baskets are usually about 12 inches (30 cm) in diameter and can accommodate enough food to feed 4. If you are cooking for 8 and need to double the recipe, it's better to cook in two batches or in 2 woks at the same time (if they fit on your grill together).

- Grill wok or basket, well oiled
- Baking sheet

1 lb	large shrimp, peeled and deveined	500 g
8 oz	sugar snap peas, trimmed	250 g
16	teardrop tomatoes (red and/or yellow)	16
½	red onion, slivered	½
¾ cup	Soy-Ginger Marinade (see recipe, page 39)	175 mL
3 cups	hot cooked white rice	750 mL

1. Rinse shrimp under cold running water and pat dry. Place shrimp, peas, tomatoes and onion in a large glass bowl. Pour in marinade, toss to coat and refrigerate for about 1 hour.

2. Meanwhile, prepare a hot fire in your grill.

3. Place prepared grill wok over the kitchen sink and pour in shrimp mixture, draining the marinade. Set wok on baking sheet and carry out to the grill.

4. Place wok on the grill. Grill, tossing with long-handled wooden spatulas every 3 to 4 minutes, for 12 to 15 minutes, or until shrimp are pink and opaque. Serve with rice.

Planked Shrimp with Garlic Chive Butter and Ciabatta

SERVES 6 TO 8 AS AN APPETIZER

This is a great appetizer to share with family and friends. The melted butter is delicious mopped up with the rustic bread.

✦ TIP ✦

Oven-baking planks are usually at least 1½-inches (4 cm) thick and have a carved shallow center that is perfect for saucing food while it sits on the plank. They should be used over indirect heat on the grill.

● Cedar oven-baking plank, soaked for at least 1 hour

1 cup	unsalted butter (2 sticks), softened	250 mL
½ cup	snipped fresh garlic chives	125 mL
1 lb	large shrimp, peeled and deveined	500 g
1	loaf ciabatta bread, sliced	1

1. In a small bowl, combine butter and garlic chives.

2. Prepare a hot indirect fire in your grill.

3. Rinse shrimp under cold running water and pat dry. Place shrimp on plank. Remove half the butter mixture and dollop over the shrimp. Reserve the other half as a finishing sauce.

4. Place plank on the indirect side of the grill. Close the lid and plank for about 30 minutes, turning shrimp once, until shrimp are pink and opaque. Serve from the plank, with bread and the reserved butter.

✦ Variation ✦

Substitute any compound butter you like.

Corncob-Smoked Shrimp with Classic Cocktail Sauce

This is a fabulous appetizer to make for guests or to bring to a gathering. In about 8 minutes, the shrimp are golden and smoky.

✦ TIPS ✦

The sauce can be stored in an airtight container in the refrigerator for up to 1 week.

If you plan to cook more than 1 lb (500 g) of shrimp in a stovetop smoker, smoking in 1-lb batches will give you optimum results.

- Stovetop smoker
- **Suggested wood:** finely ground corncob for the stovetop smoker

Classic Cocktail Sauce

1½ cups	chili sauce	375 mL
2 tbsp	prepared horseradish (or to taste)	25 mL
	Grated zest and juice of 1 lemon	
1 lb	large shrimp, peeled and deveined	500 g
	Extra-virgin olive oil	
	Kosher salt	

1. *Prepare the sauce:* In a bowl, combine chili sauce, horseradish, lemon zest and lemon juice. Refrigerate until ready to use.

2. Set up stovetop smoker using 1½ tbsp (22 mL) corncob.

3. Rinse shrimp under cold running water and pat dry. Brush shrimp with olive oil and season to taste with salt.

4. Place shrimp in a single layer on the grill rack. Close the lid almost all the way and turn the burner to high heat. When a wisp of smoke appears, close the lid. Reduce heat to medium-high and smoke for 6 minutes, or until shrimp are golden, almost opaque and somewhat firm to the touch. Turn off heat and keep the lid closed for 2 or 3 minutes, until shrimp are opaque.

5. Serve warm with sauce on the side. Or let cool, refrigerate for up to 1 week and serve cold with sauce on the side.

Grilled Spot Prawns in Garlic-Wine Marinade with Zesty Peanut Sauce

Spot prawns are large and plump, making them perfect for grilling. As soon as they become opaque, remove them from the grill — they will continue to cook for another 5 minutes.

● Perforated grill rack, oiled

Garlic-Wine Marinade

½ cup	unsalted butter	125 mL
4	green onions, chopped	4
1	clove garlic, minced	1
1 cup	dry white wine	250 mL
2 tbsp	chopped fresh parsley	25 mL
	Grated zest and juice of 1 lemon	
3 lbs	spot prawns or jumbo shrimp, peeled and deveined	1.5 kg

Zesty Peanut Sauce

¼ cup	unsalted butter	50 mL
1	onion, minced	1
1½ cups	chunky peanut butter	375 mL
1 cup	chicken stock	250 mL
1 tbsp	packed brown sugar	15 mL
1 tbsp	freshly squeezed lemon juice	15 mL
½ tsp	kosher salt	2 mL
¼ tsp	hot pepper flakes	1 mL

1. *Prepare the marinade:* In a saucepan, melt butter over medium heat. Sauté green onions and garlic for 2 minutes, until softened. Stir in wine, parsley, lemon zest and lemon juice. Let cool.

2. Rinse prawns under cold running water and pat dry. Place prawns in a large glass bowl and pour in marinade. Cover and refrigerate for at least 1 hour or up to 2 hours.

3. *Prepare the sauce:* In a saucepan, melt butter over medium heat. Sauté onion for 3 to 4 minutes, until softened. Stir in peanut butter. Add chicken stock, brown sugar, lemon juice, salt and hot pepper flakes; simmer, stirring frequently, for 15 minutes. If sauce is too thick, add water a little bit at a time to thin. Remove from heat and set aside.

4. Prepare a hot fire in your grill.

5. Remove prawns from marinade, discarding marinade. Arrange prawns on grill rack and place rack on the grill. Grill for 3 to 4 minutes per side, turning once, until prawns are pink and opaque. Serve with peanut sauce on the side.

Wood-Grilled Crab Cakes with Lemon Chive Butter

The best way to get wood flavor for these tender crab cakes is with a charcoal fire.

- Perforated grill rack, oiled
- **Suggested wood: oak, mesquite or alder**

Lemon Chive Butter

½ cup	unsalted butter, softened	125 mL
¼ cup	snipped fresh chives	50 mL
	Grated zest of 1 lemon	

Crab Cakes

1	egg, beaten	1
8 oz	backfin (lump) crabmeat, shells picked out	250 g
⅔ cup	fresh bread crumbs	150 mL
¼ cup	sliced green onion	50 mL
1 tbsp	Dijon mustard	15 mL
½ tsp	dried tarragon	2 mL
¼ tsp	hot pepper flakes	1 mL

1. *Prepare the butter:* In a small bowl, combine butter, chives and lemon zest. Set aside.

2. *Prepare the crab cakes:* In a bowl, combine egg, crabmeat, bread crumbs, green onion, mustard, tarragon and hot pepper flakes. Form into eight ½-inch (1 cm) thick patties. Cover and refrigerate for about 30 minutes, until firm.

3. Meanwhile, prepare a hot fire with a kiss of smoke in your grill. Place grill rack over the fire and let heat for 3 to 4 minutes.

4. When you see the first wisp of smoke from the wood, place crab cakes on the grill rack. Close the lid and grill for 4 to 5 minutes per side, turning once, until patties are crisp on the outside and hot in the center.

5. Serve 2 crab cakes per person, with a dollop of Lemon Chive Butter atop each.

✦ Variations ✦

For a beautiful presentation, serve with sliced yellow and red tomatoes.

Make crab cake sandwiches with aïoli on artisan buns.

Champagne-Buttered Lobster Tails with Mâche Florets

SERVES 4

Definitely sip on the remaining chilled Champagne while enjoying this French version of grilled lobster tails.

◆ TIP ◆

If you don't have lemon balm, substitute 1 tbsp (15 mL) grated lemon zest (or to taste).

4	rock lobster tails (each about 8 oz/250 g)	4
¼ cup	unsalted butter, melted	50 mL

Champagne Butter

1 cup	unsalted butter	250 mL
½ cup	Champagne	125 mL
¼ cup	chopped fresh lemon balm leaves	50 mL
8 oz	mâche florets (about 4 cups/1 L)	250 g
1 tbsp	freshly squeezed lemon juice	15 mL
1	loaf crusty French bread, warmed	1

1. Prepare a medium-hot fire in your grill.

2. Using kitchen shears or a cleaver, cut the lobster tails in half lengthwise. Brush lobster meat with melted butter.

3. *Prepare the Champagne butter:* In a small saucepan, melt butter over medium heat. Stir in Champagne and lemon balm. Remove from heat and keep warm.

4. Place lobster tails cut side down on the grill. Grill for 2 to 3 minutes to lightly char the meat. Turn and grill on the shell side for 7 to 9 minutes, or until meat is opaque and just firm to the touch (the shell may char).

5. Dress mâche with lemon juice and place in the center of each plate. Set a lobster tail on each portion of mâche. Serve with Champagne butter on the side for dipping and crusty French bread for sopping.

Venetian Grilled Lobster

So simple, yet so incredibly good. You grill the lobster just enough to slightly caramelize the sweet meat and lend a hint of wood smoke to the flavor.

✦ TIP ✦

If desired, place live lobsters in the freezer for about 15 minutes to numb them, then plunge them into the pot of boiling water.

● **Suggested wood: oak**

4	live lobsters	4
	Olive oil	
	Lemon wedges	
	Chopped fresh flat-leaf (Italian) parsley	

1. Prepare a hot fire with a kiss of smoke in your grill.

2. Bring a large pot of salted water to a boil over high heat. Plunge lobsters into water, cover and boil for 2 to 3 minutes, or until lobsters turn red. Using tongs, immediately remove lobsters, run under cold water and transfer to a cutting board. Using a large, sharp knife, cut off the claws and head. Discard the head. Split the lobster tail in half lengthwise. Brush the claws and tail on all sides with olive oil.

3. When you see the first wisp of smoke from the wood, place lobster claws and tails on the grill. Close the lid and grill for 2 minutes. Turn, close the lid and grill for 2 minutes, until meat is opaque. Serve drizzled with olive oil and lemon juice and sprinkled with parsley.

✦ Variation ✦

This lobster is delicious as is, but it's also wonderful served with many of the sauces in this book, such as Pancetta and Basil Aïoli (page 113), Warm Lime-Gingerroot Vinaigrette (page 110), Romesco Sauce (page 51) or Aji-li-Mojili (page 42).

Aussie Grilled Shellfish Salad with Lemon Dill Rémoulade

Make this a show-stopper and use grilled lobster, scallops and whole shrimp, with the heads on.

✦ Variation ✦

Any grilled fish would be delicious on this platter.

Lemon Dill Rémoulade

1 cup	mayonnaise	250 mL
1 tsp	chopped fresh dill	5 mL
1 tsp	snipped fresh chives	5 mL
1 tsp	chopped fresh parsley	5 mL
1 tsp	drained capers	5 mL
1 tsp	Dijon mustard	5 mL
	Grated zest of 1 lemon	
1	head butter lettuce	1
2	grilled lobster tails, meat removed and sliced	2
1 lb	shrimp, grilled	500 g
1 lb	sea scallops, grilled	500 g
3	lemons, halved	3
3	hard-cooked eggs, halved	3
1	bouquet of fresh herbs, tied with strands of fresh chives	1

1. *Prepare the rémoulade:* In a serving bowl, combine mayonnaise, dill, chives, parsley, capers, mustard and lemon zest. Cover and refrigerate until ready to use, for up to 3 days.

2. Arrange lettuce on a large platter. Arrange lobster meat in the center, with shrimp on one side and scallops on the other. Nestle the bowl of rémoulade into a lettuce leaf. Place 3 lemon halves and 3 egg halves on each side of the platter. Set the bouquet of herbs attractively on the platter.

Char-Grilled Squid and Octopus Tapas in Peppered Sherry Marinade

Both squid and octopus are usually sold already cleaned, or ask your fishmonger to do so. Rinse them again before marinating.

• Perforated grill rack, oiled

Peppered Sherry Marinade

6	cloves garlic, minced	6
1/4 cup	olive oil	50 mL
1/4 cup	dry sherry	50 mL
1 tbsp	dried oregano	15 mL
1 tsp	hot pepper flakes	5 mL
1 tsp	smoked Spanish paprika	5 mL
1/2 tsp	kosher salt	2 mL
16	baby squid (up to 3 inches/ 7.5 cm long), cleaned	16
1 1/2 lbs	small octopus, cleaned	750 g
	Finely chopped fresh flat-leaf (Italian) parsley	

1. *Prepare the marinade:* In a small bowl, combine garlic, olive oil, sherry, oregano, hot pepper flakes, paprika and salt.

2. Place squid and octopus in a large sealable plastic bag and pour in marinade. Seal, toss to coat and refrigerate for at least 3 hours or up to 4 hours.

3. Meanwhile, prepare a hot fire in your grill.

4. Remove squid and octopus from marinade, discarding marinade, and arrange on grill rack. Place grill rack over the fire. Grill octopus for about 2 minutes per quarter turn, until opaque and firm in the thickest part, with a bit of char. Grill squid for 1 to 2 minutes per side, turning once, until opaque, with a bit of char.

5. Transfer octopus to a cutting board. Using a chef's knife, chop octopus into small pieces and arrange on a serving platter. Arrange squid on the platter and garnish with parsley.

Poultry

Sicilian Grill-Roasted Chicken 139

Vineyard Smoked Chicken with Lemon Tarragon
   Cream Sauce 140

Smoky Chicken and Poblano Chowder. *141*

Waltzing Matilda Chicken with Lemon-Garlic Wine Sauce 142

Argentinean Chicken Asado 144

Jamaican Jerk Chicken 145

Chicken Agliata. 146

Grilled Bone-In Chicken Breasts with Lemon Caper Sauce . . . 148

Chicken Breast Stuffed with Brie and Black Olive Tapenade . . . 149

Indonesian Chicken with Chile-Ginger Sambal 150

Vietnamese Grilled Chicken Sandwiches with
   Carrot and Daikon Relish *151*

Grilled Chicken Paillards with Work of Art Drizzle 152

Tandoori Chicken on a Plank 153

Wasabi-Slathered Chicken on an Alder Plank 154

Stir-Grilled Chicken with Sugar Snap Peas
   and Grape Tomatoes 155

Stir-Grilled Peppadew Chicken in Baby Pineapple Halves 156

Stir-Grilled Chicken Fajitas 157

Peruvian Grilled Chicken Skewers in Mango Chipotle Mojo. . . 158

Chopsticks Chicken with Gingered Teriyaki Glaze 159

Thai Chicken Skewers 160

Yakitori-Style Chicken Skewers over Soba Noodles 161

Sizzling Pecorino Romano Chicken Thighs 162

Moroccan Chicken with Apricot and Pistachio Couscous 163

Grilled Miso Chicken. 164

Chicken Shawarma 165

Red-Hot Grilled Wings with Cold Blue Cheese
   Dipping Sauce 166

continued on next page...

Chinese-Style Barbecued Wings 167

Barbecue-Basted Wings. 168

Pancetta-Wrapped Cornish Game Hens. 169

Bourbon-Brined Pecan-Smoked Turkey 170

Herb Butter–Basted Turkey on a Spit 172

Tarragon Vinegar Grilled Turkey Breast 173

Smoked Prosciutto-Wrapped Turkey Breast 174

Grilled Turkey Steak Piccata 175

County Fair Barbecued Turkey Legs 176

Chicken, done to a burnished gold on the grill or smoker, turns out finger-lickin' good. Chicken is probably the most versatile protein to barbecue — you can skewer, plank, leaf-wrap, rotisserie-cook, grill, stir-grill, grill-roast or slow-smoke it.

The sweet, mild flavor of poultry goes well with citrus, herbs, fruits, wine, spices and vegetables, as long as the companion flavors don't overwhelm.

Poultry tastes best with mild to medium wood smoke flavors, especially fruitwoods such as apple, cherry and peach.

The best cuts of poultry for direct grilling are boneless skinless chicken and turkey breasts; the best cuts for indirect grilling are bone-in chicken and turkey pieces; and the best cuts for smoking are whole birds and bone-in pieces.

✦ Poultry Cuts and Best Barbecue Methods ✦

Boneless skinless breasts: Grill, skewer, herb-grill, indirect grill, plank, stir-grill

Boneless skinless thighs: Grill, skewer, herb-grill, indirect grill, plank, stir-grill

Turkey breast steak: Grill, indirect grill, smoke

Bone-in pieces: Grill, indirect grill, leaf-wrap, smoke

Whole bird: Grill, indirect grill, grill-roast, rotisserie, herb-grill, smoke

Sicilian Grill-Roasted Chicken

The sunny garlic-lemon-herb flavors of these juicy birds will have you crooning along with Dean Martin to "That's Amore." If you like, brush the chickens with olive oil and grill baby eggplant, pattypan squash and small tomatoes on the vine to round out the meal — and create a beautiful presentation on the platter.

✦ Variation ✦

If you prefer, you can grill the chickens over a hot indirect fire instead of using the rotisserie. Place the chickens on the indirect side of the grill. Close the lid and grill for 3 to 4 hours, basting with the reserved slather halfway through, until a meat thermometer inserted in the thickest part of a thigh registers 165°F (74°C) and the leg joint moves easily.

● Rotisserie

Slather

6	cloves garlic, minced	6
½ cup	finely chopped fresh flat-leaf (Italian) parsley	125 mL
¼ cup	freshly squeezed lemon juice	50 mL
¼ cup	olive oil	50 mL
2 tsp	ground fennel seeds	10 mL
2	whole chickens (each 3 to 4 lbs/1.5 to 2 kg), giblets and necks removed	2
	Kosher salt and freshly ground black pepper	

1. *Prepare the slather:* In a bowl, whisk together garlic, parsley, lemon juice, olive oil and fennel. Transfer ¼ cup (50 mL) of the slather to another bowl; cover and refrigerate.

2. Rinse chickens under cold running water and pat dry. Place in a large dish and brush with the remaining slather, coating evenly. Cover with plastic wrap and refrigerate for at least 30 minutes or up to 8 hours.

3. Meanwhile, set up your grill for rotisserie cooking.

4. Season chickens inside and out with salt and pepper. Tie the legs together with soaked kitchen string. Attach chickens to the spit (see page 24), leaving about 6 inches (15 cm) between the birds. Heat the grill to medium-high. Close the lid and grill for 3 to 4 hours, basting with the reserved slather halfway through, until an instant-read thermometer inserted in the thickest part of a thigh registers 165°F (74°C) and the leg joint moves easily. Transfer chickens to serving platters, tent with foil and let rest for 15 minutes.

5. Carve chickens and arrange the pieces attractively on a platter.

Vineyard Smoked Chicken with Lemon Tarragon Cream Sauce

SERVES 8		

Grapevine cuttings and rosemary branches add a special fragrance to your backyard and this chicken. The sauce is divine. Serve the same kind of dry white wine with the meal as you use in the marinade and sauce. Sauvignon Blanc, Viognier, Chardonnay or Pinot Grigio would all be good choices.

● **Suggested wood:** grapevine cuttings or wine barrel wood and fresh rosemary branches, soaked for at least 1 hour

2	whole chickens (each 3½ to 4 lbs/1.75 to 2 kg), giblets and necks removed	2
4	sprigs fresh tarragon	4
3	cloves garlic, sliced	3
1	large onion, slivered	1
1 cup	dry white wine	250 mL
1 cup	grape tomatoes, halved	250 mL
1 cup	drained kalamata olives	250 mL
1 cup	crumbled feta cheese	250 mL
1	recipe Lemon Tarragon Cream Sauce (page 50), warmed	1
	Additional sprigs fresh tarragon	

1. Rinse chickens inside and out under cold running water and pat dry. Place each chicken in a large sealable plastic bag. Add tarragon, garlic, onion and wine, dividing them evenly between the bags. Seal, toss to coat and refrigerate for at least 30 minutes or up to 8 hours, tossing occasionally.

2. Meanwhile, prepare an indirect fire for smoking in your grill or smoker.

3. Remove chickens from marinade, discarding marinade, and place breast side up on the indirect side of the grill. Close the lid and smoke for 3 to 4 hours, or until a meat thermometer inserted in the thickest part of a thigh registers 165°F (74°C) and the leg joint moves easily. Let rest for 5 minutes.

4. Carve chickens and arrange the pieces attractively on a platter. Scatter with tomatoes and olives and top with feta. Spoon warm sauce over chicken and serve garnished with tarragon sprigs.

Smoky Chicken and Poblano Chowder

On a cold winter day, make this chowder to warm body and soul.

✦ TIPS ✦

Look for canned fire-roasted tomatoes (such as Muir Glen or Hunt's) in health food stores or the organic section of well-stocked supermarkets.

Be an efficient barbecuer. Wrap and freeze leftover smoked or grilled chicken for later use in dishes like this one.

2 tbsp	olive oil	25 mL
3	poblano peppers, seeded and chopped	3
2	onions, chopped	2
2	cloves garlic, minced	2
2 cups	canned fire-roasted diced tomatoes (see tip, at left), with juice	500 mL
2 cups	quartered husked tomatillos	500 mL
2 cups	chopped smoked chicken	500 mL
6 cups	rich chicken stock (see tip, page 213)	1.5 L
2 cups	fruity white wine (such as Riesling)	500 mL
1 cup	drained canned white hominy	250 mL
1 tbsp	dried oregano	15 mL
1 tsp	ground cumin	5 mL
1 tsp	chipotle powder	5 mL
½ tsp	whole fennel seeds	2 mL
	Kosher salt and freshly ground black pepper	
	Diced avocado, chopped fresh cilantro and lime wedges	

1. In a large pot, heat olive oil over medium-high heat. Sauté poblanos, onions and garlic for about 10 minutes, or until tender. Add tomatoes with juice, tomatillos, chicken, chicken stock, wine, hominy, oregano, cumin, chipotle powder and fennel seeds; reduce heat and simmer for about 30 minutes, until flavors have blended. Season to taste with salt and pepper.

2. Ladle into bowls and garnish with avocado, cilantro and lime wedges to squeeze over top.

Waltzing Matilda Chicken with Lemon-Garlic Wine Sauce

Just as in the song, everyone will have a good time eating this smoky succulent bird. Serve an Australian Chardonnay or a New Zealand Sauvignon Blanc and any variety of Foster's beer and turn on the tunes. The addition of wood to the fire gives the chicken a kiss of smoke.

- 2 vertical chicken roasters
- **Suggested wood: pecan**

2	whole chickens (each 3½ to 4 lbs/1.75 to 2 kg), giblets and necks removed	2
1	bottle (750 mL) dry white wine (preferably Australian)	1
	Fresh herb sprigs, kiwifruit slices and lemon wedges	

Lemon-Garlic Wine Sauce

8 to 10	cloves garlic, minced	8 to 10
¾ cup	olive oil	175 mL
¾ cup	dry white wine	175 mL
¾ cup	freshly squeezed lemon juice	175 mL

1. Rinse chickens inside and out under cold running water and pat dry. Place each chicken in a large sealable plastic bag.

2. *Prepare the sauce:* In a bowl, whisk together garlic, olive oil, wine and lemon juice. Add ½ cup (125 mL) to each bag of chicken. Seal, toss to coat and refrigerate for at least 1 hour and preferably overnight, tossing occasionally. Cover and refrigerate the remaining sauce until ready to use.

3. Meanwhile, prepare a medium-hot indirect fire with a kiss of smoke in your grill.

4. Fill each roaster cylinder with half the wine. Remove chicken from marinade, discarding marinade, and position a chicken on top of each roaster, following the manufacturer's instructions.

If the chicken starts to get too brown, tent it with foil.

To cook on a can instead of a roaster, lower the chicken cavity onto the liquid-filled can. Pull the chicken legs forward to balance the bird so that it stands upright. Removing the chicken from the can is a bit trickier than from the roaster. Wear a heat-resistant mitt and hold on to the can while lifting the chicken off with tongs.

5. When you see the first wisp of smoke from the wood, set roasters on the indirect side of the grill. Close the lid and grill for 3 to 4 hours, basting occasionally with half the reserved sauce, until a meat thermometer inserted into the thickest part of a thigh registers 165°F (74°C) and the leg joint moves easily. Using tongs, carefully remove chickens from roasters. Let rest for 5 minutes. Discard juices from roaster.

6. Meanwhile, warm the remaining sauce.

7. Carve chickens and arrange the pieces attractively on a platter. Stuff sprigs of herbs around the platter for garnish, along with kiwi slices and lemon wedges. Drizzle chicken with sauce.

Argentinean Chicken Asado

A typical asado always has beef, but chicken, goat, lamb and pork find their way to the open fire too. Preparation is fairly simple, and large cuts of meat such as whole or half chickens are the mandate.

✦ TIPS ✦

If you don't have time to let the chimichurri stand for a day, transfer it to a small saucepan and warm over low heat to about 120°F (50°C) for 1 to 2 minutes, then let stand for about 1 hour to blend.

The chimichurri can be stored in the refrigerator for up to 2 weeks.

An asado always includes bread, a simple *mixta* salad of lettuce, tomato and onions, a cubed potato and hard-boiled egg salad, and chimichurri.

● **Suggested wood:** oak

Chimichurri

12	cloves garlic, chopped	12
1½ cups	olive oil	375 mL
1½ cups	red wine vinegar	375 mL
¾ cup	chopped fresh parsley	175 mL
2 tsp	dried oregano	10 mL
2 tsp	hot pepper flakes	10 mL
1 tsp	kosher salt	5 mL
1 tsp	freshly ground black pepper	5 mL
2	whole chickens, halved lengthwise (each half 1½ to 2 lbs/750 g to 1 kg)	2

1. *Prepare the chimichurri:* In a bowl, combine garlic, olive oil, vinegar, parsley, oregano, hot pepper flakes, salt and black pepper. Cover and let stand at room temperature for 1 day.

2. Rinse chickens under cold running water, pat dry and place in an extra-large sealable plastic bag. Add 1 cup (250 mL) of the chimichurri. Seal, toss to coat and refrigerate for at least 30 minutes or up to 8 hours, tossing occasionally. Refrigerate the remaining chimichurri until ready to use.

3. Meanwhile, prepare a dual-heat fire, hot on one side and medium-low on the other, in your grill. Add the wood to the hot fire when ready to grill.

4. Remove chicken from marinade, discarding marinade, and place cavity side down over the hot fire. Grill for about 6 minutes, or until starting to brown. Turn and grill for 6 minutes. Baste with 1 cup (250 mL) of the reserved chimichurri. Move chicken over the medium-low fire and close the lid. Grill for 1 to 2 hours, basting with chimichurri every 10 to 15 minutes, until a meat thermometer inserted in the thickest part of a thigh registers 165°F (74°C) and the leg joint moves easily. Let rest for 5 minutes.

5. Carve chickens and arrange attractively on a platter. Serve with the remaining chimichurri on the side.

Jamaican Jerk Chicken

Authentic jerk chicken means a whole chicken, cut up and on the bone. Since it's a slow-smoked dish, the dark meat of the thighs and drumsticks is moister and more flavorful than the white meat, so pull the white meat off the smoker first to avoid overcooking it.

● **Suggested wood:** oak, hickory or apple

Jerk Marinade

2	large onions, quartered	2
1	hot chile pepper (such as jalapeño, serrano or habanero)	1
½ cup	soy sauce	125 mL
¼ cup	vegetable oil	50 mL
¼ cup	cider vinegar	50 mL
1 tbsp	granulated sugar	15 mL
1 tbsp	ground allspice (preferably Jamaican)	15 mL
2 tsp	ground nutmeg	10 mL
2 tsp	ground cinnamon	10 mL
2 tsp	kosher salt	10 mL
1 tsp	hot pepper flakes	5 mL
4	sprigs fresh thyme	4
6 to 7 lbs	bone-in chicken pieces	3 to 3.5 kg

1. *Prepare the marinade:* In a food processor, combine onions, chile pepper, soy sauce, oil, vinegar, sugar, allspice, nutmeg, cinnamon, salt and hot pepper flakes; pulse until smooth. Add thyme sprigs.

2. Rinse chicken under cold running water and pat dry. Place in a large dish and pour in half the marinade, turning chicken to coat each piece. Cover and refrigerate for at least 4 hours or up to 6 hours, turning occasionally. Transfer the remaining marinade to a small bowl, cover and refrigerate until ready to grill.

3. Meanwhile, prepare an indirect fire for smoking in your grill or smoker.

4. Remove chicken from marinade, discarding marinade, and place skin side down on the indirect side of the grill. Close the lid and smoke for 1½ to 2 hours, turning and basting with the reserved marinade every 10 minutes, until a meat thermometer inserted in the thickest part registers 165°F (74°C).

Chicken Agliata

Agliata is a wonderful creamy condiment that comes from the French-speaking part of the Italian Alps, around Aosta. This Alpine herbal pesto is a stunning color and is absolutely delicious. Adding a little wood to the fire gives this dish a kiss of smoke.

● **Suggested wood: oak**

2	whole chickens, halved lengthwise (each half 1½ to 2 lbs/ 750 g to 1 kg)	2
2 tbsp	chopped fresh parsley	25 mL
3 tbsp	olive oil	45 mL
	Grated zest and juice of 2 lemons	
	Kosher salt and freshly ground black pepper	
1	loaf rustic Italian bread, sliced	1

Agliata

10	fresh basil leaves	10
5	fresh celery leaves	5
2	cloves garlic	2
1 cup	packed fresh parsley	250 mL
2 tbsp	freshly squeezed lemon juice	25 mL
½ tsp	olive oil	2 mL
8 oz	double-cream Brie or robioletta cheese (see tip, at right), cut into cubes	250 g
	Kosher salt and freshly ground black pepper	

1. Rinse chickens under cold running water, pat dry and place in an extra-large sealable plastic bag. Add parsley, olive oil, lemon zest and lemon juice. Season to taste with salt and pepper. Seal, toss to coat and refrigerate for at least 30 minutes or up to 8 hours, tossing occasionally.

2. *Prepare the agliata:* In a large mortar and pestle, pound basil, celery leaves, garlic and parsley to a paste. Add lemon juice and olive oil; mix well. Add cheese, 2 to 3 cubes at a time, mashing until blended. Season to taste with salt and pepper. Taste and add garlic, lemon juice, oil, salt and/or pepper as desired. Cover and refrigerate for 1 hour.

3. Meanwhile, prepare a dual-heat fire, hot on one side and medium-low on the other, with a kiss of smoke on the hot side.

4. Remove chicken from marinade, discarding marinade. When you see the first wisp of smoke from the wood, place chicken cavity side down over the hot fire. Grill for about 6 minutes, or until starting to brown. Turn and grill for 6 minutes. Move chicken over the medium-low fire and close the lid. Grill for 1 to 2 hours, until a meat thermometer inserted in the thickest part of a thigh registers 165°F (74°C) and the leg joint moves easily. Let rest for 5 minutes.

5. Carve chickens and arrange the pieces attractively on a platter. Serve with Italian bread and a communal bowl of agliata.

Grilled Bone-In Chicken Breasts with Lemon Caper Sauce

So easy, but so good. An indirect fire lets you sear the chicken on the hot side, then finish cooking it on the lower-heat side. Crisp the skin again on the hot side right before serving. With pasta and a green salad, this makes a great meal.

Lemon Caper Sauce

¼ cup	unsalted butter	50 mL
1 tbsp	drained capers	15 mL
1 tbsp	freshly squeezed lemon juice	15 mL
4	bone-in chicken breasts	4
	Olive oil	
	Kosher salt and freshly ground black pepper	

1. *Prepare the sauce:* In a saucepan, melt butter over medium heat. Whisk in capers and lemon juice. Remove from heat and keep warm.

2. Prepare a hot indirect fire in your grill.

3. Rinse chicken under cold running water and pat dry. Brush with olive oil and season to taste with salt and pepper. Place over the hot fire. Grill for 2 to 3 minutes per side, turning once, until seared on both sides. Move to the indirect side of the grill and close the lid. Grill for 25 to 35 minutes, or until a meat thermometer inserted in the thickest part of a breast registers 165°F (74°C). Serve drizzled with sauce.

Chicken Breast Stuffed with Brie and Black Olive Tapenade

Let this recipe be your blueprint to create variations: feta and roasted red bell peppers, Cheddar and bacon, and chopped green onions and Boursin are all delicious stuffing alternatives.

✦ TIP ✦

Serve sliced rounds of the stuffed chicken with a cold salad the next day. Refrigerate the cooked chicken without slicing, so it firms up. When ready to serve, cut into 1/4-inch (0.5 cm) slices and arrange on the salad of your choice.

6	boneless skinless chicken breasts	6
6	1/4-inch (0.5 cm) slices Brie cheese	6
3 tbsp	black olive tapenade	45 mL
	Olive oil	
	Kosher salt and freshly ground black pepper	

1. Rinse chicken under cold running water and pat dry. Slit a lengthwise pocket horizontally along the side of each chicken breast and stuff each with 1 slice of Brie and 1 1/2 tsp (7 mL) tapenade. Lightly coat chicken with olive oil and season to taste with salt and pepper.

2. Prepare a medium-hot fire in your grill.

3. Grill chicken for 6 to 7 minutes per side, turning once, or until a meat thermometer inserted in the thickest part of a breast (but not in the stuffing) registers 165°F (74°C). Let rest for 5 minutes, then cut into 1/2-inch (1 cm) slices on the diagonal.

✦ Variation ✦

Make roulades by pounding chicken breasts to 1/2 inch (1 cm) thick. Place Brie and tapenade down the center of each flattened chicken breast. Roll up and secure with soaked toothpicks. Grill for about the same amount of time, but with the lid closed.

Indonesian Chicken
with Chile-Ginger Sambal

SERVES 4

Adapted from a Singaporean street food recipe, this is a bold-flavored dish designed to be cooked fast.

Chile-Ginger Sambal

12	red serrano peppers, stemmed	12
5	cloves garlic	5
1	shallot	1
2 tbsp	grated gingerroot	25 mL
2 tsp	granulated sugar (or to taste)	10 mL
1 tsp	kosher salt	5 mL
4 tsp	freshly squeezed lime juice	20 mL
1 tsp	seasoned rice vinegar	5 mL
4	boneless skinless chicken breasts	4
	Vegetable oil	
	Kosher salt and freshly ground black pepper	
	Sliced cucumber and green onions	
	Steamed rice	

1. *Prepare the sambal:* In a small saucepan of boiling water, blanch serranos for 1 minute. Drain and transfer to a food processor. Add garlic, shallot, ginger, sugar, salt, lime juice and vinegar; purée until smooth.

2. Prepare a medium-hot fire in your grill.

3. Rinse chicken under cold running water and pat dry. Brush with oil and season to taste with salt and pepper. Grill for 4 to 5 minutes per side, turning once, or until a meat thermometer inserted in the thickest part of a breast registers 165°F (74°C). Serve with sambal, cucumber, green onions and steamed rice.

Vietnamese Grilled Chicken Sandwiches with Carrot and Daikon Relish

From Vancouver to San Diego, these sandwiches (known as banh mi ga*) have developed a devoted following. True fusion food from the French occupation of Indochina, the combination of French bread, grilled chicken, a sweet-and-sour crunchy relish (known as* do chua*) and aromatic cilantro make this an ideal hot-weather dish.*

✦ TIP ✦

Be an efficient barbecuer. Wrap and freeze leftover grilled chicken for later use in dishes like this one.

Carrot and Daikon Relish

½ cup	rice vinegar	125 mL
1 tbsp	granulated sugar	15 mL
½ tsp	salt	2 mL
1	carrot, julienned	1
1	small daikon radish, peeled and julienned	1
4	10-inch (25 cm) baguettes, sliced almost in half lengthwise	4
	Softened butter or mayonnaise	
4	grilled chicken breasts, sliced	4
1	jalapeño pepper, seeded and very thinly sliced lengthwise into strips	1
8	sprigs fresh cilantro	8

1. *Prepare the relish:* In a bowl, whisk together vinegar, sugar and salt. Stir in carrot and radish. Let stand at room temperature for 30 minutes.

2. Spread the cut sides of each baguette with butter. Arrange chicken on one half of the baguette and top with relish, jalapeño and cilantro. Close the baguette and press gently so that the juices permeate the bread. Serve immediately.

Grilled Chicken Paillards with Work of Art Drizzle

"Paillard" is a French term meaning a very thin boneless skinless piece of meat. You can have chicken, veal, lamb and even pork paillards. Pounded to just ½-inch (1 cm) thickness, paillards grill in just 5 minutes over a hot fire. That's real fast food!

♦ TIP ♦

Arrange crisp romaine lettuce on plates, ready for the sizzling chicken and the potent finishing drizzle of lemon, garlic and olive oil.

4	boneless skinless chicken breasts	4
	Olive oil	
	Kosher salt and freshly ground black pepper	
1	recipe Work of Art Drizzle (page 41)	1

1. Rinse chicken under cold running water and pat dry. If chicken breasts are thick, slice in half lengthwise. Place each piece between two sheets of plastic wrap and pound to ½-inch (1 cm) thickness.

2. Prepare a hot fire in your grill.

3. Brush chicken with olive oil and season to taste with salt and pepper. Grill for 2½ minutes per side, turning once, or until chicken is no longer pink inside. Serve immediately, with about 2 tbsp (25 mL) drizzle over each portion.

Tandoori Chicken on a Plank

The earthy spiciness of tandoori is delicious and beautiful when used as a topping for planked chicken. The yogurt mixture turns a light golden brown from the heat and produces moist, delectable chicken.

✦ TIP ✦

Tandoori chicken is delicious served cold over a salad or chopped up for a pita sandwich.

● Cedar or oak plank, soaked for at least 1 hour

4	boneless skinless chicken breasts	4
2 tsp	olive oil	10 mL
2 tsp	lemon pepper	10 mL
2	cloves garlic, minced	2
1	2-inch (5 cm) piece gingerroot, chopped	1
1 cup	plain yogurt	250 mL
2 tsp	ground cumin	10 mL
2 tsp	ground coriander	10 mL
1 tsp	cayenne pepper	5 mL
1 tsp	kosher salt	5 mL

1. Rinse chicken under cold running water and pat dry. Place on plank, leaving a bit of space between each piece. Lightly brush the top of the chicken with olive oil and season with lemon pepper.

2. In a food processor, combine garlic, ginger, yogurt, cumin, coriander, cayenne and salt; process until smooth. Spread evenly over chicken and around the edges, touching the plank to seal the chicken.

3. Prepare a dual-heat fire, hot on one side and medium-low on the other, in your grill.

4. Place plank over the hot fire for 3 to 4 minutes, or until plank begins to smoke and pop. Move plank over the medium-low fire and close the lid. Plank for 20 to 30 minutes, or until a meat thermometer inserted in the thickest part of a breast registers 165°F (74°C).

✦ Variation ✦

Instead of a dual-heat fire, prepare a hot indirect fire in your grill. Place plank on the indirect side, close the lid and plank for about 30 minutes.

Wasabi-Slathered Chicken on an Alder Plank

Serve this moist, juicy chicken with noodles or fried rice and thick slices of fresh garden tomatoes drizzled with an Asian vinaigrette.

● Alder, cedar or oak plank, soaked for at least 1 hour

Wasabi Slather

4	green onions, chopped	4
1 cup	mayonnaise	250 mL
2 tsp	freshly grated gingerroot	10 mL
2 tsp	wasabi paste	10 mL
2 tsp	soy sauce	10 mL
2 tsp	freshly squeezed lemon juice	10 mL
4	boneless skinless chicken breasts	4

1. *Prepare the slather:* In a food processor, combine green onions, mayonnaise, ginger, wasabi paste, soy sauce and lemon juice; pulse until smooth.

2. Rinse chicken under cold running water and pat dry. Place on plank, leaving a bit of space between each piece. Spread slather evenly over chicken and around the edges, touching the plank to seal the chicken.

3. Prepare a dual-heat fire, hot on one side and medium-low on the other, in your grill.

4. Place plank over the hot fire for 3 to 4 minutes, or until plank begins to smoke and pop. Move plank over the medium-low fire and close the lid. Plank for 20 to 30 minutes, or until a meat thermometer inserted in the thickest part of a breast registers 165°F (74°C).

Stir-Grilled Chicken with Sugar Snap Peas and Grape Tomatoes

A big-flavored, good-for-you one-dish meal! Serve with steamed rice, if you like.

 ◆ TIP ◆

If it is a cool, windy day, the chicken may need to grill longer, and you may want to close the lid when you're not stirring.

- Grill wok or basket
- Baking sheet

1 lb	boneless skinless chicken breasts, cut into 2-inch (5 cm) pieces	500 g
1	red onion, cut into small wedges	1
1 cup	grape or small cherry tomatoes	250 mL
1 cup	sugar snap peas	250 mL
1 cup	zesty Italian-style vinaigrette	250 mL

1. Place chicken, red onion, tomatoes and peas in a sealable plastic bag and pour in vinaigrette. Seal, toss to coat and refrigerate for at least 30 minutes or up to 1 hour.

2. Meanwhile, prepare a hot fire in your grill.

3. Place grill wok over the kitchen sink and pour in chicken mixture, draining the marinade. Set wok on baking sheet and carry out to the grill.

4. Place wok on the grill. Grill, tossing with long-handled wooden spatulas every 3 to 4 minutes, for 16 to 18 minutes, or until chicken is no longer pink inside.

Stir-Grilled Peppadew Chicken in Baby Pineapple Halves

In South Africa, a barbecue is known as a brai, and just might feature small, slightly sweet bottled red peppers known as peppadews, along with baby pineapples. Use any leftover peppadews in foil packet potatoes on the grill.

◆ TIPS ◆

You can find peppadews in many grocery store olive bars.

If you can't find baby pineapples, simply brush fresh pineapple rings with vegetable oil and grill them along with the chicken for 2 to 3 minutes per side, then serve the chicken on the grilled pineapple rings.

- Grill wok or basket
- Baking sheet

Worcestershire Marinade

2	cloves garlic, minced	2
¼ cup	Worcestershire sauce	50 mL
¼ cup	vegetable oil	50 mL
½ tsp	granulated sugar	2 mL
1 lb	boneless skinless chicken breasts, cut into ½-inch (1 cm) strips	500 g
1 cup	drained peppadews	250 mL
1 cup	chopped green onions	250 mL
4	baby pineapples, halved lengthwise and cores removed	4

1. *Prepare the marinade:* In a small bowl, whisk together garlic, Worcestershire sauce, oil and sugar.

2. Place chicken, peppadews and green onions in a sealable plastic bag and pour in marinade. Seal, toss to coat and refrigerate for at least 30 minutes or up to 1 hour.

3. Meanwhile, prepare a hot fire in your grill.

4. Place grill wok over the kitchen sink and pour in chicken mixture, draining the marinade. Set wok on baking sheet and carry out to the grill.

5. Place wok on the grill. Grill, tossing with long-handled wooden spatulas every 3 or 4 minutes, for 16 to 18 minutes, or until chicken is no longer pink inside.

6. Meanwhile, place pineapple halves cut side down on the grill. Grill for 2 or 3 minutes, or until slightly charred and warmed them.

7. Place 2 pineapple halves on each plate and top with chicken mixture.

Stir-Grilled Chicken Fajitas

This salsa is an adaptation of a traditional Mexican pipian sauce. Mexican pumpkin seeds, known as pepitas, are widely available in North America, in the organic section of well-stocked grocery stores, often in bulk.

✦ TIP ✦

If it is a cool, windy day, the chicken may need to grill longer, and you may want to close the lid when you're not stirring.

- Grill wok or basket
- Baking sheet

Marinade

4	green onions, chopped	4
2	cloves garlic, minced	2
	Grated zest of 2 limes	
¼ cup	freshly squeezed lime juice	50 mL
¼ cup	olive oil	50 mL
¼ cup	chopped fresh cilantro	50 mL
	Kosher salt	
4	boneless skinless chicken breasts, cut into ½-inch (1 cm) strips	4
4	red bell peppers, cut into strips	4
2	green bell peppers, cut into strips	2
1	large red onion, cut into slivers	1
6 to 8	large flour tortillas	6 to 8
2 cups	Pumpkin Seed Salsa (see recipe, page 60)	500 mL

1. *Prepare the marinade:* In a bowl, combine green onions, garlic, lime zest, lime juice, olive oil, cilantro and salt to taste.

2. Place chicken, red peppers, green peppers and red onion in a sealable plastic bag and pour in marinade. Seal, toss to coat and refrigerate for at least 1 hour or up to 2 hours.

3. Meanwhile, prepare a hot fire in your grill.

4. Place grill wok over the kitchen sink and pour in chicken mixture, draining the marinade. Set wok on baking sheet and carry out to the grill.

5. Place wok on the grill. Grill, tossing with long-handled wooden spatulas every 3 to 4 minutes, for 16 to 18 minutes, or until chicken is no longer pink inside.

6. Meanwhile, wrap tortillas in foil and warm on the grill for 5 minutes.

7. Serve chicken with warm tortillas and Pumpkin Seed Salsa on the side.

Peruvian Grilled Chicken Skewers in Mango Chipotle Mojo

SERVES 4 AS A MAIN COURSE, 8 AS AN APPETIZER

To be authentic, grill and serve these anticuchos de pollo on sugarcane skewers. You can find them at Hispanic markets; simply peel off the tough outer skin, then cut the cane into skewers. There's no need to soak fresh sugarcane.

◆ TIP ◆

If you use fresh sugarcane (available at Hispanic markets), make sure it has not been treated with chemicals. You may need to pierce the chicken first with a sharp skewer, then thread it onto the sugarcane skewers.

- Sixteen 12-inch (30 cm) fresh sugarcane skewers, or flat bamboo skewers, soaked for at least 30 minutes

Mango Chipotle Mojo

2	chipotle peppers in adobo sauce	2
2 cups	mango nectar	500 mL
2 tbsp	tomato-based barbecue sauce	25 mL
1 tbsp	freshly squeezed lime juice (or to taste)	15 mL
	Kosher salt and freshly ground black pepper	
2 lbs	boneless skinless chicken breasts, cut into 2-inch (5 cm) pieces	1 kg

1. *Prepare the mojo:* In a food processor or blender, purée chipotles, mango nectar, barbecue sauce and lime juice until smooth. Season to taste with salt and pepper. Taste and add more lime juice, if desired.

2. Place chicken in a large sealable plastic bag and pour in half the mojo. Seal, toss to coat and refrigerate for at least 30 minutes or up to 8 hours, tossing occasionally. Transfer the remaining mojo to a bowl, cover and refrigerate until ready to serve.

3. Meanwhile, prepare a medium-hot fire in your grill.

4. Remove chicken from mojo, discarding mojo, and thread onto skewers, leaving space between pieces. Grill for 3 to 4 minutes per side, turning once, until chicken is no longer pink inside and has good grill marks. Serve with the reserved mojo.

Chopsticks Chicken with Gingered Teriyaki Glaze

Sustainable, renewable bamboo is everywhere these days — in good-luck indoor plants, cutting boards, chopsticks and classic skewers for grilling. The teriyaki sauce in this dish gets extra flavor from fresh ginger, and it adds a burnished sheen to the food. Grill rings of fresh pineapple, brushed with oil, along with the skewers for an inspired pairing.

✦ TIPS ✦

If you use fresh bamboo shoots (available at Asian markets), make sure they have not been treated with chemicals. You may need to pierce the chicken first with a sharp skewer, then thread it onto the bamboo shoots.

It's always a good idea to oil the grill rack well before heating up the grill, but it's especially important when you're grilling foods with a sweet glaze or baste, so they don't stick.

● Twelve 12-inch (30 cm) flat bamboo skewers, soaked for at least 30 minutes, or fresh bamboo shoots

Gingered Teriyaki Glaze

½ cup	teriyaki sauce (store-bought or see recipe, page 252)	125 mL
2 tbsp	vegetable oil	25 mL
2 tsp	finely grated gingerroot	10 mL
2 lbs	boneless skinless chicken breasts, cut into 2-inch (5 cm) pieces	1 kg

1. *Prepare the glaze:* In a small bowl, whisk together teriyaki sauce, oil and ginger. Pour half into another bowl and refrigerate until ready to use.

2. Thread chicken onto skewers, leaving space between pieces, and brush with half the glaze. Refrigerate, uncovered, for 30 minutes. Discard any unused glaze.

3. Meanwhile, prepare a medium-hot fire in your grill.

4. Grill skewers for 3 to 4 minutes per side, turning once and brushing with the reserved glaze, until chicken is no longer pink inside. Serve hot.

Thai Chicken Skewers

SERVES 4

Grill the chicken and fruit on separate skewers, so everything cooks evenly. Then enjoy both with steamed rice flavored with lime juice and cilantro. The marinade does triple duty as a marinade, baste and finishing sauce.

✦ TIP ✦

If you use fresh bamboo shoots (available at Asian markets), make sure they have not been treated with chemicals. You may need to pierce the chicken first with a sharp skewer, then thread it onto the bamboo shoots.

• Twelve 12-inch (30 cm) flat bamboo skewers, soaked for at least 30 minutes, or fresh bamboo shoots

Coconut Curry Marinade

1	can (14 oz/400 mL) coconut milk	1
2 tsp	finely grated orange zest	10 mL
½ cup	freshly squeezed orange juice	125 mL
1 tbsp	Thai red curry paste	15 mL
4	boneless skinless chicken breasts, cut into 2-inch (5 cm) pieces	4
1 cup	cubed fresh pineapple (2-inch/5 cm cubes)	250 mL
1 cup	cubed fresh mango (2-inch/5 cm cubes)	250 mL
1 cup	seedless green grapes	250 mL
	Orange or lime wedges	

1. *Prepare the marinade:* In a bowl, combine coconut milk, orange zest, orange juice and curry paste.

2. Place chicken in a large sealable plastic bag and pour in half the marinade. Seal, toss to coat and refrigerate for at least 30 minutes or up to 8 hours, tossing occasionally. Cover and refrigerate the remaining marinade until ready to use.

3. Meanwhile, prepare a medium-hot fire in your grill.

4. Remove chicken from marinade, discarding marinade, and thread onto 8 skewers, leaving space between pieces. Thread pineapple, mango and grapes onto the remaining skewers and brush with some of the reserved marinade.

5. Grill chicken skewers for 3 to 4 minutes per side, turning once, until chicken is no longer pink inside and has good grill marks.

6. Meanwhile, grill fruit skewers for 2 to 3 minutes per side, turning once, until fruit has good grill marks.

7. Serve chicken and fruit skewers drizzled with the remaining marinade and garnished with orange wedges.

Yakitori-Style Chicken Skewers over Soba Noodles

**SERVES 4 AS
A MAIN COURSE,
8 AS AN APPETIZER**

*Traditionally eaten
as snacks in open-air
markets or izakayas
(Japanese pubs), these
chicken skewers can
be appetizers or main
dish fare.*

● Sixteen 12-inch (30 cm) flat bamboo skewers, soaked
for at least 30 minutes

Soba Noodles

1 lb	soba noodles, cooked and drained	500 g
½ cup	minced green onions	125 mL
¼ cup	rice vinegar	50 mL
1 tbsp	wasabi powder	15 mL
3 tbsp	soy sauce	45 mL
2 tbsp	toasted sesame oil	25 mL
¼ cup	toasted sesame oil	50 mL
¼ cup	soy sauce	50 mL
2 lbs	boneless skinless chicken breasts, cut into 2-inch (5 cm) pieces	1 kg

1. *Prepare the noodles:* Place noodles in a large bowl. In a small bowl, whisk together green onions, vinegar, wasabi powder, soy sauce and sesame oil. Pour over noodles and toss to coat. Set aside.

2. In a small bowl, whisk together sesame oil and soy sauce. Thread chicken onto skewers, leaving space between pieces, and brush with sesame oil mixture.

3. Prepare a medium-hot fire in your grill.

4. Grill skewers for 3 to 4 minutes per side, turning once, until chicken is no longer pink inside and has good grill marks. Serve skewers over noodles.

Sizzling Pecorino Romano Chicken Thighs

The key to this delicious recipe is to top the hot chicken with the hot butter and sprinkles of cheese as soon as it comes off the grill.

2 lbs	boneless skinless chicken thighs	1 kg
1 cup	Italian-style vinaigrette	250 mL
	Grated zest and juice of 1 lemon	

Sage Butter

½ cup	unsalted butter	125 mL
3 to 4	fresh sage leaves	3 to 4
½ cup	grated Pecorino Romano cheese	125 mL

1. Rinse chicken under cold running water and pat dry. Place in a large sealable plastic bag and add vinaigrette, lemon zest and lemon juice. Seal, toss to coat and refrigerate for at least 1 hour or up to 2 hours.

2. *Meanwhile, prepare the butter:* In a small saucepan, melt butter over medium-low heat. Add sage and cook until butter browns and is infused with sage flavor, about 20 minutes. Keep hot.

3. Prepare a hot fire in your grill.

4. Remove chicken from marinade, discarding marinade. Grill for 15 to 18 minutes, turning every 3 to 4 minutes, until juices run clear when chicken is pierced. Transfer to a platter, drizzle with hot sage butter and sprinkle with cheese.

✦ Variation ✦

If using bone-in, skin-on thighs, cook for about 10 minutes longer, or until a meat thermometer inserted in the thickest part of a thigh registers 170°F (77°C).

Moroccan Chicken with Apricot and Pistachio Couscous

Honey-sweet and savory with spice, this chicken dish is a meal in minutes. Just add a green salad. The marinade is multi-functional: one half flavors the chicken, the other half dresses the couscous. Here's looking at you, kid.

✦ TIP ✦

It's always a good idea to oil the grill rack well before heating up the grill, but it's especially important when you're grilling foods that have been marinated in a sweet mixture, so they don't stick.

Marinade

2	cloves garlic, minced	2
1	bunch green onions, chopped (about 1 cup/250 mL)	1
½ cup	dry white wine	125 mL
3 tbsp	liquid honey	45 mL
2 tbsp	olive oil	25 mL
2 tsp	ground cumin	10 mL
2 tsp	ground coriander	10 mL
½ tsp	ground cinnamon	2 mL
1 lb	boneless skinless chicken thighs	500 g
½ cup	dried apricots, snipped into small pieces	125 mL
½ cup	hot water	125 mL
1⅔ cups	instant couscous	400 mL
½ cup	shelled roasted pistachios	125 mL

1. *Prepare the marinade:* In a bowl, whisk together garlic, green onions, wine, honey, olive oil, cumin, coriander and cinnamon.

2. Rinse chicken under cold running water and pat dry. Place in a large sealable plastic bag and pour in half the marinade. Seal, toss to coat and refrigerate for at least 30 minutes or up to 8 hours, tossing occasionally. Cover and refrigerate the remaining marinade until ready to use.

3. Meanwhile, prepare a medium-hot fire in your grill.

4. Place apricots in a small bowl, pour in hot water and let soften.

5. Remove chicken from marinade, discarding marinade. Grill for 18 to 20 minutes, turning every 3 to 4 minutes, until juices run clear when chicken is pierced.

6. Meanwhile, prepare couscous according to package directions. Drain apricots. Toss couscous with the reserved marinade, apricots and pistachios. Serve with chicken.

Grilled Miso Chicken

**SERVES 4 AS
A MAIN COURSE,
8 AS AN APPETIZER**

*This recipe is great
for urban loft dwellers
with a balcony big
enough for a small
grill, for sophisticated
tailgaters or for
suburban backyarders
wanting to make a
tasty appetizer. In
cold weather, serve
with warm sake; in
warmer weather, with
a Japanese beer such
as Sapporo, Kirin,
Suntory or the harder-
to-find Asahi.*

Marinade

4	green onions, finely chopped	4
2	cloves garlic, minced	2
½ cup	Japanese or lager-style beer	125 mL
¼ cup	soy sauce	50 mL
¼ cup	light miso	50 mL
2 tsp	finely grated gingerroot	10 mL
2 lbs	bone-in chicken wings, legs or thighs	1 kg

1. *Prepare the marinade:* In a small bowl, whisk together green onions, garlic, beer, soy sauce, miso and ginger.

2. Rinse chicken under cold running water and pat dry. Place in a large sealable plastic bag and pour in marinade. Seal, toss to coat and refrigerate for at least 30 minutes or up to 8 hours, tossing occasionally.

3. Meanwhile, prepare a medium-hot fire in your grill.

4. Remove chicken from marinade, discarding marinade. Grill, turning often, until browned and crisp and juices run clear when chicken is pierced, about 20 minutes for wings, 30 minutes for legs or thighs.

Chicken Shawarma

This Middle Eastern sandwich is popular in Syria, Turkey and Iran and is similar to Greek gyros. "Shawarma" is an anglicization of a Turkish word that means "turning," as the meat for shawarma is grilled on a spit or on skewers.

✦ TIPS ✦

Soak the skewers in water for at least 30 minutes.

If desired, sprinkle the cooked chicken with tart ground sumac (a lemony seasoning made from ground sumac berries) or freshly squeezed lemon juice.

- Eight 12-inch (30 cm) flat bamboo skewers, soaked

Marinade

2	cloves garlic, minced	2
1 cup	plain yogurt	250 mL
1/4 cup	cider vinegar	50 mL
1/2 tsp	each ground cardamom and allspice	2 mL
	Kosher salt and freshly ground black pepper	
1 lb	boneless skinless chicken thighs, cut into 2-inch (5 cm) pieces	500 g
1	recipe Lemon Tahini (page 54)	1
8	pitas	8
	Olive oil	
	Thinly sliced cucumber, chopped tomato and chopped green onion	

1. *Prepare the marinade:* In a bowl, whisk together garlic, yogurt, vinegar, cardamom and allspice. Season to taste with salt and pepper.

2. Place chicken in a large sealable plastic bag and pour in half the marinade. Seal, toss to coat and refrigerate for at least 30 minutes or up to 8 hours, tossing occasionally. Cover and refrigerate the remaining marinade until ready to use.

3. Prepare a medium-hot fire in your grill.

4. Remove chicken from marinade, discarding marinade, and thread onto skewers, leaving space between pieces. Grill for 3 to 4 minutes per side, turning once, or until juices run clear when chicken is pierced and chicken has good grill marks.

5. Meanwhile, brush pitas with olive oil. Grill for about 1 minute per side, turning once, until warmed through but not crispy.

6. Remove chicken from skewers and arrange in the center of pitas, dividing evenly. Drizzle with the reserved marinade and top with cucumber, tomato and green onions. Fold pitas around filling into a half-moon shape.

Red-Hot Grilled Wings with Cold Blue Cheese Dipping Sauce

With a pungent blue cheese dressing that's a great dipping sauce for chicken wings or raw or grilled vegetables, this is tasty party fare. The dressing is also superb served over a crisp wedge of iceberg lettuce.

✦ TIPS ✦

If you prefer a thinner consistency for the dipping sauce, increase the vinegar by 2 to 3 tbsp (25 to 45 mL).

The dipping sauce can be stored in an airtight container in the refrigerator for up to 2 weeks.

Blue Cheese Dipping Sauce

8 oz	blue cheese (such as Maytag), crumbled	250 g
2 cups	sour cream	500 mL
⅔ cup	mayonnaise	150 mL
3 tbsp	cider vinegar	45 mL
1 tsp	hot pepper flakes	5 mL
	Onion salt	
	Worcestershire sauce	
3 lbs	chicken wings, cut at joints, tips discarded	1.5 kg
¼ cup	vegetable oil	50 mL
⅓ cup	Red-Hot Rub (approx.; see recipe, page 36)	75 mL

1. *Prepare the dipping sauce:* In a bowl, whisk together blue cheese, sour cream, mayonnaise, vinegar and hot pepper flakes. Season to taste with onion salt and Worcestershire sauce. Cover and refrigerate for 24 hours.

2. Rinse wings under cold running water and pat dry. Place in a large sealable plastic bag and add oil. Seal and turn several times to coat. Add rub, seal and toss to coat. (Add more rub if needed to coat all the wings.) Refrigerate for at least 3 hours or overnight.

3. Meanwhile, prepare a medium-hot fire in your grill.

4. Remove wings from marinade, discarding marinade. Grill for about 20 minutes, turning often, until juices run clear when chicken is pierced. Serve on a platter, with dipping sauce on the side.

Chinese-Style Barbecued Wings

**SERVES 6 AS
A MAIN COURSE,
12 AS AN APPETIZER**

Chicken wings are perfect for a casual supper. Add a salad or slaw dressed with wasabi vinaigrette, grilled or sautéed broccoli florets with butter and toasted sesame seeds, a French baguette and a bottle or two of Kirin beer. Have plenty of napkins or damp towelettes for everyone's sticky fingers.

Marinade

3 to 4	cloves garlic, minced	3 to 4
1	1-inch (2.5 cm) piece gingerroot, sliced	1
1 cup	soy sauce	250 mL
⅓ cup	toasted sesame oil	75 mL
3 lbs	chicken wings, cut at joints, tips discarded	1.5 kg
1	recipe Asian Barbecue Sauce (page 64)	1

1. *Prepare the marinade:* In a bowl, combine garlic, ginger, soy sauce and sesame oil.

2. Rinse wings under cold running water and pat dry. Place in a large sealable plastic bag and pour in marinade. Seal, toss to coat and refrigerate for at least 30 minutes or up to 8 hours, tossing occasionally.

3. Meanwhile, prepare a medium-hot fire in your grill.

4. Remove wings from marinade, discarding marinade. Grill for about 20 minutes, turning often and basting with some of the barbecue sauce during the last 5 minutes, until juices run clear when chicken is pierced. Serve on a platter, with a bowl of the remaining sauce on the side.

✦ Variation ✦

Grill whole chicken wings if you prefer, adding a couple of minutes to the cooking time. The joints should move easily when the wings are done.

Barbecue-Basted Wings

**SERVES 6 AS
A MAIN COURSE,
12 AS AN APPETIZER**

Coated in a zesty spice mixture, then basted with barbecue sauce while being slow-smoked, these wings make a mighty tasty appetizer.

● **Suggested wood:** hickory, oak, apple or mesquite

Blue Ribbon Wing Rub

½ cup	packed light brown sugar	125 mL
2 tbsp	chili powder	25 mL
2 tbsp	garlic salt	25 mL
2 tbsp	freshly ground black pepper	25 mL
2 tbsp	sweet Hungarian paprika	25 mL
2 tbsp	celery salt	25 mL
3 lbs	chicken wings, cut at joints, tips discarded	1.5 kg
2 cups	tomato-based barbecue sauce	500 mL

1. *Prepare the rub:* In a small bowl, combine brown sugar, chili powder, garlic salt, pepper, paprika and celery salt.

2. Rinse wings under cold running water and pat dry. Place in a large sealable plastic bag. Add rub, seal and toss until well coated.

3. Prepare an indirect fire for smoking in your grill or smoker.

4. Place wings on the indirect side of the grill. Close the lid and smoke for about 1 hour, basting with some of the barbecue sauce during the last 15 minutes, until juices run clear when chicken is pierced. Serve on a platter, with a bowl of the remaining sauce on the side.

Pancetta-Wrapped Cornish Game Hens

With adjusted cooking times, this recipe can also be used for quail, pheasant, chukar and chicken.

● **Suggested wood: apple, cherry or grape**

Marinade

2	cloves garlic, minced	2
½ cup	soy sauce	125 mL
¼ cup	olive oil	50 mL
¼ cup	Marsala	50 mL
	Grated zest and juice of 1 orange	
4	Cornish game hens, split in half	4
16	slices pancetta or bacon	16
	Olive oil	

1. *Prepare the marinade:* In a bowl, combine garlic, soy sauce, olive oil, Marsala, orange zest and orange juice.

2. Rinse hens under cold running water, pat dry and place in a large sealable plastic bag. Pour in marinade, seal, toss to coat and refrigerate for at least 30 minutes or up to 8 hours, tossing occasionally.

3. Meanwhile, prepare a medium-hot fire with a kiss of smoke in your grill.

4. Remove hens from marinade, discarding marinade. Wrap hens with pancetta, securing with soaked toothpicks if necessary.

5. When you see the first wisp of smoke from the wood, grill hens for 20 to 30 minutes, turning and basting with olive oil every 5 minutes, until a meat thermometer inserted in the thickest part of a thigh registers 165°F (74°C) and hens are no longer pink inside. Let rest for 5 minutes.

Bourbon-Brined Pecan-Smoked Turkey

SERVES 8 TO 10

Why wait till Thanksgiving for moist, succulent smoked turkey? Make this seasonal favorite all year long.

- **Large cooler**
- **Suggested wood: pecan**

Bourbon Brine

1	onion, chopped	1
1	bunch fresh flat-leaf (Italian) parsley, chopped (about 2 cups/500 mL)	1
1	lemon, quartered	1
4 cups	bourbon	1 L
4 cups	water	1 L
½ cup	kosher salt	125 mL
½ cup	packed dark brown sugar	125 mL
1 tbsp	whole black peppercorns	15 mL
1	whole turkey (10 to 12 lbs/5 to 6 kg), giblets and neck removed	1
	Ice cubes	
	Olive oil	

1. *Prepare the brine:* In an extra-large bowl, combine onion, parsley, lemon, bourbon, water, salt, sugar and peppercorns, stirring until salt and sugar are dissolved.

2. Rinse turkey inside and out under cold running water and pat dry. Place 2 to 3 bucketfuls of ice in the bottom of a large cooler. Place turkey in a large plastic bag (such as a food-safe garbage bag) and set on top of the ice. Pour in brine and close bag with a twist tie. Add ice as needed to keep cool and brine for at least 8 hours or up to 12 hours.

Brining with water, salt and sugar increases the meat protein's ability to hold water, making meat moister and more tender. Brining is particularly effective with very lean meat, so wild game and poultry are perfect candidates. Brine recipes that have lots of additional flavorings are actually more marinades than brines. Either way, they add moisture, tenderness and flavor to the meat.

3. Meanwhile, prepare an indirect fire for smoking in your grill or smoker.

4. Remove turkey from brine, discarding brine. Rinse thoroughly with cold water and pat dry. Lightly coat turkey with olive oil.

5. Place turkey breast side up on the indirect side of the grill. Close the lid and smoke for 4 to 5 hours, or until a meat thermometer inserted in the thickest part of a thigh registers 165°F (74°C), turkey is golden brown on the outside and meat is slightly pink. Transfer turkey to a serving platter, tent with foil and let rest for 10 to 15 minutes.

6. Carve turkey into thick pieces and arrange attractively on a platter.

Herb Butter–Basted Turkey on a Spit

SERVES 8 TO 10

Rotisserie turkey is wonderful any time. But it's really special at Thanksgiving, served with cranberry relish and all the traditional trimmings.

✦ TIP ✦

Thick slices of turkey stay warmer and moister than thin slices.

- Foil pan
- Rotisserie

1	whole turkey (10 to 12 lbs/5 to 6 kg), giblets and neck removed	1
3 tbsp	olive oil	45 mL
3 tbsp	smoked Spanish paprika	45 mL
2 tbsp	kosher salt	25 mL
2 tbsp	lemon pepper	25 mL

Herb Butter

½ cup	unsalted butter, softened	125 mL
1 tbsp	chopped fresh parsley	15 mL
1 tsp	dried oregano	5 mL
1 tsp	dried basil	5 mL
	Kosher salt	

1. Rinse turkey inside and out under cold running water and pat dry. Place in foil pan and coat lightly with oil.

2. In a glass jar with a tight-fitting lid, combine paprika, salt and lemon pepper; cover and shake to blend. Sprinkle on turkey, inside and out. Let stand for 20 minutes.

3. Meanwhile, set up your grill for rotisserie cooking.

4. *Prepare the butter:* In a bowl, combine butter, parsley, oregano and basil. Season to taste with salt.

5. Tie turkey legs together with soaked kitchen string. Attach turkey to the spit (see page 24). Heat grill to medium-high. Close the lid and grill for about 4 hours, basting lightly with butter every 30 minutes, until a meat thermometer inserted in the thickest part of a thigh registers 165°F (74°C) and juices run clear when a thigh is pierced. Transfer turkey to a serving platter, tent with foil and let rest for 10 to 15 minutes.

6. Carve turkey into thick pieces and arrange attractively on a platter.

Tarragon Vinegar Grilled Turkey Breast

Carolina-style barbecue gets an update in this recipe, with tarragon vinegar adding lots of tangy flavor to the bird. You need to tend to the turkey during the entire grilling process, so serve with make-ahead side dishes.

✦ TIPS ✦

Serve this tangy turkey with shredded red and green cabbage dressed with some of the reserved marinade. Grill whole ears of corn, basting them with the marinade too.

When grilling or smoking 2 turkey breasts (or roasts or briskets), make sure both pieces of meat weigh about the same, so that the cooking time will be similar.

● **Suggested wood:** hickory

Tarragon Vinegar Marinade

⅓ cup	dry white wine	75 mL
⅓ cup	tarragon-flavored vinegar	75 mL
⅓ cup	peanut oil	75 mL
1 tbsp	poultry seasoning	15 mL
1 tbsp	freshly ground black pepper	15 mL
2 tsp	garlic salt	10 mL
2 tsp	dried tarragon	10 mL
1 tsp	hot pepper sauce	5 mL
1 tsp	freshly squeezed lemon juice	5 mL
2	bone-in turkey breasts (each about 4 lbs/2 kg)	2

1. *Prepare the marinade:* In a bowl, whisk together wine, vinegar, peanut oil, poultry seasoning, black pepper, garlic salt, tarragon, hot pepper sauce and lemon juice.

2. Rinse turkey under cold running water and pat dry. Place in a sealable plastic bag and pour in half the marinade. Seal, toss to coat and refrigerate for at least 30 minutes or up to 8 hours, tossing occasionally. Cover and refrigerate the remaining marinade until ready to use.

3. Meanwhile, prepare a hot fire with a kiss of smoke in your grill.

4. Remove turkey from marinade, discarding marinade. When you see the first wisp of smoke from the wood, place turkey on the grill. Grill for 45 to 60 minutes, turning and basting with the reserved marinade every 5 minutes, until a meat thermometer inserted in the thickest part of a breast registers 165°F (74°C). Let rest for 5 minutes before slicing.

Smoked Prosciutto-Wrapped Turkey Breast

SERVES 4

Wrapping the turkey breast in prosciutto helps keep the meat perfectly moist.

✦ TIP ✦

You can use store-bought roasted peppers in a jar or roast your own. To roast peppers, preheat broiler or your grill to high. Broil or grill whole peppers until blackened, blistered and tender. Place peppers in a brown paper bag and close the top. Set aside for about 5 minutes, until cool. Slice peppers open to remove the core and seeds. Rub excess char off the skins. Use immediately or store in an airtight container in the refrigerator for up to 2 days.

- Foil pan
- **Suggested wood: oak, apple or pecan**

2	boneless turkey breasts (each about 3 lbs/1.5 kg)	2
6	slices Monterey Jack cheese	6
4	strips bacon, cooked crisp	4
2	canned large artichoke hearts, quartered	2
1	roasted red bell pepper (see tip, at left), cut into strips	1
1 tbsp	olive oil	15 mL
4 oz	prosciutto, thinly sliced	125 g

1. Prepare an indirect fire for smoking in your grill or smoker.

2. Rinse turkey under cold running water and pat dry. Slit a lengthwise pocket horizontally along the side of each turkey breast and stuff each with half the cheese, bacon, artichoke hearts and roasted pepper. Lightly coat turkey with olive oil and wrap each breast with half the prosciutto, securing with soaked toothpicks if necessary. Place turkey in foil pan.

3. Place pan on the indirect side of the grill. Close the lid and smoke for 1½ to 2 hours, or until a meat thermometer inserted in the thickest part of a breast (but not in the stuffing) registers 165°F (74°C). Let rest for 10 minutes, then cut into ⅜-inch (0.75 cm) thick slices. Serve warm or let cool, refrigerate for up to 3 days and serve cold.

Grilled Turkey Steak Piccata

This is a variation on classic sautéed chicken piccata with a sauce of white wine, capers and butter. For the grill, the sauce is made in a skillet on a side burner or directly over the heat of the grill.

✦ TIP ✦

Grilled asparagus and garlic mashed potatoes would be superb with this dish. Double the sauce recipe so there's plenty to drizzle over the turkey and side dishes.

● **Baking sheet**

½ cup	all-purpose flour	125 mL
⅓ cup	freshly grated Parmesan cheese	75 mL
1 tsp	kosher salt	5 mL
1 tsp	freshly ground black pepper	5 mL
4	turkey breast steaks (each about 6 oz/175 g and ½ inch/1 cm thick)	4
	Olive oil	
½ cup	dry white wine or chicken stock	125 mL
¼ cup	drained capers	50 mL
¼ cup	butter	50 mL
3 tbsp	freshly squeezed lemon juice	45 mL
¼ cup	fresh chopped parsley	50 mL

1. In a shallow bowl, combine flour, cheese, salt and pepper.

2. Rinse turkey under cold running water and pat dry. Lightly coat with olive oil and dredge in seasoned flour. Place on baking sheet and drizzle with olive oil on both sides. Discard any excess flour mixture.

3. Prepare a hot fire in your grill (if you don't have a side burner, prepare a dual-heat fire, hot on one side and medium-hot on the other).

4. In a small skillet, combine wine, capers, butter and lemon juice. Carry out to the grill with the turkey.

5. Grill turkey over the hot fire for 6 to 8 minutes, turning once, until turkey is no longer pink.

6. Meanwhile, on a side burner over medium-high heat, or over the medium-hot fire, heat sauce until bubbly.

7. Serve turkey drizzled with sauce and sprinkled with parsley.

County Fair Barbecued Turkey Legs

At county fairs, Renaissance festivals and summer gatherings throughout North America, barbecued turkey legs help provide a sense of occasion. You can get the same feeling — without the long lines and funnel cakes — by making these in your own backyard.

● **Suggested wood:** oak, pecan or apple

4	turkey drumsticks	4
	Olive oil	
3 tbsp	sweet Hungarian paprika	45 mL
2 tbsp	fine sea salt	25 mL
2 tbsp	lemon pepper	25 mL

1. Rinse turkey under cold running water and pat dry. Brush with olive oil and sprinkle with paprika, salt and lemon pepper.

2. Prepare an indirect fire for smoking in your grill or smoker.

3. Place turkey on the indirect side of the grill. Close the lid and smoke for 3 to 4 hours, or until a meat thermometer inserted in the thickest part of a thigh registers 165°F (74°C). Let rest for 5 minutes.

Pork

Blue Ribbon Pulled Pork 179

BBQ Poutine *180*

Memphis Piggy Sandwiches with Vinegar Coleslaw *181*

Smoked Pork and Black-Eyed Pea Gumbo for a Crowd *182*

Cuban Barbecued Pork Shoulder 184

Cherry-Smoked Crown Roast of Pork 185

Mayan-Style Pit Pork 186

Spit-Roasted Pork Loin in Maple Mustard Brine 188

Guava-Glazed Rotisserie Pork Loin Roast 189

Apple-Smoked Roasted Pork Loin with
    Apple Chutney Stuffing 190

Graisse de Roti 192

Tuscan Rolled Pork Loin Stuffed with Rosemary and Garlic . . . 193

Mustard-Grilled Pork Paillards with Tarragon Mustard Drizzle . . . 194

Hawaiian Pork Skewers with Pineapple Rum Glaze 195

Raspberry-Glazed Pork Tenderloin with
    Spicy Raspberry Jalapeño Barbecue Sauce 196

Sesame-Soy Marinated Pork Tenderloin
    with Asian Dipping Sauce 197

Aussie Paperbark Pork with Lemon Myrtle Chutney 198

Grilled Pork and Mango Skewers with Mango
    Chipotle Barbecue Sauce 199

Wood-Grilled Filipino Pork Steaks with
    Pineapple Tangerine Glaze 200

Grilled Double Pork Chops 201

Hickory-Grilled Double Pork Chops with
    Fire-Roasted Tomato and Bacon Vinaigrette 202

Maple Ginger Butterflied Pork Chops 203

Hickory Pork Burgers with Carolina Mustard Barbecue Sauce . . 204

Kiss of Smoke Indoor/Outdoor Ribs 205

Sweet, Smoky, Sticky Baby Back Ribs 206

Championship BBQ Spareribs 207

Charcoal-Grilled Ribs, Florentine-Style 208

continued on next page...

Country-Style Raspberry Ribs. 209
Honey-Basted Asian-Style Ribs 210
Rotisserie Cola-Mopped Ham with Cherry Barbecue Glaze . . .211
Double-Smoked Ham. 212
Double-Smoked Ham and Wild Rice Soup *213*
Grilled Ham Steaks with Bourbon Cider Glaze 214
Italian Sausage with Stir-Grilled Peppers,
    Onions and Potatoes 215
Oktoberfest Grillwurst. 216

Whether grilled, smoked, spit-roasted or skewered, pork is a natural on the grill. Pork's natural richness marries well with tart and tangy vinegar, herbs, savory spices, fruits of all kinds, mustard, tomato, beer, wine, cider and spirits.

Almost any wood flavor goes well with pork, although mesquite can sometimes be too overpowering and alder too light.

The best cuts of pork for grilling are chops, tenderloin, pork steaks, baby back ribs, country-style ribs, crown roast, pork loin, ham steaks and sausage. The best cuts of pork for smoking are thicker chops, tenderloin (grill-marked first), pork steaks, baby back ribs, spareribs (side ribs), country-style ribs, crown roast, pork butt or shoulder and whole hog (see page 309).

✦ Pork Cuts and Best Barbecue Methods ✦

Chop: Grill, herb-grill, indirect grill, smoke, plank

Tenderloin: Grill, skewer, stir-grill, herb-grill, indirect grill, smoke, plank

Pork steak: Grill, indirect grill, smoke

Pork loin: Grill, indirect grill, rotisserie, herb-grill, smoke

Baby back ribs: Grill, smoke

Spareribs (side ribs): Smoke

Country-style ribs: Grill, smoke

Pork butt: Smoke, leaf-wrap

Crown roast: Indirect grill, grill-roast, smoke

Whole hog: Smoke

Blue Ribbon Pulled Pork

Pork butt, or shoulder blade, is a tough piece of meat that really benefits from spicy flavorings and low, slow cooking over a wood fire, making it one of the glories of barbecue. You can buy the roast bone-in or boneless and tied; either way, it should shred apart in moist, delicious morsels when you're done.

✦ TIPS ✦

Size matters: slow-smoking two smaller pork butts will take significantly less time than smoking one large roast. And boneless roasts take about 1 hour less to smoke than bone-in.

To test whether pork is fork-tender, stick a fork in a section of meat and twist. If the meat twists, it's tender enough.

- Foil pan
- Plastic spray bottle
- **Suggested wood:** hickory

2	boneless pork shoulder blade roasts (each about 3½ lbs/1.75 kg)	2
1 cup	prepared mustard	250 mL
1 cup	Blue Ribbon Rub (see recipe, page 34)	250 mL
2 cups	apple juice	500 mL

1. Slather pork with mustard, then sprinkle with rub. Place pork in foil pan. Let stand for 15 to 30 minutes, or until the surface of the meat is tacky to the touch.

2. Meanwhile, prepare an indirect fire for smoking in your grill or smoker.

3. Fill spray bottle with apple juice. Place pork on the indirect side of the grill. Close the lid and smoke for about 6 hours, spraying with juice every 30 minutes for the last 2 hours, until pork is fork-tender. Pull meat apart while still hot and arrange on a platter.

✦ Variation ✦

To create a bark, or dark exterior, on your pork butt, first slather it with mustard and then dust with a dry rub. Start it out at a higher temperature on your grill or smoker — about 350°F (180°C) — for about 30 minutes. Then lower the temperature to 225°F to 250°F (110°F to 120°C) and slow-smoke for the remaining time.

BBQ Poutine

In the 1950s, or so the legend goes, someone walked into a restaurant in Quebec and ordered fries topped with beef gravy and cheese curds. "That's a real mess," someone said in Québécois slang — "poutine." And so this dish was born. The BBQ poutine on the menu at Memphis Blues barbecue restaurant in Vancouver features pulled pork and barbecue sauce over fries, topped with cheese. Here's our version.

- Deep fryer, electric skillet or large skillet
- Candy/deep-fry thermometer

	Vegetable oil	
4	baking potatoes, peeled and cut into ½-inch (1 cm) wide fries	4
	Kosher or sea salt	
2 cups	Blue Ribbon Pulled Pork (see recipe, page 179)	500 mL
1 cup	tomato-based barbecue sauce	250 mL
1 cup	fresh cheese curds, queso fresco or shredded Monterey Jack cheese	250 mL

1. In deep fryer, heat 2 inches (5 cm) of oil over medium heat until it registers 350°F (180°C) on thermometer. Add potatoes, in batches, and fry, stirring frequently, for 8 to 10 minutes per batch, or until golden. Remove with a slotted spoon to a plate lined with paper towels. Season to taste with salt.

2. Portion fries among plates and top with pulled pork, sauce and cheese.

Memphis Piggy Sandwiches with Vinegar Coleslaw

Pulled or chopped pork piled on a bun, sauced with Vinegar Barbecue Sauce and topped with a big spoonful of vinegar coleslaw — this is what's called living high off the hog.

✦ TIP ✦

Be an efficient barbecuer. Wrap and freeze leftover smoked meats for later use.

Vinegar Coleslaw

¼ cup	vegetable oil	50 mL
¼ cup	white vinegar	50 mL
1½ tsp	granulated sugar	7 mL
½ tsp	celery seeds	2 mL
½ tsp	kosher salt	2 mL
1	package (16 oz/454 g) coleslaw mix	1
4 cups	pulled or chopped cooked pork (see recipe, page 179)	1 L
1 cup	Vinegar Barbecue Sauce (see recipe, page 62)	250 mL
4	hamburger buns, split	4

1. *Prepare the coleslaw:* In a bowl, combine oil, vinegar, sugar, celery seeds and salt. Add coleslaw and toss to coat. Set aside.

2. In a bowl, toss pork with ½ cup (125 mL) of the barbecue sauce.

3. Arrange meat on bottom halves of buns and drizzle with barbecue sauce, if desired. Spoon coleslaw over the meat and cover with top halves. Serve any remaining sauce and coleslaw on the side.

Smoked Pork and Black-Eyed Pea Gumbo for a Crowd

Adapted from a recipe served at Cochon in New Orleans, this is a great way to use extra barbecued pork butt. With steamed rice, it's mighty fine cold-weather food, perfect for a casual supper around the fireplace or tailgating at the big game.

Roux

½ cup	vegetable oil	125 mL
½ cup	all-purpose flour	125 mL
2	cloves garlic, chopped	2
1 cup	collard or mustard greens, steamed and chopped	250 mL
½ cup	diced onion	125 mL
½ cup	diced celery	125 mL
½ cup	diced green bell pepper	125 mL
6 cups	chicken stock (approx.)	1.5 L
1	recipe Cajun Spice Rub (page 35)	1
2 tbsp	vegetable oil or lard	25 mL
12 oz	fresh or frozen and thawed okra, trimmed and cut into ½-inch (1 cm) rounds	375 g
3 to 4 cups	Blue Ribbon Pulled Pork (see recipe, page 179)	750 mL to 1 L
1 cup	cooked black-eyed peas	250 mL
1 tbsp	cider vinegar (or to taste)	15 mL
1 tsp	hot pepper sauce (or to taste)	5 mL
	Steamed white rice	

1. *Prepare the roux:* In a cast-iron or other heavy pot, heat ½ cup (125 mL) oil over medium-high heat and stir in flour to make a paste. Cook for about 8 minutes, whisking often, until reddish-brown but not dark. Carefully stir in garlic, collard greens, onion, celery and green pepper; cook, stirring, for 1 minute. Gradually stir in chicken stock and spice rub. Reduce heat, partially cover and simmer for 1 hour

to blend the flavors, stirring occasionally and adding water if necessary.

2. Meanwhile, in a skillet, heat 2 tbsp (25 mL) oil over medium-high heat. Sear okra until well browned. Remove okra with a slotted spoon and add to the roux, along with pork and peas. Add water, if necessary, to make a mixture halfway between a soup and a stew. Simmer until pork is hot. Season to taste with vinegar and hot pepper sauce. Serve over steamed rice.

Cuban Barbecued Pork Shoulder

SERVES 10 TO 12

From start to finish, this barbecued pork dish is infused with the flavor of tangy citrus, for succulent results. To get the marinade deep into the meat, use a culinary injector.

✦ TIPS ✦

As a shortcut, you could use bottled mojo (we like Goya Criollo) in place of the homemade marinade.

To test whether pork is fork-tender, stick a fork in a section of meat and twist. If the meat twists, it's tender enough.

If you're only serving 4 to 6 people, let leftovers cool and freeze in a sealable freezer bag for up to 6 months.

- Culinary injector (optional)
- 2 foil pans
- Plastic spray bottle
- **Suggested wood:** oak

1 cup	Sour Orange Marinade (see recipe, page 38), strained	250 mL
2	boneless pork shoulder blade roasts (each about 3½ lbs/1.75 kg)	2
2 cups	unsweetened pineapple juice	500 mL
1	recipe Aji-li-Mojili (page 42)	1

1. Fill a culinary injector with marinade. Set pork in a large dish and inject with marinade, refilling the injector until all the marinade is used. Cover with plastic wrap and refrigerate for at least 4 hours or up to 24 hours. (Or place each roast in a large sealable plastic bag and pour in marinade, dividing evenly between bags. Seal, toss to coat and refrigerate.)

2. Meanwhile, prepare an indirect fire for smoking in your grill or smoker.

3. Fill spray bottle with pineapple juice. Remove pork from marinade, if necessary, discarding marinade. Place pork butts in foil pans and place pans on the indirect side of the grill. Close the lid and smoke for about 6 hours, spraying with juice every 30 minutes for the last 2 hours, until pork is fork-tender. Let rest for 10 minutes. Pull meat apart while still hot and arrange on a platter.

Cherry-Smoked
Crown Roast of Pork

SERVES 8 TO 10

*Crown roast of pork
— a rack of pork tied
to form a circular
shape — looks and
tastes festive. With a
savory slather and a
spell on the smoker,
this dish will be tender
and flavorful. If you
like, fill the cavity
with your favorite
cornbread stuffing
or an autumn fruit
compote before
serving. Finish it off
with an easy Brandied
Cherry Sauce (page 52).*

- Foil pan
- Plastic spray bottle
- **Suggested wood:** cherry, apple, hickory or pecan

1	pork crown roast (about 10 lbs/5 kg)	1
1 cup	Dijon mustard	250 mL
1 cup	Cajun Spice Rub (see recipe, page 35)	250 mL
1 cup	apple juice	250 mL

1. Rinse pork under cold running water and pat dry. Place in foil pan. Using a brush or spatula, spread mustard over the meaty part of the rack, then sprinkle with rub. Cover and refrigerate for at least 2 hours or overnight.

2. Meanwhile, prepare an indirect fire for smoking in your grill or smoker.

3. Fill spray bottle with apple juice. Place pork on the indirect side of the grill. Close the lid and smoke for about 5 hours, spraying with juice every 30 minutes for the last 4 hours, until a meat thermometer inserted in the thickest part of the meat registers 150°F (65°C) for medium, or until desired doneness. Let rest for 10 to 15 minutes before slicing.

Mayan-Style Pit Pork

SERVES 4 TO 6

Before the Spanish invasion (and the pigs they brought), native Mayans cooked wild rainforest game using this method. Serve with warm corn tortillas and salsa.

✦ TIPS ✦

You'll need 1 to 2 sour oranges to make ½ cup (125 mL) juice. If you can't find sour oranges, use 2 tbsp (25 mL) freshly squeezed Valencia orange juice mixed with 6 tbsp (90 mL) freshly squeezed lime juice (from 4 to 5 limes).

You'll find fresh banana leaves and achiote paste at Hispanic or Asian markets. Look for frozen banana leaves at larger grocery stores catering to an ethnic population or at www.goya.com.

Mayan Marinade

2	cloves garlic, minced	2
4 oz	achiote paste (about ½ cup/125 mL packed)	125 g
½ cup	freshly squeezed sour orange juice (see tip, at left)	125 mL
1 tsp	white wine vinegar	5 mL
Pinch	dried Mexican or Italian oregano	Pinch
1	boneless pork shoulder blade roast (about 3½ lbs/1.75 kg), trimmed	1
	Kosher or sea salt and freshly ground black pepper	
1	large banana leaf, fresh or frozen and thawed (see tip, at left)	1

1. *Prepare the marinade:* In a glass bowl, combine garlic, achiote paste, sour orange juice, vinegar and oregano.

2. Season pork with salt and pepper, place in a large sealable plastic bag and pour in marinade. Seal, toss to coat and refrigerate for at least 2 hours or overnight.

3. Meanwhile, prepare a hot indirect fire in your grill.

4. For a fresh banana leaf, remove center core and discard. Run the leaf under hot water until pliable. Pat leaf dry with paper towels and cut in half horizontally; overlap the two pieces of leaf so that they will cover the pork. (For a frozen and thawed banana leaf, separate sections of the leaf and overlap them so that they will cover the pork.)

Butts in a Bag! You'll need 2 medium brown paper grocery bags. Slide pork butt into a grocery bag, then double-bag it by sliding the open end into the second grocery bag, completely enclosing the pork butt. Do not use this technique if the bag is at all close to a live flame; make sure to place the wrapped pork on the indirect side of the grill.

5. Remove pork from marinade, discarding marinade. Place pork on the banana leaves, fold in the left and right sides and roll up like a burrito, completely covering the pork.

6. Place pork on the indirect side of the grill, with the seam of the banana leaves facing down. Close the lid and grill for about 6 hours, or until pork is fork-tender. During the last hour, carefully remove the top wrapping to let pork develop a crust. Let rest for 10 minutes.

7. Unwrap pork and discard banana leaves. Using two forks, shred meat onto a serving platter.

Spit-Roasted Pork Loin in Maple Mustard Brine

SERVES 6 TO 8

Here's a deliciously easy way to prepare a traditional pork loin roast with a sweet and smoky twist. Brining helps give the meat a buttery texture.

◆ TIPS ◆

Grade B, or medium, maple syrup is darker and more flavorful than the sweeter Grade A, and makes brines, marinades and sauces more robust.

If you prefer, you can grill the pork over a hot indirect fire instead of using the rotisserie. Place pork on the indirect side of the grill, close the lid and grill for about 1½ hours, basting several times with sauce, until a meat thermometer inserted in the center registers 150°F (65°C).

● Rotisserie

| 1 | boneless pork loin roast (about 3 lbs/1.5 kg) | 1 |
| 1 | recipe Maple Mustard Brine (page 37) | 1 |

Maple Apricot Barbecue Sauce

1 cup	tomato-based barbecue sauce	250 mL
1 cup	apricot preserves or jam	250 mL
¼ cup	pure maple syrup (Grade B/medium is ideal)	50 mL
	Juice of 1 lemon	

1. Place pork in a large sealable plastic bag and pour in brine. Seal, toss to coat and refrigerate for at least 3 hours or overnight.

2. *Prepare the sauce:* In a bowl, whisk together barbecue sauce, preserves, maple syrup and lemon juice. Transfer 1 cup (250 mL) to another bowl to use for basting. Reserve the rest for the table.

3. Set up your grill for rotisserie cooking.

4. Remove pork from brine, discarding brine. Rinse pork well under cold running water and pat dry.

5. Attach pork to the spit (see page 24). Heat the grill to medium-high. Close the lid and grill for about 1½ hours, basting several times with sauce, until an instant-read thermometer inserted in the thickest part of the meat registers 150°F (65°C) for medium, or until desired doneness. Transfer to a cutting board, tent with foil and let rest for 15 minutes before slicing. Pass the reserved sauce at the table.

Guava-Glazed Rotisserie Pork Loin Roast

SERVES 6 TO 8

The guava fruit is rich in vitamin C, with a flavor that hints of honey, melon and strawberries. It's native to South America, Australia, Hawaii and the Caribbean. Serve rum-flavored cocktails when this is on your menu.

● Rotisserie

Guava Glaze

¾ cup	guava jelly	175 mL
1 tbsp	grated gingerroot	15 mL
2 tbsp	dark rum	25 mL
3 tbsp	freshly squeezed lemon juice	45 mL
1	boneless pork loin roast (3 to 4 lbs/1.5 to 2 kg)	1
	Garlic salt and freshly ground black pepper	

1. *Prepare the glaze:* In a small saucepan, heat guava jelly, ginger and rum over medium heat, stirring occasionally, until jelly melts. Whisk in lemon juice. Transfer half the glaze to a bowl and set aside to use as a finishing sauce. Keep the remaining glaze warm by the grill.

2. Set up your grill for rotisserie cooking.

3. Sprinkle pork with garlic salt and pepper and attach to the spit (see page 24). Heat the grill to medium-high. Close the lid and grill for about 2 hours, basting lightly with glaze every 30 minutes, until an instant-read thermometer inserted in the thickest part of the meat registers 150°F (65°C) for medium, or until desired doneness. Transfer to a cutting board, tent with foil and let rest for 15 minutes before slicing. Serve with the reserved glaze on the side.

Apple-Smoked Roasted Pork Loin with Apple Chutney Stuffing

SERVES 6 TO 8

Butterfly the roast or have your butcher do it for you. Smoking first, then roasting gives this pork loin plenty of smokiness and a nice crusty exterior in less time than slow-smoking alone.

- Foil pan
- **Suggested wood: apple or cherry**

Apple Chutney Stuffing

2 tbsp	unsalted butter	25 mL
4	tart cooking apples, peeled and chopped	4
4	stalks celery, diced	4
1	onion, diced	1
¼ cup	golden raisins	50 mL
1 tbsp	chopped fresh rosemary	15 mL
½ tsp	ground nutmeg	2 mL
½ tsp	ground allspice	2 mL
4	slices crusty bread, crumbled (approx.)	4
1	boneless pork loin roast (3 to 4 lbs/1.5 to 2 kg), butterflied	1
½ tsp	kosher or sea salt (or to taste)	2 mL
½ tsp	freshly ground white pepper (or to taste)	2 mL
2 tbsp	freshly ground black pepper	25 mL
2 tsp	garlic salt	10 mL
3 cups	apple juice, divided	750 mL
2	onions, halved	2

1. Prepare an indirect fire for smoking in your grill or smoker.

2. *Prepare the stuffing:* In a large skillet, melt butter over medium heat. Add apples, celery, onion, raisins, rosemary, nutmeg and allspice. Cook, stirring often, for 6 to 8 minutes, or until onion is translucent. Stir in enough bread crumbs to bind the mixture together. Remove from heat.

3. Lay pork cut side up on a work surface and season with salt and white pepper. Spread stuffing over the meat and, starting with a long side, roll up jellyroll-style. Tie the roll together at intervals with kitchen string. Sprinkle with black pepper and garlic salt. Place in foil pan with 2 cups (500 mL) of the apple juice and the onion halves.

4. Place pan on the indirect side of the grill. Close the lid and smoke for 1 hour.

5. Meanwhile, preheat oven to 400°F (200°C).

6. Transfer roast to the oven and baste with the remaining apple juice. Roast for about 30 minutes, or until a meat thermometer inserted in the thickest part of the meat (but not in the stuffing) registers 150°F (65°C) for medium, or until desired doneness. Transfer to a cutting board, tent with foil and let rest for 10 minutes before slicing.

✦ Variation ✦

Leave the bread crumbs out of the stuffing recipe, and you'll have a great fruit chutney to use as a side relish. Store chutney in an airtight container in the refrigerator for up to 1 week.

Graisse de Roti

We give the pork loin a kiss of smoke for a barbecued version of authentic Quebec daube. The graisse de roti, made from the meat drippings (similar to gravy), is served cold on toast. Serve slices of the cold smoky pork beside it.

✦ TIP ✦

Serve with chow chow relish and pickles.

- Foil pan
- **Suggested wood: maple**

1	boneless pork loin roast (3 to 4 lbs/1.5 to 2 kg)	1
4	cloves garlic, halved	4
1 tsp	dry mustard	5 mL
1 tsp	dried savory	5 mL
	Kosher salt and freshly ground black pepper	
1 cup	boiling water	250 mL

1. Prepare an indirect fire for smoking in your grill or smoker.

2. Make 8 incisions in the roast and place half a garlic clove in each slit. Rub meat with mustard and savory. Season to taste with salt and pepper. Set roast fat side up in foil pan.

3. Place pan on the indirect side of the grill. Close the lid and smoke for about 1½ hours, or until pork has become nicely burnished. Cover tightly with foil and continue to cook, without adding any more wood, for 30 to 60 minutes, or until a meat thermometer inserted in the thickest part of the meat registers 150°F (65°C) for medium, or until desired doneness.

4. Remove roast from pan and set on a plate to cool. Wrap roast in foil and refrigerate until ready to serve. Add boiling water to the pan drippings, scraping the bottom of the pan. Transfer to an airtight container and refrigerate for at least 4 hours or for up to 24 hours. If necessary, remove some of the solidified fat from the top of the graisse de roti before serving.

5. Spoon cold graisse de roti over toast and serve with cold pork on the side.

Vietnamese Grilled Chicken Sandwiches with
Carrot and Daikon Relish (page 151)

Grilled Pork and Mango Skewers
with Mango Chipotle Barbecue Sauce (page 109)

Wood-Grilled Filipino Pork Steaks
with Pineapple Tangerine Glaze (page 200)

Honey-Basted Asian-Style Flank Steak (210)

Steakhouse Filets with Fried Onion Slivers
and Béarnaise Sauce (page 234)

Cowboy Steaks with Two-Steppin' Rub (page 241)

Tropical Lamb Burgers with
Fresh Mango Chutney (page 283)

Souvlaki with Grilled Pita (page 281)

Tuscan Rolled Pork Loin Stuffed with Rosemary and Garlic

This recipe for pork loin with herbs and garlic is a staple in Tuscany. Traditionally, the loin rib roast is cooked over a wood fire, then served cold, which is the way the Tuscans prefer it. This version is a bit easier and still very tasty. You choose whether to serve it hot or cold; either way is delicious.

✦ TIP ✦

Use an assortment of Italian herbs rather than just the rosemary. Serve with roasted potatoes and tomatoes, which can be prepared in the smoker along with the roast.

- Foil pan
- Kitchen string, soaked
- **Suggested wood:** oak

1	boneless pork loin roast (3 to 4 lbs/1.5 to 2 kg), butterflied	1
	Kosher salt and freshly ground black pepper	
4	cloves garlic, slivered	4
2 tbsp	chopped fresh rosemary	25 mL

1. Prepare an indirect fire for smoking in your grill or smoker.

2. Lay pork cut side up on a work surface and season with salt and pepper. Arrange garlic evenly over meat and sprinkle with rosemary. Starting with a long side, roll up jellyroll-style. Tie the roll together at intervals with soaked kitchen string. Season to taste with salt and pepper. Place in foil pan.

3. Place pan on the indirect side of the grill. Close the lid and smoke for about 2 hours, or until a meat thermometer inserted in the thickest part of the meat registers 150°F (65°C) for medium, or until desired doneness. Transfer to a cutting board, tent with foil and let rest for 10 minutes before slicing and serving hot. Or let cool, refrigerate for up to 2 days and serve cold.

Mustard-Grilled Pork Paillards with Tarragon Mustard Drizzle

"Paillard" is a French term meaning a very thin boneless, skinless piece of meat. On French bistro menus, you usually see chicken paillards, but at home you can easily make pork paillards from the loin. Cut ½ inch (1 cm) thick, pork paillards grill in just 5 minutes over a hot fire.

✦ TIP ✦

As a do-along side dish, grill wedges of cabbage, brushed with oil on the cut sides, until they have good grill marks. Slice cabbage into fine shreds, then dress with extra drizzle.

● Baking sheet

Tarragon Mustard Drizzle

½ cup	vegetable oil	125 mL
½ cup	tarragon-flavored vinegar	125 mL
¼ cup	granulated sugar	50 mL
1 tbsp	chopped fresh tarragon	15 mL
2 tbsp	Dijon mustard	25 mL
2 lbs	boneless pork loin, cut into ½-inch (1 cm) steaks	1 kg

1. *Prepare the drizzle:* In a bowl, whisk together oil, vinegar, sugar, tarragon and mustard.

2. Place pork on baking sheet. Remove up to half the drizzle and brush pork on both sides. Reserve the remaining drizzle as a finishing sauce.

3. Prepare a hot fire in your grill.

4. Grill pork for 5 minutes, turning once, until just a hint of pink remains inside. Serve drizzled with the reserved sauce.

Hawaiian Pork Skewers with Pineapple Rum Glaze

SERVES 4

Your taste buds will hula-hula when you take a bite.

◆ TIPS ◆

If you use fresh bamboo shoots (available at Asian markets), make sure they have not been treated with chemicals. You may need to pierce the pork first with a sharp skewer, then thread it onto the bamboo shoots.

It's always a good idea to oil the grill rack well before heating the grill, but it's especially important when you're grilling foods with a sweet glaze or baste, so they don't stick.

● Twelve 12-inch (30 cm) flat bamboo skewers, soaked for at least 30 minutes, or fresh bamboo shoots

Pineapple Rum BBQ Glaze

1	can (8 oz/227 mL) crushed pineapple, drained	1
½ cup	tomato-based barbecue sauce	125 mL
2 tbsp	light or dark rum	25 mL
1 tbsp	soy sauce	15 mL
1	large sweet potato, peeled and cut into 2-inch (5 cm) pieces	1
1 lb	boneless pork loin, cut into 2-inch (5 cm) pieces	500 g
1 cup	cubed fresh pineapple (2-inch/5 cm cubes)	250 mL

1. *Prepare the glaze:* In a small saucepan, bring pineapple, barbecue sauce, rum and soy sauce to a boil over medium-high heat. Reduce heat and simmer for 10 minutes.

2. Meanwhile, place sweet potato in a microwave-safe bowl and microwave on High for 5 minutes, or until almost tender.

3. Thread pork onto 8 skewers, leaving space between pieces. Thread pineapple and sweet potato onto the remaining skewers. Remove half the glaze and brush first the fruit skewers, then the pork. Reserve the remaining glaze as a finishing sauce.

4. Prepare a medium-hot fire in your grill.

5. Grill pork skewers for 3 to 4 minutes per side, turning once, until pork has good grill marks and just a hint of pink remains inside.

6. Meanwhile, grill fruit skewers for 2 to 3 minutes per side, turning once, until fruit has good grill marks.

7. Serve skewers drizzled with the reserved glaze.

Raspberry-Glazed Pork Tenderloin with Spicy Raspberry Jalapeño Barbecue Sauce

A little bit sweet and a little bit tart, this fruity version of grilled pork tenderloin is a winner. Serve with grilled summer squash and a salad dressed with raspberry vinaigrette.

✦ TIP ✦

It's always a good idea to oil the grill rack well before heating the grill, but it's especially important when you're grilling foods with a sweet glaze or baste, so they don't stick.

4	pork tenderloins (each about 12 oz/375 g)	4
¼ cup	spicy barbecue seasoning (such as Cajun Spice Rub, page 35)	50 mL
1½ cups	Spicy Raspberry Jalapeño Barbecue Sauce (see recipe, page 66)	375 mL

1. Sprinkle pork with barbecue seasoning and let stand at room temperature for 30 minutes.

2. Meanwhile, prepare a hot fire in your grill.

3. Grill pork for 3 to 4 minutes per quarter turn, basting with some of the barbecue sauce during the last 5 minutes, until a meat thermometer inserted in the thickest part of a tenderloin registers 130°F (54°C) for rare, or until desired doneness. Let rest for 5 minutes. Serve with the remaining sauce on the side.

Sesame-Soy Marinated Pork Tenderloin with Asian Dipping Sauce

Serve this succulent tenderloin with steamed spinach or kale.

✦ TIPS ✦

The sauce can be stored in an airtight container in the refrigerator for up to 10 days.

When serving pork tenderloin as an entrée, cut the meat into ½- to ¾-inch (1 to 1.5 cm) thick slices. The meat will stay hotter and moister than it would with thin slices.

This recipe also works well as an appetizer, with one tenderloin serving 8 to 10 people. Cut the tenderloin into thin slices and serve hot or cold with hot Chinese mustard and Asian Dipping Sauce.

Asian Dipping Sauce

2	cloves garlic, minced	2
1 tbsp	minced gingerroot	15 mL
½ cup	hoisin sauce	125 mL
¼ cup	plum sauce	50 mL
2 tbsp	soy sauce	25 mL
2 tbsp	liquid honey	25 mL
2 tbsp	rice vinegar	25 mL
½ tsp	five-spice powder	2 mL
4	pork tenderloins (each about 12 oz/375 g)	4
3	cloves garlic, minced	3
1 tbsp	chopped gingerroot	15 mL
1 cup	soy sauce	250 mL
⅓ cup	toasted sesame oil	75 mL

1. *Prepare the sauce:* In a bowl, combine garlic, ginger, hoisin, plum sauce, soy sauce, honey, vinegar and five-spice powder. Cover and refrigerate until ready to serve.

2. Place pork in a large sealable plastic bag and add garlic, ginger, soy sauce and sesame oil. Seal, toss to coat and refrigerate for at least 2 hours or overnight, tossing occasionally.

3. Meanwhile, prepare a hot fire in your grill.

4. Remove pork from marinade, discarding marinade. Grill pork for about 5 minutes per quarter turn, or until a meat thermometer inserted in the thickest part of a tenderloin registers 130°F (54°C) for rare, or until desired doneness. Let rest for 5 minutes. Serve with sauce on the side.

Aussie Paperbark Pork with Lemon Myrtle Chutney

Paperbark is indigenous to Australia and comes from the melaleuca tree. It imparts a delicate smokiness from the oils that are released when it is heated. Cedar wraps may be substituted.

✦ TIPS ✦

Other flavors of wood paper wraps are available at kitchen and gourmet stores and online. They range from 6 inches (15 cm) to 9 inches (23 cm) square (or sometimes oblong).

Mountain pepper is a pepper plant native to the cooler areas of southern Australia. It is similar to regular black pepper, but has an added herbal dimension. It is available at some specialty stores and at www.salttraders.com

Lemon myrtle chutney may be difficult to find, but dried lemon myrtle is available online at places like Amazon.com. Buy a fruit chutney or applesauce and add dried lemon myrtle to taste or the grated zest of 1 lemon and 1 lime.

- 15- by 8-inch (38 by 20 cm) piece of paperbark or 2 to 3 cedar wraps, soaked for at least 1 hour
- Kitchen string, soaked
- Metal paper clips
- Griddle

¼ cup	vegetable oil	50 mL
2	pork tenderloins (each about 12 oz/375 g), butterflied lengthwise	2
¼ cup	lemon myrtle chutney (see tip, at left)	50 mL
1	red bell pepper, julienned	1
	Kosher salt and mountain pepper or freshly ground black pepper	

1. Prepare a hot fire in your grill. Place griddle over the fire until hot.

2. Choose the side of paperbark that has the least amount of stringy fiber. Brush that side with oil so the meat does not stick to the bark.

3. Lay tenderloins cut side up on a work surface and spoon chutney down the center of each. Top with red pepper. Sprinkle with salt and pepper to taste. Starting with a long side, roll up jellyroll-style. Tie the rolls together at intervals with soaked kitchen string. Wrap with paperbark and secure with paper clips.

4. Place pork on griddle and grill for 18 to 20 minutes, turning several times, until bark is blackened and smoking and a meat thermometer inserted in the thickest part of a tenderloin registers 130°F (54°C) for rare, or until desired doneness. Let rest for 5 to 10 minutes. Unwrap pork and slice.

Grilled Pork and Mango Skewers with Mango Chipotle Barbecue Sauce

If you haven't eaten mangoes before, be sure to give this recipe a try. They are perfect paired with pork, and you'll love the sweet, hot sauce.

✦ TIP ✦

Another way to grill with skewers is to thread all like food onto individual skewers. When each skewer is done, unthread the food into a big glass bowl. Toss and serve from the bowl.

● Twelve 12-inch (30 cm) flat bamboo skewers, soaked for at least 30 minutes, or flat metal skewers

2	pork tenderloins (each about 12 oz/375 g), cut into ¾-inch (2 cm) cubes	2
3	firm ripe mangoes, peeled and cut into 1-inch (2.5 cm) cubes	3
2	red bell peppers, cut into 1-inch (2.5 cm) squares	2
1	recipe Mango Chipotle Barbecue Sauce (page 66)	1

1. Prepare a medium-hot fire in your grill.

2. Thread pork, mangoes and red bell peppers onto skewers, leaving space between pieces. Grill skewers for 2 minutes per quarter turn. Baste with some of the barbecue sauce and grill for 2 minutes per quarter turn, basting after each turn, until just a hint of pink remains inside pork. Serve with the remaining sauce on the side.

Wood-Grilled Filipino Pork Steaks with Pineapple Tangerine Glaze

SERVES 6

This delicious fruity glaze works well with thin-cut pork steaks or chops. Serve simply with white rice and Pineapple Mandarin Salsa (page 61) on the side.

● **Suggested wood:** oak, apple or orange

Pineapple Tangerine Glaze

3	cloves garlic	3
1 tsp	minced gingerroot	5 mL
2/3 cup	freshly squeezed tangerine juice	150 mL
1/3 cup	crushed pineapple	75 mL
1/3 cup	soy sauce	75 mL
1/4 tsp	hot pepper flakes	1 mL
6	thin-cut boneless pork steaks or chops (each about 1/2 inch/ 1 cm thick)	6

1. *Prepare the glaze:* In a bowl, combine garlic, ginger, tangerine juice, pineapple, soy sauce and hot pepper flakes.

2. Place pork in a large sealable plastic bag and pour in half the glaze. Seal, toss to coat and refrigerate for at least 30 minutes or up to 2 hours. Cover and refrigerate the remaining glaze until ready to use.

3. Meanwhile, prepare a medium-hot indirect fire with a kiss of smoke in your grill.

4. Remove pork from marinade, discarding marinade. When you see the first wisp of smoke from the wood, place pork over the hot fire. Grill for 2 minutes per side. Move to the indirect side of the grill, overlapping steaks if necessary, and baste with some of the reserved glaze. Close the lid and grill for 30 to 45 minutes, occasionally basting with glaze and moving the steaks around on the grill for even heat, until just a hint of pink remains inside.

Grilled Double Pork Chops

SERVES 4

A feast fit for an emperor — or empress. After soaking in a flavorful Asian marinade, these thick, bone-in chops are seared over a medium-hot fire, then finished on the indirect side. Special-order these chops from your butcher, buy them online or substitute the thickest pork chops you can find.

✦ TIP ✦

These are delicious served with Creamy Mustard Sauce (page 49).

Asian Marinade

2	green onions, finely chopped	2
2	cloves garlic, minced	2
2 tsp	granulated sugar	10 mL
1 tsp	grated gingerroot	5 mL
¾ cup	hoisin sauce	175 mL
2 tbsp	rice vinegar	25 mL
1 tbsp	tamari or soy sauce	15 mL
	Kosher or sea salt and finely ground white pepper	
4	double bone-in pork chops (each about 10 oz/300 g), trimmed and bones frenched	4

1. *Prepare the marinade:* In a bowl, whisk together green onions, garlic, sugar, ginger, hoisin, vinegar and tamari. Season to taste with salt and pepper.

2. Place pork in a sealable plastic bag and pour in half the marinade. Seal, toss to coat and refrigerate for at least 3 hours or up to 8 hours, tossing occasionally. Cover and refrigerate the remaining marinade until ready to use.

3. Meanwhile, prepare a medium-hot indirect fire in your grill.

4. Remove pork from marinade, discarding marinade. Grill for 5 minutes per side, rotating a quarter turn after 2½ minutes on each side for crosshatch grill marks. Move to the indirect side of the grill and baste with some of the reserved marinade. Close the lid and grill for 20 minutes, basting with marinade after 10 minutes, until a meat thermometer inserted in the thickest part of a chop registers 150°F (65°C) for medium, or until desired doneness. Serve drizzled with the remaining marinade.

Hickory-Grilled Double Pork Chops with Fire-Roasted Tomato and Bacon Vinaigrette

SERVES 4

You need medium-hot heat to produce flavorful and just done, yet still juicy, thick-cut pork chops. A marinade bath beforehand helps too. Serve the chops with mashed potatoes and drizzle the vinaigrette over all.

✦ TIP ✦

Look for canned fire-roasted tomatoes (such as Muir Glen or Hunt's) in health food stores or the organic section of well-stocked supermarkets.

● **Suggested wood:** hickory

Fire-Roasted Tomato and Bacon Vinaigrette

3	slices smoked bacon, diced	3
1	small shallot, sliced	1
½ cup	canned fire-roasted tomatoes (see tip, at left), chopped	125 mL
2 tbsp	red wine vinegar	25 mL
	Fine kosher or sea salt and freshly ground black pepper	
	Granulated sugar	
4	boneless center-cut pork chops (1 inch/2.5 cm thick)	4
	Fine kosher or sea salt and freshly ground black pepper	

1. *Prepare the vinaigrette:* In a small skillet, sauté bacon until starting to brown. Add shallot and sauté until bacon is crisp. Stir in tomatoes and vinegar. Season to taste with salt, pepper and sugar. Keep warm.

2. Place pork in a sealable plastic bag and add ½ cup (125 mL) of the vinaigrette. Seal, toss to coat and refrigerate for at least 30 minutes or up to 60 minutes.

3. Meanwhile, prepare a medium-hot fire with a kiss of smoke in your grill.

4. Remove pork from vinaigrette, discarding vinaigrette. When you see the first wisp of smoke from the wood, place pork on the grill. Grill for about 10 minutes per side, until a meat thermometer inserted in the thickest part of a chop registers 150°F (65°C) for medium, or until desired doneness. Season with salt and pepper and drizzle with the remaining vinaigrette.

Maple Ginger Butterflied Pork Chops

SERVES 4

Make sure you don't over-grill these boneless pork chops. Their internal temperature will continue to rise after you pull them off the grill.

Maple Ginger Sauce

1	clove garlic, minced	1
1 tbsp	minced gingerroot	15 mL
½ cup	pure maple syrup	125 mL
2 tbsp	cider vinegar	25 mL
4	boneless pork chops, butterflied	4

1. Prepare a hot fire in your grill.
2. *Prepare the sauce:* In a small bowl, combine garlic, ginger, maple syrup and vinegar.
3. Grill pork for 2 minutes per side. Baste with some of the sauce and grill for about 2 minutes per side, or until just a hint of pink remains inside. Serve with the remaining sauce on the side.

✦ Variation ✦

Grilled Pork Chop Sandwiches: Pound chops to about ¼ inch (0.5 cm) thick. Grill for 2 to 3 minutes per side, basting with some of the sauce, until just a hint of pink remains inside. Brush cut sides of sandwich buns with sauce and grill until toasted. Garnish with thinly sliced red onion and the remaining sauce.

Hickory Pork Burgers with Carolina Mustard Barbecue Sauce

SERVES 8

Juicy and smoky, this pork burger might convert you away from beef.

✦ Variation ✦

Hickory Pork Meatloaf: Prepare an indirect fire for smoking in your grill or smoker, using hickory wood. Form the pork mixture into a large loaf, place in a doubled foil pan and pour Carolina Mustard Barbecue Sauce over the loaf. Place pan on the indirect side of the grill. Close the lid and smoke for 2 to 3 hours, spooning sauce over meatloaf every 30 minutes, until a meat thermometer inserted in the center of the loaf registers 160°F (71°C). Let rest for 10 to 15 minutes before slicing.

● **Suggested wood: hickory**

3	cloves garlic, minced	3
2 lbs	lean ground pork	1 kg
¼ cup	finely chopped onion	50 mL
¼ cup	buttermilk	50 mL
1½ tsp	seasoned salt	7 mL
1 tsp	coarsely ground black pepper	5 mL
1 tsp	dried oregano	5 mL
8	hamburger buns, split	8
	Olive oil	
	Sliced red onion, lettuce, dill pickles, sliced cheese and sliced tomato	
2 cups	Carolina Mustard Barbecue Sauce (see recipe, page 69)	500 mL

1. Prepare a medium-hot fire with a kiss of smoke in your grill.

2. In a bowl, using your hands, combine garlic, pork, onion, buttermilk, seasoned salt, pepper and oregano. Form into eight ½-inch (1 cm) thick patties.

3. When you see the first wisp of smoke from the wood, grill burgers for 4 to 5 minutes per side, turning once, until a meat thermometer inserted in the center of a burger registers 160°F (71°C).

4. Meanwhile, brush the insides of buns with olive oil. Grill cut side down for 2 minutes, or until lightly browned.

5. Serve burgers with assorted garnishes and barbecue sauce on the side.

Kiss of Smoke Indoor/Outdoor Ribs

Preparing four or more racks, layered on top of each other and rotated during the oven-roasting process, keeps the meat moist. Start these indoors, then finish them on the grill.

✦ TIP ✦

After step 1, the ribs can be cooled, wrapped in foil and refrigerated for up to 2 days. Let stand at room temperature for 30 minutes before grilling.

- Preheat oven to 350°F (180°C)
- Rimmed baking sheet, covered with foil
- **Suggested wood:** hickory

1 cup	Blue Ribbon Rub (see recipe, page 34)	250 mL
4	racks baby back ribs (each about 1½ lbs/750 g), trimmed and membrane removed	4
2 cups	barbecue sauce	500 mL

1. Sprinkle rub evenly over both sides of ribs. Stack ribs meaty side up in two piles of two on prepared baking sheet. Roast in preheated oven for about 2½ hours, rotating ribs every 30 to 45 minutes, until fork-tender.

2. Prepare a medium-hot fire with a kiss of smoke in your grill.

3. When you see the first wisp of smoke from the wood, place ribs on the grill. Grill, turning several times, for 10 to 15 minutes. Baste the meaty side of the ribs with sauce, close the lid and grill for 10 minutes, until sauce is caramelized.

✦ Variation ✦

For indoor ribs, layer ribs and roast in preheated oven for 2 hours. Baste the meaty side of the ribs with sauce, spread ribs in a single layer and roast for 15 to 30 minutes, until sauce is caramelized and meat pulls away from the ends of the bones.

Sweet, Smoky, Sticky Baby Back Ribs

These sweet and sticky ribs are the archetype of those served in backyards all over North America. The celery flavor is typical of Kansas City–style barbecue rubs.

✦ TIP ✦

Use needle-nose pliers to grab the membrane on the underside of each rack of ribs and pull it off in one motion. This is easiest to do when the ribs are cold. Once they warm up, the membrane breaks apart, making it an exasperating task.

• **Suggested wood:** hickory, oak, apple or maple

¼ cup	granulated sugar	50 mL
2 tbsp	garlic salt	25 mL
2 tbsp	freshly ground black pepper	25 mL
2 tbsp	paprika	25 mL
2 tbsp	celery salt	25 mL
3	racks baby back ribs (each about 1½ lbs/750 g), trimmed and membrane removed	3
¾ cup	liquid honey, warmed	175 mL
1	can (12 oz/341 mL) beer	1
3 cups	spicy tomato barbecue sauce	750 mL

1. In a bowl, combine sugar, garlic salt, pepper, paprika and celery salt. Sprinkle over the meaty side of the ribs. Cover and refrigerate overnight.

2. Prepare an indirect fire for smoking in your grill or smoker.

3. Place ribs meaty side up on the indirect side of the grill. Close the lid and smoke for 1½ hours. Baste the meaty side with honey, close the lid and smoke for about 30 minutes, or until meat pulls about ½ inch (1 cm) away from the ends of the bones. Baste the meaty side with beer, close the lid and smoke for 1 hour, basting with beer every 10 to 15 minutes (the more moisture, the better the ribs). Baste the meaty side with barbecue sauce, close the lid and smoke for 30 minutes, basting every 10 to 15 minutes with sauce, until meat is fork-tender.

Championship BBQ Spareribs

SERVES 6

Memphis is the barbecue pork competition capital of North America. In Memphis, "dry" ribs are preferred to "wet" (sauced) ribs.

● **Suggested wood:** hickory or oak

Memphis-Style Dry Rub

1/2 cup	paprika	125 mL
3 tbsp	dry mustard	45 mL
3 tbsp	granulated garlic	45 mL
1 1/2 tbsp	onion salt	22 mL
1 1/2 tbsp	dried basil	22 mL
1 1/2 tbsp	cayenne pepper	22 mL
1 tbsp	coarsely ground black pepper	15 mL
3	racks baby back ribs (each about 1 1/2 lbs/750 g), trimmed and membrane removed	3

Memphis Mop

2 cups	tomato-based barbecue sauce	500 mL
1 cup	cider vinegar	250 mL
1 cup	vegetable oil	250 mL
1/4 cup	freshly squeezed lemon juice	50 mL

1. *Prepare the rub:* In a bowl, combine paprika, mustard, garlic, onion salt, basil, cayenne and black pepper.

2. Sprinkle half the rub over the meaty side of the ribs. Cover and refrigerate overnight. Reserve the remaining rub.

3. *Prepare the mop:* In a stainless steel bowl, combine barbecue sauce, vinegar, oil and lemon juice. Refrigerate until ready to use.

4. Prepare an indirect fire for smoking in your grill or smoker.

5. Place ribs meaty side up on the indirect side of the grill. Close the lid and smoke for about 1 1/2 hours, or until meat begins to pull away from the ends of the bones. Baste the meaty side with mop, close the lid and smoke for 1 1/2 hours, basting every 10 to 15 minutes, until meat is fork-tender.

6. Sprinkle ribs with the reserved rub and serve dry, or offer sauce to those who prefer wet.

Charcoal-Grilled Ribs, Florentine-Style

We call these ribs Florentine-style because we adapted them from a recipe by Tuscan chef and restaurateur Pino Luongo. For authentic Tuscan flavor, use a charcoal grill.

✦ TIP ✦

After rubbing the meat with the head of garlic, roast the garlic alongside the ribs over indirect heat. It will taste great spread on the grilled bread!

6	racks baby back ribs (each about 1½ lbs/750 g), trimmed and membrane removed	6
1	large head of garlic, cut in half horizontally	1
	Coarse kosher salt and freshly ground black pepper	
6	sprigs fresh rosemary, finely chopped	6
	Italian bread, thickly sliced	
	Extra-virgin olive oil	

1. Rub meaty side of ribs with the cut side of the garlic and sprinkle generously with salt and pepper. Sprinkle with rosemary and let stand at room temperature for 30 minutes.

2. Prepare a medium-hot fire in your charcoal grill.

3. Grill ribs for 40 to 45 minutes, turning every 8 to 10 minutes, until meat pulls away from the ends of the bones.

4. Meanwhile, brush bread with olive oil. Grill for about 1 minute per side, turning once, until warmed through and light golden brown.

5. Cut racks into double-rib sections and arrange on a platter with the grilled bread.

Country-Style Raspberry Ribs

SERVES 4

In this recipe, thick, meaty country-style ribs are slathered with a hot, tangy sauce and grilled with a kiss of smoke to sticky, finger-lickin' perfection.

✦ TIP ✦

Before brushing the ribs with the barbecue sauce, divide it into two portions: one for basting and one to serve at the table.

- Foil pan
- Plastic spray bottle
- **Suggested wood:** apple, cherry, hickory or oak

2 lbs	country-style pork ribs	1 kg
	Kosher or sea salt and freshly ground black pepper	
1	recipe Spicy Raspberry Jalapeño Barbecue Sauce (page 66), divided	1
1 cup	cranberry juice	250 mL

1. Prepare a medium-hot indirect fire with a kiss of smoke in your grill.

2. Place ribs in foil pan and season to taste with salt and pepper.

3. Fill spray bottle with cranberry juice. When you see the first wisp of smoke from the wood, place pan on the indirect side of the grill. Close the lid and grill for 2 hours, spraying with juice every 30 minutes. Brush with 1 cup (250 mL) of the sauce, close the lid and grill for about 60 minutes, or until fork-tender. Serve with the remaining sauce on the side.

✦ Variation ✦

You can also slow-smoke these ribs for about 3 hours, spraying with cranberry juice every 30 minutes and basting with sauce for the last 30 minutes, until fork-tender.

Honey-Basted Asian-Style Ribs

SERVES 8

Delicious and meaty, country-style ribs are great grilled with a lick of fire to caramelize the meat, then slow-cooked until fork-tender. The Hoisin Chili Marinade is a stand-out recipe that can be used on any cut of poultry or pork.

● Large foil pan

Hoisin Chili Marinade

2	cloves garlic, minced	2
½ cup	hoisin sauce	125 mL
¼ cup	chili sauce	50 mL
¼ cup	rice vinegar	50 mL
¼ cup	soy sauce	50 mL
¼ cup	liquid honey	50 mL
1 tbsp	toasted sesame oil	15 mL
1 tsp	kosher salt	5 mL
	Red food coloring	
4 lbs	country-style pork ribs	2 kg

1. *Prepare the marinade:* In a bowl, combine garlic, hoisin, chili sauce, vinegar, soy sauce, honey, sesame oil and salt. Stir in enough red food coloring to lightly tint the mixture.

2. Place ribs in a large sealable plastic bag and pour in half the marinade. Seal, toss to coat and refrigerate for at least 4 hours or up to 8 hours, tossing occasionally. Cover and refrigerate the remaining marinade until ready to use.

3. Meanwhile, prepare a medium-hot indirect fire in your grill.

4. Remove ribs from marinade, discarding marinade. Place ribs over the hot fire. Grill for 20 to 30 minutes, turning several times and basting with some of the reserved marinade, until sauce is caramelized. Place ribs in foil pan, drizzle with the remaining marinade and cover tightly with foil. Place pan on the indirect side of the grill. Close the lid and grill for 2½ to 3 hours, or until fork-tender.

Rotisserie Cola-Mopped Ham with Cherry Barbecue Glaze

Check the maximum weight your rotisserie motor can handle before buying your ham. Don't need a whole ham? You can always freeze part of it for another tasty meal at a later date.

● Rotisserie

1	boneless ham (5 to 7 lbs/2.5 to 3.5 kg)	1
1	bottle or can (12 oz or 355 mL) cola	1
1½ cups	Cherry Barbecue Glaze (see recipe, page 52)	375 mL

1. Set up your grill for rotisserie cooking.
2. Attach ham to the spit (see page 24). Heat the grill to medium-high. Close the lid and grill for 1½ hours, mopping with cola every 15 minutes, then basting with glaze for the last 20 to 30 minutes, until an instant-read thermometer inserted in the center registers 140°F (60°C) and ham is a beautiful burnished brown. Serve hot, or let cool, refrigerate for up to 1 week and serve cold.

✦ Variation ✦

Nowadays, ham often comes with a packet of glaze. Use it as is, or doctor it up with a little vinegar to cut the sweetness.

Double-Smoked Ham

SERVES 8 TO 10

Spiral-sliced ham allows smoke to penetrate farther into the meat in a shorter amount of time — 1 to 2 hours is just fine — even tented with foil in a stovetop smoker. Don't cook it too long or the sliced meat will dry out.

- Foil pan
- **Suggested wood:** apple, hickory, pecan or oak (or a combination)

1 cup	apricot preserves or jam	250 mL
2 tbsp	cider vinegar	25 mL
1 tsp	hot pepper flakes	5 mL
1	cooked spiral-sliced ham (5 to 7 lbs/2.5 to 3.5 kg)	1

1. Prepare an indirect fire for smoking in your grill or smoker.

2. In a bowl, combine apricot preserves, vinegar and red pepper flakes. Set aside.

3. Place ham in foil pan and place pan on the indirect side of the grill. Close the lid and smoke for 1 hour. Baste with preserves mixture and pan juices, close the lid and smoke for 1 to 2 hours, or until ham is bronzed and reaches the desired smokiness.

✦ Variation ✦

If you want a mahogany-colored ham with lots of smoke, and you have some time on your hands, choose a country-cured or precooked whole ham rather than the spiral-cut. The outside "rind" on a whole ham keeps the inner meat from drying out. Smoke for 2 to 6 hours, depending on the desired smokiness.

Double-Smoked Ham and Wild Rice Soup

The smokiness of the ham is sublime in this soup. Serve hot, with crusty bread.

✦ TIP ✦

You can make a rich, smoky chicken stock from the leftover bones of smoked or rotisserie-cooked half or whole chickens. After cutting the meat from the bones, pull the carcass apart and place the bones in a stockpot. Cover with water and add a quartered peeled onion and a couple of celery stalks. Cover and bring to a boil over high heat. Reduce heat to medium-low, remove the lid and cook for 2 to 3 hours, or until liquid is reduced by half. Discard the bones and vegetables. Place a double layer of cheesecloth over a strainer and strain stock into a clean bowl. Stock can be stored in an airtight container in the refrigerator for up to 10 days or in the freezer for up to 3 months.

½ cup	unsalted butter	125 mL
2	stalks celery, chopped	2
1	small onion, chopped	1
¾ cup	all-purpose flour	175 mL
3 cups	rich chicken stock (see tip, at left)	750 mL
1 cup	water	250 mL
3 cups	cooked wild rice	750 mL
1 cup	finely chopped smoked ham	250 mL
1 cup	finely chopped carrots	250 mL
1 cup	half-and-half (10%) cream	250 mL
½ cup	shredded Cheddar cheese	125 mL
⅓ cup	dry sherry	75 mL
1½ tsp	curry powder	7 mL
1 tsp	freshly ground white pepper	5 mL
¼ tsp	kosher salt	1 mL

1. In a large pot, melt butter over medium heat. Sauté celery and onion for 5 minutes, or until tender. Add flour and cook for 5 minutes, stirring constantly, until it begins to bubble and brown. Stir in stock 1 cup (250 mL) at a time. Increase heat to medium-high and stir in water. Cook for about 30 minutes, stirring once or twice, until thickened. Add wild rice, ham, carrots, cream, cheese, sherry, curry powder, pepper and salt; reduce heat to medium-low and cook for 30 minutes, stirring frequently. Do not let boil.

✦ Variation ✦

Smoked Duck Soup: Substitute beef consommé for the chicken stock and smoked duck for the ham.

Grilled Ham Steaks
with Bourbon Cider Glaze

Because ham is precooked, ham steaks are so simple to prepare on the grill. Just add a bit of smoke and a tasty glaze, heat the ham through and you've got dinner. Because the steaks grill so quickly, we prefer to use charcoal for the most flavor.

✦ TIPS ✦

This glaze would also be delicious on any type of pork or on chicken.

It's always a good idea to oil the grill rack well before heating the grill, but it's especially important when you're grilling foods with a sweet glaze or baste, so they don't stick.

● **Suggested wood: apple or pecan**

Bourbon-Cider Glaze

1 cup	apple cider	250 mL
¼ cup	bourbon	50 mL
¼ cup	packed dark brown sugar	50 mL
¼ cup	butter	50 mL
4	ham slices (½ inch/1 cm thick)	4

1. *Prepare the glaze:* In a small saucepan, combine cider and bourbon; boil over high heat until reduced by almost half. Add brown sugar and butter, stirring until sugar is dissolved. Remove from heat and keep warm.

2. Prepare a hot fire with a kiss of smoke in your charcoal grill.

3. When you see the first wisp of smoke from the wood, place ham on the grill. Close the lid and grill for about 2 minutes per side, turning once, or until ham has good grill marks and is heated through. Brush with glaze and grill, turning once, until caramelized on both sides. Serve with any remaining glaze on the side.

✦ Variation ✦

Add ¼ cup (50 mL) of your favorite fruit preserves or jam, such as apricot or cherry, to the glaze. The pectin in the preserves helps to gel the sauce.

Italian Sausage with Stir-Grilled Peppers, Onions and Potatoes

This is a grilled version of a classic Italian home cooking tradition.

✦ Variations ✦

To stir-grill the sausages and potato mixture together, first slice the sausages about 1 inch (2.5 cm) thick. Place in the wok and stir-grill for 7 to 10 minutes, or until crispy. Add the veggies and stir-grill until slightly charred and warmed through and sausage is no longer pink inside. Serve over creamy polenta.

Prepare the stir-grilled sausage mixture above and use as a topping for grilled pizza.

- Grill wok or basket, oiled
- Baking sheet

1 lb	fingerling potatoes, halved lengthwise	500 g
4	bell peppers (a mix of red, yellow and green), cut into strips	4
1	large red onion, cut into 8 wedges	1
2 tbsp	olive oil (approx.)	25 mL
	Kosher salt and freshly ground black pepper	
6	Italian sausages (each 8 oz/250 g)	6
	Shaved Parmesan cheese	

1. Place potatoes in a microwave-safe bowl and microwave on High for 2 minutes. Toss and microwave on High for 2 minutes, or until they can be pierced with a fork.

2. In a large bowl, combine potatoes, peppers and onion. Drizzle with olive oil and toss to coat, adding a little more oil if necessary to coat well. Season to taste with salt and pepper.

3. Prepare a hot fire in your grill.

4. Transfer vegetables to prepared grill wok. Set wok and sausages on baking sheet and carry out to the grill.

5. Place wok on the grill. Grill, tossing with long-handled wooden spatulas every 2 minutes, for 15 minutes, or until vegetables have browned and softened.

6. Meanwhile, prick sausages lightly with a fork. Grill for 10 to 15 minutes, turning to brown all over, until no longer pink inside.

7. Serve sausages with the vegetable medley on the side. Sprinkle vegetables with Parmesan.

Oktoberfest Grillwurst

Prepare an assortment of German sausages, such as bockwurst, bratwurst, frankfurters, knockwurst, weinerwurst and weisswurst. Raw sausages need to be fully cooked; precooked or smoked sausages can be warmed on the grill. To complete the party atmosphere, offer steins of cold German beer.

✦ TIPS ✦

Perk up the flavor of store-bought sauerkraut with a pinch of lightly toasted caraway seeds.

20 to 24	assorted German sausages	20 to 24
8 cups	prepared sauerkraut	2 L
2	loaves bread (black bread and rye)	2
	Assorted rolls (sourdough, caraway and poppy seed)	
	Assorted German mustards	

1. Prepare a medium fire in your grill.

2. In a large saucepan, warm sauerkraut over medium heat. Keep warm.

3. Prick sausages lightly with a fork. Grill for 10 to 15 minutes, turning several times, until golden brown and no longer pink inside. Serve with a bowl of warm sauerkraut and assorted bread, rolls and mustards on the side.

Beef

Texas-Style Beef Brisket with Brazos Mop
  and Smoked Chile Barbecue Sauce 220

Kansas City Hickory-Smoked Brisket Flats 222

Smoked Brisket Soup. 224

Burnt-End Sandwiches with Caramelized Onions 225

Provençal Beef Daube with a Double Kiss of Smoke. 226

Old-Fashioned Chuck Roast with a Kiss of Smoke 228

Santa Maria Tri-Tip 229

Cherry-Smoked Rib Roast with Horseradish Crème Fraîche . . . 230

Calgary Stampede Spitted Beef Roast 231

Grill-Roasted Tenderloin with Bacon Mushroom Sauce 232

Grilled Cuban Beef Medallions in Cumin-Lime Marinade 233

Steakhouse Filets with Fried Onion Slivers
  and Béarnaise Sauce 234

Kansas City Strip Steaks with Stir-Grilled Vegetables 235

Black and Bleu Sirloin Served over Greens
  with Tarragon Vinaigrette 236

Tagliata Steak Salad with Shaved Parmesan. 237

Mesquite-Grilled Sirloin with Shortcut Mexican Mole. 238

Black Pepper–Rubbed Sirloin with Horseradish Butter 239

Branding Iron Beef with Smoked Chile Drizzle. 240

Cowboy Steaks with Two-Steppin' Rub 241

Down Under Rib Eye with Ginger-Lime Hollandaise 242

Pecan-Grilled Porterhouse with Cambozola Butter 243

Thai Marinated Beef in Lettuce Cups 244

Grilled Flank Steak with Smoked Garlic Cream Sauce 245

Carne Asada with Poblano and Onion Rajas. 246

continued on next page…

Lime-Grilled Skirt Steak Fajitas with
Charred Tomato Chipotle Salsa 248

Sriracha, Soy and Sesame Hanger Steak 250

Salt and Pepper Ranch Steaks with
Stir-Grilled Onion Slivers 251

Bamboo Beef with Homemade Teriyaki Sauce 252

Korean Bulgogi with Kimchee 253

Vietnamese Grilled Beef Skewers in Pho 254

Greek Kofta Kabobs 256

Grilled Short Ribs with Mestiza 257

Flame-Licked Beef Short Ribs with
Bourbon Barbecue Sauce 258

Rosemary-Grilled Veal Chops with Garlic Rosemary Butter . . . 259

Bistro Burger 260

The deep, rich flavor of beef takes well to the grill, rotisserie or smoker. Grilled beef skewers, burgers, steaks and tenderloin develop a dark crust while remaining juicy and tender inside. Large roasts turn slowly on a spit and brisket slow-smokes to fork-tender deliciousness.

When building barbecue flavor, try umami flavors (mushroom, soy, miso, etc.) and the heavier tastes of tomato, spices, peppers, wine, beer and bourbon in marinades, rubs and sauces.

Medium to heavy wood smoke, especially cherry, hickory, oak, pecan and mesquite, also helps accentuate beef's robust flavor.

✦ Beef Cuts and Best Barbecue Methods ✦

Burgers: Grill

Steaks: Grill, indirect grill, smoke

Boneless beef: Grill, skewer, herb-grill, plank, stir-grill, leaf-wrap

Stewing beef: Smoke-braise, smoke

Roasts: Indirect grill, grill-roast, rotisserie, smoke

✦ Steak Your Claim ✦

Steak Type	Best Barbecue Methods
Boneless flat steak (flank, hanger, flat-iron, bavette)	Marinate, grill to medium-rare over a hot fire, slice on the diagonal, finish with sauce
Boneless steak (sirloin, rib eye, strip)	Season with rub or flavoring paste, grill to medium-rare over a hot fire, finish with sauce
Filet mignon (tenderloin)	Season with rub or flavoring paste, grill to medium-rare over a hot fire using a cast-iron skillet or piastra, finish with sauce
Bone-in steak (rib eye, porterhouse, strip)	Season with rub, sear over a hot fire, grill to medium-rare on the indirect side, finish with sauce
Thick-cut steak (sirloin, porterhouse, tri-tip)	Season with rub or flavoring paste, grill "black and bleu" over a hot fire, slice and serve over greens

Texas-Style Beef Brisket with Brazos Mop and Smoked Chile Barbecue Sauce

SERVES 12 TO 16, PLUS LEFTOVERS

Here's a tried-and-true way to cook brisket Texas-style: grill for 1 hour per pound (500 g) of meat, plus a little more in case the fire gets too low or the meat is tough and stubborn.

◆ TIPS ◆

Before barbecuing, cut a notch or V shape into the brisket indicating the direction of the grain of the meat; this will help you slice it properly after it is cooked.

To test whether brisket is fork-tender, stick a fork in a section of meat and twist. If the meat twists, it's tender enough.

- Baking sheet
- **Suggested wood: oak or mesquite**

1	beef brisket (10 lbs/5 kg)	1
½ cup	Brisket Rub (see recipe, page 35)	125 mL

Brazos Mop

¾ cup	unsalted butter	175 mL
¾ cup	packed brown sugar	175 mL
¾ cup	cider vinegar	175 mL
¾ cup	tequila	175 mL
2 tbsp	canned chipotle chile purée	25 mL
1	recipe Smoked Chile Barbecue Sauce (page 63), divided	1
	Dill pickle slices, sliced onion and pickled jalapeños	

1. Place brisket on baking sheet and generously coat all sides with rub. Cover with plastic wrap and let stand for 30 minutes.

2. Meanwhile, prepare an indirect fire for smoking in your grill or smoker.

3. Place brisket on the indirect side of the grill. Close the lid and smoke for 2 hours.

4. *Meanwhile, prepare the mop:* In a saucepan, melt butter over medium heat. Add brown sugar, vinegar, tequila and chile purée. Simmer, stirring occasionally, for about 10 minutes to blend the flavors.

Perfectly cooked brisket has an internal temperature of 185°F to 200°F (90°C to 100°C). If the meat registers more than that, it will be too dry. Remember that the internal temperature will rise at least another 5°F (3°C) once the meat is removed from the grill.

In Canada, brisket is available mainly in urban areas with a Jewish population. For those who cannot easily come by brisket, try substituting a bottom round roast or top sirloin. These cuts are a bit more tender than brisket, so the cooking time will be slightly shorter.

5. Brush brisket with mop, close the lid and smoke for about 7 hours, basting with mop every hour. Remove brisket from the grill and place on a large piece of heavy-duty foil. Pour 1 cup (250 mL) of the barbecue sauce over the brisket, wrap tightly and return to the grill. Close the lid and smoke for 1 hour, or until fork-tender. Let rest for 20 minutes. Transfer to a cutting board, trim off the fat and carve across the grain into thin slices.

6. Serve with the remaining barbecue sauce, pickles, onion and jalapeños on the side.

✦ Variation ✦

To make burnt ends, cut off the thin end portion of the smoked brisket. Cut into cubes, baste with mop and smoke for 1 to 2 hours, or until dark on all sides.

Stack several slices of brisket in a sandwich bun spread lightly with barbecue sauce.

Kansas City Hickory-Smoked Brisket Flats

SERVES 8 TO 10

If you're new to slow-smoking, a brisket flat is easier and quicker than smoking a whole brisket, and still gives you succulent beef with the wonderful flavor of smoke. This Kansas City–style brisket is richly flavored and slightly chewy.

✦ TIPS ✦

Before barbecuing, cut a notch or V shape into the brisket indicating the direction of the grain of the meat; this will help you slice it properly after it is cooked.

To test whether brisket is fork-tender, stick a fork in a section of meat and twist. If the meat twists, it's tender enough.

- Baking sheet
- **Suggested wood:** hickory, apple, oak or pecan

Rub

2 tbsp	sweet Hungarian paprika	25 mL
2 tbsp	granulated garlic	25 mL
2 tbsp	onion salt	25 mL
1 tbsp	freshly ground black pepper	15 mL
1	boneless beef brisket flat (5 lbs/2.5 kg)	1
1 cup	prepared yellow mustard	250 mL
	Tomato-based barbecue sauce	

Kansas City Brisket Mop

1½ cups	beef stock	375 mL
½ cup	Worcestershire sauce	125 mL
¼ cup	tomato-based barbecue sauce	50 mL
	Additional tomato-based barbecue sauce	

1. *Prepare the rub:* In a small bowl, combine paprika, garlic, onion salt and pepper.
2. Place brisket on baking sheet, slather all over with mustard and sprinkle with rub. Let stand until coating is just tacky.
3. Meanwhile, prepare an indirect fire for smoking in your grill or smoker.
4. Place brisket on the indirect side of the grill. Close the lid and smoke for 2½ hours.

A whole brisket is really two pieces of meat; the "flat" is the narrower, thinner section. Have your butcher cut it for you.

Granulated garlic is available at well-stocked grocery stores or online.

5. *Meanwhile, prepare the mop:* In a bowl, combine beef stock, Worcestershire sauce and barbecue sauce.

6. Brush brisket with mop, close the lid and smoke for $2\frac{1}{2}$ hours, basting with mop every hour. Remove brisket from the grill and place on a large piece of heavy-duty foil. Slather with barbecue sauce, wrap tightly and return to the grill. Close the lid and smoke for $1\frac{1}{2}$ hours, or until fork-tender. Let rest for 15 minutes. Transfer to a cutting board, trim off any fat and carve across the grain into thin slices. Serve with barbecue sauce.

✦ Variations ✦

To make burnt ends, cut off the thin end portion of the smoked brisket flat. Cut into cubes, baste with mop and smoke for 1 to 2 hours, or until dark on all sides.

For Texas-style brisket, substitute Two-Steppin' Rub (page 241), use a half-quantity of mesquite wood and smoke for 1 to 2 hours longer in step 4, so it's very tender.

Smoked Brisket Soup

This recipe makes it clear why you want to smoke a big brisket: so you'll have leftovers to make this hearty, satisfying soup. Leftovers never tasted so good.

✦ TIPS ✦

Be an efficient barbecuer. Wrap and freeze leftover smoked meats for later use in dishes like this one.

The soup can be served immediately or cooled and refrigerated overnight, then reheated the next day. The soup will actually be more delicious the second day!

12 cups	beef consommé	3 L
4 cups	tomato sauce	1 L
8 oz	sliced baby bella mushrooms	250 g
3 cups	shredded smoked brisket	750 mL
2 cups	chopped roasted red bell peppers (see tip, page 174)	500 mL
2 cups	chopped carrots	500 mL
½ cup	brandy or cognac	125 mL
1 tsp	freshly ground white pepper	5 mL
1 tsp	smoked Spanish paprika	5 mL
	Grated zest and juice of 1 lemon	
	Kosher salt	

1. In a large pot, bring consommé and tomato sauce to a boil. Add mushrooms, brisket, roasted peppers, carrots, brandy, pepper, paprika, lemon zest, lemon juice and salt to taste; bring to a boil. Reduce heat to low and simmer for at least 1 hour to blend the flavors.

✦ Variation ✦

Leftover grilled or smoked duck would be a great substitute for the brisket.

Burnt-End Sandwiches with Caramelized Onions

Traditional burnt ends are a signature dish in Kansas City. The thinnest ends of the brisket are chopped, dressed with tangy barbecue sauce and seasoned with an all-purpose rub. Then they are wrapped tightly in foil and thrown back on the grill to cook slowly for a couple of hours. This version uses more of the meat from the brisket flat.

◆ TIP ◆

Be an efficient barbecuer. Wrap and freeze leftover smoked meats for later use.

● Foil pan

3 lbs	smoked brisket flat meat (see recipe, page 222), chopped	1.5 kg
3 cups	Kansas City–Style Smoky Tomato Barbecue Sauce (page 70), divided	750 mL
1½ tbsp	All-Purpose Barbecue Rub (see recipe, page 34)	22 mL
8 to 10	Kaiser rolls or other buns, split and wrapped in foil	8 to 10

Caramelized Onions

4	onions, thinly sliced	4
3 tbsp	packed dark brown sugar	45 mL
3 tbsp	bourbon	45 mL
1 tsp	kosher salt	5 mL

1. Prepare a medium-hot indirect fire in your grill.

2. Place brisket meat in foil pan and add half the barbecue sauce and the rub. Toss to coat and cover tightly with foil. Place pan on the indirect side of the grill and grill for about 2 hours, or until meat has charred and sauce has caramelized. Place rolls on top of the brisket for the last 20 minutes.

3. *Meanwhile, prepare the onions:* In a large skillet, over medium heat, sauté onions and sugar for 20 to 25 minutes, or until onions are golden brown. Add bourbon and salt; cook until bourbon is absorbed.

4. Set out warm buns, burnt ends, caramelized onions and the remaining barbecue sauce for everyone to make their own sandwiches.

Provençal Beef Daube
with a Double Kiss of Smoke

SERVES 8 TO 10

This daube is best made 2 days ahead. Smoke for 1½ hours and marinate overnight the first day, braise in a fragrant, smoky broth the second day, then let cool and refrigerate. Reheat the third day and serve with crusty bread and butter and a hearty glass of red wine. It is worth the effort, and is perfect as a make-ahead dish for company.

◆ TIP ◆

Look for canned fire-roasted tomatoes (such as Muir Glen or Hunt's) in health food stores or the organic section of well-stocked supermarkets.

- **Large foil pan**
- **Suggested wood:** oak, pecan or apple

4 lbs	boneless beef chuck (blade) roast, cut into 3-inch (7.5 cm) cubes	2 kg
4	onions, thinly sliced	4
5	whole cloves	5
5	whole allspice	5
5	bay leaves	5
5	sprigs thyme	5
2 tsp	liquid smoke	10 mL
4 cups	dry red wine	1 L
¼ cup	olive oil (approx.)	50 mL
	Kosher salt and freshly ground black pepper	
1	can (28 oz/796 mL) fire-roasted whole tomatoes (see tip, at left), with juice	1
1	jar (15 oz/426 mL) chopped roasted red bell peppers, drained	1
4	cloves garlic, minced	4
2 tbsp	drained capers	25 mL

1. Prepare an indirect fire for smoking in your grill or smoker.

2. Arrange beef in foil pan and place on the indirect side of the grill. Close the lid and smoke for 1½ hours.

3. Transfer beef to a large stainless steel bowl. Cover with onions and add cloves, allspice, bay leaves, thyme and liquid smoke. Pour red wine over all. Cover and refrigerate for 20 to 24 hours. Strain beef mixture, reserving the marinade.

4. In a Dutch oven, heat oil over high heat. Sauté onions for 10 minutes, or until translucent. Remove with a slotted spoon to a plate and set aside.

5. Add oil to the pan if necessary and, working in three to four batches, brown beef over medium heat, adding oil as necessary between batches. Season with salt and pepper, remove with a slotted spoon to a plate and set aside.

6. Pour marinade into the pan and bring to a boil. Reduce heat to medium-low and add tomatoes with juice, roasted peppers, garlic and capers. Return onions, beef and any accumulated juices to the pan. Cover and simmer for at least 2 hours, or until beef is fork-tender. Remove lid and let cool for at least 1 hour. Cover and refrigerate overnight.

7. Reheat daube and ladle into bowls.

Old-Fashioned Chuck Roast with a Kiss of Smoke

SERVES 8 TO 10

Simple and delicious equals a winning combination that can't be beat.

✦ TIPS ✦

To test whether roast is fork-tender, stick a fork in a section of meat and twist. If the meat twists, it's tender enough.

You can either slice the meat or, if making sandwiches, pull it apart in chunks and chop the chunks.

Serve this luscious fall-apart roast with garlic mashed potatoes and roasted carrots.

- **Large foil pan**
- **Suggested wood: oak, hickory or apple**

4 lbs	boneless beef chuck (blade) roast	2 kg
	Kosher salt and freshly ground black pepper	
½ cup	grainy mustard	125 mL

1. Prepare an indirect fire for smoking in your grill or smoker.
2. Season roast with salt and pepper, slather with mustard and place in foil pan. Place pan on the indirect side of the grill. Close the lid and smoke for 2 hours. Cover with foil, add 1 inch (2.5 cm) of water to keep the meat from getting dry and smoke for 1½ to 2 hours, or until beef is fork-tender. Transfer to a cutting board, tent with foil and let rest for about 10 minutes before slicing.

Santa Maria Tri-Tip

Santa Maria, California, is the home of tri-tip roast (the butt, or bottom, of the sirloin) grilled over regional red oak hardwood on brazier-style grills. For authentic flavor, grill this beef with a kiss of smoke on a charcoal grill.

✦ TIPS ✦

Before barbecuing, cut a notch or V shape into the roast indicating the direction of the grain of the meat; this will help you slice it properly after it is cooked.

Serve with your favorite salsa and grilled garlic bread.

● **Suggested wood: oak**

Santa Maria Mop

¼ cup	olive oil	50 mL
¼ cup	balsamic vinegar	50 mL
¼ cup	freshly squeezed orange juice	50 mL
¼ cup	freshly squeezed lemon juice	50 mL
1 tbsp	garlic salt	15 mL
1 tbsp	lemon pepper	15 mL
1 tbsp	dry mustard	15 mL
2 tsp	ground dried rosemary	10 mL
½ tsp	hot pepper flakes	2 mL
1	beef tri-tip roast (about 3 lbs/1.5 kg)	1
4	cloves garlic, slivered	4
2 tbsp	olive oil	25 mL
2 tsp	coarse kosher salt	10 mL
2 tsp	freshly ground black pepper	10 mL
1 tsp	each dried rosemary and oregano	5 mL

1. *Prepare the mop:* In a bowl, combine olive oil, vinegar, orange juice, lemon juice, garlic salt, lemon pepper, mustard, rosemary and hot pepper flakes. Cover and refrigerate until ready to use.

2. With a sharp paring knife, make several small slits in the roast and insert the garlic slivers. Lightly coat roast with olive oil.

3. In a bowl, combine salt, pepper, rosemary and oregano. Sprinkle over roast. Set aside.

4. Prepare a medium-hot fire with a kiss of smoke in your grill.

5. When you see the first wisp of smoke from the wood, place roast on the grill. Close the lid and grill for 40 to 45 minutes, turning and basting with mop every 5 minutes, until a meat thermometer inserted in the thickest part of the roast registers 130°F (54°C) for medium-rare, or until desired doneness. Let rest for 15 minutes before carving across the grain into thin slices.

Cherry-Smoked Rib Roast with Horseradish Crème Fraîche

Once you've smoked a rib roast, you'll never go back to the oven method. The beef still gets that characteristic dark crustiness, but it also has a wonderful smoky aroma. If you like, cut off some of the fat for Yorkshire pudding before you put the beef on the smoker.

● **Suggested wood:** cherry, pecan, hickory or a combination of mesquite and apple

Horseradish Crème Fraîche

1 cup	sour cream	250 mL
1 cup	whipping (35%) cream	250 mL
2 tbsp	prepared horseradish (or to taste)	25 mL
1 tbsp	snipped fresh chives	15 mL
1	boneless prime rib roast (about 4 lbs/2 kg)	1
	Granulated garlic, kosher salt and freshly ground black pepper	

1. *Prepare the crème fraîche:* In a small bowl, whisk together sour cream, whipping cream, horseradish and chives. Cover and refrigerate until ready to serve.

2. Prepare an indirect fire for smoking in your grill or smoker.

3. Sprinkle roast with garlic, salt and pepper to taste. Place on the indirect side of the grill. Close the lid and smoke for 2 hours, or until a meat thermometer inserted in the thickest part of the roast registers 130°F (54°C) for medium-rare, or until desired doneness. Let rest for 15 minutes before carving. Pass the crème fraîche at the table.

Calgary Stampede Spitted Beef Roast

Beef ranching on the North American prairie extends from the southern tip of Texas to the tundra of northern Saskatchewan, Manitoba and Alberta. The week-long Calgary Stampede, which takes place in mid-July, celebrates beef in all its glory. So rustle up all your friends and family for this great grub.

- **Rotisserie**
- **Suggested wood:** mesquite, cherry, pecan or hickory

Dry Rub

2 tbsp	sweet Hungarian paprika	25 mL
2 tbsp	garlic powder	25 mL
1 tbsp	dry mustard	15 mL
1 tbsp	chili powder	15 mL
1 tbsp	onion salt	15 mL
1 tbsp	freshly ground black pepper	15 mL
1	boneless prime rib roast (about 6 lbs/3 kg)	1

1. *Prepare the rub:* In a small bowl, combine paprika, garlic powder, mustard, chili powder, onion salt and pepper.
2. Season roast all over with rub and set aside.
3. Set up your grill for rotisserie cooking.
4. Attach roast to the spit (see page 24). Heat the grill to medium-high and add a kiss of smoke. When you see the first wisp of smoke from the wood, close the lid and grill for 2 to 2½ hours, until an instant-read thermometer inserted in the thickest part of the roast registers 130°F (54°C) for medium-rare, or until desired doneness. Let rest for 15 minutes before carving.

✦ Variation ✦

If you prefer, you can grill the roast over a hot indirect fire instead of using the rotisserie. Place the roast in a foil pan and place the pan on the indirect side of the grill. Close the lid and grill for 2 to 2½ hours, turning the roast every 30 minutes.

Grill-Roasted Tenderloin with Bacon Mushroom Sauce

Grill the tenderloin with a little char on the exterior, leaving the interior rosy and juicy. You'll need a really hot fire, preferably one made with mesquite charcoal, though you can still have a mighty fine tenderloin on a gas grill.

✦ TIPS ✦

You can get extra savings on beef tenderloin if you trim it yourself, which is easy to do. The whole tenderloin will have a thick end and will taper down to a thin end. Trim off any fat and silverskin. Cut the size tenderloin you want to grill whole, then slice the rest into 1-inch (2.5 cm) thick steaks. Cut the tapered end into chunks for kabobs. Wrap well and freeze for up to 3 months.

The blend of apple and hickory wood is especially nice with beef. Another great wood combination is cherry and oak.

● **Suggested wood:** apple and hickory

Bacon Mushroom Sauce

12 oz	thick-sliced bacon	375 g
4 oz	mushrooms, sliced	125 g
1½ cups	sour cream	375 mL
2 tbsp	finely chopped fresh flat-leaf (Italian) parsley	25 mL
1 tbsp	grated onion	15 mL
2 tsp	prepared horseradish	10 mL
1	beef tenderloin (6 to 8 lbs/3 to 4 kg), trimmed	1
3 tbsp	melted unsalted butter	45 mL
	Coarse kosher salt and freshly ground black pepper	

1. *Prepare the sauce:* In a large skillet over high heat, cook bacon until crisp. Transfer to a plate lined with paper towels. Pour off all but 2 tbsp (25 mL) of the bacon fat and sauté mushrooms until softened, 3 to 5 minutes. Transfer to a bowl and let cool. Crumble bacon and add to bowl with sour cream, parsley, onion and horseradish. Cover and refrigerate until ready to use.

2. Brush tenderloin with butter and season to taste with salt and pepper. Set aside.

3. Prepare a hot fire with a kiss of smoke in your grill.

4. When you see the first wisp of smoke from the wood, place tenderloin on the grill. Close the lid and grill for 20 to 22 minutes, turning a quarter turn every 5 minutes and brushing with butter halfway through, until a meat thermometer inserted in the thickest part of the tenderloin registers 130°F (54°C) for medium-rare, or until desired doneness. Let rest for 5 minutes before slicing. Serve with sauce.

Grilled Cuban Beef Medallions in Cumin-Lime Marinade

SERVES 6

This barrio, or neighborhood, dish, adapted from a recipe by Aaron Sanchez of Paladar in New York, is delicious served with mashed potatoes, but it also makes addictive steak sandwiches. The marinade is good with any type of steak.

◆ TIP ◆

These medallions can also be cooked indoors in a grill pan.

Cumin-Lime Marinade

2	large cloves garlic, minced	2
1 tbsp	chopped fresh oregano	15 mL
1/2 tsp	ground cumin	2 mL
2 tbsp	freshly squeezed lime juice	25 mL
1 1/2 tbsp	olive oil	22 mL
1	eye of round roast (2 to 2 1/2 lbs/1 to 1.25 kg)	1
1 1/2 tbsp	olive oil	22 mL
1	large onion, thinly sliced	1
1/4 cup	chopped fresh flat-leaf (Italian) parsley	50 mL
	Kosher salt and freshly ground black pepper	

1. *Prepare the marinade:* In a small bowl, combine garlic, oregano, cumin, lime juice and olive oil.

2. Cut beef across the grain into 1/2-inch (1 cm) thick slices. Place each slice between two pieces of plastic wrap and pound to 1/4 inch (0.5 cm) thick. Place in a shallow dish, overlapping as necessary, and pour in marinade. Cover and refrigerate for 1 hour.

3. Meanwhile, in a skillet, heat oil over medium-high heat. Sauté onion for 15 to 20 minutes, or until caramelized. Stir in parsley and season to taste with salt and pepper. Set aside and keep warm.

4. Meanwhile, prepare a medium-hot fire in your grill.

5. Remove beef from marinade, discarding marinade, and pat dry. Grill beef for 3 minutes per side, turning once. Season to taste with salt and pepper. Serve topped with caramelized onion.

Steakhouse Filets with Fried Onion Slivers and Béarnaise Sauce

SERVES 4

Add a side of creamed spinach and you've got the classic steakhouse entrée! Steakhouses have commercial equipment that cranks out the BTUs for high, high heat, but you can achieve a charry exterior and tender, juicy interior with a cast-iron skillet, grill pan or griddle.

✦ TIPS ✦

Use a mandoline slicer for paper-thin onion slivers.

If you prefer, you can cook the steaks inside on the stovetop over high heat. You'll still need to heat the skillet first.

- Candy/deep-fry thermometer
- Cast-iron skillet, grill pan or griddle

Fried Onion Slivers

1	large onion, sliced paper-thin	1
½ cup	all-purpose flour	125 mL
3 cups	peanut oil	750 mL
	Kosher salt	
4	filets mignons (each 8 oz/250 g and 2 inches/5 cm thick)	4
	Olive oil	
	Kosher salt and freshly ground black pepper	
1	recipe Béarnaise Sauce (page 55)	1

1. *Prepare the onion slivers:* Toss onion in flour until well coated. In a deep saucepan or an electric skillet, heat peanut oil over medium heat until it registers 350°F (180°C) on thermometer. Add onion, in batches, and fry, stirring frequently, for 7 to 8 minutes, or until golden. Remove with a slotted spoon to a plate lined with paper towels. Season to taste with salt. Set aside and keep warm.

2. Prepare a hot fire in your grill. Heat skillet until the inside bottom begins to turn gray, about 20 minutes.

3. Brush steaks with olive oil. Grill for 2 to 3 minutes per side, turning once, until dark and crusty on the outside and a meat thermometer inserted in the thickest part of a steak registers 130°F (54°C) for medium-rare, or until desired doneness. Season to taste with salt and pepper. Serve with fried onions and Béarnaise Sauce.

Kansas City Strip Steaks with Stir-Grilled Vegetables

With the Parmesan-sprinkled vegetables, this is an Italian take on grilled steak. If you like, spoon a little of the Parmesan mixture over the steaks before serving. Serve garlic bread toasted on the grill for a great side.

✦ TIP ✦

Other names for Kansas City strip steaks are top loin steaks, New York strip steaks and strip loin steaks.

✦ Variation ✦

Stir-grilled vegetables are all about color, so add yellow teardrop tomatoes, red grape tomatoes and sugar snap peas to this medley for a spectacular combination of good-for-you vegetables.

● Grill wok or basket, oiled

3	cloves garlic, minced	3
3 tbsp	ground dried basil	45 mL
1 tbsp	freshly ground black pepper	15 mL
4	Kansas City strip steaks (each about 10 oz/300 g)	1
½ cup	freshly grated Parmesan cheese	125 mL
¼ cup	olive oil	50 mL
¼ cup	red wine vinegar	50 mL
2	large red onions, cut into ½-inch (1 cm) slices	2
3	bell peppers (preferably a mix of colors), quartered	3

1. In a bowl, combine garlic, basil and pepper. Rub each steak with 2 tsp (10 mL) of the mixture. Set aside.

2. In a small bowl, combine cheese, olive oil, vinegar and the remaining seasoning mixture. Set aside.

3. Place onions in a microwave-safe bowl and microwave on High for 1½ to 2 minutes, or until slightly softened. Transfer to prepared wok and add bell peppers.

4. Prepare a dual-heat fire, hot on one side and medium-hot on the other, in your grill.

5. Place wok over the medium-hot fire. Grill vegetables for 5 minutes, tossing once or twice with long-handled wooden spatulas. Add cheese mixture and grill, tossing every 3 to 4 minutes, for 7 to 10 minutes, or until vegetables are softened to your liking and heated all the way through.

6. Meanwhile, place steaks over the hot fire and grill for 7 to 8 minutes per side, turning once, until a meat thermometer inserted in the thickest part of a steak registers 130°F (54°C) for medium-rare, or until desired doneness.

Black and Bleu Sirloin Served over Greens with Tarragon Vinaigrette

SERVES 8 TO 12

The term "black and bleu" refers to a steak that is charred on the outside and rare on the inside. You'll need a hotter than hot fire or a really hot seasoned cast-iron skillet, grill pan or griddle.

✦ TIP ✦

KISS (keep it simple, stupid) could be the slogan for this type of steak. Grill one huge slab of beef, then slice it and serve. It's easier to cook a thick-cut steak just right, as there is a greater margin of error than with a thinner steak. Grill a thick steak for a minute or two longer, and it's no big deal.

Tarragon Vinaigrette

½ cup	olive oil	125 mL
½ cup	tarragon-flavored vinegar	125 mL
1 tbsp	granulated sugar	15 mL
1 tsp	kosher salt	5 mL
1	sirloin steak (about 4 lbs/2 kg and 2 inches/5 cm thick)	1
2 tbsp	olive oil or melted butter	25 mL
	Coarse kosher salt and freshly ground black pepper	
1 lb	mixed salad greens, including baby spinach and arugula	500 g
	Pecorino Romano cheese shavings	

1. *Prepare the vinaigrette:* In a bowl, whisk together olive oil, vinegar, sugar and salt. Set aside.

2. Brush steak with olive oil and season to taste with salt and pepper. Set aside.

3. Prepare a very hot fire in your grill.

4. Grill steak for about 7 minutes per side, turning once, until a meat thermometer inserted in the thickest part of the steak registers 120°F (50°C). Transfer to a cutting board, tent with foil and let rest for 10 to 15 minutes before slicing across the grain.

5. Place greens in a large bowl, add vinaigrette and toss to coat.

6. Divide greens among plates, top with steak slices and sprinkle with cheese.

✦ Variation ✦

Serve the steak with your favorite barbecue sauce on grill-toasted ciabatta rolls or a crusty Italian loaf.

Tagliata Steak Salad with Shaved Parmesan

Tagliata is an Italian dish featuring a thick steak seared until charry on the outside but rare on the inside, served sliced over greens.

8 oz	mixed salad greens, including baby spinach and arugula	250 g
1 cup	cherry or grape tomatoes	250 mL
½ cup	thinly sliced red onion	125 mL
2 lbs	black and bleu grilled sirloin steak, sliced	1 kg
	Balsamic vinaigrette	
	Shaved Parmigiano-Reggiano cheese	

1. In a large bowl, combine greens, tomatoes and red onion. Portion onto plates or mound on a platter. Arrange steak over salad. Drizzle with vinaigrette and garnish with cheese.

Mesquite-Grilled Sirloin with Shortcut Mexican Mole

SERVES 6

Mesquite grows abundantly in the southwest U.S. and Mexico. It burns hot, giving steak an excellent char, so this recipe is for a charcoal grill only. Doctoring up prepared mole with a few ingredients is a big time-saver versus making it from scratch — and it tastes great.

✦ TIPS ✦

Any kind of pepper can be roasted over a hot fire. Grill, turning often, until the skin is charred, then place in a paper bag, close the bag and let cool for 5 to 10 minutes. Rub a little of the skin off and remove stem and seeds.

The mole can be stored in an airtight container in the refrigerator for up to 2 weeks.

✦ Variation ✦

Mole is also great with grilled lamb, pork and chicken.

- Baking sheet
- Mesquite lump charcoal

Shortcut Mexican Mole

2 cups	canned fire-roasted diced tomatoes (see tip, page 226), with juice	500 mL
1½ cups	chopped roasted red bell peppers (store-bought or see tip, at left)	375 mL
1 cup	prepared mole	250 mL
1 tbsp	packed dark brown sugar	15 mL
1 tbsp	peanut butter	15 mL
	Kosher salt	
6	pieces sirloin steak (each about 8 oz/250 g)	6
2 tbsp	olive oil	25 mL
1 tbsp	garlic salt	15 mL
1 tbsp	cracked black pepper	15 mL

1. *Prepare the mole:* In a food processor, purée tomatoes, roasted peppers, mole, brown sugar, peanut butter and salt to taste.

2. Transfer to a saucepan and bring to a simmer over medium-low heat. Reduce heat to low, cover and keep warm until ready to use.

3. Place steaks on baking sheet and brush both sides with olive oil. In a small bowl, combine garlic salt and pepper. Sprinkle over both sides of steaks.

4. Prepare a hot fire in your charcoal grill, using mesquite charcoal.

5. Grill steaks for 5 minutes per side, turning once, until a meat thermometer inserted in the thickest part of a steak registers 130°F (54°C) for medium-rare, or until desired doneness.

6. Spoon mole onto each plate and place steaks on the sauce.

Black Pepper–Rubbed Sirloin with Horseradish Butter

Creamy mashed potatoes and caramelized onions would complement the robust flavors of this dish.

✦ TIP ✦

The horseradish butter can be stored in the refrigerator for up to 5 days, or wrapped in additional freezer plastic or paper and stored in the freezer for up to 2 weeks. Let thaw, then slice into rounds while still cold.

Horseradish Butter

6 tbsp	butter, softened	90 mL
3 tbsp	prepared horseradish	45 mL
½ tsp	kosher salt	2 mL
6	pieces sirloin steak (each about 8 oz/250 g)	6
3	cloves garlic, minced	3
3 tbsp	cracked black pepper	45 mL
2 tbsp	coarse kosher salt	25 mL

1. *Prepare the butter:* In a small bowl, whisk together butter, horseradish and salt. Spoon onto a piece of waxed paper and roll into a log about 3 inches (7.5 cm) long. Wrap in plastic wrap and refrigerate for about 1 hour, or until firm.

2. Coat steaks with garlic. In a shallow dish, combine pepper and salt. Press steaks into the salt and pepper mixture, coating both sides. Let stand for 20 minutes.

3. Meanwhile, prepare a hot fire in your grill.

4. Grill steaks for 4 to 5 minutes per side, turning once, until a meat thermometer inserted in the thickest part of a steak registers 130°F (54°C) for medium-rare, or until desired doneness. Serve each steak topped with a slice of horseradish butter.

Branding Iron Beef with Smoked Chile Drizzle

A version of beef carpaccio made famous at Harry's Bar in Venice, this thinly sliced appetizer gets a little tasty char around the outside, is very rare inside and has a smoky sauce to finish. The key is a cast-iron skillet and a hot fire.

- Plastic squeeze bottle
- Cast-iron skillet, grill pan or griddle

Smoked Chile Drizzle

1 cup	mayonnaise	250 mL
¼ cup	bottled smoked chipotle pepper sauce	50 mL
1 lb	boneless sirloin tip steak	500 g
	Olive oil	
¼ cup	drained capers	50 mL

1. *Prepare the drizzle:* In a small bowl, whisk together mayonnaise and chipotle pepper sauce until smooth. Transfer to squeeze bottle and set aside.

2. Place 8 appetizer plates in the refrigerator to chill.

3. Prepare a hot fire in your grill. Heat skillet for 20 to 30 minutes.

4. Brush steak with olive oil. Grill for about 1 minute per side, turning once, until blackened on both sides. Let cool to room temperature. Cover with plastic wrap and place in the freezer for 20 minutes.

5. Using a mandoline or a very sharp knife, cut beef across the grain into paper-thin slices and arrange on chilled plates. Drizzle with sauce, making a crosshatch pattern, and scatter with capers.

Cowboy Steaks with Two-Steppin' Rub

Everything's bigger in Texas, including rib eyes with the bone in, called cowboy rib eyes. A cowboy rib eye requires an indirect fire so you can sear over high heat, then finish cooking the steak over lower heat, a treatment that works for any bone-in steak. As for the rub, it's a simple blend of salt and pepper, but it will dance in your mouth.

● Cast-iron skillet or foil pan

Two-Steppin' Rub

¼ cup	coarse kosher or smoked salt	50 mL
¼ cup	whole black peppercorns	50 mL
4	bone-in rib eye steaks (each about 18 oz/550 g and 1 inch/2.5 cm thick), bones frenched	4
	Olive oil	

1. Prepare a dual-heat fire, hot on one side and medium on the other, in your grill.

2. *Prepare the rub:* Place salt and peppercorns in skillet and toast over the hot fire, stirring occasionally, until spices exude a warm aroma. Let cool slightly. Transfer to a clean coffee grinder or spice mill and grind.

3. Brush steaks with olive oil and sprinkle with rub. Place over the hot fire and grill for 3 to 4 minutes per side, turning once, until charred. Move over the medium fire, close the lid and grill for 2 to 3 minutes, turning once, until a meat thermometer inserted in the thickest part of a steak registers 130°F (54°C) for medium-rare, or until desired doneness. Let rest for 5 minutes.

Down Under Rib Eye
with Ginger-Lime Hollandaise

Almost anything grilled — vegetables, chicken, lamb, fish, shellfish — tastes wonderful with this Asian-style hollandaise, a reflection of the Pacific Rim cuisine of Australia and New Zealand, but well-marbled rib eye is especially tasty.

✦ TIP ✦

The hollandaise recipe contains raw egg yolks. If the food safety of raw eggs is a concern for you, use pasteurized eggs. Many grocery stores now carry pasteurized eggs in their shells. Alternatively, use ¼ cup (50 mL) pasteurized liquid whole egg; the hollandaise won't be quite as rich.

Ginger-Lime Hollandaise

1 cup	unsalted butter, divided	250 mL
½ tsp	finely grated gingerroot	2 mL
4	egg yolks	4
½ tsp	grated lime zest	2 mL
3 tbsp	freshly squeezed lime juice	45 mL
2 tbsp	chopped fresh cilantro (optional)	25 mL
	Kosher salt and freshly ground black pepper	
4	boneless rib eye steaks (each about 8 oz/250 g and 1 inch/2.5 cm thick)	4
	Olive oil	

1. *Prepare the sauce:* In a saucepan, melt 2 tbsp (25 mL) of the butter over medium-high heat. Sauté ginger for 2 minutes. Add the remaining butter and heat until very hot but not browning. Remove from heat.

2. In a food processor or blender, process egg yolks and lime juice for 30 seconds. With the motor running, through the feed tube, gradually add hot butter and lime zest, processing until thickened. Add cilantro and pulse to blend. Transfer to a bowl and season to taste with salt and pepper. Keep warm over hot water.

3. Prepare a medium-hot fire in your grill.

4. Brush steaks with olive oil. Grill for 3 minutes per side, turning once, until a meat thermometer inserted in the thickest part of a steak registers 130°F (54°C) for medium-rare, or until desired doneness. Serve each steak with a dollop of sauce.

Pecan-Grilled Porterhouse with Cambozola Butter

Adding pecan wood chips to the fire for a kiss of smoke gives this steak a smoky hit, and the savory Cambozola Butter makes it even more luscious.

✦ TIPS ✦

German Cambozola cheese blends the creaminess of Camembert and the sharpness of Gorgonzola; if you like, use half Camembert or Brie and half blue cheese in place of Cambozola.

If not serving the Cambozola butter immediately, spoon into a ramekin and cover with plastic wrap. (Or spoon onto a piece of waxed paper, roll into a log and wrap in plastic wrap.) Store in the refrigerator for up to 1 week or wrap in additional freezer plastic or paper and freeze for up to 3 months. Let thaw, then slice into rounds while still cold.

● **Suggested wood:** pecan, mesquite, oak or maple

Cambozola Butter

4	large cloves garlic, minced	4
6 oz	Cambozola cheese, at room temperature	175 g
½ cup	unsalted butter, at room temperature	125 mL
1 tbsp	snipped fresh chives	15 mL
1 tbsp	anchovy paste	15 mL
2	porterhouse steaks (each 1 to 1½ lbs/500 to 750 g and 1½ inches/4 cm thick)	2
	Olive oil	
	Kosher salt and freshly ground black pepper	

1. *Prepare the butter:* In a small bowl, using a fork, combine garlic, cheese, butter, chives and anchovy paste. Cover and let stand at room temperature for 1 hour.

2. Meanwhile, prepare a dual-heat fire, hot on one side and medium on the other, with a kiss of smoke on the hot side.

3. Brush steaks with olive oil and season to taste with salt and pepper. When you see the first wisp of smoke from the wood, place steaks over the hot fire. Grill for 4 to 5 minutes per side, turning once, until charred. Move over the medium fire, close the lid and grill for 2 to 3 minutes, turning once, until a meat thermometer inserted in the thickest part of a steak registers 130°F (54°C) for medium-rare, or until desired doneness. Let rest for 5 minutes. Serve topped with Cambozola butter.

Thai Marinated Beef in Lettuce Cups

✦ TIP ✦

After the grilled steak has cooled, it can be stored in an airtight container in the refrigerator for up to 2 days.

Marinade

2 cups	coconut milk (regular or light)	500 mL
¼ cup	seasoned rice vinegar	50 mL
2 tbsp	Thai green curry paste	25 mL
1½ lb	flank steak, trimmed	750 g
36	Bibb, butter or Sweet Gem lettuce leaves (from about 6 heads)	36
	Fresh Thai basil leaves, cilantro leaves and chopped green onions	

1. *Prepare the marinade:* In a small bowl, combine coconut milk, vinegar and curry paste.

2. Place steak in a large sealable plastic bag and pour in half the marinade. Seal, toss to coat and refrigerate for at least 3 hours or overnight, tossing occasionally. Cover and refrigerate the remaining marinade until ready to use.

3. Meanwhile, prepare a hot fire in your grill.

4. Remove steak from marinade, discarding marinade, and pat dry. Grill steak for 2½ to 3 minutes per side, turning once, until a meat thermometer inserted in the thickest part of the steak registers 130°F (54°C) for medium-rare, or until desired doneness. Transfer to a cutting board. Let cool to room temperature, then slice across the grain and on the diagonal at a 45-degree angle into very thin slices. Cut each slice into bite-size pieces.

5. Place a bite-size piece of steak in the center of each cupped lettuce leaf. Drizzle each piece with ½ tsp (2 mL) of the reserved marinade and garnish with basil, cilantro and green onions.

Grilled Flank Steak with Smoked Garlic Cream Sauce

Flank steak has a chewy texture but great beef flavor. Tenderize it either by marinating it for at least 1 hour (and preferably 8 hours) or by pounding it with a meat tenderizer or mallet.

✦ TIPS ✦

Have your butcher run the steak through the cuber once or twice to tenderize it.

Any thin marinating steak, such as hanger, skirt, charcoal or flat-iron, can be used for this recipe.

Smoking garlic is so easy: just prepare your grill for smoking, place the whole head of garlic on the indirect side of the grill and smoke for 25 to 30 minutes. If you don't want to use smoked garlic, substitute 2 cloves garlic, minced; the flavor will be sharper, but still delicious.

1½ lb	flank steak, trimmed	750 g
1 cup	Italian vinaigrette or marinade	250 mL

Smoked Garlic Cream Sauce

6	cloves garlic, smoked and peeled (see tip, at left)	6
1	poblano or jalapeño pepper, roasted (see tip, page 238)	1
2 cups	whipping (35%) cream	500 mL
½ cup	unsalted butter, cut into pieces	125 mL
1 tbsp	freshly squeezed lemon or lime juice	15 mL
	Kosher salt and freshly ground black pepper	

1. Place steak in a large sealable plastic bag and pour in vinaigrette. Seal, toss to coat and refrigerate for at least 1 hour or up to 8 hours, tossing occasionally.

2. Meanwhile, prepare a hot fire in your grill.

3. *Prepare the sauce:* In a heavy saucepan, combine garlic, poblano and cream; bring to a simmer over medium heat. Simmer, stirring occasionally, until reduced by half, about 15 minutes. Strain and discard garlic and poblano. Return to the pan and, over low heat, whisk in butter, one piece at a time, whisking until sauce is smooth. Stir in lemon juice and season to taste with salt and pepper. Remove from heat and keep warm.

4. Remove steak from vinaigrette, discarding vinaigrette, and pat dry. Grill steak for 2 to 3 minutes per side, turning once, until a meat thermometer inserted in the thickest part of the steak registers 130°F (54°C) for medium-rare, or until desired doneness. Let rest for 5 minutes, then slice across the grain, on the diagonal and at a 45-degree angle, into slices about ¼ inch (0.5 cm) thick.

5. Spoon sauce onto each plate and arrange steak slices on the sauce.

Carne Asada with Poblano and Onion Rajas

While many Mexican dishes are slow-simmered, carne asada ("grilled meat") with seasoned poblano and onion strips delivers a bolder flavor. The grilling paste imparts flavor and helps tenderize the steak. Use skirt, hanger or flank for a beefy steak meant to be served in slices.

✦ TIPS ✦

For a more tender steak, ask the butcher to run it through the cuber once.

Try a variety of fesh chiles for grilling rajas: Anaheim, Guero, jalapeño, Mirasol and New Mexico chiles all work in place of poblanos.

● Baking sheet

Flavoring Paste

3	cloves garlic	1
1	small onion	1
3 tbsp	freshly squeezed lime juice	45 mL
¼ tsp	ground cumin	1 mL
1 lb	skirt, hanger or flank steak, trimmed	500 g
3	poblano peppers	3
	Olive oil	
1	large onion, cut into ½-inch (1 cm) slices	1
	Kosher salt and freshly ground black pepper	
12	small corn tortillas, warmed	12
	Lime wedges	

1. *Prepare the paste:* In a food processor or blender, purée garlic, onion, lime juice and cumin.

2. Place steak on baking sheet. With a spatula, spread paste over both sides of the steak. Cover with plastic wrap and refrigerate for at least 1 hour or up to 8 hours.

3. Meanwhile, prepare a medium-hot fire in your grill.

4. Brush poblanos with olive oil. Grill for 8 to 10 minutes, turning often, until the skins blister and burn. Transfer to a sealable plastic bag, seal and let steam and soften until cool enough to handle. Remove the stems, papery skin and seeds, then slice into thin strips.

Before barbecuing, cut a notch or V shape into the steak indicating the direction of the grain of the meat; this will help you slice it properly after it is cooked.

5. Meanwhile, brush onion slices with olive oil. Grill for about 10 minutes, turning once, until onions have good grill marks on both sides. Cut onion slices in half and, using a fork, break into strands.

6. In a bowl, combine poblanos and onions. Season to taste with salt and pepper. Keep warm.

7. Gently shake excess paste from the steak. Brush steak with olive oil. Grill for 2 to 3 minutes per side, turning once, until a meat thermometer inserted in the thickest part of the steak registers 130°F (54°C) for medium-rare, or until desired doneness. Season to taste with salt and pepper. Transfer to a cutting board, tent with foil and let rest for 5 to 10 minutes, then thinly slice across the grain.

8. Arrange steak slices, poblanos and onions on a platter. Serve with tortillas and lime wedges.

Lime-Grilled Skirt Steak Fajitas with Charred Tomato Chipotle Salsa

Mmmmmm. Just the thought of these smoky beef fajitas makes us hungry. If you can't find skirt steak, flank steak is a good alternative.

◆ TIPS ◆

Look for canned fire-roasted tomatoes (such as Muir Glen or Hunt's) in health food stores or the organic section of well-stocked supermarkets.

If you prefer, you can grill your own tomatoes for the salsa instead of using canned. Simply grill a large tomato over a hot fire until charry, then dice.

The salsa can be stored in an airtight container in the refrigerator for up to 5 days.

Charred Tomato Chipotle Salsa

4	green onions, chopped	4
2	chipotle peppers, with 1 tbsp (15 mL) adobo sauce	2
2	cloves garlic, minced	2
1	can (15½ oz/440 mL) fire-roasted diced tomatoes (see tip, at left), with juice	1
2 tsp	freshly squeezed lime juice	10 mL

Marinade

2	cloves garlic, minced	2
3 tbsp	freshly squeezed lime juice	45 mL
3 tbsp	olive oil	45 mL
1 lb	skirt or flank steak, trimmed	500 g
	Large flour tortillas, warmed	
	Guacamole, sour cream, pico de gallo and shredded cheese	

1. *Prepare the salsa:* In a bowl, combine green onions, chipotles with sauce, garlic, tomatoes and lime juice. Cover and refrigerate until ready to use.

2. *Prepare the marinade:* In a small bowl, whisk together garlic, lime juice and olive oil.

3. Place steak in a large sealable plastic bag and pour in marinade. Seal, toss to coat and refrigerate for at least 30 minutes or overnight, tossing occasionally.

Before barbecuing, cut a notch or V shape into the steak indicating the direction of the grain of the meat; this will help you slice it properly after it is cooked.

4. Meanwhile, prepare a hot fire in your grill.

5. Remove steak from marinade, discarding marinade, and pat dry. Grill steak for $2\frac{1}{2}$ to 3 minutes per side, turning once, until a meat thermometer inserted in the thickest part of the steak registers 130°F (54°C) for medium-rare, or until desired doneness. Transfer to a cutting board. Let cool to room temperature, then slice across the grain and on the diagonal at a 45-degree angle into very thin slices.

6. Serve steak slices on tortillas, with bowls of salsa, guacamole, sour cream, pico de gallo and cheese for diners to add as desired.

◆ Variation ◆

The marinade and salsa are also delicious on grilled chicken paillards, pork tenderloin, shellfish and fish fillets, but only marinate for 30 minutes.

Sriracha, Soy and Sesame Hanger Steak

Marinade

2	cloves garlic, minced	2
¼ cup	sriracha or bottled puréed red chili sauce	50 mL
¼ cup	soy sauce	50 mL
2 tbsp	packed brown sugar	25 mL
1 tbsp	toasted sesame oil	15 mL
4	pieces hanger steak (each about 8 oz/250 g), trimmed	4

1. *Prepare the marinade:* In a small bowl, combine garlic, chili sauce, soy sauce, brown sugar and sesame oil.

2. With a sharp skewer or a meat fork, poke holes all over each steak. Place steaks in a large sealable plastic bag and pour in marinade. Seal, toss to coat and refrigerate for at least 1 hour or up to 8 hours, tossing occasionally.

3. Meanwhile, prepare a medium-hot fire in your grill.

4. Remove steaks from marinade, discarding marinade, and pat dry. Grill steaks for 3 to 5 minutes per side, turning once, until a meat thermometer inserted in the thickest part of a steak registers 130°F (54°C) for medium-rare, or until desired doneness.

Salt and Pepper Ranch Steaks with Stir-Grilled Onion Slivers

SERVES 4	

"Ranch steak" is another name for a center-cut steak from the boneless chuck shoulder. It is very flavorful but a bit tough, so it is best grilled like hanger, flank or skirt steaks: seared quickly on both sides to medium-rare.

- Grill basket or wok
- Baking sheet

4	boneless chuck (cross-rib) or ranch steaks (each 10 oz/300 g and ¾ inch/2 cm thick)	4
¼ cup	olive oil, divided	50 mL
	Coarse kosher salt and freshly ground black pepper	
2	large red onions, halved and slivered	2

1. Lightly coat steaks with half the olive oil and season to taste with salt and pepper.

2. In a bowl, toss onions with the remaining olive oil and season to taste with salt and pepper. Transfer to grill wok, set wok and steaks on baking sheet and carry out to the grill.

3. Prepare a hot fire in your grill.

4. Place wok on the grill. Grill onions, tossing with long-handled wooden spatulas every 2 minutes, for 6 to 8 minutes, or until softened.

5. Meanwhile, grill steaks for about 3 minutes per side, turning once, until medium-rare, or until desired doneness.

6. Serve each steak with a spoonful of grilled onion slivers on top.

Bamboo Beef with Homemade Teriyaki Sauce

Strips of beef grilled on bamboo skewers get their flavor and sheen from easy-to-make teriyaki sauce. In Japanese, teri *means "glaze" and* yaki *means "grill" or "broil." Use teriyaki as a marinade, glaze or finishing sauce.*

✦ TIPS ✦

Mirin is a pale gold, sweet Japanese wine; look for the Takara Shuzo brand.

It's always a good idea to oil the grill rack well before heating the grill, but it's especially important when you're grilling foods that have marinated in a sweet mixture, so they don't stick.

If you use fresh bamboo shoots (available at Asian markets), make sure they have not been treated with chemicals. You may need to pierce the steak first with a sharp skewer, then thread it onto the bamboo shoots.

● Twelve 12-inch (30 cm) flat bamboo skewers, soaked for at least 30 minutes, or fresh bamboo shoots

Homemade Teriyaki Sauce

½ cup	soy sauce	125 mL
½ cup	mirin	125 mL
2 tbsp	granulated sugar	25 mL
1 lb	boneless beef sirloin (about 1 inch/2.5 cm thick), cut across the grain into 1-inch (2.5 cm) strips	500 g

1. *Prepare the sauce:* In a small bowl, whisk together soy sauce, mirin and sugar.

2. Place steak in a large sealable plastic bag and pour in sauce. Seal, toss to coat and refrigerate for at least 30 minutes or up to 8 hours, tossing occasionally.

3. Meanwhile, prepare a medium-hot fire in your grill.

4. Remove steak from marinade, discarding marinade, and thread steak lengthwise onto skewers, leaving space between pieces. Grill for 5 to 7 minutes, turning often, or until cooked to medium.

Korean Bulgogi with Kimchee

In Korea, bulgogi ("fire meat") is cooked on a metal plate over charcoal in the center of the table. In North America, you can buy an electric teppanyaki, or Korean-style table grill, or simply use the backyard grill or a hibachi. The thinly sliced beef is usually seasoned with soy sauce, sugar, sesame oil, doenjang (fermented soybean paste, more easily found here as miso), garlic, ginger, gochujang (red chili paste) and green onions, for a trip around all the taste buds. The traditional banchans (side dishes) are kimchee (fermented napa cabbage in chili paste) and steamed rice.

It's always a good idea to oil the grill rack well before heating the grill, but it's especially important when you're grilling foods that have marinated in a sweet mixture, so they don't stick.

Marinade

4	green onions, cut into 1-inch (2.5 cm) pieces	4
4	cloves garlic, minced	4
1 cup	water	250 mL
1/3 cup	granulated sugar	75 mL
1/3 cup	soy sauce	75 mL
1 tbsp	grated gingerroot	15 mL
1 tbsp	miso or fermented soybean paste	15 mL
2 tsp	toasted sesame oil	10 mL
2 tsp	red chili paste	10 mL
1 lb	boneless rib eye or sirloin steak, very thinly sliced across the grain	500 g
	Prepared kimchee, green onions and steamed rice	

1. *Prepare the marinade:* In a bowl, whisk together green onions, garlic, water, sugar, soy sauce, ginger, miso, sesame oil and chili paste.

2. Place steak in a large sealable plastic bag and pour in marinade. Seal, toss to coat and refrigerate for at least 30 minutes or up to 8 hours, tossing occasionally.

3. Meanwhile, prepare a medium-hot fire in your grill.

4. Remove steak from marinade, discarding marinade. Grill steak for 2 minutes per side, turning once, or until caramelized on the outside. Serve with kimchee, green onions and steamed rice.

✦ Variations ✦

You can also serve bulgogi in lettuce cups.

Substitute baby squid, large shrimp or thinly sliced chicken or pork for the beef.

Vietnamese Grilled Beef Skewers in Pho

Pho is a fragrant sweet-and-sour broth that gets even better with the addition of grill-charred gingerroot and onion. Each diner makes his or her own additions to create a customized dish.

- Foil pan
- Cheesecloth
- Sixteen 6-inch (15 cm) flat bamboo skewers, soaked for at least 30 minutes, or fresh bamboo shoots

4	whole cloves	4
4	whole star anise	4
½ tsp	whole black peppercorns	2 mL
1	2-inch (5 cm) piece gingerroot, slightly flattened with the side of a chef's knife	1
1	small onion, peeled	1
6 cups	good-quality canned pho stock or chicken stock	1.5 L
1½ cups	water	375 mL
1 tbsp	granulated sugar	15 mL
3 tbsp	nam pla (fish sauce)	45 mL
1 lb	boneless beef sirloin, cut lengthwise into 16 strips	500 g
1 lb	thin Thai rice noodles, cooked	500 g
	Lime wedges, chopped fresh Thai basil, chopped fresh cilantro, bean sprouts, chopped Thai chile peppers and chopped green onions	

1. Prepare a medium-hot fire in your grill.
2. Place cloves, star anise and peppercorns in foil pan. Place pan on the grill. Grill for 4 to 5 minutes, or until spices are warmed and give off a toasted aroma. Transfer spices to a cheesecloth bag.
3. Grill ginger and onion for 10 to 12 minutes, or until blistered and blackened on all sides (if necessary, skewer them so they don't fall through the grill grates).

4. In a saucepan, combine the bag of whole spices, charred ginger and onion, pho stock, water, sugar and nam pla; bring to a boil over medium-high heat. Reduce heat and simmer while you grill the beef.

5. Thread beef strips lengthwise onto skewers. Grill for 3 to 5 minutes, turning often, or until medium-rare.

6. Divide noodles among 4 bowls. Ladle broth over noodles and lay beef skewers across each bowl. Pass lime wedges, basil, cilantro, bean sprouts, Thai chile peppers and green onions at the table so that diners can add their favorite garnishes.

Greek Kofta Kabobs

SERVES 6

Koftas are like hamburgers on a stick, but oh what flavor they have compared to traditional burgers. What makes them so sublime? Fragrant spices such as cumin, coriander and cinnamon are paired with fresh cilantro, red onions and tzatziki, a Greek yogurt sauce enlivened with garlic, cucumber and dill.

✦ TIP ✦

If your grill is an open brazier without a lid, you'll need to cook the kabobs for a couple of minutes longer.

✦ Variation ✦

Substitute ground lamb for the ground beef, or combine them half and half.

- Six 12-inch (30 cm) flat bamboo skewers, soaked for at least 30 minutes
- Perforated grill rack, oiled

Kofta Kabobs

1	egg	1
1	onion, grated	1
1½ lbs	lean ground beef	750 g
½ cup	finely chopped fresh cilantro	125 mL
2 tsp	ground coriander	10 mL
2 tsp	ground cumin	10 mL
2 tsp	sweet paprika	10 mL
1 tsp	chili powder	5 mL
½ tsp	ground turmeric	2 mL
½ tsp	ground cinnamon	2 mL
6	pitas	6
	Olive oil	
1	recipe Tzatziki (page 57)	1
2	tomatoes, sliced	2
1	red onion, sliced	1

1. *Prepare the kabobs:* In a bowl, using your hands, combine egg, onion, beef, cilantro, coriander, cumin, paprika, chili powder, turmeric and cinnamon. Form into sausage shapes around skewers and flatten slightly.

4. Prepare a medium-hot indirect fire in your grill.

5. Place skewers on prepared grill rack and place over the fire. Grill for 4 minutes per quarter turn, or until medium-well. Transfer to the indirect side of the grill.

6. Brush pitas with olive oil. Place over the fire and grill for about 1 minute per side, turning once, until warmed through but not crispy.

7. Serve kabobs and pitas with tzatziki, tomatoes and onion.

Grilled Short Ribs with Mestiza

SERVES 4

Known as tablones, these indirect-grilled short ribs with a kiss of smoke create a fiesta in your mouth when served with mestiza (a "mixed color" sauce featuring green tomatillos and red tomatoes). Accompany with rajas (page 246), if you like, and warm flour tortillas.

✦ TIPS ✦

The mestiza can be stored in an airtight container in the refrigerator for up to 2 days.

Use needle-nose pliers or strong tweezers to remove the membrane (silverskin) from the back of the ribs.

If space on your grill is at a premium, stack the ribs one rack on top of another. Rotate which ribs are on top during grilling and add 30 to 60 minutes to the cooking time.

- Perforated grill rack, oiled
- Suggested wood: mesquite, pecan or oak

Mestiza

4	tomatillos (unhusked)	4
4	plum (Roma) or small tomatoes	4
4	garlic cloves, threaded onto a skewer	4
1	small onion, peeled	1
½ cup	packed fresh cilantro	125 mL
2 tbsp	bottled smoked chipotle sauce	25 mL
2 tbsp	olive oil	25 mL
½ tsp	granulated sugar (or to taste)	2 mL
2	racks beef short ribs (each about 4 lbs/2 kg), trimmed and membrane removed	2
	Kosher salt, granulated garlic and freshly ground black pepper	
	Olive oil	

1. Prepare a hot indirect fire with a kiss of smoke in your grill.

2. *Prepare the mestiza:* Place tomatillos, tomatoes, garlic and onion on prepared grill rack and place over the fire. Grill for about 10 minutes, turning often, until vegetables have blackened and blistered all over. Husk the tomatillos.

3. In a food processor or blender, chop tomatillos, tomatoes, garlic and onion. Add cilantro, chipotle sauce, olive oil and sugar; pulse until well blended but chunky. Set aside.

4. Season the meaty side of the ribs with salt, granulated garlic and pepper to taste.

5. When you see the first wisp of smoke from the wood, place ribs meaty side up on the indirect side of the grill. Close the lid and grill for 30 minutes. Brush with olive oil, close the lid and grill for 30 minutes, turning ribs if they get too browned near the fire, until meat pulls away from the ends of the bones. Cut ribs into individual portions and serve with mestiza.

Flame-Licked Beef Short Ribs with Bourbon Barbecue Sauce

SERVES 8

The key to this recipe is rendering enough of the fat from the short ribs during the oven-roasting process. Finish them on the grill with a lick of flame for caramelization.

✦ TIPS ✦

For maximum flavor, the ribs can be sprinkled with the paprika, garlic salt and lemon pepper up to 1 day before. Wrap well and store in the refrigerator.

After step 1, the ribs can be cooled, wrapped in foil and refrigerated for up to 2 days. Let stand at room temperature for 30 minutes before grilling.

The sauce can be stored in an airtight container in the refrigerator for up to 3 months.

- Preheat oven to 350°F (180°C)
- Baking sheet, lined with foil
- Baking racks

½ cup	smoked paprika	125 mL
2 tbsp	garlic salt	25 mL
2 tbsp	lemon pepper	25 mL
4 lbs	beef short ribs, trimmed and membrane removed	2 kg

Bourbon Barbecue Sauce

1½ cups	ketchup	375 mL
1½ cups	chili sauce	375 mL
½ cup	packed dark brown sugar	125 mL
½ cup	apple- or fig-flavored balsamic vinegar	125 mL
¼ cup	dry mustard	50 mL
¼ cup	bourbon	50 mL
¼ cup	water	50 mL
1 tbsp	celery salt	15 mL
1 tbsp	liquid smoke	15 mL

1. In a bowl, combine paprika, garlic salt and lemon pepper. Sprinkle evenly over both sides of ribs. Place ribs on baking racks set on baking sheet. Bake in preheated oven for about 2½ hours, or until meat pulls away from the ends of the bones.

2. *Meanwhile, prepare the sauce:* In a large saucepan, combine ketchup, chili sauce, brown sugar, vinegar, mustard, bourbon, water, celery salt and liquid smoke; bring to a simmer over medium-low heat. Simmer for 45 to 60 minutes, stirring occasionally, until slightly thickened.

3. Prepare a medium-hot fire in your grill.

4. Place ribs meaty side down on the grill. Grill for 7 to 10 minutes, or until meat is a nice burnished color. Turn ribs and slather the meaty side with sauce. Grill for 7 to 10 minutes, or until sauce is caramelized.

Rosemary-Grilled Veal Chops with Garlic Rosemary Butter

SERVES 4

Flavored butters can do double duty as a finishing sauce for the meat and a spread for crusty artisan bread.

✦ TIP ✦

If not serving the garlic rosemary butter immediately, spoon into a ramekin and cover with plastic wrap. (Or spoon onto a piece of waxed paper, roll into a log and wrap in plastic wrap.) Store in the refrigerator for up to 1 week or wrap in additional freezer plastic or paper and freeze for up to 3 months. Bring to room temperature before using.

● Baking sheet

Garlic Rosemary Butter

2	cloves garlic, minced	2
½ cup	butter	125 mL
1 tsp	ground dried rosemary	5 mL
4	veal loin chops (each about 8 oz/250 g)	4
¼ cup	extra-virgin olive oil	50 mL
16	sprigs fresh rosemary	16
	Coarse kosher salt and freshly cracked black pepper	

1. *Prepare the butter:* In a small bowl, combine garlic, butter and rosemary. Cover with plastic wrap until ready to use.

2. Place veal on baking sheet. Brush both sides of veal with olive oil and press 2 rosemary sprigs into each side of each chop. Cover with plastic wrap and refrigerate for at least 30 minutes or up to 1 hour.

3. Meanwhile, prepare a medium-hot fire in your grill.

4. Grill veal for 4 minutes per side, turning once, until lightly charred and a meat thermometer inserted in the thickest part of a chop registers 130°F (54°C) for medium-rare. Discard rosemary sprigs and season to taste with salt and pepper. Serve topped with a dollop of butter.

✦ Variation ✦

Substitute your favorite herb for the rosemary in the butter.

Bistro Burger

SERVES 4

Ooh-la-la! Your guests will storm your backyard to get a taste of this fabulously decadent burger, replete with all things French: béarnaise sauce, purple shallots and Roquefort. Just make sure the quality of beef you use is worthy.

1 tbsp	butter	15 mL
1 cup	sliced purple shallots	250 mL
	Kosher salt and freshly ground black pepper	
1 lb	ground tenderloin and strip steak or sirloin	500 g
4 oz	Roquefort or other blue cheese, crumbled	125 g
4	brioche or hamburger buns	4
½ cup	béarnaise sauce (prepared from a mix or see recipe, page 55) or Mustard-Cornichon Butter Sauce (see recipe, page 56)	125 mL

1. Prepare a medium-hot fire in your grill.

2. In a skillet, melt butter over medium-high heat. Sauté shallots until softened, about 5 minutes. Season to taste with salt and pepper. Remove from heat and keep warm.

3. Form ground beef into four ¾-inch (2 cm) thick patties.

4. Grill burgers for 4 to 5 minutes per side, turning once, or until a meat thermometer inserted in the center of a burger registers 160°F (71°C). Sprinkle burgers with cheese and grill until cheese melts.

5. Spread the inside of each roll with béarnaise sauce and place a burger on the bottom half of each roll. Spoon shallots over each burger and cover with the top half of the roll.

Lamb

Lavender-Smoked Rack of Lamb 263

Turkish Rack of Lamb with Charry Eggplant
    Tarragon Sauce 264

Down Under Grilled Lamb Chops with Prickly Ash Rub 266

Grill-Roasted Lamb Loin with Mustard-Cornichon
    Butter Sauce 267

Grilled Lamb Steak with Sauce Paloise 268

Guava-Glazed Rotisserie Lamb 269

Down Under Fire-Kissed Lamb 270

Tequila-Chile Lamb Shanks 271

Rolled Stuffed Leg of Lamb 272

Catalan-Style Leg of Lamb with Mediterranean
    Vegetables and Romesco 273

Leg of Lamb Fattoush 274

Grilled Lamb and Nopales with Fire-Roasted
    Tomato Mint Salsa 275

Singaporean Lamb Satay 276

Kentucky-Style Smoked Lamb 277

Smoky Lamb You Can Eat with a Spoon 278

Kabuli Lamb Kebabs 280

Souvlaki with Grilled Pita 281

Spanish-Style Lamb Ribs Pimenton 282

Tropical Lamb Burgers with Fresh Mango Chutney 283

Moroccan Lamb Burgers 284

Since ancient times, lamb has been a favorite food to cook over the embers. Spit-roasted, grilled or smoked, lamb is sweetly succulent when done to medium-rare.

The distinctive taste of lamb stands up to the robust flavors of garlic, Dijon mustard, citrus, wine vinegar, wine, spices and piquant herbs such as rosemary, mint and tarragon.

Mild to medium hardwood flavors work best with lamb, especially fruitwoods such as apple, cherry and peach.

✦ Lamb Cuts and Best Barbecue Methods ✦

Breast or shoulder: Indirect grill, smoke

Boneless meat: Skewer, stir-grill, leaf-wrap, smoke/braise

Burgers: Grill, skewer

Chops: Grill, herb-grill, indirect grill, griddle

Leg: Grill, herb-grill, indirect grill, rotisserie, smoke, leaf-wrap

Rack: Grill, indirect grill, grill-roast, smoke

Steak: Grill

Tenderloin: Grill, indirect grill, grill-roast, rotisserie, herb-grill, smoke

Lavender-Smoked Rack of Lamb

SERVES 2 TO 4

With this aromatic lamb, a crisp rosé wine, a crusty baguette and a salad of mixed baby greens, you'll get a taste of southern France. We use dried lavender sticks (the stem and aromatic bud) from our gardens, but you can also buy the sticks at barbecue and grill shops or use fresh stems from a plant you buy at a garden nursery (just make sure it hasn't been sprayed).

✦ TIP ✦

Ask your butcher to french the racks of lamb for the grill. This process removes excess fat from the bones, and some from the meat, too.

● **Suggested wood:** 1½ to 2 oz (45 to 60 g) dried lavender sticks

2	racks of lamb (each about 1½ lbs/750 g), fat removed and bones frenched	2
1	recipe Provençal Flavoring Paste (page 45)	1

1. Slather lamb with flavoring paste. Set aside.
2. Prepare a hot indirect fire with a kiss of smoke in your grill.
3. Place lamb over the fire and sear on all sides. Transfer to the indirect side of the grill. When the lavender starts to smolder, close the lid and grill for 15 to 20 minutes, until a meat thermometer inserted in the thickest part of a rack registers 130°F (54°C) for medium-rare, or until desired doneness. Transfer to a cutting board, tent with foil and let rest for 10 minutes before slicing.

✦ Variation ✦

Prepare this dish in a stovetop smoker. Place a heaping tablespoon (15 mL) dried lavender buds in the bottom of the smoker. Place the tray on top, then the rack. Place lamb on the rack and cover tightly with foil. Place smoker over medium-high heat. When you see the first wisp of smoke from the lavender, set the timer for 15 minutes. Carefully remove the smoker from the burner and remove the foil to check the lamb's internal temperature. If a meat thermometer inserted in the thickest part of a rack registers 130°F (54°C) for medium-rare, the lamb is done. If not, replace the foil, put the lamb back on the burner and smoke for another 5 minutes.

Turkish Rack of Lamb with Charry Eggplant Tarragon Sauce

SERVES 4

Pomegranates and eggplant are abundant in the Mediterranean, and especially at Turkish markets. This recipe makes use of both, for true Turkish flair. Serve with grilled flatbread.

Pomegranate Marinade

1 cup	pomegranate juice	250 mL
1 cup	orange juice	250 mL
2 tbsp	liquid honey	25 mL
1 tbsp	freshly squeezed lemon juice	15 mL
1 tsp	fine kosher or sea salt	5 mL
4	racks of lamb (each about 1½ lbs/750 g), fat removed and bones frenched	4
	Olive oil	
	Kosher salt and freshly ground white pepper	

Charry Eggplant Tarragon Sauce

1 lb	eggplant, trimmed and cut into ½-inch (1 cm) slices	500 g
	Olive oil	
	Kosher salt and freshly ground black pepper	
2	cloves garlic, minced	2
½ cup	olive oil (approx.)	125 mL
1 tbsp	chopped fresh tarragon	15 mL
1 tbsp	freshly squeezed lemon juice (approx.)	15 mL

1. *Prepare the marinade:* In a bowl, whisk together pomegranate juice, orange juice, honey, lemon juice and salt.

2. Place lamb in two extra-large sealable plastic bags. Pour in marinade, dividing evenly. Seal, toss to coat and refrigerate for at least 4 hours or up to 12 hours, tossing occasionally.

3. Meanwhile, prepare a medium-hot fire in your grill.

4. Remove lamb from marinade, discarding marinade, and pat dry. Brush lamb with olive oil and season to taste with salt and white pepper. Place lamb on the grill, close the lid and grill for about 45 minutes, turning every 15 minutes, until a meat thermometer inserted in the thickest part of a rack registers 130°F (54°C) for medium-rare, or until desired doneness. Transfer to a cutting board, tent with foil and let rest for 10 minutes before slicing.

5. *Meanwhile, prepare the sauce:* Brush eggplant with olive oil and season to taste with salt and black pepper. Grill for 3 to 4 minutes per side, turning once, until well browned on both sides.

6. In a food processor, combine grilled eggplant, garlic, olive oil, tarragon and lemon juice; purée until smooth. Taste and adjust seasoning with lemon juice, salt and black pepper, if desired. For a thinner sauce, add more olive oil.

7. Spoon some of the sauce onto plates and place lamb chops on top. Serve additional sauce on the side.

✦ Variation ✦

For a kiss of smoke, use pecan or apple wood.

Down Under Grilled Lamb Chops with Prickly Ash Rub

SERVES 4

Prickly ash is an Australian shrub that produces a fruit similar to Szechuan pepper (known in Japanese as sansho). The outer husk of the berry has a slightly lemony taste that can make your tongue tingle. When you warm the spices before grinding them, you release the essential oils and increase the flavor in this simply seasoned dish.

✦ TIP ✦

Flare-ups can actually add a bit of flavorful char to your food, but if things get out of hand, here's what to do:

- To manage flare-ups on a charcoal grill, douse coals with a squeeze bottle filled with water, or simply close the grill lid and vents.

- To manage flare-ups on a gas grill, move flaming food to a cooler spot and close the grill lid.

Prickly Ash Rub

3 tbsp	coarse kosher or sea salt	45 mL
1 tbsp	prickly ash or Szechuan pepper	15 mL
12	thin boneless lamb loin or shoulder chops, pounded to ½ inch (1 cm) thick	12
	Olive oil	
	Lemon wedges and fresh rosemary branches	

1. *Prepare the rub:* In a dry heavy skillet, over medium-high heat, toast salt and prickly ash, shaking the pan, for 2 to 3 minutes, or until very aromatic. Coarsely grind spices in a clean coffee or spice grinder or with a mortar and pestle.

2. Prepare a hot fire in your grill.

3. Brush lamb with olive oil and season with rub. Grill for 1 to 2 minutes per side, turning once, until medium-rare, or until desired doneness. Garnish with lemon wedges and rosemary branches.

✦ Variation ✦

A squeeze of lemon and a drizzle of extra-virgin olive oil would be a simple and delicious finish to this dish, but a dollop or two of Sauce Paloise (variation, page 55), Béarnaise Sauce (page 55) or Charry Eggplant Tarragon Sauce (page 264) would not go amiss, either.

Grill-Roasted Lamb Loin with Mustard-Cornichon Butter Sauce

Slathered with an easy grilling paste, the lamb stays moist and delicious as it grills. The French sauce that accompanies it sounds fancy, but it's quite easy to make.

● Baking sheet

Tarragon Mustard Slather

½ cup	Dijon mustard	125 mL
½ cup	mayonnaise	125 mL
2 tsp	dried tarragon	10 mL
	Kosher or sea salt and freshly ground black pepper	
1	boneless lamb loin (about 4 lbs/2 kg), trimmed and tied	1
1	recipe Mustard-Cornichon Butter Sauce (page 56)	1

1. *Prepare the slather:* In a small bowl, combine mustard, mayonnaise and tarragon. Season to taste with salt and pepper.

2. Place lamb on baking sheet and brush all over with slather. Cover with plastic wrap and refrigerate for at least 1 hour or up to 24 hours.

3. Meanwhile, prepare a hot indirect fire in your grill.

4. Place lamb on the indirect side of the grill. Close the lid and grill for 15 minutes. Rotate the lamb so the sides will brown evenly, then close the lid and grill for 15 minutes, or until a meat thermometer inserted in the thickest part of the lamb registers 130°F (54°C) for medium-rare, or until desired doneness. Transfer to a cutting board, tent with foil and let rest for 5 minutes before slicing.

Grilled Lamb Steak with Sauce Paloise

SERVES 4

Chill a crisp, Provençal rosé wine, warm a loaf of crusty bread, grill fresh asparagus along with the lamb, and you'll have a fresh-tasting, summery meal to remember. Sauce Paloise is a version of the classic béarnaise, made with fresh mint instead of tarragon.

4	boneless lamb leg steaks (about ¾ inch/2 cm thick)	4
	Olive oil	
	Kosher salt and freshly ground pepper	
1	recipe Sauce Paloise (variation, page 55)	1

1. Prepare a hot fire in your grill.
2. Brush steaks with olive oil and season to taste with salt and pepper. Grill for 2 minutes per side, turning once, until medium-rare, or until desired doneness. Serve with Sauce Paloise.

Guava-Glazed Rotisserie Lamb

Although native to Mexico and South America, the tropical guava is now grown throughout Asia. In Hawaii, guava wood is used for slow-smoking. In this recipe, a boneless leg of lamb is slathered with an aromatic guava glaze, then spit-roasted on the grill.

- Baking sheet
- Rotisserie

Guava Glaze

4	cloves garlic, minced	4
1½ cups	guava jelly	375 mL
¼ cup	dark rum	50 mL
2 tbsp	grated gingerroot	25 mL
2 tbsp	freshly squeezed lime juice	25 mL
1	boneless leg of lamb (3 to 4 lbs/ 1.5 to 2 kg), rolled and tied	1

1. *Prepare the glaze:* In a small saucepan, over medium heat, whisk together garlic, guava jelly, rum and ginger until jelly melts. Whisk in lime juice.
2. Place lamb on baking sheet. Remove half the glaze and brush over lamb. Reserve the remaining glaze for basting.
3. Set up your grill for rotisserie cooking.
4. Attach lamb to the spit (see page 24). Heat the grill to medium-high. Close the lid and grill for 1½ to 2 hours, basting with the reserved glaze halfway through, until an instant-read thermometer inserted in the thickest part of the lamb registers 130°F (54°C) for medium-rare, or until desired doneness. Transfer to a cutting board, tent with foil and let rest for 15 minutes before slicing.

✦ Variation ✦

If you prefer, you can grill the lamb over a hot indirect fire instead of using the rotisserie. Place lamb in a foil pan and place on the indirect side of the grill. Close the lid and grill for 1½ to 2 hours, basting with the reserved glaze halfway through, until a meat thermometer inserted in the thickest part of the lamb registers 130°F (54°C) for medium-rare, or until desired doneness.

Down Under Fire-Kissed Lamb

SERVES 6

Ask your butcher to cut boneless lamb rumps for you. These are also known as top round roasts and come from the top part of the leg. Serve the sumptuous slices of lamb with crusty bread slathered with Cilantro Butter (page 53).

✦ TIP ✦

The yogurt marinade is equally good on poultry, pork and fish.

● Baking sheet

Spiced Yogurt Marinade

1 tsp	cardamom pods	5 mL
1 tsp	whole cloves	5 mL
1 tsp	whole black peppercorns	5 mL
1 tsp	whole white peppercorns	5 mL
1 tsp	ground turmeric	5 mL
1 tsp	ground cumin	5 mL
½ tsp	kosher salt	2 mL
½ tsp	hot pepper flakes	2 mL
3	cloves garlic, minced	3
1½ cups	plain yogurt	375 mL
1 cup	chopped fresh cilantro	250 mL
6	boneless lamb rumps (each 8 oz/250 g)	6

1. *Prepare the marinade:* In a dry heavy skillet, over medium-high heat, toast cardamom, cloves and black and white peppercorns, shaking the pan, for 2 to 3 minutes, or until very aromatic. (Be careful not to let them burn.) Grind spices in a clean spice grinder or with a mortar and pestle.

2. In a food processor, combine ground roasted spices, turmeric, cumin, salt and hot pepper flakes; pulse to blend. Add garlic, yogurt and cilantro; pulse to blend.

3. Place lamb on baking sheet and coat all over with marinade. Cover with plastic wrap and refrigerate for at least 12 hours or overnight.

4. Meanwhile, prepare a hot fire in your grill.

5. Remove lamb from marinade, lightly scraping off and discarding excess marinade. Grill lamb for 10 to 14 minutes, turning to char all sides, until a meat thermometer inserted in the thickest part of the lamb registers 130°F (54°C) for medium-rare, or until desired doneness. Transfer to a cutting board, tent with foil and let rest for 15 minutes before slicing.

Tequila-Chile Lamb Shanks

This succulent Mexican dish, known as mixiote de borrego asado, *gets even more flavorful when left to braise until tender.*

✦ TIP ✦

If you can't find pasilla chiles, guajillo chiles and chiles de arbol, use a mixture of whatever dried Mexican chiles you can find.

- Preheat oven to 350°F (180°C)
- Baking sheet
- Deep foil pan
- **Suggested wood: mesquite**

4 oz	dried pasilla chile peppers, stemmed	125 g
4 oz	dried guajillo chile peppers, stemmed	125 g
2	dried chiles de arbol, stemmed	2
3	large cloves garlic, minced	3
½ cup	tequila	125 mL
½ cup	freshly squeezed lemon juice	125 mL
1 tsp	ground cumin	5 mL
	Kosher or sea salt and freshly ground pepper	
4	lamb shanks, trimmed	4

1. Place pasilla chiles, guajillo chiles and chiles de arbol on baking sheet. Toast in preheated oven for 2 minutes. Transfer to a bowl and pour in enough hot water to cover; soak for about 1 hour, or until soft. Strain, reserving the soaking water.

2. In a food processor, combine chiles and enough soaking water to purée into a thick, smooth paste. Add garlic, tequila, lemon juice and cumin; pulse to blend. Season to taste with salt and pepper.

3. Place lamb in foil pan and brush with paste. Cover with plastic wrap and refrigerate for at least 4 hours or up to 24 hours.

4. Meanwhile, prepare an indirect fire for smoking in your grill or smoker.

5. Add 1 cup (250 mL) hot water to the foil pan and cover with foil. Place pan on the indirect side of the grill. Close the lid and smoke for 2 to 3 hours, or until meat is almost falling off the bone. Transfer lamb to a platter and keep warm.

6. Skim any excess fat from the sauce in the pan and whisk sauce until smooth, adding up to ½ cup (125 mL) hot water as needed to make a rich sauce. Spoon some sauce onto each plate and place a lamb shank on top.

Rolled Stuffed Leg of Lamb

SERVES 6 TO 8

Stuffed leg of lamb takes on a whole new flavor with a kiss of smoke.

✦ Variation ✦

For a French twist on the stuffing, use the same amount of spinach, oil, garlic and bread crumbs. Add 4 oz (125 g) goat cheese, ¼ cup (50 mL) chopped sun-dried tomatoes and ¼ cup (50 mL) chopped fresh mixed herbs, such as tarragon, chives and parsley. Season to taste with salt and pepper.

- Kitchen string, soaked
- Suggested wood: oak, pecan or fruitwood

1 lb	spinach, stemmed	500 g
3 tbsp	olive oil	45 mL
3	cloves garlic, minced	3
4 to 6 oz	feta cheese, crumbled	125 to 175 g
½ cup	fresh bread crumbs	125 mL
¼ cup	chopped kalamata olives	50 mL
¼ cup	pine nuts	50 mL
¼ cup	chopped fresh oregano	50 mL
½ tsp	coarse kosher salt	2 mL
¼ tsp	freshly ground black pepper	1 mL
1	boneless leg of lamb (3 to 4 lbs/ 1.5 to 2 kg), trimmed and butterflied	1

1. Prepare an indirect fire for smoking in your grill or smoker.

2. Pat spinach dry on paper towels. Stack 10 to 12 large leaves, roll into a cigar shape and cut crosswise into ⅛-inch (0.25 cm) shreds (chiffonade). Repeat with the remaining spinach.

3. In a skillet, heat olive oil over high heat. Stir in spinach and garlic and cook, stirring often, for 2 minutes, or until the moisture has evaporated.

4. Transfer spinach mixture to a bowl and let cool. Stir in feta cheese to taste, bread crumbs, olives, pine nuts, oregano, salt and pepper.

5. Lay lamb cut side up on a work surface and spread with the spinach mixture. Starting with a long side, roll up jellyroll-style. Tie the roll together at intervals with soaked kitchen string.

6. Place lamb on the indirect side of the grill. Close the lid and smoke for 5 to 6 hours, until a meat thermometer inserted in the thickest part of the lamb (but not in the stuffing) registers 130°F (54°C) for medium-rare, or until desired doneness. Transfer to a cutting board, tent with foil and let rest for 15 minutes before slicing.

Catalan-Style Leg of Lamb with Mediterranean Vegetables and Romesco

SERVES 8

This celebratory leg of lamb *a la brasa bathes in a sherry marinade first. The escalivada, or mixture of vegetables, grills right along with the lamb. Then it's all finished off with romesco sauce.*

1	boneless leg of lamb (3 to 4 lbs/ 1.5 to 2 kg), trimmed and butterflied	1
1	recipe Sherry Marinade (page 38)	1
4	large bell peppers (any color), quartered	1
2	large red onions, cut into 1-inch (2.5 cm) slices	2
1	baby or Japanese eggplant (about 2 lbs/1 kg)	1
	Olive oil	
	Kosher salt and freshly ground black pepper	
1	recipe Romesco Sauce (page 51)	1
	Chopped fresh flat-leaf (Italian) parsley	

1. Place lamb in an extra-large sealable plastic bag and pour in marinade. Seal, toss to coat and refrigerate for at least 4 hour or up to 24 hours, tossing occasionally.

2. Meanwhile, prepare a medium-hot fire in your grill.

3. Remove lamb from marinade, discarding marinade. Grill lamb for 15 minutes per side, turning once, until a meat thermometer inserted in the thickest part of the lamb registers 130°F (54°C) for medium-rare, or until desired doneness. Transfer to a cutting board, tent with foil and let rest for 10 minutes before slicing.

4. Meanwhile, brush bell peppers, red onions and eggplant with olive oil and season to taste with salt and pepper. Grill vegetables for about 20 minutes, turning often, until blistered and softened.

5. Arrange lamb slices on a platter and surround with vegetables. Drizzle with sauce and garnish with parsley.

Leg of Lamb Fattoush

Fattoush is a Middle Eastern salad made with fresh garden vegetables, torn mint leaves and toasted pieces of pita bread.

Don't add the pitas until you're ready to serve the salad, or they will get soggy.

For a colorful heirloom fattoush, use red, orange and yellow heirloom tomatoes and a yellow, orange or red bell pepper.

Marinade

1/3 cup	olive oil	75 mL
1/3 cup	freshly squeezed lemon juice	75 mL
1 tsp	kosher salt	5 mL
1 tsp	ground cumin	5 mL
2 lb	boneless leg of lamb, trimmed and butterflied	1 kg

Fattoush

6	green onions, sliced	6
3	large tomatoes, diced	3
3	cloves garlic, minced	3
1	cucumber, peeled, seeded and diced	1
1	green bell pepper, diced	1
1	red onion, chopped	1
1/2 cup	chopped fresh mint	125 mL
1/4 cup	chopped fresh flat-leaf (Italian) parsley	50 mL
4	toasted pitas, torn into pieces	4

1. *Prepare the marinade:* In a bowl, combine olive oil, lemon juice, salt and cumin.

2. Place lamb in a glass dish and lightly drizzle with about one-third of the marinade. Set aside. Reserve the remaining marinade as a finishing sauce.

3. Prepare a hot fire in your grill.

4. *Prepare the fattoush:* In a large bowl, combine green onions, tomatoes, garlic, cucumber, green pepper, red onion, mint and parsley. Set aside.

5. Grill lamb for about 10 minutes per side, turning once, until a meat thermometer inserted in the thickest part of the lamb registers 130°F (54°C) for medium-rare, or until desired doneness. Transfer to a cutting board, tent with foil and let rest for 10 minutes before slicing against the grain.

6. Mix pita pieces into the fattoush and divide among plates. Top with lamb slices and drizzle with the reserved marinade.

Grilled Lamb and Nopales with Fire-Roasted Tomato Mint Salsa

SERVES 4

This recipe evokes the flavors of la parilla, *the Mexican grill with nopal cactus leaves and a minty salsa also known as* recado.

✦ TIPS ✦

Look for canned fire-roasted tomatoes (such as Muir Glen or Hunt's) in health food stores or the organic section of well-stocked supermarkets.

The salsa is best served the day it is made.

If you like a drier salsa, drain off some of the tomato juice before adding the tomatoes.

For a more finely chopped salsa, pulse the ingredients in a food processor.

Fire-Roasted Tomato Mint Salsa

1	onion, diced	1
1½ cups	diced canned fire-roasted tomatoes (see tip, at left), with juice	375 mL
½ cup	chopped fresh mint	125 mL
½ cup	chopped fresh cilantro	125 mL
1 tsp	kosher salt	5 mL
1 tsp	freshly ground black pepper	5 mL
4	small nopales, spines removed	4
1	boneless leg of lamb (about 2 lbs/1 kg), trimmed and butterflied	1
3 tbsp	olive oil	45 mL
1 tsp	onion salt	5 mL
	Freshly ground black pepper	

1. *Prepare the salsa:* In a bowl, combine onion, tomatoes, mint, cilantro, salt and pepper. Set aside.

2. Prepare a hot fire in your grill.

3. Lightly brush nopales and lamb with olive oil and sprinkle with onion salt and pepper to taste.

4. Grill lamb for about 10 minutes per side, turning once, until a meat thermometer inserted in the thickest part of the lamb registers 130°F (54°C) for medium-rare, or until desired doneness. Transfer to a cutting board, tent with foil and let rest for 10 minutes before slicing across the grain into thin slices.

5. Meanwhile, grill nopales for about 5 minutes per side, turning once, until browned and soft.

6. Serve lamb and nopales with salsa on the side.

Singaporean Lamb Satay

*Grilled lamb skewers,
flavored with tropical
tamarind and
lemongrass, make
a wonderful grilled
appetizer or main
dish. Serve with Satay
Sauce (page 50) for
dipping, if you like.*

✦ TIPS ✦

Tamarind paste is
available at Asian
markets.

Crush the fennel seeds
in a mortar and pestle
or with a meat mallet.

The grilling paste is also
delicious with chicken,
fish, shellfish and pork.

- Sixteen 12-inch (30 cm) flat bamboo skewers, soaked for at least 30 minutes

Tamarind and Lemongrass Grilling Paste

½ cup	hot water	125 mL
1 tbsp	tamarind paste or freshly squeezed lime juice	15 mL
2	stalks lemongrass, chopped (or 1 tsp/5 mL grated lemon zest)	2
1 tbsp	grated gingerroot	15 mL
1 tbsp	ground coriander	15 mL
2 tsp	packed light brown sugar	10 mL
1 tsp	ground turmeric	5 mL
½ tsp	crushed fennel seeds	2 mL
½ tsp	ground cumin	2 mL
½ tsp	salt	2 mL
1 lb	boneless leg of lamb, cut into 1½-inch (4 cm) strips	500 g

1. *Prepare the paste:* In a small bowl, combine hot water and tamarind paste, stirring until well blended. Strain into a food processor and add lemongrass, ginger, coriander, sugar, turmeric, fennel, cumin and salt; purée until smooth.

2. Place lamb in a sealable plastic bag and spoon in paste. Seal, toss to coat and refrigerate for at least 4 hours or up to 12 hours, tossing occasionally.

3. Meanwhile, prepare a hot fire in your grill.

4. Remove lamb from paste, lightly scraping off and discarding excess paste. Thread lamb onto skewers, leaving space between pieces. Grill skewers for 2 to 3 minutes per side, turning once, until lamb has good grill marks.

Kentucky-Style Smoked Lamb

The western part of bluegrass Kentucky, around Owensboro, was a wool-producing region in the early 1800s, so their barbecue of choice was mutton, accompanied by a Worcestershire-laced "black sauce." Susan Goss, co-owner of West Town Tavern in Chicago, turned that style of barbecue into a more sophisticated restaurant dish featuring a stack of mashed potatoes, tarragon slaw and a final crown of slow-smoked lamb. We tried it, and it was love at first bite. Here's our version.

✦ TIP ✦

Wait to toss the cabbage with the dressing until just before you're ready to serve.

- Large, deep foil pan
- Plastic spray bottle
- **Suggested wood: hickory**

3 lbs	boneless lamb shoulder or leg, cut into 3-inch (7.5 cm) cubes	1.5 kg
1 cup	Worcestershire sauce	250 mL
½ cup	All-Purpose Barbecue Rub (see recipe, page 34)	125 mL
1 cup	unsweetened pineapple juice	250 mL

Tarragon Slaw

4 cups	finely chopped cabbage	1 L
¼ cup	mayonnaise	50 mL
1 tbsp	granulated sugar	15 mL
2 tbsp	tarragon-flavored vinegar	25 mL
1 tsp	dried tarragon	5 mL
	Kosher or sea salt and freshly ground black pepper	
1	recipe Kentucky-Style Black Barbecue Sauce (page 67)	1

1. Place lamb in foil pan. Pour in Worcestershire sauce and sprinkle with rub; toss to coat. Cover and refrigerate for at least 4 hours or overnight, tossing occasionally.

2. Meanwhile, prepare an indirect fire for smoking in your grill or smoker.

3. Fill spray bottle with pineapple juice. Place pan on the indirect side of the grill. Close the lid and smoke for 2 to 3 hours, spraying with juice every 30 minutes, until lamb is fork-tender.

4. *Prepare the slaw:* Place cabbage in a large bowl. In another bowl, whisk together mayonnaise, sugar, vinegar and tarragon. Season to taste with salt and pepper. Pour dressing over cabbage and toss to coat.

5. Divide slaw among plates, top with lamb and drizzle with barbecue sauce.

Smoky Lamb
You Can Eat with a Spoon

SERVES 8

Fall-apart tender, this lamb has the ancient flavor of the hearth, but using the smoker as your oven. Use a good-quality (but not expensive) dry red wine, such as a Cabernet, Pinot Noir or Burgundy.

✦ TIP ✦

Do not overcrowd the pan when browning the lamb, or it will not brown properly.

- **Large foil pan**
- **Suggested wood: mesquite, hickory, pecan, apple or oak**

3 tbsp	olive oil (approx.)	45 mL
3 lbs	boneless lamb shoulder, cut into ½-inch (1 cm) cubes	1.5 kg
2 tbsp	water	25 mL
3	sprigs fresh thyme	3
2	shallots, diced	2
1	carrot, diced	1
1	small stalk celery, diced	1
1	head garlic, cloves separated and peeled	1
2 tbsp	all-purpose flour	25 mL
1	bottle (750 mL) medium- to full-bodied dry red wine	1
1 tsp	red wine vinegar	5 mL
	Additional fresh thyme sprigs (optional)	

1. Prepare an indirect fire for smoking in your grill or smoker.

2. In a wide-bottomed pot, heat olive oil over medium-high heat until smoking. Working in batches, sauté lamb for 8 to 10 minutes, or until browned on all sides, adding oil as necessary between batches. Transfer to foil pan.

3. Add water to pot, scraping up any browned bits from the bottom of the pot. Pour pan juices into foil pan. Stir in thyme, shallots, carrot, celery and garlic. Whisk in flour, then stir in wine.

4. Place pan on the indirect side of the grill. Close the lid and smoke for 1 hour. Stir, cover with foil, close the lid and smoke for 1 hour, or until lamb is fork-tender. Using a slotted spoon, remove lamb to a platter and keep warm.

5. Transfer contents of the pan to a food processor or blender, discarding thyme, and purée. Stir in vinegar.

6. Pour sauce over lamb and garnish with thyme sprigs, if desired.

✦ Variation ✦

Any type of shoulder meat, such as beef chuck or pork shoulder blade (butt), can be cooked this way. Just smoke until fork-tender.

Kabuli Lamb Kebabs

SERVES 4 TO 6

Afghan cooks grill over charcoal, usually in a separate outbuilding in the family's courtyard. They rinse and salt raw onion to extract the fiery juice, then blend it with fresh tomato and herbs for a quick relish known as salata. Served with grilled flatbread, the kebabs and relish make for a fresh-tasting, casual meal.

✦ TIPS ✦

Soak the skewers in water for at least 30 minutes.

Instead of the pitas, you could use 2 to 3 large Afghan flatbreads, halved.

● Twelve 12-inch (30 cm) flat bamboo skewers, soaked

Salata

1	large onion, thinly sliced	1
¼ tsp	kosher or sea salt	1 mL
	Juice of 1 lemon	
2	large tomatoes, thinly sliced	2
¼ cup	finely chopped fresh cilantro	50 mL
1½ lbs	boneless lamb shoulder or leg, cut into 2-inch (2.5 cm) cubes	750 g
3	cloves garlic, minced	3
¼ cup	finely chopped fresh cilantro	50 mL
½ tsp	kosher or sea salt	2 mL
¼ tsp	cayenne pepper	1 mL
	Juice of 1 lemon	
	Olive oil	
4 to 6	pitas	4 to 6

1. *Prepare the salata:* In a colander, rinse onion with cold water and drain. In a bowl, combine onion, salt and lemon juice. Let stand for at least 1 hour or overnight.

2. Place lamb in a sealable plastic bag and add garlic, cilantro, salt, cayenne and lemon juice. Seal, toss to coat and refrigerate for at least 1 hour or up to 2 hours, tossing occasionally.

3. Meanwhile, prepare a hot fire in your grill.

4. Remove lamb from marinade, discarding marinade. Thread lamb onto skewers, leaving space between pieces, and brush with olive oil. Grill skewers for 2 to 3 minutes per quarter turn, or until lamb has good grill marks.

5. Meanwhile, brush pitas with olive oil. Grill for 1 to 2 minutes per side, turning once, until pitas have good grill marks.

6. Drain the onion and combine with tomatoes and cilantro to complete the *salata*.

7. Place a pita on each plate and top each with 2 to 3 skewers. Pass the *salata* at the table.

Souvlaki with Grilled Pita

Greek street food is perfect for a backyard barbecue.

• Twenty-four 12-inch (30 cm) flat bamboo skewers, soaked for at least 30 minutes, or flat metal skewers

Marinade

2	cloves garlic, minced	2
¼ cup	freshly squeezed lemon juice	50 mL
¼ cup	olive oil	50 mL
1 tbsp	ground dried oregano	15 mL
½ tsp	onion salt	2 mL
½ tsp	freshly ground white pepper	2 mL
2 lbs	boneless lamb, trimmed and cut into 1-inch (2.5 cm) strips	1 kg
8 to 12	pitas	8 to 12
	Olive oil	
1	large white onion, thinly sliced	1
8 to 12	lemon wedges	8 to 12
	Tzatziki (see recipe, page 57)	

1. *Prepare the marinade:* In a bowl, combine garlic, lemon juice, olive oil, oregano, onion salt and white pepper.

2. Place lamb in a large sealable plastic bag and pour in marinade. Seal, toss to coat and refrigerate for at least 2 hours or up to 12 hours, tossing occasionally.

3. Meanwhile, prepare a hot fire in your grill.

4. Remove lamb from marinade, discarding marinade, and thread lamb lengthwise onto skewers, leaving space between pieces. Grill skewers for 2 to 3 minutes per side, turning once, until lamb has good grill marks.

5. Meanwhile, lightly brush pitas with olive oil. Grill for about 1 minute per side, turning once, until warmed through but not crispy.

6. Holding a pita in one hand and 2 to 3 skewers in the other, pull the meat from the skewers into the pita. Repeat with the remaining skewers and pitas. Divide onion among pitas, add a squeeze of lemon juice and top with tzatziki. Serve immediately.

Spanish-Style Lamb Ribs Pimenton

Pimenton, or smoked paprika, is now more widely available in North America at spice emporia and gourmet shops. In this recipe, its smoky, spicy flavor blends with olive oil, garlic, oregano and parsley in a savory grilling paste that is also good on beef or pork. A kiss of smoke builds even more flavor until the final flourish: a taste of honey.

✦ TIP ✦

For easier basting, use a squeeze bottle of honey. Squeeze the honey onto the ribs and brush onto the meat with a grilling brush.

● **Suggested wood: oak, pecan, apple or hickory**

Pimenton Grilling Paste

6	cloves garlic, minced	6
2 tbsp	chopped fresh flat-leaf (Italian) parsley	25 mL
1 tbsp	smoked or sweet Hungarian paprika	15 mL
2 tbsp	red wine vinegar	25 mL
2 tbsp	olive oil	25 mL
1 tsp	kosher or sea salt	5 mL
1 tsp	dried oregano	5 mL
¼ tsp	hot pepper flakes	1 mL
4 lbs	Denver lamb ribs or lamb spare ribs, trimmed	2 kg
½ cup	liquid honey	125 mL

1. *Prepare the paste:* In a bowl, whisk together garlic, parsley, paprika, vinegar, olive oil, salt, oregano and hot pepper flakes.

2. Prepare a hot indirect fire with a kiss of smoke in your grill.

3. Slather meaty side of ribs with paste. When you see the first wisp of smoke from the wood, place ribs meaty side up on the indirect side of the grill. Close the lid and grill for 1 hour. Baste meaty side with honey, close the lid and smoke for about 1½ hours, basting with honey every 15 minutes, until meat pulls away from the ends of the bones. Slice into individual ribs and serve on a platter.

Tropical Lamb Burgers with Fresh Mango Chutney

SERVES 4

Eaten open-faced or on grilled flatbread, these burgers feature the tastes of the tropics, from sweet mango and coconut to mellow cashews, tart tamarind and fiery chiles.

✦ TIP ✦

Tamarind paste is available at Asian markets.

Fresh Mango Chutney

¼ cup	hot water	50 mL
1 tbsp	tamarind paste or freshly squeezed lime juice	15 mL
2	cloves garlic, minced	2
2	small red or green hot chile peppers, seeded and finely chopped	1
2 cups	thinly sliced ripe mango	500 mL
¼ cup	finely chopped fresh cilantro	50 mL
½ tsp	ground cumin	2 mL
½ tsp	ground coriander	2 mL
¼ tsp	ground turmeric	1 mL
2	small red or green hot chile peppers, seeded and finely chopped	2
2	cloves garlic, minced	2
1	egg	1
1 lb	ground lamb (from shoulder or leg)	500 g
½ cup	roasted salted cashews, coarsely chopped	125 mL
½ cup	unsweetened shredded coconut	125 mL

1. *Prepare the chutney:* In a small bowl, combine hot water and tamarind paste. Stir to blend, then strain into another bowl. Stir in garlic, chiles, mango, cilantro, cumin, coriander and turmeric. Set aside.

2. In a large bowl, combine chiles, garlic, egg, lamb, cashews and coconut. Add 1 tbsp (15 mL) warm water if mixture is too dry. Form into four ½-inch (1 cm) thick patties. Cover and refrigerate for 1 hour.

3. Meanwhile, prepare a medium-hot fire in your grill.

4. Grill burgers for 3 to 4 minutes per side, turning once, or until a meat thermometer inserted in the center of a burger registers 160°F (71°C). Serve each burger topped with chutney.

Moroccan Lamb Burgers

For a bold burger, you can't beat this one, with its Moroccan spices and fiery topping.

Harissa Mayonnaise

¼ cup	mayonnaise	50 mL
1 tbsp	chopped fresh cilantro	15 mL
1 tbsp	harissa (or to taste)	15 mL
	Freshly squeezed lemon juice (optional)	
1 lb	lean ground lamb	500 g
3 tbsp	fine dry bread crumbs	45 mL
2 tbsp	finely chopped green onion	25 mL
1 tsp	ground cumin	5 mL
1 tsp	ground coriander	5 mL
1 tsp	ground turmeric	5 mL
½ tsp	ground cinnamon	2 mL
4	Kaiser rolls, hamburger buns or pita breads	4
	Leaf lettuce and sliced tomato, cucumber and onion	

1. *Prepare the mayonnaise:* In a small bowl, whisk together mayonnaise, cilantro and harissa. Taste and add lemon juice, if desired. Set aside.

2. Prepare a medium-hot fire in your grill.

3. In a large bowl, using your hands, combine lamb, bread crumbs, green onion, cumin, coriander, turmeric and cinnamon. Form into four ½-inch (1 cm) thick patties.

4. Grill burgers for 3 to 4 minutes per side, turning once, or until a meat thermometer inserted in the center of a burger registers 160°F (71°C).

5. Place each burger on a roll, top with harissa mayonnaise and garnish with lettuce, tomato, cucumber and onion.

Specialty Meats

Grilled Spatchcocked Quail 287

Persian Grilled Quail Breasts. 288

Grilled Grouse with Lemon-Caper Herb Broth
   and Shaved Parmigiano-Reggiano 289

Prosciutto-Wrapped Smoked Pheasant Breasts 290

Apricot Cognac–Glazed Whole Smoked Duck 291

Hickory-Grilled Rotisserie Duck with Rosemary Fennel Rub . . . 292

Wood-Fired Duck Breasts with Blackberry Vinaigrette. 293

Szechuan Tea-Smoked Duck Breasts. 294

Smoke-Roasted Goose 296

Herbs de Provence Wood-Grilled Rabbit 297

Venison Steaks with Blackberry Brandy Beurre Blanc 298

Seared Elk Strip Loin with Huckleberry Port Wine Sauce 299

Rotisserie-Grilled Elk Tenderloin with Smoky
   Poblano Cream Sauce 300

Pepper-Crusted Bison Tenderloin
   with Point Reyes Blue Cheese Sauce 302

Mesquite-Grilled Bison Steak with Italian Parsley Pesto 303

Stuffed Bison Meatloaf 304

Prairie-Style Smoked Bison Chili. 305

Cabrito en Adobo. 306

Cuban-Style Suckling Pig 307

North Carolina Pig Pickin'. 308

Memphis in May Whole Hog. 309

Greek-Style Spitted Lamb with Rosemary Garlic Baste. 310

Every once in a while, the avid barbecuer can be called upon to do something out of the ordinary: grill or smoke wild game, spit-roast a lamb for a holiday or barbecue a whole hog for an old-fashioned pig-pickin'.

Each type of specialty meat has its own unique techniques. With lean and meaty game, the emphasis is on keeping the meat moist until it's tender. With larger cuts, it's getting everything done evenly and in a timely manner.

Because lean game meat has very little fat, it gets tough and dry when overcooked. When grilling, aim for rare to medium-rare; when spit-roasting or slow-smoking, baste and mop frequently until cooked to a tender well-done.

✦ Specialty Meats and Best Barbecue Methods ✦

Frog legs: Grill or smoke

Whole foie gras: Indirect grill

Skin-on boneless duck breast: Indirect grill (sear on hot side, finish over indirect side)

Pheasant breast: Wrap and indirect grill or slow-smoke

Whole game birds: Indirect grill, spit-roast or slow-smoke with frequent basting

Small game birds: Grill

Bone-in small game: Indirect grill

Steaks (elk, bison, venison): Direct grill to rare or medium-rare

Larger cuts of game: Indirect grill, spit-roast or slow-smoke

Whole hog: Slow-smoke

Grilled Spatchcocked Quail

Spatchcocked (flattened) birds look great on a plate or platter. Flattening the birds also makes for easier and more even grilling. Spatchcock the birds yourself by cutting through and removing the backbone with kitchen scissors and pushing the birds down with the heel of your hand to flatten.

● Sixteen 12-inch (30 cm) flat bamboo skewers (not soaked)

Marinade

2	cloves garlic, minced	2
1	onion, diced	1
½ cup	soy sauce	125 mL
¼ cup	liquid honey	50 mL
1 tbsp	toasted sesame oil	15 mL
8	quail	8
3 to 4	oranges, cut into thick slices	3 to 4
	Olive oil	

1. *Prepare the marinade:* In a bowl, combine garlic, onion, soy sauce, honey and sesame oil.

2. Remove the backbones from the quail by cutting either side with a pair of strong kitchen scissors. Flatten the birds with the heel of your palm and thread 2 bamboo skewers through each bird, forming an X. Arrange quail on a large shallow platter and pour half the marinade over them. Cover with plastic wrap and refrigerate for at least 2 hours or overnight. Cover and refrigerate the remaining marinade until ready to use.

3. Meanwhile, prepare a hot indirect fire in your grill.

4. Remove quail from marinade, discarding marinade. Place quail over the hot fire and grill for about 4 minutes per side, turning once, until juices run clear when quail is pierced. Stack quail on the indirect side of the grill.

5. Brush orange slices with oil and place over the hot fire. Grill for about 2 minutes per side, turning once, until lightly charred.

6. Arrange orange slices around the edges of a platter. Place quail down the center. Spoon some of the reserved marinade over oranges and quail. Serve the remaining marinade on the side.

Persian Grilled Quail Breasts

*Quail breasts are
very small but oh
so delicious. Serve
two breast halves
per person for an
appetizer and four
breast halves per
person for an entrée.*

- Perforated grill rack, oiled

3 tbsp	balsamic vinegar	45 mL
2 tbsp	olive oil	25 mL
1 tbsp	walnut oil	15 mL
4 cups	mixed salad greens	1 L
½ cup	sliced mushrooms	125 mL
¼ cup	walnut halves, toasted	50 mL
8	quail breast halves	8
¼ cup	butter, melted	50 mL
½ tsp	ground cumin	2 mL
½ tsp	ground coriander	2 mL
	Kosher salt and freshly ground black pepper	

1. Prepare a hot fire in your grill.

2. In a small bowl, whisk together vinegar, olive oil and walnut oil. Set aside.

3. In a large bowl, combine greens, mushrooms and walnuts. Set aside.

4. Brush quail with butter and sprinkle with cumin, coriander and salt and pepper to taste. Place on prepared grill rack and place rack on the grill. Grill for about 3 minutes per side, turning once and brushing with any remaining butter, until juices run clear when quail is pierced.

5. Toss greens with vinaigrette and divide among plates. Top with quail.

Szechuan Tea-Smoked Duck Breasts (page 294)

Mesquite-Grilled Bison Steak with Italian Parsley Pesto (page 303)

Argentinean Grilled Vegetable Platter with Chimichurri (page 348)

Provençal Tomatoes on the Vine (page 345)

Grilled Pears with Gorgonzola and Drizzled Honey (page 355)

Grilled Peaches with
Buttery Amaretto Glaze

Naan with Coconut Chutney (page 390)

Grilled Salmon Niçoise Salad (page 384)

Grilled Grouse with Lemon-Caper Herb Broth and Shaved Parmigiano-Reggiano

SERVES 6

Spoon the savory sauce into a shallow bowl, then place the grilled grouse on top for a great presentation. Crusty bread for sopping up the sauce is a must.

✦ TIP ✦

There are several kinds of grouse. Ruffed grouse and spruce grouse are tasty birds similar to quail. The ruffed has whitish meat; the spruce has darkish meat. Both are a bit bigger than quail, weighing in at 12 to 16 oz (375 to 500 g) dressed. If preparing spruce grouse, in step 3, after grilling for 3 to 4 minutes, move to the indirect side of the grill, close the lid and grill for about 1 hour, or until tender.

Lemon-Caper Herb Broth

2 tbsp	unsalted butter	25 mL
2 tbsp	all-purpose flour	25 mL
¾ cup	chicken stock	175 mL
¼ cup	snipped chives or chopped green onions	50 mL
2 tbsp	drained capers	25 mL
	Grated zest and juice of 1 lemon	
6	ruffed grouse (each about 12 oz/ 375 g)	6
	Olive oil	
	Kosher salt and freshly ground black pepper	
	Parmigiano-Reggiano cheese shavings	

1. Prepare a medium-hot indirect fire in your grill.

2. *Prepare the broth:* In a large saucepan, melt butter over medium heat. Stir in flour to form a paste. Gradually stir in chicken stock and cook for 4 to 5 minutes, or until starting to thicken. Stir in chives, capers, lemon zest and lemon juice. Remove from heat and keep warm.

3. Lightly brush grouse with olive oil and season to taste with salt and pepper. Place over the hot fire. Grill for 3 to 4 minutes per side, turning once and brushing with oil if necessary, until a meat thermometer inserted in the thickest part of a thigh registers 165°F (74°C). If not quite tender, stack grouse on the indirect side of the grill, close the lid and grill for 5 to 10 minutes.

4. Divide sauce among plates and place grouse on top. Sprinkle with cheese.

Prosciutto-Wrapped Smoked Pheasant Breasts

SERVES 4

The key to smoking is not looking. When you open the lid to take a peek, the heat escapes and you'll need to add 5 to 10 minutes to compensate. The smoke also escapes... so don't peek.

✦ TIP ✦

The Brie will soften and begin to seep out of the breasts while they cook, but the foil pan will keep the yummy cheese from getting away.

- Foil pan
- **Suggested wood:** oak, apple, maple or pecan

4	boneless skinless pheasant breasts	4
4 oz	Brie cheese, sliced	125 g
8	basil leaves	8
4	slices prosciutto	4
2 tbsp	olive oil	25 mL

1. Prepare an indirect fire for smoking in your grill or smoker.

2. Using a meat mallet, pound pheasant to ½-inch (1 cm) thickness. Place on a work surface, smooth side down. Place 1 oz (30 g) of Brie and 2 basil leaves in the middle of each breast. Fold the sides over to enclose the cheese, tucking a little bit of the ends inward too. Wrap each with a slice of prosciutto and lightly coat with olive oil. Place in foil pan.

3. Place pan on the indirect side of the grill. Close the lid and smoke for 45 to 55 minutes, or until a meat thermometer inserted in the thickest part of a breast registers 165°F (74°C). Transfer to a cutting board, tent with foil and let rest for 10 minutes. Slice crosswise into slightly less than 1-inch (2.5 cm) thick slices.

Apricot Cognac–Glazed Whole Smoked Duck

Smoked duck is a great addition to soups, casseroles and salads. If you are using a wild duck, the legs will probably be too tough to eat, but the breast meat will have a wonderful smokiness.

✦ TIP ✦

The smoking process can dry out a duck that isn't very fatty, especially lean wild ducks. If this is a concern, cut 2 to 3 pieces of bacon in half and drape over the breasts to help them retain moisture. Baste on top of the bacon. Discard the bacon before serving, if desired.

- Shallow foil pan
- **Suggested wood: oak, mesquite, maple or fruitwood**

2	ducks (each about 2 lbs/1 kg)	2
2 tsp	olive oil	10 mL
	Kosher salt and freshly ground black pepper	

Apricot Cognac Glaze

1 cup	apricot preserves or jam	250 mL
¼ cup	orange juice	50 mL
¼ cup	cognac or brandy	50 mL

1. Place ducks in foil pan and rub with olive oil. Sprinkle inside and out with salt and pepper.

2. Prepare an indirect fire for smoking in your grill or smoker.

3. *Prepare the glaze:* In a saucepan, bring apricot preserves, orange juice and cognac to a boil over high heat, stirring constantly. Remove from heat.

4. Place pan on the indirect side of the grill. Close the lid and smoke for 1½ to 2 hours, brushing with glaze during the last 30 minutes, until a meat thermometer inserted in the thickest part of a thigh registers 165°F (74°C). Transfer to a cutting board, tent with foil and let rest for 5 to 10 minutes before slicing.

✦ Variation ✦

Combine ¼ cup (50 mL) maple syrup and ¼ cup (50 mL) spicy barbecue sauce; use in place of the apricot glaze.

Hickory-Grilled Rotisserie Duck with Rosemary Fennel Rub

The ducks cook uniformly on the spit, but if you don't have a rotisserie, try placing each duck over a can of beer set over a hot indirect fire. The moistness from the beer will keep the ducks from drying out.

✦ TIP ✦

Grind rosemary and fennel seeds in a spice grinder or a clean coffee grinder.

- Rotisserie
- Foil pan
- **Suggested wood:** hickory or oak

Rosemary Fennel Rub

2 tbsp	dried rosemary, ground	25 mL
2 tbsp	fennel seeds, ground	25 mL
2 tbsp	coarse kosher salt	25 mL
2	ducks (each about 2 lbs/1 kg), cleaned	2
	Olive oil	

1. *Prepare the rub:* In a small bowl, combine rosemary, fennel and salt.

2. Set up your grill for rotisserie cooking with a kiss of smoke.

3. Lightly brush ducks with olive oil and sprinkle inside and out with rub. Attach ducks to the spit (see page 24). Heat grill to medium-high and place a foil pan filled with 3 to 4 cups (750 mL to 1 L) water over the fire. Close the lid and grill for 1 to 1½ hours, basting with olive oil for the last 20 to 30 minutes, until an instant-read thermometer inserted in the thickest part of a thigh registers 165°F (74°C). Transfer to a cutting board, tent with foil and let rest for 5 to 10 minutes before slicing.

Wood-Fired Duck Breasts with Blackberry Vinaigrette

Wild mallard duck breasts are very small, about 6 oz (175 g). Domestic muscovy or Long Island duck breasts are about 8 oz (250 g), while moulard duck breasts can weigh up to 1 lb (500 g)! If you use larger duck breasts, grill them longer, with your meat thermometer at the ready. You're aiming for 150°F (65°C) for medium-rare.

✦ Variation ✦

For a more casual duck supper, make duck sandwiches. Buy some good-quality hoagies, butter each side and toast. Slather with the spread of your choice or a drizzle of the blackberry vinaigrette. Place a grilled duck breast on each roll and top with thinly sliced red onion and crumbled feta or blue cheese.

● **Suggested wood:** fruitwood, oak, pecan or walnut

4	boneless skinless mallard duck breasts	4
1 tbsp	olive oil	15 mL
1 tsp	coarse kosher salt	5 mL
1 tsp	freshly cracked black pepper	5 mL

Blackberry Vinaigrette

½ cup	blackberry jam	125 mL
2	cloves garlic, minced	2
⅓ cup	red wine vinegar	75 mL
⅓ cup	olive oil	75 mL
1 tsp	dry mustard	5 mL
½ tsp	ground cloves	2 mL
½ tsp	freshly ground black pepper	2 mL
¼ tsp	kosher salt	1 mL

1. Using a meat mallet, pound duck to ¾-inch (2 cm) thickness. Lightly coat with olive oil and sprinkle with salt and pepper. Set aside.

2. Prepare a medium-hot fire with a kiss of smoke in your grill.

3. *Prepare the vinaigrette:* In a small saucepan, gently heat jam over medium-low heat until dissolved. Remove from heat and whisk in garlic, vinegar, olive oil, mustard, cloves, pepper and salt. Set aside.

4. Grill duck for 3 to 3½ minutes per side, turning once, until a meat thermometer inserted in the thickest part of a breast registers 150°F (65°C) for medium-rare, or until desired doneness. Transfer to a cutting board, tent with foil and let rest for 5 to 10 minutes before slicing. Serve drizzled with vinaigrette.

Szechuan Tea-Smoked Duck Breasts

Tea-smoked duck is one of the most famous dishes of Szechuan Province. Originally, smoking was a way to preserve foods, but it later came to be used as a flavor enhancer.

◆ TIPS ◆

Other wood chips could substitute for the mesquite. Try oak, sugar maple or any fruitwood.

Try tea-smoking other skin-on poultry, such as chicken thighs or breasts, quail, pheasant or turkey.

This marinade can also be used for poultry, pork, fish and shellfish.

● Stovetop smoker

Marinade

2 tbsp	sake	25 mL
1 tbsp	soy sauce	15 mL
1 tsp	liquid honey	5 mL
½ tsp	grated gingerroot	2 mL
2	boneless muscovy or moulard duck breasts (with skin)	2
1 tbsp	whole Szechuan peppercorns	15 mL
1 tsp	coarse kosher salt	5 mL
1 tsp	five-spice powder	5 mL
1	cinnamon stick (6 inches/15 cm), broken into small pieces	1
2 tbsp	loose black tea leaves	25 mL
1 tbsp	dry mesquite wood chips for the stovetop smoker	15 mL
½ tsp	dried orange peel	2 mL
½ tsp	vegetable oil	2 mL

1. *Prepare the marinade:* In a bowl, combine sake, soy sauce, honey and ginger.

2. With a sharp knife, make scores in duck skin, through the fat (do not cut into meat), about ½ inch (1 cm) apart in a crosshatch pattern. Place duck in a large sealable plastic bag and pour in marinade. Seal, toss to coat and refrigerate for at least 2 hours or up to 4 hours, tossing occasionally.

3. In a heavy skillet, over medium-low heat, stir peppercorns and salt for 3 to 5 minutes, or until peppercorns are toasted and fragrant. Coarsely grind in a clean coffee or spice grinder. Stir in five-spice powder.

4. Remove duck from marinade, discarding marinade, and lightly pat dry. Sprinkle duck with pepper mixture.

5. Line the bottom of the stovetop smoker with a double layer of heavy-duty foil, leaving a 3-inch (7.5 cm) overhang along the edges.

6. In a bowl, combine cinnamon, tea leaves, mesquite and orange peel. Pour into the center of the smoker and spread out evenly to ¼ inch (0.5 cm) thick in the middle of the bottom pan. Place the drip pan over the mixture and set the grill rack in the smoker.

7. In a skillet, heat oil over high heat. Place duck skin side down and sear for 2 to 3 minutes, or until a deep golden brown.

8. Transfer duck to the grill rack. Fold the foil inward and slip on the smoker cover, closing it almost all the way. Heat over high heat for 5 to 10 minutes, or until steady wisps of smoke appear. Close the lid and reduce heat to medium. Smoke duck for 8 minutes. Turn off heat and let duck stand in smoker for 10 minutes, until a meat thermometer inserted in the thickest part of a breast registers 150°F (65°C) for medium-rare, or until desired doneness. Carefully open the smoker and transfer duck to a cutting board. Transfer to a cutting board, tent with foil and let rest for 5 to 10 minutes before slicing. Serve warm or at room temperature.

Smoke-Roasted Goose

SERVES 4 TO 6

Smoke-roasting is a technique that gives a kiss of smoke at higher temperatures. The goose infuses with smoke for an hour, then roasts in a 350°F (180°C) oven to crisp the skin.

- Foil pan
- **Suggested wood:** oak, pecan or fruitwood

Marinade

1 cup	dry red wine	250 mL
¼ cup	red wine vinegar	50 mL
¼ cup	barbecue seasoning	50 mL
1	goose (4 to 6 lbs/2 to 3 kg)	1
3	strips bacon	3

1. *Prepare the marinade:* In a bowl, combine wine, vinegar and barbecue seasoning.
2. Place goose in a large sealable plastic bag and pour in marinade. Seal, toss to coat and refrigerate for at least 2 hours or up to 3 hours.
3. Prepare a hot indirect fire with a kiss of smoke in your grill.
4. Remove goose from marinade, discarding marinade, and place in foil pan. Place pan on the indirect side of the grill and lay bacon over the breasts. Close the lid and smoke for 1 hour.
5. Meanwhile, preheat oven to 350°F (180°C).
6. Cover goose tightly with foil and roast in the oven for 1 to 1½ hours, removing the foil for the last 15 minutes, until a meat thermometer inserted in the thickest part of a thigh registers 165°F (74°C). Transfer to a cutting board, tent with foil and let rest for 15 minutes before carving.

✦ Variation ✦

If you want to smoke just goose breasts, wrap them with prosciutto and place in the foil pan. Smoke for about 45 minutes, or until a thermometer inserted in the thickest part of a breast registers 165°F (74°C).

Herbs de Provence Wood-Grilled Rabbit

SERVES 4

Soaking wild rabbit in milk eliminates any gaminess. If the rabbit is domestic, no presoaking is necessary.

● **Suggested wood: oak, pecan or fruitwood**

1	wild or domestic rabbit (about 3 lbs/1.5 kg), cut into 8 pieces	1
2 cups	milk (optional)	500 mL
2 tbsp	olive oil	25 mL
2 tbsp	dried herbes de Provence	25 mL

1. If using wild rabbit, place in a large bowl and add milk. Cover and refrigerate for at least 4 hours or overnight. Remove rabbit from milk, discarding milk, and pat dry.

2. Place rabbit in a shallow dish, rub with olive oil and sprinkle with herbes de Provence. Cover and refrigerate for 2 hours.

3. Meanwhile, prepare a medium-hot fire with a kiss of smoke in your grill.

4. When you see the first wisp of smoke from the wood, place rabbit on the grill. Close the lid and grill for 8 to 10 minutes per side, turning once, until a meat thermometer inserted in the thickest part of a rabbit piece registers 160°F (71°C).

Venison Steaks with Blackberry Brandy Beurre Blanc

Venison steaks are a coveted cut from deer and elk. If you don't have time to make the sauce, simply grill them with the olive oil, salt and pepper. But once you taste the sauce, you'll find time to make it.

✦ TIP ✦

The beurre blanc is also delicious with grilled beef tenderloin and chicken breasts.

Blackberry Brandy Beurre Blanc

1	clove garlic, minced	1
1 cup	blackberry brandy	250 mL
1/4 cup	freshly squeezed lemon juice	50 mL
1 tbsp	minced shallot	15 mL
1 cup	whipping (35%) cream	250 mL
1/4 cup	cold unsalted butter, cut into pieces	50 mL
1 cup	fresh or frozen blackberries	250 mL
8	deer or elk tenderloin steaks (each about 4 oz/125 g and 1/2 inch/1 cm thick)	8
2 tbsp	olive oil	25 mL
	Coarse kosher salt and freshly cracked black pepper	

1. *Prepare the beurre blanc:* In a small saucepan, combine garlic, brandy, lemon juice and shallot; bring to a boil over medium-high heat. Boil, stirring often, until reduced to about 1/4 cup (50 mL), about 5 minutes. Add cream and return to a boil. Boil until reduced by half, about 5 minutes. Remove from heat and whisk in butter, one piece at a time, whisking until sauce glistens and thickens. Stir in blackberries and keep warm.

2. Prepare a hot fire in your grill.

3. Lightly brush steaks with olive oil and season to taste with salt and pepper. Grill for about 2 minutes per side, turning once, until medium-rare, or until desired doneness. Serve with beurre blanc.

Seared Elk Strip Loin with Huckleberry Port Wine Sauce

Strip loin steaks are excellent for the grill and can also be pan-seared restaurant-style over very high heat. Cook to medium-rare for optimum results.

✦ TIP ✦

The sauce can be stored in an airtight container in the refrigerator for up to 5 days. Reheat gently before serving.

Huckleberry Port Wine Sauce

1 cup	port wine	250 mL
2 tbsp	granulated sugar	25 mL
1 tsp	grated lemon zest	5 mL
1 tsp	freshly squeezed lemon juice	5 mL
Pinch	kosher salt	Pinch
1 lb	huckleberries, stemmed	500 g
1 tsp	grated orange zest	5 mL
Pinch	freshly ground black pepper	Pinch
4	boneless elk strip loin or other prime steaks (about ¾ inch/2 cm thick)	4
	Olive oil	
	Kosher salt and freshly ground black pepper	

1. *Prepare the sauce:* In a saucepan, combine port, sugar, lemon juice and salt; bring to a boil over high heat. Reduce heat to medium and simmer, stirring occasionally, until syrupy. Gently stir in huckleberries, lemon zest, orange zest and pepper. Remove from heat and keep warm.

2. Prepare a hot fire in your grill.

3. Brush steaks with olive oil and season to taste with salt and pepper. Grill for 2 to 3 minutes per side, turning once, until a meat thermometer inserted in the thickest part of a steak registers 130°F (54°C) for medium-rare, or until desired doneness. Serve with sauce on the side.

✦ Variations ✦

Increase the granulated sugar in the sauce to ½ cup (125 mL) and serve drizzled over desserts such as cheesecake, pound cake or ice cream.

If you can't find huckleberries, substitute blueberries and reduce the sugar to 1 tbsp (15 mL), or to taste.

Rotisserie-Grilled Elk Tenderloin with Smoky Poblano Cream Sauce

Invite a crowd over for this delicious meat, slow-cooked on a spit. Figure 8 oz (250 g) meat per person.

✦ TIPS ✦

You can smoke as many as 12 poblano peppers at a time. Use your favorite wood, such as oak or apple, and smoke for 35 to 45 minutes, or until supple. Use right away or place each pepper in a freezer bag and freeze for up to 6 months.

If you can't find a fresh poblano, substitute a jalapeño.

- Rotisserie
- **Suggested wood: very fine oak chips**

1	elk tenderloin, trimmed	1
2 cups	Italian vinaigrette	500 mL
1 cup	cider vinegar	250 mL

Baste

2	cloves garlic, minced	2
1 cup	butter, melted	250 mL
2 tbsp	soy sauce	25 mL

Smoky Poblano Cream Sauce

1	poblano pepper, smoked (see tips, at left)	1
2 cups	whipping (35%) cream	500 mL
½ cup	unsalted butter, cut into pieces	125 mL
	Kosher or sea salt and freshly ground black pepper	

1. Place tenderloin in a large roasting pan and pour in vinaigrette and vinegar. Cover and refrigerate for at least 4 hours or up to 24 hours.

2. Set up your grill for rotisserie cooking.

3. *Prepare the baste:* In a bowl, combine garlic, butter and soy sauce.

4. Remove tenderloin from marinade, discarding marinade, rinse well and pat dry. Attach tenderloin to the spit (see page 24). Preheat the grill to medium-high. Close the lid and grill for 20 to 25 minutes per lb (500 g), basting every 15 minutes, until an instant-read thermometer inserted in the thickest part of the tenderloin registers 130°F (54°C) for medium-rare, or until desired doneness. Transfer to a cutting board, tent with foil and Let rest for 15 minutes.

5. *Meanwhile, prepare the sauce:* In a heavy saucepan, bring poblano and cream to a simmer over medium heat. Simmer, stirring constantly, until reduced by half, about 15 minutes. Strain, discarding poblano, and return cream to the pan over low heat. Whisk in butter, one piece at a time, whisking until sauce is smooth. Season to taste with salt and pepper.

6. Slice meat across the grain and serve drizzled with sauce.

✦ Variations ✦

Substitute beef tenderloin or any venison tenderloin.

Instead of using the rotisserie, grill the tenderloin directly over a hot fire for 15 to 20 minutes per lb (500 g), turning every 5 to 7 minutes to sear all sides, until medium-rare, or until desired doneness.

Pepper-Crusted Bison Tenderloin with Point Reyes Blue Cheese Sauce

The distinct flavor of Point Reyes blue cheese comes from cows that are grass-fed on certified organic green pastures, with coastal fog and salty ocean breezes. In a pinch, substitute any good-quality blue cheese you like.

1	bison tenderloin (about 4 lbs/2 kg)	1
	Olive oil	
	Coarse kosher salt and coarsely ground black pepper	

Point Reyes Blue Cheese Sauce

¾ cup	crumbled Point Reyes blue cheese	175 mL
½ cup	whipping (35%) cream	125 mL
2 tbsp	dry white wine	25 mL

1. Brush tenderloin with olive oil and season to taste with salt and pepper.

2. Prepare a hot fire in your grill.

3. Grill tenderloin for 20 to 30 minutes, turning often, until a meat thermometer inserted in the thickest part of the tenderloin registers 130°F (54°C) for medium-rare, or until desired doneness. Transfer to a cutting board, tent with foil and let rest for 5 to 10 minutes.

4. *Meanwhile, prepare the sauce:* In a saucepan, over medium heat, combine blue cheese, cream and wine, stirring until smooth. Remove from heat.

5. Slice meat and serve with warm sauce on the side.

Mesquite-Grilled Bison Steak with Italian Parsley Pesto

Italian Parsley Pesto

2	cloves garlic, crushed or roughly chopped	2
2 cups	chopped fresh flat-leaf (Italian) parsley	500 mL
½ cup	walnut halves, toasted	125 mL
¾ cup	extra-virgin olive oil	175 mL
½ cup	freshly grated Parmesan or Romano cheese	125 mL
	Kosher or sea salt and freshly ground black pepper	
4	bison steaks (about 1 inch/ 2.5 cm thick)	4
	Extra-virgin olive oil	
	Coarse kosher salt and freshly ground black pepper	

1. *Prepare the pesto:* In a food processor, combine garlic, parsley and walnuts; process to a smooth paste. With the motor running, through the feed tube, gradually add olive oil in a slow, steady stream until thickened. Add Parmesan and salt and pepper to taste; pulse to combine. Set aside.

2. Prepare a hot fire in your grill.

3. Brush steaks with olive oil and season to taste with salt and pepper. Grill for 2 to 3 minutes per side, turning once, until a meat thermometer inserted in the thickest part of a steak registers 130°F (54°C) for medium-rare, or until desired doneness. Serve each steak with a dollop of pesto on top.

Stuffed Bison Meatloaf

This meatloaf, made with lean, flavorful bison, is fit for company. Serve with a Caesar salad and garlic mashed potatoes. Don't forget to fill the wine glasses with the remaining merlot.

You can use store-bought roasted peppers in a jar or roast your own. To roast peppers, preheat broiler or your grill to high. Broil or grill whole peppers until blackened, blistered and tender. Place peppers in a brown paper bag and close the top. Set aside for about 5 minutes, until cool. Slice peppers open to remove the core and seeds. Rub excess char off the skins. Use immediately or store in an airtight container in the refrigerator for up to 2 days.

- Doubled foil pan
- **Suggested wood:** oak, mesquite, sugar maple or fruitwood

2	eggs, beaten	2
1	onion, chopped	1
2 lbs	ground bison	1 kg
1 lb	ground beef sirloin	500 g
1½ cups	spaghetti sauce, divided	375 mL
1 cup	chopped roasted red bell pepper (see tip, at left)	250 mL
1 cup	ricotta cheese	250 mL
¾ cup	dry Italian-style bread crumbs	175 mL
2 tbsp	dried Italian herb seasoning, crushed	25 mL
	Kosher salt and seasoned pepper (such as McCormick Seasoned Pepper Blend or Lawry's Seasoned Pepper)	
4	slices mozzarella (about 8 oz/250 g)	4
½ cup	dry red wine (such as Merlot)	125 mL

1. Prepare an indirect fire for smoking in your grill or smoker.

2. In a large bowl, using your hands, combine eggs, onion, bison, beef, ½ cup (125 mL) of the spaghetti sauce, roasted pepper, ricotta, bread crumbs and Italian herb seasoning. Season to taste with salt and seasoned pepper.

3. Divide meat mixture in half and form each half into a flat loaf about 2 inches (5 cm) high and 12 inches (30 cm) long. Place one loaf in foil pan and layer mozzarella evenly over top. Cover with the other loaf and smooth the meat mixture together to form a completed meatloaf. Pour wine and the remaining spaghetti sauce over meatloaf.

4. Place pan on the indirect side of the grill. Close the lid and smoke for 3 hours, spooning sauce over meatloaf every 30 minutes, until a meat thermometer inserted in the center of the loaf registers 160°F (71°C). Let rest for 10 to 15 minutes before slicing.

Prairie-Style Smoked Bison Chili

SERVES 4 TO 6

This chili is made sublime by the smoky flavor of outdoor cooking. Serve with cornbread.

✦ TIPS ✦

Smoking ground meat is pretty simple. Try smoking ground beef, turkey or sausage for use in other soups.

Look for canned fire-roasted tomatoes (such as Muir Glen or Hunt's) in health food stores or the organic section of well-stocked supermarkets.

- Foil pan
- **Suggested wood: oak, mesquite or apple**

1 lb	ground bison	500 g
1 tbsp	vegetable oil	15 mL
2	cloves garlic, minced	2
1	large onion, chopped	1
2	bay leaves	2
1	roasted red bell pepper (see tip, page 304), chopped	1
1	can (14 to 19 oz/398 to 540 mL) black beans, rinsed and drained	1
2 cups	canned fire-roasted diced tomatoes (see tip, at left), with juice	500 mL
2 cups	water	500 mL
½ cup	chopped celery	125 mL
2 tsp	dried thyme	10 mL
1 tsp	freshly ground black pepper	5 mL
½ cup	sour cream	125 mL

1. Prepare an indirect fire for smoking in your grill or smoker.

2. Spread bison in foil pan. Place pan on the indirect side of the grill, close the lid and smoke for 1 hour.

3. In a large stockpot, heat oil over medium-low heat. Sauté garlic and onion for 6 to 8 minutes, or until softened. Add smoked bison, bay leaves, roasted pepper, beans, tomatoes with juice, water, celery, thyme and pepper; bring to a boil over medium-high heat. Reduce heat, cover partially and simmer, stirring frequently, for 30 minutes, or until chili is very thick but not dried out.

4. Ladle into bowls and top each with a dollop of sour cream.

Cabrito en Adobo

Cabrito (young goat) is a popular barbecue dish in Texas and Mexico, where it is colored by achiote paste and seasoned with adobo seasoning, then slow-smoked until tender.

✦ TIPS ✦

You can special-order cabrito, usually from May through October, from a butcher shop or grocery store catering to an Hispanic clientele.

Adobo seasoning — a blend of granulated garlic, dried Mexican oregano, ground cumin, cayenne pepper and black pepper — can be found in the spice section of well-stocked grocery stores or at Hispanic markets.

● **Suggested wood:** oak or mesquite

Cabrito Mop

1	can or bottle (12 oz/341 mL) beer	1
¼ cup	Worcestershire sauce	50 mL
¼ cup	freshly squeezed lime juice	50 mL
1 cup	achiote paste	250 mL
1 cup	orange juice	250 mL
½ cup	freshly squeezed lime juice	125 mL
1	cabrito hind leg (about 5 lbs/2.5 kg)	1
1 cup	adobo seasoning	250 mL
	Tomato-based barbecue sauce	

1. *Prepare the mop:* In a bowl, combine beer, Worcestershire sauce and lime juice.

2. In another bowl, combine achiote paste, orange juice and lime juice.

3. Place cabrito in a roasting pan, brush all over with the achiote mixture and sprinkle with adobo seasoning.

4. Prepare an indirect fire for smoking in your grill or smoker.

5. Remove cabrito from pan and place on the indirect side of the grill. Close the lid and smoke for 3 to 3½ hours, mopping every 30 minutes, until a meat thermometer inserted in the thickest part of the cabrito registers 165°F (74°C) and the meat is tender. Transfer to a cutting board, tent with foil and let rest for 10 minutes before slicing. Serve with barbecue sauce.

✦ Variation ✦

For rainforest-style cabrito, smoke it wrapped in a banana leaf. Follow the instructions in the Mayan-Style Pit Pork recipe (page 186) for wrapping the meat, and smoke as above, omitting the mop.

Cuban-Style Suckling Pig

Lechon asado *(grilled suckling pig) is a traditional dish on Christmas Eve in the Caribbean. The pork is flavored with a sour orange marinade, then cooked slowly until moist and delicious. Garnish the platter with fruits of the season. You'll need about 30 lbs (14 kg) of charcoal. Use wood for the first 3 hours only.*

◆ TIPS ◆

Order a dressed pig from your butcher at least 1 week before you need it.

For a festive look, place an apple in the smoked pig's mouth and surround it with an abundance of fresh fruit: green and purple grapes, halved lemons and limes, Seckel pears, crabapples — whatever looks good.

- Large roasting pan or food-safe plastic bag
- Cheesecloth
- Plastic spray bottle
- **Suggested wood: apple, cherry or oak**

Marinade

4	cloves garlic, minced	4
1 cup	sour orange juice (see tip, page 38)	250 mL
1 tbsp	white wine vinegar	15 mL
1 tsp	dried Mexican or Italian oregano	5 mL
1	suckling pig (about 20 lbs/10 kg)	1
2 cups	unsweetened pineapple juice	500 mL
	Kosher or sea salt, granulated garlic and freshly ground black pepper	
	Fruits of the season	
1	recipe Aji-li-Mojili (page 42)	1

1. *Prepare the marinade:* In a bowl, combine garlic, sour orange juice, vinegar and oregano.

2. Place pig in roasting pan or food-safe plastic bag. Pour in marinade, cover or seal and refrigerate for at least 8 hours or overnight, turning occasionally.

3. Meanwhile, prepare an indirect fire for smoking in your grill or smoker.

4. Fill spray bottle with pineapple juice. Remove pig from marinade, discarding marinade, and pat dry. Season inside and out with salt, granulated garlic and pepper. Place a ball of foil in the mouth. Place pig cavity side down on the indirect side of the grill. Drape with cheesecloth and spray with pineapple juice. Close the lid and smoke for 10 to 12 hours, spraying with juice every hour, until a meat thermometer inserted in the thickest part of the pig registers 180°F (82°C) and the meat is tender. Transfer to a large platter, tent with foil and let rest for 15 to 30 minutes. Remove the cheesecloth and ball of foil.

5. Arrange fruits around the pig. Carve portions of the meat at the table and serve with Aji-li-Mojili.

North Carolina Pig Pickin'

SERVES 50

A pig pickin' is a traditional festival food, often associated with political rallies or church gatherings, dating back to the 19th century in the American South. Today, it's the province of barbecue contests and backyard barbecues for a crowd. Everyone seems to have their own "secret" sauce. Since we're giving ours away, it's "not-so-secret." You'll need at least 60 lbs (27 kg) of charcoal. Use wood for the first 3 hours only. And, of course, you'll need a smoker large enough to hold a 50-lb (23 kg) pig, and enough strong people to handle it.

✦ TIPS ✦

Order a dressed pig from your butcher at least 1 week before you need it. Have the butcher skin and trim the pig for you.

You'll need a large commercial-size pit smoker to smoke a whole pig or other large pieces of meat.

Whole pig is usually "picked" and the pieces served on platters.

- Cheesecloth
- Plastic spray bottle
- **Suggested wood: hickory**

3 cups	prepared mustard	750 mL
½ cup	liquid amber honey	125 mL
1	pig (about 50 lbs/23 kg), skinned and exterior fat trimmed to ¼-inch (0.5 cm) thickness	1
3 cups	All-Purpose Barbecue Rub (see recipe, page 34)	750 mL
4 cups	apple juice	1 L
1	recipe Not-So-Secret Sauce (page 64)	1

1. In a large bowl, combine mustard and honey.

2. Using a hose or a pitcher of cold water, rinse the inside of the pig and pat dry. Using a sharp knife, peel all the membranes out of the cavity and trim off as much of the fat as possible. Brush the cavity with some of the mustard mixture and sprinkle with some of the rub. Brush the exterior with the remaining mustard mixture and sprinkle with the remaining rub. Let stand at room temperature for 1 hour, until the surface is tacky.

3. Meanwhile, prepare an indirect fire for smoking in your grill or smoker.

4. Fill spray bottle with apple juice. Place pig cavity side down on the indirect side of the grill and spread out as much as possible. Drape with cheesecloth and spray with apple juice. Close the lid and smoke for 6 to 8 hours, spraying with juice every hour, until pig is beginning to burnish. Remove cheesecloth, spray with juice, close the lid and smoke for 3 hours, spraying with juice every 30 minutes, until a meat thermometer inserted in the thickest part of the pig registers 180°F (82°C) and the meat is tender. Let rest for 30 minutes.

5. Place pig on a covered table and carve, or let guests pick the pig. Serve with Not-So-Secret Sauce.

Memphis in May Whole Hog

SERVES 75

Memphis in May is an annual barbecue contest that inspires a perfect storm of pork, spice and smoke. Contestants are judged not only on their food, but also on their rigs and the overall ambience of their prep area, so there's lots of over-the-top barbecue setups and plenty of sippin' whiskey. The result is plenty of fun and great-tasting barbecue. You'll need at least 60 lbs (27 kg) of charcoal. Use wood for the first 3 hours only.

✦ TIPS ✦

Order a dressed hog from your butcher at least 1 week before you need it. Have the butcher skin and trim the hog for you.

You'll need a large commercial-size pit smoker to smoke a whole hog or other large pieces of meat.

Whole hog is usually "picked" and the pieces served on platters.

- Culinary injector
- Cheesecloth
- Plastic spray bottle
- **Suggested wood:** hickory

1	recipe Sour Orange Marinade (page 38)	1
1	hog (about 75 lbs/34 kg), skinned and exterior fat trimmed to ¼-inch (0.5 cm) thickness	1
3 cups	All-Purpose Barbecue Rub (see recipe, page 34)	750 mL
4 cups	unsweetened pineapple juice	1 L
1	recipe Nectar of the BBQ Gods (page 65) or Not-So-Secret Sauce (page 64)	1

1. Strain marinade through a fine-mesh sieve.

2. Using a hose or a pitcher of cold water, rinse the inside of the hog and pat dry. Using a sharp knife, peel the membranes out of the cavity and trim off as much fat as possible. Fill the injector with some of the marinade and inject the hog all over, refilling the injector until all the marinade is used. Sprinkle inside and out with rub. Let stand at room temperature for 1 hour, until the surface is tacky.

3. Meanwhile, prepare an indirect fire for smoking in your grill or smoker.

4. Fill spray bottle with pineapple juice. Place hog cavity side down on the indirect side of the grill and spread out as much as possible. Drape with cheesecloth and spray with pineapple juice. Close the lid and smoke for 9 to 11 hours, spraying with juice every hour, until hog is beginning to burnish. Remove cheesecloth, spray with juice, close the lid and smoke for 3 hours, spraying with juice every 30 minutes, until a meat thermometer inserted in the thickest part of the hog registers 180°F (82°C) and the meat is tender. Let rest for 30 minutes.

5. Place hog on a covered table and carve, or let guests pick the pig. Serve with the sauce of your choice.

Greek-Style Spitted Lamb with Rosemary Garlic Baste

SERVES 20 TO 24

Reminiscent of herb-covered hilltops on tiny, sun-baked isles, this dish is traditionally served at Greek weddings and church festivals, and on Easter.

✦ TIPS ✦

Order a dressed lamb from your butcher at least 1 week before you need it. Have the butcher skin and trim the lamb for you.

For the best result, the spit rod should extend 10 inches (25 cm) on either side of the lamb. If this is not possible, make sure the hottest fire is under the thickest part of the lamb, the shoulder area.

If you prefer, you can grill the lamb over a hot indirect fire with a kiss of smoke instead of using the rotisserie. Place lamb on the indirect side of the grill, close the lid and grill for 4 to 5 hours, basting every 30 minutes, until a meat thermometer inserted in the thickest part of the thigh registers 150°F (65°C).

- Rotisserie
- **Suggested wood: olive, oak or apple**

Rosemary Garlic Baste

8	cloves garlic, minced	8
¼ cup	fresh rosemary	50 mL
2 tsp	fine kosher or sea salt	10 mL
2 cups	olive oil	500 mL
	Juice of 4 lemons	
	Freshly ground black pepper	
1	lamb (20 to 22 lbs/10 to 11 kg)	1

1. *Prepare the baste:* In a food processor, pulse garlic, rosemary and salt until finely minced. With the motor running, through the feed tube, gradually add olive oil in a steady stream. Add lemon juice and pulse to blend. Season to taste with pepper.

2. Set up your grill for rotisserie cooking with a kiss of smoke.

3. Brush the interior of the lamb with some of the baste and attach to the spit (see page 24). Brush the exterior of the lamb with baste. Heat the grill to medium-high. Close the lid and grill for 4 to 5 hours, basting every 30 minutes, until an instant-read thermometer inserted in the thickest part of the thigh registers 150°F (65°C). Let rest for 15 minutes before carving.

✦ Variation ✦

Substitute two boneless legs of lamb (each about 5 lbs/2.5 kg), rolled and tied, for the whole lamb. Attach both to the spit, leaving about 6 inches (15 cm) between them. Reduce the grilling time to about 2½ hours. Serves 16 to 20 people.

Vegetables

Grilled Baby Artichokes with Balsamic Olive Oil Drizzle 313

Grilled Asparagus with Asian Dipping Sauce. 314

Brazilian Grilled Avocados with Caipirinha Glaze 315

Stir-Grilled Green Beans with Lemon Verbena Pesto. 316

Grilled Fava Beans in the Pod with Fresh Pecorino 317

Barbecued White Beans with Bacon and Pear 318

Texas Cowpoke Pintos with Jalapeño Peppers. 319

Calico Smoked Beans 320

Stir-Grilled Baby Beets with Green Onions
   and Lemon-Herb Butter. 321

Grilled Baby Bok Choy with Gingered Soy Sauce 322

Stir-Grilled Brussels Sprouts 323

Grilled Blue Cheese Coleslaw 324

Stir-Grilled Minted Baby Carrots 325

Smoked Corn in the Husk with Hot Pepper Herb Butter 326

Smoked Corn and Chorizo Casserole. *327*

Grilled Corn in the Husk with Smoked Paprika Butter 328

Grilled Eggplant with Gruyère and Sun-Dried Tomatoes 329

Smoked Garlic Custards. 330

Grilled Endive and Escarole with Persian Feta
   and Walnut Vinaigrette 331

Char-Grilled Hearts of Romaine with Goat Cheese
   and Pinot Grigio Vinaigrette 332

Brie and Pepper–Stuffed Portobellos 333

Wok-Grilled Greek Taverna Olives. 334

Grilled Onions with Thyme-Scented Cream. 335

Foil-Wrapped Pepper Strips in Aji-li-Mojili 336

Stuffed Smoked Peppers 337

Grill-Smoked Jalapeño Poppers 338

Tapas-Style Grilled Fingerlings with Portuguese Aïoli. 339

Smoked Potato Casserole 340

Smoked Sweet Potato Casserole with Ginger,
   Lime and Brown Sugar. 341

continued on next page…

Stir-Grilled Shallots with Tarragon Butter 342
Grilled Tomato Slices and Mozzarella 343
Planked Goat Cheese–Topped Beefsteak Tomatoes 344
Provençal Tomatoes on the Vine 345
Sicilian Grill-Roasted Tomatoes 346
Smoked Garlic Aïoli Platter of Roasted Root Vegetables 347
Argentinean Grilled Vegetable Platter with Chimichurri 348
Vegetable Kebabs with Za'atar 349
Teriyaki Vegetable Skewers 350

Vegetables add color, texture and flavor to any meal — especially if they're barbecued. In this chapter, we offer vegetables you can grill or smoke along with the main course, or by themselves. Because vegetables vary so much in flavor, a whole cupboard of condiments, herbs and spices comes into use in rubs, marinades, drizzles, flavored butters and sauces for the grilled veggies.

Grilled vegetables have the added benefit of retaining their color and flavor the day after cooking, so extras are great for use in salads, pastas or sandwiches. Smoked vegetables such as shallots, onions, garlic, bell peppers and tomatoes can be frozen for later use in dishes such as sauces, gumbo, stews, soups and flavored butters.

Most vegetables respond well to medium woods, such as apple, hickory, oak and pecan, but if you're smoking your veggies along with a main course, don't worry if the wood you're using doesn't fit into this category — the veggies will still taste great!

✦ Vegetables for Grilling, Skewering, Stir-Grilling and Grill-Roasting ✦

Artichokes, asparagus, avocados, baby beets, bell peppers, bok choy, Brussels sprouts, cabbage, baby carrots, chile peppers, corn, eggplant, escarole, fava beans, green beans, green onions, mushrooms, onions, potatoes, romaine lettuce, sweet potatoes, tomatoes, winter squash, yellow summer squash, zucchini

✦ Vegetables for Smoking ✦

Bell peppers, chile peppers, corn, dried beans (in a casserole), mushrooms, onions, potatoes, sweet potatoes, tomatoes, winter squash

✦ Vegetables for Planking ✦

Bell peppers, chile peppers, mushrooms, onions, tomatoes

Grilled Baby Artichokes with Balsamic Olive Oil Drizzle

SERVES 4

Whenever baby artichokes are available, grab them and make this dish, as tasty as it is pretty.

8	baby artichokes	8
	Grated zest and juice of 1 lemon	
	Kosher salt	
1	clove garlic, minced	1
½ cup	extra-virgin olive oil	125 mL
⅓ cup	balsamic vinegar	75 mL
	Freshly ground black pepper	

1. Remove the bottom outer leaves from the artichokes and trim off stems. Slice artichokes in half lengthwise. Trim about 1 inch (2.5 cm) off the tops. Snip off the tops of the remaining outer leaves. With the tip of a teaspoon, remove the hairy chokes and discard.

2. In a large non-reactive pot, bring 1 inch (2.5 cm) of water, lemon zest, lemon juice and several shakes of salt to a boil. Add artichokes, cover and cook for 5 to 6 minutes, or until artichoke bottoms are tender when pierced with a small knife. Drain well and set aside.

3. Prepare a medium-hot fire in your grill.

4. In a small bowl, combine garlic, olive oil, vinegar and salt and pepper to taste. Brush artichokes with some of the dressing.

5. Grill artichokes for about 5 minutes, turning a couple of times, until lightly charred. Transfer to a platter and serve hot or warm with the remaining dressing on the side.

Grilled Asparagus with Asian Dipping Sauce

Prepare this recipe during the height of asparagus season, from April through June, for the most flavorful results.

Tamarind juice is available in cans or bottles in some grocery stores and Asian markets.

To make sure you don't lose any spears through the grill grates, thread asparagus crosswise onto two parallel skewers, leaving space between the spears.

Asian Dipping Sauce

3	cloves garlic, minced	3
1 cup	tamarind juice (see tip, at left)	250 mL
1/2 cup	firmly packed brown sugar	125 mL
1/2 cup	soy sauce	125 mL
1/2 cup	nam pla (fish sauce)	125 mL
1 tbsp	grated gingerroot	15 mL
2 tsp	toasted sesame oil	10 mL
	Grated zest and juice of 1 lime	
2 lbs	asparagus, trimmed	1 kg

1. *Prepare the sauce:* In a bowl, combine garlic, tamarind juice, brown sugar, soy sauce, nam pla, ginger, sesame oil, lime zest and lime juice, stirring until sugar is dissolved.

2. Lay asparagus in a shallow glass dish and pour in half the sauce. Set aside.

3. Prepare a medium-hot fire in your grill.

4. Place asparagus perpendicular to the grill rack. Grill for 8 to 10 minutes, turning often, until asparagus is tender-crisp. Transfer to a platter and serve hot or at room temperature with the remaining sauce on the side.

Brazilian Grilled Avocados with Caipirinha Glaze

4	ripe but firm Hass avocados	4
	Freshly squeezed lemon juice	
	Olive oil	
	Kosher or sea salt and freshly ground black pepper	
1	recipe Caipirinha Glaze (page 88)	1

1. Prepare a medium-hot fire in your grill.

2. Halve avocados and remove the pits. Drizzle with lemon juice, then brush with olive oil and season to taste with salt and pepper.

3. Place avocados cut side down on the grill. Grill for 2 to 3 minutes, or until avocados have good grill marks. Turn cut side up and brush with some of the glaze, letting it pool in the cavities. Close the lid and grill for 2 to 3 minutes, or until glaze is shiny. Serve drizzled with the remaining glaze and give diners spoons to scoop out the flesh.

Stir-Grilled Green Beans with Lemon Verbena Pesto

Fragrant lemon verbena is excellent paired with the freshest beans you can get.

✦ TIPS ✦

This recipe makes about 1 cup (250 mL) pesto. The extra is delicious served as an appetizer with crusty bread or dolloped on grilled chicken or fish. It can be stored in an airtight container in the refrigerator for up to 3 weeks or in the freezer for up to 3 months.

Asparagus beans are also known as yard-long beans. If you prefer, you may cut the beans into smaller lengths, but the long beans are very attractive served on a platter with the pesto on the side.

● Grill wok or basket, oiled

Lemon Verbena Pesto

2	cloves garlic, chopped or minced	2
1 cup	lightly packed fresh lemon verbena or lemon balm leaves	250 mL
¼ cup	freshly grated Parmesan cheese	50 mL
¼ cup	pine nuts	50 mL
½ cup	olive oil	125 mL
	Kosher salt and freshly ground black pepper	
2 lbs	asparagus green beans (or regular green beans)	1 kg
2 tsp	olive oil	10 mL

1. *Prepare the pesto:* In a food processor, purée garlic, lemon verbena, Parmesan and pine nuts. With the motor running, through the feed tube, gradually add olive oil in a steady stream. Season to taste with salt and pepper and process until smooth. Set aside.

2. Prepare a hot fire in your grill. Set prepared grill wok over the fire.

3. In a bowl, toss beans with olive oil. Transfer to the wok and stir-grill for 5 to 8 minutes, or until tender.

4. Toss beans with ¼ cup (50 mL) of the pesto. Serve warm or let cool, refrigerate for up to 3 days and serve cold.

Grilled Fava Beans in the Pod with Fresh Pecorino

SERVES 4

If you're lucky enough to know an Italian gardener, ask for fava beans in the pod. Brushed with a little olive oil, seasoned to taste and simply grilled, they're wonderful served with fresh pecorino.

✦ TIP ✦

If fresh fava bean pods are not to be found, do the same with sugar snap peas, snow peas or edamame in the pod (do not try to eat the edamame pod). Reduce the cooking time for sugar snap peas and snow peas to 6 to 8 minutes.

1 lb	fava beans in the pod	500 g
	Olive oil	
	Kosher or sea salt and freshly ground black pepper	
8 oz	fresh pecorino cheese (or other soft sheep's or goat's milk cheese)	250 g

1. Prepare a medium-hot fire in your grill.

2. Brush bean pods with olive oil and season to taste with salt and pepper. Grill for 10 to 12 minutes, turning often, until pods have good grill marks.

3. Divide bean pods and cheese among plates. Try eating them pod and all, but if the pods are too tough, open them and scoop out the beans to eat with cheese and a little olive oil.

Barbecued White Beans with Bacon and Pear

Any type of pork and bean dish tastes so much smokier and richer right off the grill. This one pairs well with grilled sausages, especially those made with veal, such as bratwurst, weisswurst or bockwurst.

- Foil pan or cast-iron pot
- **Suggested wood:** apple, hickory or pear

4	large pears, peeled and diced	4
1 lb	dry white navy beans, soaked in water overnight, drained and rinsed	500 g
1 lb	smoked bacon, diced and cooked crisp	500 g
3 cups	beer (preferably a pale lager)	750 mL
¼ cup	light (fancy) molasses or pure maple syrup	50 mL
1 tsp	kosher or sea salt	5 mL
½ tsp	freshly ground black pepper	2 mL

1. In foil pan, combine pears, beans, bacon, beer, molasses, salt and pepper. Set aside.

2. Prepare a hot indirect fire with a kiss of smoke in your grill.

3. When you see the first wisp of smoke from the wood, place pan on the indirect side of the grill. Close the lid and grill for 1 to 1¼ hours, adding a little water if necessary, until beans have softened and thickened and have a good smoky aroma.

✦ Variation ✦

You can also smoke this dish. Simply prepare an indirect fire for smoking in your grill or smoker, close the lid and smoke for 2½ to 3 hours, or until beans are tender.

Texas Cowpoke Pintos with Jalapeño Peppers

These spicy beans dole out big flavor.

✦ TIPS ✦

For extra smokiness, add 1 to 2 tsp (5 to 10 mL) hickory-flavored liquid smoke. Liquid smoke has a bad rap from people using way too much of it, so use it sparingly.

This recipe can also be prepared on the stovetop. Leave the bean mixture in the pot and simmer for 5 to 6 hours.

● Foil pan

3	jalapeño peppers, sliced	3
2	cans (each 20 oz/568 mL) diced tomatoes with chiles	2
1	onion, diced	1
1 lb	dry pinto beans, soaked in water overnight, drained and rinsed	500 g
8 oz	bacon, chopped	250 g
½ tsp	ground cumin	2 mL
½ tsp	chili powder	2 mL
½ tsp	smoked paprika	2 mL
¼ tsp	cayenne pepper	1 mL
¼ tsp	dried basil	1 mL
	Kosher salt and freshly ground black pepper	

1. In a large pot, combine jalapeños, tomatoes with chiles, onion, beans, bacon, cumin, chili powder, paprika, cayenne and basil. Add enough water to cover and bring to a boil.

2. Meanwhile, prepare a hot indirect fire in your grill.

3. Transfer bean mixture to foil pan. Place on the indirect side of the grill and cook for 5 to 6 hours, stirring frequently, until beans are soft and liquid has thickened. Season to taste with salt and pepper.

Calico Smoked Beans

SERVES 10 TO 12

Hearty appetites will love these baked beans. Cook them on the smoker, in a slow cooker or in the oven.

✦ Variations ✦

To prepare the beans in a slow cooker, transfer the mixture to a slow cooker at the end of step 2, cover and cook on High for 4 hours, or until bubbling and heated all the way through.

To bake the beans, transfer the mixture to a large casserole dish at the end of step 2 and bake in a 350°F (180°C) oven for 45 to 60 minutes, or until bubbling and heated all the way through.

- Doubled foil pan
- **Suggested wood: apple**

8 oz	bacon	250 g
8 oz	lean ground beef	250 g
1	onion, chopped	1
1	clove garlic, minced	1
1	can (28 oz/796 mL) baked beans	1
1	can (14 to 19 oz/398 to 540 mL) chickpeas, drained and rinsed	1
1	can (14 to 19 oz/398 to 540 mL) kidney beans, drained and rinsed	1
1	can (14 to 19 oz/398 to 540 mL) lima beans, drained and rinsed	1
½ cup	ketchup	125 mL
½ cup	packed brown sugar	125 mL
2 tbsp	Worcestershire sauce	25 mL
1½ tbsp	cider vinegar	22 mL
1 tbsp	prepared mustard	15 mL
1 tsp	kosher salt	5 mL

1. In a large skillet, over high heat, cook bacon until crisp. Transfer to a plate lined with paper towels, let cool and crumble.

2. In the same skillet, sauté ground beef and onion until beef is no longer pink. Drain off fat and stir in bacon, garlic, baked beans, chickpeas, kidney beans, lima beans, ketchup, brown sugar, Worcestershire sauce, vinegar, mustard and salt. Transfer to foil pan and set aside.

3. Prepare an indirect fire for smoking in your grill or smoker.

4. Place pan on the indirect side of the grill. Close the lid and smoke for 2 hours, until smoky and bubbling. Add a small amount of water if the mixture gets too thick.

Stir-Grilled Baby Beets with Green Onions and Lemon-Herb Butter

Fresh beets are sweet and delicious. The contrast in color with the green onions is very pretty.

- Grill wok or basket, oiled
- Baking sheet

12	baby beets, trimmed	12
	Kosher salt and freshly ground black pepper	
8	green onions, cut into 3-inch (7.5 cm) pieces	8

Lemon-Herb Butter

½ cup	unsalted butter, softened	125 mL
2	cloves garlic, minced	2
2 tbsp	chopped fresh herbs (such as dill, oregano, thyme or parsley)	25 mL
2 tsp	freshly squeezed lemon juice	10 mL

1. In a pot of boiling water, boil beets for 10 to 15 minutes, or until tender enough to just pierce with a fork. Drain, rinse in cold water and pat dry. Set aside.

2. *Prepare the butter:* In a small saucepan, melt butter over medium-high heat. Sauté garlic for 1 minute, or until fragrant. Remove from heat and stir in herbs and lemon juice. Set aside.

3. Prepare a hot fire in your grill.

4. Place beets in prepared grill wok and set wok on baking sheet. Drizzle beets with some of the butter, tossing to coat. Season to taste with salt and pepper.

5. Place wok on the grill. Stir-grill for about 8 minutes, basting occasionally with butter, until beets are charred. Add green onions and stir-grill for 4 minutes, basting with butter, until onions are charred. Transfer to a platter and serve with the remaining butter on the side.

Grilled Baby Bok Choy with Gingered Soy Sauce

Late spring or early summer is when small heads of bok choy are most available. The smaller they are, the sweeter for grilling.

✦ TIP ✦

Just about any grilled vegetable will taste sensational with Gingered Soy Sauce, but especially asparagus, eggplant, mushrooms or zucchini.

Gingered Soy Sauce

1	clove garlic, minced	1
¼ cup	unsalted butter, melted	50 mL
2 tbsp	olive oil	25 mL
2 tsp	minced gingerroot	10 mL
2 tsp	soy sauce	10 mL
2	small heads bok choy, trimmed and halved lengthwise	2

1. *Prepare the sauce:* In a bowl, whisk together garlic, butter, olive oil, ginger and soy sauce. Place bok choy in a shallow dish and brush with some of the sauce. Set aside.

2. Prepare a medium-hot fire in your grill.

3. Place bok choy cut side down on the grill. Grill for about 10 minutes, or until fork-tender. Turn and baste with sauce. Grill for about 10 minutes, basting occasionally, until tender.

Stir-Grilled Brussels Sprouts

Brussels sprouts are perfect for the grill. They will be tender-crisp, not overcooked and mushy, as so many people cook them on the stovetop.

● Grill wok or basket, oiled

1½ lbs	small Brussels sprouts, trimmed	750 g
2 tbsp	butter	25 mL
1	clove garlic, minced	1
2 oz	feta cheese, crumbled	60 g

1. In a pot of boiling water, blanch Brussels sprouts for 3 to 4 minutes, or until tender enough to just pierce with a fork. Using a strainer, remove from boiling water and immediately plunge into cold water; let stand until cold. Drain well and set aside.

2. In a saucepan, melt butter over medium-high heat. Sauté garlic for 1 minute, or until fragrant. Remove from heat and set aside.

3. Prepare a hot fire in your grill.

4. Place Brussels sprouts in prepared grill wok and place wok on the grill. Stir-grill for 8 to 10 minutes, or until charred and tender-crisp. Transfer to a platter, drizzle with butter and sprinkle with feta.

✦ Variation ✦

Substitute chopped cabbage for the Brussels sprouts and omit step 1. Stir-grill for 6 to 8 minutes, or until charred and tender.

Grilled Blue Cheese Coleslaw

Grilled coleslaw? You bet! Grilled cabbage wedges acquire terrific flavor while retaining their crunchiness.

✦ TIPS ✦

Place the onions perpendicular to the grill grates so they don't fall through.

Grill the onions and cabbage when you're also grilling a steak, pork tenderloin, chicken, or fish.

8	green onions, tops trimmed	8
1	large head cabbage, tough outer leaves removed, cut into 8 wedges	1
	Vegetable oil	
8 oz	blue cheese, crumbled	250 g
2	cloves garlic, minced	2
¾ cup	vegetable oil	175 mL
⅓ cup	cider vinegar	75 mL
1 tsp	celery seeds	5 mL
1 tsp	kosher or sea salt	5 mL
½ tsp	freshly ground black pepper	2 mL
¼ tsp	dry mustard	1 mL

1. Prepare a hot fire in your grill.
2. Brush green onions and cut sides of cabbage with oil. Grill for 2 to 3 minutes per side, turning once, until vegetables have good grill marks on both sides.
3. Finely chop cabbage, coarsely chop green onions and combine in a large bowl. Let cool, then stir in blue cheese.
4. In another bowl, whisk together garlic, ¾ cup (175 mL) oil, vinegar, celery seeds, salt, pepper and mustard. Pour over cabbage mixture and toss to coat.

✦ Variation ✦

You can also make this with raw chopped cabbage and green onions. Dress the coleslaw right before serving, as the dressing makes the cabbage wilt.

Stir-Grilled Minted Baby Carrots

Carrots seem to be the forgotten vegetable, perhaps because they are often overcooked. When grilled, they get a little bit of flavorful char. The beautiful orange color is unequaled, and the interior crunch is great.

✦ TIP ✦

If you are using fresh garden carrots, peel them and cut into even pieces.

- Grill wok or basket, oiled
- Baking sheet

¼ cup	finely chopped fresh mint	50 mL
2 tbsp	unsalted butter, melted	25 mL
4 cups	baby carrots	1 L

1. Prepare a hot fire in your grill.
2. In a large bowl, combine mint and butter. Add carrots and toss to coat. Transfer to prepared grill wok and place on a baking sheet to carry out to the grill.
3. Place wok on the grill. Stir-grill for 15 to 20 minutes, or until tender.

✦ Variation ✦

Think color. Add 1 small yellow summer squash or zucchini, cubed with the skin on, to the wok for the last 10 to 12 minutes of cooking.

Smoked Corn in the Husk with Hot Pepper Herb Butter

SERVES 12

Corn smoked in the husk stays moist, and the silks come right off, so don't bother to remove them ahead of time.

✦ TIP ✦

If you make lots of this recipe, cut the excess corn off the cob, place in an airtight container and freeze for up to 2 months. The smoked corn can be added to dips, soups and stews.

● **Suggested wood:** apple, cherry, oak or pecan

12	ears corn, in the husk	12
	Kosher salt and freshly ground black pepper	

Hot Pepper Herb Butter

¾ cup	butter, softened	175 mL
¼ cup	chopped fresh herbs (such as mint, cilantro or parsley)	50 mL
½ tsp	hot pepper flakes	2 mL

1. Soak corn in a large container of cold water for 1 to 2 hours. Drain well.

2. Meanwhile, prepare an indirect fire for smoking in your grill or smoker.

3. Place corn on the indirect side of the grill. Close the lid and smoke for about 1 hour, or until tender. Let cool slightly.

4. *Meanwhile, prepare the butter:* In a small bowl, combine butter, herbs and hot pepper flakes.

5. Pull a long piece of husk off each ear of corn, then pull back the husks and tie them together with the long piece. The silks should fall off. Serve with the butter and salt and pepper.

Smoked Corn and Chorizo Casserole

Corn pudding made with fresh sweet corn is a memory-maker. The chorizo contrasts nicely with the corn.

- Preheat oven to 350°F (180°C)
- 8-cup (2 L) casserole dish, buttered
- 13- by 9-inch (3 L) baking pan

8 oz	cooked chorizo	250 g
2 cups	smoked corn kernels (about 4 ears)	500 mL
¼ cup	chopped green onions	50 mL
1½ tbsp	all-purpose flour	22 mL
1 tbsp	minced red bell pepper	15 mL
2 tsp	granulated sugar	10 mL
¼ tsp	salt	1 mL
¼ tsp	cornstarch	1 mL
2	eggs, beaten	2
1 cup	whipping (35%) cream	250 mL
Pinch	cayenne pepper	Pinch

1. In a large bowl, combine chorizo, corn, green onions, flour, red pepper, sugar, salt and cornstarch, stirring well.

2. In another bowl, whisk together eggs and cream. Add to corn mixture and stir in cayenne.

3. Spoon corn mixture into prepared casserole dish. Place in baking pan and add water to a depth of 1 inch (2.5 cm). Bake in preheated oven for 1 hour, or until a knife inserted in the center comes out clean. Serve hot.

◆ Variation ◆

Omit the sausage for a vegetarian corn casserole.

Grilled Corn in the Husk with Smoked Paprika Butter

SERVES 6

Pulling the leaves back on the corn creates a natural handle to hold onto while you devour the corn.

◆ TIP ◆

If you love the Smoked Paprika Butter, make twice as much and serve it with warm crusty bread, too.

6	ears corn, in the husk	6

Smoked Paprika Butter

1	clove garlic, minced	1
¼ cup	unsalted butter, softened	50 mL
½ tsp	smoked paprika (or to taste)	2 mL

1. Peel back corn husks, taking care not to pull them off. Remove silks and pull husks back over corn, tying securely with kitchen string. Soak in cold water for 15 minutes. Drain well.

2. *Meanwhile, prepare the butter:* In a bowl, combine garlic, butter and paprika. Set aside.

3. Prepare a hot fire in your grill.

4. Grill corn for 10 to 12 minutes, turning often, until husks are slightly charred. Let cool slightly, then pull husks back and brush corn with the butter.

Grilled Eggplant with Gruyère and Sun-Dried Tomatoes

This is a superb grilled version of eggplant Parmesan.

Eggplant seems to suck up olive oil, and it doesn't even look like you oiled it, but refrain from adding too much oil. For best results, oil the eggplant right before you grill it.

Sun-dried tomatoes are available in sealable bags or in jars with olive oil. We prefer the bagged variety, as they are nice and supple and very flavorful.

2	small eggplants	2
	Kosher salt	
1	clove garlic, finely minced	1
½ cup	extra-virgin olive oil	125 mL
2 tbsp	dried oregano, crumbled	25 mL
¼ cup	chopped sun-dried tomatoes	50 mL
½ cup	shredded Gruyère cheese	125 mL

1. Slice the ends off the eggplants, but do not peel. Cut lengthwise into ½-inch (1 cm) slices and lightly salt. Place in colander and let drain for at least 30 minutes to remove excess water. Pat dry.

2. Meanwhile, prepare a medium-hot fire in your grill.

3. In a bowl, combine garlic, olive oil and oregano. Brush on both sides of eggplant slices.

4. Grill eggplant for about 10 minutes, turning once, until tender. Sprinkle with sun-dried tomatoes and cheese for the last 2 minutes.

Smoked Garlic Custards

SERVES 8

Make this elegant yet easy side dish to go along with Cherry-Smoked Crown Roast of Pork (page 185) or Cherry-Smoked Rib Roast with Horseradish Crème Fraîche (page 230). It's also delicious as a quiche-like main dish or to float atop a puréed squash or pumpkin soup as a final flourish.

✦ TIP ✦

Be an efficient barbecuer. Smoke cloves of garlic, peppers, and onions when you're already smoking something else. Then wrap and freeze the vegetables for later use in sauces and side dishes.

- Foil pan
- 8 custard cups, buttered
- 13- by 9-inch (3 L) baking pan
- **Suggested wood: cherry, hickory, oak or pecan**

30	cloves garlic, peeled	30
	Olive oil	
7	egg yolks	7
2 cups	milk	500 mL
1 tsp	kosher or sea salt	5 mL
1 tsp	freshly ground white pepper	5 mL

1. Prepare an indirect fire for smoking in your grill or smoker.

2. Place garlic in foil pan and drizzle with olive oil. Place pan on the indirect side of the grill. Close the lid and smoke for about 1 hour, or until tender.

3. Meanwhile, preheat oven to 300°F (150°C).

4. Place prepared custard cups in baking pan and fill pan with enough water to come halfway up the sides of the cups.

5. In a food processor, purée the smoked garlic. Add egg yolks, milk, salt and pepper; process until well blended. Strain into a 4-cup (1 L) glass measuring cup. Pour batter into custard cups.

6. Bake for 35 to 45 minutes, or until set. Let cool for 2 to 3 minutes. Run a knife around the inside of each custard cup to loosen, and invert custards onto plates.

✦ Variation ✦

Smoked Garlic Crème Brûlée: After baking, top each custard with a sprinkling of freshly grated Parmesan cheese. Broil for 3 minutes, until cheese has formed a crust on top.

Grilled Endive and Escarole with Persian Feta and Walnut Vinaigrette

SERVES 4

Grilled greens are delicious, always a welcome surprise to people who have never tasted them before. They are charry on the outside and still crisp inside, with a combination of flavor and texture that can't be beat.

◆ TIP ◆

Persian feta is soft and creamy. If you can't find it, try a creamy goat cheese.

4	small heads Belgian endive, outer leaves trimmed	4
4	small heads escarole, outer leaves trimmed	4
¼ cup	extra-virgin olive oil	50 mL
½ cup	crumbled Persian feta cheese	125 mL
	Kosher salt and freshly ground black pepper	
½ cup	Walnut Vinaigrette (see recipe, page 40)	125 mL

1. Prepare a hot fire in your grill.

2. Brush endive and escarole with olive oil. Grill for 5 to 8 minutes, turning every 2 minutes, until nicely charred.

3. Place greens on a platter and sprinkle with feta. Season lightly with salt and pepper and drizzle with vinaigrette.

Char-Grilled Hearts of Romaine with Goat Cheese and Pinot Grigio Vinaigrette

SERVES 6

The little bit of char on the romaine gives it an enormous flavor leap. It's perfect for a summer salad.

✦ TIP ✦

Do not trim the core of the lettuce, or several of the outer leaves will fall off.

Pinot Grigio Vinaigrette

1½ cups	Pinot Grigio	375 mL
2	shallots, minced	2
2 tsp	rice vinegar	10 mL
	Grated zest and juice of 1 lemon	
¾ cup	olive oil	175 mL
	Kosher salt and freshly ground black pepper	
3	hearts of romaine, halved lengthwise	3
	Extra-virgin olive oil	
4 oz	goat cheese, crumbled	125 g
1 cup	garlic-flavored croutons	250 mL

1. *Prepare the vinaigrette:* In a small saucepan, bring wine to a simmer over medium heat; simmer until reduced by half. Add shallots, vinegar, lemon zest and lemon juice. Gradually whisk in olive oil, then season to taste with salt and pepper. Set aside.

2. Prepare a hot fire in your grill.

3. Brush cut side of romaine with olive oil. Place cut side down on the grill. Grill for 3 to 4 minutes, or until outer lettuce leaves are charred and there are good grill marks on the cut side. (Do not close the grill lid or lettuce will wilt.)

4. Serve each half romaine sprinkled with crumbled goat cheese and croutons and drizzled with vinaigrette.

Brie and Pepper–Stuffed Portobellos

A grilled portobello brushed with olive oil and seasoned with salt and pepper is a simple pleasure. When you add a little extra oomph of flavor, it's divine.

✦ TIP ✦

You can use store-bought roasted peppers in a jar or roast your own. To roast peppers, preheat broiler or your grill to high. Broil or grill whole peppers until blackened, blistered and tender. Place peppers in a brown paper bag and close the top. Set aside for about 5 minutes, until cool. Slice peppers open to remove the core and seeds. Rub excess char off the skins. Use immediately or store in an airtight container in the refrigerator for up to 2 days.

● **Baking sheet**

4	portobello mushrooms, stemmed	4
¼ cup	extra-virgin olive oil	50 mL
4 oz	Brie cheese, cut into slices	125 g
2	roasted red bell peppers (see tip, at left), sliced	2
	Kosher salt and freshly ground black pepper	

1. Prepare a hot fire in your grill.

2. Place mushrooms on baking sheet and brush both sides with olive oil. Turn stem side up and evenly distribute cheese and peppers among the mushrooms. Season to taste with salt and pepper.

3. Place mushrooms on the grill. Close the lid and grill for 8 to 10 minutes, or until mushrooms are softened.

Wok-Grilled
Greek Taverna Olives

*What a difference a
little sizzle on the grill
can make! Serve with
grilled flatbread for
an easy appetizer.*

✦ TIPS ✦

Select your favorite
olive varieties from your
grocery store olive bar.

For an extra-special
appetizer, serve with
grilled haloumi cheese
as well as the flatbread.

- Grill wok or basket
- Baking sheet

4 cups	drained mixed black and green olives (both brine- and oil-cured)	1 L
	Olive oil	
	Hot pepper flakes and fresh rosemary (optional)	
	Flatbread	

1. Prepare a medium-hot fire in your grill.
2. Place olives in a bowl and drizzle with olive oil. Sprinkle to taste with hot pepper flakes and rosemary, if desired. Toss to coat.
3. Place grill wok over the kitchen sink and pour in olives, draining any extra oil. Set wok on baking sheet and carry out to the grill.
4. Place wok on the grill. Stir-grill for 6 to 8 minutes, or until olives are heated through.
5. Meanwhile, brush flatbread with olive oil. Grill for about 1 minute per side, turning once, until warmed through but not crispy.
6. Serve olives with flatbread.

Grilled Onions with Thyme-Scented Cream

These make a fabulous accompaniment to grilled steaks or pork chops. If grilling them at the same time, you'll need a hot fire for the meat but a cooler spot for the onions — perhaps along the perimeter of the grill or on an elevated rack. Or you can grill these alone over a medium fire.

6 to 8	small yellow or white onions, peeled	6 to 8
	Olive oil	
2	cloves garlic, minced	2
1 cup	whipping (35%) cream	250 mL
1 tsp	fresh thyme leaves (or ½ tsp/2 mL dried)	5 mL
½ tsp	fine kosher or sea salt	2 mL
½ tsp	freshly ground black pepper	2 mL

1. Prepare a medium fire in your grill.

2. Using a grapefruit spoon or paring knife, cut out a 1-inch (2.5 cm) diameter core from the top of each onion. Brush the bottoms with olive oil.

3. In a bowl, whisk together garlic, cream, thyme, salt and pepper. Spoon about 1 tbsp (15 mL) into each onion, letting some drizzle down the sides. Reserve the remaining cream mixture.

4. Place onions on the grill. Close the lid and grill for 10 to 15 minutes. Baste with some of the cream mixture, close the lid and grill for 10 minutes, or until onions are browned and softened. Serve with the remaining cream spooned on top.

Foil-Wrapped Pepper Strips in Aji-li-Mojili

This big-flavor side dish goes well with grilled steaks, pork chops, fish and chicken.

1	red bell pepper, seeded and cut into thin strips	1
1	yellow bell pepper, seeded and cut into thin strips	1
1	orange bell pepper, seeded and cut into thin strips	1
1	green bell pepper, seeded and cut into thin strips	1

Aji-li-Mojili

2	cloves garlic, minced	2
1/4 cup	olive oil	50 mL
2 tbsp	freshly squeezed lime juice	25 mL
1/2 tsp	kosher or sea salt	2 mL
1/4 tsp	hot pepper flakes	1 mL

1. Prepare a medium-hot fire in your grill.

2. Lay a large sheet of foil on a flat surface. Arrange red, yellow, orange and green peppers over half the foil.

3. *Prepare the Aji-li-Mojili:* In a bowl, whisk together garlic, olive oil, lime juice, salt and hot pepper flakes. Drizzle over peppers. Fold foil over pepper mixture and crimp all around to seal.

4. Place foil package on the grill. Grill for 15 minutes. Turn and grill for 10 minutes, or until tender and hot. Carefully open the foil and spoon peppers and sauce onto plates.

Stuffed Smoked Peppers

**SERVES 4 AS
A LIGHT ENTRÉE
OR SIDE DISH**

In hilltop villages in southern Italy, France and Spain, the baker's wood-fired oven was often pressed into service to wood-roast stuffed summer vegetable dishes like this one.

✦ Variations ✦

Substitute finely chopped cooked ham or baby shrimp for the bacon.

Instead of bell peppers, use zucchini or summer squash. Cut in half lengthwise, scoop out some of the flesh, chop and add to the filling. Stuff zucchini halves with filling and place in foil pan. Smoke for 30 minutes, or until tender.

• Foil pan
• **Suggested wood:** hickory, oak or pecan

4	large green, red, yellow or orange bell peppers (or one of each)	4
8	strips bacon	8
1	large onion, diced	1
8	slices country-style bread, cubed	8
1	can (14 oz/398 mL) diced tomatoes, with juice	1
1 cup	shredded cheese (such as Cheddar, fontina or Gruyère)	250 mL
	Kosher or sea salt and freshly ground black pepper	

1. Stem and hollow out each pepper. If necessary, trim the bottoms so they will stand upright in foil pan. Set aside.

2. In a skillet, over high heat, cook bacon until crisp. Transfer to a plate lined with paper towels.

3. Add onion to the fat remaining in the skillet and sauté for about 5 minutes, or until transparent. Remove with a slotted spoon to a plate lined with paper towels.

4. Crumble bacon into a large bowl. Add onion, bread cubes, tomatoes with juice, and cheese. Season to taste with salt and pepper. Stuff peppers with this mixture. Set aside.

5. Prepare an indirect fire for smoking in your grill or smoker.

6. Place pan on the indirect side of the grill. Close the lid and smoke for about 1 hour, or until peppers are tender but still upright.

Grill-Smoked Jalapeño Poppers

- Metal jalapeño popper rack or paper pulp egg carton
- 12 toothpicks, soaked
- **Suggested wood:** apple, hickory, mesquite, oak or pecan

12	large jalapeño peppers	12
8 oz	cream cheese or queso blanco, softened	250 g
6	strips bacon, halved horizontally	6

1. Prepare a hot indirect fire with a kiss of smoke in your grill.

2. Using a paring knife, stem each pepper and scoop out the seeds. Stuff peppers with cheese. Wrap each with half a bacon slice to cover the filling and secure with a soaked toothpick. Place peppers in popper rack.

3. When you see the first wisp of smoke from the wood, place popper rack on the indirect side of the grill. Close the lid and grill for about 1 hour, or until peppers are softened and bacon is crisp.

◆ Variation ◆

Smoked Chiles Rellenos: For the stuffing, use Mexican panela (a ricotta-like cheese), Oaxaca or Chihuahua cheese, if you can find it. Or simply cut a piece of Monterey Jack into small wedges that will fit inside each pepper. Omit the bacon and secure the openings with soaked toothpicks. Grill for about 45 minutes, or until peppers are softened. Serve with your favorite salsa.

Tapas-Style Grilled Fingerlings with Portuguese Aïoli

SERVES 8

Simply grilled fingerling potatoes, paired with a zesty dipping sauce, make an appetizer perfect for entertaining.

✦ TIPS ✦

The aïoli can be stored in an airtight container in the refrigerator for up to 6 days.

If you like, partially cook the potatoes first in the microwave or oven, then finish them on the grill.

Portuguese Aïoli

2	cloves garlic, minced	2
1 cup	good-quality mayonnaise	250 mL
1 tsp	grated orange zest	5 mL
2 tbsp	freshly squeezed orange juice	25 mL
1 tbsp	tomato purée	15 mL
½ tsp	cayenne pepper	2 mL
½ tsp	smoked or sweet Hungarian paprika	2 mL
	Kosher or sea salt and freshly ground black pepper	
4 lbs	fingerling or new potatoes, pierced all over with a fork	2 kg
	Olive oil	
	Kosher or sea salt and freshly ground black pepper	

1. *Prepare the aïoli:* In a bowl, whisk together garlic, mayonnaise, orange zest, orange juice, tomato purée, cayenne and paprika. Season to taste with salt and black pepper. Cover and refrigerate until ready to serve.

2. Prepare a medium-hot fire in your grill.

3. Brush potatoes with olive oil and season to taste with salt and black pepper. Place potatoes, in batches as necessary, on the grill. Grill for about 15 minutes, turning often, until fork-tender. Serve hot with aïoli.

✦ Variation ✦

Serve with Romesco Sauce (page 51) instead of the aïoli.

Smoked Potato Casserole

Who can resist a potato casserole with the flavor of the hearth? Not us!

✦ TIPS ✦

Put your potatoes on to smoke when you're already smoking something else.

If you're in a hurry, partially cook pierced potatoes in the microwave on High for 7 minutes, then smoke for about 30 minutes, or until fork-tender.

You can assemble the casserole up to 3 days ahead. Cover and refrigerate until ready to bake. Increase the baking time by 10 to 15 minutes.

- 8-cup (2 L) casserole dish, buttered
- **Suggested wood:** hickory, oak or pecan

5 lbs	baking potatoes, pierced all over with a fork	2.5 kg
1 lb	cream cheese, softened	500 g
1 cup	half-and-half (10%) or light (5%) cream	250 mL
½ cup	unsalted butter	125 mL
2 tsp	onion powder	10 mL
	Kosher or sea salt and freshly ground black pepper	
	Chopped fresh flat-leaf (Italian) parsley	

1. Prepare an indirect fire for smoking in your grill or smoker.

2. Place potatoes on the indirect side of the grill. Close the lid and smoke for 1 to 1½ hours, or until fork-tender.

3. Meanwhile, preheat oven to 350°F (180°C).

4. Peel potatoes, cut into chunks and place in a large bowl. Add cream cheese, cream and butter; mash until chunky. Stir in onion powder and season to taste with salt and pepper. Spoon into prepared casserole dish.

5. Bake for about 30 minutes, or until browned and bubbling. Serve hot, sprinkled with parsley.

Smoked Sweet Potato Casserole with Ginger, Lime and Brown Sugar

SERVES 8

There are two ways to make this low-fat side dish, depending on the size of your smoker and your timing: either smoke the sweet potatoes first, then make the casserole, or bake the sweet potatoes, assemble the casserole and put the casserole on the smoker (see the variation).

● **Suggested wood:** hickory, oak, or pecan

5 lbs	large sweet potatoes (about 6), pierced all over with a fork	2.5 kg
1	1-inch (2.5 cm) piece gingerroot, grated	1
½ cup	firmly packed brown sugar	125 mL
	Juice of 1 lime	

1. Prepare an indirect fire for smoking in your grill or smoker.

2. Place sweet potatoes on the indirect side of the grill. Close the lid and smoke for 1 to 1½ hours, or until fork-tender.

3. Cut potatoes in half and scoop the flesh into a food processor. Add ginger, brown sugar and lime juice; purée until smooth.

> ### ✦ Variation ✦
>
> Bake pierced sweet potatoes in a 350°F (180°C) oven for about 1 hour, or until fork-tender. Meanwhile, prepare an indirect fire in your grill or smoker. Cut potatoes in half and scoop the flesh into a food processor. Add ginger, brown sugar and lime juice; purée until smooth. Spoon into a foil pan. Place pan on the indirect side of the grill. Close the lid and smoke for 1 hour, or until the casserole has a smoky aroma.

Stir-Grilled Shallots with Tarragon Butter

SERVES 6 TO 8

Make the full recipe even if you are dining with fewer people. Leftover grilled shallots can be chopped and served over any meat dish or added to salads, soups and pizzas.

✦ TIP ✦

Use these shallots as a topping for the Bistro Burger (page 260), in place of the shallots and Béarnaise Sauce.

• Grill wok or basket, oiled

| 10 to 12 | shallots | 10 to 12 |
| | Kosher salt and freshly ground black pepper | |

Tarragon Butter

1	clove garlic, minced	1
½ cup	unsalted butter, softened	125 mL
1 tbsp	chopped fresh tarragon	15 mL
1 tsp	tarragon-flavored vinegar	5 mL
1	loaf crusty French bread	1

1. Prepare a hot fire in your grill.
2. Pull shallot sections apart if necessary, but do not peel. Place in prepared grill wok and season to taste with salt and pepper. Set aside.
3. *Prepare the butter:* In a small bowl, combine garlic, butter, tarragon and vinegar. Set aside.
4. Place wok on the grill. Stir-grill for about 15 minutes, or until skins are charred and some of the flesh is exposed and golden, with a bit of caramel ooze. Let cool for 3 to 4 minutes, then slip off the skins.
5. Meanwhile, wrap bread in foil and heat on the grill for about 2 minutes per side.
6. Place shallots in a shallow dish, add some of the butter and toss to coat. Serve with bread and the remaining butter.

Grilled Tomato Slices and Mozzarella

SERVES 6 TO 8

A grilled insalata caprese *is perfect for the middle of summer, when the tomatoes are vine-ripened and oozing with flavor. The trick to grilling tomatoes is to grill one side only.*

◆ TIP ◆

The mozzarella does not have to go on the grill. If it is room temperature and placed between the hot slices of tomato, it will warm and be perfect for eating.

2 to 3	large tomatoes (such as beefsteak), sliced medium-thick	2 to 3
	Extra-virgin olive oil	
8 oz	good-quality mozzarella cheese, at room temperature	250 g
1 cup	chopped fresh basil	250 mL
2 tbsp	drained capers	25 mL
	Coarse kosher salt and freshly ground black pepper	

1. Prepare a hot fire in your grill.

2. Lightly brush one side of each tomato slice with olive oil. Place tomatoes oiled side down on the grill. Grill for about 3 minutes, or until the oiled side is beautifully charred.

3. Cut mozzarella into enough slices that there is one slice of cheese for every slice of tomato.

4. Arrange tomatoes on plates, with the charred side up. Tuck cheese slices between the tomato slices so that they overlap slightly. Sprinkle with basil and capers. Season to taste with salt and pepper and drizzle with olive oil.

Planked Goat Cheese–Topped Beefsteak Tomatoes

SERVES 6 TO 8

Planking vegetables is so very easy, because you usually aren't cooking them, merely heating them through and letting them sit on the warmed plank to pick up a bit of its woody flavor.

- 1 to 2 oak, cedar or maple planks, soaked for at least 1 hour

2 to 3	large tomatoes (such as beefsteak), sliced medium-thick	2 to 3
	Kosher salt and freshly ground black pepper	
	Extra-virgin olive oil	
4 oz	goat cheese	125 g
¼ cup	chopped fresh herbs (such as chives, oregano, parsley or basil)	50 mL
	Balsamic vinegar	

1. Prepare a medium-hot indirect fire in your grill.

2. Arrange tomato slices on plank(s). Season lightly with salt and pepper and drizzle with olive oil. Crumble goat cheese over each tomato slice.

3. Place plank(s) on the indirect side of the grill. Close the lid and plank for about 15 minutes, or until tomatoes are warmed through and cheese is soft. Serve on the plank(s) with a sprinkle of fresh herbs and a drizzle of balsamic vinegar.

✦ Variations ✦

Prepare a variety of colorful heirloom tomatoes. Slice larger tomatoes, quarter smaller ones and halve cherry tomatoes. Arrange on the plank(s) and follow the rest of the steps above.

Use crumbled blue cheese or feta or shredded Cheddar cheese in place of the goat cheese.

Provençal Tomatoes on the Vine

SERVES 6 TO 8

Many grocery stores offer clusters of tomatoes on the vine. They are very pretty and hold together well, making them a snap to throw on the grill, and they won't roll all around.

✦ TIPS ✦

Serve with a side of aïoli (pages 46–48).

If you grow your own tomatoes, plant cluster tomatoes or cherry or grape tomatoes to replicate this recipe. The smaller grape or cherry tomatoes would be lovely on a cheese platter.

1	cluster of tomatoes on the vine	1
	Extra-virgin olive oil	
	Kosher salt and freshly ground pepper	

1. Prepare a hot fire in your grill.

2. Brush tomatoes with olive oil and season to taste with salt and pepper. Place on the grill with the vine side up and away from the heat. Grill for 1 or 2 minutes, or until charred. Turn the tomatoes to char the sides. Do not let tomatoes get mushy. Use a spatula to remove the tomatoes from the grill so that they do not fall off the vine. Serve hot or at room temperature.

Sicilian Grill-Roasted Tomatoes

SERVES 6

These robustly flavored stuffed tomatoes taste great with grilled fish, shellfish, chicken, lamb or beef with a Mediterranean flair. Start the tomatoes on the indirect side, then grill the meat on the direct side, and voila — dinner's ready!

● Foil pan

12	ripe but firm tomatoes	12
2 tbsp	salted capers	25 mL
¼ cup	olive oil	50 mL
⅓ cup	minced onion	75 mL
6	salted anchovies, rinsed and boned	6
2 cups	lightly toasted fresh bread crumbs	500 mL
1 tbsp	finely chopped garlic	15 mL
1 tbsp	finely chopped fresh flat-leaf (Italian) parsley	15 mL

1. Core the tomatoes. With the tip of a spoon, remove as many of the seeds as you can while leaving the pulp intact. Turn tomatoes upside down to drain on paper towels.

2. In a bowl, cover capers with warm water. Let soak for 10 minutes; drain well.

3. In a skillet, heat olive oil over medium heat. Sauté onion until golden, about 5 minutes. Add anchovies and stir until dissolved. Remove from heat and stir in bread crumbs, garlic, parsley and capers.

4. Place tomatoes right side up in foil pan and stuff with the bread crumb mixture. Set aside.

5. Prepare a hot indirect fire in your grill.

6. Place pan on the indirect side of the grill. Close the lid and grill for 20 to 30 minutes, or until tomatoes are softened and tops are browned. Serve hot or at room temperature.

Smoked Garlic Aïoli Platter of Roasted Root Vegetables

SERVES 6 TO 8

Tender root vegetables with a kiss of smoke are delectable, and become sublime when served with smoked garlic aïoli.

✦ TIPS ✦

Sometimes the simplest things pack the most flavor. This is the case with smoked garlic, which can be used to make smoked garlic aïoli, smoked garlic butter, smoked garlic and tomato gazpacho and so forth.

The combination of oak and apple woods gives this recipe a depth of smoky flavor. Other wood combinations you could try are mesquite and pear or maple and pecan.

● **Suggested wood: oak and apple**

4 lbs	mixed root vegetables (such as sweet potatoes, white potatoes, carrots, turnips, onions and garlic)	2 kg
	Extra-virgin olive oil	
	Coarse kosher salt and freshly ground black pepper	
1	recipe Smoked Garlic Aïoli (variation, page 46)	1

1. Prepare a medium-hot indirect fire with a kiss of smoke in your grill.

2. Scrub potatoes, leaving skin on. Rinse and peel carrots, turnips and onions. Leave carrots whole and cut turnips and onions into 1-inch (2.5 cm) thick slices. Leave garlic whole, with the skin on. Brush vegetables with olive oil.

3. When you see the first wisp of smoke from the wood, place vegetables on the indirect side of the grill. Close the lid and grill for about 2 hours, or until vegetables are fork-tender.

4. Slice potatoes into wedges. Arrange vegetables on a platter, season to taste with salt and pepper and drizzle lightly with olive oil. Serve with aïoli on the side.

✦ Variation ✦

Winter squash (such as acorn or butternut), while not root vegetables, would be a nice addition to this medley of underground growers. Peel and cut into 1-inch (2.5 cm) thick strips.

Argentinean Grilled Vegetable Platter with Chimichurri

Chimichurri gives Argentinean distinction to this platter of seasonal grilled vegetables.

Grill all the vegetables simultaneously, timing it so that they all come off the grill at the same time.

4 lbs	mixed seasonal garden vegetables (such as zucchini, yellow summer squash, romaine, tomatoes, eggplant and onions)	2 kg
	Olive oil	
	Sea salt and freshly ground black pepper	
1	recipe Chimichurri (page 144)	1

1. Halve zucchini, squash and romaine lengthwise. Cut tomatoes, eggplant and onions into 1-inch (2.5 cm) thick slices. Brush the cut side of the romaine with olive oil. Brush the other vegetables with oil on both sides. Season to taste with salt and pepper. Set aside.

2. Prepare a hot fire in your grill.

3. Grill eggplant and onions for 3 to 4 minutes per side, turning once, until charred on both sides.

4. Place zucchini, squash and romaine cut side down on the grill. Grill for about 4 minutes, until the cut side is charred and has nice grill marks.

5. Grill tomatoes on one side for 3 to 4 minutes, until charred.

6. Arrange vegetables on a platter and drizzle with chimichurri.

Vegetable Kebabs with Za'atar

*Mediterranean
vegetables get a
dusting of sour za'atar,
a Middle Eastern
seasoning blend of
dried sumac, ground
sesame seeds, thyme
and salt. Grill these
skewers along with
flatbread brushed
with olive oil, and
serve with hummus.*

✦ TIPS ✦

Grind sesame seeds in a
spice grinder or a clean
coffee grinder.

If you prefer, you can
purchase za'atar at
better spice emporia.

- Twelve 12-inch (30 cm) flat bamboo skewers, soaked
  for at least 30 minutes

Za'atar

2 tsp	ground sesame seeds	10 mL
1 tsp	ground sumac or dried lemon peel	5 mL
1 tsp	dried thyme	5 mL
1 tsp	fine kosher or sea salt	5 mL
2	lemons, each cut into 6 wedges	2
2	zucchini, trimmed and cut into 1-inch (2.5 cm) pieces	2
2	yellow summer squash, trimmed and cut into 1-inch (2.5 cm) pieces	2
1	red bell pepper, cut into 1-inch (2.5 cm) pieces	1
½ cup	pitted drained brine-cured kalamata or niçoise olives	125 mL
1 cup	cherry tomatoes	250 mL
	Olive oil	
4	pitas	4
	Prepared hummus	

1. *Prepare the za'atar:* In a bowl, combine sesame seeds, sumac, thyme and salt.

2. Thread lemon wedges, zucchini, squash, red pepper, olives and tomatoes onto skewers, leaving space between pieces. Brush with olive oil and dust with za'atar.

3. Prepare a medium-hot fire in your grill.

4. Grill skewers for 3 to 4 minutes per side, turning once, until vegetables have good grill marks.

5. Meanwhile, brush pitas with olive oil. Grill for about 1 minute per side, turning once, until warmed through but not crispy.

6. Cut pitas into triangles and remove vegetables from skewers. Arrange pitas and vegetables on a platter, with a bowl of hummus on the side. Squeeze the lemon wedges over the vegetables and hummus.

Teriyaki Vegetable Skewers

SERVES 6

Almost any vegetable would work on these easy skewers, but the ones used here replicate authentic Japanese cuisine. If you're not preparing a vegetarian meal, these are delicious with grilled fish, chicken or beef.

◆ TIPS ◆

If you like, serve with steamed rice and drizzle with any remaining teriyaki sauce.

If you use fresh bamboo shoots (available at Asian markets), make sure they have not been treated with chemicals. You may need to pierce the vegetables first with a sharp skewer, then thread onto the bamboo shoots.

It's always a good idea to oil the grill rack well before heating the grill, but it's especially important when you're grilling foods with a sweet glaze or baste, so they don't stick.

● Twelve 12-inch (30 cm) flat bamboo skewers, soaked for at least 30 minutes, or fresh bamboo shoots

1 cup	teriyaki sauce (store-bought or see recipe, page 252)	250 mL
12	green onions, trimmed to a 6-inch (15 cm) length	12
12	pickled plums	12
6	Japanese eggplants, trimmed and halved	6
1	small cabbage, cut into 12 wedges, each wedge halved horizontally	1
1 lb	firm tofu, cut into 2-inch (5 cm) squares	500 g
	Vegetable oil	

1. Pour teriyaki sauce into a large sealable plastic bag. Add green onions, plums, eggplants, cabbage and tofu. Seal, toss to coat and refrigerate for at least 30 minutes or up to 4 hours, tossing occasionally.

2. Meanwhile, prepare a medium-hot fire in your grill.

3. Remove vegetables and tofu from teriyaki sauce, reserving sauce. Thread vegetables and tofu onto skewers, leaving space between pieces. Brush with oil. Grill skewers for 3 to 4 minutes per side, turning 3 to 4 times and basting with sauce, until eggplant is softened and vegetables have good grill marks.

Fruit

Grilled Apple Rings with Cider Bourbon Cream Sauce 354

Grilled Pears with Gorgonzola and Drizzled Honey 355

Grilled Grape Clusters with Brown Sugar Crème Fraîche 356

Grilled Figs with Warm Smoked Goat Cheese. 357

Prosciutto-Wrapped Grilled Figs with Orange
  and Honey Drizzle. 358

Planked Brie and Apricots with Ice Wine. 359

Grilled Apricot and Plum Skewers with Almond Cream 360

Freeform Grilled Plum Pastries 361

Grilled Peaches with Buttery Amaretto Baste 362

Catalan-Style Planked Peaches with Pork,
  Almond and Brandy Filling 363

Grilled Avocados, Tomatoes and Lemons. 364

Sicilian Grilled Blood Oranges with Honey Orange Drizzle . . . 365

Grilled Pound Cake with Amaretto Cream, Grilled Orange
  Slices and Crimson Jam. 366

Blistered Bananas with Puerto Rican Brown Sugar Butter. . . . 368

Grilled Mango Boats with Strawberry-Cilantro Salsa
  and Blue Cheese 369

Island Grilled Papaya 370

Char-Grilled Pineapple 370

Grilled Pineapple Rings with Pineapple Sorbet 371

Caipiroska-Glazed Tropical Fruit Skewers 372

✦ ◆ ✦

Grilling fruit intensifies its flavor and sweetness. The look of grilled fruit is appealing, too, with charry grill marks that add caramelization and a rustic appearance.

Like vegetables on the grill, you don't want fruit to be overcooked and mushy, so use ripe-but-firm fruit. Underripe fruit is not a good choice, as it does not have optimum flavor.

Size matters when grilling fruit. Large fruit, halved or cut into wedges, may be fine placed directly on the grill grates, but if the fruit is smaller, skewer it or use a grill rack, wok or basket.

Naturally soft fruits, such as bananas, plantains, apricots, peaches, pears, plums, figs, guavas, mangoes, papayas, nectarines, kiwis and star fruit (carambola), are best grilled cut in half. If you're using skewers or a grill rack, wok or basket, some of these fruits can be grilled in thick slices. Firmer fruits, such as apples, melon slices with the rind on, and oranges, lemons, limes and grapefruit with the rind on, can be cut in half, sliced or cut into wedges for grilling. Peeled melon slices or wedges are delicious wrapped in prosciutto. Clusters of grilled grapes make a wonderful addition to a cheese platter. Even strawberries threaded onto skewers can be quickly grilled.

The simplest way to prepare whole or cut fruit for grilling is to brush it with mild olive oil (not extra-virgin), grapeseed oil or other vegetable oil. Melted butter is also delicious; it shouldn't burn, because you grill fruit for only a few minutes per cut side.

✦ ◆ ✦

✦ Fruits and Best Barbecue Methods ✦

Apples: Grill, indirect grill, grill-roast, plank

Apricots: Grill, skewer, leaf-wrap, stir-grill, plank

Bananas: Grill in a foil packet, grill in skins

Cherries: Skewer, plank

Citrus Fruits: Grill

Figs: Grill, skewer, plank

Grapes: Grill in clusters

Kiwis: Grill

Mangoes/Papayas: Grill, skewer, stir-grill, plank

Melons: Grill, skewer, stir-grill, plank

Nectarines/Peaches: Grill, skewer, leaf-wrap, stir-grill, plank

Pears: Grill, indirect grill, grill-roast, plank

Pineapple: Grill, skewer, stir-grill, plank

Plums: Grill, skewer, stir-grill, plank

Strawberries: Skewer

Grilled Apple Rings with Cider Bourbon Cream Sauce

SERVES 4

For eating out of hand, you want a crisp, tart apple. But for grilling, you want a softer, sweeter apple, such as a Golden Delicious, that will soften but not crack or fall apart. These grilled apple slices go well with grilled or smoked game birds, poultry or pork.

✦ TIP ✦

It's always a good idea to oil the grill rack well before heating the grill, but it's especially important when you're grilling foods with a sweet glaze or baste, so they don't stick.

- Baking sheet

Cider Bourbon Cream Sauce

½ cup	apple cider	125 mL
½ cup	whipping (35%) cream	125 mL
1 tbsp	bourbon (or to taste)	15 mL
4	Golden Delicious apples	4

1. *Prepare the sauce:* In a small saucepan, bring cider to a boil over high heat; boil until reduced by half, about 4 minutes. Remove from heat and stir in cream and bourbon. Set aside.

2. Prepare a medium-hot fire in your grill.

3. Using an apple corer, remove cores from apples. Cut apples crosswise into 1-inch (1 cm) thick rings. Place on baking sheet and brush one side with some of the sauce. Place apples basted side down on the grill. Grill for 5 to 7 minutes, basting with sauce and turning once, until apples have good grill marks on both sides. Serve warm or at room temperature.

✦ Variation ✦

Pears, nectarines, plums and peaches are also good grilled with this sauce. Simply pit the fruit, cut it into quarters, brush with sauce and grill.

Grilled Pears with Gorgonzola and Drizzled Honey

Ripe, fresh pears and pungent blue cheese make a delicious combination. Grilled, they're spectacular. Serve as a salad over dressed greens, as part of a cheese course or as a dessert.

◆ TIP ◆

Purple-skinned Bosc pears look fabulous prepared this way.

4	ripe but somewhat firm Bartlett or Bosc pears (unpeeled), halved lengthwise	4
	Melted unsalted butter	
½ cup	Gorgonzola or other creamy blue cheese	125 mL
	Liquid honey	
	Toasted chopped hazelnuts	

1. Prepare a hot indirect fire in your grill.

2. Using a melon baller, core and scoop out a small cavity in each pear half. Brush both sides of each pear half with melted butter.

3. Place pears cut side down over the hot fire. Grill for about 2 minutes, or until fruit is blistered. Move to the indirect side of the grill and place skin side down. Mound 1 tbsp (15 mL) cheese in the cavity of each pear. Close the lid and grill for about 8 minutes, or until pears are blistered and cheese is melted. Serve drizzled with honey and garnished with hazelnuts.

Grilled Grape Clusters with Brown Sugar Crème Fraîche

So easy and so good! Serve the clusters on a big platter, arranged around a bowl of the crème fraîche.

Brown Sugar Crème Fraîche

1 cup	whipping (35%) cream	250 mL
1 cup	sour cream	250 mL
2 tbsp	packed brown sugar	25 mL
2 lbs	seedless green and purple grape clusters	1 kg
	Melted unsalted butter	

1. *Prepare the crème fraîche:* In a bowl, stir together cream, sour cream and brown sugar. Let stand at room temperature for at least 1 hour or up to 6 hours.
2. Meanwhile, prepare a hot fire in your grill.
3. Brush grapes with butter. Grill for 4 to 5 minutes, turning often, until grapes have good grill marks or scorching. Serve with crème fraîche.

Grilled Figs with Warm Smoked Goat Cheese

- **Foil pan**
- **Perforated grill rack, greased**
- **Suggested wood:** apple or other fruitwood

4 oz	goat cheese, softened	125 g
	Olive oil	
16	fresh Mission figs	16
16	thin slices pancetta (or 8 thin slices prosciutto, halved lengthwise)	16
	Liquid lavender honey	

1. Prepare an indirect fire for smoking in your grill or smoker.
2. Spread goat cheese in foil pan. Drizzle lightly with olive oil, spreading the oil with a brush or your fingers. Place pan on the indirect side of the grill. Close the lid and smoke for 45 to 60 minutes, or until cheese has a smoky aroma.
3. Prepare a hot fire in your grill.
4. Slice an X in the top of each fig, without cutting all the way through. Stuff figs with smoked goat cheese. Wrap a slice of pancetta around each fig to hold the goat cheese in place.
5. Place prepared grill rack over the fire and place figs on the rack. Grill for 6 to 8 minutes, turning often, until pancetta is crispy on all sides.
6. Transfer figs to a platter and drizzle with honey.

✦ Variation ✦

Grilled prosciutto-wrapped cantaloupe slices are delicious. Grill for 2 to 3 minutes per side to crisp the prosciutto. You won't need a grill rack, because the melon slices are big enough that they won't fall through the grates. Serve cantaloupe with a spoonful of smoked goat cheese on the side and drizzle all with honey.

Prosciutto-Wrapped Grilled Figs with Orange and Honey Drizzle

SERVES 4

The pretty green Calimyrna figs are especially nice for this dish.

● Perforated grill rack, greased

¼ cup	liquid wildflower honey	50 mL
	Grated zest of 1 orange	
10	fresh Calimyrna or Mission figs, halved lengthwise	10
4 oz	prosciutto, thinly sliced	125 g
2 tsp	chopped fresh rosemary	10 mL
4	sprigs fresh rosemary	4

1. Prepare a hot fire in your grill.

2. In a bowl, combine honey and orange zest. Set aside.

3. Wrap each fig half with a small slice of prosciutto.

4. Place prepared grill rack over the fire and place figs on the rack. Grill for 6 to 8 minutes, turning often, until prosciutto is crispy on all sides.

5. Divide figs among plates and drizzle with orange honey. Sprinkle with chopped rosemary and garnish each plate with a rosemary sprig.

✦ Variations ✦

Nectarines, peaches, apples and pears would all be interesting substitutes for the figs. Pit or core the fruit and cut into quarters. Increase the amount of prosciutto accordingly.

Pears, nectarines, plums and peaches are also good grilled with this sauce. Simply pit the fruit, cut it into quarters, brush with sauce and grill.

Planked Brie and Apricots with Ice Wine

SERVES 12

Planked Brie or Camembert in its soft white rind looks stunning. The cheese can be dressed up with savory onions and peppers or sweet fruits. Colorful toppings are the most eye-catching.

✦ TIPS ✦

An oven-baking plank is thicker than a grilling plank and has a concave indentation that keeps sauce on the board. If you use a grilling plank, transfer the cheese to a platter before topping with sauce.

Most varieties of ice wine have fruit notes: apricot, peach, pear, mango, green apple — even fig with honey. So experiment with different fruits in this recipe.

● Oak or cedar oven-baking plank or grilling plank, soaked for at least 1 hour

½ cup	ice wine (Eiswein) or other sweet dessert wine	125 mL
¼ cup	apricot preserves or chutney	50 mL
6	apricots, sliced	6
1	wheel baby Brie or Camembert (about 12 oz/375 g)	1

1. Prepare a hot indirect fire in your grill.

2. In a small saucepan, bring ice wine and apricot preserves to a simmer over medium-low heat. Add apricots and simmer for 3 to 4 minutes, until just tender. Remove from heat and keep warm.

3. Place Brie on plank and set plank on the indirect side of the grill. Close the lid and plank for about 20 minutes, or until Brie is soft and warmed through.

4. Serve cheese on the plank, with apricot mixture spooned on top.

✦ Variation ✦

The cheese can be planked in a 350°F (180°C) oven instead of on the grill.

Grilled Apricot and Plum Skewers with Almond Cream

● 4 campfire sticks or sturdy twigs about 8 inches (20 cm) long (see tip, at left)

Almond Cream

1 cup	whipping (35%) cream	250 mL
2 tbsp	granulated sugar	25 mL
½ tsp	almond extract	2 mL
8	firm apricots, halved	8
8	small firm purple plums, halved	8
	Melted butter	
1 cup	blackberries	250 mL

1. Prepare a medium-hot fire in your grill.

2. *Prepare the cream:* Using an electric mixer, beat cream, sugar and almond extract until stiff peaks form. Set aside.

3. Thread apricots and plums on sticks so that they look like whole fruit, two cut sides together, leaving space between fruits. Brush with butter.

4. Grill skewers for 6 to 8 minutes, turning often, until fruit begins to soften and has a scorched exterior. Serve each skewer with a dollop of cream and a scattering of blackberries.

Freeform Grilled Plum Pastries

SERVES 6

Shards of nut-crusted puff pastry top sweet grilled plums for a deconstructed pastry.

✦ TIPS ✦

The pastries can be baked up to 3 days in advance and stored at room temperature in an airtight container.

It's always a good idea to oil the grill rack well before heating the grill, but it's especially important when you're grilling foods with a sweet glaze or baste, so they don't stick.

- Preheat oven to 400°F (200°C)
- Baking sheet, greased

1 cup	granulated sugar, divided	250 mL
1 tbsp	ground cinnamon	15 mL
½ cup	pecans or walnuts	125 mL
1	9-inch (23 cm) square sheet frozen puff pastry, thawed	1
12	plums, halved	12
	Melted butter	
	Whipped cream	

1. In a small bowl, combine sugar and cinnamon.

2. In a food processor, finely grind pecans with half the cinnamon sugar.

3. Place puff pastry on a floured surface and press half the nut mixture into one side. Turn and press the remaining half into the other side. Roll out into a 15- by 12-inch (38 by 30 cm) rectangle. Cut into 6 rectangles, and cut each rectangle into 2 triangles. Place on baking sheet and prick the surface of each triangle all over with a fork.

4. Bake in preheated oven for about 15 minutes, or until golden brown and puffed.

5. Meanwhile, prepare a medium-hot fire in your grill.

6. Brush plums all over with butter and sprinkle with the remaining cinnamon sugar. Place cut side up on the grill. Grill for 4 to 5 minutes, turning once, until plums are tender and blistered.

7. Place 4 plum halves on each plate and top with 2 pastry triangles. Garnish with rosettes of whipped cream.

Grilled Peaches with Buttery Amaretto Baste

Fresh, juicy peaches are one of summer's true pleasures. We take them a step further by placing them on the grill for warmth and caramelization. The almond-flavored butter baste is simply divine.

Buttery Amaretto Baste

¼ cup	unsalted butter	50 mL
¼ cup	amaretto	50 mL
Pinch	sea salt	Pinch
4	large firm peaches or nectarines (unpeeled), halved	4
	Crème fraîche or whipped cream	
	Blackberries, raspberries or blueberries	

1. *Prepare the baste:* In a small saucepan, melt butter over medium heat. Remove from heat and stir in amaretto and salt. Keep warm.

2. Prepare a medium-hot fire in your grill.

3. Brush peaches all over with baste. Place cut side down on the grill. Grill for 4 to 6 minutes, turning and basting once, until peaches are tender and blistered.

4. Arrange peaches on a platter or portion onto plates. Dollop with crème fraîche and scatter with berries.

Catalan-Style Planked Peaches with Pork, Almond and Brandy Filling

A fruitier take on stuffed peppers, this is a great summer dish for brunch, lunch or dinner. Plus, you get the aromatic flavor of the wood plank.

✦ TIP ✦

Use a food processor or mini-chopper to finely grind the almonds.

● Cedar or oak plank, soaked for at least 1 hour

Filling

1	egg, lightly beaten	1
8 oz	lean ground pork	250 g
1/3 cup	toasted blanched almonds or Marcona almonds, finely ground	75 mL
2 tbsp	finely minced fresh herbs (such as thyme, oregano and parsley)	25 mL
	Kosher or sea salt and freshly ground white pepper	
4	large firm peaches or nectarines (unpeeled), halved	4
1/4 cup	brandy or amaretto	50 mL

1. *Prepare the filling:* In a bowl, combine egg, pork, ground almonds and herbs. Season to taste with salt and pepper.

2. Prepare a dual-heat fire, hot on one side and medium-low on the other, in your grill.

3. Place peaches cut side up on plank and fill cavities with pork mixture. Drizzle with brandy. Place plank over the medium-low fire. Close the lid and plank for 35 to 40 minutes, or until filling is no longer pink and peaches are tender when pierced with a knife. Arrange peaches on a platter or portion onto plates.

Grilled Avocados, Tomatoes and Lemons

SERVES 6 TO 8

Yes, avocados are a fruit — and technically tomatoes are too, because they have seeds. But our palates are used to savory preparations of these two fruits. Make sure to use ripe or almost ripe avocados and tomatoes; overly ripe fruits will get mushy when cooked.

✦ TIP ✦

To add the dimension of smoke to this dish, substitute a smoked salt for the kosher salt.

4	avocados (unpeeled), halved	4
3	lemons, halved	3
¼ cup	extra-virgin olive oil	50 mL
2	large ripe tomatoes, thickly sliced	2
1	small red onion, thinly sliced	1
1 tbsp	drained capers	15 mL
	Coarse kosher salt and freshly ground black pepper	

1. Prepare a hot fire in your grill.
2. Lightly brush the cut side of the avocados and lemons with olive oil. Place cut side down on the grill. Grill for 1 to 2 minutes, or until the skins begin to brown. Let cool.
3. Lightly brush one side of the tomato slices with olive oil. Place oiled side down on the grill. Grill for about 2 minutes, or until the oiled side is charred. Arrange on a platter, with some slices grilled side up.
4. Slip skins off avocados and cut flesh into quarters. Arrange on top of the tomatoes. Squeeze juice from half a grilled lemon over avocados. Scatter red onion and capers over all. Season to taste with salt and pepper. Squeeze more lemon juice over top and arrange the remaining grilled lemon halves on the platter as garnish.

✦ Variations ✦

Grill the onions too, if you like. Brush the slices with oil on both sides and grill for 3 to 4 minutes per side, turning once, until charred on both sides. Sprinkle crumbled feta cheese over all.

Smoke some corn (see Smoked Corn in the Husk with Hot Pepper Herb Butter, page 326), cut it off the cob and sprinkle over all for smoke and color.

Sicilian Grilled Blood Oranges with Honey Orange Drizzle

SERVES 8

Blood oranges are available from late winter through spring, so shovel a path out to your grill or use a grill pan indoors for this dish. It's fabulous as a brunch dish or dessert.

✦ TIP ✦

When blood oranges are out of season, you can use Valencia or navel oranges.

8	blood oranges	8
	Melted unsalted butter	
1	recipe Honey Orange Drizzle (page 41), made with blood orange zest and juice	1

1. Prepare a hot fire in your grill.
2. Trim the ends off the oranges (but do not peel), then cut crosswise into ½-inch (1 cm) thick slices. Brush both sides with butter.
3. Grill orange slices for 1 minute per side, turning once, until lightly browned on both sides. Arrange on a platter or portion onto plates and drizzle with sauce.

Grilled Pound Cake with Amaretto Cream, Grilled Orange Slices and Crimson Jam

| SERVES 8 TO 12 |

This dessert is perfect in the summer. You'll feel like it's Christmas in July!

◆ TIPS ◆

When cranberries are in season, during the fall and winter months, buy several bags to keep in the freezer for use at other times of the year.

The sauce and the jam can each be stored in an airtight container in the refrigerator for up to 1 week.

Amaretto Cream Sauce

1 cup	granulated sugar	250 mL
¾ cup	water	175 mL
1 tsp	vanilla extract	5 mL
1 cup	whipping (35%) cream	250 mL
¼ cup	amaretto	50 mL

Crimson Jam

1	bag (12 oz/375 g) frozen cranberries, thawed	1
¾ cup	granulated sugar	175 mL
1 tbsp	water	15 mL
1	package (10 oz/300 g) frozen strawberries	1
1	pound cake (store-bought or homemade), cut into ½-inch (1 cm) thick slices	1
¼ cup	vegetable oil	50 mL
2 to 3	oranges, cut into ½-inch (1 cm) thick slices	2 to 3

1. *Prepare the sauce:* In a saucepan, over medium heat, combine sugar, water and vanilla, stirring until sugar dissolves. Increase heat to medium-high and boil, without stirring, until golden brown, about 10 minutes. Remove from heat and gradually whisk in cream. Return to medium-low heat and stir until thickened. Remove from heat and stir in amaretto.

2. *Prepare the jam:* In another saucepan, over medium-high heat, combine cranberries, sugar and water. Cook for 5 to 7 minutes, stirring occasionally, until cranberries start to pop and bubble. Add strawberries and cook until thawed.

3. Prepare a medium-hot fire in your grill.

4. Brush pound cake lightly with oil on both sides. Grill for 2 to 3 minutes, turning once, until light golden brown on both sides.

5. Meanwhile, brush orange slices with oil on both sides. Grill for 1 minute per side, turning once, until lightly browned on both sides. Cut slices in half.

6. Spoon sauce onto each plate and arrange pound cake over sauce. Arrange orange slices, overlapping each other, around the cake. Spoon jam over cake.

✦ Variation ✦

Substitute angel food cake for the pound cake. The angel food cake will get nice grill marks in 1 to 2 minutes. For a simpler presentation, serve it with vanilla bean ice cream and a store-bought strawberry or raspberry sauce.

Blistered Bananas with Puerto Rican Brown Sugar Butter

Classic Bananas Foster adapts beautifully to the grill. Plantains could be substituted for the bananas, if desired.

4	bananas (unpeeled), halved lengthwise	4
2 tbsp	butter	25 mL
2 tbsp	packed brown sugar	25 mL
2 tbsp	dark rum	25 mL
2 tsp	freshly squeezed lime juice	10 mL
1 tsp	ground cinnamon	5 mL
4 cups	vanilla ice cream	1 L

1. Prepare a hot fire in your grill.

2. Place bananas cut side down on the grill. Grill for 2 to 3 minutes, until bananas have grill marks. Let cool.

3. In a small saucepan, melt butter over medium heat. Add brown sugar, rum, lime juice and cinnamon; bring to a boil. Reduce heat and simmer, stirring, for 1 to 2 minutes, or until smooth and creamy. Remove from heat.

4. Peel bananas, cut in half crosswise and place in shallow bowls. Scoop ice cream into the center of each bowl and spoon sauce over top.

✦ Variation ✦

Offer a variety of ice creams to jazz up the flavor. Try coconut, chocolate and butter pecan.

Grilled Mango Boats with Strawberry-Cilantro Salsa and Blue Cheese

SERVES 4

Choose mangoes that are just ripe enough. Mangoes that are too ripe will get mushy on the grill.

✦ TIP ✦

When preparing a sweet salsa, if it needs a bit of a lift, try adding a pinch of salt or a little hot pepper.

Strawberry-Cilantro Salsa

2 cups	chopped strawberries	500 mL
2 tbsp	chopped fresh cilantro	25 mL
2 tsp	granulated sugar (or to taste)	10 mL
	Grated zest and juice of 1 lime	
4	ripe mangoes (unpeeled), halved lengthwise	4
1 tsp	vegetable oil	5 mL
1 oz	blue cheese, crumbled	30 g

1. Prepare a hot fire in your grill.

2. *Prepare the salsa:* In a bowl, combine strawberries, cilantro, sugar, lime zest and lime juice; toss to coat. Set aside.

3. Lightly brush the cut side of the mangoes with oil. Place cut side down on the grill. Grill for about 2 minutes, or until the cut side has good grill marks.

4. Place two mango halves cut side up on each plate. Spoon salsa over mangoes and sprinkle with blue cheese.

Island Grilled Papaya

SERVES 6 TO 8

This simple yet sophisticated side dish, brunch offering or dessert looks great on a white platter.

¼ cup	unsalted butter, melted	50 mL
Pinch	cayenne pepper	Pinch
	Grated zest and juice of 1 lime	
2	large papayas, peeled and cut into 2-inch (5 cm) wedges	2
	Fresh lime wedges	

1. Prepare a hot fire in your grill.
2. In a bowl, combine butter, cayenne, lime zest and lime juice.
3. Brush papaya all over with butter mixture. Grill for 4 to 5 minutes, turning often, until papaya has good grill marks. Serve with lime wedges on the side.

Char-Grilled Pineapple

SERVES 8 TO 10

This recipe makes extra papaya butter, which is wonderful spread on toast the next morning.

Papaya Butter

½ cup	chopped papaya	125 mL
½ cup	unsalted butter, softened	125 mL
1 tbsp	freshly squeezed lemon juice	15 mL
2	pineapples, peeled, cored and cut into medium-thick spears	2
1	recipe Sugar & Spice Rub (page 36)	1

1. Prepare a medium-hot fire in your grill.
2. *Prepare the butter:* In a food processor, purée papaya, butter and lemon juice until smooth. Spoon into a microwave-safe bowl and set aside.
3. Grill pineapple spears for about 2 minutes per side, turning once, until pineapple has nice char marks. Arrange on a platter and sprinkle with some of the rub.
4. If necessary, microwave papaya butter on High for 5 to 10 seconds, or until soft. Spoon over pineapple and dust with a little more of the rub.

Grilled Pineapple Rings with Pineapple Sorbet

This is the easiest sorbet you will ever make. It tastes terrific and is so pretty spooned in the middle of the pineapple rings.

Pineapple Sorbet

1	can (19 oz/540 mL) crushed pineapple in heavy syrup, frozen and unopened	1
3 tbsp	dark rum	45 mL
3 tbsp	canned cream of coconut	45 mL
1	large pineapple, peeled and cored	1

1. *Prepare the sorbet:* Submerge the can of frozen pineapple in hot water for 1 minute. Open the can and pour the syrup into a food processor. Cut the frozen fruit into chunks, add to the processor and purée until smooth. Transfer to a bowl and stir in rum and cream of coconut. Cover and store in the freezer until ready to serve or for up to 8 hours.

2. Prepare a medium-hot fire in your grill.

3. Cut pineapple into eight 1-inch (2.5 cm) thick rings. Grill for about 2 minutes per side, turning once, until pineapple is browned and softened.

4. Place a pineapple ring on each plate and scoop sorbet into the center of each ring.

✦ Variation ✦

Spoon Pineapple Mandarin Salsa (page 61) over the sorbet.

Caipiroska-Glazed Tropical Fruit Skewers

SERVES 8

A cocktail — or dessert — on a stick! A Caipiroska is a Caipirinha made with vodka instead of cachaça; here, it does triple duty as a marinade, baste and finishing sauce. If possible, use a mix of unusual tropical fruits on the skewers, but fresh pineapple is always a good fallback.

✦ TIP ✦

It's always a good idea to oil the grill rack well before heating the grill, but it's especially important when you're grilling foods with a sweet glaze or baste, so they don't stick.

● Eight 12-inch (30 cm) flat bamboo skewers, soaked for at least 30 minutes

Caipiroska Glaze

2	limes, cut into 6 wedges	2
2 tsp	superfine sugar	10 mL
¼ cup	vodka	50 mL
16	fresh lychees, shelled and seeded, or whole kumquats	16
4	limes, quartered	4
2	large star fruit (carambola), cut into 1-inch (2.5 cm) thick stars	2
1	mango, cut into 2-inch (5 cm) chunks	1

1. *Prepare the glaze:* In a bowl, muddle limes and sugar with a wooden spoon or muddler. Stir in vodka. Strain into a large sealable plastic bag.

2. Add lychees, limes, star fruit and mango to the glaze. Seal, toss to coat and let stand at room temperature for 30 minutes.

3. Meanwhile, prepare a medium-hot fire in your grill.

4. Remove fruit from glaze, reserving glaze. Thread star fruit slices onto skewers lengthwise, piercing the skin at one point of the star and going through the soft middle and a point of the star on the other end. Alternate the other fruits, leaving space between pieces and ending with a lime wedge.

5. Grill skewers for about 2 minutes per side, turning often, until fruit is blistered.

6. Arrange skewers on a platter and baste fruit with glaze. Drizzle any remaining glaze over the fruit.

Soups, Salads, Breads and Sandwiches

Grilled Vegetable Gazpacho with Assorted Condiments 376

Smoked Tomato and Basil Bisque 377

Smoked Italian Sausage and Tortellini Soup 378

Char-Grilled Romaine, Bacon, Tomato
    and Blue Cheese Salad 379

Grilled Haloumi, Artichoke and Olive Salad
    with Lemony Za'atar Vinaigrette 380

Flame-Seared Potato and Fennel Salad 381

Grilled Panzanella 382

Stir-Grilled Jamaican Shrimp and Vegetable Salad 383

Grilled Salmon Niçoise Salad 384

Leaf-Wrapped Breadsticks 386

Grilled Bread with Serrano Ham and Manchego Cheese 386

Portuguese Country Bread with Green Olive Relish 387

Grilled Afghan Bread 388

Aussie Herbed Damper on a Stick 389

Naan with Coconut Chutney 390

Grilled Red Pepper Piada 391

continued on next page...

Grilled Dark Chocolate Crostini 392

Barbecued Shrimp Quesadillas 393

Toasted Croissants with Boursin, Grilled Tomatoes
   and Bacon 394

Grilled Italian Garden Sandwiches 395

Montreal Smoked Meat Sandwiches 396

Churrasco-Style Steak Sandwiches 398

Panini Caprese 400

Soups, salads and sandwiches with an element of something grilled, whether it's a vegetable, fish or meat, are de rigueur on restaurant menus. And you can follow suit at home by creating deliciously smoky soups, salads with great char-grilled flavor and fabulous panini. Try pairing Grilled Vegetable Gazpacho with Assorted Condiments (page 376) with Panini Caprese (page 400) for a great cross-cultural lunch or supper.

As we've suggested in previous chapters, grilling and/or smoking foods to have on hand as "frozen assets" can really pay off. You'll make the most of your time at the grill or smoker, and enjoy the flavor of the hearth in soups, sandwiches and even salads. When tomatoes are at their peak, for example, enjoy them fresh by all means, but also slow-smoke a few to add to Smoky Tomato and Basil Bisque (page 377) or your favorite vegetable soup or chili.

Breads of all kinds taste even better with the added flavor they get from grilling. Most world cuisines include some kind of bread — usually a flatbread — that was originally baked over coals or on the hearth. Today, we can enjoy pitas, naan, pizzas and piadine, as well as baguettes, round artisan loaves and breadsticks, from the grill.

To grill breads, whether from dough or fully baked, first slather them with olive oil or get more fancy with a flavored butter. Uncooked dough performs on the grill as pancakes do on a griddle: when you place the dough on the grill, it will bubble up. When the underside has browned, in a minute or two, turn the dough with tongs or a spatula and grill the other side. It's simply delicious! Just as with any grilled food, you can add a kiss of smoke for even more flavor.

Prebaked breads, such as baguettes, can be grilled in two different ways: you can brush slices with olive oil and grill until the edges are lightly charred, or you can cut the loaf in half lengthwise, layer on sandwich fillings or slather the cut sides with a flavorful mixture, then wrap the loaf in foil and grill to warm, crusty perfection.

Use the bread recipes in this chapter as your blueprint to create your own signature breads, flatbreads and pizzas on the grill.

Grilled Vegetable Gazpacho with Assorted Condiments

If you love gazpacho, you'll adore this version, with the fresh taste of garden vegetables and the flavor of the grill.

✦ TIP ✦

You can also use smoked tomatoes in this gazpacho.

4	large beefsteak tomatoes, sliced	4
2	red bell peppers, halved lengthwise and seeded	2
1	large red onion, sliced	1
	Olive oil	
½ cup	extra-virgin olive oil	125 mL
¼ cup	red wine vinegar	50 mL
2 tbsp	Worcestershire sauce	25 mL
1 tsp	kosher salt	5 mL
1 tsp	hot pepper sauce	5 mL
1	cucumber, peeled, seeded and diced	1
1	bunch green onions, chopped (about 1½ cups/375 mL)	1
1 cup	cherry tomatoes, halved	250 mL
½ cup	snipped fresh chives	125 mL
½ cup	sour cream	125 mL
½ cup	pesto	125 mL

1. Prepare a hot fire in your grill.

2. Brush beefsteak tomatoes, red peppers and red onions with olive oil. Grill for 8 to 10 minutes, turning once, until nicely charred on both sides. (The tomatoes may need to come off the grill a bit sooner, so they do not get mushy and fall through the grates.)

3. Transfer grilled vegetables to a food processor and pulse until finely chopped. Add extra-virgin olive oil, vinegar, Worcestershire sauce, salt and hot pepper sauce; purée until smooth. Serve immediately or refrigerate until chilled.

4. Set up a condiment bar with bowls of cucumber, green onions, cherry tomatoes, chives, sour cream and pesto. Ladle gazpacho into bowls and let guests help themselves to condiments.

Smoked Tomato and Basil Bisque

SERVES 4

We think a stash of smoked tomatoes is a frozen asset everyone should have — especially when you want to serve this delicious soup.

✦ TIP ✦

Be an efficient barbecuer. Wrap and freeze leftover smoked tomatoes for later use in dishes like this one.

● **Suggested wood: corncob, mesquite, oak or sugar maple**

8	plum (Roma) tomatoes	8
2 cups	chicken stock	500 mL
1 cup	whipping (35%) cream	250 mL
4 oz	goat cheese, crumbled	125 g
2 tbsp	freshly squeezed lemon juice	25 mL
	Kosher salt and freshly ground black pepper	
1 to 2 tbsp	olive oil	15 to 25 mL
1 cup	fresh bread crumbs	250 mL
1 cup	chopped fresh basil	250 mL

1. Prepare a hot indirect fire with a kiss of smoke in your grill.

2. When you see the first wisp of smoke from the wood, place tomatoes on the indirect side of the grill. Close the lid and grill for about 30 minutes, or until skin breaks apart on the tomatoes. Let cool, peel and chop.

3. In a large saucepan, heat chicken stock and cream over medium heat, stirring constantly until just beginning to boil. Add goat cheese and stir until melted. Add tomatoes and lemon juice; cook until heated through. Season to taste with salt and pepper.

4. In a skillet, heat olive oil. Add bread crumbs and toast until nicely browned.

5. Ladle soup into bowls and garnish with bread crumbs and basil.

Smoked Italian Sausage and Tortellini Soup

Here's a smoky twist on an Italian favorite.

✦ TIP ✦

When making soup, have a lemon and hot pepper sauce or flakes at the ready. A squeeze of lemon juice or a sprinkle of something hot can be just what the soup needs to lift it from ordinary to sublime.

● Foil pan
● **Suggested wood:** oak, pecan, or apple

1 lb	spicy Italian sausage (bulk or casings removed)	500 g
6 cups	chicken stock	1.5 L
1 lb	small cheese tortellini	500 g
2	carrots, chopped	2
1	onion, chopped	1
1	zucchini, chopped	1
2 cups	freshly grated Romano cheese	500 mL

1. Prepare a hot indirect fire with a kiss of smoke in your grill.

2. Spread sausage in foil pan. When you see the first wisp of smoke from the wood, place pan on the indirect side of the grill. Close the lid and grill for about 1 hour, or until no longer pink.

3. In a large pot, bring chicken stock to a boil. Add tortellini and cook until tender to the bite. Using a slotted spoon, remove tortellini to a bowl.

4. Add smoked sausage, carrots, onion and zucchini to the pot; bring to a boil. Reduce heat and simmer for about 10 minutes to blend the flavors. Return tortellini to the soup and simmer until heated through.

5. Ladle soup into bowls and sprinkle with lots of cheese.

Char-Grilled Romaine, Bacon, Tomato and Blue Cheese Salad

You can make a meal of this salad, served with crusty bread.

✦ TIPS ✦

The vinaigrette can be stored in the refrigerator for up to 2 weeks.

Do not trim the core of the lettuce, or several of the outer leaves will fall off.

✦ Variation ✦

To turn the vinaigrette into a creamy blue cheese dressing, add ½ cup (125 mL) mayonnaise and ½ cup (125 mL) crumbled blue cheese; stir to blend. Try using this dressing on other salads too!

As Simple As It Gets Vinaigrette

¾ cup	vegetable oil	175 mL
¼ cup	white vinegar	50 mL
1 tbsp	granulated sugar	15 mL
1 tsp	Dijon mustard	5 mL
1 tsp	kosher salt	5 mL
3	hearts of romaine, halved	3
	Olive oil	
	Kosher salt and freshly ground black pepper	
12	strips bacon, cooked crisp and crumbled	12
3 cups	halved cherry tomatoes	750 mL
6 oz	blue cheese, crumbled	175 g

1. *Prepare the vinaigrette:* In a glass jar with a tight-fitting lid, combine oil, vinegar, sugar, mustard and salt; cover and shake to blend.

2. Prepare a hot fire in your grill.

3. Brush cut side of romaine with olive oil and season with salt and pepper. Place cut side down on the grill. Grill for 3 or 4 minutes, or until outer lettuce leaves are charred and there are good grill marks on the cut side. (Do not close the grill lid or lettuce will wilt.)

4. Portion romaine among plates and sprinkle with salt and pepper. Top with bacon, tomatoes and blue cheese. Drizzle with vinaigrette.

Grilled Haloumi, Artichoke and Olive Salad with Lemony Za'atar Vinaigrette

SERVES 4

Haloumi is a sheep's milk cheese similar in flavor to feta, and it's made for the grill. This deconstructed dish is great warm-weather food when you want a dish that practically makes itself.

✦ TIP ✦

Za'atar is a Middle Eastern spice blend that combines sumac (a lemony dried herb), thyme, salt and sesame seed.

✦ Variation ✦

Make this indoors, using a ridged griddle or grill pan to sizzle the cheese and pitas.

Lemony Za'atar Vinaigrette

1	clove garlic, minced	1
¼ cup	olive oil	50 mL
½ tsp	fine sea salt	2 mL
½ tsp	ground sumac	2 mL
¼ tsp	dried thyme	1 mL
	Juice of ½ lemon	
1 lb	haloumi cheese, cut into 8 slices	500 g
4	pitas	4
	Olive oil	
1	recipe Grilled Baby Artichokes (page 313)	1
1 cup	sliced cucumber	250 mL
1 cup	cherry or grape tomatoes	250 mL
½ cup	drained brine- or oil-cured black olives	125 mL
1 tbsp	toasted sesame seeds	15 mL

1. *Prepare the vinaigrette:* In a bowl, whisk together garlic, olive oil, salt, sumac, thyme and lemon juice.

2. Prepare a hot fire in your grill.

3. Brush cheese and pitas with oil. Grill for 1 to 2 minutes per side, turning once, until cheese and pitas have good grill marks.

4. Portion cheese, pitas, artichokes, cucumber, tomatoes and olives among plates. Drizzle vegetables with vinaigrette and sprinkle with sesame seeds.

Flame-Seared Potato and Fennel Salad

SERVES 10 TO 12

When fennel is grilled, it caramelizes beautifully and gives off a wonderful licorice aroma.

✦ Variation ✦

Grilled Fennel Salad with Arugula and Goat Cheese: Grill fennel as above. Toss 6 cups (1.5 L) arugula with your favorite vinaigrette. Plate the arugula, top with grilled fennel and drizzle with a little more vinaigrette. Sprinkle with 4 oz (125 g) crumbled goat cheese.

- Perforated grill rack, oiled

4	green onions, thinly sliced	4
2	cloves garlic, minced	2
1½ cups	mayonnaise	375 mL
	Grated zest of 1 lemon	
	Kosher salt and freshly ground black pepper	
¼ cup	freshly squeezed lemon juice	50 mL
4	baking potatoes, thinly sliced lengthwise	4
	Olive oil	
2	fennel bulbs, cut lengthwise into ¼-inch (0.5 cm) slices	2

1. Prepare a hot fire in your grill. Set grill rack directly over the fire.

2. In a bowl, whisk together green onions, garlic, mayonnaise, lemon zest and lemon juice. Season to taste with salt and pepper. Set aside.

3. Brush potatoes with olive oil and season to taste with salt and pepper. Arrange on grill rack, close the lid and grill for 2 to 3 minutes per side, turning once, until fork-tender. Remove grill rack and keep potatoes warm.

4. Brush fennel with olive oil and season to taste with salt and pepper. Grill for 2 to 3 minutes per side, turning once, until fork-tender.

5. Arrange fennel in the middle of a large platter, with potatoes on either side. Drizzle with sauce. Serve any remaining sauce in a bowl on the side.

Grilled Panzanella

SERVES 8

This is the perfect salad when you have lots of ripe, juicy tomatoes. Grilling the bread adds extra crunch, char flavor and color.

✦ TIP ✦

The tomatoes will produce more juice once they are tossed with the other ingredients.

5	slices crusty rustic bread (¾-inch/2 cm slices)	5
	Olive oil	
2	yellow bell peppers, halved lengthwise and seeded	2
1	red onion, cut into ½-inch (1 cm) slices	1
4	large tomatoes, coarsely chopped	4
1	small cucumber, seeded and chopped	1
3 tbsp	drained capers	45 mL
2 tbsp	extra-virgin olive oil	25 mL
2 tbsp	red wine vinegar	25 mL
⅓ cup	packed fresh basil leaves, roughly torn	75 mL
	Kosher salt and freshly ground black pepper	

1. Prepare a hot fire in your grill.

2. Brush both sides of bread with olive oil. Grill for 1 to 2 minutes per side, turning once, until toasted. Let cool.

3. Brush the skin side of yellow peppers with olive oil. Grill skin side down for 5 to 7 minutes, until skin is blackened. Let cool.

4. Brush both sides of onion slices with olive oil. Grill for about 5 minutes per side, turning once, until charred on both sides. Let cool.

5. Cut bread into ¾-inch (2 cm) cubes and coarsely chop peppers and onion. Place in a large bowl and add tomatoes, cucumber, capers, oil and vinegar. Add basil and toss well. Season to taste with salt and pepper. Let stand for 15 to 20 minutes to let flavors blend.

Stir-Grilled Jamaican Shrimp and Vegetable Salad

This is great as a one-dish meal, or add rice or couscous as a side.

- Grill wok or basket, oiled
- Baking sheet

1 lb	large shrimp, peeled and deveined	500 g
1	small red onion, slivered	1
1	small zucchini, sliced	1
5 oz	sugar snap peas	150 g
1 cup	grape or cherry tomatoes	250 mL
1 cup	Italian-style vinaigrette	250 mL
1 tbsp	jerk seasoning	15 mL
	Grated zest and juice of 1 lime	
	Kosher salt and freshly ground black pepper	

1. Rinse shrimp under cold running water and pat dry. In a large bowl, combine shrimp, red onion, zucchini, peas and tomatoes. Add vinaigrette and toss to coat. Sprinkle with jerk seasoning and stir in lime zest and lime juice. Season to taste with salt and pepper. Cover and refrigerate for about 30 minutes.

2. Meanwhile, prepare a hot fire in your grill.

3. Place prepared grill wok over the kitchen sink and pour in shrimp mixture, draining most of the vinaigrette. Set wok on baking sheet and carry out to the grill.

4. Place wok on the grill. Grill, tossing with long-handled wooden spatulas every 3 to 4 minutes, for 12 to 15 minutes, or until shrimp are pink and opaque.

✦ Variation ✦

Substitute salmon pieces or scallops for the shrimp and change the vegetables as you like.

Grilled Salmon Niçoise Salad

In this favorite summer dish from the south of France, we've punched up the flavor by grilling a salmon fillet instead of tuna. Instead of boiled potatoes, serve crusty bread to mop up the delicious vinaigrette. With a chilled bottle of dry rosé, you're ready for summer.

1	salmon fillet (about 3 lbs/1.5 kg), skin on or off	1
1	recipe Provençal Flavoring Paste (page 45)	1

Red Wine Vinaigrette

1	large clove garlic, minced	1
1 cup	extra-virgin olive oil	250 mL
¼ cup	red wine vinegar	50 mL
2 tbsp	minced shallot	25 mL
1½ tbsp	finely chopped fresh basil	22 mL
1 tbsp	Dijon mustard	15 mL
1 tsp	anchovy paste	5 mL
½ tsp	dried herbes de Provence or thyme	2 mL
	Kosher or sea salt and freshly ground black pepper	
12 oz	thin green beans or haricots verts (fresh or frozen and thawed), trimmed	375 g
6 cups	leafy greens (such as Boston lettuce)	1.5 L
2 cups	cherry or grape tomatoes	500 mL
3	hard-cooked eggs, quartered	3
1 cup	drained brine- or oil-cured niçoise olives	250 mL
	Kosher or sea salt and freshly ground black pepper	

1. Prepare a hot fire in your grill.

2. Rinse salmon and pat dry with paper towels. Brush flesh side with paste. Place flesh side down on the grill. Grill for 10 minutes per inch (2.5 cm) of thickness, turning once, until fish is opaque and flakes easily with a fork. Keep warm.

3. *Prepare the vinaigrette:* In a bowl, whisk together garlic, olive oil, vinegar, shallot, basil, mustard, anchovy paste and herbes de Provence. Season to taste with salt and pepper. Set aside.

Frozen thin French beans are now readily available if you can't find fresh.

You can grill the salmon the day before; let cool, place in a sealable plastic bag and store in the refrigerator.

4. Bring a large saucepan of water to a boil over high heat. Cook beans for 3 to 4 minutes, or until tender-crisp. Drain and refresh with cold water. Pat dry with paper towels. Set aside.

5. In a large bowl, toss greens with 2 tbsp (25 mL) of the vinaigrette. Arrange greens on a large platter and top with salmon. Place beans in the large bowl and toss with 1 tbsp (15 mL) of the vinaigrette. Arrange on the platter. Place tomatoes in the bowl and toss with 1 tbsp (15 mL) of the vinaigrette. Arrange on the platter. Arrange eggs and olives on the platter. Pass the remaining vinaigrette at the table.

✦ Variation ✦

Prepare this recipe indoors, using a ridged griddle to grill the salmon.

Leaf-Wrapped Breadsticks

Talk about a rustic appetizer with wow factor! Originally an oven-baked Russian-Mennonite recipe from the Canadian prairie, these breadsticks taste even better on the grill. Surprisingly, the chard leaves wrapped around the breadsticks taste like black olives.

✦ TIP ✦

Serve the breadsticks on a round platter, arranged like the spokes of a wheel, with a bowl of olive oil, Lemon Tahini (page 54) or another dip in the center.

● Baking sheet

12	frozen unbaked yeast rolls, thawed	12
12	fresh Swiss chard or beet leaves, long stems trimmed	12
	Olive oil	
	Kosher salt	

1. Roll each yeast roll into a breadstick about 1 inch (2.5 cm) in diameter. Carefully wrap a Swiss chard leaf loosely around each breadstick. Brush with olive oil and place on baking sheet to rise in a warm place until doubled in bulk, about 45 minutes.

2. Prepare a hot indirect fire in your grill.

3. Place breadsticks perpendicular to the grates on the indirect side of the grill. Close the lid and grill for 15 to 20 minutes, or until breadsticks are puffed and browned. Brush with olive oil and sprinkle with salt.

Grilled Bread with Serrano Ham and Manchego Cheese

SERVES 8

This very simple appetizer relies entirely on the quality of the ingredients. To be authentic, serve each slice atop a glass of chilled fino sherry — or serve on a platter for a cocktail party.

1	baguette, sliced on the diagonal	1
	Olive oil	
8 oz	Manchego cheese, thinly sliced	250 g
8 oz	serrano ham, sliced paper thin	250 g

1. Prepare a hot indirect fire in your grill.

2. Brush both sides of baguette slices with olive oil. Grill for about 3 minutes on one side, until it has good grill marks. Turn grilled side up, move to the indirect side and top with cheese and ham. Cover and grill for 10 to 15 minutes, or until cheese is melted and ham is lightly browned.

Portuguese Country Bread with Green Olive Relish

A twist on garlic bread, this recipe features a crusty country loaf spread with Portuguese Aïoli and grilled, then topped with a bold-flavored olive relish. It's perfect to nibble on while you're sipping a chilled white wine or fino sherry.

✦ Variation ✦

This is also delicious accompanied by or topped with grilled shrimp.

● **Suggested wood: oak**

Portuguese Aïoli

1	clove garlic, minced	1
1 cup	good-quality mayonnaise	250 mL
1 tbsp	tomato purée or ketchup	15 mL
1 tsp	grated orange zest	5 mL
½ tsp	smoked paprika	2 mL
	Freshly squeezed orange juice	

Green Olive Relish

1 cup	drained pimento-stuffed olives, roughly chopped	250 mL
½ cup	fresh flat-leaf (Italian) parsley, chopped	125 mL
1 tbsp	drained capers	15 mL
1	round loaf artisan bread	1
	Olive oil	

1. *Prepare the aïoli:* In a bowl, whisk together garlic, mayonnaise, tomato purée, orange zest and paprika. Stir in orange juice to taste. Set aside.

2. Prepare a hot indirect fire with a kiss of smoke in your grill.

3. *Prepare the relish:* In a bowl, combine olives, parsley and capers. Set aside.

4. Cut bread into ½-inch (1 cm) slices. Cut large slices in half. Brush both sides with olive oil.

5. Grill bread over the hot fire for 1 to 2 minutes per side, turning once, until bread has good grill marks. Brush one side of each slice with aïoli and move to the indirect side. When you see the first wisp of smoke from the wood, close the lid and grill for 10 to 15 minutes, or until aïoli has a burnished appearance. Serve topped with relish.

Grilled Afghan Bread

1 lb	frozen pizza or bread dough, thawed	500 g
1	small jalapeño or serrano pepper, seeded and finely chopped	1
1 cup	finely chopped green onions	250 mL
1 cup	finely chopped fresh cilantro	250 mL
¼ tsp	fine kosher or sea salt	1 mL
	Olive oil	

1. Place dough in a large bowl and set in a warm place to rise according to package directions.

2. In a bowl, combine jalapeño, green onions, cilantro and salt. Transfer to a sieve placed over a bowl and let drain for 15 minutes.

3. Meanwhile, prepare a medium-hot fire in your grill.

4. Divide dough into 4 portions. Roll or pat each portion into a ½-inch (1 cm) thick oval. Place one-quarter of the jalapeño mixture on half of each oval, leaving a ½-inch (1 cm) border around the edge. Brush the perimeter of each oval with water and fold over, pressing the edges together. Brush with olive oil.

5. Grill for 3 to 4 minutes per side, turning once, until bread is golden and has some grill marks.

Aussie Herbed Damper on a Stick

Damper is a biscuit-like dough that is either baked in the coals or wrapped around a campfire stick and grilled. It tastes great with Leaf-Wrapped Barramundi on the Barbie (page 74), Down Under Grilled Lamb Chops with Prickly Ash Rub (page 266) or any simply grilled food.

✦ TIP ✦

Make sure your sticks are fresh and green inside so they don't burn; if they are dry, soak them for 30 minutes before wrapping the dough around them.

● **4 campfire sticks (see tip, at left)**

1 cup	self-rising flour or biscuit mix	250 mL
1 tsp	ground prickly ash or Szechuan pepper	5 mL
1 tsp	chopped fresh rosemary	5 mL
2 tbsp	butter, softened	25 mL
1 cup	milk	250 mL
2 tbsp	sour cream	25 mL
	Olive oil	
	Additional butter (optional)	

1. Prepare a medium-hot fire in your grill.

2. In a bowl, combine flour, prickly ash and rosemary. Using your fingers, work in butter until mixture resembles coarse crumbs. Using a fork, stir in milk and sour cream.

3. Transfer dough to a floured surface and divide into 4 portions. Roll each portion into a rope about ½ inch (1 cm) in diameter. Wrap each rope in a spiral around a campfire stick and brush with olive oil.

4. Grill damper for about 10 minutes, turning often, until browned and golden. Gently slide damper from the stick and serve with butter or olive oil.

Naan with Coconut Chutney

SERVES 8

Northern tandoori and tropical southern India meet in this irresistible flatbread. Clarified butter, or ghee, is the traditional slather for naan, but you can also use vegetable oil if you want to stay true to the southern Indian vegetarian way. A little bit of the chutney goes a long way.

✦ TIPS ✦

This bread is oh so good with any type of skewered and grilled food.

You can also grill store-bought naan. Just brush it with clarified butter and grill for 1 minute per side, until warmed through and golden.

- Baking sheet

½ cup	unsalted butter	125 mL
3 cups	all-purpose flour (approx.)	750 mL
1½ tsp	instant or bread machine yeast	7 mL
1½ tsp	granulated sugar	7 mL
1 tsp	salt	5 mL
3 tbsp	plain yogurt	45 mL
1 cup	warm water	250 mL
1 tbsp	black nigella or onion seeds (optional)	15 mL
1	recipe Coconut Chutney (page 58)	1

1. In a saucepan, melt butter over medium heat. Line a sieve with cheesecloth and place over a microwave-safe bowl. Pour hot butter through the sieve. Discard milk solids in cheesecloth; reserve clarified butter.

2. In a large bowl, combine flour, yeast, sugar and salt. Stir in 3 tbsp (45 mL) of the clarified butter and the yogurt. Stir in warm water until a smooth dough forms.

3. Turn dough out onto a floured surface and knead for about 5 minutes, adding more flour if necessary, until dough is smooth and elastic. Place in an oiled bowl and turn to coat. Cover and let rise in a warm place until doubled in bulk, about 1½ hours.

4. Punch dough down and divide into 8 portions. Roll each portion into a ball. Roll or pat each ball into a circle, then gently stretch into a ½-inch (1 cm) thick oval.

5. Prepare a medium-hot fire in your grill.

6. Microwave the remaining clarified butter until melted. Brush naan with butter and sprinkle with nigella (if using). Place on baking sheet to carry outside.

7. Place naan on grill, close the lid and grill for about 2 minutes per side, turning once, until naan is puffed and golden and has a few grill marks. Serve warm, with chutney.

Grilled Red Pepper Piada

Piada (also known as piadina) is similar to pizza dough but just a bit thicker and softer. A little bit of lemon juice helps to keep the dough tender. A piada tastes best when eaten fresh, the same day. Piadas are also great for making a fold-over sandwich with delicious fillings.

✦ TIPS ✦

Piada dough can be made up to 3 days ahead, wrapped in plastic wrap and stored in the refrigerator. Let warm to room temperature before shaping.

Once it is rolled out and grilled, wrap the unused portion tightly in plastic wrap and use within 1 day.

1½ cups	unbleached all-purpose flour (approx.)	375 mL
½ cup	water	125 mL
2 tbsp	extra-virgin olive oil	25 mL
1 tsp	hot pepper flakes	5 mL
1 tsp	freshly squeezed lemon juice	5 mL
½ tsp	salt	2 mL
	Additional olive oil	

1. In a food processor fitted with a plastic dough blade, combine flour, water, olive oil, hot pepper flakes, lemon juice and salt, pulsing until dough comes together. Continue to pulse in quick bursts for about 3 minutes.

2. Turn dough out onto a floured surface and knead for about 8 minutes, adding more flour if necessary, until dough is soft, smooth and firm. Form into a ball and brush lightly with olive oil. Wrap in plastic wrap and let rest at room temperature for about 30 minutes.

3. Divide dough into 4 portions. Roll each portion into an 8-inch (20 cm) round.

4. Prepare a hot fire in your grill.

5. Grill dough for about 1 minute, or until bubbles form on the surface. Turn with grill tongs. The grilled side should have charred little bubbles. Grill the other side for 1 minute, until lightly browned. Stack piadas on a clean towel and wrap so they stay warm. For best results, serve within 30 minutes of cooking.

Grilled Dark Chocolate Crostini

MAKES 16 CROSTINI

This is a grown-up variation of s'mores for the grill. Serve with a bowl of juicy strawberries.

✦ TIP ✦

Please everyone's palates by offering semisweet, bittersweet and milk chocolate.

1	10-inch (25 cm) baguette	1
	Extra-virgin olive oil	
8 oz	good-quality semisweet chocolate, in bar form	250 g
	Coarse kosher or sea salt	

1. Prepare a medium-hot indirect fire in your grill.

2. Slice off the ends of the bread, then slice bread on the diagonal into 16 slices, each about ½ inch (1 cm) thick. Drizzle one side of each bread slice with olive oil.

3. Break or cut chocolate into 16 pieces.

4. Place bread oiled side down over the fire. Grill for 1 to 2 minutes, or until browned on the oiled side. Turn bread over and move to the indirect side. Place a piece of chocolate on each slice. Close the lid and grill for 2 minutes to warm the chocolate. Transfer crostini to a serving dish and sprinkle with a tiny bit of salt.

Barbecued Shrimp Quesadillas

Quesadillas are like Mexican pizzas, but you don't have to make pizza dough — store-bought flour tortillas make them quick and easy.

◆ TIP ◆

Try serving these with Grilled Guacamole (page 62), Pumpkin Seed Salsa (page 60) and/or Golden Papaya Salsa (page 61).

● Six 12-inch (30 cm) flat bamboo skewers, soaked for at least 30 minutes

1 lb	large shrimp, peeled and deveined	500 g
1 cup	chipotle barbecue sauce, divided	250 mL
8	10-inch (25 cm) flour tortillas	8
2 cups	shredded Monterey Jack cheese	500 mL
	Sour cream, guacamole and/or salsa	

1. Prepare a medium-hot fire in your grill.

2. Rinse shrimp under cold running water and pat dry. Thread shrimp onto skewers, leaving space between pieces. Remove half the barbecue sauce and brush shrimp on both sides.

3. Grill skewers for about 5 minutes, turning often, until shrimp are pink and opaque.

4. Place 4 of the tortillas on a work surface and divide shrimp among them. Drizzle with the remaining barbecue sauce and sprinkle with cheese. Top each with another tortilla.

5. Grill tortillas for 3 to 4 minutes per side, turning once, until bread is golden and cheese is melted.

6. Using a sharp knife or pizza wheel, cut quesadillas into triangles. Serve with sour cream, guacamole and/or salsa.

Toasted Croissants with Boursin, Grilled Tomatoes and Bacon

Ooh-la-la! Croissants toasted on the grill seem so decadent.

✦ TIP ✦

Choose tomatoes that are ripe but still firm. Overly ripe tomatoes get too mushy when grilled.

4	croissants, halved	4
	Extra-virgin olive oil	
3	tomatoes, cut into ⅜-inch (0.75 cm) thick slices	3
	Kosher salt and freshly ground black pepper	
½ cup	Boursin cheese	125 mL
4 tsp	olive paste	20 mL
8	strips bacon, cooked crisp	8
8 to 12	fresh basil leaves	8 to 12
1	bunch fresh chives (about 2 oz/60 g)	1

1. Prepare a medium-hot indirect fire in your grill.

2. Brush cut side of croissants with olive oil. Place croissants cut side down over the fire. Grill for 1 to 2 minutes, until browned. Move to the indirect side.

3. Brush both sides of tomatoes with olive oil and sprinkle with salt and pepper. Place tomatoes over the fire. Grill on one side for 2 to 3 minutes, until tomatoes have grill marks.

4. Spread 2 tbsp (25 mL) of the cheese on the bottom halves of croissants and 1 tsp (5 mL) olive paste on the top halves. On bottom halves, layer with grilled tomatoes, bacon, basil and chives. Cover with top halves and serve warm.

✦ Variation ✦

Use other types of bread, such as ciabatta, challah or sourdough, and cut them into ½-inch (1 cm) thick slices.

Grilled Italian Garden Sandwiches

SERVES 4 TO 6

Here's a good-for-you sandwich that everyone will love.

✦ TIPS ✦

You can use store-bought roasted peppers in a jar or roast your own. To roast peppers, preheat broiler or your grill to high. Broil or grill whole peppers until blackened, blistered and tender. Place peppers in a brown paper bag and close the top. Set aside for about 5 minutes, until cool. Slice peppers open to remove the core and seeds. Rub excess char off the skins. Use immediately or store in an airtight container in the refrigerator for up to 2 days.

Be an efficient barbecuer. Wrap and freeze leftover grilled vegetables for later use in dishes like this one.

1	loaf Italian bread, halved lengthwise	1
⅓ cup	Sun-Dried Tomato Pesto (see recipe, page 42)	75 mL
9 oz	soft goat cheese	275 g
4	plum (Roma) tomatoes, sliced	4
	Kosher salt and freshly ground black pepper	
¾ cup	roasted red bell pepper strips (see tip, at left)	175 mL
½ cup	chopped drained canned or marinated artichoke hearts	125 mL
¼ cup	chopped drained pickled pepperoncini peppers	50 mL
2 tbsp	toasted pine nuts	25 mL
	Olive oil	

1. Prepare a medium-hot indirect fire in your grill.
2. Hollow out about one-third of the top half of the bread. Lightly brush the inside of both halves with olive oil. Spread pesto on the top half and goat cheese on the bottom half. On the bottom half, layer with tomatoes and season to taste with salt and pepper. Layer with roasted peppers, artichoke hearts, pepperoncini and pine nuts. Cover with the top half. Brush sandwich all over with olive oil and wrap in foil.
3. Grill sandwich over the fire for about 5 minutes per side, turning once, until heated through. Move to the indirect side, close the lid and grill for 10 minutes.
4. Cut sandwich into 4 or 6 slices and serve warm or at room temperature.

✦ Variation ✦

Use leftover grilled vegetables to fill the sandwich and add slices of your favorite cheese.

Montreal Smoked Meat Sandwiches

SERVES 6

Schwartz's in Montreal sets the bar high for the ultimate Montreal smoked meat sandwich, but we like to think this recipe comes close.

✦ TIP ✦

Before barbecuing, cut a notch or V shape into the brisket indicating the direction of the grain of the meat; this will help you slice it properly after it is cooked.

- Cast-iron skillet
- Doubled foil pan
- **Suggested wood:** maple, cherry or apple

Montreal Spice Seasoning

2	allspice berries	2
2 tsp	whole black peppercorns	10 mL
2 tsp	fennel seeds	10 mL
1 tsp	coriander seeds	5 mL
1 tsp	cumin seeds	5 mL
1 tsp	mustard seeds	5 mL
2	cloves garlic, minced	2
2 tbsp	packed brown sugar	25 mL
1 tbsp	celery seeds	15 mL
1 tbsp	smoked paprika	15 mL
1 tbsp	kosher salt	15 mL
3 lbs	beef brisket	1.5 kg
1 cup	dry red wine	250 mL
3	strips double-smoked bacon	3
1	loaf deli rye bread	1
	Mustard and dill pickles	

1. *Prepare the seasoning:* In cast-iron skillet, over medium heat, toast allspice, peppercorns, fennel seeds, coriander seeds, cumin seeds and mustard seeds, stirring constantly, for 5 to 7 minutes, until fragrant. Coarsely grind spices in a mortar and pestle or a spice grinder.

2. In a bowl, combine ground spices, brown sugar, celery seeds, paprika and salt.

3. Place brisket in foil pan and rub all sides with seasoning. Pour wine over brisket. Cover and refrigerate for at least 4 hours or overnight.

4. Meanwhile, prepare an indirect fire for smoking in your grill or smoker.

5. Lay bacon strips over brisket, wrap pan loosely with foil and place pan on the indirect side of the grill. Close the lid and smoke for 2 hours. Crimp foil tightly around the pan and smoke for about 1 hour, or until brisket is fork-tender. Let rest for 30 minutes. Discard bacon and pan juices. Transfer brisket to a cutting board, trim off the fat and carve across the grain into thin slices.

6. Slather bread with mustard, layer with sliced meat and garnish with pickles.

Churrasco-Style Steak Sandwiches

Traditionally, churrasco is skewered beef, cooked over a hot fire. In modern churrasco steakhouses, it's an elaborate system of skewers set on a rotating spit and cooked over flames.

◆ TIP ◆

It's traditional to use cilantro in the marinade and the chimichurri, but if it isn't your favorite herb, you can substitute a combination of snipped chives and chopped fresh flat-leaf (Italian) parsley, mint or basil.

Marinade

4	cloves garlic, minced	4
1	red onion, chopped	1
1 cup	white vinegar	250 mL
½ cup	chopped fresh cilantro	125 mL
½ cup	olive oil	125 mL
1 tbsp	ground cumin	15 mL
1 tbsp	fresh oregano leaves	15 mL
1 tbsp	fresh thyme leaves	15 mL
1 tbsp	coarsely ground black pepper	15 mL
1 tbsp	coarse kosher salt	15 mL
4 lbs	boneless beef sirloin steak (about 1½ inches/4 cm thick)	2 kg
8	good-quality bakery rolls, split	8
	Olive oil	
1	recipe Chimichurri (page 144)	1

1. *Prepare the marinade:* In a bowl, combine garlic, red onion, vinegar, cilantro, olive oil, cumin, oregano, thyme, pepper and salt.

2. Place steak in a large sealable plastic bag and pour in marinade. Seal, toss to coat and refrigerate for at least 4 hours or overnight, tossing occasionally.

3. Meanwhile, prepare a hot fire in your grill.

4. Remove steak from marinade, discarding marinade. Grill steak for about 5 minutes per side, turning once, until a meat thermometer inserted in the thickest part of the steak registers 130°F (54°C) for medium-rare, or until desired doneness. Transfer to a cutting board, tent with foil and let rest for 5 minutes.

Be an efficient barbecuer. Wrap and freeze leftover grilled steak for later use in dishes like this one.

If you use leftover grilled steak for these sandwiches, warm it first by wrapping it in foil and heating it on the indirect side of the grill, with the lid closed, until heated through, about 5 minutes.

5. Meanwhile, brush the cut sides of rolls with olive oil. Grill cut side down for 1 to 2 minutes, until browned. Transfer to a basket.

6. Thinly slice steak across the grain and on the diagonal and arrange on a platter. Spoon some of the chimichurri over the steak. Serve the remaining chimichurri on the side, along with the basket of rolls.

✦ Variation ✦

Substitute other cuts of steak, such as tenderloin, skirt or flank steak. Or try making these sandwiches with grilled chicken, shrimp, fish or sausage.

Panini Caprese

SERVES 4

The most divine salad of the summer? Home-grown tomatoes with the best-quality mozzarella and fresh-from-the-garden basil. We've made it into a fabulous grilled sandwich, flattened with a brick.

- Baking sheet
- 4 bricks, covered with foil

8	slices Italian bread (½-inch/1 cm slices)	8
	Extra-virgin olive oil	
½ cup	pesto	125 mL
3	large tomatoes, cut into ½-inch (1 cm) thick slices	3
	Kosher salt and freshly ground black pepper	
8	slices mozzarella cheese	8
1	small red onion, very thinly sliced	1
¼ cup	packed large fresh basil leaves	50 mL

1. Prepare a medium-hot fire in your grill.

2. Brush both sides of bread with olive oil. Spread one side of top halves with pesto. Place bottom halves on baking sheet, layer with tomatoes and season to taste with salt and pepper. Layer with mozzarella, red onion and basil. Cover with top halves, pesto side down.

3. Place sandwiches on the grill and place a brick on top of each sandwich. Grill for 3 to 4 minutes, until bread is golden brown. Turn sandwiches over and weigh down with bricks. Grill for 3 to 4 minutes, until bread is golden brown. Cut in half and serve warm.

✦ Variation ✦

For a taste of New Orleans, make a muffuletta panini. The filling includes 8 thin slices each of provolone cheese, hard salami and mortadella or ham, as well as 1 cup (250 mL) chopped olive salad, divided evenly among the 4 sandwiches. If you can't find olive salad, make your own by combining ¾ cup (175 mL) assorted cured chopped olives, ¼ cup (50 mL) roasted red pepper strips and 1 tbsp (15 mL) capers.

Glossary

Achiote paste: A dark red coloring and flavoring paste made from annatto seed, used in East Indian (tandoori), Spanish and Latin American barbecue.

Across the grain: The correct way to slice chewy steaks, such as bavette, flank, flat-iron and hanger, as well as brisket. These cuts of beef have a pronounced and identifiable "grain." Cutting across, or against, the grain gives a more tender result. Cutting with the grain gives a chewy, elastic result.

Asado: A Spanish term for roasted, broiled or grilled foods.

Baby back ribs: Pork ribs cut from the rib area closest to the backbone. Baby back ribs are more tender than spareribs and can be grilled or smoked. They may be labeled simply as "back ribs."

Barbacoa: A pit barbecue style indigenous to Central America and the Caribbean in which meats are wrapped in banana or maguey leaves, then placed in a pit, covered and left to cook and steam until done.

Barbe-a-queue: A French term meaning "from beard to tail," indicating meat cooked on a spit.

Barbecue: (Also known as barbeque, BBQ, Bar-B-Q, Bar-B-Que, Bar-B-Cue, 'cue, 'que.) Technically, to cook meat using indirect heat in an enclosed space over smoldering hardwoods. However "barbecue" and "grill" have become synonymous, both meaning to cook food directly over intense heat, usually outdoors using natural woods, charcoal or gas, on a grill, in an open pit or on a spit.

Barbecue sauce: North American barbecue sauces range from white with mayonnaise to bright yellow with mustard to bright red from ketchup. Some are tart and vinegary, some are sweet, some are very spicy and some are aromatic and savory with green herbs. Most are tomato- or ketchup-based. The best sauces complement the meat flavor without burying it.

Barbie: Australian slang for the barbecue grill.

Bark: A brown, crunchy crust that forms on some barbecued foods, created by seasonings and higher heat for 30 minutes or more.

Baste: To brush a seasoned liquid over a food surface, adding moisture and flavor.

Bavette: A thin, chewy, French-style beef steak, cut from the flap of the loin, grilled rare and usually served with *pommes frites* on bistro menus.

Big Green Egg: A ceramic, egg-shaped grill.

Brai, braai: The South African (Afrikaans) term for a barbecue.

Brasa: A Spanish term for a live coal used for grilling. *A la brasa* means grilled over charcoal. *Alla brache* is the Italian term for the same technique.

Brazier: See Grill.

Brine: A salty liquid that may have other flavoring agents. Soaking meats in brine can, by chemical magic, ensure a moister result after cooking.

Brochette: A French term for a kabob (*en brochette*), food cooked on a skewer. Also a metal skewer.

BTUs: British thermal units, units of energy used in gas grilling. The more BTUs your gas grill has — we recommend 40,000 BTUs, not including side burners — the hotter it will get.

Burnt ends, brownies: The thin end of a slow-smoked beef brisket that is cut into chunks and put back on the smoker for a little longer.

Cabinet smokers: Rectangular upright smoking units with front doors, like a refrigerator. These are fueled by wood, charcoal, gas or electricity. The front door makes loading the smoker with wood or food fairly easy. They usually have four or five racks that are all adjustable.

Carolina-style barbecue: A regional barbecue style from North and South Carolina, emphasizing pork smoked with hickory and accompanied by vinegar- or mustard-based barbecue sauces.

Ceramic briquettes: Radiant materials compacted into a brick shape, used in gas grills. Ceramic briquettes don't burn completely like charcoal. Lava rocks and metal plates are similar alternatives.

Charcoal briquettes: Ground charcoal, coal dust and starch compacted into a brick shape and used as fuel in charcoal grills.

Charcoal grate: The rack that holds charcoal in the firebox.

Charcoal grill: A grill that uses charcoal briquettes as its principal fuel.

Charwood: (Also known as lump charcoal or chunk charwood.) Charcoal made by burning whole logs or large pieces of wood in a kiln without oxygen. This type of charcoal is pure and burns very hot.

Chimney starter: (Also known as a charcoal chimney.) A cylinder-shaped metal container used to start a charcoal fire. Newspaper stuffed underneath is set alight, which in turn lights the charcoal.

Churrasco: Brazilian barbecue, done over a wood fire with meats on large spits or skewers.

Coconut husk charcoal: Used for grilling in Vietnam. This charcoal is made by slowly smoldering coconut husks until they are of a uniform size.

Cold smoking: Smoke is applied to food at a low temperature, usually between 90°F (32°C) and 120°F (50°C). Cheese, some spices and some fish are good when cold-smoked. Cold smoking must be done carefully, because microbes thrive at these temperatures. Fish and meats are often cured first to remove moisture. You need specialized equipment for cold smoking.

Composition briquettes: Made from wood scraps and/or coal dust, and bound by paraffin or petroleum. These briquettes do not burn cleanly.

Cowboy steak: A bone-in beef rib eye steak (mainly on restaurant menus).

Direct grilling: A method of quickly cooking food by placing it on the grill grate directly over the heat. Food is most often cooked uncovered on a charcoal grill, but covered on a gas grill.

Drip pan: A metal or foil pan placed under food to catch drippings when grilling. A drip pan can also be made from heavy-duty foil.

Dry aging: A technique that adds flavor and increases tenderness in beef. During the dry-aging process, beef is kept on racks in a climate- and humidity-controlled area in which air circulates. Dry-aged beef may lose up to 25% of its weight, which is why dry-aged steaks are more expensive.

Electric grill: A small electric tabletop grill. Also, many high-end range tops include a grate or grill insert and a built-in exhaust fan for smokeless indoor grilling.

Electric starter: A metal loop that heats up when the starter is plugged in. You bury the loop beneath the mound of charcoal, then plug in the starter. When the coals at the core of the mound are red hot, unplug and remove the starter. Make sure to place it on a non-flammable surface and let it cool.

Firebox: The area at the bottom of the grill that holds the fire or heat.

Flake: To test the flesh of a fish to see if it is done by using a fork to break away a small piece.

Flare-ups: Flames caused by fat dripping onto hot coals or lava rocks.

Flat-iron steak: A chewy, whole-muscle steak cut from the beef shoulder.

Flat-top grill: A grill with a griddle-like cooking surface.

Gas grill: A grill that uses gas from a propane tank or a natural gas line for fuel.

Glaze: To form a glossy, flavorful coating on food as it cooks, usually by basting it. Glazes get their sheen from sugar. Some sauces are also glazes. A gorgeous glaze can be created simply by brushing food with honey.

Granulated garlic: Dried garlic in granule form, often used by barbecuers for rubs and seasonings. It mixes better with other seasonings than the finer garlic salt or powder.

Griddle: A flat piece of steel or cast iron that is heated from beneath.

Grill: (Also known as a brazier.) A grill is constructed so the food sits on a grate above the flame, directly exposed to the heat. Hibachis and kettle grills are good examples. Grilling is usually done at temperatures of 300°F (150°C) or higher, and some grills can reach more than 600°C (316°C). It is important to differentiate between grills/braziers and smokers/barbecues; it may seem like a minor semantic difference, but the different techniques make a huge difference in flavor.

Grill basket: A hinged wire basket that is used to hold fish or vegetables for grilling.

Grill grate: (Also known as a grid.) The latticework of metal rods that holds food on a grill.

Grill wok: A wok that is made specifically for grilling. With its sloped sides and numerous perforations, it makes small pieces of vegetables, meat or shellfish easy to stir-grill.

Grilling: To cook food directly over intense heat on a grate over hot coals, natural wood or gas. Grilling is "hot and fast."

Hanger steak: A thin, chewy cut of beef steak so named because it "hangs" from the diaphragm of the steer.

Hibachi: A small, portable, uncovered grill often made of cast iron.

Indirect grilling: A method of cooking food slowly, off to one side of the heat source, usually over a drip pan in a covered grill.

Infrared: A gas grill technology in which the gas heats a ceramic tile, which then gives off infrared radiation, cooking food faster.

Jerk: A Jamaican seasoning (which has given its name to the method involved) including Scotch bonnet (habanero) chiles, allspice and herbs used on foods that have been previously marinated in lime juice or vinegar. Traditional jerk foods (pork, chicken and fish) are then grilled on skewers made from the allspice tree.

Kabobs, kebabs: Pieces of meat, poultry, seafood and/or vegetables threaded on skewers and grilled.

Kansas City–style barbecue: A regional barbecue style from Missouri, emphasizing pork and beef smoked with hickory, oak and/or apple and accompanied by a smoky, sweet, tomato-based barbecue sauce.

Kettle grill: A round charcoal grill with a heavy cover. It usually stands on three legs and can be used for either direct or indirect grilling.

Korean table grill: A small, round charcoal or electric grill placed in the center of the table for grilling thin strips of bulgogi and other thin or small foods.

Lava rock: A natural rock made from volcanic lava, used as an alternative to ceramic briquettes in gas or electric grills. It can be used many times but eventually needs to be replaced.

Liquid smoke: A bottled flavoring agent made from hardwood condensates — usually hickory, mesquite, pecan and sometimes alder and apple.

Low 'n' slow: The quintessential slow-smoking technique. By keeping the heat low (under 250°C/120°C) and taking your time, the fats and collagens in the meat melt, making the end product juicy and flavorful.

Lump charcoal: (Also known as hardwood lump charcoal or chunk charwood.) Charcoal made by burning whole logs or large pieces of wood in a kiln without oxygen. This type of charcoal is pure and burns very hot.

Marinade: A flavoring liquid used to soak food before cooking. In order for it to penetrate — and it doesn't penetrate very far — the marinade needs acidity from fruit juice, wine or vinegar.

Marinate: To soak food in a flavorful liquid mixture before it is cooked.

Membrane: (Also known as silverskin.) This thin, tough sheath must be removed from meats, especially tenderloin and ribs, before grilling or smoking.

Memphis-style barbecue: A regional barbecue style from Tennessee, emphasizing pork smoked with hickory and accompanied by tomato-based barbecue sauces. Ribs are offered "wet" (with sauce) or "dry" (no sauce and with extra rub sprinkled on the ribs before serving).

Mop or mop sauce: A thin sauce brushed on meat while it is cooking, especially on an old-fashioned direct-heat pit. A mop keeps the surface cool and adds flavor and moisture. The classic mop is vinegar-based, with black pepper, hot pepper flakes and hot pepper sauce. Modern variations include beer, apple juice and even soft drinks such as Dr. Pepper.

Natural briquettes: Briquettes made from pulverized wood held together with natural starches. Used in charcoal grills.

Notching: The practice of cutting a notch or V shape in a brisket, flank steak or hangar steak, indicating the direction of the grain of the meat, before barbecuing, so that the meat may be sliced properly after it is cooked.

Offset (side) firebox: A very popular smoker design with two sealed boxes or tubes connected on one side. One box is for a charcoal or wood fire; the heat and smoke drain into the other box (the oven), which is set a little higher.

Paillard: A thin, boneless piece of meat or poultry, usually pounded thin. A paillard pounded to ½-inch (1 cm) thickness will grill perfectly over a hot fire in 2½ minutes per side.

Parilla: A Spanish term for a charcoal grill grate or a rare steak cooked on one. *A la parilla* means charcoal-grilled.

Perforated grill rack: A perforated or metal-wire rack placed on top of the grill grate to hold small pieces of food that might fall through the grates.

Piastra: An Italian stone griddle. Foods cooked *alla piastra* require the griddle to be very, very hot.

Pig pickin': A meal in which a whole pig or hog is served and people pluck the meat off whatever part they wish.

Pit: Originally, a pit was a hole in the ground lined with logs burned down to charcoal. In recent years, the word "pit" has become more generic and now means just about any device for slow smoking.

Pit master: An experienced barbecue cook, a skilled craftsman, who watches over the pit and can tell by sight, sound, smell and touch if it is running too hot or too cold, when it needs fuel, when to add wood, when to add sauce and when the meat is ready.

Planking: A native American barbecue method, originally used with salmon and halibut in the Pacific Northwest and shad in the northern Atlantic coastal regions. The fish were cleaned, butterflied and lashed to hardwood planks placed upright around a hardwood fire. Regional woods — alder and cedar in the Pacific Northwest and hickory, maple or oak in the Atlantic — lent an aromatic wood flavor to the fish. Today, planks can be purchased at barbecue and grill shops and some supermarkets.

Pound: To use a heavy mallet or frying pan to flatten meat or poultry, often between sheets of waxed paper. Pounding helps tenderize meat and poultry.

Prepare fire (preheat): On gas grills, this means setting to a certain temperature 15 to 20 minutes before grilling. With charcoal grills, it means lighting coals 15 to 20 minutes before grilling.

Reduce: To boil a sauce to reduce its volume and intensify its flavor.

Rest: To let beef, steak, chicken — almost anything you grill — stand for a few minutes before serving. Resting allows meat juices, driven to the center of the cut by searing heat, to return to the surface, resulting in a juicier, more flavorful piece of meat.

Robatayaki: A Japanese grilling style, often at better restaurants, in which food is grilled at the table on hibachis.

Rodizio: A Brazilian grill used for spit-roasting.

Rotisserie: The spit or long metal skewer that suspends and rotates food over the grill's heat source.

Rub: A blend of herbs and/or spices that is rubbed on meat before grilling. Typical Southern barbecue rubs include paprika, salt, sugar, garlic, black pepper and chile pepper in varying amounts. Some rubs are applied thick, some thin; some overnight, some just before cooking. Even if left on overnight, they do not penetrate far into the meat but provide a "bark" and the initial flavor.

Santa Maria–style barbecue: A regional barbecue style from California, emphasizing beef tri-tip seasoned with a simple salt, granulated garlic and black pepper rub, grilled over red oak and served with toasted French bread and slow-simmered pinquito beans.

Satay (also saté): An Indonesian dish in which thin bamboo skewers are threaded with meat, fish or poultry and grilled. Satay is often accompanied by a peanut-based satay sauce.

Sear: To brown the surface, usually of meat, by a brief exposure to high heat.

Shiner: A pejorative term for a sparerib, raw or cooked, that has been cut so that the bone shows — a no-no on the barbecue contest circuit.

Shred: To cut or tear food into thin strips, a technique used with pulled pork or chicken.

Skewer: A long, narrow metal or wooden stick that can be inserted through pieces of meat or vegetables for grilling. Skewers can also be made from shards of sugar cane, rosemary branches, fresh bamboo, lemongrass, hardwood campfire sticks or any other sturdy, non-toxic plant.

Spareribs: Pork ribs cut from the midsection. The St. Louis cut is squared off; the Kansas City cut is fuller and may have flap meat attached.

Smoker box: A small, perforated steel or cast-iron container placed on a gas grill's lava rocks or ceramic briquettes, or on the grill rack, to hold wood chips and provide smoke. Some gas grills have a built-in smoker box fixed to one side of the grill grate.

Smoke ring: A dark pink ribbon of color, usually about ⅛ inch (0.25 cm) wide, just below the surface of smoked meats, created when myoglobin in the meat contacts moist nitrogen dioxide formed during combustion of the wood. The use of green wood is believed to enhance the smoke ring because it has more moisture and produces more nitrogen dioxide. Propane cookers with wood chips, chunks or pellets and a water pan are especially good at producing a smoke ring. A smoke ring used to be a judging criterion in barbecue contests but has fallen out of favor because the same visual effect can be achieved with curing salts.

Smoking: Cooking in an atmosphere infused with smoke from cellulosic materials, usually wood. Hot smoking is the method used for most of what we call barbecue, at a temperature between 225°F (110°C) and 250°C (120°C). The food is cooked by the heat, and when it is finished it is free of harmful living microbes. Hot smoking is relatively easy to do on backyard grills and smokers. Cold smoking is usually done at temperatures under 120°F (50°C). The food is heavily infused with smoke flavor, but is not cooked.

Spatchcock: To cut out the backbone of a chicken or Cornish game hen and spread the bird out flat for grilling. Some chefs run a skewer through the thighs to keep the drumsticks secure and fold the wings under.

Stovetop smoker: A metal pan with a cover in which fine wood chips are smoldered over a stovetop burner to cook and smoke food.

Tandoori: A high-heat Indian grilling/roasting/baking technique that uses a charcoal fire contained in a tandoori oven, usually made of clay. Temperatures might reach 800°F (427°C). Flatbreads, such as naan, and chicken or fish slathered with paste are typical tandoori foods.

Teppanyaki: A Japanese term referring to food cooked on a cast-iron griddle over a charcoal or gas fire.

Texas-style barbecue: A regional barbecue style from Texas, emphasizing beef — especially brisket and clod (shoulder) — smoked over mesquite or oak.

Tongs: The most essential tool in a griller's toolbox. Long-handled tongs enable you to turn foods without stabbing them or burning yourself.

Tuscan grill: A metal grill grate on legs, meant for fireplace use — you place the Tuscan grill over glowing embers. Restaurants in Tuscany use long grates on legs with hot coals and wood underneath.

Twist: A test to see if a beef brisket or pork butt is fork-tender. Stick a fork in a section of meat and twist. If the meat twists, it's tender enough.

Vents: Holes in a grill cover or firebox that open and close. When open, air circulates through, increasing the heat of a fire.

Water smoker: A bullet-shaped smoker with the heat source on the lowest level, a water pan on the middle level and the food placed on the top level. Water smokers can be heated by charcoal, gas or electricity.

Yakitori: Yakitori parlors are small Japanese eateries, often market stalls, that offer grilled foods on skewers.

Library and Archives Canada Cataloguing in Publication

Adler, Karen
   300 big & bold barbecue & grilling recipes / Karen Adler, Judith Fertig.

Includes index.
ISBN 978-0-7788-0212-9

   1. Barbecue cookery. I. Fertig, Judith M. II. Title. III. Title: Three hundred big and bold barbecue and grilling recipes.

TX840.B3A45 2009   641.5'784   C2008-907404-1

Index

Afghan Bread, Grilled, 388
aïoli, 32, 46–48
Aji-li-Mojili, 42
Alabama White Sauce, 68
All-Purpose Barbecue Rub, 34
All-Purpose Lemon Brine, 37
appetizers
    Balinese Shrimp Satay on
        Lemongrass Stalks, 121
    Bamboo Beef with Homemade
        Teriyaki Sauce, 252
    Barbecue-Basted Wings, 168
    Branding Iron Beef with Smoked
        Chile Drizzle, 240
    Chinese-Style Barbecued Wings,
        167
    Corncob-Smoked Shrimp with
        Classic Cocktail Sauce, 129
    Grilled Miso Chicken, 164
    Harissa-Rubbed Snapper Skewers
        with Golden Papaya Salsa, 92
    Korean Bulgogi with Kimchee,
        253
    Orange-Basted Shrimp on the
        Barbie, 122
    Persian Grilled Quail Breasts, 288
    Peruvian Grilled Chicken
        Skewers in Mango Chipotle
        Mojo, 158
    Planked and Pepper-Crusted
        Maple-Glazed Salmon, 91
    Planked Shrimp with Garlic Chive
        Butter and Ciabatta, 128
    Red-Hot Grilled Wings with Cold
        Blue Cheese Dipping Sauce, 166
    Sea Scallops Wrapped in
        Radicchio and Prosciutto, 114
    Singaporean Lamb Satay, 276
    Smoked Scallops with Smoked
        Chile Butter Drizzle, 119
    Stir-Grilled Coconut Shrimp, 126
    Thai Marinated Beef in Lettuce
        Cups, 244
    Thai-Style Halibut on Lemongrass
        Skewers, 80
    Vegetable Kebabs with Za'atar,
        349
    Wasabi Grilled Scallops with
        Japanese Beans, 115
    Wok-Grilled Greek Taverna
        Olives, 334
    Wood-Grilled Clams with Piquillo
        Pepper Butter, 111
    Wood-Grilled Oysters with
        Pancetta and Basil Aïoli, 113
    Yakitori-Style Chicken Skewers
        over Soba Noodles, 161
Apple Rings with Cider Bourbon
    Cream Sauce, Grilled, 354

Apple-Smoked Roasted Pork Loin
    with Apple Chutney Stuffing,
    190
Apricot and Plum Skewers with
    Almond Cream, Grilled, 360
Apricot Cognac–Glazed Whole
    Smoked Duck, 291
Arctic Char with Grilled Lemon
    Halves, 78
Argentinean Chicken Asado, 144
Argentinean Grilled Vegetable
    Platter with Chimichurri, 348
Asian Barbecue Sauce, 64
Asparagus with Asian Dipping
    Sauce, Grilled, 314
Aussie Grilled Shellfish Salad with
    Lemon Dill Rémoulade, 135
Aussie Herbed Damper on a Stick,
    389
Aussie Paperbark Pork with Lemon
    Myrtle Chutney, 198
Avocados, Tomatoes and Lemons,
    Grilled, 364

Baby Artichokes with Balsamic
    Olive Oil Drizzle, Grilled, 313
Baby Beets with Green Onions and
    Lemon-Herb Butter, Stir-Grilled,
    321
Baby Bok Choy with Gingered Soy
    Sauce, Grilled, 322
bacon. See also pancetta
    Apricot Cognac–Glazed Whole
        Smoked Duck (tip), 291
    Barbecued White Beans with
        Bacon and Pear, 318
    Calico Smoked Beans, 320
    Char-Grilled Romaine, Bacon,
        Tomato and Blue Cheese Salad,
        379
    Grill-Roasted Tenderloin with
        Bacon Mushroom Sauce, 232
    Grill-Smoked Jalapeño Poppers,
        338
    Hickory-Grilled Double Pork
        Chops with Fire-Roasted
        Tomato and Bacon Vinaigrette,
        202
    Montreal Smoked Meat
        Sandwiches, 396
    Smoke-Roasted Goose, 296
    Texas Cowpoke Pintos with
        Jalapeño Peppers, 319
    Toasted Croissants with Boursin,
        Grilled Tomatoes and Bacon,
        394
    Wood-Grilled Trout (variation), 99
Baja Fish Tacos with Napa Slaw
    and Guacamole, 106

Balinese Shrimp Satay on
    Lemongrass Stalks, 121
Bamboo Beef with Homemade
    Teriyaki Sauce, 252
Barbecue-Basted Wings, 168
barbecue sauces, 32, 62–70
Barbecued Shrimp Quesadillas, 393
Barbecued White Beans with Bacon
    and Pear, 318
barbecuing. See also grilling; smoking
    doneness in, 12, 13
    flavor elements of, 27–28
bastes, 32
BBQ Poutine, 180
beans and peas. See also vegetables
    Barbecued White Beans with
        Bacon and Pear, 318
    Calico Smoked Beans, 320
    Prairie-Style Smoked Bison Chili,
        305
    Smoked Pork and Black-Eyed
        Pea Gumbo for a Crowd, 182
    Texas Cowpoke Pintos with
        Jalapeño Peppers, 319
Béarnaise Sauce, 55
beef, 218–19
    Bamboo Beef with Homemade
        Teriyaki Sauce, 252
    Bistro Burger, 260
    Black and Bleu Sirloin Served
        over Greens with Tarragon
        Vinaigrette, 236
    Black Pepper–Rubbed Sirloin
        with Horseradish Butter, 239
    Branding Iron Beef with Smoked
        Chile Drizzle, 240
    Burnt-End Sandwiches with
        Caramelized Onions, 225
    Calgary Stampede Spitted Beef
        Roast, 231
    Calico Smoked Beans, 320
    Carne Asada with Poblano and
        Onion Rajas, 246
    Cherry-Smoked Rib Roast with
        Horseradish Crème Fraîche, 230
    Chuck Roast with a Kiss of
        Smoke, Old-Fashioned, 228
    Churrasco-Style Steak
        Sandwiches, 398
    Cowboy Steaks with Two-
        Steppin' Rub, 241
    Down-Under Rib Eye with
        Ginger-Lime Hollandaise, 242
    Flame-Licked Beef Short Ribs
        with Bourbon Barbecue Sauce,
        258
    Greek Kofta Kabobs, 256
    Grill-Roasted Tenderloin with
        Bacon Mushroom Sauce, 232

Grilled Cuban Beef Medallions in Cumin-Lime Marinade, 233
Grilled Flank Steak with Smoked Garlic Cream Sauce, 245
Grilled Short Ribs with Mestiza, 257
Kansas City Hickory-Smoked Brisket Flats, 222
Kansas City Strip Steaks with Stir-Grilled Vegetables, 235
Korean Bulgogi with Kimchee, 253
Lime-Grilled Skirt Steak Fajitas with Charred Tomato Chipotle Salsa, 248
Mesquite-Grilled Sirloin with Shortcut Mexican Mole, 238
Montreal Smoked Meat Sandwiches, 396
Pecan-Grilled Porterhouse with Cambozola Butter, 243
Provençal Beef Daube with a Double Kiss of Smoke, 226
Rotisserie-Grilled Elk Tenderloin with Smoky Poblano Cream Sauce (variation), 300
Salt and Pepper Ranch Steaks with Stir-Grilled Onion Slivers, 251
Santa Maria Tri-Tip, 229
Smoked Brisket Soup, 224
Smoky Lamb You Can Eat with a Spoon (variation), 278
Sriracha, Soy and Sesame Hanger Steak, 250
Steakhouse Filets with Fried Onion Slivers and Béarnaise Sauce, 234
Stuffed Bison Meatloaf, 304
Tagliata Steak Salad with Shaved Parmesan, 237
Texas-Style Beef Brisket with Brazos Mop and Smoked Chile Barbecue Sauce, 220
Thai Marinated Beef in Lettuce Cups, 244
Vietnamese Grilled Beef Skewers in Pho, 254
bison
Mesquite-Grilled Bison Steak with Italian Parsley Pesto, 303
Pepper-Crusted Bison Tenderloin with Point Reyes Blue Cheese Sauce, 302
Prairie-Style Smoked Bison Chili, 305
Stuffed Bison Meatloaf, 304
Bistro Burger, 260
Black and Bleu Sirloin Served over Greens with Tarragon Vinaigrette, 236
Black Pepper–Rubbed Sirloin with Horseradish Butter, 239
Blackened Redfish, Grilled, 86

Blistered Bananas with Puerto Rican Brown Sugar Butter, 368
Bloody Mary Salsa, 59
Blue Cheese Coleslaw, Grilled, 324
Blue Ribbon Pulled Pork, 179
Blue Ribbon Rub, 34
Bourbon-Brined Pecan-Smoked Turkey, 170
Brandied Cherry Sauce, 52
Branding Iron Beef with Smoked Chile Drizzle, 240
Brazilian Grilled Avocados with Caipirinha Glaze, 315
breads, 374–75, 386–91. See also pitas; tortillas
Brie and Pepper–Stuffed Portobellos, 333
brines, 32, 37
Brisket Rub, 35
Brisket Soup, Smoked, 224
Brussels Sprouts, Stir-Grilled, 323
burgers, 204, 260, 283–84
Burnt-End Sandwiches with Caramelized Onions, 225
butters (compound), 32, 33, 53–54

Cabrito en Adobo, 306
Caesar Butter, 54
Caesar Dressing, 40
Caipirinha-Glazed Salmon, 88
Caipiroska-Glazed Tropical Fruit Skewers, 372
Cajun Spice Rub, 35
Calgary Stampede Spitted Beef Roast, 231
Calico Smoked Beans, 320
Carne Asada with Poblano and Onion Rajas, 246
Carolina Mustard Barbecue Sauce, 69
Catalan-Style Leg of Lamb with Mediterranean Vegetables and Romesco, 273
Catalan-Style Planked Peaches with Pork, Almond and Brandy Filling, 363
Cedar-Planked Fish with Mustard-Mayo Slather, 104
Champagne-Buttered Lobster Tails with Mâche Florets, 133
Championship BBQ Spareribs, 207
Char-Grilled Hearts of Romaine with Goat Cheese and Pinot Grigio Vinaigrette, 332
Char-Grilled Pineapple, 370
Char-Grilled Romaine, Bacon, Tomato and Blue Cheese Salad, 379
Char-Grilled Salmon Patties, 87
Char-Grilled Squid and Octopus Tapas in Peppered Sherry Marinade, 136
Charcoal-Grilled Ribs, Florentine-Style, 208
charcoal grills, 6–7, 8–10, 14

cheese
Barbecued Shrimp Quesadillas, 393
BBQ Poutine, 180
Brie and Pepper–Stuffed Portobellos, 333
Caesar Dressing, 40
Char-Grilled Hearts of Romaine with Goat Cheese and Pinot Grigio Vinaigrette, 332
Char-Grilled Romaine, Bacon, Tomato and Blue Cheese Salad, 379
Chicken Agliata, 146
Chicken Breast Stuffed with Brie and Black Olive Tapenade, 149
Flame-Seared Potato and Fennel Salad (variation), 381
Four-Herb Pesto, 43
Grill-Smoked Jalapeño Poppers, 338
Grilled Avocados, Tomatoes and Lemons (variation), 364
Grilled Blue Cheese Coleslaw, 324
Grilled Bread with Serrano Ham and Manchego Cheese, 386
Grilled Eggplant with Gruyère and Sun-Dried Tomatoes, 329
Grilled Endive and Escarole with Persian Feta and Walnut Vinaigrette, 331
Grilled Fava Beans in the Pod with Fresh Pecorino, 317
Grilled Figs with Warm Smoked Goat Cheese, 357
Grilled Haloumi, Artichoke and Olive Salad with Lemony Za'atar Vinaigrette, 380
Grilled Italian Garden Sandwiches, 395
Grilled Mango Boats with Strawberry-Cilantro Salsa and Blue Cheese, 369
Grilled Pears with Gorgonzola and Drizzled Honey, 355
Grilled Tomato Slices and Mozzarella, 343
Panini Caprese, 400
Pecan-Grilled Porterhouse with Cambozola Butter, 243
Pepper-Crusted Bison Tenderloin with Point Reyes Blue Cheese Sauce, 302
Planked Brie and Apricots with Ice Wine, 359
Planked Goat Cheese–Topped Beefsteak Tomatoes, 344
Red-Hot Grilled Wings with Cold Blue Cheese Dipping Sauce, 166
Rolled Stuffed Leg of Lamb, 272
Sizzling Pecorino Romano Chicken Thighs, 162

cheese (*continued*)
  Smoked Garlic Custards (variation), 330
  Smoked Italian Sausage and Tortellini Soup, 378
  Smoked Potato Casserole, 340
  Smoked Prosciutto-Wrapped Turkey Breast, 174
  Stuffed Bison Meatloaf, 304
  Stuffed Smoked Peppers, 337
  Toasted Croissants with Boursin, Grilled Tomatoes and Bacon, 394
  Vineyard Smoked Chicken with Lemon Tarragon Cream Sauce, 140
Cherry Barbecue Glaze, 52
Cherry-Smoked Crown Roast of Pork, 185
Cherry-Smoked Rib Roast with Horseradish Crème Fraîche, 230
chicken
  Argentinean Chicken Asado, 144
  Baja Fish Tacos with Napa Slaw and Guacamole (variation), 106
  Barbecue-Basted Wings, 168
  Chicken Agliata, 146
  Chicken Breast Stuffed with Brie and Black Olive Tapenade, 149
  Chicken Shawarma, 165
  Chinese-Style Barbecued Wings, 167
  Chopsticks Chicken with Gingered Teriyaki Glaze, 159
  Churrasco-Style Steak Sandwiches (variation), 398
  Grilled Bone-In Chicken Breasts with Lemon Caper Sauce, 148
  Grilled Chicken Paillards with Work of Art Drizzle, 152
  Grilled Miso Chicken, 164
  Indonesian Chicken with Chile-Ginger Sambal, 150
  Jamaican Jerk Chicken, 145
  Korean Bulgogi with Kimchee (variation), 253
  Lime-Grilled Skirt Steak Fajitas with Charred Tomato Chipotle Salsa (variation), 248
  Mesquite-Grilled Sirloin with Shortcut Mexican Mole (variation), 238
  Moroccan Chicken with Apricot and Pistachio Couscous, 163
  Peruvian Grilled Chicken Skewers in Mango Chipotle Mojo, 158
  Red-Hot Grilled Wings with Cold Blue Cheese Dipping Sauce, 166
  Sicilian Grill-Roasted Chicken, 139
  Sizzling Pecorino Romano Chicken Thighs, 162
  Smoky Chicken and Poblano Chowder, 141
  Stir-Grilled Chicken Fajitas, 157
  Stir-Grilled Chicken with Sugar Snap Peas and Grape Tomatoes, 155
  Stir-Grilled Peppadew Chicken in Baby Pineapple Halves, 156
  Tandoori Chicken on a Plank, 153
  Thai Chicken Skewers, 160
  Vietnamese Grilled Chicken Sandwiches with Carrot and Daikon Relish, 151
  Vineyard Smoked Chicken with Lemon Tarragon Cream Sauce, 140
  Waltzing Matilda Chicken with Lemon-Garlic Wine Sauce, 142
  Wasabi-Slathered Chicken on an Alder Plank, 154
  Yakitori-Style Chicken Skewers over Soba Noodles, 161
chickpeas. *See* beans and peas
Chilled Grilled Shrimp with Jalapeño Slaw and Bloody Mary Salsa, 124
Chinese-Style Barbecued Wings, 167
Chopsticks Chicken with Gingered Teriyaki Glaze, 159
Chuck Roast with a Kiss of Smoke, Old-Fashioned, 228
Churrasco-Style Steak Sandwiches, 398
Cilantro Butter, 53
Clams with Piquillo Pepper Butter, Wood-Grilled, 111
Clams with Warm Lime-Gingerroot Vinaigrette, Grilled, 110
coconut
  Coconut Chutney, 58
  Grilled Pineapple Rings with Pineapple Sorbet, 371
  Satay Sauce, 50
  Stir-Grilled Coconut Shrimp, 126
  Thai Chicken Skewers, 160
  Thai Marinated Beef in Lettuce Cups, 244
  Thai-Style Halibut on Lemongrass Skewers, 80
  Tropical Lamb Burgers with Fresh Mango Chutney, 283
Corn and Chorizo Casserole, Smoked, 327
Corn in the Husk with Hot Pepper Herb Butter, Smoked, 326
Corn in the Husk with Smoked Paprika Butter, Grilled, 328
Corncob-Smoked Shrimp with Classic Cocktail Sauce, 129
Country-Style Raspberry Ribs, 209
County Fair Barbecued Turkey Legs, 176
Cowboy Steaks with Two-Steppin' Rub, 241
Crab Cakes with Lemon Chive Butter, Wood-Grilled, 132
Creamy Mustard Sauce, 49
Cuban Barbecued Pork Shoulder, 184
Cuban Beef Medallions in Cumin-Lime Marinade, Grilled, 233
Cuban-Style Suckling Pig, 307

Dark Chocolate Crostini, Grilled, 392
deer. *See* venison
The Doctor Is In Easy Aïoli, 47
Double Pork Chops, Grilled, 201
Double-Smoked Ham, 212
Double-Smoked Ham and Wild Rice Soup, 213
Down-Under Fire-Kissed Lamb, 270
Down-Under Grilled Lamb Chops with Prickly Ash Rub, 266
Down-Under Rib Eye with Ginger-Lime Hollandaise, 242
drizzles, 32, 40–41
duck, 286
  Apricot Cognac–Glazed Whole Smoked Duck, 291
  Double-Smoked Ham and Wild Rice Soup (variation), 213
  Hickory-Grilled Rotisserie Duck with Rosemary Fennel Rub, 292
  Smoked Brisket Soup (variation), 224
  Szechuan Tea-Smoked Duck Breasts, 294
  Wood-Fired Duck Breasts with Blackberry Vinaigrette, 293

Eggplant with Gruyère and Sun-Dried Tomatoes, Grilled, 329
elk. *See* venison
Endive and Escarole with Persian Feta and Walnut Vinaigrette, Grilled, 331

Fava Beans in the Pod with Fresh Pecorino, Grilled, 317
Fennel Salad with Arugula and Goat Cheese, Grilled, 381
Figs with Warm Smoked Goat Cheese, Grilled, 357
Filipino Pork Steaks with Pineapple Tangerine Glaze, Wood-Grilled, 200
fish, 72, 73. *See also* salmon; shellfish
  Aussie Grilled Shellfish Salad with Lemon Dill Rémoulade (variation), 135
  Baja Fish Tacos with Napa Slaw and Guacamole, 106
  Cedar-Planked Fish with Mustard-Mayo Slather, 104
  Churrasco-Style Steak Sandwiches (variation), 398

Flame-Kissed Ahi Tuna Steaks with Wasabi Vinaigrette, 102

Grenada-Style Grouper with Lemon Pomegranate Beurre Blanc, 79

Grill-Roasted Monkfish with Roasted Red Pepper Shatta, 85

Grill-Smoked Trout with Cilantro Gremolata, 100

Grill-Smoked Whitefish with Horseradish Sauce, 103

Grilled Blackened Redfish, 86

Grilled Halibut with Red Pepper Aïoli, 81

Grilled Monkfish with Rouille, 84

Grilled Swordfish Steaks with Lemon Truffle Oil, 97

Grilled Swordfish with Sun-Dried Tomato Relish, 96

Harissa-Rubbed Snapper Skewers with Golden Papaya Salsa, 92

Herb-Rubbed Tilapia with Cucumber Relish, 98

Leaf-Wrapped Barramundi on the Barbie, 74

Lime-Grilled Skirt Steak Fajitas with Charred Tomato Chipotle Salsa (variation), 248

Macadamia-Buttered Mahi Mahi, 83

Mesquite-Grilled Snapper with Avocado Corn Salsa, 93

Sea Bass Tandoori-Style, 75

Smoked Trout with Lemon Caper Butter, 101

Stir-Grilled Sea Bass with Orange-Basil Cream Sauce, 76

Thai-Style Halibut on Lemongrass Skewers, 80

Vietnamese Grilled Fish and Cellophane Noodle Salad, 105

Wood-Grilled Trout, 99

Flame-Kissed Ahi Tuna Steaks with Wasabi Vinaigrette, 102

Flame-Licked Beef Short Ribs with Bourbon Barbecue Sauce, 258

Flame-Seared Potato and Fennel Salad, 381

Flank Steak with Smoked Garlic Cream Sauce, Grilled, 245

flavoring pastes, 32, 44–45

Foil-Wrapped Pepper Strips in Aji-li-Mojili, 336

Food Processor Aïoli, 46

Four-Herb Pesto, 43

Freeform Grilled Plum Pastries, 361

Fresh Herb Aïoli, 47

Fresh Herb Paste for Poultry, Pork and Fish, 44

frog legs, 286

fruit, 352–53

Aji-li-Mojili, 42

All-Purpose Lemon Brine, 37

Barbecued White Beans with Bacon and Pear, 318

Blistered Bananas with Puerto Rican Brown Sugar Butter, 368

Brandied Cherry Sauce, 52

Caipiroska-Glazed Tropical Fruit Skewers, 372

Catalan-Style Planked Peaches with Pork, Almond and Brandy Filling, 363

Char-Grilled Pineapple, 370

Cherry Barbecue Glaze, 52

Freeform Grilled Plum Pastries, 361

Golden Papaya Salsa, 61

Grilled Apple Rings with Cider Bourbon Cream Sauce, 354

Grilled Apricot and Plum Skewers with Almond Cream, 360

Grilled Avocados, Tomatoes and Lemons, 364

Grilled Figs with Warm Smoked Goat Cheese, 357

Grilled Grape Clusters with Brown Sugar Crème Fraîche, 356

Grilled Mango Boats with Strawberry-Cilantro Salsa and Blue Cheese, 369

Grilled Peaches with Buttery Amaretto Baste, 362

Grilled Pears with Gorgonzola and Drizzled Honey, 355

Grilled Pineapple Rings with Pineapple Sorbet, 371

Grilled Pound Cake with Amaretto Cream, Grilled Orange Slices and Crimson Jam, 366

Honey Orange Drizzle, 41

Island Grilled Papaya, 370

Lemon Tarragon Cream Sauce, 50

Nectar of the BBQ Gods, 65

Pineapple Mandarin Salsa, 61

Planked Brie and Apricots with Ice Wine, 359

Prosciutto-Wrapped Grilled Figs with Orange and Honey Drizzle, 358

Sicilian Grilled Blood Oranges with Honey Orange Drizzle, 365

Sour Orange Marinade, 38

Spicy Raspberry Jalapeño Barbecue Sauce, 66

Stir-Grilled Peppadew Chicken in Baby Pineapple Halves, 156

game, 286. See also bison; venison
Herbs de Provence Wood-Grilled Rabbit, 297

game birds, 286. See also duck
Grilled Grouse with Lemon-Caper Herb Broth and Shaved Parmigiano-Reggiano, 289

Grilled Spatchcocked Quail, 287

Pancetta-Wrapped Cornish Game Hens, 169

Persian Grilled Quail Breasts, 288

Prosciutto-Wrapped Smoked Pheasant Breasts, 290

Smoke-Roasted Goose, 296

gas grills, 7, 10–11, 14

gingerroot
Chopsticks Chicken with Gingered Teriyaki Glaze, 159

Down-Under Rib Eye with Ginger-Lime Hollandaise, 242

Grilled Clams with Warm Lime-Gingerroot Vinaigrette, 110

Indonesian Chicken with Chile-Ginger Sambal, 150

Maple Ginger Butterflied Pork Chops, 203

Sea Bass Tandoori-Style, 75

Smoked Sweet Potato Casserole with Ginger, Lime and Brown Sugar, 341

Soy-Ginger Marinade, 39

Tandoori Chicken on a Plank, 153

Vietnamese Grilled Beef Skewers in Pho, 254

glazes, 32, 52

Golden Papaya Salsa, 61

Graisse de Roti, 192

Grape Clusters with Brown Sugar Crème Fraîche, Grilled, 356

Greek Kofta Kabobs, 256

Greek-Style Spitted Lamb with Rosemary Garlic Baste, 310

Green Beans with Lemon Verbena Pesto, Stir-Grilled, 316

Grenada-Style Grouper with Lemon Pomegranate Beurre Blanc, 79

Grill-Roasted Lamb Loin with Mustard-Cornichon Butter Sauce, 267

Grill-Roasted Monkfish with Roasted Red Pepper Shatta, 85

Grill-Roasted Northwest King Salmon with Honey Soy Glaze, 90

Grill-Roasted Tenderloin with Bacon Mushroom Sauce, 232

Grill-Smoked Jalapeño Poppers, 338

Grill-Smoked Trout with Cilantro Gremolata, 100

Grill-Smoked Whitefish with Horseradish Sauce, 103

grilling, 6–13, 19–25

Grouse with Lemon-Caper Herb Broth and Shaved Parmigiano-Reggiano, Grilled, 289

Guacamole, Grilled, 62
Guava-Glazed Rotisserie Lamb, 269
Guava-Glazed Rotisserie Pork Loin Roast, 189

Halibut with Red Pepper Aïoli, Grilled, 81
Haloumi, Artichoke and Olive Salad with Lemony Za'atar Vinaigrette, Grilled, 380
ham. *See also* prosciutto
   Double-Smoked Ham, 212
   Double-Smoked Ham and Wild Rice Soup, 213
   Grilled Bread with Serrano Ham and Manchego Cheese, 386
   Grilled Ham Steaks with Bourbon Cider Glaze, 214
   Panini Caprese (variation), 400
   Rotisserie Cola-Mopped Ham with Cherry Barbecue Glaze, 211
   Stuffed Smoked Peppers (variation), 337
Harissa-Rubbed Snapper Skewers with Golden Papaya Salsa, 92
Hawaiian Pork Skewers with Pineapple Rum Glaze, 195
Hearts of Romaine with Goat Cheese and Pinot Grigio Vinaigrette, Char-Grilled, 332
Herb Butter–Basted Turkey on a Spit, 172
Herb-Rubbed Tilapia with Cucumber Relish, 98
Herbs de Provence Wood-Grilled Rabbit, 297
Hickory-Grilled Double Pork Chops with Fire-Roasted Tomato and Bacon Vinaigrette, 202
Hickory-Grilled Rotisserie Duck with Rosemary Fennel Rub, 292
Hickory Pork Burgers with Carolina Mustard Barbecue Sauce, 204
Honey-Basted Asian-Style Ribs, 210
Honey Orange Drizzle, 41
Hot Pepper Mint Butter, 53

Indonesian Chicken with Chile-Ginger Sambal, 150
Island Grilled Papaya, 370
Italian Garden Sandwiches, Grilled, 395
Italian Sausage and Tortellini Soup, Smoked, 378
Italian Sausage with Stir-Grilled Peppers, Onions and Potatoes, 215

Jamaican Jerk Chicken, 145
Jamaican Shrimp and Vegetable Salad, Stir-Grilled, 383

Kabuli Lamb Kebabs, 280
Kansas City Hickory-Smoked Brisket Flats, 222
Kansas City Strip Steaks with Stir-Grilled Vegetables, 235
Kansas City–Style Smoky Tomato Barbecue Sauce, 70
Kentucky-Style Black Barbecue Sauce, 67
Kentucky-Style Smoked Lamb, 277
kiss of smoke, 8–11
Kiss of Smoke Indoor/Outdoor Ribs, 205
Korean Bulgogi with Kimchee, 253

lamb and goat, 262
   Cabrito en Adobo, 306
   Catalan-Style Leg of Lamb with Mediterranean Vegetables and Romesco, 273
   Down-Under Fire-Kissed Lamb, 270
   Down-Under Grilled Lamb Chops with Prickly Ash Rub, 266
   Greek Kofta Kabobs (variation), 256
   Greek-Style Spitted Lamb with Rosemary Garlic Baste, 310
   Grill-Roasted Lamb Loin with Mustard-Cornichon Butter Sauce, 267
   Grilled Lamb and Nopales with Fire-Roasted Tomato Mint Salsa, 275
   Grilled Lamb Steak with Sauce Paloise, 268
   Guava-Glazed Rotisserie Lamb, 269
   Kabuli Lamb Kebabs, 280
   Kentucky-Style Smoked Lamb, 277
   Lavender-Smoked Rack of Lamb, 263
   Leg of Lamb Fattoush, 274
   Mesquite-Grilled Sirloin with Shortcut Mexican Mole (variation), 238
   Moroccan Lamb Burgers, 284
   Rolled Stuffed Leg of Lamb, 272
   Singaporean Lamb Satay, 276
   Smoky Lamb You Can Eat with a Spoon, 278
   Souvlaki with Grilled Pita, 281
   Spanish-Style Lamb Ribs Pimenton, 282
   Tequila-Chile Lamb Shanks, 271
   Tropical Lamb Burgers with Fresh Mango Chutney, 283
   Turkish Rack of Lamb with Charry Eggplant Tarragon Sauce, 264
Lavender-Smoked Rack of Lamb, 263

Leaf-Wrapped Barramundi on the Barbie, 74
Leaf-Wrapped Breadsticks, 386
leaf-wrapping, 21, 22
Leg of Lamb Fattoush, 274
Lemon Tarragon Cream Sauce, 50
Lime-Grilled Skirt Steak Fajitas with Charred Tomato Chipotle Salsa, 248

Macadamia-Buttered Mahi Mahi, 83
Mackerel with Savory Lemon Chutney, Grilled, 82
Mango Boats with Strawberry-Cilantro Salsa and Blue Cheese, Grilled, 369
Mango Chipotle Barbecue Sauce, 66
Maple Ginger Butterflied Pork Chops, 203
Maple Mustard Brine, 37
marinades, 32, 38–39
Martini Smoked Salmon, 89
Mayan-Style Pit Pork, 186
meatloaf, 204, 304
Memphis in May Whole Hog, 309
Memphis Piggy Sandwiches with Vinegar Coleslaw, 181
Mesquite-Grilled Bison Steak with Italian Parsley Pesto, 303
Mesquite-Grilled Sirloin with Shortcut Mexican Mole, 238
Mesquite-Grilled Snapper with Avocado Corn Salsa, 93
Miso Chicken, Grilled, 164
Monkfish with Roasted Red Pepper Shatta, Grill-Roasted, 85
Monkfish with Rouille, Grilled, 84
Montreal Smoked Meat Sandwiches, 396
Moroccan Chicken with Apricot and Pistachio Couscous, 163
Moroccan Lamb Burgers, 284
Mustard-Cornichon Butter Sauce, 56
Mustard-Grilled Pork Paillards with Tarragon Mustard Drizzle, 194
Mustard-Mayonnaise Slather, 45
Mustard Seed Sauce, 49

Naan with Coconut Chutney, 390
Nectar of the BBQ Gods, 65
noodles and pasta
   Grilled Shrimp and Pasta Soup with Roasted Red Peppers, 123
   Smoked Italian Sausage and Tortellini Soup, 378
   Vietnamese Grilled Beef Skewers in Pho, 254
   Vietnamese Grilled Fish and Cellophane Noodle Salad, 105
   Yakitori-Style Chicken Skewers over Soba Noodles, 161

North Carolina Pig Pickin', 308
Northwest King Salmon with Honey Soy Glaze, Grill-Roasted, 90
Not-So-Secret Sauce, 64

Oktoberfest Grillwurst, 216
Old-Fashioned Chuck Roast with a Kiss of Smoke, 228
olives
  Chicken Breast Stuffed with Brie and Black Olive Tapenade, 149
  Grilled Haloumi, Artichoke and Olive Salad with Lemony Za'atar Vinaigrette, 380
  Grilled Salmon Niçoise Salad, 384
  Panini Caprese (variation), 400
  Portuguese Country Bread with Green Olive Relish, 387
  Vegetable Kebabs with Za'atar, 349
  Vineyard Smoked Chicken with Lemon Tarragon Cream Sauce, 140
  Wok-Grilled Greek Taverna Olives, 334
Onions with Thyme-Scented Cream, Grilled, 335
Orange-Basted Shrimp on the Barbie, 122
Oysters with Pancetta and Basil Aïoli, Wood-Grilled, 113

pancetta. See also bacon
  Grilled Figs with Warm Smoked Goat Cheese, 357
  Pancetta-Wrapped Cornish Game Hens, 169
  Sea Scallops Wrapped in Radicchio and Prosciutto (variation), 114
  Wood-Grilled Oysters with Pancetta and Basil Aïoli, 113
  Wood-Grilled Trout (variation), 99
Panini Caprese, 400
Panzanella, Grilled, 382
pasta. See noodles and pasta
Peaches with Buttery Amaretto Baste, Grilled, 362
Pears with Gorgonzola and Drizzled Honey, Grilled, 355
Pecan-Grilled Porterhouse with Cambozola Butter, 243
Peppadew Chicken in Baby Pineapple Halves, Stir-Grilled, 156
Pepper-Crusted Bison Tenderloin with Point Reyes Blue Cheese Sauce, 302
Persian Grilled Quail Breasts, 288
Peruvian Grilled Chicken Skewers in Mango Chipotle Mojo, 158

pesto, 42–43, 60
Pesto Aïoli, 47
Pineapple Mandarin Salsa, 61
Pineapple Rings with Pineapple Sorbet, Grilled, 371
Pistachio-Buttered Scallops on a Plank, 117
pitas
  Chicken Shawarma, 165
  Greek Kofta Kabobs, 256
  Grilled Haloumi, Artichoke and Olive Salad with Lemony Za'atar Vinaigrette, 380
  Kabuli Lamb Kebabs, 280
  Leg of Lamb Fattoush, 274
  Moroccan Lamb Burgers, 284
  Souvlaki with Grilled Pita, 281
  Vegetable Kebabs with Za'atar, 349
plank-cooking, 23–24
Planked and Pepper-Crusted Maple-Glazed Salmon, 91
Planked Brie and Apricots with Ice Wine, 359
Planked Goat Cheese–Topped Beefsteak Tomatoes, 344
Planked Shrimp with Garlic Chive Butter and Ciabatta, 128
pork, 178, 286. See also bacon; ham; sausage
  Apple-Smoked Roasted Pork Loin with Apple Chutney Stuffing, 190
  Aussie Paperbark Pork with Lemon Myrtle Chutney, 198
  BBQ Poutine, 180
  Blue Ribbon Pulled Pork, 179
  Catalan-Style Planked Peaches with Pork, Almond and Brandy Filling, 363
  Championship BBQ Spareribs, 207
  Charcoal-Grilled Ribs, Florentine-Style, 208
  Cherry-Smoked Crown Roast of Pork, 185
  Country-Style Raspberry Ribs, 209
  Cuban Barbecued Pork Shoulder, 184
  Cuban-Style Suckling Pig, 307
  Graisse de Roti, 192
  Grilled Double Pork Chops, 201
  Grilled Pork and Mango Skewers with Mango Chipotle Barbecue Sauce, 199
  Guava-Glazed Rotisserie Pork Loin Roast, 189
  Hawaiian Pork Skewers with Pineapple Rum Glaze, 195
  Hickory-Grilled Double Pork Chops with Fire-Roasted Tomato and Bacon Vinaigrette, 202

Hickory Pork Burgers with Carolina Mustard Barbecue Sauce, 204
Honey-Basted Asian-Style Ribs, 210
Kiss of Smoke Indoor/Outdoor Ribs, 205
Korean Bulgogi with Kimchee (variation), 253
Lime-Grilled Skirt Steak Fajitas with Charred Tomato Chipotle Salsa (variation), 248
Maple Ginger Butterflied Pork Chops, 203
Mayan-Style Pit Pork, 186
Memphis in May Whole Hog, 309
Memphis Piggy Sandwiches with Vinegar Coleslaw, 181
Mesquite-Grilled Sirloin with Shortcut Mexican Mole (variation), 238
Mustard-Grilled Pork Paillards with Tarragon Mustard Drizzle, 194
North Carolina Pig Pickin', 308
Raspberry-Glazed Pork Tenderloin with Spicy Raspberry Jalapeño Barbecue Sauce, 196
Sesame-Soy Marinated Pork Tenderloin with Asian Dipping Sauce, 197
Smoked Pork and Black-Eyed Pea Gumbo for a Crowd, 182
Smoky Lamb You Can Eat with a Spoon (variation), 278
Spit-Roasted Pork Loin in Maple Mustard Brine, 188
Sweet, Smoky, Sticky Baby Back Ribs, 206
Tuscan Rolled Pork Loin Stuffed with Rosemary and Garlic, 193
Wood-Grilled Filipino Pork Steaks with Pineapple Tangerine Glaze, 200
Portuguese Country Bread with Green Olive Relish, 387
Potato and Fennel Salad, Flame-Seared, 381
Potato Casserole, Smoked, 340
poultry, 138. See also chicken; duck; game birds; turkey
  Smoke-Roasted Goose, 296
Pound Cake with Amaretto Cream, Grilled Orange Slices and Crimson Jam, Grilled, 366
Prairie-Style Smoked Bison Chili, 305
prosciutto. See also ham
  Grilled Figs with Warm Smoked Goat Cheese, 357
  Prosciutto-Wrapped Grilled Figs with Orange and Honey Drizzle, 358

prosciutto (*continued*)
  Prosciutto-Wrapped Smoked Pheasant Breasts, 290
  Scallops alla Piastra with Lemony Prosciutto Crumb Topping, 118
  Sea Scallops Wrapped in Radicchio and Prosciutto, 114
  Smoke-Roasted Goose (variation), 296
  Smoked Prosciutto-Wrapped Turkey Breast, 174
Provençal Beef Daube with a Double Kiss of Smoke, 226
Provençal Flavoring Paste, 45
Provençal Tomatoes on the Vine, 345
Pulled Pork, Blue Ribbon, 179
Pumpkin Seed Salsa, 60

Raspberry-Glazed Pork Tenderloin with Spicy Raspberry Jalapeño Barbecue Sauce, 196
Red-Hot Grilled Wings with Cold Blue Cheese Dipping Sauce, 166
Red-Hot Rub, 36
Red Pepper Piada, Grilled, 391
rice and wild rice
  Double-Smoked Ham and Wild Rice Soup, 213
  Stir-Grilled Coconut Shrimp, 126
  Wok-Grilled Shrimp with Sugar Snap Peas, Teardrop Tomatoes and Red Onion Slivers, 127
Roasted Red Pepper Aïoli, 47
Rolled Stuffed Leg of Lamb, 272
Romesco Sauce, 51
Rotisserie Cola-Mopped Ham with Cherry Barbecue Glaze, 211
rotisserie cooking, 24–25
Rotisserie-Grilled Elk Tenderloin with Smoky Poblano Cream Sauce, 300
rubs, 32, 34–36

salad dressings, 39–40
salads, 135, 237, 379–85
salmon
  Caipirinha-Glazed Salmon, 88
  Char-Grilled Salmon Patties, 87
  Grill-Roasted Northwest King Salmon with Honey Soy Glaze, 90
  Grilled Salmon Niçoise Salad, 384
  Martini Smoked Salmon, 89
  Planked and Pepper-Crusted Maple-Glazed Salmon, 91
  Stir-Grilled Jamaican Shrimp and Vegetable Salad (variation), 383
salsas, 59–61, 83, 97
Salt and Pepper Ranch Steaks with Stir-Grilled Onion Slivers, 251

sandwiches, 151, 181, 225, 293, 392–400. *See also* burgers
Santa Maria Tri-Tip, 229
Satay Sauce, 50
Sauce Paloise, 55
sauces, 32, 49–52, 54–57, 95
  barbecue, 62–70
sausage
  Churrasco-Style Steak Sandwiches (variation), 398
  Italian Sausage with Stir-Grilled Peppers, Onions and Potatoes, 215
  Oktoberfest Grillwurst, 216
  Panini Caprese (variation), 400
  Smoked Corn and Chorizo Casserole, 327
  Smoked Italian Sausage and Tortellini Soup, 378
scallops
  Pistachio-Buttered Scallops on a Plank, 117
  Scallops alla Piastra with Lemony Prosciutto Crumb Topping, 118
  Sea Scallops Wrapped in Radicchio and Prosciutto, 114
  Smoked Scallops with Smoked Chile Butter Drizzle, 119
  Stir-Grilled Jamaican Shrimp and Vegetable Salad (variation), 383
  Stir-Grilled Scallops with Snow Peas and Red Pepper Strips, 116
  Wasabi Grilled Scallops with Japanese Beans, 115
Sea Bass Tandoori-Style, 75
Sea Bass with Orange-Basil Cream Sauce, Stir-Grilled, 76
Sea Scallops Wrapped in Radicchio and Prosciutto, 114
Seared Elk Strip Loin with Huckleberry Port Wine Sauce, 299
Sesame-Soy Marinated Pork Tenderloin with Asian Dipping Sauce, 197
Shallots with Tarragon Butter, Stir-Grilled, 342
shellfish, 72, 73, 108, 109. *See also* scallops; shrimp
  Aussie Grilled Shellfish Salad with Lemon Dill Rémoulade, 135
  Champagne-Buttered Lobster Tails with Mâche Florets, 133
  Char-Grilled Squid and Octopus Tapas in Peppered Sherry Marinade, 136
  Grilled Clams with Warm Lime-Gingerroot Vinaigrette, 110
  Grilled Spot Prawns in Garlic-Wine Marinade with Zesty Peanut Sauce, 130

Grilled Yabbies with Cilantro Lime Sauce, 120
Korean Bulgogi with Kimchee (variation), 253
Lime-Grilled Skirt Steak Fajitas with Charred Tomato Chipotle Salsa (variation), 248
Venetian Grilled Lobster, 134
Warm Smoked Mussels with Curried Onion Butter, 112
Wood-Grilled Clams with Piquillo Pepper Butter, 111
Wood-Grilled Crab Cakes with Lemon Chive Butter, 132
Wood-Grilled Oysters with Pancetta and Basil Aïoli, 113
Sherry Marinade, 38
Short Ribs with Mestiza, Grilled, 257
shrimp
  Aussie Grilled Shellfish Salad with Lemon Dill Rémoulade, 135
  Balinese Shrimp Satay on Lemongrass Stalks, 121
  Barbecued Shrimp Quesadillas, 393
  Chilled Grilled Shrimp with Jalapeño Slaw and Bloody Mary Salsa, 124
  Churrasco-Style Steak Sandwiches (variation), 398
  Corncob-Smoked Shrimp with Classic Cocktail Sauce, 129
  Grilled Shrimp and Pasta Soup with Roasted Red Peppers, 123
  Grilled Spot Prawns in Garlic-Wine Marinade with Zesty Peanut Sauce, 130
  Grilled Yabbies with Cilantro Lime Sauce, 120
  Korean Bulgogi with Kimchee (variation), 253
  Orange-Basted Shrimp on the Barbie, 122
  Planked Shrimp with Garlic Chive Butter and Ciabatta, 128
  Portuguese Country Bread with Green Olive Relish (variation), 387
  Stir-Grilled Coconut Shrimp, 126
  Stir-Grilled Jamaican Shrimp and Vegetable Salad, 383
  Stuffed Smoked Peppers (variation), 337
  Wok-Grilled Shrimp with Sugar Snap Peas, Teardrop Tomatoes and Red Onion Slivers, 127
Sicilian Grill-Roasted Chicken, 139
Sicilian Grill-Roasted Tomatoes, 346
Sicilian Grilled Blood Oranges with Honey Orange Drizzle, 365

Singaporean Lamb Satay, 276
Sizzling Pecorino Romano Chicken
    Thighs, 162
slathers, 32, 45
Smoke-Roasted Goose, 296
smokers, bullet, 15
smoking, 13–20, 21, 26–27
Smoky Chicken and Poblano
    Chowder, 141
Smoky Lamb You Can Eat with a
    Spoon, 278
soups, 123, 141, 213, 224, 376–78
Sour Orange Marinade, 38
Souvlaki with Grilled Pita, 281
Soy-Ginger Marinade, 39
Spanish-Style Lamb Ribs Pimenton,
    282
Spatchcocked Quail, Grilled, 287
Spicy Raspberry Jalapeño Barbecue
    Sauce, 66
Spit-Roasted Pork Loin in Maple
    Mustard Brine, 188
Spot Prawns in Garlic-Wine
    Marinade with Zesty Peanut
    Sauce, Grilled, 130
Squid and Octopus Tapas in
    Peppered Sherry Marinade,
    Char-Grilled, 136
Sriracha, Soy and Sesame Hanger
    Steak, 250
Steakhouse Filets with Fried Onion
    Slivers and Béarnaise Sauce,
    234
Stir-Grilled Baby Beets with Green
    Onions and Lemon-Herb
    Butter, 321
Stir-Grilled Brussels Sprouts, 323
Stir-Grilled Chicken Fajitas, 157
Stir-Grilled Chicken with Sugar
    Snap Peas and Grape
    Tomatoes, 155
Stir-Grilled Coconut Shrimp, 126
Stir-Grilled Green Beans with
    Lemon Verbena Pesto, 316
Stir-Grilled Jamaican Shrimp and
    Vegetable Salad, 383
Stir-Grilled Minted Baby Carrots,
    325
Stir-Grilled Peppadew Chicken in
    Baby Pineapple Halves, 156
Stir-Grilled Scallops with Snow
    Peas and Red Pepper Strips,
    116
Stir-Grilled Sea Bass with Orange-
    Basil Cream Sauce, 76
Stir-Grilled Shallots with Tarragon
    Butter, 342
Stuffed Bison Meatloaf, 304
Stuffed Smoked Peppers, 337
Sturgeon with Charred Chile Salsa,
    Grilled, 94
Sugar & Spice Rub, 36
Sun-Dried Tomato Aïoli, 47
Sun-Dried Tomato Pesto, 42

Sweet, Smoky, Sticky Baby Back
    Ribs, 206
Sweet Potato Casserole with
    Ginger, Lime and Brown Sugar,
    Smoked, 341
Swordfish Steaks with Lemon
    Truffle Oil, Grilled, 97
Swordfish with Sun-Dried Tomato
    Relish, Grilled, 96
Szechuan Tea-Smoked Duck
    Breasts, 294

Tagliata Steak Salad with Shaved
    Parmesan, 237
Tandoori Chicken on a Plank, 153
Tapas-Style Grilled Fingerlings
    with Portuguese Aïoli, 339
Tarragon Vinegar Grilled Turkey
    Breast, 173
Tequila-Chile Lamb Shanks, 271
Teriyaki Vegetable Skewers, 350
Texas Cowpoke Pintos with
    Jalapeño Peppers, 319
Texas-Style Beef Brisket with
    Brazos Mop and Smoked Chile
    Barbecue Sauce, 220
Thai Chicken Skewers, 160
Thai Marinated Beef in Lettuce
    Cups, 244
Thai-Style Halibut on Lemongrass
    Skewers, 80
Toasted Croissants with Boursin,
    Grilled Tomatoes and Bacon,
    394
tomatoes
    Argentinean Grilled Vegetable
        Platter with Chimichurri, 348
    Bloody Mary Salsa, 59
    Char-Grilled Romaine, Bacon,
        Tomato and Blue Cheese Salad,
        379
    The Doctor Is In Easy Aïoli
        (variation), 47
    Grilled Avocados, Tomatoes and
        Lemons, 364
    Grilled Eggplant with Gruyère
        and Sun-Dried Tomatoes, 329
    Grilled Italian Garden
        Sandwiches, 395
    Grilled Lamb and Nopales with
        Fire-Roasted Tomato Mint
        Salsa, 275
    Grilled Panzanella, 382
    Grilled Short Ribs with Mestiza, 257
    Grilled Swordfish with Sun-Dried
        Tomato Relish, 96
    Grilled Tomato Slices and
        Mozzarella, 343
    Grilled Vegetable Gazpacho with
        Assorted Condiments, 376
    Hickory-Grilled Double Pork
        Chops with Fire-Roasted
        Tomato and Bacon Vinaigrette,
        202

Leg of Lamb Fattoush, 274
Lime-Grilled Skirt Steak Fajitas
    with Charred Tomato Chipotle
    Salsa, 248
Panini Caprese, 400
Planked Goat Cheese–Topped
    Beefsteak Tomatoes, 344
Provençal Tomatoes on the
    Vine, 345
Sicilian Grill-Roasted Tomatoes,
    346
Smoked Tomato and Basil
    Bisque, 377
Stir-Grilled Chicken with
    Sugar Snap Peas and Grape
    Tomatoes, 155
Sun-Dried Tomato Pesto, 42
Texas Cowpoke Pintos with
    Jalapeño Peppers, 319
Toasted Croissants with Boursin,
    Grilled Tomatoes and Bacon,
    394
Wok-Grilled Shrimp with
    Sugar Snap Peas, Teardrop
    Tomatoes and Red Onion
    Slivers, 127
tortillas
    Baja Fish Tacos with Napa Slaw
        and Guacamole, 106
    Barbecued Shrimp Quesadillas,
        393
    Carne Asada with Poblano and
        Onion Rajas, 246
    Lime-Grilled Skirt Steak Fajitas
        with Charred Tomato Chipotle
        Salsa, 248
    Stir-Grilled Chicken Fajitas, 157
Tropical Lamb Burgers with Fresh
    Mango Chutney, 283
Trout with Cilantro Gremolata,
    Grill-Smoked, 100
Trout with Lemon Caper Butter,
    Smoked, 101
Trout, Wood-Grilled, 99
turkey
    Bourbon-Brined Pecan-Smoked
        Turkey, 170
    County Fair Barbecued Turkey
        Legs, 176
    Grilled Turkey Steak Piccata,
        175
    Herb Butter–Basted Turkey on
        a Spit, 172
    Smoked Prosciutto-Wrapped
        Turkey Breast, 174
    Tarragon Vinegar Grilled Turkey
        Breast, 173
Turkish Rack of Lamb with
    Charry Eggplant Tarragon
    Sauce, 264
Tuscan Rolled Pork Loin Stuffed
    with Rosemary and Garlic,
    193
Tzatziki, 57

Veal Chops with Garlic Rosemary Butter, Rosemary-Grilled, 259
vegetables, 312. *See also* beans and peas; tomatoes
Argentinean Grilled Vegetable Platter with Chimichurri, 348
Bloody Mary Salsa, 59
Brazilian Grilled Avocados with Caipirinha Glaze, 315
Brie and Pepper–Stuffed Portobellos, 333
Char-Grilled Hearts of Romaine with Goat Cheese and Pinot Grigio Vinaigrette, 332
Char-Grilled Romaine, Bacon, Tomato and Blue Cheese Salad, 379
The Doctor Is In Easy Aïoli, 47
Flame-Seared Potato and Fennel Salad, 381
Foil-Wrapped Pepper Strips in Aji-li-Mojili, 336
Food Processor Aïoli, 46
Grill-Smoked Jalapeño Poppers, 338
Grilled Asparagus with Asian Dipping Sauce, 314
Grilled Avocados, Tomatoes and Lemons, 364
Grilled Baby Artichokes with Balsamic Olive Oil Drizzle, 313
Grilled Baby Bok Choy with Gingered Soy Sauce, 322
Grilled Blue Cheese Coleslaw, 324
Grilled Corn in the Husk with Smoked Paprika Butter, 328
Grilled Eggplant with Gruyère and Sun-Dried Tomatoes, 329
Grilled Fava Beans in the Pod with Fresh Pecorino, 317
Grilled Guacamole, 62
Grilled Haloumi, Artichoke and Olive Salad with Lemony Za'atar Vinaigrette, 380
Grilled Italian Garden Sandwiches, 395
Grilled Onions with Thyme-Scented Cream, 335
Grilled Panzanella, 382

Grilled Vegetable Gazpacho with Assorted Condiments, 376
Leaf-Wrapped Breadsticks, 386
Mustard-Mayonnaise Slather (variation), 45
Pumpkin Seed Salsa, 60
Romesco Sauce, 51
Sherry Marinade, 38
Smoked Chile Barbecue Sauce, 63
Smoked Corn and Chorizo Casserole, 327
Smoked Corn in the Husk with Hot Pepper Herb Butter, 326
Smoked Garlic Aïoli Platter of Roasted Root Vegetables, 347
Smoked Garlic Custards, 330
Smoked Potato Casserole, 340
Smoked Sweet Potato Casserole with Ginger, Lime and Brown Sugar, 341
Spicy Raspberry Jalapeño Barbecue Sauce, 66
Stir-Grilled Baby Beets with Green Onions and Lemon-Herb Butter, 321
Stir-Grilled Brussels Sprouts, 323
Stir-Grilled Green Beans with Lemon Verbena Pesto, 316
Stir-Grilled Minted Baby Carrots, 325
Stuffed Smoked Peppers, 337
Sun-Dried Tomato Pesto, 42
Tapas-Style Grilled Fingerlings with Portuguese Aïoli, 339
Teriyaki Vegetable Skewers, 350
Tzatziki, 57
Vegetable Kebabs with Za'atar, 349
White Truffle Aïoli, 48
Venetian Grilled Lobster, 134
venison
Rotisserie-Grilled Elk Tenderloin with Smoky Poblano Cream Sauce, 300
Seared Elk Strip Loin with Huckleberry Port Wine Sauce, 299
Venison Steaks with Blackberry Brandy Beurre Blanc, 298

Vietnamese Grilled Beef Skewers in Pho, 254
Vietnamese Grilled Chicken Sandwiches with Carrot and Daikon Relish, 151
Vietnamese Grilled Fish and Cellophane Noodle Salad, 105
Vinegar Barbecue Sauce, 62
Vineyard Smoked Chicken with Lemon Tarragon Cream Sauce, 140

Walnut Vinaigrette, 40
Waltzing Matilda Chicken with Lemon-Garlic Wine Sauce, 142
Warm Smoked Mussels with Curried Onion Butter, 112
Wasabi Grilled Scallops with Japanese Beans, 115
Wasabi-Slathered Chicken on an Alder Plank, 154
Wasabi Vinaigrette, 39
Whitefish with Horseradish Sauce, Grill-Smoked, 103
White Truffle Aïoli, 48
wild rice. *See* rice and wild rice
Wok-Grilled Greek Taverna Olives, 334
Wok-Grilled Shrimp with Sugar Snap Peas, Teardrop Tomatoes and Red Onion Slivers, 127
Wood-Fired Duck Breasts with Blackberry Vinaigrette, 293
Wood-Grilled Clams with Piquillo Pepper Butter, 111
Wood-Grilled Crab Cakes with Lemon Chive Butter, 132
Wood-Grilled Filipino Pork Steaks with Pineapple Tangerine Glaze, 200
Wood-Grilled Oysters with Pancetta and Basil Aïoli, 113
Wood-Grilled Trout, 99
Work of Art Drizzle, 41

Yabbies with Cilantro Lime Sauce, Grilled, 120
Yakitori-Style Chicken Skewers over Soba Noodles, 161

	AVERAGE HOUSEHOLD SPENDING	BEST CUSTOMERS (index)	BIGGEST CUSTOMERS (market share)
HOUSEHOLD INCOME			
Average household	**$26.49**	**100**	**100.0%**
Under $20,000	17.39	66	14.3
$20,000 to $39,999	21.53	81	18.6
$40,000 to $49,999	22.51	85	8.0
$50,000 to $69,999	24.85	94	13.5
$70,000 to $79,999	28.66	108	6.5
$80,000 to $99,999	38.27	144	12.0
$100,000 or more	42.30	160	27.4
HOUSEHOLD TYPE			
Average household	**26.49**	**100**	**100.0**
Married couples	34.38	130	64.0
Married couples, no children	25.62	97	20.5
Married couples, with children	41.19	155	36.2
Oldest child under age 6	28.23	107	4.6
Oldest child aged 6 to 17	44.57	168	19.8
Oldest child aged 18 or older	42.78	161	11.7
Single parent with child under age 18	24.57	93	5.5
Single person	13.08	49	14.5
RACE AND HISPANIC ORIGIN			
Average household	**26.49**	**100**	**100.0**
Asian	14.69	55	2.4
Black	24.11	91	11.1
Hispanic	24.22	91	11.1
Non-Hispanic white and other	27.23	103	77.9
REGION			
Average household	**26.49**	**100**	**100.0**
Northeast	30.46	115	21.1
Midwest	29.71	112	25.0
South	21.91	83	30.4
West	27.53	104	23.5
EDUCATION			
Average household	**26.49**	**100**	**100.0**
Less than high school graduate	23.80	90	12.8
High school graduate	25.88	98	24.9
Some college	25.07	95	19.9
Associate's degree	26.51	100	9.5
Bachelor's degree or more	29.26	110	32.8
Bachelor's degree	25.51	96	18.2
Master's, professional, doctoral degree	36.64	138	15.0

Note: Market shares may not sum to 100.0 because of rounding and missing categories by household type. "Asian" and "black" include Hispanics and non-Hispanics who identify themselves as being of the respective race alone. "Hispanic" includes people of any race who identify themselves as Hispanic. "Other" includes people who identify themselves as non-Hispanic and as Alaska Native, American Indian, Asian (who are also included in the "Asian" row), or Native Hawaiian or other Pacific Islander as well as non-Hispanics reporting more than one race.

Source: Calculations by New Strategist based on the Bureau of Labor Statistics' 2010 Consumer Expenditure Survey

Lettuce

Best customers: **Householders aged 35 to 54**
Married couples with school-aged or older children at home
Asians
Households in the Northeast

Customer trends: **Average household spending on lettuce may stabilize as the baby boom exits the best customer lifestage and household size shrinks.**

The best customers of lettuce are the largest households. Married couples with school-aged or older children at home spend 42 to 49 percent more than the average household on lettuce. Householders aged 35 to 54, most with children, spend 17 to 21 percent more than the average household on this item. Asians spend 38 percent more than average on lettuce. In the Northeast, household spending on lettuce is 24 percent above average.

Average household spending on lettuce climbed 14 percent between 2000 and 2010, after adjusting for inflation. One factor behind the growth was the attempt to eat a healthier diet and the convenience of bagged lettuce available in the grocery store. Average household spending on lettuce may stabilize as the baby boom exits the best customer lifestage and household size shrinks.

Table 9.49 Lettuce

Total household spending $3,641,687,490.00
Average household spends 30.07

	AVERAGE HOUSEHOLD SPENDING	BEST CUSTOMERS (index)	BIGGEST CUSTOMERS (market share)
AGE OF HOUSEHOLDER			
Average household	**$30.07**	**100**	**100.0%**
Under age 25	18.40	61	4.1
Aged 25 to 34	27.73	92	15.4
Aged 35 to 44	35.32	117	21.3
Aged 45 to 54	36.26	121	24.9
Aged 55 to 64	30.00	100	17.6
Aged 65 to 74	28.82	96	10.3
Aged 75 or older	20.21	67	6.4

	AVERAGE HOUSEHOLD SPENDING	BEST CUSTOMERS (index)	BIGGEST CUSTOMERS (market share)
HOUSEHOLD INCOME			
Average household	**$30.07**	**100**	**100.0%**
Under $20,000	18.39	61	13.3
$20,000 to $39,999	26.11	87	19.9
$40,000 to $49,999	26.61	88	8.4
$50,000 to $69,999	30.71	102	14.6
$70,000 to $79,999	29.85	99	5.9
$80,000 to $99,999	33.58	112	9.3
$100,000 or more	50.29	167	28.7
HOUSEHOLD TYPE			
Average household	**30.07**	**100**	**100.0**
Married couples	37.92	126	62.2
Married couples, no children	32.54	108	23.0
Married couples, with children	41.60	138	32.2
Oldest child under age 6	32.22	107	4.6
Oldest child aged 6 to 17	42.63	142	16.7
Oldest child aged 18 or older	44.87	149	10.8
Single parent with child under age 18	21.86	73	4.3
Single person	18.41	61	17.9
RACE AND HISPANIC ORIGIN			
Average household	**30.07**	**100**	**100.0**
Asian	41.40	138	5.9
Black	23.95	80	9.7
Hispanic	28.95	96	11.7
Non-Hispanic white and other	31.23	104	78.7
REGION			
Average household	**30.07**	**100**	**100.0**
Northeast	37.14	124	22.7
Midwest	32.02	106	23.7
South	24.48	81	29.9
West	31.50	105	23.7
EDUCATION			
Average household	**30.07**	**100**	**100.0**
Less than high school graduate	25.95	86	12.3
High school graduate	25.23	84	21.4
Some college	24.82	83	17.4
Associate's degree	32.75	109	10.3
Bachelor's degree or more	39.07	130	38.6
Bachelor's degree	36.85	123	23.1
Master's, professional, doctoral degree	43.44	144	15.6

Note: Market shares may not sum to 100.0 because of rounding and missing categories by household type. "Asian" and "black" include Hispanics and non-Hispanics who identify themselves as being of the respective race alone. "Hispanic" includes people of any race who identify themselves as Hispanic. "Other" includes people who identify themselves as non-Hispanic and as Alaska Native, American Indian, Asian (who are also included in the "Asian" row), or Native Hawaiian or other Pacific Islander as well as non-Hispanics reporting more than one race.

Source: Calculations by New Strategist based on the Bureau of Labor Statistics' 2010 Consumer Expenditure Survey

Lunch Meats (Cold Cuts)

Best customers:	Householders aged 35 to 54
	Married couples with school-aged or older children at home
	Households in the Northeast
Customer trends:	Average household spending on lunch meats will continue to decline as more boomers become empty-nesters.

The best customers of lunch meats are the largest households. Married couples with school-aged or older children at home spend 54 to 66 percent more than the average household on this item. Householders aged 35 to 54, most with children, spend 17 to 27 percent more than average on lunch meats. Households in the Northeast outspend the average by 18 percent.

Average household spending on lunch meats fell 5 percent between 2000 and 2006, after adjusting for inflation, and has remained stable since then. Behind the earlier decline was the substitution of fast food for brown-bag lunches. Average household spending on lunch meats should resume its decline as more boomers become empty-nesters.

Table 9.50 Lunch meats (cold cuts)

Total household spending	$9,906,552,600.00
Average household spends	81.80

	AVERAGE HOUSEHOLD SPENDING	BEST CUSTOMERS (index)	BIGGEST CUSTOMERS (market share)
AGE OF HOUSEHOLDER			
Average household	**$81.80**	**100**	**100.0%**
Under age 25	45.64	56	3.7
Aged 25 to 34	71.91	88	14.6
Aged 35 to 44	95.89	117	21.2
Aged 45 to 54	103.90	127	26.3
Aged 55 to 64	83.87	103	18.1
Aged 65 to 74	75.59	92	9.9
Aged 75 or older	51.86	63	6.0

	AVERAGE HOUSEHOLD SPENDING	BEST CUSTOMERS (index)	BIGGEST CUSTOMERS (market share)
HOUSEHOLD INCOME			
Average household	**$81.80**	**100**	**100.0%**
Under $20,000	52.06	64	13.9
$20,000 to $39,999	63.65	78	17.8
$40,000 to $49,999	69.92	85	8.1
$50,000 to $69,999	88.70	108	15.6
$70,000 to $79,999	108.65	133	8.0
$80,000 to $99,999	101.12	124	10.3
$100,000 or more	126.74	155	26.6
HOUSEHOLD TYPE			
Average household	**81.80**	**100**	**100.0**
Married couples	104.37	128	62.9
Married couples, no children	80.44	98	20.9
Married couples, with children	122.10	149	34.7
Oldest child under age 6	84.27	103	4.4
Oldest child aged 6 to 17	126.03	154	18.1
Oldest child aged 18 or older	135.60	166	12.0
Single parent with child under age 18	79.54	97	5.7
Single person	44.10	54	15.8
RACE AND HISPANIC ORIGIN			
Average household	**81.80**	**100**	**100.0**
Asian	43.49	53	2.3
Black	64.57	79	9.7
Hispanic	76.27	93	11.4
Non-Hispanic white and other	85.40	104	79.2
REGION			
Average household	**81.80**	**100**	**100.0**
Northeast	96.17	118	21.6
Midwest	84.84	104	23.1
South	74.63	91	33.5
West	78.76	96	21.8
EDUCATION			
Average household	**81.80**	**100**	**100.0**
Less than high school graduate	70.99	87	12.4
High school graduate	76.75	94	24.0
Some college	80.37	98	20.7
Associate's degree	91.15	111	10.5
Bachelor's degree or more	88.94	109	32.3
Bachelor's degree	86.50	106	20.0
Master's, professional, doctoral degree	93.75	115	12.4

Note: Market shares may not sum to 100.0 because of rounding and missing categories by household type. "Asian" and "black" include Hispanics and non-Hispanics who identify themselves as being of the respective race alone. "Hispanic" includes people of any race who identify themselves as Hispanic. "Other" includes people who identify themselves as non-Hispanic and as Alaska Native, American Indian, Asian (who are also included in the "Asian" row), or Native Hawaiian or other Pacific Islander as well as non-Hispanics reporting more than one race.

Source: Calculations by New Strategist based on the Bureau of Labor Statistics' 2010 Consumer Expenditure Survey

Margarine

Best customers: **Householders aged 35 to 74**
                              Married couples without children at home
                              Married couples with school-aged or older children at home

Customer trends: **Average household spending on margarine in the coming years may depend more**
                             on marketing than demographics.

Margarine's fortunes were waning as the reputation of butter improved. In 2000, the average household spent 68 percent as much on margarine as it did on butter. By 2010, the figure had fallen to 43 percent. Many of the best customers of margarine are older householders. Householders ranging in age from 35 to 74 spend more than average on margarine. Married couples without children at home (most of them empty-nesters) spend 12 percent more than the average household on this item. Couples with school-aged or older children at home spend 36 to 47 percent more than average on margarine.

Average household spending on margarine fell 33 percent between 2000 and 2010, after adjusting for inflation. Behind the downward slide were health warnings about transfats in margarine and the improving reputation of butter. Average household spending on margarine in the coming years may depend more on marketing than demographics.

Table 9.51 Margarine

| Total household spending | $1,201,381,440.00 |
| Average household spends | 9.92 |

	AVERAGE HOUSEHOLD SPENDING	BEST CUSTOMERS (index)	BIGGEST CUSTOMERS (market share)
AGE OF HOUSEHOLDER			
Average household	**$9.92**	**100**	**100.0%**
Under age 25	3.89	39	2.6
Aged 25 to 34	7.72	78	13.0
Aged 35 to 44	11.87	120	21.6
Aged 45 to 54	10.08	102	21.0
Aged 55 to 64	11.54	116	20.5
Aged 65 to 74	11.05	111	12.0
Aged 75 or older	9.69	98	9.3

	AVERAGE HOUSEHOLD SPENDING	BEST CUSTOMERS (index)	BIGGEST CUSTOMERS (market share)
HOUSEHOLD INCOME			
Average household	**$9.92**	**100**	**100.0%**
Under $20,000	7.11	72	15.6
$20,000 to $39,999	9.24	93	21.4
$40,000 to $49,999	12.25	123	11.7
$50,000 to $69,999	8.67	87	12.5
$70,000 to $79,999	10.66	107	6.4
$80,000 to $99,999	10.22	103	8.6
$100,000 or more	13.69	138	23.7
HOUSEHOLD TYPE			
Average household	**9.92**	**100**	**100.0**
Married couples	12.04	121	59.9
Married couples, no children	11.15	112	23.9
Married couples, with children	12.57	127	29.5
Oldest child under age 6	5.88	59	2.5
Oldest child aged 6 to 17	13.53	136	16.0
Oldest child aged 18 or older	14.55	147	10.6
Single parent with child under age 18	9.02	91	5.4
Single person	5.59	56	16.5
RACE AND HISPANIC ORIGIN			
Average household	**9.92**	**100**	**100.0**
Asian	7.37	74	3.2
Black	9.49	96	11.7
Hispanic	10.42	105	12.8
Non-Hispanic white and other	9.92	100	75.8
REGION			
Average household	**9.92**	**100**	**100.0**
Northeast	10.55	106	19.5
Midwest	10.00	101	22.5
South	9.29	94	34.4
West	10.37	105	23.7
EDUCATION			
Average household	**9.92**	**100**	**100.0**
Less than high school graduate	10.85	109	15.6
High school graduate	9.56	96	24.6
Some college	10.01	101	21.2
Associate's degree	11.63	117	11.1
Bachelor's degree or more	9.18	93	27.5
Bachelor's degree	9.14	92	17.4
Master's, professional, doctoral degree	9.26	93	10.1

Note: Market shares may not sum to 100.0 because of rounding and missing categories by household type. "Asian" and "black" include Hispanics and non-Hispanics who identify themselves as being of the respective race alone. "Hispanic" includes people of any race who identify themselves as Hispanic. "Other" includes people who identify themselves as non-Hispanic and as Alaska Native, American Indian, Asian (who are also included in the "Asian" row), or Native Hawaiian or other Pacific Islander as well as non-Hispanics reporting more than one race.

Source: Calculations by New Strategist based on the Bureau of Labor Statistics' 2010 Consumer Expenditure Survey

Milk, Fresh

Best customers: **Householders aged 35 to 54**
                                            Married couples with children at home

Customer trends: **Average household spending on milk may stabilize as the large millennial**
                                              generation enters the best-customer lifestage.

The best customers of milk are the largest households. Married couples with children at home spend 59 percent more than the average household on this item. Householders aged 35 to 54, most with children, spend 16 to 26 percent more than average on milk.

Average household spending on milk purchased at grocery or convenience stores declined 20 percent between 2000 and 2010, after adjusting for inflation, as the large baby-boom generation left the best-customer lifestage, replaced by the small generation X. Average household spending on milk may stabilize in the years ahead as the millennial generation replaces generation X in the married-with-children demographic.

Table 9.52 Milk, fresh

Total household spending $14,657,580,210.00
Average household spends   121.03

	AVERAGE HOUSEHOLD SPENDING	BEST CUSTOMERS (index)	BIGGEST CUSTOMERS (market share)
AGE OF HOUSEHOLDER			
Average household	**$121.03**	**100**	**100.0%**
Under age 25	78.70	65	4.3
Aged 25 to 34	118.71	98	16.3
Aged 35 to 44	152.82	126	22.8
Aged 45 to 54	140.10	116	23.9
Aged 55 to 64	116.38	96	17.0
Aged 65 to 74	101.66	84	9.0
Aged 75 or older	83.39	69	6.6

	AVERAGE HOUSEHOLD SPENDING	BEST CUSTOMERS (index)	BIGGEST CUSTOMERS (market share)
HOUSEHOLD INCOME			
Average household	**$121.03**	**100**	**100.0%**
Under $20,000	84.98	70	15.3
$20,000 to $39,999	103.84	86	19.7
$40,000 to $49,999	113.07	93	8.8
$50,000 to $69,999	124.67	103	14.8
$70,000 to $79,999	130.65	108	6.5
$80,000 to $99,999	151.75	125	10.5
$100,000 or more	173.80	144	24.6
HOUSEHOLD TYPE			
Average household	**121.03**	**100**	**100.0**
Married couples	157.66	130	64.3
Married couples, no children	112.41	93	19.7
Married couples, with children	192.81	159	37.1
Oldest child under age 6	179.52	148	6.4
Oldest child aged 6 to 17	201.67	167	19.6
Oldest child aged 18 or older	186.39	154	11.1
Single parent with child under age 18	103.96	86	5.1
Single person	61.77	51	15.0
RACE AND HISPANIC ORIGIN			
Average household	**121.03**	**100**	**100.0**
Asian	160.45	133	5.6
Black	90.63	75	9.2
Hispanic	151.14	125	15.2
Non-Hispanic white and other	121.20	100	75.9
REGION			
Average household	**121.03**	**100**	**100.0**
Northeast	132.83	110	20.1
Midwest	115.02	95	21.2
South	115.70	96	35.1
West	126.23	104	23.6
EDUCATION			
Average household	**121.03**	**100**	**100.0**
Less than high school graduate	122.80	101	14.5
High school graduate	117.59	97	24.8
Some college	107.29	89	18.6
Associate's degree	124.21	103	9.7
Bachelor's degree or more	132.21	109	32.5
Bachelor's degree	127.38	105	19.9
Master's, professional, doctoral degree	141.72	117	12.7

Note: Market shares may not sum to 100.0 because of rounding and missing categories by household type. "Asian" and "black" include Hispanics and non-Hispanics who identify themselves as being of the respective race alone. "Hispanic" includes people of any race who identify themselves as Hispanic. "Other" includes people who identify themselves as non-Hispanic and as Alaska Native, American Indian, Asian (who are also included in the "Asian" row), or Native Hawaiian or other Pacific Islander as well as non-Hispanics reporting more than one race.

Source: Calculations by New Strategist based on the Bureau of Labor Statistics' 2010 Consumer Expenditure Survey

Nondairy Cream and Imitation Milk

Best customers: **Householders aged 45 to 54**
Married couples

Customer trends: **Average household spending on nondairy cream and imitation milk may continue**
to rise in the years ahead as soy products become more commonly consumed.

Older householders and the largest households are the biggest spenders on nondairy cream and imitation milk. Married couples with children at home spend 42 percent more than average on this item, the figure peaking at 84 percent above average among couples with adult children at home. Married couples without children at home, most of them empty-nesters, spend 18 percent more than average. Householders aged 45 to 54, many with (adult) children at home, spend 42 percent more than average on nondairy cream and imitation milk.

Average household spending on nondairy cream and imitation milk grew by an enormous 46 percent between 2000 and 2010, after adjusting for inflation. Behind the increase was the growing popularity of soy products. Average household spending on nondairy cream and imitation milk may continue to rise in the years ahead as soy products become more commonly consumed.

Table 9.53 Nondairy cream and imitation milk

Total household spending   **$2,053,974,720.00**
Average household spends   **16.96**

	AVERAGE HOUSEHOLD SPENDING	BEST CUSTOMERS (index)	BIGGEST CUSTOMERS (market share)
AGE OF HOUSEHOLDER			
Average household	**$16.96**	**100**	**100.0%**
Under age 25	9.31	55	3.6
Aged 25 to 34	14.82	87	14.6
Aged 35 to 44	18.53	109	19.8
Aged 45 to 54	24.03	142	29.3
Aged 55 to 64	17.17	101	17.9
Aged 65 to 74	15.07	89	9.6
Aged 75 or older	9.04	53	5.1

	AVERAGE HOUSEHOLD SPENDING	BEST CUSTOMERS (index)	BIGGEST CUSTOMERS (market share)
HOUSEHOLD INCOME			
Average household	**$16.96**	**100**	**100.0%**
Under $20,000	10.04	59	12.9
$20,000 to $39,999	14.46	85	19.5
$40,000 to $49,999	15.83	93	8.8
$50,000 to $69,999	18.82	111	15.9
$70,000 to $79,999	17.45	103	6.2
$80,000 to $99,999	23.89	141	11.7
$100,000 or more	24.44	144	24.7
HOUSEHOLD TYPE			
Average household	**16.96**	**100**	**100.0**
Married couples	22.53	133	65.5
Married couples, no children	19.94	118	25.0
Married couples, with children	24.08	142	33.0
Oldest child under age 6	19.19	113	4.8
Oldest child aged 6 to 17	21.01	124	14.6
Oldest child aged 18 or older	31.17	184	13.3
Single parent with child under age 18	12.78	75	4.4
Single person	8.33	49	14.4
RACE AND HISPANIC ORIGIN			
Average household	**16.96**	**100**	**100.0**
Asian	14.05	83	3.5
Black	9.85	58	7.1
Hispanic	16.93	100	12.2
Non-Hispanic white and other	18.07	107	80.8
REGION			
Average household	**16.96**	**100**	**100.0**
Northeast	18.25	108	19.7
Midwest	17.27	102	22.7
South	15.46	91	33.5
West	18.05	106	24.1
EDUCATION			
Average household	**16.96**	**100**	**100.0**
Less than high school graduate	14.96	88	12.6
High school graduate	16.66	98	25.1
Some college	16.01	94	19.8
Associate's degree	22.25	131	12.4
Bachelor's degree or more	17.01	100	29.8
Bachelor's degree	16.37	97	18.2
Master's, professional, doctoral degree	18.26	108	11.6

Note: Market shares may not sum to 100.0 because of rounding and missing categories by household type. "Asian" and "black" include Hispanics and non-Hispanics who identify themselves as being of the respective race alone. "Hispanic" includes people of any race who identify themselves as Hispanic. "Other" includes people who identify themselves as non-Hispanic and as Alaska Native, American Indian, Asian (who are also included in the "Asian" row), or Native Hawaiian or other Pacific Islander as well as non-Hispanics reporting more than one race.

Source: Calculations by New Strategist based on the Bureau of Labor Statistics' 2010 Consumer Expenditure Survey

Nuts

Best customers: Householders aged 45 to 64
Married couples without children at home
Married couples with school-aged or older children at home
Households in the Northeast

Customer trends: Average household spending on nuts will continue to climb as boomers age.

Older Americans are the biggest spenders on nuts. Householders aged 45 to 64 spend 25 percent more than the average household on nuts and control 48 percent of the market. Married couples without children at home (most of them older) spend 40 percent more than average on nuts, while those with school-aged or older children at home (the largest households) spend 41 to 50 percent more. Households in the Northeast outspend the average by 24 percent.

Average household spending on nuts increased 28 percent between 2000 and 2010, after adjusting for inflation. Behind the increase was the aging of the baby-boom generation into the best-customer age groups, as well as the increased attention to the health benefits of nut consumption. Average household spending on nuts should continue to climb as boomers age.

Table 9.54 Nuts

Total household spending $4,075,250,550.00
Average household spends 33.65

AGE OF HOUSEHOLDER	AVERAGE HOUSEHOLD SPENDING	BEST CUSTOMERS (index)	BIGGEST CUSTOMERS (market share)
Average household	**$33.65**	**100**	**100.0%**
Under age 25	14.71	44	2.9
Aged 25 to 34	21.43	64	10.6
Aged 35 to 44	35.03	104	18.8
Aged 45 to 54	42.01	125	25.8
Aged 55 to 64	42.23	125	22.1
Aged 65 to 74	38.66	115	12.4
Aged 75 or older	25.30	75	7.2

	AVERAGE HOUSEHOLD SPENDING	BEST CUSTOMERS (index)	BIGGEST CUSTOMERS (market share)
HOUSEHOLD INCOME			
Average household	**$33.65**	**100**	**100.0%**
Under $20,000	18.30	54	11.9
$20,000 to $39,999	21.67	64	14.8
$40,000 to $49,999	29.83	89	8.4
$50,000 to $69,999	31.41	93	13.4
$70,000 to $79,999	37.61	112	6.7
$80,000 to $99,999	50.22	149	12.4
$100,000 or more	64.29	191	32.8
HOUSEHOLD TYPE			
Average household	**33.65**	**100**	**100.0**
Married couples	45.99	137	67.4
Married couples, no children	46.95	140	29.6
Married couples, with children	45.48	135	31.4
Oldest child under age 6	29.84	89	3.8
Oldest child aged 6 to 17	47.52	141	16.6
Oldest child aged 18 or older	50.43	150	10.8
Single parent with child under age 18	17.69	53	3.1
Single person	20.24	60	17.6
RACE AND HISPANIC ORIGIN			
Average household	**33.65**	**100**	**100.0**
Asian	30.51	91	3.9
Black	19.45	58	7.1
Hispanic	25.37	75	9.2
Non-Hispanic white and other	37.18	110	83.8
REGION			
Average household	**33.65**	**100**	**100.0**
Northeast	41.82	124	22.8
Midwest	36.05	107	23.9
South	26.65	79	29.1
West	36.08	107	24.3
EDUCATION			
Average household	**33.65**	**100**	**100.0**
Less than high school graduate	23.41	70	9.9
High school graduate	26.31	78	20.0
Some college	29.22	87	18.3
Associate's degree	31.92	95	9.0
Bachelor's degree or more	48.45	144	42.8
Bachelor's degree	44.93	134	25.2
Master's, professional, doctoral degree	55.37	165	17.8

Note: Market shares may not sum to 100.0 because of rounding and missing categories by household type. "Asian" and "black" include Hispanics and non-Hispanics who identify themselves as being of the respective race alone. "Hispanic" includes people of any race who identify themselves as Hispanic. "Other" includes people who identify themselves as non-Hispanic and as Alaska Native, American Indian, Asian (who are also included in the "Asian" row), or Native Hawaiian or other Pacific Islander as well as non-Hispanics reporting more than one race.

Source: Calculations by New Strategist based on the Bureau of Labor Statistics' 2010 Consumer Expenditure Survey

Olives, Pickles, and Relishes

Best customers:	Householders aged 45 to 54
	Married couples without children at home
	Married couples with school-aged or older children at home
	Households in the Northeast
Customer trends:	Average household spending on olives, pickles, and relishes should stabilize now that boomers are beginning to exit the best-customer lifestage.

The best customers of olives, pickles, and relishes are the largest households and older householders. Couples with school-aged children spend 64 percent more than the average household on this item, and those with adult children at home, 56 percent. Married couples without children at home, most empty-nesters, outspend the average for this item by 23 percent. Householders aged 45 to 54 spend 22 more than average on olives, pickles, and relishes. Households in the Northeast spend 26 percent more than average.

Average household spending on olives, pickles, and relishes increased 20 percent between 2000 and 2010, after adjusting for inflation. Behind the increase is the greater availability of fresh olives and relishes in grocery stores. Average household spending on olives, pickles, and relishes should stabilize now that boomers are beginning to exit the best-customer lifestage.

Table 9.55 Olives, pickles, and relishes

Total household spending $1,799,650,020.00
Average household spends 14.86

	AVERAGE HOUSEHOLD SPENDING	BEST CUSTOMERS (index)	BIGGEST CUSTOMERS (market share)
AGE OF HOUSEHOLDER			
Average household	**$14.86**	**100**	**100.0%**
Under age 25	9.96	67	4.4
Aged 25 to 34	13.00	87	14.6
Aged 35 to 44	16.02	108	19.5
Aged 45 to 54	18.06	122	25.1
Aged 55 to 64	14.57	98	17.3
Aged 65 to 74	16.09	108	11.7
Aged 75 or older	11.32	76	7.3

	AVERAGE HOUSEHOLD SPENDING	BEST CUSTOMERS (index)	BIGGEST CUSTOMERS (market share)
HOUSEHOLD INCOME			
Average household	**$14.86**	**100**	**100.0%**
Under $20,000	10.47	70	15.4
$20,000 to $39,999	10.06	68	15.5
$40,000 to $49,999	11.79	79	7.5
$50,000 to $69,999	15.53	105	15.0
$70,000 to $79,999	14.46	97	5.8
$80,000 to $99,999	19.44	131	10.9
$100,000 or more	26.36	177	30.4
HOUSEHOLD TYPE			
Average household	**14.86**	**100**	**100.0**
Married couples	20.04	135	66.5
Married couples, no children	18.34	123	26.2
Married couples, with children	21.95	148	34.4
Oldest child under age 6	12.68	85	3.7
Oldest child aged 6 to 17	24.31	164	19.2
Oldest child aged 18 or older	23.19	156	11.3
Single parent with child under age 18	10.75	72	4.3
Single person	7.82	53	15.4
RACE AND HISPANIC ORIGIN			
Average household	**14.86**	**100**	**100.0**
Asian	13.11	88	3.8
Black	9.76	66	8.0
Hispanic	8.77	59	7.2
Non-Hispanic white and other	16.60	112	84.7
REGION			
Average household	**14.86**	**100**	**100.0**
Northeast	18.65	126	23.0
Midwest	16.34	110	24.5
South	11.89	80	29.4
West	15.14	102	23.1
EDUCATION			
Average household	**14.86**	**100**	**100.0**
Less than high school graduate	10.85	73	10.4
High school graduate	14.52	98	24.9
Some college	13.69	92	19.4
Associate's degree	16.31	110	10.4
Bachelor's degree or more	17.30	116	34.6
Bachelor's degree	15.60	105	19.8
Master's, professional, doctoral degree	20.64	139	15.0

Note: Market shares may not sum to 100.0 because of rounding and missing categories by household type. "Asian" and "black" include Hispanics and non-Hispanics who identify themselves as being of the respective race alone. "Hispanic" includes people of any race who identify themselves as Hispanic. "Other" includes people who identify themselves as non-Hispanic and as Alaska Native, American Indian, Asian (who are also included in the "Asian" row), or Native Hawaiian or other Pacific Islander as well as non-Hispanics reporting more than one race.

Source: Calculations by New Strategist based on the Bureau of Labor Statistics' 2010 Consumer Expenditure Survey

Oranges

Best customers: **Householders aged 35 to 54**
Married couples with school-aged or older children at home
Single parents
Asians and Hispanics
Households in the Northeast and West

Customer trends: **Average household spending on oranges may continue to rise due to the growth of the Asian and Hispanic populations, but the baby-boom generation's exit from the best-customer lifestage may limit gains.**

The biggest spenders on oranges are the largest households. Married couples with school-aged or older children at home spend 50 to 55 percent more than average on oranges. Householders aged 35 to 54, many with children at home, spend 15 to 30 percent more than average on this item. Single parents, whose spending is well below average on most items, spend 16 percent more than average on oranges. Asians spend 55 percent more than average, and Hispanics, who have the largest families, spend 38 percent more than the average household on oranges. Households in the West, where many Asians and Hispanics reside, outspend the average by 23 percent. In the Northeast, average household spending on oranges is 16 percent above average.

Average household spending on oranges grew 3 percent between 2000 and 2010, after adjusting for inflation. Behind the increase was the rapid growth in the Asian and Hispanic populations. Spending on oranges may continue to rise due to the ongoing increases in those populations, but the baby-boom generation's exit from the best-customer lifestage may limit gains.

Table 9.56 Oranges

Total household spending $2,993,765,040.00
Average household spends   24.72

	AVERAGE HOUSEHOLD SPENDING	BEST CUSTOMERS (index)	BIGGEST CUSTOMERS (market share)
AGE OF HOUSEHOLDER			
Average household	**$24.72**	**100**	**100.0%**
Under age 25	15.98	65	4.3
Aged 25 to 34	24.36	99	16.4
Aged 35 to 44	32.06	130	23.5
Aged 45 to 54	28.40	115	23.8
Aged 55 to 64	23.56	95	16.8
Aged 65 to 74	21.59	87	9.4
Aged 75 or older	15.24	62	5.9

	AVERAGE HOUSEHOLD SPENDING	BEST CUSTOMERS (index)	BIGGEST CUSTOMERS (market share)
HOUSEHOLD INCOME			
Average household	**$24.72**	**100**	**100.0%**
Under $20,000	16.45	67	14.5
$20,000 to $39,999	21.77	88	20.2
$40,000 to $49,999	23.15	94	8.9
$50,000 to $69,999	21.98	89	12.8
$70,000 to $79,999	26.25	106	6.4
$80,000 to $99,999	32.04	130	10.8
$100,000 or more	38.52	156	26.7
HOUSEHOLD TYPE			
Average household	**24.72**	**100**	**100.0**
Married couples	30.34	123	60.5
Married couples, no children	22.38	91	19.2
Married couples, with children	35.72	144	33.6
Oldest child under age 6	26.43	107	4.6
Oldest child aged 6 to 17	37.13	150	17.7
Oldest child aged 18 or older	38.36	155	11.2
Single parent with child under age 18	28.66	116	6.8
Single person	12.72	51	15.1
RACE AND HISPANIC ORIGIN			
Average household	**24.72**	**100**	**100.0**
Asian	38.31	155	6.6
Black	25.55	103	12.6
Hispanic	34.21	138	16.9
Non-Hispanic white and other	23.13	94	70.9
REGION			
Average household	**24.72**	**100**	**100.0**
Northeast	28.60	116	21.2
Midwest	23.78	96	21.4
South	19.98	81	29.7
West	30.32	123	27.8
EDUCATION			
Average household	**24.72**	**100**	**100.0**
Less than high school graduate	27.98	113	16.2
High school graduate	21.42	87	22.1
Some college	18.08	73	15.4
Associate's degree	22.60	91	8.6
Bachelor's degree or more	31.73	128	38.1
Bachelor's degree	28.07	114	21.4
Master's, professional, doctoral degree	38.95	158	17.0

Note: Market shares may not sum to 100.0 because of rounding and missing categories by household type. "Asian" and "black" include Hispanics and non-Hispanics who identify themselves as being of the respective race alone. "Hispanic" includes people of any race who identify themselves as Hispanic. "Other" includes people who identify themselves as non-Hispanic and as Alaska Native, American Indian, Asian (who are also included in the "Asian" row), or Native Hawaiian or other Pacific Islander as well as non-Hispanics reporting more than one race.

Source: Calculations by New Strategist based on the Bureau of Labor Statistics' 2010 Consumer Expenditure Survey

Pasta, Cornmeal, and Other Cereal Products

Best customers:	Householders aged 35 to 54
	Married couples with school-aged or older children at home
	Asians
	Households in the Northeast

Customer trends:	Average household spending on pasta should resume its decline as more boomers become empty-nesters and household size shrinks.

The biggest spenders on pasta, cornmeal, and other cereal products are households with children. Married couples with school-aged children spend 71 percent more than the average household on this item, and those with adult children at home, 59 percent. Householders aged 35 to 54, most with children at home, spend 21 to 24 percent more than average on pasta. Asians spend 55 percent more than average on this item. Households in the Northeast outspend the average for pasta by one-quarter.

Average household spending on pasta, cornmeal, and other cereal products fell 28 percent between 2000 and 2006, after adjusting for inflation, then grew 29 percent between 2006 and 2010. Behind the earlier decline was the growing propensity of consumers to eat out rather than cook a meal at home. Efforts at belt tightening and a renewed surge of home cooking may have been responsible for the ensuing rise in average household spending on pasta. Average household spending on pasta should resume its decline as more boomers become empty-nesters and household size shrinks.

Table 9.57 Pasta, cornmeal, and other cereal products

Total household spending $4,107,949,440.00
Average household spends 33.92

	AVERAGE HOUSEHOLD SPENDING	BEST CUSTOMERS (index)	BIGGEST CUSTOMERS (market share)
AGE OF HOUSEHOLDER			
Average household	**$33.92**	**100**	**100.0%**
Under age 25	19.18	57	3.8
Aged 25 to 34	32.44	96	15.9
Aged 35 to 44	41.18	121	22.0
Aged 45 to 54	41.92	124	25.6
Aged 55 to 64	34.23	101	17.8
Aged 65 to 74	28.55	84	9.1
Aged 75 or older	20.87	62	5.9

	AVERAGE HOUSEHOLD SPENDING	BEST CUSTOMERS (index)	BIGGEST CUSTOMERS (market share)
HOUSEHOLD INCOME			
Average household	**$33.92**	**100**	**100.0%**
Under $20,000	20.78	61	13.4
$20,000 to $39,999	26.71	79	18.0
$40,000 to $49,999	30.23	89	8.4
$50,000 to $69,999	37.91	112	16.0
$70,000 to $79,999	31.87	94	5.6
$80,000 to $99,999	39.63	117	9.7
$100,000 or more	57.20	169	28.9
HOUSEHOLD TYPE			
Average household	**33.92**	**100**	**100.0**
Married couples	44.35	131	64.5
Married couples, no children	33.46	99	21.0
Married couples, with children	52.39	154	35.9
Oldest child under age 6	33.31	98	4.2
Oldest child aged 6 to 17	57.98	171	20.1
Oldest child aged 18 or older	53.83	159	11.5
Single parent with child under age 18	27.30	80	4.7
Single person	17.56	52	15.2
RACE AND HISPANIC ORIGIN			
Average household	**33.92**	**100**	**100.0**
Asian	52.67	155	6.6
Black	26.10	77	9.4
Hispanic	33.07	97	11.9
Non-Hispanic white and other	35.32	104	78.9
REGION			
Average household	**33.92**	**100**	**100.0**
Northeast	42.52	125	23.0
Midwest	34.33	101	22.6
South	28.52	84	30.9
West	35.33	104	23.6
EDUCATION			
Average household	**33.92**	**100**	**100.0**
Less than high school graduate	31.28	92	13.2
High school graduate	29.89	88	22.5
Some college	28.86	85	17.9
Associate's degree	34.34	101	9.6
Bachelor's degree or more	42.15	124	36.9
Bachelor's degree	41.67	123	23.2
Master's, professional, doctoral degree	43.09	127	13.7

Note: Market shares may not sum to 100.0 because of rounding and missing categories by household type. "Asian" and "black" include Hispanics and non-Hispanics who identify themselves as being of the respective race alone. "Hispanic" includes people of any race who identify themselves as Hispanic. "Other" includes people who identify themselves as non-Hispanic and as Alaska Native, American Indian, Asian (who are also included in the "Asian" row), or Native Hawaiian or other Pacific Islander as well as non-Hispanics reporting more than one race.

Source: Calculations by New Strategist based on the Bureau of Labor Statistics' 2010 Consumer Expenditure Survey

Peanut Butter

Best customers: **Householders aged 35 to 64**
Married couples with children at home
Households in the Midwest

Customer trends: **Average household spending on peanut butter may decline because the small**
generation X is in the best-customer lifestage.

Married couples with children at home spend the most on peanut butter, 58 percent more than average. The figure peaks among those with school-aged children at 67 percent above average. Householders aged 35 to 64, many with children, spend 13 to 34 percent more than the average household on peanut butter. Households in the Midwest outspend the average by 19 percent.

Average household spending on peanut butter fell 19 percent between 2000 and 2006, after adjusting for inflation, then rebounded 27 percent between 2006 and 2010. Behind the rebound was belt-tightening by parents who substituted homemade sandwiches for school-bought meals in an effort to cut costs. Average household spending on peanut butter may decline because the small generation X is in the best-customer lifestage.

Table 9.58 Peanut butter

Total household spending $1,872,314,220.00
Average household spends 15.46

	AVERAGE HOUSEHOLD SPENDING	BEST CUSTOMERS (index)	BIGGEST CUSTOMERS (market share)
AGE OF HOUSEHOLDER			
Average household	**$15.46**	**100**	**100.0%**
Under age 25	9.69	63	4.2
Aged 25 to 34	13.05	84	14.1
Aged 35 to 44	18.01	116	21.1
Aged 45 to 54	20.64	134	27.6
Aged 55 to 64	17.43	113	19.9
Aged 65 to 74	9.34	60	6.5
Aged 75 or older	10.73	69	6.6

	AVERAGE HOUSEHOLD SPENDING	BEST CUSTOMERS (index)	BIGGEST CUSTOMERS (market share)
HOUSEHOLD INCOME			
Average household	**$15.46**	**100**	**100.0%**
Under $20,000	9.86	64	13.9
$20,000 to $39,999	11.36	73	16.8
$40,000 to $49,999	15.24	99	9.3
$50,000 to $69,999	15.41	100	14.3
$70,000 to $79,999	14.42	93	5.6
$80,000 to $99,999	23.29	151	12.6
$100,000 or more	25.18	163	27.9
HOUSEHOLD TYPE			
Average household	**15.46**	**100**	**100.0**
Married couples	20.53	133	65.5
Married couples, no children	16.98	110	23.3
Married couples, with children	24.47	158	36.8
Oldest child under age 6	19.10	124	5.3
Oldest child aged 6 to 17	25.77	167	19.6
Oldest child aged 18 or older	25.28	164	11.8
Single parent with child under age 18	10.67	69	4.1
Single person	8.14	53	15.4
RACE AND HISPANIC ORIGIN			
Average household	**15.46**	**100**	**100.0**
Asian	13.39	87	3.7
Black	10.36	67	8.2
Hispanic	8.97	58	7.1
Non-Hispanic white and other	17.28	112	84.7
REGION			
Average household	**15.46**	**100**	**100.0**
Northeast	16.74	108	19.9
Midwest	18.37	119	26.5
South	13.52	87	32.1
West	14.68	95	21.5
EDUCATION			
Average household	**15.46**	**100**	**100.0**
Less than high school graduate	11.48	74	10.6
High school graduate	12.69	82	21.0
Some college	15.50	100	21.1
Associate's degree	15.85	103	9.7
Bachelor's degree or more	19.50	126	37.5
Bachelor's degree	17.92	116	21.9
Master's, professional, doctoral degree	22.62	146	15.8

Note: Market shares may not sum to 100.0 because of rounding and missing categories by household type. "Asian" and "black" include Hispanics and non-Hispanics who identify themselves as being of the respective race alone. "Hispanic" includes people of any race who identify themselves as Hispanic. "Other" includes people who identify themselves as non-Hispanic and as Alaska Native, American Indian, Asian (who are also included in the "Asian" row), or Native Hawaiian or other Pacific Islander as well as non-Hispanics reporting more than one race.

Source: Calculations by New Strategist based on the Bureau of Labor Statistics' 2010 Consumer Expenditure Survey

Pies, Tarts, and Turnovers

Best customers:	Householders aged 45 to 54
	Married couples with school-aged or older children at home
	Households in the Northeast and West

Customer trends:	Average household spending on pies, tarts, and turnovers is likely to stabilize as the small generation X enters the best-customer lifestage.

The best customers of pies, tarts, and turnovers are households with children. Married couples with school-aged or older children at home spend 60 to 67 percent more than average on pies. Householders aged 45 to 54, many with children, spend 32 percent more than average on this item and control 27 percent of the market. Households in the Northeast and West spend, respectively, 20 and 15 percent more than average on pies, tarts, and turnover.

Average household spending on pies, tarts, and turnovers fell 10 percent between 2000 and 2006, after adjusting for inflation, then rebounded by 8 percent between 2006 and 2010. Behind the decline in the earlier part of the decade was the growing propensity of consumers to eat out, and the increase since 2006 is due to more meals eaten at home because of Great Recession belt-tightening. Spending on pies, tarts, and turnovers is likely to stabilize as the small generation X enters the best-customer lifestage.

Table 9.59 Pies, tarts, and turnovers

Total household spending $1,974,044,100.00
Average household spends 16.30

	AVERAGE HOUSEHOLD SPENDING	BEST CUSTOMERS (index)	BIGGEST CUSTOMERS (market share)
AGE OF HOUSEHOLDER			
Average household	**$16.30**	**100**	**100.0%**
Under age 25	9.80	60	4.0
Aged 25 to 34	12.78	78	13.1
Aged 35 to 44	17.46	107	19.4
Aged 45 to 54	21.44	132	27.2
Aged 55 to 64	16.73	103	18.1
Aged 65 to 74	17.28	106	11.4
Aged 75 or older	11.44	70	6.7

	AVERAGE HOUSEHOLD SPENDING	BEST CUSTOMERS (index)	BIGGEST CUSTOMERS (market share)
HOUSEHOLD INCOME			
Average household	**$16.30**	**100**	**100.0%**
Under $20,000	11.06	68	14.8
$20,000 to $39,999	11.70	72	16.4
$40,000 to $49,999	15.03	92	8.7
$50,000 to $69,999	17.52	107	15.4
$70,000 to $79,999	19.02	117	7.0
$80,000 to $99,999	19.73	121	10.1
$100,000 or more	26.48	162	27.9
HOUSEHOLD TYPE			
Average household	**16.30**	**100**	**100.0**
Married couples	20.21	124	61.2
Married couples, no children	14.92	92	19.4
Married couples, with children	24.73	152	35.3
Oldest child under age 6	15.74	97	4.1
Oldest child aged 6 to 17	26.09	160	18.8
Oldest child aged 18 or older	27.30	167	12.1
Single parent with child under age 18	13.95	86	5.0
Single person	9.45	58	17.0
RACE AND HISPANIC ORIGIN			
Average household	**16.30**	**100**	**100.0**
Asian	17.23	106	4.5
Black	11.41	70	8.6
Hispanic	14.03	86	10.5
Non-Hispanic white and other	17.44	107	81.1
REGION			
Average household	**16.30**	**100**	**100.0**
Northeast	19.63	120	22.1
Midwest	16.59	102	22.7
South	12.95	79	29.2
West	18.82	115	26.2
EDUCATION			
Average household	**16.30**	**100**	**100.0**
Less than high school graduate	14.15	87	12.4
High school graduate	15.92	98	24.9
Some college	16.45	101	21.2
Associate's degree	17.64	108	10.2
Bachelor's degree or more	17.04	105	31.1
Bachelor's degree	15.91	98	18.4
Master's, professional, doctoral degree	19.27	118	12.8

Note: Market shares may not sum to 100.0 because of rounding and missing categories by household type. "Asian" and "black" include Hispanics and non-Hispanics who identify themselves as being of the respective race alone. "Hispanic" includes people of any race who identify themselves as Hispanic. "Other" includes people who identify themselves as non-Hispanic and as Alaska Native, American Indian, Asian (who are also included in the "Asian" row), or Native Hawaiian or other Pacific Islander as well as non-Hispanics reporting more than one race.

Source: Calculations by New Strategist based on the Bureau of Labor Statistics' 2010 Consumer Expenditure Survey

Pork Chops

Best customers:	**Householders aged 35 to 54** **Married couples with school-aged or older children at home** **Hispanics and blacks** **Householders without a high school diploma**
Customer trends:	**Average household spending on pork chops will continue to decline as more boomers become empty-nesters and prepared food claims a growing share of the food dollar, but growth of minority populations may limit the drop.**

Households with children and households headed by blacks and Hispanics are the biggest spenders on pork chops. Married couples with school-aged or older children at home spend 20 to 58 percent more than average on this item. Householders aged 35 to 54, most with children, spend 25 to 26 percent more. Hispanic and black households spend, respectively, 31 and 28 percent more than average on pork chops and account for one-third of the market. Households in the South represent 41 percent of the market for pork chops. Householders without a high school diploma spend 38 percent more on pork chops than the average household.

Average household spending on pork chops fell by a steep 54 percent between 2000 and 2010, after adjusting for inflation. Spending on pork chops is declining as Americans substitute fast food and deli items for home-cooked meals. Average household spending on pork chops is likely to continue to decline as more boomers become empty-nesters and prepared food claims a growing share of the food dollar, but growth of minority populations may limit the drop.

Table 9.60 Pork chops

Total household spending	$2,878,713,390.00
Average household spends	23.77

	AVERAGE HOUSEHOLD SPENDING	BEST CUSTOMERS (index)	BIGGEST CUSTOMERS (market share)
AGE OF HOUSEHOLDER			
Average household	**$23.77**	**100**	**100.0%**
Under age 25	17.83	75	5.0
Aged 25 to 34	16.31	69	11.4
Aged 35 to 44	29.80	125	22.7
Aged 45 to 54	29.96	126	26.1
Aged 55 to 64	22.81	96	16.9
Aged 65 to 74	20.53	86	9.3
Aged 75 or older	21.44	90	8.6

	AVERAGE HOUSEHOLD SPENDING	BEST CUSTOMERS (index)	BIGGEST CUSTOMERS (market share)
HOUSEHOLD INCOME			
Average household	**$23.77**	**100**	**100.0%**
Under $20,000	17.21	72	15.8
$20,000 to $39,999	21.15	89	20.4
$40,000 to $49,999	27.42	115	10.9
$50,000 to $69,999	25.06	105	15.1
$70,000 to $79,999	25.53	107	6.4
$80,000 to $99,999	28.50	120	10.0
$100,000 or more	29.58	124	21.3
HOUSEHOLD TYPE			
Average household	**23.77**	**100**	**100.0**
Married couples	29.22	123	60.6
Married couples, no children	26.31	111	23.5
Married couples, with children	30.38	128	29.7
Oldest child under age 6	21.88	92	3.9
Oldest child aged 6 to 17	28.57	120	14.1
Oldest child aged 18 or older	37.44	158	11.4
Single parent with child under age 18	20.18	85	5.0
Single person	12.29	52	15.1
RACE AND HISPANIC ORIGIN			
Average household	**23.77**	**100**	**100.0**
Asian	12.28	52	2.2
Black	30.50	128	15.7
Hispanic	31.15	131	16.0
Non-Hispanic white and other	21.69	91	69.2
REGION			
Average household	**23.77**	**100**	**100.0**
Northeast	26.60	112	20.5
Midwest	20.76	87	19.5
South	26.59	112	41.1
West	19.87	84	18.9
EDUCATION			
Average household	**23.77**	**100**	**100.0**
Less than high school graduate	32.70	138	19.7
High school graduate	24.36	102	26.2
Some college	18.40	77	16.3
Associate's degree	26.46	111	10.5
Bachelor's degree or more	22.31	94	27.9
Bachelor's degree	21.12	89	16.8
Master's, professional, doctoral degree	24.65	104	11.2

Note: Market shares may not sum to 100.0 because of rounding and missing categories by household type. "Asian" and "black" include Hispanics and non-Hispanics who identify themselves as being of the respective race alone. "Hispanic" includes people of any race who identify themselves as Hispanic. "Other" includes people who identify themselves as non-Hispanic and as Alaska Native, American Indian, Asian (who are also included in the "Asian" row), or Native Hawaiian or other Pacific Islander as well as non-Hispanics reporting more than one race.

Source: Calculations by New Strategist based on the Bureau of Labor Statistics' 2010 Consumer Expenditure Survey

Potato Chips and Other Snacks

Best customers: **Householders aged 35 to 54**
Married couples with children at home
Single parents

Customer trends: **Average household spending on potato chips and other snacks may decline as more boomers become empty-nesters.**

The best customers of potato chips and other snacks are households with children. Married couples with children at home spend 69 percent more than the average household on this item, the figure peaking among those with school-aged children at 89 percent above average. Single parents, whose spending approaches average on only a few items, spend 2 percent more than average on potato chips. Householders aged 35 to 54, most with children at home, spend 26 to 33 percent more than average on potato chips and other snacks and control half the market.

Average household spending on potato chips and other snacks increased by 9 percent between 2000 and 2010, after adjusting for inflation. Americans' penchant for snack food was behind the increase, as was the growing variety of snacks on grocery store shelves. Average household spending on potato chips and other snacks may decline in the years ahead as more boomers become empty-nesters.

Table 9.61 Potato chips and other snacks

Total household spending $12,028,347,240.00
Average household spends 99.32

	AVERAGE HOUSEHOLD SPENDING	BEST CUSTOMERS (index)	BIGGEST CUSTOMERS (market share)
AGE OF HOUSEHOLDER			
Average household	**$99.32**	**100**	**100.0%**
Under age 25	60.24	61	4.0
Aged 25 to 34	95.72	96	16.0
Aged 35 to 44	132.23	133	24.1
Aged 45 to 54	124.99	126	26.0
Aged 55 to 64	93.42	94	16.6
Aged 65 to 74	68.95	69	7.5
Aged 75 or older	59.71	60	5.7

	AVERAGE HOUSEHOLD SPENDING	BEST CUSTOMERS (index)	BIGGEST CUSTOMERS (market share)
HOUSEHOLD INCOME			
Average household	**$99.32**	**100**	**100.0%**
Under $20,000	54.63	55	12.0
$20,000 to $39,999	73.86	74	17.0
$40,000 to $49,999	90.05	91	8.6
$50,000 to $69,999	102.02	103	14.7
$70,000 to $79,999	113.81	115	6.9
$80,000 to $99,999	139.76	141	11.7
$100,000 or more	170.11	171	29.4
HOUSEHOLD TYPE			
Average household	**99.32**	**100**	**100.0**
Married couples	131.73	133	65.4
Married couples, no children	91.99	93	19.7
Married couples, with children	167.56	169	39.2
Oldest child under age 6	116.88	118	5.0
Oldest child aged 6 to 17	187.63	189	22.2
Oldest child aged 18 or older	163.57	165	11.9
Single parent with child under age 18	100.83	102	6.0
Single person	49.57	50	14.6
RACE AND HISPANIC ORIGIN			
Average household	**99.32**	**100**	**100.0**
Asian	86.38	87	3.7
Black	70.57	71	8.7
Hispanic	88.06	89	10.8
Non-Hispanic white and other	105.56	106	80.6
REGION			
Average household	**99.32**	**100**	**100.0**
Northeast	93.01	94	17.2
Midwest	106.37	107	23.9
South	94.04	95	34.8
West	106.05	107	24.2
EDUCATION			
Average household	**99.32**	**100**	**100.0**
Less than high school graduate	76.02	77	10.9
High school graduate	92.82	93	23.9
Some college	90.25	91	19.1
Associate's degree	101.81	103	9.7
Bachelor's degree or more	121.10	122	36.2
Bachelor's degree	121.00	122	23.0
Master's, professional, doctoral degree	121.29	122	13.2

Note: Market shares may not sum to 100.0 because of rounding and missing categories by household type. "Asian" and "black" include Hispanics and non-Hispanics who identify themselves as being of the respective race alone. "Hispanic" includes people of any race who identify themselves as Hispanic. "Other" includes people who identify themselves as non-Hispanic and as Alaska Native, American Indian, Asian (who are also included in the "Asian" row), or Native Hawaiian or other Pacific Islander as well as non-Hispanics reporting more than one race.

Source: Calculations by New Strategist based on the Bureau of Labor Statistics' 2010 Consumer Expenditure Survey

Potatoes, Fresh

Best customers: Householders aged 35 to 74
                       Married couples
                       Asians

Customer trends: Average household spending on potatoes may resume its decline as home cooking
                       becomes less common, but only if discretionary income grows.

Families that cook meals from scratch are the best customers of fresh potatoes. Married couples with children at home spend 34 percent more than average on potatoes, the figure peaking among those with adult children at 48 percent above average. Householders ranging in age from 35 to 74 spend 5 to 17 percent more than average on this item. Married couples without children at home outspend the average by 19 percent. Asian householders spend 29 percent more than average on potatoes.

After declining 5 percent between 2000 and 2006, average household spending on potatoes grew 7 percent between 2006 and 2010, after adjusting for inflation. Behind the increase is the renewed surge of home cooking in an effort to control spending. Average household spending on potatoes may resume its decline as home cooking becomes less common, but only if discretionary income grows.

Table 9.62 Potatoes, fresh

Total household spending $4,373,173,770.00
Average household spends   36.11

	AVERAGE HOUSEHOLD SPENDING	BEST CUSTOMERS (index)	BIGGEST CUSTOMERS (market share)
AGE OF HOUSEHOLDER			
Average household	**$36.11**	**100**	**100.0%**
Under age 25	19.86	55	3.6
Aged 25 to 34	29.46	82	13.6
Aged 35 to 44	39.87	110	20.0
Aged 45 to 54	42.12	117	24.1
Aged 55 to 64	37.93	105	18.5
Aged 65 to 74	42.17	117	12.6
Aged 75 or older	28.26	78	7.5

	AVERAGE HOUSEHOLD SPENDING	BEST CUSTOMERS (index)	BIGGEST CUSTOMERS (market share)
HOUSEHOLD INCOME			
Average household	**$36.11**	**100**	**100.0%**
Under $20,000	23.42	65	14.2
$20,000 to $39,999	31.24	87	19.8
$40,000 to $49,999	29.44	82	7.7
$50,000 to $69,999	38.35	106	15.2
$70,000 to $79,999	34.91	97	5.8
$80,000 to $99,999	46.28	128	10.7
$100,000 or more	56.01	155	26.6
HOUSEHOLD TYPE			
Average household	**36.11**	**100**	**100.0**
Married couples	47.26	131	64.6
Married couples, no children	43.02	119	25.3
Married couples, with children	48.44	134	31.2
Oldest child under age 6	41.63	115	4.9
Oldest child aged 6 to 17	47.46	131	15.5
Oldest child aged 18 or older	53.39	148	10.7
Single parent with child under age 18	23.42	65	3.8
Single person	18.32	51	14.9
RACE AND HISPANIC ORIGIN			
Average household	**36.11**	**100**	**100.0**
Asian	46.66	129	5.5
Black	30.48	84	10.3
Hispanic	37.63	104	12.7
Non-Hispanic white and other	36.73	102	77.1
REGION			
Average household	**36.11**	**100**	**100.0**
Northeast	39.17	108	19.9
Midwest	36.86	102	22.8
South	34.69	96	35.3
West	35.16	97	22.1
EDUCATION			
Average household	**36.11**	**100**	**100.0**
Less than high school graduate	35.31	98	14.0
High school graduate	35.54	98	25.1
Some college	32.95	91	19.2
Associate's degree	36.00	100	9.4
Bachelor's degree or more	39.30	109	32.3
Bachelor's degree	36.29	100	19.0
Master's, professional, doctoral degree	45.22	125	13.5

Note: Market shares may not sum to 100.0 because of rounding and missing categories by household type. "Asian" and "black" include Hispanics and non-Hispanics who identify themselves as being of the respective race alone. "Hispanic" includes people of any race who identify themselves as Hispanic. "Other" includes people who identify themselves as non-Hispanic and as Alaska Native, American Indian, Asian (who are also included in the "Asian" row), or Native Hawaiian or other Pacific Islander as well as non-Hispanics reporting more than one race.

Source: Calculations by New Strategist based on the Bureau of Labor Statistics' 2010 Consumer Expenditure Survey

Poultry Other than Chicken

Best customers:
Householders aged 35 to 54
Married couples with children at home
Blacks

Customer trends:
Average household spending on poultry other than chicken should continue its fall as home cooking becomes less common.

Families with children spend the most on poultry other than chicken (primarily turkey). Married couples with school-aged children spend 51 percent more than the average household on this item. Householders ranging in age from 35 to 54, most with children at home, spend 15 to 17 percent more than average on this item and control 45 percent of the market. Blacks spend 26 percent more than the average household on other poultry.

Average household spending on poultry other than chicken tumbled 28 percent between 2000 and 2010, after adjusting for inflation. Behind the decline was Americans' waning interest in cooking from scratch. Average household spending on poultry other than chicken should continue its decline as home cooking becomes less common.

Table 9.63 Poultry other than chicken

Total household spending $3,374,041,020.00
Average household spends 27.86

	AVERAGE HOUSEHOLD SPENDING	BEST CUSTOMERS (index)	BIGGEST CUSTOMERS (market share)
AGE OF HOUSEHOLDER			
Average household	**$27.86**	**100**	**100.0%**
Under age 25	13.70	49	3.3
Aged 25 to 34	29.31	105	17.5
Aged 35 to 44	31.99	115	20.8
Aged 45 to 54	32.58	117	24.2
Aged 55 to 64	26.11	94	16.5
Aged 65 to 74	30.01	108	11.6
Aged 75 or older	17.76	64	6.1

	AVERAGE HOUSEHOLD SPENDING	BEST CUSTOMERS (index)	BIGGEST CUSTOMERS (market share)
HOUSEHOLD INCOME			
Average household	**$27.86**	**100**	**100.0%**
Under $20,000	13.79	50	10.8
$20,000 to $39,999	24.60	88	20.2
$40,000 to $49,999	24.60	88	8.3
$50,000 to $69,999	28.94	104	14.9
$70,000 to $79,999	28.62	103	6.1
$80,000 to $99,999	35.15	126	10.5
$100,000 or more	47.25	170	29.1
HOUSEHOLD TYPE			
Average household	**27.86**	**100**	**100.0**
Married couples	35.99	129	63.7
Married couples, no children	30.37	109	23.2
Married couples, with children	38.91	140	32.5
Oldest child under age 6	34.38	123	5.3
Oldest child aged 6 to 17	41.99	151	17.7
Oldest child aged 18 or older	36.64	132	9.5
Single parent with child under age 18	26.75	96	5.7
Single person	12.89	46	13.6
RACE AND HISPANIC ORIGIN			
Average household	**27.86**	**100**	**100.0**
Asian	22.33	80	3.4
Black	35.17	126	15.4
Hispanic	27.37	98	12.0
Non-Hispanic white and other	26.86	96	73.1
REGION			
Average household	**27.86**	**100**	**100.0**
Northeast	31.50	113	20.8
Midwest	24.27	87	19.4
South	27.41	98	36.1
West	29.26	105	23.8
EDUCATION			
Average household	**27.86**	**100**	**100.0**
Less than high school graduate	22.42	80	11.5
High school graduate	24.46	88	22.4
Some college	28.18	101	21.3
Associate's degree	28.48	102	9.7
Bachelor's degree or more	32.83	118	35.0
Bachelor's degree	29.95	108	20.3
Master's, professional, doctoral degree	38.49	138	14.9

Note: Market shares may not sum to 100.0 because of rounding and missing categories by household type. "Asian" and "black" include Hispanics and non-Hispanics who identify themselves as being of the respective race alone. "Hispanic" includes people of any race who identify themselves as Hispanic. "Other" includes people who identify themselves as non-Hispanic and as Alaska Native, American Indian, Asian (who are also included in the "Asian" row), or Native Hawaiian or other Pacific Islander as well as non-Hispanics reporting more than one race.

Source: Calculations by New Strategist based on the Bureau of Labor Statistics' 2010 Consumer Expenditure Survey

Prepared Food (except Desserts, Frozen Meals, and Salads)

Best customers:	**Householders aged 35 to 54** **Married couples with children at home** **Single parents** **Asians and Hispanics** **Households in the West**
Customer trends:	**Average household spending on prepared foods should continue to grow as grocery stores compete with restaurants for customers.**

Grocery stores increasingly offer fresh prepared foods as they compete with fast-food restaurants for customers. Americans have responded, with households spending an average of $147 on prepared foods (not including desserts, frozen meals, or salads) in 2010. The biggest spenders on prepared foods are the busiest—households with children. Married couples with children at home spend 49 percent more than average on this item. Householders aged 35 to 54, most with children, spend 15 to 19 percent more than average on prepared foods. Single parents, whose spending is well below average on most items, spend 6 percent more than average on prepared food. Hispanic households, which tend to include more children than average, spend 18 percent more than average on prepared food. Asian householders spend 20 percent above average on this item. Households in the West spend one-third more than average on prepared food.

Average household spending on prepared foods from grocery stores rose by a substantial 57 percent between 2000 and 2010, after adjusting for inflation, and is now the third-largest grocery category. Behind the increase were consumers looking for eat-and-run convenience and the growing variety of prepared food offered by grocery store delis. Average household spending on prepared foods should continue to grow as grocery stores compete with restaurants for customers.

Table 9.64 Prepared food (except desserts, frozen meals, and salads)

Total household spending	$17,773,663,320.00
Average household spends	146.76

	AVERAGE HOUSEHOLD SPENDING	BEST CUSTOMERS (index)	BIGGEST CUSTOMERS (market share)
AGE OF HOUSEHOLDER			
Average household	**$146.76**	**100**	**100.0%**
Under age 25	100.42	68	4.5
Aged 25 to 34	134.53	92	15.3
Aged 35 to 44	175.02	119	21.6
Aged 45 to 54	168.06	115	23.7
Aged 55 to 64	159.36	109	19.2
Aged 65 to 74	124.98	85	9.2
Aged 75 or older	101.35	69	6.6

	AVERAGE HOUSEHOLD SPENDING	BEST CUSTOMERS (index)	BIGGEST CUSTOMERS (market share)
HOUSEHOLD INCOME			
Average household	**$146.76**	**100**	**100.0%**
Under $20,000	91.99	63	13.7
$20,000 to $39,999	108.75	74	17.0
$40,000 to $49,999	150.94	103	9.7
$50,000 to $69,999	146.84	100	14.3
$70,000 to $79,999	159.73	109	6.5
$80,000 to $99,999	195.31	133	11.1
$100,000 or more	240.05	164	28.0
HOUSEHOLD TYPE			
Average household	**146.76**	**100**	**100.0**
Married couples	185.95	127	62.5
Married couples, no children	150.24	102	21.7
Married couples, with children	218.54	149	34.6
Oldest child under age 6	171.21	117	5.0
Oldest child aged 6 to 17	226.21	154	18.1
Oldest child aged 18 or older	231.33	158	11.4
Single parent with child under age 18	155.91	106	6.3
Single person	78.91	54	15.8
RACE AND HISPANIC ORIGIN			
Average household	**146.76**	**100**	**100.0**
Asian	175.74	120	5.1
Black	114.21	78	9.5
Hispanic	172.89	118	14.4
Non-Hispanic white and other	147.84	101	76.4
REGION			
Average household	**146.76**	**100**	**100.0**
Northeast	135.20	92	16.9
Midwest	136.90	93	20.8
South	128.64	88	32.2
West	196.10	134	30.3
EDUCATION			
Average household	**146.76**	**100**	**100.0**
Less than high school graduate	126.44	86	12.3
High school graduate	131.45	90	22.9
Some college	130.25	89	18.7
Associate's degree	151.15	103	9.7
Bachelor's degree or more	179.75	122	36.4
Bachelor's degree	174.48	119	22.5
Master's, professional, doctoral degree	190.12	130	14.0

Note: Market shares may not sum to 100.0 because of rounding and missing categories by household type. "Asian" and "black" include Hispanics and non-Hispanics who identify themselves as being of the respective race alone. "Hispanic" includes people of any race who identify themselves as Hispanic. "Other" includes people who identify themselves as non-Hispanic and as Alaska Native, American Indian, Asian (who are also included in the "Asian" row), or Native Hawaiian or other Pacific Islander as well as non-Hispanics reporting more than one race.

Source: Calculations by New Strategist based on the Bureau of Labor Statistics' 2010 Consumer Expenditure Survey

Prepared Food, Frozen (Other than Meals)

Best customers:	**Householders aged 25 to 54** **Married couples with children at home** **Single parents** **Households in the Midwest**
Customer trends:	**Average household spending on frozen prepared food other than meals will continue to fall because of the growing preference for fresh food.**

The biggest spenders on frozen prepared food other than meals are the busiest households—parents with children. Married couples with children at home spend two-thirds more than average on this item. The figure peaks at 73 percent more than average among parents with school-aged children. Single parents spend an unusually high 31 percent more. Householders ranging in age from 25 to 54, most with children, spend 18 to 28 percent more than average on frozen prepared food. Households in the Midwest outspend the average by 18 percent.

Average household spending on frozen prepared food declined slowly over the entire decade, ending up 9 percent lower in 2010 than 2000, after adjusting for inflation. One factor behind the decline is the growing availability of fresh rather than frozen prepared food. Average household spending on frozen prepared food will continue to fall because of consumers' preference for fresh food.

Table 9.65 Prepared food, frozen (other than meals)

Total household spending	$8,619,185,190.00
Average household spends	71.17

	AVERAGE HOUSEHOLD SPENDING	BEST CUSTOMERS (index)	BIGGEST CUSTOMERS (market share)
AGE OF HOUSEHOLDER			
Average household	**$71.17**	**100**	**100.0%**
Under age 25	67.07	94	6.3
Aged 25 to 34	84.32	118	19.7
Aged 35 to 44	90.82	128	23.1
Aged 45 to 54	87.23	123	25.4
Aged 55 to 64	55.67	78	13.8
Aged 65 to 74	46.67	66	7.1
Aged 75 or older	35.13	49	4.7

	AVERAGE HOUSEHOLD SPENDING	BEST CUSTOMERS (index)	BIGGEST CUSTOMERS (market share)
HOUSEHOLD INCOME			
Average household	**$71.17**	**100**	**100.0%**
Under $20,000	48.59	68	14.9
$20,000 to $39,999	62.71	88	20.2
$40,000 to $49,999	65.33	92	8.7
$50,000 to $69,999	72.89	102	14.7
$70,000 to $79,999	98.15	138	8.3
$80,000 to $99,999	91.60	129	10.7
$100,000 or more	93.22	131	22.5
HOUSEHOLD TYPE			
Average household	**71.17**	**100**	**100.0**
Married couples	88.26	124	61.2
Married couples, no children	53.37	75	15.9
Married couples, with children	118.42	166	38.7
Oldest child under age 6	114.41	161	6.9
Oldest child aged 6 to 17	123.38	173	20.4
Oldest child aged 18 or older	113.06	159	11.5
Single parent with child under age 18	93.49	131	7.7
Single person	36.76	52	15.1
RACE AND HISPANIC ORIGIN			
Average household	**71.17**	**100**	**100.0**
Asian	57.19	80	3.4
Black	45.08	63	7.8
Hispanic	66.20	93	11.3
Non-Hispanic white and other	76.17	107	81.1
REGION			
Average household	**71.17**	**100**	**100.0**
Northeast	60.79	85	15.7
Midwest	84.26	118	26.4
South	67.52	95	34.8
West	72.48	102	23.1
EDUCATION			
Average household	**71.17**	**100**	**100.0**
Less than high school graduate	68.49	96	13.7
High school graduate	64.08	90	23.0
Some college	71.05	100	21.0
Associate's degree	72.98	103	9.7
Bachelor's degree or more	78.07	110	32.6
Bachelor's degree	81.18	114	21.5
Master's, professional, doctoral degree	71.93	101	10.9

Note: Market shares may not sum to 100.0 because of rounding and missing categories by household type. "Asian" and "black" include Hispanics and non-Hispanics who identify themselves as being of the respective race alone. "Hispanic" includes people of any race who identify themselves as Hispanic. "Other" includes people who identify themselves as non-Hispanic and as Alaska Native, American Indian, Asian (who are also included in the "Asian" row), or Native Hawaiian or other Pacific Islander as well as non-Hispanics reporting more than one race.

Source: Calculations by New Strategist based on the Bureau of Labor Statistics' 2010 Consumer Expenditure Survey

Prepared Meals, Frozen

Best customers: Householders aged 45 to 54
Married couples with children at home
Single parents

Customer trends: Average household spending on frozen meals is likely to continue to decline as grocery stores offer more of the fresh variety.

The biggest spenders on frozen meals are householders who want the least bother. Some are buying low-fat or low-carb frozen meals as part of a dietary regimen. Others are on the go and do not want to take the time to cook or stop at a restaurant. Married couples with school-aged or older children at home spend the most on frozen meals, 27 percent more than the average household. Even single parents, whose spending on most items is well below average, spend 11 percent more than average on this item. Spending on frozen prepared meals is 14 percent above average among householders aged 45 to 54.

Average household spending on frozen meals more than doubled between 2000 and 2006, after adjusting for inflation. It then fell 18 percent from 2006 to 2010. The earlier rapid increase occurred as consumers demanded greater convenience in meal preparation and as the variety of frozen meals—including many ethnic options—expanded. Average household spending on frozen meals is likely to continue to decline as grocery stores offer more of the fresh variety.

Table 9.66 Prepared meals, frozen

Total household spending $7,381,471,650.00
Average household spends   60.95

	AVERAGE HOUSEHOLD SPENDING	BEST CUSTOMERS (index)	BIGGEST CUSTOMERS (market share)
AGE OF HOUSEHOLDER			
Average household	**$60.95**	**100**	**100.0%**
Under age 25	36.70	60	4.0
Aged 25 to 34	61.07	100	16.7
Aged 35 to 44	65.46	107	19.4
Aged 45 to 54	69.66	114	23.6
Aged 55 to 64	60.29	99	17.4
Aged 65 to 74	50.21	82	8.9
Aged 75 or older	63.66	104	10.0

	AVERAGE HOUSEHOLD SPENDING	BEST CUSTOMERS (index)	BIGGEST CUSTOMERS (market share)
HOUSEHOLD INCOME			
Average household	**$60.95**	**100**	**100.0%**
Under $20,000	39.18	64	14.0
$20,000 to $39,999	49.90	82	18.8
$40,000 to $49,999	62.60	103	9.7
$50,000 to $69,999	62.57	103	14.7
$70,000 to $79,999	54.83	90	5.4
$80,000 to $99,999	81.50	134	11.1
$100,000 or more	93.13	153	26.2
HOUSEHOLD TYPE			
Average household	**60.95**	**100**	**100.0**
Married couples	70.84	116	57.3
Married couples, no children	64.41	106	22.4
Married couples, with children	76.15	125	29.1
Oldest child under age 6	69.92	115	4.9
Oldest child aged 6 to 17	77.27	127	14.9
Oldest child aged 18 or older	77.69	127	9.2
Single parent with child under age 18	67.65	111	6.5
Single person	43.95	72	21.1
RACE AND HISPANIC ORIGIN			
Average household	**60.95**	**100**	**100.0**
Asian	44.20	73	3.1
Black	61.57	101	12.4
Hispanic	35.47	58	7.1
Non-Hispanic white and other	64.79	106	80.6
REGION			
Average household	**60.95**	**100**	**100.0**
Northeast	53.51	88	16.1
Midwest	66.59	109	24.4
South	58.83	97	35.4
West	64.83	106	24.1
EDUCATION			
Average household	**60.95**	**100**	**100.0**
Less than high school graduate	43.18	71	10.1
High school graduate	52.13	86	21.8
Some college	51.46	84	17.7
Associate's degree	83.82	138	13.0
Bachelor's degree or more	75.80	124	36.9
Bachelor's degree	75.13	123	23.3
Master's, professional, doctoral degree	77.13	127	13.7

Note: Market shares may not sum to 100.0 because of rounding and missing categories by household type. "Asian" and "black" include Hispanics and non-Hispanics who identify themselves as being of the respective race alone. "Hispanic" includes people of any race who identify themselves as Hispanic. "Other" includes people who identify themselves as non-Hispanic and as Alaska Native, American Indian, Asian (who are also included in the "Asian" row), or Native Hawaiian or other Pacific Islander as well as non-Hispanics reporting more than one race.

Source: Calculations by New Strategist based on the Bureau of Labor Statistics' 2010 Consumer Expenditure Survey

Rice

Best customers:
Householders aged 35 to 54
Married couples with children at home
Asians, Hispanics, and blacks
Households in the West and Northeast
Householders without a high school diploma

Customer trends:
Average household spending on rice should resume its decline as prepared food claims a bigger share of the food dollar, but growing minority populations may limit the drop.

Asian householders are the biggest spenders on rice by far—they spend over five times the average. Hispanics, who tend to have large families, spend 57 percent more, and blacks, 23 percent more. Together the three groups, which represent 29 percent of the population, account for 57 percent of the market for rice. Married couples with children of any age at home spend 56 percent more than the average household on this item. Householders aged 35 to 54, most with children, spend 17 to 34 percent more than average on rice. Households in the Northeast outspend the average by 21 percent, and those in the West do so by 31 percent. Spending on rice by householders who did not complete high school is one-third above average.

Average household spending on rice grew 31 percent between 2006 and 2010, after adjusting for inflation, completely making up for its 23 percent decline from 2000 to 2006. Behind the recent increase are growing Asian and Hispanic populations and a renewed surge of home cooking in an effort to rein in household spending because of the Great Recession. Spending on rice should resume its decline as prepared food claims a growing share of the food dollar, but growing minority populations may limit the drop.

Table 9.67 Rice

Total household spending $2,993,765,040.00
Average household spends   24.72

	AVERAGE HOUSEHOLD SPENDING	BEST CUSTOMERS (index)	BIGGEST CUSTOMERS (market share)
AGE OF HOUSEHOLDER			
Average household	**$24.72**	**100**	**100.0%**
Under age 25	17.14	69	4.6
Aged 25 to 34	24.35	99	16.4
Aged 35 to 44	33.06	134	24.2
Aged 45 to 54	28.91	117	24.2
Aged 55 to 64	26.17	106	18.7
Aged 65 to 74	17.03	69	7.4
Aged 75 or older	11.71	47	4.5

	AVERAGE HOUSEHOLD SPENDING	BEST CUSTOMERS (index)	BIGGEST CUSTOMERS (market share)
HOUSEHOLD INCOME			
Average household	$24.72	100	100.0%
Under $20,000	18.86	76	16.6
$20,000 to $39,999	23.23	94	21.5
$40,000 to $49,999	19.77	80	7.6
$50,000 to $69,999	26.86	109	15.6
$70,000 to $79,999	19.03	77	4.6
$80,000 to $99,999	28.56	116	9.6
$100,000 or more	35.98	146	25.0
HOUSEHOLD TYPE			
Average household	24.72	100	100.0
Married couples	31.21	126	62.3
Married couples, no children	18.00	73	15.5
Married couples, with children	38.46	156	36.2
Oldest child under age 6	33.22	134	5.8
Oldest child aged 6 to 17	34.23	138	16.3
Oldest child aged 18 or older	47.45	192	13.9
Single parent with child under age 18	20.73	84	4.9
Single person	10.30	42	12.2
RACE AND HISPANIC ORIGIN			
Average household	24.72	100	100.0
Asian	132.07	534	22.7
Black	30.32	123	15.0
Hispanic	38.88	157	19.2
Non-Hispanic white and other	21.59	87	66.2
REGION			
Average household	24.72	100	100.0
Northeast	29.84	121	22.2
Midwest	17.73	72	16.0
South	21.84	88	32.4
West	32.35	131	29.6
EDUCATION			
Average household	24.72	100	100.0
Less than high school graduate	32.28	131	18.7
High school graduate	20.50	83	21.2
Some college	21.19	86	18.0
Associate's degree	23.35	94	8.9
Bachelor's degree or more	28.10	114	33.8
Bachelor's degree	29.37	119	22.4
Master's, professional, doctoral degree	25.62	104	11.2

Note: Market shares may not sum to 100.0 because of rounding and missing categories by household type. "Asian" and "black" include Hispanics and non-Hispanics who identify themselves as being of the respective race alone. "Hispanic" includes people of any race who identify themselves as Hispanic. "Other" includes people who identify themselves as non-Hispanic and as Alaska Native, American Indian, Asian (who are also included in the "Asian" row), or Native Hawaiian or other Pacific Islander as well as non-Hispanics reporting more than one race.

Source: Calculations by New Strategist based on the Bureau of Labor Statistics' 2010 Consumer Expenditure Survey

Salad Dressing

Best customers: **Householders aged 35 to 54**
Married couples without children at home
Married couples with school-aged or older children at home

Customer trends: **Average household spending on salad dressing may resume its fall as more**
boomers become empty-nesters and household size shrinks.

Middle-aged married couples with children spend the most on salad dressing. Householders aged 35 to 54, many with children at home, spend 16 to 19 percent more than average on this item. Married couples with school-aged children spend 43 percent more than the average household on salad dressing, while those with adult children at home spend 54 percent more than average. Married couples without children at home (most empty-nesters) outspend the average on salad dressing by 21 percent.

Average household spending on salad dressing fell 18 percent between 2000 and 2006, after adjusting for inflation, but has stabilized since then. The growing popularity of prepared and fast food cut spending on this item. Average household spending on salad dressing may resume its decline as more boomers become empty-nesters and household size shrinks.

Table 9.68 **Salad dressing**

Total household spending   **$3,484,248,390.00**
Average household spends   **28.77**

	AVERAGE HOUSEHOLD SPENDING	BEST CUSTOMERS (index)	BIGGEST CUSTOMERS (market share)
AGE OF HOUSEHOLDER			
Average household	**$28.77**	**100**	**100.0%**
Under age 25	17.60	61	4.1
Aged 25 to 34	23.60	82	13.7
Aged 35 to 44	34.23	119	21.5
Aged 45 to 54	33.36	116	24.0
Aged 55 to 64	30.31	105	18.6
Aged 65 to 74	28.59	99	10.7
Aged 75 or older	22.48	78	7.5

	AVERAGE HOUSEHOLD SPENDING	BEST CUSTOMERS (index)	BIGGEST CUSTOMERS (market share)
HOUSEHOLD INCOME			
Average household	**$28.77**	**100**	**100.0%**
Under $20,000	17.24	60	13.1
$20,000 to $39,999	22.86	79	18.2
$40,000 to $49,999	28.59	99	9.4
$50,000 to $69,999	31.07	108	15.5
$70,000 to $79,999	34.60	120	7.2
$80,000 to $99,999	33.55	117	9.7
$100,000 or more	45.22	157	27.0
HOUSEHOLD TYPE			
Average household	**28.77**	**100**	**100.0**
Married couples	37.49	130	64.3
Married couples, no children	34.84	121	25.7
Married couples, with children	39.77	138	32.2
Oldest child under age 6	27.25	95	4.1
Oldest child aged 6 to 17	41.00	143	16.8
Oldest child aged 18 or older	44.34	154	11.1
Single parent with child under age 18	25.62	89	5.3
Single person	14.00	49	14.3
RACE AND HISPANIC ORIGIN			
Average household	**28.77**	**100**	**100.0**
Asian	12.71	44	1.9
Black	23.39	81	9.9
Hispanic	25.78	90	10.9
Non-Hispanic white and other	30.07	105	79.2
REGION			
Average household	**28.77**	**100**	**100.0**
Northeast	30.36	106	19.4
Midwest	31.44	109	24.4
South	25.54	89	32.6
West	30.07	105	23.7
EDUCATION			
Average household	**28.77**	**100**	**100.0**
Less than high school graduate	24.00	83	11.9
High school graduate	28.77	100	25.5
Some college	27.94	97	20.4
Associate's degree	33.70	117	11.1
Bachelor's degree or more	29.83	104	30.8
Bachelor's degree	29.54	103	19.4
Master's, professional, doctoral degree	30.40	106	11.4

Note: Market shares may not sum to 100.0 because of rounding and missing categories by household type. "Asian" and "black" include Hispanics and non-Hispanics who identify themselves as being of the respective race alone. "Hispanic" includes people of any race who identify themselves as Hispanic. "Other" includes people who identify themselves as non-Hispanic and as Alaska Native, American Indian, Asian (who are also included in the "Asian" row), or Native Hawaiian or other Pacific Islander as well as non-Hispanics reporting more than one race.

Source: Calculations by New Strategist based on the Bureau of Labor Statistics' 2010 Consumer Expenditure Survey

Salads, Prepared

Best customers:	**Householders aged 45 to 64** **Married couples without children at home** **Married couples with school-aged or older children at home** **Households in the West**
Customer trends:	**Average household spending on prepared salads will continue to rise as consumers look for healthy, convenient meal options.**

The best customers of prepared salads are older married couples. Householders aged 45 to 64 spend one-fifth more than the average household on this item. Married couples with adult children at home spend 61 percent more than average on prepared salads. Those with school-aged children outspend the average by 29 percent. Couples without children at home (most of them empty-nesters) spend 15 percent above average on prepared salads. Spending on prepared salads by households in the West is 19 percent higher than average.

Average household spending on prepared salads rose by a stunning 51 percent between 2000 and 2010, after adjusting for inflation. Behind the gain was Americans' growing demand for the convenience and quality of fresh prepared food. Average household spending on prepared salads may continue to rise in the years ahead as consumers look for healthy, convenient meal options.

Table 9.69 Salads, prepared

Total household spending	$4,290,821,010.00
Average household spends	35.43

	AVERAGE HOUSEHOLD SPENDING	BEST CUSTOMERS (index)	BIGGEST CUSTOMERS (market share)
AGE OF HOUSEHOLDER			
Average household	**$35.43**	**100**	**100.0%**
Under age 25	16.88	48	3.2
Aged 25 to 34	28.09	79	13.2
Aged 35 to 44	35.01	99	17.9
Aged 45 to 54	42.04	119	24.5
Aged 55 to 64	42.57	120	21.2
Aged 65 to 74	38.72	109	11.8
Aged 75 or older	30.17	85	8.1

	AVERAGE HOUSEHOLD SPENDING	BEST CUSTOMERS (index)	BIGGEST CUSTOMERS (market share)
HOUSEHOLD INCOME			
Average household	**$35.43**	**100**	**100.0%**
Under $20,000	19.64	55	12.1
$20,000 to $39,999	25.10	71	16.2
$40,000 to $49,999	33.18	94	8.9
$50,000 to $69,999	36.99	104	15.0
$70,000 to $79,999	40.00	113	6.8
$80,000 to $99,999	41.99	119	9.9
$100,000 or more	65.47	185	31.7
HOUSEHOLD TYPE			
Average household	**35.43**	**100**	**100.0**
Married couples	43.95	124	61.2
Married couples, no children	40.88	115	24.5
Married couples, with children	47.69	135	31.3
Oldest child under age 6	34.66	98	4.2
Oldest child aged 6 to 17	45.86	129	15.2
Oldest child aged 18 or older	57.09	161	11.6
Single parent with child under age 18	32.62	92	5.4
Single person	23.21	66	19.2
RACE AND HISPANIC ORIGIN			
Average household	**35.43**	**100**	**100.0**
Asian	29.87	84	3.6
Black	26.27	74	9.1
Hispanic	20.09	57	6.9
Non-Hispanic white and other	39.27	111	84.0
REGION			
Average household	**35.43**	**100**	**100.0**
Northeast	36.88	104	19.1
Midwest	33.35	94	21.0
South	31.89	90	33.0
West	42.16	119	27.0
EDUCATION			
Average household	**35.43**	**100**	**100.0**
Less than high school graduate	20.26	57	8.2
High school graduate	29.34	83	21.1
Some college	31.12	88	18.5
Associate's degree	37.15	105	9.9
Bachelor's degree or more	50.04	141	42.0
Bachelor's degree	45.26	128	24.1
Master's, professional, doctoral degree	59.44	168	18.2

Note: Market shares may not sum to 100.0 because of rounding and missing categories by household type. "Asian" and "black" include Hispanics and non-Hispanics who identify themselves as being of the respective race alone. "Hispanic" includes people of any race who identify themselves as Hispanic. "Other" includes people who identify themselves as non-Hispanic and as Alaska Native, American Indian, Asian (who are also included in the "Asian" row), or Native Hawaiian or other Pacific Islander as well as non-Hispanics reporting more than one race.

Source: Calculations by New Strategist based on the Bureau of Labor Statistics' 2010 Consumer Expenditure Survey

Salt, Spices, and Other Seasonings

Best customers: **Householders aged 35 to 54**
Married couples with school-aged or older children at home
Asians and Hispanics

Customer trends: **Average household spending on salt, spices, and other seasonings may decline as household size shrinks with the aging of the population.**

The biggest spenders on salt, spices, and other seasonings are households most likely to cook from scratch—married couples with children. Married couples with adult children at home spend 57 percent more than average on this item, and those with school-aged children, 43 percent more. Householders aged 35 to 54 spend 17 to 19 percent more than average on salt and spices. Asians outspend the average by 38 percent and Hispanics do so by 20 percent.

Average household spending on salt, spices, and other seasonings grew 24 percent between 2000 and 2010, after adjusting for inflation—despite the growing propensity of Americans to substitute prepared food for home-cooked meals. Behind the increase were changing tastes, with specialty flavorings growing in popularity. Spending on salt, spices, and other seasonings may decline in the years ahead as household size shrinks along with the aging of the population.

Table 9.70 **Salt, spices, and other seasonings**

| Total household spending | $3,934,766,430.00 | | |
| Average household spends | 32.49 | | |

	AVERAGE HOUSEHOLD SPENDING	BEST CUSTOMERS (index)	BIGGEST CUSTOMERS (market share)
AGE OF HOUSEHOLDER			
Average household	**$32.49**	**100**	**100.0%**
Under age 25	22.99	71	4.7
Aged 25 to 34	31.44	97	16.1
Aged 35 to 44	38.81	119	21.6
Aged 45 to 54	37.93	117	24.2
Aged 55 to 64	34.20	105	18.6
Aged 65 to 74	27.62	85	9.1
Aged 75 or older	19.32	59	5.7

	AVERAGE HOUSEHOLD SPENDING	BEST CUSTOMERS (index)	BIGGEST CUSTOMERS (market share)
HOUSEHOLD INCOME			
Average household	**$32.49**	**100**	**100.0%**
Under $20,000	22.45	69	15.1
$20,000 to $39,999	25.27	78	17.8
$40,000 to $49,999	26.81	83	7.8
$50,000 to $69,999	34.01	105	15.0
$70,000 to $79,999	30.52	94	5.6
$80,000 to $99,999	41.33	127	10.6
$100,000 or more	54.10	167	28.6
HOUSEHOLD TYPE			
Average household	**32.49**	**100**	**100.0**
Married couples	40.99	126	62.2
Married couples, no children	34.45	106	22.5
Married couples, with children	46.09	142	33.0
Oldest child under age 6	35.32	109	4.7
Oldest child aged 6 to 17	46.46	143	16.8
Oldest child aged 18 or older	51.05	157	11.3
Single parent with child under age 18	31.15	96	5.7
Single person	16.90	52	15.2
RACE AND HISPANIC ORIGIN			
Average household	**32.49**	**100**	**100.0**
Asian	44.68	138	5.8
Black	28.54	88	10.7
Hispanic	38.95	120	14.6
Non-Hispanic white and other	32.07	99	74.8
REGION			
Average household	**32.49**	**100**	**100.0**
Northeast	35.90	110	20.3
Midwest	32.73	101	22.5
South	28.91	89	32.7
West	35.36	109	24.7
EDUCATION			
Average household	**32.49**	**100**	**100.0**
Less than high school graduate	34.00	105	15.0
High school graduate	28.99	89	22.8
Some college	28.57	88	18.5
Associate's degree	33.30	102	9.7
Bachelor's degree or more	37.48	115	34.3
Bachelor's degree	35.62	110	20.7
Master's, professional, doctoral degree	41.13	127	13.7

Note: Market shares may not sum to 100.0 because of rounding and missing categories by household type. "Asian" and "black" include Hispanics and non-Hispanics who identify themselves as being of the respective race alone. "Hispanic" includes people of any race who identify themselves as Hispanic. "Other" includes people who identify themselves as non-Hispanic and as Alaska Native, American Indian, Asian (who are also included in the "Asian" row), or Native Hawaiian or other Pacific Islander as well as non-Hispanics reporting more than one race.

Source: Calculations by New Strategist based on the Bureau of Labor Statistics' 2010 Consumer Expenditure Survey

Sauces and Gravies

Best customers: **Householders aged 35 to 54**
                        Married couples with children at home
                        Single parents

Customer trends: **Average household spending on sauces and gravies is likely to decline as boomers become empty-nesters and prepared food claims a growing share of the food dollar.**

Married couples with children at home, the householders most likely to cook from scratch, are the best customers of sauces and gravies. They spend 53 percent more than average on this item. Householders aged 35 to 54, most with children, spend 26 to 31 percent more than average on sauces and gravies. Sauces and gravies are one of the relatively few items on which single parents, with their lower incomes, spend an average amount.

Average household spending on sauces and gravies increased 11 percent between 2000 and 2010, after adjusting for inflation. Behind the increase are changing tastes, with specialty sauces growing in popularity. Average household spending on this item is likely to decline in the years ahead as more boomers become empty-nesters and prepared food claims a growing share of the food dollar.

Table 9.71 Sauces and gravies

Total household spending $6,350,851,080.00
Average household spends   52.44

AGE OF HOUSEHOLDER	AVERAGE HOUSEHOLD SPENDING	BEST CUSTOMERS (index)	BIGGEST CUSTOMERS (market share)
Average household	**$52.44**	**100**	**100.0%**
Under age 25	36.48	70	4.6
Aged 25 to 34	51.35	98	16.3
Aged 35 to 44	68.65	131	23.7
Aged 45 to 54	65.97	126	26.0
Aged 55 to 64	48.26	92	16.2
Aged 65 to 74	40.21	77	8.3
Aged 75 or older	26.62	51	4.8

	AVERAGE HOUSEHOLD SPENDING	BEST CUSTOMERS (index)	BIGGEST CUSTOMERS (market share)
HOUSEHOLD INCOME			
Average household	**$52.44**	**100**	**100.0%**
Under $20,000	29.83	57	12.4
$20,000 to $39,999	37.16	71	16.2
$40,000 to $49,999	53.41	102	9.6
$50,000 to $69,999	59.07	113	16.2
$70,000 to $79,999	56.00	107	6.4
$80,000 to $99,999	64.78	124	10.3
$100,000 or more	88.44	169	28.9
HOUSEHOLD TYPE			
Average household	**52.44**	**100**	**100.0**
Married couples	68.91	131	64.8
Married couples, no children	53.59	102	21.7
Married couples, with children	80.45	153	35.7
Oldest child under age 6	70.85	135	5.8
Oldest child aged 6 to 17	82.87	158	18.6
Oldest child aged 18 or older	81.75	156	11.3
Single parent with child under age 18	52.76	101	5.9
Single person	24.09	46	13.5
RACE AND HISPANIC ORIGIN			
Average household	**52.44**	**100**	**100.0**
Asian	54.88	105	4.5
Black	45.71	87	10.7
Hispanic	52.96	101	12.3
Non-Hispanic white and other	53.40	102	77.2
REGION			
Average household	**52.44**	**100**	**100.0**
Northeast	57.62	110	20.2
Midwest	51.40	98	21.8
South	46.48	89	32.5
West	59.08	113	25.5
EDUCATION			
Average household	**52.44**	**100**	**100.0**
Less than high school graduate	42.32	81	11.5
High school graduate	46.13	88	22.5
Some college	50.86	97	20.4
Associate's degree	61.24	117	11.0
Bachelor's degree or more	60.67	116	34.4
Bachelor's degree	59.68	114	21.5
Master's, professional, doctoral degree	62.61	119	12.9

Note: Market shares may not sum to 100.0 because of rounding and missing categories by household type. "Asian" and "black" include Hispanics and non-Hispanics who identify themselves as being of the respective race alone. "Hispanic" includes people of any race who identify themselves as Hispanic. "Other" includes people who identify themselves as non-Hispanic and as Alaska Native, American Indian, Asian (who are also included in the "Asian" row), or Native Hawaiian or other Pacific Islander as well as non-Hispanics reporting more than one race.

Source: Calculations by New Strategist based on the Bureau of Labor Statistics' 2010 Consumer Expenditure Survey

Sausage

Best customers:
      Householders aged 45 to 54
      Married couples with school-aged or older children at home
      Blacks
      Households in the South

Customer trends:
      Average household spending on sausage should continue to decline now that the
      small generation X is in the best-customer lifestage.

Households with children are the biggest spenders on sausage. Married couples school-aged or older children at home spend 40 to 57 percent more than average on this item. Householders aged 45 to 54, many with children at home, spend 25 percent more than average on sausage. Blacks spend 38 percent more than average on this item. Spending on sausage by households in the South, where many blacks reside, is 17 percent above average.

Average household spending on sausage declined 18 percent between 2000 and 2010, after adjusting for inflation. The growing popularity of fast-food breakfasts rather than home-cooked meals during the period leading up to the Great Recession was one factor behind the drop in spending. Average household spending on sausage should continue to decline now that the small generation X is in the best-customer lifestage.

Table 9.72 Sausage

Total household spending $3,164,525,910.00
Average household spends   26.13

	AVERAGE HOUSEHOLD SPENDING	BEST CUSTOMERS (index)	BIGGEST CUSTOMERS (market share)
AGE OF HOUSEHOLDER			
Average household	**$26.13**	**100**	**100.0%**
Under age 25	12.92	49	3.3
Aged 25 to 34	24.47	94	15.6
Aged 35 to 44	25.24	97	17.5
Aged 45 to 54	32.73	125	25.9
Aged 55 to 64	26.64	102	18.0
Aged 65 to 74	29.30	112	12.1
Aged 75 or older	20.66	79	7.5

	AVERAGE HOUSEHOLD SPENDING	BEST CUSTOMERS (index)	BIGGEST CUSTOMERS (market share)
HOUSEHOLD INCOME			
Average household	**$26.13**	**100**	**100.0%**
Under $20,000	18.44	71	15.4
$20,000 to $39,999	23.33	89	20.5
$40,000 to $49,999	26.50	101	9.6
$50,000 to $69,999	27.01	103	14.8
$70,000 to $79,999	35.16	135	8.1
$80,000 to $99,999	28.99	111	9.3
$100,000 or more	34.25	131	22.5
HOUSEHOLD TYPE			
Average household	**26.13**	**100**	**100.0**
Married couples	33.57	128	63.4
Married couples, no children	28.69	110	23.3
Married couples, with children	36.07	138	32.1
Oldest child under age 6	24.25	93	4.0
Oldest child aged 6 to 17	36.71	140	16.5
Oldest child aged 18 or older	41.15	157	11.4
Single parent with child under age 18	20.93	80	4.7
Single person	13.19	50	14.8
RACE AND HISPANIC ORIGIN			
Average household	**26.13**	**100**	**100.0**
Asian	25.93	99	4.2
Black	36.06	138	16.9
Hispanic	27.06	104	12.6
Non-Hispanic white and other	24.40	93	70.8
REGION			
Average household	**26.13**	**100**	**100.0**
Northeast	25.84	99	18.1
Midwest	24.22	93	20.7
South	30.60	117	43.0
West	20.94	80	18.2
EDUCATION			
Average household	**26.13**	**100**	**100.0**
Less than high school graduate	28.15	108	15.4
High school graduate	28.38	109	27.7
Some college	23.10	88	18.6
Associate's degree	32.22	123	11.7
Bachelor's degree or more	23.43	90	26.6
Bachelor's degree	21.16	81	15.3
Master's, professional, doctoral degree	27.90	107	11.6

Note: Market shares may not sum to 100.0 because of rounding and missing categories by household type. "Asian" and "black" include Hispanics and non-Hispanics who identify themselves as being of the respective race alone. "Hispanic" includes people of any race who identify themselves as Hispanic. "Other" includes people who identify themselves as non-Hispanic and as Alaska Native, American Indian, Asian (who are also included in the "Asian" row), or Native Hawaiian or other Pacific Islander as well as non-Hispanics reporting more than one race.

Source: Calculations by New Strategist based on the Bureau of Labor Statistics' 2010 Consumer Expenditure Survey

Soups, Canned and Packaged

Best customers: Householders aged 35 to 54
Married couples with school-aged or older children at home

Customer trends: Average household spending on soup may rise again if the product promotes itself
as an inexpensive convenience food.

Families with children are the best customers of soup. Couples with school-aged or older children at home spend 35 to 52 percent more than average on soup. Householders aged 35 to 54, most with children, spend 13 to 17 percent more than average on soup.

Average household spending on soup fell 6 percent between 2000 and 2010, after adjusting for inflation. Spending on soup may rise again if the product promotes itself as an inexpensive convenience food.

Table 9.73 Soups, canned and packaged

Total household spending $5,122,826,100.00
Average household spends 42.30

	AVERAGE HOUSEHOLD SPENDING	BEST CUSTOMERS (index)	BIGGEST CUSTOMERS (market share)
AGE OF HOUSEHOLDER			
Average household	**$42.30**	**100**	**100.0%**
Under age 25	24.65	58	3.9
Aged 25 to 34	35.70	84	14.1
Aged 35 to 44	47.69	113	20.4
Aged 45 to 54	49.42	117	24.2
Aged 55 to 64	40.58	96	16.9
Aged 65 to 74	43.27	102	11.0
Aged 75 or older	42.42	100	9.6

	AVERAGE HOUSEHOLD SPENDING	BEST CUSTOMERS (index)	BIGGEST CUSTOMERS (market share)
HOUSEHOLD INCOME			
Average household	**$42.30**	**100**	**100.0%**
Under $20,000	28.06	66	14.5
$20,000 to $39,999	34.69	82	18.8
$40,000 to $49,999	39.33	93	8.8
$50,000 to $69,999	41.24	97	14.0
$70,000 to $79,999	46.06	109	6.5
$80,000 to $99,999	53.19	126	10.5
$100,000 or more	67.16	159	27.2
HOUSEHOLD TYPE			
Average household	**42.30**	**100**	**100.0**
Married couples	53.31	126	62.2
Married couples, no children	47.63	113	23.9
Married couples, with children	56.73	134	31.2
Oldest child under age 6	41.48	98	4.2
Oldest child aged 6 to 17	56.93	135	15.8
Oldest child aged 18 or older	64.24	152	11.0
Single parent with child under age 18	34.95	83	4.9
Single person	27.30	65	18.9
RACE AND HISPANIC ORIGIN			
Average household	**42.30**	**100**	**100.0**
Asian	48.72	115	4.9
Black	30.26	72	8.8
Hispanic	35.74	84	10.3
Non-Hispanic white and other	45.22	107	81.0
REGION			
Average household	**42.30**	**100**	**100.0**
Northeast	46.85	111	20.3
Midwest	44.69	106	23.6
South	38.37	91	33.3
West	42.61	101	22.8
EDUCATION			
Average household	**42.30**	**100**	**100.0**
Less than high school graduate	36.31	86	12.3
High school graduate	40.61	96	24.5
Some college	39.77	94	19.8
Associate's degree	48.48	115	10.8
Bachelor's degree or more	46.20	109	32.4
Bachelor's degree	43.89	104	19.6
Master's, professional, doctoral degree	50.74	120	13.0

Note: Market shares may not sum to 100.0 because of rounding and missing categories by household type. "Asian" and "black" include Hispanics and non-Hispanics who identify themselves as being of the respective race alone. "Hispanic" includes people of any race who identify themselves as Hispanic. "Other" includes people who identify themselves as non-Hispanic and as Alaska Native, American Indian, Asian (who are also included in the "Asian" row), or Native Hawaiian or other Pacific Islander as well as non-Hispanics reporting more than one race.

Source: Calculations by New Strategist based on the Bureau of Labor Statistics' 2010 Consumer Expenditure Survey

Sports Drinks

Best customers:
Householders aged 25 to 54
Married couples with children at home
Single parents
Hispanics
Households in the Midwest

Customer trends:
Average household spending on sports drinks should rise in the years ahead because they are being marketed as a healthy alternative to sodas.

The biggest spenders on sports drinks are the largest households. Married couples with children at home spend 60 percent more than average on this item. Householders aged 25 to 54, most of them parents, spend 26 to 47 percent more than average on sports drinks and account for three-quarters of the market. Single parents, whose spending approaches average on only a few items, spend 19 percent more than average on sports drinks. Hispanics, who have the largest families, outspend the average by 34 percent. Households in the Midwest spend 13 percent more than average on sports drinks.

Sports drinks is a recently added category in the Consumer Expenditure Survey, and there are no comparative spending data from 2000 or 2006. Average household spending on sports drinks should rise in the years ahead because they are being marketed as a healthy alternative to sodas.

Table 9.74 Sports drinks

| Total household spending | $2,314,354,770.00 |
| Average household spends | 19.11 |

	AVERAGE HOUSEHOLD SPENDING	BEST CUSTOMERS (index)	BIGGEST CUSTOMERS (market share)
AGE OF HOUSEHOLDER			
Average household	**$19.11**	**100**	**100.0%**
Under age 25	11.52	60	4.0
Aged 25 to 34	24.05	126	21.0
Aged 35 to 44	28.18	147	26.7
Aged 45 to 54	24.74	129	26.8
Aged 55 to 64	15.31	80	14.1
Aged 65 to 74	8.48	44	4.8
Aged 75 or older	5.41	28	2.7

	AVERAGE HOUSEHOLD SPENDING	BEST CUSTOMERS (index)	BIGGEST CUSTOMERS (market share)
HOUSEHOLD INCOME			
Average household	**$19.11**	**100**	**100.0%**
Under $20,000	8.57	45	9.8
$20,000 to $39,999	15.91	83	19.1
$40,000 to $49,999	16.70	87	8.3
$50,000 to $69,999	21.76	114	16.3
$70,000 to $79,999	18.94	99	5.9
$80,000 to $99,999	25.03	131	10.9
$100,000 or more	33.19	174	29.8
HOUSEHOLD TYPE			
Average household	**19.11**	**100**	**100.0**
Married couples	23.82	125	61.5
Married couples, no children	16.23	85	18.0
Married couples, with children	30.65	160	37.3
Oldest child under age 6	26.40	138	5.9
Oldest child aged 6 to 17	28.48	149	17.5
Oldest child aged 18 or older	36.05	189	13.6
Single parent with child under age 18	22.66	119	7.0
Single person	9.25	48	14.2
RACE AND HISPANIC ORIGIN			
Average household	**19.11**	**100**	**100.0**
Asian	15.87	83	3.5
Black	16.55	87	10.6
Hispanic	25.53	134	16.3
Non-Hispanic white and other	18.53	97	73.5
REGION			
Average household	**19.11**	**100**	**100.0**
Northeast	16.90	88	16.2
Midwest	21.52	113	25.1
South	19.33	101	37.1
West	18.11	95	21.5
EDUCATION			
Average household	**19.11**	**100**	**100.0**
Less than high school graduate	15.84	83	11.8
High school graduate	14.70	77	19.6
Some college	20.64	108	22.7
Associate's degree	22.80	119	11.3
Bachelor's degree or more	22.07	115	34.3
Bachelor's degree	22.95	120	22.7
Master's, professional, doctoral degree	20.34	106	11.5

Note: Market shares may not sum to 100.0 because of rounding and missing categories by household type. "Asian" and "black" include Hispanics and non-Hispanics who identify themselves as being of the respective race alone. "Hispanic" includes people of any race who identify themselves as Hispanic. "Other" includes people who identify themselves as non-Hispanic and as Alaska Native, American Indian, Asian (who are also included in the "Asian" row), or Native Hawaiian or other Pacific Islander as well as non-Hispanics reporting more than one race.

Source: Calculations by New Strategist based on the Bureau of Labor Statistics' 2010 Consumer Expenditure Survey

Sugar

Best customers:
Householders aged 35 to 54
Married couples with school-aged or older children at home
Hispanics and blacks
Householders without a high school diploma

Customer trends:
Average household spending on sugar is likely to resume its decline as more boomers become empty-nesters and household size shrinks.

The biggest spenders on sugar are households that do the most cooking from scratch, typically families with children. Couples with school-aged or older children at home spend 43 to 86 percent more than average on sugar. Householders aged 35 to 54, most with children, spend 23 to 33 percent more than average on this item and control half the market. Hispanics, who tend to have large families, spend 39 percent more than average on sugar, and blacks spend 17 percent more. Spending on sugar by householders without a high school diploma is 49 percent higher than average.

Average household spending on sugar fell 16 percent between 2000 and 2006, after adjusting for inflation, then grew 27 percent between 2006 and 2010. Behind the earlier decline was the rise in popularity of prepared food as busy families found less time to cook from scratch. The rise since 2006 is due in part to more home cooking in the aftermath of the Great Recession. Average household spending on sugar is likely to resume its decline as more boomers become empty-nesters and household size shrinks.

Table 9.75 Sugar

| Total household spending | $2,756,395,320.00 |
| Average household spends | 22.76 |

	AVERAGE HOUSEHOLD SPENDING	BEST CUSTOMERS (index)	BIGGEST CUSTOMERS (market share)
AGE OF HOUSEHOLDER			
Average household	**$22.76**	**100**	**100.0%**
Under age 25	14.87	65	4.3
Aged 25 to 34	20.98	92	15.3
Aged 35 to 44	27.93	123	22.2
Aged 45 to 54	30.17	133	27.4
Aged 55 to 64	17.79	78	13.8
Aged 65 to 74	22.99	101	10.9
Aged 75 or older	14.14	62	5.9

	AVERAGE HOUSEHOLD SPENDING	BEST CUSTOMERS (index)	BIGGEST CUSTOMERS (market share)
HOUSEHOLD INCOME			
Average household	**$22.76**	**100**	**100.0%**
Under $20,000	19.67	86	18.9
$20,000 to $39,999	21.38	94	21.5
$40,000 to $49,999	21.81	96	9.1
$50,000 to $69,999	22.26	98	14.0
$70,000 to $79,999	26.02	114	6.8
$80,000 to $99,999	24.19	106	8.9
$100,000 or more	27.96	123	21.1
HOUSEHOLD TYPE			
Average household	**22.76**	**100**	**100.0**
Married couples	28.58	126	61.9
Married couples, no children	21.82	96	20.4
Married couples, with children	34.22	150	35.0
Oldest child under age 6	23.39	103	4.4
Oldest child aged 6 to 17	32.44	143	16.8
Oldest child aged 18 or older	42.41	186	13.5
Single parent with child under age 18	20.58	90	5.3
Single person	10.15	45	13.1
RACE AND HISPANIC ORIGIN			
Average household	**22.76**	**100**	**100.0**
Asian	16.54	73	3.1
Black	26.58	117	14.3
Hispanic	31.75	139	17.0
Non-Hispanic white and other	20.75	91	69.1
REGION			
Average household	**22.76**	**100**	**100.0**
Northeast	22.48	99	18.1
Midwest	24.86	109	24.3
South	21.99	97	35.5
West	22.15	97	22.0
EDUCATION			
Average household	**22.76**	**100**	**100.0**
Less than high school graduate	33.96	149	21.3
High school graduate	23.89	105	26.8
Some college	18.35	81	16.9
Associate's degree	22.35	98	9.3
Bachelor's degree or more	20.16	89	26.3
Bachelor's degree	20.95	92	17.4
Master's, professional, doctoral degree	18.59	82	8.8

Note: Market shares may not sum to 100.0 because of rounding and missing categories by household type. "Asian" and "black" include Hispanics and non-Hispanics who identify themselves as being of the respective race alone. "Hispanic" includes people of any race who identify themselves as Hispanic. "Other" includes people who identify themselves as non-Hispanic and as Alaska Native, American Indian, Asian (who are also included in the "Asian" row), or Native Hawaiian or other Pacific Islander as well as non-Hispanics reporting more than one race.

Source: Calculations by New Strategist based on the Bureau of Labor Statistics' 2010 Consumer Expenditure Survey

Sweetrolls, Coffee Cakes, and Doughnuts

Best customers:	**Married couples with school-aged or older children at home** **Hispanics**
Customer trends:	**Average household spending on sweetrolls, coffee cakes, and doughnuts may continue to decline in the years ahead as the baby-boom generation exits the best-customer lifestage.**

The biggest spenders on sweetrolls, coffee cakes, and doughnuts are households with children. Married couples with school-aged or older children at home spend 39 to 56 percent more than average on this item. Hispanics spend 18 percent more than average on sweetrolls, coffee cakes, and doughnuts.

Average household spending on sweetrolls, coffee cakes, and doughnuts fell 22 percent between 2000 and 2010, after adjusting for inflation. Behind the spending decline is the growing propensity of Americans to grab snacks from restaurants rather than grocery stores. Average household spending on sweetrolls, coffee cakes, and doughnuts may continue to decline in the years ahead as the baby-boom generation exits the best-customer lifestage.

Table 9.76 Sweetrolls, coffee cakes, and doughnuts

Total household spending	$2,698,263,960.00
Average household spends	22.28

	AVERAGE HOUSEHOLD SPENDING	BEST CUSTOMERS (index)	BIGGEST CUSTOMERS (market share)
AGE OF HOUSEHOLDER			
Average household	**$22.28**	**100**	**100.0%**
Under age 25	14.16	64	4.2
Aged 25 to 34	18.99	85	14.2
Aged 35 to 44	23.54	106	19.1
Aged 45 to 54	22.42	101	20.8
Aged 55 to 64	24.95	112	19.7
Aged 65 to 74	21.75	98	10.5
Aged 75 or older	26.74	120	11.4

	AVERAGE HOUSEHOLD SPENDING	BEST CUSTOMERS (index)	BIGGEST CUSTOMERS (market share)
HOUSEHOLD INCOME			
Average household	**$22.28**	**100**	**100.0%**
Under $20,000	14.40	65	14.1
$20,000 to $39,999	21.20	95	21.8
$40,000 to $49,999	21.98	99	9.3
$50,000 to $69,999	21.41	96	13.8
$70,000 to $79,999	22.53	101	6.1
$80,000 to $99,999	31.63	142	11.8
$100,000 or more	29.49	132	22.7
HOUSEHOLD TYPE			
Average household	**22.28**	**100**	**100.0**
Married couples	28.47	128	63.0
Married couples, no children	24.57	110	23.4
Married couples, with children	31.01	139	32.4
Oldest child under age 6	23.62	106	4.5
Oldest child aged 6 to 17	31.07	139	16.4
Oldest child aged 18 or older	34.70	156	11.2
Single parent with child under age 18	20.50	92	5.4
Single person	13.97	63	18.4
RACE AND HISPANIC ORIGIN			
Average household	**22.28**	**100**	**100.0**
Asian	15.82	71	3.0
Black	15.01	67	8.2
Hispanic	26.21	118	14.3
Non-Hispanic white and other	22.79	102	77.5
REGION			
Average household	**22.28**	**100**	**100.0**
Northeast	23.40	105	19.3
Midwest	24.45	110	24.5
South	20.69	93	34.1
West	21.76	98	22.1
EDUCATION			
Average household	**22.28**	**100**	**100.0**
Less than high school graduate	20.89	94	13.4
High school graduate	23.06	104	26.4
Some college	21.06	95	19.9
Associate's degree	20.40	92	8.7
Bachelor's degree or more	23.71	106	31.6
Bachelor's degree	21.00	94	17.8
Master's, professional, doctoral degree	29.04	130	14.1

Note: Market shares may not sum to 100.0 because of rounding and missing categories by household type. "Asian" and "black" include Hispanics and non-Hispanics who identify themselves as being of the respective race alone. "Hispanic" includes people of any race who identify themselves as Hispanic. "Other" includes people who identify themselves as non-Hispanic and as Alaska Native, American Indian, Asian (who are also included in the "Asian" row), or Native Hawaiian or other Pacific Islander as well as non-Hispanics reporting more than one race.

Source: Calculations by New Strategist based on the Bureau of Labor Statistics' 2010 Consumer Expenditure Survey

Tea

Best customers:
Householders aged 45 to 54
Married couples with school-aged or older children at home
Households in the Northeast

Customer trends:
Average household spending on tea may continue to rise because of the introduction of new products and tea's touted health benefits.

Although the media frequently tout the nutritional benefits of tea, Americans still spend far less on tea than on coffee. But tea is closing in. In 2010, the average household spent 48 percent as much on tea ($29.20) as on coffee ($60.25), up from 37 percent in 2000. Middle-aged householders are the best customers of tea, those aged 45 to 54 spending 26 percent more than average on this item. Married couples with school-aged children spend 36 percent more than average tea, while those with adult children at home spend 79 percent more than average on this item. Households in the Northeast spend 29 percent more than average on tea.

Average household spending on tea purchased at grocery or convenience stores rose by a substantial 47 percent between 2000 and 2010, after adjusting for inflation. Behind the rise in spending on tea are the health and nutritional claims for green and black tea, as well as the greater variety of tea available in grocery stores. Average household spending on tea may continue to rise because of the introduction of new products and tea's touted health benefits.

Table 9.77 Tea

| Total household spending | $3,536,324,400.00 |
| Average household spends | 29.20 |

	AVERAGE HOUSEHOLD SPENDING	BEST CUSTOMERS (index)	BIGGEST CUSTOMERS (market share)
AGE OF HOUSEHOLDER			
Average household	**$29.20**	**100**	**100.0%**
Under age 25	14.81	51	3.4
Aged 25 to 34	24.48	84	14.0
Aged 35 to 44	31.74	109	19.7
Aged 45 to 54	36.72	126	26.0
Aged 55 to 64	32.73	112	19.8
Aged 65 to 74	29.23	100	10.8
Aged 75 or older	19.27	66	6.3

	AVERAGE HOUSEHOLD SPENDING	BEST CUSTOMERS (index)	BIGGEST CUSTOMERS (market share)
HOUSEHOLD INCOME			
Average household	**$29.20**	**100**	**100.0%**
Under $20,000	17.77	61	13.3
$20,000 to $39,999	23.76	81	18.6
$40,000 to $49,999	29.84	102	9.7
$50,000 to $69,999	30.91	106	15.2
$70,000 to $79,999	31.17	107	6.4
$80,000 to $99,999	36.39	125	10.4
$100,000 or more	44.95	154	26.4
HOUSEHOLD TYPE			
Average household	**29.20**	**100**	**100.0**
Married couples	36.57	125	61.8
Married couples, no children	30.80	105	22.4
Married couples, with children	40.69	139	32.4
Oldest child under age 6	21.36	73	3.1
Oldest child aged 6 to 17	39.62	136	16.0
Oldest child aged 18 or older	52.19	179	12.9
Single parent with child under age 18	20.39	70	4.1
Single person	16.69	57	16.7
RACE AND HISPANIC ORIGIN			
Average household	**29.20**	**100**	**100.0**
Asian	30.29	104	4.4
Black	28.88	99	12.1
Hispanic	30.78	105	12.8
Non-Hispanic white and other	28.99	99	75.3
REGION			
Average household	**29.20**	**100**	**100.0**
Northeast	37.60	129	23.6
Midwest	26.51	91	20.2
South	28.67	98	36.0
West	25.89	89	20.1
EDUCATION			
Average household	**29.20**	**100**	**100.0**
Less than high school graduate	27.54	94	13.5
High school graduate	29.02	99	25.4
Some college	27.11	93	19.5
Associate's degree	31.04	106	10.0
Bachelor's degree or more	30.98	106	31.5
Bachelor's degree	28.47	98	18.4
Master's, professional, doctoral degree	35.94	123	13.3

Note: Market shares may not sum to 100.0 because of rounding and missing categories by household type. "Asian" and "black" include Hispanics and non-Hispanics who identify themselves as being of the respective race alone. "Hispanic" includes people of any race who identify themselves as Hispanic. "Other" includes people who identify themselves as non-Hispanic and as Alaska Native, American Indian, Asian (who are also included in the "Asian" row), or Native Hawaiian or other Pacific Islander as well as non-Hispanics reporting more than one race.

Source: Calculations by New Strategist based on the Bureau of Labor Statistics' 2010 Consumer Expenditure Survey

Tomatoes

Best customers:
Householders aged 35 to 64
Married couples with children at home
Asians and Hispanics
Households in the Northeast and West

Customer trends:
Average household spending on tomatoes may continue to rise along with the
Asian and Hispanic populations.

The best customers of fresh tomatoes are the largest households. Married couples with children at home spend 37 percent more than average on tomatoes. Householders ranging in age from 35 to 64, many with children, spend 7 to 16 percent more than average on tomatoes. Asians spend 71 percent more than the average on this item, and Hispanics—who have the largest families— spend 57 percent more than average on this item. Households in the West, where many Asians and Hispanics live, spend 26 percent more than average on tomatoes. Those in the Northeast spend 11 percent more.

Average household spending on fresh tomatoes grew 5 percent between 2000 and 2010, after adjusting for inflation. Behind the increase was rapid growth of the Asian and Hispanic populations. Average household spending on tomatoes may continue to rise along with the Asian and Hispanic populations.

Table 9.78 Tomatoes

Total household spending $4,757,082,960.00
Average household spends   39.28

	AVERAGE HOUSEHOLD SPENDING	BEST CUSTOMERS (index)	BIGGEST CUSTOMERS (market share)
AGE OF HOUSEHOLDER			
Average household	**$39.28**	**100**	**100.0%**
Under age 25	30.56	78	5.2
Aged 25 to 34	39.49	101	16.7
Aged 35 to 44	43.36	110	20.0
Aged 45 to 54	45.44	116	23.9
Aged 55 to 64	41.85	107	18.8
Aged 65 to 74	30.99	79	8.5
Aged 75 or older	28.29	72	6.9

	AVERAGE HOUSEHOLD SPENDING	BEST CUSTOMERS (index)	BIGGEST CUSTOMERS (market share)
HOUSEHOLD INCOME			
Average household	**$39.28**	**100**	**100.0%**
Under $20,000	24.44	62	13.6
$20,000 to $39,999	34.69	88	20.2
$40,000 to $49,999	39.55	101	9.5
$50,000 to $69,999	37.40	95	13.7
$70,000 to $79,999	37.92	97	5.8
$80,000 to $99,999	46.15	117	9.8
$100,000 or more	63.00	160	27.5
HOUSEHOLD TYPE			
Average household	**39.28**	**100**	**100.0**
Married couples	50.62	129	63.6
Married couples, no children	42.73	109	23.1
Married couples, with children	53.79	137	31.9
Oldest child under age 6	49.16	125	5.4
Oldest child aged 6 to 17	53.54	136	16.0
Oldest child aged 18 or older	56.53	144	10.4
Single parent with child under age 18	29.57	75	4.4
Single person	21.88	56	16.3
RACE AND HISPANIC ORIGIN			
Average household	**39.28**	**100**	**100.0**
Asian	67.34	171	7.3
Black	28.08	71	8.7
Hispanic	61.74	157	19.1
Non-Hispanic white and other	37.50	95	72.4
REGION			
Average household	**39.28**	**100**	**100.0**
Northeast	43.63	111	20.4
Midwest	35.48	90	20.1
South	33.19	84	31.0
West	49.59	126	28.6
EDUCATION			
Average household	**39.28**	**100**	**100.0**
Less than high school graduate	44.77	114	16.3
High school graduate	34.97	89	22.7
Some college	32.16	82	17.2
Associate's degree	39.22	100	9.4
Bachelor's degree or more	45.83	117	34.7
Bachelor's degree	42.60	108	20.5
Master's, professional, doctoral degree	52.18	133	14.4

Note: Market shares may not sum to 100.0 because of rounding and missing categories by household type. "Asian" and "black" include Hispanics and non-Hispanics who identify themselves as being of the respective race alone. "Hispanic" includes people of any race who identify themselves as Hispanic. "Other" includes people who identify themselves as non-Hispanic and as Alaska Native, American Indian, Asian (who are also included in the "Asian" row), or Native Hawaiian or other Pacific Islander as well as non-Hispanics reporting more than one race.

Source: Calculations by New Strategist based on the Bureau of Labor Statistics' 2010 Consumer Expenditure Survey

Vegetable Juice, Fresh and Canned

Best customers:
Householders aged 35 to 54
Married couples with school-aged or older children at home
Single parents
Hispanics

Customer trends:
Average household spending on vegetable juice may continue to rise in the years ahead as the large millennial generation has children.

The biggest spenders on vegetable juice are households with children. Married couples with school-aged children spend 71 percent more than average on vegetable juice, and those with adult children at home, 72 percent. Householders aged 35 to 54, most of them parents, spend 20 to 30 percent more than average on vegetable juice. Single parents, whose spending approaches average on only a few items, spend 12 percent more than the average household on vegetable juice. Hispanics, who have the largest families, outspend the average by 36 percent.

Average household spending on vegetable juice purchased at grocery or convenience stores rose 29 percent between 2000 and 2010, after adjusting for inflation. One factor behind the increase is the growing Hispanic population. Spending on vegetable juice may continue to increase in the years ahead as the large millennial generation has children.

Table 9.79 Vegetable juice, fresh and canned

| Total household spending | $1,833,559,980.00 |
| Average household spends | 15.14 |

	AVERAGE HOUSEHOLD SPENDING	BEST CUSTOMERS (index)	BIGGEST CUSTOMERS (market share)
AGE OF HOUSEHOLDER			
Average household	**$15.14**	**100**	**100.0%**
Under age 25	11.20	74	4.9
Aged 25 to 34	16.05	106	17.7
Aged 35 to 44	19.65	130	23.5
Aged 45 to 54	18.20	120	24.9
Aged 55 to 64	12.45	82	14.5
Aged 65 to 74	11.99	79	8.5
Aged 75 or older	9.63	64	6.1

	AVERAGE HOUSEHOLD SPENDING	BEST CUSTOMERS (index)	BIGGEST CUSTOMERS (market share)
HOUSEHOLD INCOME			
Average household	$15.14	100	100.0%
Under $20,000	10.12	67	14.6
$20,000 to $39,999	14.03	93	21.2
$40,000 to $49,999	13.18	87	8.2
$50,000 to $69,999	14.94	99	14.2
$70,000 to $79,999	16.28	108	6.4
$80,000 to $99,999	18.60	123	10.2
$100,000 or more	22.05	146	25.0
HOUSEHOLD TYPE			
Average household	15.14	100	100.0
Married couples	18.97	125	61.8
Married couples, no children	12.68	84	17.8
Married couples, with children	24.29	160	37.3
Oldest child under age 6	16.42	108	4.6
Oldest child aged 6 to 17	25.84	171	20.1
Oldest child aged 18 or older	26.01	172	12.4
Single parent with child under age 18	16.95	112	6.6
Single person	8.61	57	16.7
RACE AND HISPANIC ORIGIN			
Average household	15.14	100	100.0
Asian	16.14	107	4.5
Black	15.00	99	12.1
Hispanic	20.59	136	16.6
Non-Hispanic white and other	14.29	94	71.6
REGION			
Average household	15.14	100	100.0
Northeast	17.35	115	21.0
Midwest	15.70	104	23.1
South	12.93	85	31.3
West	16.40	108	24.5
EDUCATION			
Average household	15.14	100	100.0
Less than high school graduate	12.09	80	11.4
High school graduate	15.18	100	25.6
Some college	15.18	100	21.1
Associate's degree	12.29	81	7.7
Bachelor's degree or more	17.38	115	34.1
Bachelor's degree	16.44	109	20.5
Master's, professional, doctoral degree	19.23	127	13.7

Note: Market shares may not sum to 100.0 because of rounding and missing categories by household type. "Asian" and "black" include Hispanics and non-Hispanics who identify themselves as being of the respective race alone. "Hispanic" includes people of any race who identify themselves as Hispanic. "Other" includes people who identify themselves as non-Hispanic and as Alaska Native, American Indian, Asian (who are also included in the "Asian" row), or Native Hawaiian or other Pacific Islander as well as non-Hispanics reporting more than one race.

Source: Calculations by New Strategist based on the Bureau of Labor Statistics' 2010 Consumer Expenditure Survey

Vegetables, Canned

Best customers: **Householders aged 35 to 54**
Married couples with school-aged or older children at home
Hispanics

Customer trends: **Average household spending on canned vegetables is likely to resume its decline**
as more boomers become empty-nesters.

The largest households spend the most on canned vegetables. Married couples with school-aged or older children at home spend 42 to 64 percent more than average on canned vegetables. Householders aged 35 to 54, most with children, spend 16 to 26 percent more than average on this item. Hispanics, who tend to have the largest families, outspend the average for canned vegetables by 15 percent.

Average household spending on canned vegetables fell 12 percent between 2000 and 2006, after adjusting for inflation, then climbed 26 percent between 2006 and 2010. Behind the decline in the earlier part of the decade was the greater propensity to eat out. The increase in spending during the later part of the decade was due to more home cooking in the aftermath of the Great Recession. Average household spending on canned vegetables is likely to resume its decline as more boomers become empty-nesters.

Table 9.80 Vegetables, canned

Total household spending $6,359,328,570.00
Average household spends   52.51

	AVERAGE HOUSEHOLD SPENDING	BEST CUSTOMERS (index)	BIGGEST CUSTOMERS (market share)
AGE OF HOUSEHOLDER			
Average household	**$52.51**	**100**	**100.0%**
Under age 25	31.53	60	4.0
Aged 25 to 34	44.86	85	14.2
Aged 35 to 44	60.76	116	20.9
Aged 45 to 54	66.05	126	26.0
Aged 55 to 64	52.18	99	17.5
Aged 65 to 74	48.88	93	10.0
Aged 75 or older	39.68	76	7.2

	AVERAGE HOUSEHOLD SPENDING	BEST CUSTOMERS (index)	BIGGEST CUSTOMERS (market share)
HOUSEHOLD INCOME			
Average household	**$52.51**	**100**	**100.0%**
Under $20,000	32.61	62	13.6
$20,000 to $39,999	46.72	89	20.4
$40,000 to $49,999	47.86	91	8.6
$50,000 to $69,999	55.56	106	15.2
$70,000 to $79,999	58.40	111	6.7
$80,000 to $99,999	61.48	117	9.8
$100,000 or more	79.23	151	25.9
HOUSEHOLD TYPE			
Average household	**52.51**	**100**	**100.0**
Married couples	66.60	127	62.6
Married couples, no children	55.51	106	22.5
Married couples, with children	74.16	141	32.9
Oldest child under age 6	50.69	97	4.1
Oldest child aged 6 to 17	74.34	142	16.6
Oldest child aged 18 or older	85.93	164	11.8
Single parent with child under age 18	49.98	95	5.6
Single person	26.22	50	14.6
RACE AND HISPANIC ORIGIN			
Average household	**52.51**	**100**	**100.0**
Asian	42.62	81	3.5
Black	50.54	96	11.8
Hispanic	60.39	115	14.0
Non-Hispanic white and other	51.58	98	74.5
REGION			
Average household	**52.51**	**100**	**100.0**
Northeast	55.93	107	19.5
Midwest	53.50	102	22.7
South	50.82	97	35.5
West	51.51	98	22.2
EDUCATION			
Average household	**52.51**	**100**	**100.0**
Less than high school graduate	56.29	107	15.3
High school graduate	49.81	95	24.2
Some college	47.78	91	19.1
Associate's degree	58.92	112	10.6
Bachelor's degree or more	54.50	104	30.8
Bachelor's degree	50.88	97	18.3
Master's, professional, doctoral degree	61.64	117	12.7

Note: Market shares may not sum to 100.0 because of rounding and missing categories by household type. "Asian" and "black" include Hispanics and non-Hispanics who identify themselves as being of the respective race alone. "Hispanic" includes people of any race who identify themselves as Hispanic. "Other" includes people who identify themselves as non-Hispanic and as Alaska Native, American Indian, Asian (who are also included in the "Asian" row), or Native Hawaiian or other Pacific Islander as well as non-Hispanics reporting more than one race.

Source: Calculations by New Strategist based on the Bureau of Labor Statistics' 2010 Consumer Expenditure Survey

Vegetables, Dried

Best customers: **Householders aged 35 to 54**
                             Married couples with children at home
                             Hispanics and Asians
                             Householders without a high school diploma

Customer trends: **Average household spending on dried vegetables could continue to increase along**
                             with the Hispanic population.

The biggest spenders on dried vegetables are Hispanics, who spend two-thirds more than the average household on this item and account for one-fifth of the market. Householders aged 35 to 54, the largest households, outspend the average by 27 to 31 percent. Married couples with children at home spend 47 percent more than the average on dried vegetables. Householders without a high school diploma, many of them Hispanic, spend 28 percent more than average on dried vegetables.

Average household spending on dried vegetables increased 37 percent between 2000 and 2010, after adjusting for inflation. Behind this increase was growth of the Hispanic population. Spending on dried vegetables could continue to increase along with the Hispanic population.

Table 9.81 **Vegetables, dried**

Total household spending $2,210,202,750.00
Average household spends   18.25

	AVERAGE HOUSEHOLD SPENDING	BEST CUSTOMERS (index)	BIGGEST CUSTOMERS (market share)
AGE OF HOUSEHOLDER			
Average household	**$18.25**	**100**	**100.0%**
Under age 25	11.88	65	4.3
Aged 25 to 34	19.03	104	17.4
Aged 35 to 44	23.09	127	22.9
Aged 45 to 54	23.83	131	27.0
Aged 55 to 64	15.74	86	15.2
Aged 65 to 74	9.68	53	5.7
Aged 75 or older	14.42	79	7.5

	AVERAGE HOUSEHOLD SPENDING	BEST CUSTOMERS (index)	BIGGEST CUSTOMERS (market share)
HOUSEHOLD INCOME			
Average household	**$18.25**	**100**	**100.0%**
Under $20,000	13.90	76	16.6
$20,000 to $39,999	16.80	92	21.1
$40,000 to $49,999	13.19	72	6.8
$50,000 to $69,999	19.46	107	15.3
$70,000 to $79,999	18.12	99	5.9
$80,000 to $99,999	19.33	106	8.8
$100,000 or more	26.80	147	25.2
HOUSEHOLD TYPE			
Average household	**18.25**	**100**	**100.0**
Married couples	24.64	135	66.6
Married couples, no children	19.55	107	22.8
Married couples, with children	26.89	147	34.3
Oldest child under age 6	20.99	115	4.9
Oldest child aged 6 to 17	27.17	149	17.5
Oldest child aged 18 or older	29.50	162	11.7
Single parent with child under age 18	16.93	93	5.5
Single person	8.75	48	14.0
RACE AND HISPANIC ORIGIN			
Average household	**18.25**	**100**	**100.0**
Asian	25.47	140	5.9
Black	16.87	92	11.3
Hispanic	30.61	168	20.4
Non-Hispanic white and other	16.56	91	68.8
REGION			
Average household	**18.25**	**100**	**100.0**
Northeast	19.17	105	19.3
Midwest	20.77	114	25.4
South	15.60	85	31.4
West	19.34	106	24.0
EDUCATION			
Average household	**18.25**	**100**	**100.0**
Less than high school graduate	23.39	128	18.3
High school graduate	18.03	99	25.2
Some college	15.16	83	17.5
Associate's degree	14.88	82	7.7
Bachelor's degree or more	19.56	107	31.8
Bachelor's degree	17.17	94	17.8
Master's, professional, doctoral degree	24.26	133	14.4

Note: Market shares may not sum to 100.0 because of rounding and missing categories by household type. "Asian" and "black" include Hispanics and non-Hispanics who identify themselves as being of the respective race alone. "Hispanic" includes people of any race who identify themselves as Hispanic. "Other" includes people who identify themselves as non-Hispanic and as Alaska Native, American Indian, Asian (who are also included in the "Asian" row), or Native Hawaiian or other Pacific Islander as well as non-Hispanics reporting more than one race.

Source: Calculations by New Strategist based on the Bureau of Labor Statistics' 2010 Consumer Expenditure Survey

Vegetables, Fresh, Total

Best customers: **Householders aged 35 to 54**
Married couples with children at home
Asians and Hispanics
Households in the Northeast and West

Customer trends: **Average household spending on fresh vegetables may continue to rise as consumers opt for fresh vegetables over frozen and canned, but prepared meals may limit the increase.**

Fresh vegetables are the second-largest grocery category in terms of household spending. The best customers of fresh vegetables are the largest households. Householders aged 35 to 54, most with children, spend 11 to 19 percent more than the average household on this item. Married couples with children at home spend 39 percent more than average on fresh vegetables. Asians spend 83 percent more than average on fresh vegetables, and Hispanics spend 21 percent more. Households in the West, where many Asians and Hispanics reside, spend one-fifth more than average on this item. Households in the Northeast spend 11 percent more.

Average household spending on fresh vegetables rose slowly but steadily over the entire 2000-to-2010 time period, after adjusting for inflation, gaining 5 percent overall. Average household spending on fresh vegetables may continue to rise as consumers opt for fresh vegetables over frozen and canned, but prepared meals may limit the increase.

Table 9.82 Vegetables, fresh, total

Total household spending $25,489,390,290.00
Average household spends   210.47

	AVERAGE HOUSEHOLD SPENDING	BEST CUSTOMERS (index)	BIGGEST CUSTOMERS (market share)
AGE OF HOUSEHOLDER			
Average household	**$210.47**	**100**	**100.0%**
Under age 25	131.03	62	4.1
Aged 25 to 34	189.80	90	15.0
Aged 35 to 44	233.45	111	20.1
Aged 45 to 54	251.02	119	24.7
Aged 55 to 64	218.35	104	18.3
Aged 65 to 74	205.83	98	10.5
Aged 75 or older	159.19	76	7.2

	AVERAGE HOUSEHOLD SPENDING	BEST CUSTOMERS (index)	BIGGEST CUSTOMERS (market share)
HOUSEHOLD INCOME			
Average household	**$210.47**	**100**	**100.0%**
Under $20,000	129.77	62	13.5
$20,000 to $39,999	171.07	81	18.6
$40,000 to $49,999	186.96	89	8.4
$50,000 to $69,999	206.67	98	14.1
$70,000 to $79,999	209.28	99	6.0
$80,000 to $99,999	262.64	125	10.4
$100,000 or more	360.86	171	29.4
HOUSEHOLD TYPE			
Average household	**210.47**	**100**	**100.0**
Married couples	274.92	131	64.4
Married couples, no children	239.52	114	24.2
Married couples, with children	292.80	139	32.4
Oldest child under age 6	251.95	120	5.1
Oldest child aged 6 to 17	293.12	139	16.4
Oldest child aged 18 or older	313.22	149	10.7
Single parent with child under age 18	138.63	66	3.9
Single person	116.36	55	16.2
RACE AND HISPANIC ORIGIN			
Average household	**210.47**	**100**	**100.0**
Asian	384.56	183	7.8
Black	156.15	74	9.1
Hispanic	255.04	121	14.8
Non-Hispanic white and other	212.14	101	76.4
REGION			
Average household	**210.47**	**100**	**100.0**
Northeast	233.04	111	20.3
Midwest	198.27	94	21.0
South	181.18	86	31.6
West	252.59	120	27.2
EDUCATION			
Average household	**210.47**	**100**	**100.0**
Less than high school graduate	197.44	94	13.4
High school graduate	180.65	86	21.9
Some college	186.97	89	18.7
Associate's degree	209.91	100	9.4
Bachelor's degree or more	259.70	123	36.7
Bachelor's degree	241.51	115	21.7
Master's, professional, doctoral degree	295.52	140	15.2

Note: Market shares may not sum to 100.0 because of rounding and missing categories by household type. "Asian" and "black" include Hispanics and non-Hispanics who identify themselves as being of the respective race alone. "Hispanic" includes people of any race who identify themselves as Hispanic. "Other" includes people who identify themselves as non-Hispanic and as Alaska Native, American Indian, Asian (who are also included in the "Asian" row), or Native Hawaiian or other Pacific Islander as well as non-Hispanics reporting more than one race.

Source: Calculations by New Strategist based on the Bureau of Labor Statistics' 2010 Consumer Expenditure Survey

Vegetables, Frozen

Best customers: **Householders aged 35 to 54**
                       Married couples with children at home

Customer trends: **Average household spending on frozen vegetables is likely to resume its decline**
                       as Americans opt for the fresh variety and prepared food claims a growing share
                       of the food dollar.

The largest households are the best customers of frozen vegetables. Married couples with children at home spend 41 percent more than average on this item. Householders aged 35 to 54, most with children, spend 13 to 34 percent more than average on frozen vegetables.

Average household spending on frozen vegetables fell by 1 percent between 2000 and 2006, after adjusting for inflation, as fewer households cooked meals at home. Then the trend reversed and spending on frozen vegetables grew 9 percent between 2006 and 2010 as household belt-tightening caused a renewed interest in home cooking. Average household spending on frozen vegetables is likely to resume its decline as Americans opt for the fresh variety and prepared food claims a growing share of the food dollar.

Table 9.83 **Vegetables, frozen**

Total household spending $4,379,229,120.00
Average household spends   36.16

	AVERAGE HOUSEHOLD SPENDING	BEST CUSTOMERS (index)	BIGGEST CUSTOMERS (market share)
AGE OF HOUSEHOLDER			
Average household	**$36.16**	**100**	**100.0%**
Under age 25	20.81	58	3.8
Aged 25 to 34	31.36	87	14.4
Aged 35 to 44	40.95	113	20.5
Aged 45 to 54	48.46	134	27.7
Aged 55 to 64	36.77	102	17.9
Aged 65 to 74	29.86	83	8.9
Aged 75 or older	24.99	69	6.6

	AVERAGE HOUSEHOLD SPENDING	BEST CUSTOMERS (index)	BIGGEST CUSTOMERS (market share)
HOUSEHOLD INCOME			
Average household	**$36.16**	**100**	**100.0%**
Under $20,000	21.40	59	12.9
$20,000 to $39,999	30.10	83	19.1
$40,000 to $49,999	44.39	123	11.6
$50,000 to $69,999	34.88	96	13.8
$70,000 to $79,999	29.16	81	4.8
$80,000 to $99,999	49.54	137	11.4
$100,000 or more	54.88	152	26.0
HOUSEHOLD TYPE			
Average household	**36.16**	**100**	**100.0**
Married couples	46.56	129	63.5
Married couples, no children	37.78	104	22.2
Married couples, with children	50.83	141	32.7
Oldest child under age 6	43.57	120	5.2
Oldest child aged 6 to 17	50.30	139	16.4
Oldest child aged 18 or older	55.35	153	11.1
Single parent with child under age 18	32.63	90	5.3
Single person	17.71	49	14.3
RACE AND HISPANIC ORIGIN			
Average household	**36.16**	**100**	**100.0**
Asian	36.57	101	4.3
Black	32.42	90	11.0
Hispanic	30.73	85	10.4
Non-Hispanic white and other	37.57	104	78.8
REGION			
Average household	**36.16**	**100**	**100.0**
Northeast	39.06	108	19.8
Midwest	33.90	94	20.9
South	38.07	105	38.6
West	32.94	91	20.6
EDUCATION			
Average household	**36.16**	**100**	**100.0**
Less than high school graduate	29.63	82	11.7
High school graduate	37.72	104	26.6
Some college	33.71	93	19.6
Associate's degree	37.18	103	9.7
Bachelor's degree or more	39.14	108	32.2
Bachelor's degree	38.64	107	20.2
Master's, professional, doctoral degree	40.11	111	12.0

Note: Market shares may not sum to 100.0 because of rounding and missing categories by household type. "Asian" and "black" include Hispanics and non-Hispanics who identify themselves as being of the respective race alone. "Hispanic" includes people of any race who identify themselves as Hispanic. "Other" includes people who identify themselves as non-Hispanic and as Alaska Native, American Indian, Asian (who are also included in the "Asian" row), or Native Hawaiian or other Pacific Islander as well as non-Hispanics reporting more than one race.

Source: Calculations by New Strategist based on the Bureau of Labor Statistics' 2010 Consumer Expenditure Survey

Water, Bottled

Best customers: **Householders aged 35 to 64**
                                     Married couples with children at home
                                     Single parents
                                     Asians, blacks, and Hispanics
                                     Households in the West

Customer trends: **Average household spending on bottled water may climb in the years ahead as Americans question the quality of tap water and search for alternatives to calorie-laden colas and fruit drinks.**

The biggest spenders on bottled water are the largest households. Householders aged 35 to 64, many with children, spend 11 to 27 percent more than average on bottled water and control 67 percent of spending on this item. Married couples with children at home spend 36 percent more than average on this item, and single parents, whose spending generally is below average on most items, spend 3 percent more than average on bottled water. Asians spend 20 percent more than average on bottled water, blacks 16 percent, and Hispanics, who have the largest families, 37 percent. Households in the West spend 25 percent more than average on bottled water.

Bottled water is a relatively new category in the Consumer Expenditure Survey, and there are no comparative spending data from 2000. From 2006 to 2010, spending on bottled water declined 13 percent, in part because less expensive alternatives entered the market and also because the Great Recession reduced household spending. Average household spending on bottled water may climb in the years ahead as Americans question the quality of tap water and search for alternatives to calorie-laden colas and fruit drinks.

Table 9.84 Water, bottled

Total household spending $6,302,408,280.00
Average household spends   52.04

	AVERAGE HOUSEHOLD SPENDING	BEST CUSTOMERS (index)	BIGGEST CUSTOMERS (market share)
AGE OF HOUSEHOLDER			
Average household	**$52.04**	**100**	**100.0%**
Under age 25	40.20	77	5.1
Aged 25 to 34	51.50	99	16.5
Aged 35 to 44	57.92	111	20.1
Aged 45 to 54	66.17	127	26.3
Aged 55 to 64	60.86	117	20.6
Aged 65 to 74	34.02	65	7.0
Aged 75 or older	22.70	44	4.2

	AVERAGE HOUSEHOLD SPENDING	BEST CUSTOMERS (index)	BIGGEST CUSTOMERS (market share)
HOUSEHOLD INCOME			
Average household	**$52.04**	**100**	**100.0%**
Under $20,000	32.74	63	13.7
$20,000 to $39,999	42.45	82	18.7
$40,000 to $49,999	49.75	96	9.0
$50,000 to $69,999	51.88	100	14.3
$70,000 to $79,999	57.76	111	6.6
$80,000 to $99,999	73.44	141	11.8
$100,000 or more	78.49	151	25.9
HOUSEHOLD TYPE			
Average household	**52.04**	**100**	**100.0**
Married couples	63.85	123	60.5
Married couples, no children	54.01	104	22.0
Married couples, with children	70.80	136	31.6
Oldest child under age 6	66.15	127	5.4
Oldest child aged 6 to 17	68.61	132	15.5
Oldest child aged 18 or older	76.45	147	10.6
Single parent with child under age 18	53.85	103	6.1
Single person	28.90	56	16.3
RACE AND HISPANIC ORIGIN			
Average household	**52.04**	**100**	**100.0**
Asian	62.37	120	5.1
Black	60.58	116	14.2
Hispanic	71.51	137	16.7
Non-Hispanic white and other	47.60	91	69.3
REGION			
Average household	**52.04**	**100**	**100.0**
Northeast	55.69	107	19.6
Midwest	42.47	82	18.2
South	48.10	92	33.9
West	65.23	125	28.4
EDUCATION			
Average household	**52.04**	**100**	**100.0**
Less than high school graduate	49.88	96	13.7
High school graduate	48.51	93	23.8
Some college	50.57	97	20.4
Associate's degree	45.40	87	8.2
Bachelor's degree or more	59.40	114	33.9
Bachelor's degree	60.75	117	22.1
Master's, professional, doctoral degree	56.73	109	11.8

Note: Market shares may not sum to 100.0 because of rounding and missing categories by household type. "Asian" and "black" include Hispanics and non-Hispanics who identify themselves as being of the respective race alone. "Hispanic" includes people of any race who identify themselves as Hispanic. "Other" includes people who identify themselves as non-Hispanic and as Alaska Native, American Indian, Asian (who are also included in the "Asian" row), or Native Hawaiian or other Pacific Islander as well as non-Hispanics reporting more than one race.

Source: Calculations by New Strategist based on the Bureau of Labor Statistics' 2010 Consumer Expenditure Survey

Chapter 10.

Health Care

Household Spending on Health Care, 2010

Out-of-pocket spending on health care by the average household has grown over the past few years as health care costs climbed and employers shifted more costs onto employees. Between 2000 and 2010, average household out-of-pocket spending on health care rose 21 percent, after adjusting for inflation. Out-of-pocket spending on health insurance ranks among the 10 biggest household expenses. It averaged $1,831 in 2010, 47 percent more than in 2000, after adjusting for inflation. Spending on Medicare premiums, the second-largest health care category, grew by an even larger 70 percent over the decade.

Prescription drugs are the third-largest health care expense for the average household. Out-of-pocket spending on prescription drugs fell 9 percent between 2000 and 2010, thanks to the introduction of the Medicare prescription drug plan in 2006. Spending on nonprescription drugs increased 9 percent, while spending on vitamins fell 22 percent during those years.

Spending on a number of other health care categories also fell between 2000 and 2010. Households spent 22 percent less on eye care services, 18 percent less on eyeglasses and contact lenses, 17 percent less on hearing aids, and 6 percent less on dental services, for example. Average household spending on commercial Medicare supplements declined 8 percent.

Older Americans are the biggest out-of-pocket spenders on health care. As the large baby-boom generation enters the older age groups, out-of-pocket spending on health care will soar.

Spending on health insurance

(average annual out-of-pocket spending by households on health insurance, 2000, 2006, and 2010; in 2010 dollars)

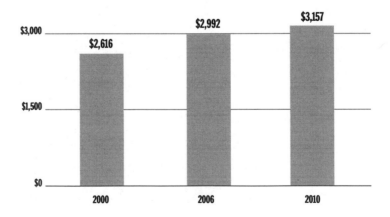

Table 10.1 Health care out-of-pocket spending, 2000 to 2010

(average annual and percent distribution of household spending on out-of-pocket health care costs by category, 2000 to 2010; percent change in spending and percentage point change in distribution, 2000–06, 2006–10, and 2000–10; in 2010 dollars; ranked by amount spent)

	2010 average household spending	2006 average household spending (in 2010$)	2000 average household spending (in 2010$)	percent change		
				2006–10	2000–06	2000–10
AVERAGE ANNUAL SPENDING						
Average household out-of-pocket spending on health care	**$3,156.88**	**$2,992.14**	**$2,615.75**	**5.5%**	**14.4%**	**20.7%**
Health insurance, including Medicare and long-term care	1,830.53	1,584.56	1,244.32	15.5	27.3	47.1
Medicare premiums	353.35	329.45	207.72	7.3	58.6	70.1
Drugs, prescription	350.07	425.05	386.44	–17.6	10.0	–9.4
Dental services	262.62	258.47	279.59	1.6	–7.6	–6.1
Physician services	183.17	181.61	170.20	0.9	6.7	7.6
Medicare supplements, commercial	154.01	148.20	167.14	3.9	–11.3	–7.9
Hospital room and services	115.48	101.47	97.61	13.8	4.0	18.3
Drugs, nonprescription	89.56	87.16	82.42	2.8	5.7	8.7
Long-term care insurance	70.67	63.81	–	10.8	–	–
Medicare prescription drug premiums	60.82	29.27	–	107.8	–	–
Eyeglasses and contact lenses	60.64	58.40	73.99	3.8	–21.1	–18.0
Nonphysician health care professional services	54.00	53.15	46.69	1.6	13.8	15.7
Vitamins, nonprescription	45.54	43.39	58.49	4.9	–25.8	–22.1
Lab tests and X-rays	44.69	46.76	25.48	–4.4	83.5	75.4
Topicals and dressings	36.17	34.71	26.58	4.2	30.6	36.1
Eye care services	34.65	41.98	44.38	–17.5	–5.4	–21.9
Hearing aids	12.38	18.32	14.92	–32.4	22.8	–17.0

| | 2006–10 | 2000–06 | 2000–10 | percentage point change | | |
				2006–10	2000–06	2000–10
PERCENT DISTRIBUTION OF SPENDING						
Average household out-of-pocket spending on health care	**100.0%**	**100.0%**	**100.0%**	–	–	–
Health insurance, including Medicare and long-term care	58.0	53.0	47.6	5.0	5.4	10.4
Medicare premiums	11.2	11.0	7.9	0.2	3.1	3.3
Drugs, prescription	11.1	14.2	14.8	–3.1	–0.6	–3.7
Dental services	8.3	8.6	10.7	–0.3	–2.1	–2.4
Physician services	5.8	6.1	6.5	–0.3	–0.4	–0.7
Medicare supplements, commercial	4.9	5.0	6.4	–0.1	–1.4	–1.5
Hospital room and services	3.7	3.4	3.7	0.3	–0.3	–0.1
Drugs, nonprescription	2.8	2.9	3.2	–0.1	–0.2	–0.3
Long-term care insurance	2.2	2.1	–	0.1	–	–
Medicare prescription drug premiums	1.9	1.0	–	0.9	–	–
Eyeglasses and contact lenses	1.9	2.0	2.8	–0.0	–0.9	–0.9
Nonphysician health care professional services	1.7	1.8	1.8	–0.1	–0.0	–0.1
Vitamins, nonprescription	1.4	1.5	2.2	–0.0	–0.8	–0.8
Lab tests and X-rays	1.4	1.6	1.0	–0.1	0.6	0.4
Topicals and dressings	1.1	1.2	1.0	–0.0	0.1	0.1
Eye care services	1.1	1.4	1.7	–0.3	–0.3	–0.6
Hearing aids	0.4	0.6	0.6	–0.2	0.0	–0.2

Note: Numbers sum to more than total because Medicare premiums and supplements and long-term care insurance are also included in health insurance total. "–" means not applicable or data are unavailable.

Source: Bureau of Labor Statistics, 2000, 2006, and 2010 Consumer Expenditure Surveys; calculations by New Strategist

Dental Services (Out-of-Pocket Expenses)

Best customers: **Householders aged 45 or older**
Married couples without children at home
Married couples with school-aged or older children at home
Households in the West

Customer trends: **Average household spending on dental services will increase as more boomers**
enter the age groups that spend the most.

The biggest out-of-pocket spenders on dental services are older Americans. Householders aged 45 or older spend 19 to 53 percent more than the average household on this item, in part because older Americans are less likely to have insurance coverage for dental care. Married couples without children at home (many of them older) spend 58 percent more than average on dental services. Couples with school-aged or older children at home spend 47 to 56 percent more than average on dental services because their households are larger than average and have more teeth that need fixing. Households in the West spend 34 percent more than average on this item. Non-Hispanic whites control 90 percent of the market for dental services.

Average out-of-pocket spending on dental services declined by 6 percent between 2000 and 2010, after adjusting for inflation. One reason for the decline in spending on dental services was belt tightening as health care costs soared. It is likely that many Americans delayed dental visits as they were forced to pay more for health insurance. Out-of-pocket spending on dental services is likely to climb in the years ahead, as boomers continue to age into the big-spending age groups.

Table 10.2 Dental services (out-of-pocket expenses)

Total household spending $31,805,120,340.00
Average household spends 262.62

	AVERAGE HOUSEHOLD SPENDING	BEST CUSTOMERS (index)	BIGGEST CUSTOMERS (market share)
AGE OF HOUSEHOLDER			
Average household	**$262.62**	**100**	**100.0%**
Under age 25	74.46	28	1.9
Aged 25 to 34	108.61	41	6.9
Aged 35 to 44	225.52	86	15.5
Aged 45 to 54	312.20	119	24.6
Aged 55 to 64	336.79	128	22.6
Aged 65 to 74	401.62	153	16.5
Aged 75 or older	331.24	126	12.0

	AVERAGE HOUSEHOLD SPENDING	BEST CUSTOMERS (index)	BIGGEST CUSTOMERS (market share)
HOUSEHOLD INCOME			
Average household	**$262.62**	**100**	**100.0%**
Under $20,000	81.79	31	6.8
$20,000 to $39,999	233.03	89	20.3
$40,000 to $49,999	193.02	73	6.9
$50,000 to $69,999	284.07	108	15.5
$70,000 to $79,999	354.78	135	8.1
$80,000 to $99,999	331.11	126	10.5
$100,000 or more	487.24	186	31.8
HOUSEHOLD TYPE			
Average household	**262.62**	**100**	**100.0**
Married couples	366.54	140	68.8
Married couples, no children	414.94	158	33.6
Married couples, with children	347.31	132	30.8
Oldest child under age 6	113.61	43	1.9
Oldest child aged 6 to 17	408.58	156	18.3
Oldest child aged 18 or older	386.10	147	10.6
Single parent with child under age 18	156.68	60	3.5
Single person	157.52	60	17.6
RACE AND HISPANIC ORIGIN			
Average household	**262.62**	**100**	**100.0**
Asian	272.75	104	4.4
Black	68.34	26	3.2
Hispanic	155.17	59	7.2
Non-Hispanic white and other	310.68	118	89.7
REGION			
Average household	**262.62**	**100**	**100.0**
Northeast	260.65	99	18.2
Midwest	254.55	97	21.6
South	212.64	81	29.7
West	353.13	134	30.5
EDUCATION			
Average household	**262.62**	**100**	**100.0**
Less than high school graduate	99.41	38	5.4
High school graduate	199.91	76	19.4
Some college	275.06	105	22.0
Associate's degree	270.85	103	9.7
Bachelor's degree or more	383.58	146	43.4
Bachelor's degree	346.38	132	24.9
Master's, professional, doctoral degree	448.54	171	18.5

Note: Market shares may not sum to 100.0 because of rounding and missing categories by household type. "Asian" and "black" include Hispanics and non-Hispanics who identify themselves as being of the respective race alone. "Hispanic" includes people of any race who identify themselves as Hispanic. "Other" includes people who identify themselves as non-Hispanic and as Alaska Native, American Indian, Asian (who are also included in the "Asian" row), or Native Hawaiian or other Pacific Islander as well as non-Hispanics reporting more than one race.

Source: Calculations by New Strategist based on the Bureau of Labor Statistics' 2010 Consumer Expenditure Survey

Drugs, Nonprescription

Best customers: **Householders aged 55 or older**
                             Married couples without children at home
                             Married couples with school-aged or older children at home

Customer trends: **Average household spending on nonprescription drugs should grow as boomers age.**

The biggest spenders on nonprescription drugs are older Americans and the largest households. Householders aged 55 or older spend 17 to 29 percent more than the average household on over-the-counter drugs. Married couples without children at home (most of them older) spend 45 more than average on this item. Couples with school-aged or older children at home spend 29 to 35 percent more because their households are larger than average.

Average household spending on nonprescription drugs rose 9 percent between 2000 and 2010, after adjusting for inflation. Average household spending on nonprescription drugs is likely to continue to climb in the years ahead as the large baby-boom generation enters the 65-or-older age group.

Table 10.3 **Drugs, nonprescription**

Total household spending $10,846,342,920.00
Average household spends 89.56

	AVERAGE HOUSEHOLD SPENDING	BEST CUSTOMERS (index)	BIGGEST CUSTOMERS (market share)
AGE OF HOUSEHOLDER			
Average household	**$89.56**	**100**	**100.0%**
Under age 25	27.25	30	2.0
Aged 25 to 34	62.16	69	11.6
Aged 35 to 44	92.41	103	18.7
Aged 45 to 54	88.16	98	20.4
Aged 55 to 64	114.14	127	22.5
Aged 65 to 74	105.01	117	12.6
Aged 75 or older	115.94	129	12.3

	AVERAGE HOUSEHOLD SPENDING	BEST CUSTOMERS (index)	BIGGEST CUSTOMERS (market share)
HOUSEHOLD INCOME			
Average household	**$89.56**	**100**	**100.0%**
Under $20,000	54.73	61	13.3
$20,000 to $39,999	63.07	70	16.1
$40,000 to $49,999	92.25	103	9.7
$50,000 to $69,999	94.92	106	15.2
$70,000 to $79,999	116.67	130	7.8
$80,000 to $99,999	108.46	121	10.1
$100,000 or more	144.36	161	27.6
HOUSEHOLD TYPE			
Average household	**89.56**	**100**	**100.0**
Married couples	121.17	135	66.7
Married couples, no children	129.58	145	30.7
Married couples, with children	113.28	126	29.4
Oldest child under age 6	93.24	104	4.5
Oldest child aged 6 to 17	115.12	129	15.1
Oldest child aged 18 or older	120.79	135	9.7
Single parent with child under age 18	61.72	69	4.1
Single person	51.56	58	16.9
RACE AND HISPANIC ORIGIN			
Average household	**89.56**	**100**	**100.0**
Asian	77.53	87	3.7
Black	54.18	60	7.4
Hispanic	74.21	83	10.1
Non-Hispanic white and other	97.68	109	82.7
REGION			
Average household	**89.56**	**100**	**100.0**
Northeast	84.59	94	17.3
Midwest	92.77	104	23.1
South	86.56	97	35.5
West	95.31	106	24.1
EDUCATION			
Average household	**89.56**	**100**	**100.0**
Less than high school graduate	70.35	79	11.2
High school graduate	78.42	88	22.4
Some college	86.22	96	20.2
Associate's degree	94.14	105	9.9
Bachelor's degree or more	108.73	121	36.1
Bachelor's degree	102.74	115	21.7
Master's, professional, doctoral degree	120.53	135	14.6

Note: Market shares may not sum to 100.0 because of rounding and missing categories by household type. "Asian" and "black" include Hispanics and non-Hispanics who identify themselves as being of the respective race alone. "Hispanic" includes people of any race who identify themselves as Hispanic. "Other" includes people who identify themselves as non-Hispanic and as Alaska Native, American Indian, Asian (who are also included in the "Asian" row), or Native Hawaiian or other Pacific Islander as well as non-Hispanics reporting more than one race.

Source: Calculations by New Strategist based on the Bureau of Labor Statistics' 2010 Consumer Expenditure Survey

Drugs, Prescription (Out-of-Pocket Expenses)

Best customers: **Householders aged 55 or older**
Married couples without children at home
Married couples with adult children at home
Non-Hispanic whites

Customer trends: **Average household spending on prescription drugs should climb as boomers fill**
the best-customer age groups.

Prescription drugs are the second-largest health care expense for the average household, trailing only health insurance spending. The biggest out-of-pocket spenders on prescription drugs are older Americans. Householders aged 55 or older spend 40 to 83 percent more than the average householder on this item and account for 61 percent of out-of-pocket spending in this market. Married couples without children at home (most of them older) spend 75 percent more than average on prescription drugs. Householders with adult children at home, whose households are larger than average, spend 47 percent more than average out-of-pocket on prescription drugs. Non-Hispanic whites outspend the minorities by a wide margin on this item and control 88 percent of the market.

Average household spending on prescription drugs, which had risen 10 percent between 2000 and 2006, fell 18 percent between 2006 and 2010, after adjusting for inflation, largely because of the introduction of the Medicare prescription drug plan. As the pharmaceutical industry introduces new and improved drugs and as the baby-boom generation ages, average household spending on prescription drugs should rise.

Table 10.4 **Drugs, prescription (out-of-pocket expenses)**

| Total household spending | $42,395,927,490.00 |
| Average household spends | 350.07 |

	AVERAGE HOUSEHOLD SPENDING	BEST CUSTOMERS (index)	BIGGEST CUSTOMERS (market share)
AGE OF HOUSEHOLDER			
Average household	**$350.07**	**100**	**100.0%**
Under age 25	65.23	19	1.2
Aged 25 to 34	107.80	31	5.1
Aged 35 to 44	219.28	63	11.3
Aged 45 to 54	357.20	102	21.1
Aged 55 to 64	491.56	140	24.8
Aged 65 to 74	618.69	177	19.0
Aged 75 or older	639.07	183	17.4

	AVERAGE HOUSEHOLD SPENDING	BEST CUSTOMERS (index)	BIGGEST CUSTOMERS (market share)
HOUSEHOLD INCOME			
Average household	**$350.07**	**100**	**100.0%**
Under $20,000	244.82	70	15.3
$20,000 to $39,999	346.82	99	22.7
$40,000 to $49,999	366.46	105	9.9
$50,000 to $69,999	361.06	103	14.8
$70,000 to $79,999	384.57	110	6.6
$80,000 to $99,999	404.89	116	9.6
$100,000 or more	431.43	123	21.1
HOUSEHOLD TYPE			
Average household	**350.07**	**100**	**100.0**
Married couples	462.84	132	65.2
Married couples, no children	612.76	175	37.2
Married couples, with children	332.69	95	22.1
Oldest child under age 6	159.68	46	2.0
Oldest child aged 6 to 17	284.98	81	9.6
Oldest child aged 18 or older	513.00	147	10.6
Single parent with child under age 18	141.29	40	2.4
Single person	245.97	70	20.6
RACE AND HISPANIC ORIGIN			
Average household	**350.07**	**100**	**100.0**
Asian	140.93	40	1.7
Black	202.08	58	7.1
Hispanic	154.96	44	5.4
Non-Hispanic white and other	404.75	116	87.7
REGION			
Average household	**350.07**	**100**	**100.0**
Northeast	328.07	94	17.2
Midwest	380.25	109	24.2
South	370.01	106	38.8
West	305.88	87	19.8
EDUCATION			
Average household	**350.07**	**100**	**100.0**
Less than high school graduate	307.72	88	12.6
High school graduate	350.38	100	25.6
Some college	330.92	95	19.9
Associate's degree	362.69	104	9.8
Bachelor's degree or more	379.70	108	32.2
Bachelor's degree	333.00	95	18.0
Master's, professional, doctoral degree	461.24	132	14.3

Note: Market shares may not sum to 100.0 because of rounding and missing categories by household type. "Asian" and "black" include Hispanics and non-Hispanics who identify themselves as being of the respective race alone. "Hispanic" includes people of any race who identify themselves as Hispanic. "Other" includes people who identify themselves as non-Hispanic and as Alaska Native, American Indian, Asian (who are also included in the "Asian" row), or Native Hawaiian or other Pacific Islander as well as non-Hispanics reporting more than one race.

Source: Calculations by New Strategist based on the Bureau of Labor Statistics' 2010 Consumer Expenditure Survey

Eye Care Services (Out-of-Pocket Expenses)

Best customers: **Householders aged 45 or older**
Married couples without children at home
Married couples with school-aged children

Customer trends: **Average household spending on eye care services is unlikely to grow until the economy recovers.**

The biggest out-of-pocket spenders on eye care services are those who need bifocals and reading glasses as they enter the second half of their life. Householders aged 45 or older spend 9 to 27 percent more than average on this item. Married couples without children at home (most of them older) spend 57 percent more than average on eye care services. Married couples with school-aged children outspend the average on this item by 53 percent because of their larger households.

Average household spending on eye care services declined 22 percent between 2000 and 2010, after adjusting for inflation. Behind the spending decline is increased health insurance coverage for this item, competition from discounters in the industry, and belt tightening as other health care costs increase. Although baby boomers are in the peak spending age group, average household spending on eye care services is unlikely to grow until the economy recovers.

Table 10.5 Eye care services (out-of-pocket expenses)

| Total household spending | $4,196,357,550.00 |
| Average household spends | 34.65 |

	AVERAGE HOUSEHOLD SPENDING	BEST CUSTOMERS (index)	BIGGEST CUSTOMERS (market share)
AGE OF HOUSEHOLDER			
Average household	**$34.65**	**100**	**100.0%**
Under age 25	21.40	62	4.1
Aged 25 to 34	21.77	63	10.5
Aged 35 to 44	33.60	97	17.5
Aged 45 to 54	37.66	109	22.5
Aged 55 to 64	44.03	127	22.4
Aged 65 to 74	38.63	111	12.0
Aged 75 or older	40.02	115	11.0

	AVERAGE HOUSEHOLD SPENDING	BEST CUSTOMERS (index)	BIGGEST CUSTOMERS (market share)
HOUSEHOLD INCOME			
Average household	**$34.65**	**100**	**100.0%**
Under $20,000	17.14	49	10.8
$20,000 to $39,999	29.94	86	19.8
$40,000 to $49,999	26.26	76	7.2
$50,000 to $69,999	21.28	61	8.8
$70,000 to $79,999	31.04	90	5.4
$80,000 to $99,999	53.20	154	12.8
$100,000 or more	71.29	206	35.3
HOUSEHOLD TYPE			
Average household	**34.65**	**100**	**100.0**
Married couples	45.92	133	65.4
Married couples, no children	54.30	157	33.3
Married couples, with children	42.26	122	28.4
Oldest child under age 6	26.51	77	3.3
Oldest child aged 6 to 17	52.98	153	18.0
Oldest child aged 18 or older	34.13	98	7.1
Single parent with child under age 18	20.16	58	3.4
Single person	23.56	68	19.9
RACE AND HISPANIC ORIGIN			
Average household	**34.65**	**100**	**100.0**
Asian	21.39	62	2.6
Black	12.51	36	4.4
Hispanic	41.38	119	14.5
Non-Hispanic white and other	37.04	107	81.0
REGION			
Average household	**34.65**	**100**	**100.0**
Northeast	30.34	88	16.1
Midwest	33.77	97	21.7
South	31.56	91	33.4
West	44.04	127	28.8
EDUCATION			
Average household	**34.65**	**100**	**100.0**
Less than high school graduate	28.90	83	11.9
High school graduate	22.69	65	16.7
Some college	31.37	91	19.0
Associate's degree	32.53	94	8.9
Bachelor's degree or more	50.71	146	43.5
Bachelor's degree	47.01	136	25.6
Master's, professional, doctoral degree	57.16	165	17.8

Note: Market shares may not sum to 100.0 because of rounding and missing categories by household type. "Asian" and "black" include Hispanics and non-Hispanics who identify themselves as being of the respective race alone. "Hispanic" includes people of any race who identify themselves as Hispanic. "Other" includes people who identify themselves as non-Hispanic and as Alaska Native, American Indian, Asian (who are also included in the "Asian" row), or Native Hawaiian or other Pacific Islander as well as non-Hispanics reporting more than one race.

Source: Calculations by New Strategist based on the Bureau of Labor Statistics' 2010 Consumer Expenditure Survey

Eyeglasses and Contact Lenses (Out-of-Pocket Expenses)

Best customers:	**Householders aged 45 to 64** **Married couples without children at home** **Married couples with school-aged or older children at home**
Customer trends:	**Average household spending on eyeglasses and contact lenses should stabilize because the large baby-boom generation has filled the prime-spending age groups.**

The biggest out-of-pocket spenders on eyeglasses and contact lenses are middle-aged and older Americans (who need bifocals) and households with children. Householders ranging in age from 45 to 64 spend 27 to 35 percent more than average on this item. Married couples with school-aged or older children at home spend 57 to 75 percent more than average because their households are relatively large. Couples without children at home (most of them older) spend 46 percent more than average out-of-pocket on eyeglasses and contact lenses.

Average household spending on eyeglasses and contact lenses fell 21 percent between 2000 and 2006, after adjusting for inflation, but has recovered some since then, rising 4 percent from 2006 to 2010. Behind the earlier decline was competition from discounters in the industry, as well as household belt tightening as other health care costs increased. Spending on eyeglasses and contact lenses should stabilize in the years ahead because the baby-boom generation will be in the prime-spending age groups.

Table 10.6 Eyeglasses and contact lenses (out-of-pocket expenses)

Total household spending	$7,343,928,480.00
Average household spends	60.64

	AVERAGE HOUSEHOLD SPENDING	BEST CUSTOMERS (index)	BIGGEST CUSTOMERS (market share)
AGE OF HOUSEHOLDER			
Average household	**$60.64**	**100**	**100.0%**
Under age 25	17.79	29	1.9
Aged 25 to 34	43.22	71	11.9
Aged 35 to 44	55.18	91	16.5
Aged 45 to 54	77.12	127	26.3
Aged 55 to 64	81.58	135	23.7
Aged 65 to 74	65.15	107	11.6
Aged 75 or older	51.71	85	8.1

	AVERAGE HOUSEHOLD SPENDING	BEST CUSTOMERS (index)	BIGGEST CUSTOMERS (market share)
HOUSEHOLD INCOME			
Average household	**$60.64**	**100**	**100.0%**
Under $20,000	22.46	37	8.1
$20,000 to $39,999	43.30	71	16.4
$40,000 to $49,999	48.42	80	7.5
$50,000 to $69,999	53.38	88	12.6
$70,000 to $79,999	72.37	119	7.1
$80,000 to $99,999	88.49	146	12.2
$100,000 or more	127.60	210	36.1
HOUSEHOLD TYPE			
Average household	**60.64**	**100**	**100.0**
Married couples	86.34	142	70.2
Married couples, no children	88.46	146	31.0
Married couples, with children	90.57	149	34.7
Oldest child under age 6	52.72	87	3.7
Oldest child aged 6 to 17	94.94	157	18.4
Oldest child aged 18 or older	105.91	175	12.6
Single parent with child under age 18	31.66	52	3.1
Single person	33.71	56	16.3
RACE AND HISPANIC ORIGIN			
Average household	**60.64**	**100**	**100.0**
Asian	52.34	86	3.7
Black	30.81	51	6.2
Hispanic	38.22	63	7.7
Non-Hispanic white and other	69.03	114	86.3
REGION			
Average household	**60.64**	**100**	**100.0**
Northeast	64.98	107	19.7
Midwest	73.72	122	27.1
South	47.61	79	28.8
West	65.38	108	24.4
EDUCATION			
Average household	**60.64**	**100**	**100.0**
Less than high school graduate	32.73	54	7.7
High school graduate	43.28	71	18.2
Some college	49.61	82	17.2
Associate's degree	72.69	120	11.3
Bachelor's degree or more	92.96	153	45.5
Bachelor's degree	87.75	145	27.3
Master's, professional, doctoral degree	102.06	168	18.2

Note: Market shares may not sum to 100.0 because of rounding and missing categories by household type. "Asian" and "black" include Hispanics and non-Hispanics who identify themselves as being of the respective race alone. "Hispanic" includes people of any race who identify themselves as Hispanic. "Other" includes people who identify themselves as non-Hispanic and as Alaska Native, American Indian, Asian (who are also included in the "Asian" row), or Native Hawaiian or other Pacific Islander as well as non-Hispanics reporting more than one race.

Source: Calculations by New Strategist based on the Bureau of Labor Statistics' 2010 Consumer Expenditure Survey

Health Insurance, Including Medicare and Supplements (Out-of-Pocket Payments)

Best customers:	Householders aged 65 or older
	Married couples without children at home
	Married couples with adult children at home

Customer trends:	Average household spending on health insurance will continue to climb steeply as health care costs rise faster than inflation and the population ages.

Not surprisingly, the only age group with universal health insurance coverage is the biggest out-of-pocket spender on health insurance. Americans aged 65 or older, covered by the federal government's Medicare program, spend 66 to 71 percent more than the average household out-of-pocket on health insurance. Married couples without children at home (most of them older) spend 63 percent more than average on this item. Those with adult children at home spend 32 percent more. Behind the higher average spending of older Americans is their nearly universal Medicare enrollment, the premiums deducted from their Social Security checks. Also, many older Americans purchase commercial Medicare supplements for additional coverage.

The average household spent $1,831 out-of-pocket on health insurance in 2010, making it the seventh-largest household expense category. Average household spending on health insurance rose 47 percent between 2000 and 2010, after adjusting for inflation. Spending on health insurance will continue to grow rapidly as health care costs rise faster than inflation and the population ages.

Table 10.7 **Health insurance, including Medicare and supplements (out-of-pocket payments)**

Total household spending	$221,689,996,710.00
Average household spends	1,830.53

	AVERAGE HOUSEHOLD SPENDING	BEST CUSTOMERS (index)	BIGGEST CUSTOMERS (market share)
AGE OF HOUSEHOLDER			
Average household	**$1,830.53**	**100**	**100.0%**
Under age 25	405.42	22	1.5
Aged 25 to 34	1,086.07	59	9.9
Aged 35 to 44	1,453.16	79	14.4
Aged 45 to 54	1,747.33	95	19.7
Aged 55 to 64	2,110.24	115	20.3
Aged 65 to 74	3,132.74	171	18.4
Aged 75 or older	3,031.46	166	15.8

	AVERAGE HOUSEHOLD SPENDING	BEST CUSTOMERS (index)	BIGGEST CUSTOMERS (market share)
HOUSEHOLD INCOME			
Average household	**$1,830.53**	**100**	**100.0%**
Under $20,000	922.91	50	11.0
$20,000 to $39,999	1,665.72	91	20.9
$40,000 to $49,999	1,791.01	98	9.2
$50,000 to $69,999	2,075.39	113	16.3
$70,000 to $79,999	2,183.42	119	7.1
$80,000 to $99,999	2,299.93	126	10.5
$100,000 or more	2,671.44	146	25.0
HOUSEHOLD TYPE			
Average household	**1,830.53**	**100**	**100.0**
Married couples	2,477.81	135	66.8
Married couples, no children	2,975.55	163	34.5
Married couples, with children	2,084.97	114	26.5
Oldest child under age 6	1,776.85	97	4.2
Oldest child aged 6 to 17	1,998.77	109	12.8
Oldest child aged 18 or older	2,408.08	132	9.5
Single parent with child under age 18	783.01	43	2.5
Single person	1,175.65	64	18.8
RACE AND HISPANIC ORIGIN			
Average household	**1,830.53**	**100**	**100.0**
Asian	1,684.90	92	3.9
Black	1,156.44	63	7.7
Hispanic	971.04	53	6.5
Non-Hispanic white and other	2,075.82	113	86.0
REGION			
Average household	**1,830.53**	**100**	**100.0**
Northeast	1,930.08	105	19.4
Midwest	1,888.06	103	23.0
South	1,797.83	98	36.0
West	1,746.23	95	21.6
EDUCATION			
Average household	**1,830.53**	**100**	**100.0**
Less than high school graduate	1,251.81	68	9.8
High school graduate	1,732.56	95	24.2
Some college	1,684.83	92	19.3
Associate's degree	1,810.68	99	9.3
Bachelor's degree or more	2,302.44	126	37.4
Bachelor's degree	2,193.93	120	22.6
Master's, professional, doctoral degree	2,491.90	136	14.7

Note: Market shares may not sum to 100.0 because of rounding and missing categories by household type. "Asian" and "black" include Hispanics and non-Hispanics who identify themselves as being of the respective race alone. "Hispanic" includes people of any race who identify themselves as Hispanic. "Other" includes people who identify themselves as non-Hispanic and as Alaska Native, American Indian, Asian (who are also included in the "Asian" row), or Native Hawaiian or other Pacific Islander as well as non-Hispanics reporting more than one race.

Source: Calculations by New Strategist based on the Bureau of Labor Statistics' 2010 Consumer Expenditure Survey

Hearing Aids

Best customers: **Householders aged 65 or older**
Married couples without children at home
Married couples with adult children at home
People who live alone
Non-Hispanic whites
Households in the Midwest

Customer trends: **Average household spending on hearing aids is likely to grow as boomers enter the best-customer age group.**

The biggest out-of-pocket spenders on hearing aids are the oldest Americans. Householders aged 75 or older spend over four times the average on hearing aids and those aged 65 to 74, nearly twice the average. Married couples without children at home (most of them older) spend one-fifth more than average on hearing aids. Married couples with adult children at home, who are older and have the largest households, spend 54 percent more than average on out-of-pocket hearing aid costs. People who live alone, whose spending is well below average on most items, spend one-third more than average on hearing aids. Non-Hispanic whites outspend minorities by a huge margin and control 95 percent of the hearing aids market. Households in the Midwest spend 63 percent more than average on hearing aids.

Average household out-of-pocket spending on hearing aids increased 23 percent between 2000 and 2006, then declined 32 percent between 2006 and 2010, after adjusting for inflation. Behind the spending decline is belt tightening as other health care costs increased, as well as competition from discounters. Average household spending on hearing aids is likely to grow as boomers enter the best-customer age group.

Table 10.8 Hearing aids

Total household spending $1,499,304,660.00
Average household spends 12.38

	AVERAGE HOUSEHOLD SPENDING	BEST CUSTOMERS (index)	BIGGEST CUSTOMERS (market share)
AGE OF HOUSEHOLDER			
Average household	**$12.38**	**100**	**100.0%**
Under age 25	–	–	–
Aged 25 to 34	0.47	4	0.6
Aged 35 to 44	4.56	37	6.7
Aged 45 to 54	11.69	94	19.5
Aged 55 to 64	9.28	75	13.2
Aged 65 to 74	21.41	173	18.6
Aged 75 or older	53.61	433	41.3

	AVERAGE HOUSEHOLD SPENDING	BEST CUSTOMERS (index)	BIGGEST CUSTOMERS (market share)
HOUSEHOLD INCOME			
Average household	**$12.38**	**100**	**100.0%**
Under $20,000	6.36	51	11.2
$20,000 to $39,999	13.55	109	25.1
$40,000 to $49,999	10.57	85	8.1
$50,000 to $69,999	7.99	65	9.3
$70,000 to $79,999	29.05	235	14.0
$80,000 to $99,999	7.94	64	5.3
$100,000 or more	19.48	157	27.0
HOUSEHOLD TYPE			
Average household	**12.38**	**100**	**100.0**
Married couples	12.87	104	51.3
Married couples, no children	14.70	119	25.2
Married couples, with children	11.98	97	22.5
Oldest child under age 6	1.29	10	0.4
Oldest child aged 6 to 17	11.51	93	10.9
Oldest child aged 18 or older	19.07	154	11.1
Single parent with child under age 18	–	–	–
Single person	16.62	134	39.3
RACE AND HISPANIC ORIGIN			
Average household	**12.38**	**100**	**100.0**
Asian	1.10	9	0.4
Black	4.86	39	4.8
Hispanic	0.19	2	0.2
Non-Hispanic white and other	15.51	125	95.0
REGION			
Average household	**12.38**	**100**	**100.0**
Northeast	15.21	123	22.5
Midwest	20.23	163	36.4
South	4.77	39	14.1
West	14.66	118	26.8
EDUCATION			
Average household	**12.38**	**100**	**100.0**
Less than high school graduate	3.48	28	4.0
High school graduate	16.93	137	34.9
Some college	16.41	133	27.9
Associate's degree	3.87	31	3.0
Bachelor's degree or more	12.59	102	30.2
Bachelor's degree	10.23	83	15.6
Master's, professional, doctoral degree	16.72	135	14.6

Note: Market shares may not sum to 100.0 because of rounding and missing categories by household type. "Asian" and "black" include Hispanics and non-Hispanics who identify themselves as being of the respective race alone, "Hispanic" includes people of any race who identify themselves as Hispanic. "Other" includes people who identify themselves as non-Hispanic and as Alaska Native, American Indian, Asian (who are also included in the "Asian" row), or Native Hawaiian or other Pacific Islander as well as non-Hispanics reporting more than one race. "–" means sample is too small to make a reliable estimate.

Source: Calculations by New Strategist based on the Bureau of Labor Statistics' 2010 Consumer Expenditure Survey

Hospital Room and Services (Out-of-Pocket Expenses)

Best customers: **Householders aged 45 to 64**
Married couples without children at home
Married couples with preschoolers

Customer trends: **Average household spending on hospital rooms and services should continue to rise as hospitals offer a greater variety of services and the population ages.**

The biggest out-of-pocket spenders on hospital rooms and services are Americans aged 45 to 64, many of whom use outpatient facilities to monitor and manage their health. These householders spend roughly one-quarter more than the average household on hospital rooms and services. Married couples without children at home spend one-third more than average because many are older empty-nesters. Couples with preschoolers spend almost three times the average on hospital room and services, primarily because of childbearing.

Average household spending on hospital rooms and services rose 18 percent between 2000 and 2010, after adjusting for inflation. Spending on this item grew because hospitals increased their offerings to include more services such as diagnostic imaging, physical therapy, and wellness clinics. As the population ages, out-of-pocket spending on hospital services should continue to rise.

Table 10.9 Hospital room and services (out-of-pocket expenses)

Total household spending $13,985,436,360.00
Average household spends 115.48

	AVERAGE HOUSEHOLD SPENDING	BEST CUSTOMERS (index)	BIGGEST CUSTOMERS (market share)
AGE OF HOUSEHOLDER			
Average household	**$115.48**	**100**	**100.0%**
Under age 25	35.63	31	2.0
Aged 25 to 34	88.81	77	12.8
Aged 35 to 44	113.19	98	17.7
Aged 45 to 54	142.93	124	25.6
Aged 55 to 64	142.24	123	21.7
Aged 65 to 74	104.49	90	9.7
Aged 75 or older	125.25	108	10.3

	AVERAGE HOUSEHOLD SPENDING	BEST CUSTOMERS (index)	BIGGEST CUSTOMERS (market share)
HOUSEHOLD INCOME			
Average household	**$115.48**	**100**	**100.0%**
Under $20,000	58.85	51	11.1
$20,000 to $39,999	79.94	69	15.9
$40,000 to $49,999	100.87	87	8.3
$50,000 to $69,999	120.08	104	14.9
$70,000 to $79,999	135.50	117	7.0
$80,000 to $99,999	139.23	121	10.1
$100,000 or more	220.70	191	32.8
HOUSEHOLD TYPE			
Average household	**115.48**	**100**	**100.0**
Married couples	153.91	133	65.7
Married couples, no children	152.38	132	28.0
Married couples, with children	163.80	142	33.0
Oldest child under age 6	320.02	277	11.9
Oldest child aged 6 to 17	132.76	115	13.5
Oldest child aged 18 or older	121.71	105	7.6
Single parent with child under age 18	106.82	93	5.5
Single person	71.32	62	18.1
RACE AND HISPANIC ORIGIN			
Average household	**115.48**	**100**	**100.0**
Asian	48.28	42	1.8
Black	40.02	35	4.2
Hispanic	109.42	95	11.5
Non-Hispanic white and other	129.35	112	84.9
REGION			
Average household	**115.48**	**100**	**100.0**
Northeast	85.74	74	13.6
Midwest	145.97	126	28.2
South	110.32	96	35.1
West	117.92	102	23.1
EDUCATION			
Average household	**115.48**	**100**	**100.0**
Less than high school graduate	100.96	87	12.5
High school graduate	75.77	66	16.8
Some college	92.64	80	16.9
Associate's degree	150.04	130	12.3
Bachelor's degree or more	161.75	140	41.6
Bachelor's degree	175.08	152	28.6
Master's, professional, doctoral degree	138.48	120	13.0

Note: Market shares may not sum to 100.0 because of rounding and missing categories by household type. "Asian" and "black" include Hispanics and non-Hispanics who identify themselves as being of the respective race alone. "Hispanic" includes people of any race who identify themselves as Hispanic. "Other" includes people who identify themselves as non-Hispanic and as Alaska Native, American Indian, Asian (who are also included in the "Asian" row), or Native Hawaiian or other Pacific Islander as well as non-Hispanics reporting more than one race.

Source: Calculations by New Strategist based on the Bureau of Labor Statistics' 2010 Consumer Expenditure Survey

Lab Tests and X-rays (Out-of-Pocket Expenses)

Best customers:	Householders aged 45 to 64
	Married couples without children at home
	Married couples with adult children at home
Customer trends:	Average household spending on lab tests and X-rays will rise as boomers age.

Householders aged 55 to 64 spend 64 percent more than the average on lab tests and X-rays and those aged 45 to 54 spend 33 percent more. Together these groups account for 56 percent of out-of-pocket spending on lab work. Married couples without children at home (most of them older) spend 57 percent more than average on this item. Married couples with adult children at home spend nearly twice the average on lab tests and X-rays because they have some of the largest households.

Average household spending on lab tests and X-rays rose by a whopping 75 percent between 2000 and 2010, after adjusting for inflation, as medical centers and physician groups nationwide installed new kinds of imaging and testing equipment and insurance copays increased. Spending in this category will continue to rise in the next few years as boomers age.

Table 10.10 **Lab tests and X-rays (out-of-pocket expenses)**

Total household spending $5,412,271,830.00
Average household spends 44.69

	AVERAGE HOUSEHOLD SPENDING	BEST CUSTOMERS (index)	BIGGEST CUSTOMERS (market share)
AGE OF HOUSEHOLDER			
Average household	**$44.69**	**100**	**100.0%**
Under age 25	12.12	27	1.8
Aged 25 to 34	22.62	51	8.4
Aged 35 to 44	45.22	101	18.3
Aged 45 to 54	59.38	133	27.5
Aged 55 to 64	73.29	164	28.9
Aged 65 to 74	42.54	95	10.2
Aged 75 or older	22.58	51	4.8

	AVERAGE HOUSEHOLD SPENDING	BEST CUSTOMERS (index)	BIGGEST CUSTOMERS (market share)
HOUSEHOLD INCOME			
Average household	**$44.69**	**100**	**100.0%**
Under $20,000	16.59	37	8.1
$20,000 to $39,999	31.52	71	16.2
$40,000 to $49,999	47.66	107	10.1
$50,000 to $69,999	46.59	104	15.0
$70,000 to $79,999	53.38	119	7.2
$80,000 to $99,999	77.61	174	14.5
$100,000 or more	75.81	170	29.1
HOUSEHOLD TYPE			
Average household	**44.69**	**100**	**100.0**
Married couples	64.89	145	71.6
Married couples, no children	70.21	157	33.4
Married couples, with children	60.87	136	31.7
Oldest child under age 6	49.10	110	4.7
Oldest child aged 6 to 17	50.51	113	13.3
Oldest child aged 18 or older	84.71	190	13.7
Single parent with child under age 18	18.49	41	2.4
Single person	23.81	53	15.6
RACE AND HISPANIC ORIGIN			
Average household	**44.69**	**100**	**100.0**
Asian	23.27	52	2.2
Black	10.82	24	3.0
Hispanic	27.23	61	7.4
Non-Hispanic white and other	52.83	118	89.6
REGION			
Average household	**44.69**	**100**	**100.0**
Northeast	35.28	79	14.5
Midwest	53.62	120	26.7
South	44.50	100	36.5
West	43.85	98	22.2
EDUCATION			
Average household	**44.69**	**100**	**100.0**
Less than high school graduate	38.13	85	12.2
High school graduate	36.03	81	20.6
Some college	42.35	95	19.9
Associate's degree	41.27	92	8.7
Bachelor's degree or more	58.05	130	38.6
Bachelor's degree	45.01	101	19.0
Master's, professional, doctoral degree	80.82	181	19.6

Note: Market shares may not sum to 100.0 because of rounding and missing categories by household type. "Asian" and "black" include Hispanics and non-Hispanics who identify themselves as being of the respective race alone. "Hispanic" includes people of any race who identify themselves as Hispanic. "Other" includes people who identify themselves as non-Hispanic and as Alaska Native, American Indian, Asian (who are also included in the "Asian" row), or Native Hawaiian or other Pacific Islander as well as non-Hispanics reporting more than one race.

Source: Calculations by New Strategist based on the Bureau of Labor Statistics' 2010 Consumer Expenditure Survey

Long-term Care Insurance

Best customers:
Householders aged 55 and older
Married couples without children at home
Asians and Non-Hispanic whites
Households in the Northeast and Midwest

Customer trends:
Average household spending on long-term care insurance will rise as boomers fill the prime-spending age groups.

The best customers of long-term care insurance are older householders worried they or a family member might require long-term care in a nursing facility. Householders aged 5 to 64 spend 57 percent more than average on this item, while those aged 65 to 74 spend more than twice the average and those aged 75 or older spend more than three times the average on long-term care insurance. Married couples without children at home (most of them older) also spend nearly three times the average on long-term care insurance and account for 59 percent of the market. Non-Hispanic whites, who account for 93 percent of spending on this category, outspend the average on long-term care insurance by 23 percent. Asian householders do so by 40 percent. Households in the Northeast and Midwest spend 26 and 22 percent, respectively, more than average on long-term care insurance.

Average household spending on long-term care insurance rose 11 percent from 2006 to 2010. (Because the item is a relatively new category in the Consumer Expenditure Survey, there are no comparison data from 2000.) Average household spending on long-term care insurance is certain to continue to rise as boomers fill the prime-spending age groups.

Table 10.11 Long-term care insurance

Total household spending $8,558,631,690.00
Average household spends 70.67

	AVERAGE HOUSEHOLD SPENDING	BEST CUSTOMERS (index)	BIGGEST CUSTOMERS (market share)
AGE OF HOUSEHOLDER			
Average household	**$70.67**	**100**	**100.0%**
Under age 25	2.26	3	0.2
Aged 25 to 34	6.51	9	1.5
Aged 35 to 44	13.14	19	3.4
Aged 45 to 54	29.52	42	8.6
Aged 55 to 64	110.76	157	27.6
Aged 65 to 74	190.37	269	29.0
Aged 75 or older	219.48	311	29.6

	AVERAGE HOUSEHOLD SPENDING	BEST CUSTOMERS (index)	BIGGEST CUSTOMERS (market share)
HOUSEHOLD INCOME			
Average household	$70.67	100	100.0%
Under $20,000	23.60	33	7.3
$20,000 to $39,999	66.80	95	21.7
$40,000 to $49,999	62.22	88	8.3
$50,000 to $69,999	73.85	104	15.0
$70,000 to $79,999	45.24	64	3.8
$80,000 to $99,999	136.03	192	16.0
$100,000 or more	114.84	163	27.9
HOUSEHOLD TYPE			
Average household	70.67	100	100.0
Married couples	105.15	149	73.4
Married couples, no children	197.17	279	59.3
Married couples, with children	40.37	57	13.3
Oldest child under age 6	20.12	28	1.2
Oldest child aged 6 to 17	29.70	42	4.9
Oldest child aged 18 or older	69.74	99	7.1
Single parent with child under age 18	4.88	7	0.4
Single person	50.02	71	20.7
RACE AND HISPANIC ORIGIN			
Average household	70.67	100	100.0
Asian	98.82	140	5.9
Black	28.58	40	4.9
Hispanic	12.25	17	2.1
Non-Hispanic white and other	86.64	123	92.9
REGION			
Average household	70.67	100	100.0
Northeast	89.29	126	23.2
Midwest	86.25	122	27.2
South	55.63	79	28.9
West	64.61	91	20.7
EDUCATION			
Average household	70.67	100	100.0
Less than high school graduate	26.08	37	5.3
High school graduate	37.23	53	13.5
Some college	59.09	84	17.6
Associate's degree	72.10	102	9.6
Bachelor's degree or more	128.60	182	54.1
Bachelor's degree	110.07	156	29.4
Master's, professional, doctoral degree	160.95	228	24.6

Note: Market shares may not sum to 100.0 because of rounding and missing categories by household type. "Asian" and "black" include Hispanics and non-Hispanics who identify themselves as being of the respective race alone. "Hispanic" includes people of any race who identify themselves as Hispanic. "Other" includes people who identify themselves as non-Hispanic and as Alaska Native, American Indian, Asian (who are also included in the "Asian" row), or Native Hawaiian or other Pacific Islander as well as non-Hispanics reporting more than one race.

Source: Calculations by New Strategist based on the Bureau of Labor Statistics' 2010 Consumer Expenditure Survey

Medicare Premiums

Best customers:　　　　**Householders aged 65 or older**
Households with incomes under $50,000
Married couples without children at home
Householders with no more than a high school education

Customer trends:　　　　**Average household spending on Medicare premiums will rise steadily along with**
the aging of the population.

Naturally, the biggest spenders on Medicare premiums are people covered by Medicare—householders aged 65 or older. On average, householders aged 65 to 74 spend $1,343 per year on Medicare premiums, and those aged 75 or older spend $1,330. Married couples without children at home (most of them older) spend more than twice the average and account for 44 percent of spending on this item. Householders with no more than a high school education and those with incomes below $50,000 are also above-average spenders on Medicare premiums because older Americans make up large percentages of these groups.

Average household spending on Medicare premiums rose 70 percent between 2000 and 2010, after adjusting for inflation. Behind the increase was the aging of the population and the rise in premiums. Average household spending on Medicare premiums will grow even faster in the future as boomers enter the eligible age group.

Table 10.12 Medicare premiums

| Total household spending | $42,793,158,450.00 |
| Average household spends | 353.35 |

	AVERAGE HOUSEHOLD SPENDING	BEST CUSTOMERS (index)	BIGGEST CUSTOMERS (market share)
AGE OF HOUSEHOLDER			
Average household	**$353.35**	**100**	**100.0%**
Under age 25	24.21	7	0.5
Aged 25 to 34	39.24	11	1.8
Aged 35 to 44	66.47	19	3.4
Aged 45 to 54	103.35	29	6.1
Aged 55 to 64	229.70	65	11.5
Aged 65 to 74	1,342.56	380	40.9
Aged 75 or older	1,329.82	376	35.9

	AVERAGE HOUSEHOLD SPENDING	BEST CUSTOMERS (index)	BIGGEST CUSTOMERS (market share)
HOUSEHOLD INCOME			
Average household	**$353.35**	**100**	**100.0%**
Under $20,000	396.90	112	24.5
$20,000 to $39,999	525.37	149	34.1
$40,000 to $49,999	383.19	108	10.2
$50,000 to $69,999	341.55	97	13.9
$70,000 to $79,999	263.68	75	4.5
$80,000 to $99,999	191.44	54	4.5
$100,000 or more	171.52	49	8.3
HOUSEHOLD TYPE			
Average household	**353.35**	**100**	**100.0**
Married couples	418.31	118	58.4
Married couples, no children	739.61	209	44.5
Married couples, with children	94.90	27	6.2
Oldest child under age 6	12.68	4	0.2
Oldest child aged 6 to 17	39.44	11	1.3
Oldest child aged 18 or older	233.99	66	4.8
Single parent with child under age 18	40.49	11	0.7
Single person	323.44	92	26.8
RACE AND HISPANIC ORIGIN			
Average household	**353.35**	**100**	**100.0**
Asian	209.39	59	2.5
Black	259.49	73	9.0
Hispanic	195.15	55	6.7
Non-Hispanic white and other	393.78	111	84.5
REGION			
Average household	**353.35**	**100**	**100.0**
Northeast	348.15	99	18.1
Midwest	357.61	101	22.6
South	371.29	105	38.6
West	324.32	92	20.8
EDUCATION			
Average household	**353.35**	**100**	**100.0**
Less than high school graduate	491.50	139	19.9
High school graduate	432.55	122	31.3
Some college	321.84	91	19.1
Associate's degree	254.96	72	6.8
Bachelor's degree or more	272.45	77	22.9
Bachelor's degree	260.59	74	13.9
Master's, professional, doctoral degree	293.15	83	9.0

Note: Market shares may not sum to 100.0 because of rounding and missing categories by household type. "Asian" and "black" include Hispanics and non-Hispanics who identify themselves as being of the respective race alone. "Hispanic" includes people of any race who identify themselves as Hispanic. "Other" includes people who identify themselves as non-Hispanic and as Alaska Native, American Indian, Asian (who are also included in the "Asian" row), or Native Hawaiian or other Pacific Islander as well as non-Hispanics reporting more than one race.

Source: Calculations by New Strategist based on the Bureau of Labor Statistics' 2010 Consumer Expenditure Survey

Medicare Prescription Drug Premiums

Best customers: **Householders aged 65 or older**
                        Households with incomes under $50,000
                        Married couples without children at home
                        People who live alone
                        Householders with no more than a high school education

Customer trends: **Average household spending on Medicare prescription drug premiums will rise**
                        steadily along with the aging of the population.

Naturally, the biggest spenders on Medicare prescription drug premiums are people covered by Medicare—householders aged 65 or older. On average, householders aged 65 to 74 spend $234 per year on Medicare prescription drug premiums, and those aged 75 or older spend a similar $229. Married couples without children at home (most of them older) account for 39 percent of spending on this item. Households with incomes under $50,000 and householders with no more than a high school diploma are also above-average spenders on Medicare prescription drug premiums because older Americans make up large percentages of these groups. People who live alone, whose spending approaches average on only a few items, outspend the average on Medicare prescription drug premiums by 15 percent.

Average household spending on Medicare prescription drug premiums more than doubled between 2006 and 2010 as more consumers signed on. (There are no comparison data from 2000 because the Medicare prescription drug plan is a new program.) Average household spending on Medicare prescription drug premiums is certain to rise as boomers fill the prime-spending age groups.

Table 10.13 **Medicare prescription drug premiums**

Total household spending $7,365,727,740.00
Average household spends   60.82

	AVERAGE HOUSEHOLD SPENDING	BEST CUSTOMERS (index)	BIGGEST CUSTOMERS (market share)
AGE OF HOUSEHOLDER			
Average household	**$60.82**	**100**	**100.0%**
Under age 25	2.16	4	0.2
Aged 25 to 34	5.45	9	1.5
Aged 35 to 44	9.77	16	2.9
Aged 45 to 54	19.82	33	6.7
Aged 55 to 64	38.62	63	11.2
Aged 65 to 74	234.33	385	41.5
Aged 75 or older	229.43	377	36.0

	AVERAGE HOUSEHOLD SPENDING	BEST CUSTOMERS (index)	BIGGEST CUSTOMERS (market share)
HOUSEHOLD INCOME			
Average household	**$60.82**	**100**	**100.0%**
Under $20,000	78.62	129	28.2
$20,000 to $39,999	85.59	141	32.2
$40,000 to $49,999	71.28	117	11.1
$50,000 to $69,999	52.25	86	12.3
$70,000 to $79,999	50.56	83	5.0
$80,000 to $99,999	32.18	53	4.4
$100,000 or more	24.01	39	6.8
HOUSEHOLD TYPE			
Average household	**60.82**	**100**	**100.0**
Married couples	67.37	111	54.6
Married couples, no children	112.27	185	39.2
Married couples, with children	17.57	29	6.7
Oldest child under age 6	–	–	–
Oldest child aged 6 to 17	4.49	7	0.9
Oldest child aged 18 or older	49.29	81	5.9
Single parent with child under age 18	1.43	2	0.1
Single person	70.02	115	33.7
RACE AND HISPANIC ORIGIN			
Average household	**60.82**	**100**	**100.0**
Asian	23.78	39	1.7
Black	52.05	86	10.5
Hispanic	33.12	54	6.6
Non-Hispanic white and other	66.95	110	83.5
REGION			
Average household	**60.82**	**100**	**100.0**
Northeast	67.52	111	20.4
Midwest	60.09	99	22.0
South	67.47	111	40.7
West	45.36	75	16.9
EDUCATION			
Average household	**60.82**	**100**	**100.0**
Less than high school graduate	91.41	150	21.5
High school graduate	74.43	122	31.2
Some college	61.15	101	21.1
Associate's degree	42.36	70	6.6
Bachelor's degree or more	40.06	66	19.6
Bachelor's degree	41.26	68	12.8
Master's, professional, doctoral degree	37.97	62	6.8

Note: Market shares may not sum to 100.0 because of rounding and missing categories by household type. "Asian" and "black" include Hispanics and non-Hispanics who identify themselves as being of the respective race alone. "Hispanic" includes people of any race who identify themselves as Hispanic. "Other" includes people who identify themselves as non-Hispanic and as Alaska Native, American Indian, Asian (who are also included in the "Asian" row), or Native Hawaiian or other Pacific Islander as well as non-Hispanics reporting more than one race. "–" means sample is too small to make a reliable estimate.

Source: Calculations by New Strategist based on the Bureau of Labor Statistics' 2010 Consumer Expenditure Survey

Medicare Supplements, Commercial

Best customers:	**Householders aged 65 or older** **Married couples without children at home**
Customer trends:	**Average household spending on commercial Medicare supplements will continue to increase in the years ahead as the baby-boom generation enters the Medicare program.**

As with Medicare premiums, the biggest spenders on commercial Medicare supplements are people covered by Medicare—householders aged 65 or older. On average, householders aged 65 to 74 spend $411 per year on Medicare supplements, which cover services not included in Medicare. Householders aged 75 or older spend $559 per year on this item. Married couples without children at home (most of them older) spend nearly twice the average on Medicare supplements and account for 40 percent of spending on this item.

Average household spending on commercial Medicare supplements fell 11 percent between 2000 and 2006, after adjusting for inflation, then rose 4 percent during the remainder of the decade. Average household spending on this item will continue to increase as aging boomers enter the Medicare program.

Table 10.14 **Medicare supplements, commercial**

Total household spending $18,651,689,070.00
Average household spends   154.01

	AVERAGE HOUSEHOLD SPENDING	BEST CUSTOMERS (index)	BIGGEST CUSTOMERS (market share)
AGE OF HOUSEHOLDER			
Average household	**$154.01**	**100**	**100.0%**
Under age 25	33.60	22	1.4
Aged 25 to 34	43.44	28	4.7
Aged 35 to 44	63.42	41	7.5
Aged 45 to 54	81.84	53	11.0
Aged 55 to 64	105.65	69	12.1
Aged 65 to 74	411.02	267	28.7
Aged 75 or older	558.64	363	34.6

	AVERAGE HOUSEHOLD SPENDING	BEST CUSTOMERS (index)	BIGGEST CUSTOMERS (market share)
HOUSEHOLD INCOME			
Average household	**$154.01**	**100**	**100.0%**
Under $20,000	111.90	73	15.9
$20,000 to $39,999	181.50	118	27.0
$40,000 to $49,999	149.29	97	9.2
$50,000 to $69,999	219.20	142	20.4
$70,000 to $79,999	190.47	124	7.4
$80,000 to $99,999	137.44	89	7.4
$100,000 or more	114.28	74	12.7
HOUSEHOLD TYPE			
Average household	**154.01**	**100**	**100.0**
Married couples	188.28	122	60.3
Married couples, no children	289.63	188	39.9
Married couples, with children	98.96	64	14.9
Oldest child under age 6	44.53	29	1.2
Oldest child aged 6 to 17	70.36	46	5.4
Oldest child aged 18 or older	177.78	115	8.3
Single parent with child under age 18	29.51	19	1.1
Single person	126.63	82	24.1
RACE AND HISPANIC ORIGIN			
Average household	**154.01**	**100**	**100.0**
Asian	101.33	66	2.8
Black	77.93	51	6.2
Hispanic	54.54	35	4.3
Non-Hispanic white and other	181.80	118	89.5
REGION			
Average household	**154.01**	**100**	**100.0**
Northeast	173.81	113	20.7
Midwest	170.59	111	24.7
South	146.65	95	34.9
West	133.59	87	19.6
EDUCATION			
Average household	**154.01**	**100**	**100.0**
Less than high school graduate	173.71	113	16.1
High school graduate	203.09	132	33.7
Some college	131.37	85	17.9
Associate's degree	122.55	80	7.5
Bachelor's degree or more	128.38	83	24.8
Bachelor's degree	123.55	80	15.2
Master's, professional, doctoral degree	136.83	89	9.6

Note: Market shares may not sum to 100.0 because of rounding and missing categories by household type. "Asian" and "black" include Hispanics and non-Hispanics who identify themselves as being of the respective race alone. "Hispanic" includes people of any race who identify themselves as Hispanic. "Other" includes people who identify themselves as non-Hispanic and as Alaska Native, American Indian, Asian (who are also included in the "Asian" row), or Native Hawaiian or other Pacific Islander as well as non-Hispanics reporting more than one race.

Source: Calculations by New Strategist based on the Bureau of Labor Statistics' 2010 Consumer Expenditure Survey

Nonphysician Health Care Professional Services (Out-of-Pocket Expenses) (Acupuncturists, Chiropractors, Nurse Practitioners, etc.)

Best customers:	**Householders aged 45 to 64** **Married couples** **Households in the West**
Customer trends:	**Average household spending on nonphysician health care professional services will rise as nonphysicians provide more health care services.**

Alternative health care has become popular over the past few decades, and millions of Americans seek the medical advice of nonphysicians such as chiropractors, acupuncturists, and nurse practitioners. The best customers of these services are householders aged 45 to 64, who spend 27 to 45 percent more than average on this item. Married couples without children at home (most of them older) spend 66 percent more than average on nonphysician services, while those with children at home spend 34 percent more, in part because their households are relatively large. Households in the West spend 63 percent more than average on this item.

Average household spending on nonphysician health care professional services rose 16 percent between 2000 and 2010, after adjusting for inflation. Behind the increase is the greater variety of services provided by these professionals, as well as the growing number of uninsured Americans seeking care outside established medical circles. Spending in this category is likely to continue to increase as nonphysicians provide more health care services.

Table 10.15 **Nonphysician health care professional services (out-of-pocket expenses) (acupuncturists, chiropractors, nurse practitioners, etc.)**

Total household spending	$6,539,778,000.00
Average household spends	54.00

	AVERAGE HOUSEHOLD SPENDING	BEST CUSTOMERS (index)	BIGGEST CUSTOMERS (market share)
AGE OF HOUSEHOLDER			
Average household	**$54.00**	**100**	**100.0%**
Under age 25	15.77	29	1.9
Aged 25 to 34	33.57	62	10.4
Aged 35 to 44	58.09	108	19.5
Aged 45 to 54	78.19	145	30.0
Aged 55 to 64	68.35	127	22.3
Aged 65 to 74	53.21	99	10.6
Aged 75 or older	30.35	56	5.4

	AVERAGE HOUSEHOLD SPENDING	BEST CUSTOMERS (index)	BIGGEST CUSTOMERS (market share)
HOUSEHOLD INCOME			
Average household	**$54.00**	**100**	**100.0%**
Under $20,000	21.44	40	8.7
$20,000 to $39,999	31.85	59	13.5
$40,000 to $49,999	33.44	62	5.9
$50,000 to $69,999	41.46	77	11.0
$70,000 to $79,999	56.40	104	6.3
$80,000 to $99,999	94.77	176	14.6
$100,000 or more	126.17	234	40.1
HOUSEHOLD TYPE			
Average household	**54.00**	**100**	**100.0**
Married couples	75.49	140	69.0
Married couples, no children	89.39	166	35.2
Married couples, with children	72.45	134	31.2
Oldest child under age 6	80.69	149	6.4
Oldest child aged 6 to 17	75.45	140	16.4
Oldest child aged 18 or older	62.67	116	8.4
Single parent with child under age 18	25.87	48	2.8
Single person	34.19	63	18.5
RACE AND HISPANIC ORIGIN			
Average household	**54.00**	**100**	**100.0**
Asian	26.38	49	2.1
Black	9.45	18	2.1
Hispanic	43.04	80	9.7
Non-Hispanic white and other	62.78	116	88.1
REGION			
Average household	**54.00**	**100**	**100.0**
Northeast	41.92	78	14.2
Midwest	35.37	66	14.6
South	50.49	94	34.3
West	87.79	163	36.8
EDUCATION			
Average household	**54.00**	**100**	**100.0**
Less than high school graduate	25.44	47	6.7
High school graduate	32.77	61	15.5
Some college	37.12	69	14.5
Associate's degree	56.85	105	9.9
Bachelor's degree or more	97.01	180	53.4
Bachelor's degree	84.36	156	29.5
Master's, professional, doctoral degree	119.09	221	23.9

Note: Market shares may not sum to 100.0 because of rounding and missing categories by household type. "Asian" and "black" include Hispanics and non-Hispanics who identify themselves as being of the respective race alone. "Hispanic" includes people of any race who identify themselves as Hispanic. "Other" includes people who identify themselves as non-Hispanic and as Alaska Native, American Indian, Asian (who are also included in the "Asian" row), or Native Hawaiian or other Pacific Islander as well as non-Hispanics reporting more than one race.

Source: Calculations by New Strategist based on the Bureau of Labor Statistics' 2010 Consumer Expenditure Survey

Physician Services (Out-of-Pocket Expenses)

Best customers: **Householders aged 45 to 64**
Married couples
Households in the West

Customer trends: **Average household out-of-pocket spending on physician services is unlikely to grow much in the years ahead because boomers will be joining Medicare, which largely covers these costs.**

The biggest out-of-pocket spenders on physician services are older married couples. Householders aged 45 to 64 spend 28 to 32 percent more than average out-of-pocket on this item. Married couples without children at home spend 36 percent more than average on physician services because most are older. Couples with children at home spend 58 percent more than average because they have the largest households. Households in the West outspend the average on physician's services by 23 percent.

Average household out-of-pocket spending on physician services grew by 8 percent between 2000 and 2010, after adjusting for inflation. Behind the increase were rising copayments. Spending in this category is unlikely to grow much in the future because boomers will soon be eligible for Medicare, which covers most physician expenses.

Table 10.16 Physician services (out-of-pocket expenses)

Total household spending $22,183,169,190.00
Average household spends   183.17

	AVERAGE HOUSEHOLD SPENDING	BEST CUSTOMERS (index)	BIGGEST CUSTOMERS (market share)
AGE OF HOUSEHOLDER			
Average household	**$183.17**	**100**	**100.0%**
Under age 25	74.85	41	2.7
Aged 25 to 34	129.48	71	11.8
Aged 35 to 44	186.82	102	18.5
Aged 45 to 54	241.11	132	27.2
Aged 55 to 64	235.14	128	22.6
Aged 65 to 74	180.55	99	10.6
Aged 75 or older	126.53	69	6.6

	AVERAGE HOUSEHOLD SPENDING	BEST CUSTOMERS (index)	BIGGEST CUSTOMERS (market share)
HOUSEHOLD INCOME			
Average household	**$183.17**	**100**	**100.0%**
Under $20,000	74.47	41	8.9
$20,000 to $39,999	134.85	74	16.9
$40,000 to $49,999	146.01	80	7.5
$50,000 to $69,999	190.96	104	15.0
$70,000 to $79,999	237.40	130	7.8
$80,000 to $99,999	277.22	151	12.6
$100,000 or more	335.41	183	31.4
HOUSEHOLD TYPE			
Average household	**183.17**	**100**	**100.0**
Married couples	259.79	142	70.0
Married couples, no children	249.39	136	28.9
Married couples, with children	289.54	158	36.8
Oldest child under age 6	320.24	175	7.5
Oldest child aged 6 to 17	282.33	154	18.1
Oldest child aged 18 or older	283.09	155	11.2
Single parent with child under age 18	120.34	66	3.9
Single person	99.69	54	15.9
RACE AND HISPANIC ORIGIN			
Average household	**183.17**	**100**	**100.0**
Asian	87.85	48	2.0
Black	76.88	42	5.1
Hispanic	95.22	52	6.3
Non-Hispanic white and other	213.96	117	88.6
REGION			
Average household	**183.17**	**100**	**100.0**
Northeast	165.30	90	16.6
Midwest	171.98	94	20.9
South	172.87	94	34.6
West	225.36	123	27.9
EDUCATION			
Average household	**183.17**	**100**	**100.0**
Less than high school graduate	94.94	52	7.4
High school graduate	140.02	76	19.5
Some college	169.65	93	19.5
Associate's degree	215.71	118	11.1
Bachelor's degree or more	261.91	143	42.5
Bachelor's degree	251.27	137	25.9
Master's, professional, doctoral degree	280.48	153	16.6

Note: Market shares may not sum to 100.0 because of rounding and missing categories by household type. "Asian" and "black" include Hispanics and non-Hispanics who identify themselves as being of the respective race alone. "Hispanic" includes people of any race who identify themselves as Hispanic. "Other" includes people who identify themselves as non-Hispanic and as Alaska Native, American Indian, Asian (who are also included in the "Asian" row), or Native Hawaiian or other Pacific Islander as well as non-Hispanics reporting more than one race.

Source: Calculations by New Strategist based on the Bureau of Labor Statistics' 2010 Consumer Expenditure Survey

Topicals and Dressings

Best customers: Householders aged 35 to 44 and 65 or older
Married couples
Households in the West

Customer trends: Average household spending on topicals and dressings is likely to grow as
boomers fill one of the best-customer age groups.

The biggest spenders on topicals and dressings are middle-aged and older married couples. Householders aged 35 to 44 spend 22 percent more than average on this item because they have young children at home. Householders aged 65 or older spend 18 to 32 percent more than average on this item. Married couples spend 28 percent more than average on topicals and dressing. Households in the West spend 36 percent more than average on this item.

Average household spending on topicals and dressings increased 36 percent between 2000 and 2010, after adjusting for inflation. Spending in this category is likely to grow as boomers fill one of the best-customer age groups.

Table 10.17 Topicals and dressings

Total household spending $4,380,440,190.00
Average household spends 36.17

	AVERAGE HOUSEHOLD SPENDING	BEST CUSTOMERS (index)	BIGGEST CUSTOMERS (market share)
AGE OF HOUSEHOLDER			
Average household	**$36.17**	**100**	**100.0%**
Under age 25	12.54	35	2.3
Aged 25 to 34	25.36	70	11.7
Aged 35 to 44	44.02	122	22.0
Aged 45 to 54	35.37	98	20.2
Aged 55 to 64	38.06	105	18.6
Aged 65 to 74	42.84	118	12.7
Aged 75 or older	47.79	132	12.6

	AVERAGE HOUSEHOLD SPENDING	BEST CUSTOMERS (index)	BIGGEST CUSTOMERS (market share)
HOUSEHOLD INCOME			
Average household	**$36.17**	**100**	**100.0%**
Under $20,000	20.09	56	12.1
$20,000 to $39,999	34.92	97	22.1
$40,000 to $49,999	28.84	80	7.5
$50,000 to $69,999	30.23	84	12.0
$70,000 to $79,999	45.73	126	7.6
$80,000 to $99,999	49.83	138	11.5
$100,000 or more	58.01	160	27.5
HOUSEHOLD TYPE			
Average household	**36.17**	**100**	**100.0**
Married couples	46.28	128	63.1
Married couples, no children	45.77	127	26.9
Married couples, with children	46.24	128	29.7
Oldest child under age 6	48.86	135	5.8
Oldest child aged 6 to 17	43.33	120	14.1
Oldest child aged 18 or older	49.22	136	9.8
Single parent with child under age 18	25.68	71	4.2
Single person	21.01	58	17.0
RACE AND HISPANIC ORIGIN			
Average household	**36.17**	**100**	**100.0**
Asian	30.58	85	3.6
Black	25.46	70	8.6
Hispanic	26.89	74	9.1
Non-Hispanic white and other	39.37	109	82.5
REGION			
Average household	**36.17**	**100**	**100.0**
Northeast	29.04	80	14.7
Midwest	33.52	93	20.7
South	33.40	92	33.9
West	49.26	136	30.9
EDUCATION			
Average household	**36.17**	**100**	**100.0**
Less than high school graduate	23.03	64	9.1
High school graduate	29.89	83	21.1
Some college	34.23	95	19.9
Associate's degree	38.15	105	10.0
Bachelor's degree or more	48.25	133	39.6
Bachelor's degree	46.91	130	24.5
Master's, professional, doctoral degree	50.88	141	15.2

Note: Market shares may not sum to 100.0 because of rounding and missing categories by household type. "Asian" and "black" include Hispanics and non-Hispanics who identify themselves as being of the respective race alone. "Hispanic" includes people of any race who identify themselves as Hispanic. "Other" includes people who identify themselves as non-Hispanic and as Alaska Native, American Indian, Asian (who are also included in the "Asian" row), or Native Hawaiian or other Pacific Islander as well as non-Hispanics reporting more than one race.

Source: Calculations by New Strategist based on the Bureau of Labor Statistics' 2010 Consumer Expenditure Survey

Vitamins, Nonprescription

Best customers: **Householders aged 55 or older**
                                   Married couples without children at home
                                   Hispanics
                                   Households in the West

Customer trends: **Average household spending on vitamins should increase as boomers age.**

As people age they become more health conscious. Consequently, older people are the best customers of vitamins. Householders aged 55 or older spend 29 to 60 percent more than average on this item and control over half the market. Married couples without children at home (most of them older) spend 27 percent more than average on vitamins. Hispanics, who have the largest families, outspend the average on vitamins by 20 percent, and households in the West, where many Hispanics reside, do so by 75 percent.

Average household spending on vitamins fell 26 percent between 2000 and 2006, after adjusting for inflation, but spending rebounded by 5 percent since then. Behind the decline was price competition from discounters, as well as belt tightening as other health care costs increased. Average household spending on vitamins should climb as boomers age and seek to prevent ailments through better nutrition.

Table 10.18 Vitamins, nonprescription

Total household spending   **$5,515,212,780.00**
Average household spends   **45.54**

	AVERAGE HOUSEHOLD SPENDING	BEST CUSTOMERS (index)	BIGGEST CUSTOMERS (market share)
AGE OF HOUSEHOLDER			
Average household	**$45.54**	**100**	**100.0%**
Under age 25	9.69	21	1.4
Aged 25 to 34	30.33	67	11.1
Aged 35 to 44	28.11	62	11.2
Aged 45 to 54	52.06	114	23.6
Aged 55 to 64	58.90	129	22.8
Aged 65 to 74	73.03	160	17.3
Aged 75 or older	59.24	130	12.4

	AVERAGE HOUSEHOLD SPENDING	BEST CUSTOMERS (index)	BIGGEST CUSTOMERS (market share)
HOUSEHOLD INCOME			
Average household	$45.54	100	100.0%
Under $20,000	27.82	61	13.3
$20,000 to $39,999	37.85	83	19.0
$40,000 to $49,999	35.57	78	7.4
$50,000 to $69,999	36.86	81	11.6
$70,000 to $79,999	58.75	129	7.7
$80,000 to $99,999	35.32	78	6.5
$100,000 or more	93.23	205	35.1
HOUSEHOLD TYPE			
Average household	45.54	100	100.0
Married couples	52.47	115	56.8
Married couples, no children	57.86	127	27.0
Married couples, with children	48.05	106	24.5
Oldest child under age 6	49.86	109	4.7
Oldest child aged 6 to 17	47.24	104	12.2
Oldest child aged 18 or older	48.34	106	7.7
Single parent with child under age 18	12.63	28	1.6
Single person	42.12	92	27.1
RACE AND HISPANIC ORIGIN			
Average household	45.54	100	100.0
Asian	35.84	79	3.3
Black	16.24	36	4.4
Hispanic	54.65	120	14.6
Non-Hispanic white and other	48.77	107	81.2
REGION			
Average household	45.54	100	100.0
Northeast	34.41	76	13.9
Midwest	39.34	86	19.3
South	34.12	75	27.5
West	79.79	175	39.7
EDUCATION			
Average household	45.54	100	100.0
Less than high school graduate	30.57	67	9.6
High school graduate	25.51	56	14.3
Some college	57.33	126	26.5
Associate's degree	38.43	84	8.0
Bachelor's degree or more	63.56	140	41.5
Bachelor's degree	62.93	138	26.1
Master's, professional, doctoral degree	64.80	142	15.4

Note: Market shares may not sum to 100.0 because of rounding and missing categories by household type. "Asian" and "black" include Hispanics and non-Hispanics who identify themselves as being of the respective race alone. "Hispanic" includes people of any race who identify themselves as Hispanic. "Other" includes people who identify themselves as non-Hispanic and as Alaska Native, American Indian, Asian (who are also included in the "Asian" row), or Native Hawaiian or other Pacific Islander as well as non-Hispanics reporting more than one race.

Source: Calculations by New Strategist based on the Bureau of Labor Statistics' 2010 Consumer Expenditure Survey

Chapter 11.

Household Services

Household Spending on Household Services, 2010

Spending on household services is dominated by day care needs. Spending on day care centers and babysitting accounted for 47 percent of the $670 the average household spent on household services in 2010. While the $239 that the average household spent on day care centers seems low, this—like all spending figures here—is an average that includes both purchasers and nonpurchasers. The 5 percent of households that paid for day care services during the average quarter of 2010 spent an average of $1,258 (see Appendix B), for an estimated annual expense of $5,032—a much more realistic figure.

The average household spent 7 percent less on household services in 2010 than in 2000, after adjusting for inflation. Average household spending on services in 2006, however, had been 7 percent higher than in 2000. Between the overall peak spending year of 2006 and 2010, spending on day care centers fell 17 percent, spending on housekeeping services declined 10 percent, and spending on gardening and lawn care services dropped 9 percent. The only household services categories to see an increase in average household spending over those years were termite and pest control services, which gained 21 percent, and security system service fee, which increased 10 percent.

Average household spending on household services should grow as the millennial generation enters the lifestage at which day care needs are greatest.

Spending on household services

(average annual spending by households on household services, 2000, 2006, and 2010; in 2010 dollars)

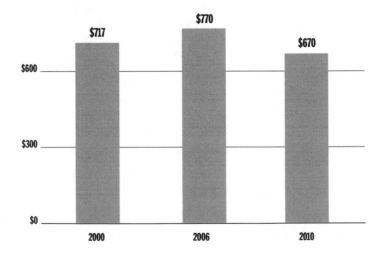

Table 11.1 Household services spending, 2000 to 2010

(average annual household spending on household services by category, 2000 to 2010; percent change and percentage point change in spending, 2000–06, 2006–10, and 2000–10; in 2010 dollars; ranked by amount spent)

	2010 average household spending	2006 average household spending (in 2010$)	2000 average household spending (in 2010$)	percent change		
				2006–10	2000–06	2000–10
AVERAGE ANNUAL SPENDING						
Average annual household spending on household services	**$670.13**	**$769.84**	**$717.19**	**–13.0%**	**7.3%**	**–6.6%**
Day care centers, nursery schools, and preschools	238.57	286.73	263.92	–16.8	8.6	–9.6
Housekeeping services	111.70	123.63	111.62	–9.6	10.8	0.1
Gardening, lawn care service	107.66	118.04	99.10	–8.8	19.1	8.6
Babysitting and childcare in own or other home	79.51	87.15	82.06	–8.8	6.2	–3.1
Moving, storage, and freight express	44.74	44.96	41.07	–0.5	9.5	8.9
Security system service fee	23.62	21.56	23.64	9.6	–8.8	–0.1
Termite and pest control services	20.97	17.26	12.12	21.5	42.5	73.0
Care for the elderly, invalids, handicapped	20.80	46.69	63.80	–55.5	–26.8	–67.4
Appliance repair, including at service center	19.02	19.45	15.93	–2.2	22.1	19.4
Water softening service	3.54	4.37	3.94	–19.0	11.0	–10.1

				percentage point change		
	2006–10	2000–06	2000–10	2006–10	2000–06	2000–10
PERCENT DISTRIBUTION OF SPENDING						
Average annual household spending on household services	**100.0%**	**100.0%**	**100.0%**	**–**	**–**	**–**
Day care centers, nursery schools, and preschools	35.6	37.2	36.8	–1.6	0.4	–1.2
Housekeeping services	16.7	16.1	15.6	0.6	0.5	1.1
Gardening, lawn care service	16.1	15.3	13.8	0.7	1.5	2.2
Babysitting and childcare in own or other home	11.9	11.3	11.4	0.5	–0.1	0.4
Moving, storage, and freight express	6.7	5.8	5.7	0.8	0.1	1.0
Security system service fee	3.5	2.8	3.3	0.7	–0.5	0.2
Termite and pest control services	3.1	2.2	1.7	0.9	0.6	1.4
Care for the elderly, invalids, handicapped	3.1	6.1	8.9	–3.0	–2.8	–5.8
Appliance repair, including at service center	2.8	2.5	2.2	0.3	0.3	0.6
Water softening service	0.5	0.6	0.5	–0.0	0.0	–0.0

Note: "–" means not applicable.

Source: Bureau of Labor Statistics, 2000, 2006, and 2010 Consumer Expenditure Surveys; calculations by New Strategist

Appliance Repair, Including at Service Center

Best customers:
Householders aged 55 to 74
Married couples without children at home
Married couples with school-aged or older children at home

Customer trends:
Average household spending on appliance repair may recover as financially strapped boomers enter the older age groups.

The best customers of appliance repair are older householders. Not only do older householders have older appliances, but their appliances are often of higher quality, which makes it costlier to replace than to repair. Householders aged 55 to 74 spend 45 to 48 percent more than the average household on appliance repair. Married couples without children at home, most older empty-nesters, spend 37 percent more than average on appliance repair, while those with school-aged or older children at home spend 50 to 97 percent more than average on this item.

Average household spending on appliance repair fell 2 percent between 2006 (the year overall household spending peaked) and 2010, after adjusting for inflation. This downturn reversed solid growth from earlier in the decade—a 22 percent increase from 2000 to 2006. Average household spending on appliance repair may recover as financially strapped boomers enter the older age groups.

Table 11.2 Appliance repair, including at service center

Total household spending $2,303,455,140.00
Average household spends   19.02

	AVERAGE HOUSEHOLD SPENDING	BEST CUSTOMERS (index)	BIGGEST CUSTOMERS (market share)
AGE OF HOUSEHOLDER			
Average household	**$19.02**	**100**	**100.0%**
Under age 25	3.52	19	1.2
Aged 25 to 34	9.46	50	8.3
Aged 35 to 44	19.21	101	18.3
Aged 45 to 54	18.89	99	20.5
Aged 55 to 64	27.63	145	25.6
Aged 65 to 74	28.19	148	15.9
Aged 75 or older	20.21	106	10.1

	AVERAGE HOUSEHOLD SPENDING	BEST CUSTOMERS (index)	BIGGEST CUSTOMERS (market share)
HOUSEHOLD INCOME			
Average household	**$19.02**	**100**	**100.0%**
Under $20,000	6.08	32	7.0
$20,000 to $39,999	13.98	74	16.8
$40,000 to $49,999	10.33	54	5.1
$50,000 to $69,999	17.69	93	13.3
$70,000 to $79,999	18.29	96	5.8
$80,000 to $99,999	30.15	159	13.2
$100,000 or more	43.00	226	38.8
HOUSEHOLD TYPE			
Average household	**19.02**	**100**	**100.0**
Married couples	27.52	145	71.4
Married couples, no children	26.06	137	29.1
Married couples, with children	28.05	147	34.3
Oldest child under age 6	11.20	59	2.5
Oldest child aged 6 to 17	28.46	150	17.6
Oldest child aged 18 or older	37.38	197	14.2
Single parent with child under age 18	7.61	40	2.4
Single person	9.19	48	14.2
RACE AND HISPANIC ORIGIN			
Average household	**19.02**	**100**	**100.0**
Asian	15.12	79	3.4
Black	11.22	59	7.2
Hispanic	10.83	57	6.9
Non-Hispanic white and other	21.54	113	85.9
REGION			
Average household	**19.02**	**100**	**100.0**
Northeast	17.97	94	17.3
Midwest	17.92	94	21.0
South	18.39	97	35.5
West	21.99	116	26.2
EDUCATION			
Average household	**19.02**	**100**	**100.0**
Less than high school graduate	11.17	59	8.4
High school graduate	16.47	87	22.1
Some college	16.20	85	17.9
Associate's degree	15.94	84	7.9
Bachelor's degree or more	27.98	147	43.7
Bachelor's degree	24.12	127	24.0
Master's, professional, doctoral degree	34.71	182	19.7

Note: Market shares may not sum to 100.0 because of rounding and missing categories by household type. "Asian" and "black" include Hispanics and non-Hispanics who identify themselves as being of the respective race alone. "Hispanic" includes people of any race who identify themselves as Hispanic. "Other" includes people who identify themselves as non-Hispanic and as Alaska Native, American Indian, Asian (who are also included in the "Asian" row), or Native Hawaiian or other Pacific Islander as well as non-Hispanics reporting more than one race.

Source: Calculations by New Strategist based on the Bureau of Labor Statistics' 2010 Consumer Expenditure Survey

Babysitting and Child Care in Own or Other Home

Best customers: **Householders aged 25 to 44**
High-income households
Married couples with children under age 18
Single parents
Asians
Households in the Northeast and West

Customer trends: **Average household spending on babysitting and child care in own or other home**
should begin to grow again as the large millennial generation has children.

Child care is one of the largest expenses parents face. Those who spend the most on babysitting (which includes arrangements from hiring a teen to be with the kids on a Saturday night to a live-in nanny) are married couples with preschoolers. This household type spends almost nine times the average on babysitting. Couples with school-aged children spend close to two-and-one-half times the average on this item, and single parents spend almost twice the average. Householders aged 25 to 44, most with children, spend over twice the average on babysitting. High-income households spend three-and-one-third times the average on this item. Asians, who have the highest incomes, spend 38 percent more than average on babysitting. Households in the Northeast outspend the average on babysitting by 61 percent, and households in the West spend 26 percent more.

Average household spending on babysitting rose 6 percent between 2000 and 2006, after adjusting for inflation. Then, between 2006 (the year overall household spending peaked) and 2010, average household spending on babysitting fell 9 percent as many families faced unemployment and had less need for babysitting services. In the years ahead, spending on babysitting should begin to grow again as the large millennial generation has children.

Table 11.3   Babysitting and child care in own or other home

Total household spending $9,629,217,570.00
Average household spends   79.51

	AVERAGE HOUSEHOLD SPENDING	BEST CUSTOMERS (index)	BIGGEST CUSTOMERS (market share)
AGE OF HOUSEHOLDER			
Average household	**$79.51**	**100**	**100.0%**
Under age 25	40.43	51	3.4
Aged 25 to 34	182.23	229	38.2
Aged 35 to 44	179.27	225	40.8
Aged 45 to 54	54.53	69	14.2
Aged 55 to 64	5.47	7	1.2
Aged 65 to 74	6.17	8	0.8
Aged 75 or older	11.95	15	1.4

	AVERAGE HOUSEHOLD SPENDING	BEST CUSTOMERS (index)	BIGGEST CUSTOMERS (market share)
HOUSEHOLD INCOME			
Average household	**$79.51**	**100**	**100.0%**
Under $20,000	20.01	25	5.5
$20,000 to $39,999	26.59	33	7.7
$40,000 to $49,999	33.08	42	3.9
$50,000 to $69,999	66.11	83	11.9
$70,000 to $79,999	30.86	39	2.3
$80,000 to $99,999	109.70	138	11.5
$100,000 or more	265.05	333	57.2
HOUSEHOLD TYPE			
Average household	**79.51**	**100**	**100.0**
Married couples	124.35	156	77.1
Married couples, no children	2.72	3	0.7
Married couples, with children	228.24	287	66.8
Oldest child under age 6	691.92	870	37.3
Oldest child aged 6 to 17	195.01	245	28.8
Oldest child aged 18 or older	7.39	9	0.7
Single parent with child under age 18	151.78	191	11.3
Single person	3.90	5	1.4
RACE AND HISPANIC ORIGIN			
Average household	**79.51**	**100**	**100.0**
Asian	109.48	138	5.9
Black	45.24	57	7.0
Hispanic	77.11	97	11.8
Non-Hispanic white and other	85.20	107	81.2
REGION			
Average household	**79.51**	**100**	**100.0**
Northeast	128.34	161	29.6
Midwest	74.10	93	20.8
South	45.37	57	20.9
West	100.58	126	28.7
EDUCATION			
Average household	**79.51**	**100**	**100.0**
Less than high school graduate	30.80	39	5.5
High school graduate	35.29	44	11.3
Some college	48.74	61	12.9
Associate's degree	65.81	83	7.8
Bachelor's degree or more	167.07	210	62.4
Bachelor's degree	88.81	112	21.1
Master's, professional, doctoral degree	303.71	382	41.3

Note: Market shares may not sum to 100.0 because of rounding and missing categories by household type. "Asian" and "black" include Hispanics and non-Hispanics who identify themselves as being of the respective race alone. "Hispanic" includes people of any race who identify themselves as Hispanic. "Other" includes people who identify themselves as non-Hispanic and as Alaska Native, American Indian, Asian (who are also included in the "Asian" row), or Native Hawaiian or other Pacific Islander as well as non-Hispanics reporting more than one race.

Source: Calculations by New Strategist based on the Bureau of Labor Statistics' 2010 Consumer Expenditure Survey

Care for the Elderly, Invalids, Handicapped, Etc.

Best customers: Householders aged 65 or older
Married couples with adult children at home
People who live alone
Non-Hispanic whites and Asians

Customer trends: Average household spending on care for the elderly, invalids, and handicapped
should rise as boomers age.

Older households spend the most on care for the elderly, invalids, and the handicapped. Householders aged 65 to 74 spend twice the average on elder care, and householders aged 75 or older spend over four-and-one-half times the average on this item, many of them caring for ailing spouses. People who live alone (many of them older) spend 40 percent more than average. Married couples with adult children at home spend almost twice the average on this item—some caring for handicapped adult children in their household. Asian households also spend nearly twice the average on this item, but non-Hispanic whites control 99 percent of the market.

Average household spending on care for the elderly, invalids, and handicapped fell by two-thirds between 2000 and 2010, after adjusting for inflation. Average household spending on this item should rise as boomers age.

Table 11.4 **Care for the elderly, invalids, handicapped, etc.**

Total household spending $2,519,025,600.00
Average household spends   20.80

	AVERAGE HOUSEHOLD SPENDING	BEST CUSTOMERS (index)	BIGGEST CUSTOMERS (market share)
AGE OF HOUSEHOLDER			
Average household	**$20.80**	**100**	**100.0%**
Under age 25	1.10	5	0.4
Aged 25 to 34	1.72	8	1.4
Aged 35 to 44	7.94	38	6.9
Aged 45 to 54	8.29	40	8.2
Aged 55 to 64	20.30	98	17.2
Aged 65 to 74	41.37	199	21.4
Aged 75 or older	97.08	467	44.5

	AVERAGE HOUSEHOLD SPENDING	BEST CUSTOMERS (index)	BIGGEST CUSTOMERS (market share)
HOUSEHOLD INCOME			
Average household	**$20.80**	**100**	**100.0%**
Under $20,000	35.75	172	37.5
$20,000 to $39,999	10.96	53	12.1
$40,000 to $49,999	21.27	102	9.7
$50,000 to $69,999	20.15	97	13.9
$70,000 to $79,999	36.34	175	10.5
$80,000 to $99,999	1.51	7	0.6
$100,000 or more	19.18	92	15.8
HOUSEHOLD TYPE			
Average household	**20.80**	**100**	**100.0**
Married couples	20.73	100	49.2
Married couples, no children	31.12	150	31.8
Married couples, with children	14.89	72	16.7
Oldest child under age 6	1.73	8	0.4
Oldest child aged 6 to 17	3.90	19	2.2
Oldest child aged 18 or older	40.58	195	14.1
Single parent with child under age 18	–	–	–
Single person	29.18	140	41.1
RACE AND HISPANIC ORIGIN			
Average household	**20.80**	**100**	**100.0**
Asian	40.00	192	8.2
Black	0.77	4	0.5
Hispanic	0.66	3	0.4
Non-Hispanic white and other	27.21	131	99.2
REGION			
Average household	**20.80**	**100**	**100.0**
Northeast	10.73	52	9.5
Midwest	6.61	32	7.1
South	12.85	62	22.7
West	55.82	268	60.8
EDUCATION			
Average household	**20.80**	**100**	**100.0**
Less than high school graduate	8.05	39	5.5
High school graduate	27.76	133	34.1
Some college	30.42	146	30.7
Associate's degree	1.82	9	0.8
Bachelor's degree or more	20.18	97	28.8
Bachelor's degree	2.49	12	2.3
Master's, professional, doctoral degree	51.06	245	26.6

Note: Market shares may not sum to 100.0 because of rounding and missing categories by household type. "Asian" and "black" include Hispanics and non-Hispanics who identify themselves as being of the respective race alone. "Hispanic" includes people of any race who identify themselves as Hispanic. "Other" includes people who identify themselves as non-Hispanic and as Alaska Native, American Indian, Asian (who are also included in the Asian column), or Native Hawaiian or other Pacific Islander as well as non-Hispanics reporting more than one race. "–" means sample is too small to make a reliable estimate.

Source: Calculations by New Strategist based on the Bureau of Labor Statistics' 2010 Consumer Expenditure Survey

Day Care Centers, Nursery Schools, and Preschools

Best customers: **Householders aged 25 to 44**
Married couples with children under age 18
Single parents
Asians

Customer trends: **Average household spending on day care centers, nursery schools, and pre-schools should rise again in the years ahead as the large millennial generation has children.**

The best customers of day care centers are married couples with preschoolers. This household type spends nine-and-one-half times the average on day care centers, nursery schools, and preschools. Married couples with school-aged children spend over twice the average on this item, as do single parents. Householders aged 25 to 44, most of them parents, also spend more than twice the average on day care centers and control 82 percent of the market. Asians spend 75 percent more than average on day care.

Average household spending on day care centers climbed 9 percent between 2000 and 2006 (the year overall household spending peaked), then fell 17 percent between 2006 and 2010, after adjusting for inflation. Behind the decline was high unemployment due to the Great Recession, which limited the need for day care. Average household spending on day care centers should rise again in the years ahead as the large millennial generation has children.

Table 11.5 Day care centers, nursery schools, and preschools

Total household spending $28,892,496,990.00
Average household spends 238.57

	AVERAGE HOUSEHOLD SPENDING	BEST CUSTOMERS (index)	BIGGEST CUSTOMERS (market share)
AGE OF HOUSEHOLDER			
Average household	**$238.57**	**100**	**100.0%**
Under age 25	112.57	47	3.1
Aged 25 to 34	572.59	240	40.0
Aged 35 to 44	547.72	230	41.5
Aged 45 to 54	125.96	53	10.9
Aged 55 to 64	45.57	19	3.4
Aged 65 to 74	21.02	9	0.9
Aged 75 or older	3.14	1	0.1

	AVERAGE HOUSEHOLD SPENDING	BEST CUSTOMERS (index)	BIGGEST CUSTOMERS (market share)
HOUSEHOLD INCOME			
Average household	**$238.57**	**100**	**100.0%**
Under $20,000	39.95	17	3.7
$20,000 to $39,999	87.23	37	8.4
$40,000 to $49,999	128.12	54	5.1
$50,000 to $69,999	193.50	81	11.6
$70,000 to $79,999	322.70	135	8.1
$80,000 to $99,999	431.51	181	15.1
$100,000 or more	668.98	280	48.1
HOUSEHOLD TYPE			
Average household	**238.57**	**100**	**100.0**
Married couples	362.45	152	74.9
Married couples, no children	13.70	6	1.2
Married couples, with children	707.40	297	69.0
Oldest child under age 6	2,266.41	950	40.7
Oldest child aged 6 to 17	529.49	222	26.1
Oldest child aged 18 or older	72.72	30	2.2
Single parent with child under age 18	544.05	228	13.4
Single person	26.44	11	3.2
RACE AND HISPANIC ORIGIN			
Average household	**238.57**	**100**	**100.0**
Asian	417.28	175	7.4
Black	209.99	88	10.8
Hispanic	185.40	78	9.5
Non-Hispanic white and other	251.88	106	80.0
REGION			
Average household	**238.57**	**100**	**100.0**
Northeast	218.53	92	16.8
Midwest	226.04	95	21.1
South	232.88	98	35.8
West	276.35	116	26.2
EDUCATION			
Average household	**238.57**	**100**	**100.0**
Less than high school graduate	47.20	20	2.8
High school graduate	119.96	50	12.8
Some college	163.99	69	14.5
Associate's degree	302.72	127	12.0
Bachelor's degree or more	464.90	195	57.9
Bachelor's degree	388.77	163	30.8
Master's, professional, doctoral degree	597.82	251	27.1

Note: Market shares may not sum to 100.0 because of rounding and missing categories by household type. "Asian" and "black" include Hispanics and non-Hispanics who identify themselves as being of the respective race alone. "Hispanic" includes people of any race who identify themselves as Hispanic. "Other" includes people who identify themselves as non-Hispanic and as Alaska Native, American Indian, Asian (who are also included in the "Asian" row), or Native Hawaiian or other Pacific Islander as well as non-Hispanics reporting more than one race.

Source: Calculations by New Strategist based on the Bureau of Labor Statistics' 2010 Consumer Expenditure Survey

Gardening and Lawn Care Services

Best customers:
Householders aged 55 or older
Married couples without children at home
Married couples with school-aged children
Asians

Customer trends:
Average household spending on gardening and lawn care services should begin to grow once again as the population ages.

Older householders are most likely to spend on gardening and lawn care services. Householders aged 55 or older, many of whom need help maintaining their lawns, spend 47 to 73 percent more than average on this item and control 58 percent of the market. Married couples without children at home (most of them older) spend 58 percent more than average on gardening and lawn care services, and those with school-aged children spend 30 percent more. Asians spend 28 percent more than average on this service.

Average household spending on gardening and lawn care services climbed 19 percent between 2000 and 2006 (the year overall household spending peaked), after adjusting for inflation. Between 2006 and 2010, spending on gardening services fell 9 percent as households tightened their belts due to the Great Recession. This category should begin to grow again as the baby-boom generation increasingly fills the best-customer age groups.

Table 11.6 Gardening and lawn care services

Total household spending $13,038,379,620.00
Average household spends 107.66

	AVERAGE HOUSEHOLD SPENDING	BEST CUSTOMERS (index)	BIGGEST CUSTOMERS (market share)
AGE OF HOUSEHOLDER			
Average household	**$107.66**	**100**	**100.0%**
Under age 25	3.47	3	0.2
Aged 25 to 34	31.35	29	4.8
Aged 35 to 44	77.23	72	13.0
Aged 45 to 54	123.14	114	23.7
Aged 55 to 64	158.43	147	26.0
Aged 65 to 74	158.72	147	15.9
Aged 75 or older	186.01	173	16.5

	AVERAGE HOUSEHOLD SPENDING	BEST CUSTOMERS (index)	BIGGEST CUSTOMERS (market share)
HOUSEHOLD INCOME			
Average household	**$107.66**	**100**	**100.0%**
Under $20,000	53.30	50	10.8
$20,000 to $39,999	57.10	53	12.2
$40,000 to $49,999	55.40	51	4.9
$50,000 to $69,999	91.66	85	12.2
$70,000 to $79,999	86.82	81	4.8
$80,000 to $99,999	102.48	95	7.9
$100,000 or more	296.39	275	47.2
HOUSEHOLD TYPE			
Average household	**107.66**	**100**	**100.0**
Married couples	140.01	130	64.1
Married couples, no children	169.98	158	33.5
Married couples, with children	124.48	116	26.9
Oldest child under age 6	80.15	74	3.2
Oldest child aged 6 to 17	140.41	130	15.3
Oldest child aged 18 or older	124.82	116	8.4
Single parent with child under age 18	51.41	48	2.8
Single person	84.83	79	23.1
RACE AND HISPANIC ORIGIN			
Average household	**107.66**	**100**	**100.0**
Asian	137.78	128	5.4
Black	56.46	52	6.4
Hispanic	51.21	48	5.8
Non-Hispanic white and other	125.07	116	88.1
REGION			
Average household	**107.66**	**100**	**100.0**
Northeast	121.46	113	20.7
Midwest	68.27	63	14.1
South	115.09	107	39.2
West	123.19	114	25.9
EDUCATION			
Average household	**107.66**	**100**	**100.0**
Less than high school graduate	28.05	26	3.7
High school graduate	63.67	59	15.1
Some college	87.08	81	17.0
Associate's degree	87.05	81	7.6
Bachelor's degree or more	204.87	190	56.5
Bachelor's degree	177.14	165	31.1
Master's, professional, doctoral degree	253.29	235	25.5

Note: Market shares may not sum to 100.0 because of rounding and missing categories by household type. "Asian" and "black" include Hispanics and non-Hispanics who identify themselves as being of the respective race alone. "Hispanic" includes people of any race who identify themselves as Hispanic. "Other" includes people who identify themselves as non-Hispanic and as Alaska Native, American Indian, Asian (who are also included in the "Asian" row), or Native Hawaiian or other Pacific Islander as well as non-Hispanics reporting more than one race.

Source: Calculations by New Strategist based on the Bureau of Labor Statistics' 2010 Consumer Expenditure Survey

Housekeeping Services

Best customers: **Householders aged 65 or older**
High-income households
Married couples without children at home
Married couples with school-aged children
Non-Hispanic whites
Households in the Northeast and West
College graduates

Customer trends: **Average household spending on housekeeping services should rise as the population ages.**

The best customers of housekeeping services are older householders and the affluent—the first group often needs such services, while the second group can afford them. Householders aged 45 or older spend at least 13 percent more than average on housekeeping services, the figure peaking at 89 percent above average among householders aged 75 or older. Households with incomes of $100,000 or more spend three-and-one-half times the average on this item. Married couples without children at home, most of them older, spend 42 percent more than average on housekeeping services, while those with school-aged children (the busiest households) spend 76 percent more. Non-Hispanic whites account for 91 percent of the market. Western householders spend 37 percent more than average on housekeeping services, and Northeastern householders, 27 percent. College graduates, who dominate the nation's affluent, spend more than twice the average on this item.

After rising 11 percent between 2000 and 2006 (the year overall household spending peaked), average household spending on housekeeping services fell 10 percent between 2006 and 2010, after adjusting for inflation. Behind the earlier increase is the aging of the baby-boom generation into the best-customer age groups, while the economic downturn is behind the more recent decline. Spending on housekeeping services should rise again in the years ahead along with the aging of the population.

Table 11.7 Housekeeping services

Total household spending: $13,527,651,900.00
Average household spends: 111.70

	AVERAGE HOUSEHOLD SPENDING	BEST CUSTOMERS (index)	BIGGEST CUSTOMERS (market share)
AGE OF HOUSEHOLDER			
Average household	**$111.70**	**100**	**100.0%**
Under age 25	11.98	11	0.7
Aged 25 to 34	38.71	35	5.8
Aged 35 to 44	108.78	97	17.6
Aged 45 to 54	126.07	113	23.3
Aged 55 to 64	127.43	114	20.1
Aged 65 to 74	149.75	134	14.4
Aged 75 or older	210.81	189	18.0

	AVERAGE HOUSEHOLD SPENDING	BEST CUSTOMERS (index)	BIGGEST CUSTOMERS (market share)
HOUSEHOLD INCOME			
Average household	**$111.70**	**100**	**100.0%**
Under $20,000	37.04	33	7.2
$20,000 to $39,999	41.36	37	8.5
$40,000 to $49,999	56.68	51	4.8
$50,000 to $69,999	63.69	57	8.2
$70,000 to $79,999	65.24	58	3.5
$80,000 to $99,999	109.70	98	8.2
$100,000 or more	388.38	348	59.6
HOUSEHOLD TYPE			
Average household	**111.70**	**100**	**100.0**
Married couples	147.47	132	65.1
Married couples, no children	158.62	142	30.2
Married couples, with children	155.19	139	32.3
Oldest child under age 6	115.26	103	4.4
Oldest child aged 6 to 17	196.16	176	20.7
Oldest child aged 18 or older	112.12	100	7.2
Single parent with child under age 18	61.39	55	3.2
Single person	84.90	76	22.3
RACE AND HISPANIC ORIGIN			
Average household	**111.70**	**100**	**100.0**
Asian	116.71	104	4.4
Black	27.88	25	3.1
Hispanic	60.66	54	6.6
Non-Hispanic white and other	133.48	119	90.6
REGION			
Average household	**111.70**	**100**	**100.0**
Northeast	141.64	127	23.3
Midwest	74.60	67	14.9
South	93.55	84	30.7
West	153.34	137	31.1
EDUCATION			
Average household	**111.70**	**100**	**100.0**
Less than high school graduate	18.29	16	2.3
High school graduate	43.24	39	9.9
Some college	74.23	66	14.0
Associate's degree	72.51	65	6.1
Bachelor's degree or more	254.42	228	67.7
Bachelor's degree	191.03	171	32.3
Master's, professional, doctoral degree	365.09	327	35.4

Note: Market shares may not sum to 100.0 because of rounding and missing categories by household type. "Asian" and "black" include Hispanics and non-Hispanics who identify themselves as being of the respective race alone. "Hispanic" includes people of any race who identify themselves as Hispanic. "Other" includes people who identify themselves as non-Hispanic and as Alaska Native, American Indian, Asian (who are also included in the "Asian" row), or Native Hawaiian or other Pacific Islander as well as non-Hispanics reporting more than one race.

Source: Calculations by New Strategist based on the Bureau of Labor Statistics' 2010 Consumer Expenditure Survey

Moving, Storage, and Freight Express

Best customers: **Householders aged 55 to 64**
Married couples with preschoolers
Single parents
Households in the West

Customer trends: **Average household spending on moving, storage, and freight express is likely to track the ups and downs of the housing market.**

The biggest spenders on moving, storage, and freight express are households that can afford to pay for moving services or that need storage space. Householders aged 55 to 64 do not move much, but when they do, many can afford to hire moving services. In addition, older householders have accumulated belongings over the years that may require additional storage space. These factors explain why householders aged 55 to 64 spend 68 percent more than average on moving and storage services. Married couples with preschoolers spend two-and-one-half times the average on this item as they move into larger homes for their expanding families. Single parents, whose spending approaches average on only a few items, somehow spend 6 percent more than average on moving, storage, and freight express. Households in the West spend 35 percent above average on this item.

After growing 9 percent between 2000 and 2006 (the year when overall household spending peaked), average household spending on moving, storage and freight express fell slightly between 2006 and 2010, after adjusting for inflation. Average household spending on this item is likely to track the ups and downs of the housing market.

Table 11.8 Moving, storage, and freight express

Total household spending $5,418,327,180.00
Average household spends   44.74

	AVERAGE HOUSEHOLD SPENDING	BEST CUSTOMERS (index)	BIGGEST CUSTOMERS (market share)
AGE OF HOUSEHOLDER			
Average household	**$44.74**	**100**	**100.0%**
Under age 25	18.76	42	2.8
Aged 25 to 34	37.18	83	13.8
Aged 35 to 44	47.59	106	19.2
Aged 45 to 54	48.25	108	22.3
Aged 55 to 64	75.38	168	29.7
Aged 65 to 74	32.34	72	7.8
Aged 75 or older	20.28	45	4.3

	AVERAGE HOUSEHOLD SPENDING	BEST CUSTOMERS (index)	BIGGEST CUSTOMERS (market share)
HOUSEHOLD INCOME			
Average household	**$44.74**	**100**	**100.0%**
Under $20,000	24.02	54	11.7
$20,000 to $39,999	20.48	46	10.5
$40,000 to $49,999	42.58	95	9.0
$50,000 to $69,999	43.23	97	13.9
$70,000 to $79,999	86.25	193	11.5
$80,000 to $99,999	48.14	108	9.0
$100,000 or more	89.81	201	34.4
HOUSEHOLD TYPE			
Average household	**44.74**	**100**	**100.0**
Married couples	52.60	118	58.0
Married couples, no children	49.87	111	23.7
Married couples, with children	54.16	121	28.2
Oldest child under age 6	109.39	245	10.5
Oldest child aged 6 to 17	45.47	102	12.0
Oldest child aged 18 or older	35.57	80	5.7
Single parent with child under age 18	47.40	106	6.2
Single person	32.63	73	21.4
RACE AND HISPANIC ORIGIN			
Average household	**44.74**	**100**	**100.0**
Asian	31.94	71	3.0
Black	27.06	60	7.4
Hispanic	14.19	32	3.9
Non-Hispanic white and other	52.41	117	88.8
REGION			
Average household	**44.74**	**100**	**100.0**
Northeast	42.79	96	17.6
Midwest	37.42	84	18.6
South	40.42	90	33.2
West	60.50	135	30.6
EDUCATION			
Average household	**44.74**	**100**	**100.0**
Less than high school graduate	7.40	17	2.4
High school graduate	26.11	58	14.9
Some college	39.73	89	18.7
Associate's degree	48.34	108	10.2
Bachelor's degree or more	81.09	181	53.8
Bachelor's degree	68.67	153	29.0
Master's, professional, doctoral degree	102.79	230	24.9

Note: Market shares may not sum to 100.0 because of rounding and missing categories by household type. "Asian" and "black" include Hispanics and non-Hispanics who identify themselves as being of the respective race alone. "Hispanic" includes people of any race who identify themselves as Hispanic. "Other" includes people who identify themselves as non-Hispanic and as Alaska Native, American Indian, Asian (who are also included in the "Asian" row), or Native Hawaiian or other Pacific Islander as well as non-Hispanics reporting more than one race.

Source: Calculations by New Strategist based on the Bureau of Labor Statistics' 2010 Consumer Expenditure Survey

Security System Service Fee

Best customers: Householders aged 55 to 74
Married couples without children at home
Married couples with school-aged children
Blacks
Households in the South

Customer trends: Average household spending on home security system service fees should continue to rise along with the aging of the population.

The best customers of home security system service fees are older married couples. Householders ranging in age from 55 to 74 spend 20 to 25 percent more than average on this item. Married couples without children at home, most of them empty-nesters, spend 33 percent more than average on security system service fees, while those with school-aged children spend 59 percent more than average. Black householders outspend the average by 60 percent. Households in the South, where many blacks reside, spend 35 percent more than average on security system service fees.

Average household spending on home security system service fees fell 9 percent between 2000 and 2006, after adjusting for inflation, but then rebounded and climbed 10 percent between 2006 and 2010. Average household spending on home security system service fees should continue to rise in the years ahead along with the aging of the population.

Table 11.9 Security system service fee

Total household spending $2,860,547,340.00
Average household spends 23.62

	AVERAGE HOUSEHOLD SPENDING	BEST CUSTOMERS (index)	BIGGEST CUSTOMERS (market share)
AGE OF HOUSEHOLDER			
Average household	**$23.62**	**100**	**100.0%**
Under age 25	3.89	16	1.1
Aged 25 to 34	17.11	72	12.1
Aged 35 to 44	28.16	119	21.6
Aged 45 to 54	24.79	105	21.7
Aged 55 to 64	29.47	125	22.0
Aged 65 to 74	28.32	120	12.9
Aged 75 or older	21.46	91	8.7

	AVERAGE HOUSEHOLD SPENDING	BEST CUSTOMERS (index)	BIGGEST CUSTOMERS (market share)
HOUSEHOLD INCOME			
Average household	**$23.62**	**100**	**100.0%**
Under $20,000	6.13	26	5.7
$20,000 to $39,999	14.26	60	13.8
$40,000 to $49,999	16.62	70	6.7
$50,000 to $69,999	19.19	81	11.7
$70,000 to $79,999	29.49	125	7.5
$80,000 to $99,999	34.61	147	12.2
$100,000 or more	58.56	248	42.5
HOUSEHOLD TYPE			
Average household	**23.62**	**100**	**100.0**
Married couples	31.41	133	65.6
Married couples, no children	31.51	133	28.3
Married couples, with children	32.66	138	32.2
Oldest child under age 6	27.01	114	4.9
Oldest child aged 6 to 17	37.62	159	18.7
Oldest child aged 18 or older	27.94	118	8.5
Single parent with child under age 18	16.03	68	4.0
Single person	14.68	62	18.2
RACE AND HISPANIC ORIGIN			
Average household	**23.62**	**100**	**100.0**
Asian	26.85	114	4.8
Black	37.69	160	19.5
Hispanic	15.79	67	8.1
Non-Hispanic white and other	22.70	96	72.9
REGION			
Average household	**23.62**	**100**	**100.0**
Northeast	18.45	78	14.3
Midwest	17.00	72	16.0
South	31.86	135	49.5
West	20.98	89	20.1
EDUCATION			
Average household	**23.62**	**100**	**100.0**
Less than high school graduate	7.65	32	4.6
High school graduate	17.76	75	19.2
Some college	18.09	77	16.1
Associate's degree	27.16	115	10.9
Bachelor's degree or more	39.12	166	49.2
Bachelor's degree	32.11	136	25.7
Master's, professional, doctoral degree	51.35	217	23.5

Note: Market shares may not sum to 100.0 because of rounding and missing categories by household type. "Asian" and "black" include Hispanics and non-Hispanics who identify themselves as being of the respective race alone. "Hispanic" includes people of any race who identify themselves as Hispanic. "Other" includes people who identify themselves as non-Hispanic and as Alaska Native, American Indian, Asian (who are also included in the "Asian" row), or Native Hawaiian or other Pacific Islander as well as non-Hispanics reporting more than one race.

Source: Calculations by New Strategist based on the Bureau of Labor Statistics' 2010 Consumer Expenditure Survey

Termite and Pest Control Products and Services

Best customers:	**Householders aged 55 or older** **Married couples without children at home** **Married couples with school-aged children** **Asians** **Households in the South**
Customer trends:	**Average household spending on termite and pest control products and services should continue to increase along with the population of the South.**

The best customers of termite and pest control products and services are older married couples in the South, where insect problems are abundant because of the warm climate. Southern households spend 71 percent more than average on this item and control 63 percent of the market. Householders aged 55 or older spend 12 to 42 percent more than average on termite and pest control. Married couples without children at home, most of them older, spend 53 percent more than average on this item. Married couples with school-aged children outspend the average for this item by 56 percent. The spending on termite and pest control by Asian householders is two-thirds higher than average.

Although the pace of growth has slowed since 2006, average household spending on termite and pest control products and services continued to rise throughout the economic downturn. Overall, spending on this item increased by a substantial 65 percent between 2000 and 2010, after adjusting for inflation. Behind the increase is the growing population of the South, where these services are often necessary. Spending on termite and pest control products and services should continue to increase along with the population of the South.

Table 11.10 Termite and pest control products and services

Total household spending	$2,539,613,790.00
Average household spends	20.97

	AVERAGE HOUSEHOLD SPENDING	BEST CUSTOMERS (index)	BIGGEST CUSTOMERS (market share)
AGE OF HOUSEHOLDER			
Average household	**$20.97**	**100**	**100.0%**
Under age 25	3.25	15	1.0
Aged 25 to 34	13.24	63	10.5
Aged 35 to 44	21.09	101	18.2
Aged 45 to 54	21.03	100	20.7
Aged 55 to 64	29.74	142	25.0
Aged 65 to 74	26.83	128	13.8
Aged 75 or older	23.58	112	10.7

	AVERAGE HOUSEHOLD SPENDING	BEST CUSTOMERS (index)	BIGGEST CUSTOMERS (market share)
HOUSEHOLD INCOME			
Average household	$20.97	100	100.0%
Under $20,000	9.65	46	10.0
$20,000 to $39,999	11.26	54	12.3
$40,000 to $49,999	11.84	56	5.3
$50,000 to $69,999	16.40	78	11.2
$70,000 to $79,999	34.10	163	9.7
$80,000 to $99,999	23.51	112	9.3
$100,000 or more	51.38	245	42.0
HOUSEHOLD TYPE			
Average household	20.97	100	100.0
Married couples	29.45	140	69.3
Married couples, no children	32.07	153	32.5
Married couples, with children	27.84	133	30.9
Oldest child under age 6	21.53	103	4.4
Oldest child aged 6 to 17	32.77	156	18.4
Oldest child aged 18 or older	23.56	112	8.1
Single parent with child under age 18	9.81	47	2.8
Single person	13.02	62	18.2
RACE AND HISPANIC ORIGIN			
Average household	20.97	100	100.0
Asian	34.84	166	7.1
Black	16.67	79	9.7
Hispanic	7.96	38	4.6
Non-Hispanic white and other	23.73	113	85.8
REGION			
Average household	20.97	100	100.0
Northeast	10.52	50	9.2
Midwest	5.49	26	5.8
South	35.92	171	62.9
West	20.43	97	22.1
EDUCATION			
Average household	20.97	100	100.0
Less than high school graduate	4.79	23	3.3
High school graduate	9.79	47	11.9
Some college	23.17	110	23.2
Associate's degree	14.98	71	6.7
Bachelor's degree or more	38.70	185	54.8
Bachelor's degree	36.68	175	33.0
Master's, professional, doctoral degree	42.22	201	21.8

Note: Market shares may not sum to 100.0 because of rounding and missing categories by household type. "Asian" and "black" include Hispanics and non-Hispanics who identify themselves as being of the respective race alone. "Hispanic" includes people of any race who identify themselves as Hispanic. "Other" includes people who identify themselves as non-Hispanic and as Alaska Native, American Indian, Asian (who are also included in the "Asian" row), or Native Hawaiian or other Pacific Islander as well as non-Hispanics reporting more than one race.

Source: Calculations by New Strategist based on the Bureau of Labor Statistics' 2010 Consumer Expenditure Survey

Water Softening Services

Best customers: **Householders aged 65 or older**
Married couples
Households in the Midwest

Customer trends: **Average household spending on water softening services should stabilize in the years ahead because boomers are solidly in the best-customer age groups.**

The biggest spenders on water softening services are older married couples in the Midwest. Householders aged 65 or older spend 22 to 75 percent more than average on this item. Married couples without children at home, most older empty-nesters, spend 44 percent more, and couples with children outspend the average by 41 percent. Households in the Midwest spend 53 percent above average on water softening services.

After rising 11 percent form 2000 to 2006, average household spending on water softening services declined 19 percent between 2006 and 2010, after adjusting for inflation. Average household spending on water softening services should stabilize in the years ahead because boomers are solidly in the best-customer age groups.

Table 11.11 Water softening service

Total household spending $428,718,780.00
Average household spends   3.54

	AVERAGE HOUSEHOLD SPENDING	BEST CUSTOMERS (index)	BIGGEST CUSTOMERS (market share)
AGE OF HOUSEHOLDER			
Average household	**$3.54**	**100**	**100.0%**
Under age 25	0.43	12	0.8
Aged 25 to 34	2.33	66	11.0
Aged 35 to 44	3.23	91	16.5
Aged 45 to 54	3.86	109	22.6
Aged 55 to 64	3.87	109	19.3
Aged 65 to 74	4.33	122	13.2
Aged 75 or older	6.19	175	16.7

	AVERAGE HOUSEHOLD SPENDING	BEST CUSTOMERS (index)	BIGGEST CUSTOMERS (market share)
HOUSEHOLD INCOME			
Average household	**$3.54**	**100**	**100.0%**
Under $20,000	1.72	49	10.6
$20,000 to $39,999	2.63	74	17.0
$40,000 to $49,999	3.16	89	8.4
$50,000 to $69,999	4.78	135	19.4
$70,000 to $79,999	3.94	111	6.7
$80,000 to $99,999	3.03	86	7.1
$100,000 or more	6.35	179	30.8
HOUSEHOLD TYPE			
Average household	**3.54**	**100**	**100.0**
Married couples	4.78	135	66.6
Married couples, no children	5.09	144	30.5
Married couples, with children	4.98	141	32.7
Oldest child under age 6	4.66	132	5.6
Oldest child aged 6 to 17	5.08	144	16.9
Oldest child aged 18 or older	5.02	142	10.2
Single parent with child under age 18	2.65	75	4.4
Single person	2.07	58	17.1
RACE AND HISPANIC ORIGIN			
Average household	**3.54**	**100**	**100.0**
Asian	2.60	73	3.1
Black	3.09	87	10.7
Hispanic	3.69	104	12.7
Non-Hispanic white and other	3.57	101	76.5
REGION			
Average household	**3.54**	**100**	**100.0**
Northeast	3.16	89	16.4
Midwest	5.42	153	34.1
South	3.30	93	34.2
West	2.38	67	15.2
EDUCATION			
Average household	**3.54**	**100**	**100.0**
Less than high school graduate	2.73	77	11.0
High school graduate	3.70	105	26.7
Some college	2.40	68	14.3
Associate's degree	4.98	141	13.3
Bachelor's degree or more	4.14	117	34.7
Bachelor's degree	4.33	122	23.1
Master's, professional, doctoral degree	3.80	107	11.6

Note: Market shares may not sum to 100.0 because of rounding and missing categories by household type. "Asian" and "black" include Hispanics and non-Hispanics who identify themselves as being of the respective race alone. "Hispanic" includes people of any race who identify themselves as Hispanic. "Other" includes people who identify themselves as non-Hispanic and as Alaska Native, American Indian, Asian (who are also included in the "Asian" row), or Native Hawaiian or other Pacific Islander as well as non-Hispanics reporting more than one race.

Source: Calculations by New Strategist based on the Bureau of Labor Statistics' 2010 Consumer Expenditure Survey

Chapter 12.

Housekeeping Supplies

Household Spending on Housekeeping Supplies, 2010

Housekeeping supplies is a catchall category that includes a variety of products such as laundry detergent, toilet paper, paper towels, vegetable seeds, insecticides, postage, stationery, and giftwrap. In 2010, the average household spent $612 on these items, just about the same as in 2000, after adjusting for inflation. Spending in this category declined 12 percent between the overall peak-spending year of 2006 and 2010.

Laundry and cleaning supplies is the largest subcategory within housekeeping supplies, accounting for 25 percent of spending in the category. Between 2000 and 2010, average household spending on laundry and cleaning supplies fell 9 percent, after adjusting for inflation. The category of cleansing and toilet tissue, paper towels, and napkins saw the largest growth in average household spending during these years, a 19 percent increase. These paper products now account for 17 percent of spending on housekeeping supplies. Lawn and garden supplies spending increased by 13 percent after adjusting for inflation. Because the primary customers of lawn and garden supplies are older householders, continued growth in the lawn and garden category is likely. Spending on postage fell 5 percent between 2000 and 2010, after adjusting for inflation, and spending on stationery, stationery supplies, and giftwrap plummeted 30 percent.

Spending on housekeeping supplies

(average annual spending by households on housekeeping supplies, 2000, 2006, and 2010; in 2010 dollars)

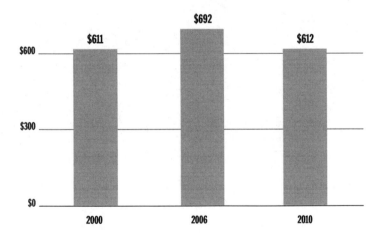

Table 12.1 Housekeeping supplies spending, 2000 to 2010

(average annual household spending on housekeeping supplies by category, 2000 to 2010; percent change and percentage point change in spending, 2000–06, 2006–10, and 2000–10; in 2010 dollars; ranked by amount spent)

	2010 average household spending	2006 average household spending (in 2010$)	2000 average household spending (in 2010$)	percent change		
				2006–10	2000–06	2000–10
AVERAGE ANNUAL SPENDING						
Average annual household spending on housekeeping supplies	**$611.58**	**$691.78**	**$610.76**	**−11.6%**	**13.3%**	**0.1%**
Laundry and cleaning supplies	150.26	163.56	165.58	−8.1	−1.2	−9.3
Cleansing and toilet tissue, paper towels, and napkins	103.41	108.01	86.68	−4.3	24.6	19.3
Lawn and garden supplies	96.09	104.97	84.80	−8.5	23.8	13.3
Postage	73.27	75.04	76.74	−2.4	−2.2	−4.5
Stationery, stationery supplies, giftwrap	56.06	92.99	80.60	−39.7	15.4	−30.4

				percentage point change		
	2006–10	2000–06	2000–10	2006–10	2000–06	2000–10
PERCENT DISTRIBUTION OF SPENDING						
Average annual household spending on housekeeping supplies	**100.0%**	**100.0%**	**100.0%**	**–**	**–**	**–**
Laundry and cleaning supplies	24.6	23.6	27.1	0.9	−3.5	−2.5
Cleansing and toilet tissue, paper towels, and napkins	16.9	15.6	14.2	1.3	1.4	2.7
Lawn and garden supplies	15.7	15.2	13.9	0.5	1.3	1.8
Postage	12.0	10.8	12.6	1.1	−1.7	−0.6
Stationery, stationery supplies, giftwrap	9.2	13.4	13.2	−4.3	0.2	−4.0

Note: Numbers do not add to total because not all categories are shown. "–" means not applicable.

Source: Bureau of Labor Statistics, 2000, 2006, and 2010 Consumer Expenditure Surveys; calculations by New Strategist

Cleansing and Toilet Tissue, Paper Towels, and Napkins

Best customers: **Householders aged 35 to 64**
Married couples with school-aged or older children at home
Hispanics

Customer trends: **Average household spending on cleansing and toilet tissue, paper towels, and
napkins is likely to continue to fall as household size declines with the aging of
the baby-boom generation.**

Because everyone buys cleansing and toilet tissue, paper towels, and napkins, there are few differences by demographic characteristic in spending on this item. Householders ranging in age from 35 to 64 spend 9 to12 percent more than average on this item. Married couples with school-aged or older children at home spend 41 to 46 percent more. The spending on toilet tissue, paper towels, and napkins by Hispanic householders, who tend to have large families, is 26 percent higher than average.

Average household spending on cleansing and toilet tissue, paper towels, and napkins rose 25 percent between 2000 and 2006, after adjusting for inflation, then dropped 4 percent over the remainder of the decade. Average household spending on this item may continue to fall in the years ahead as boomers age and average household size resumes its long-term decline.

Table 12.2   Cleansing and toilet tissue, paper towels, and napkins

Total household spending $12,523,674,870.00
Average household spends   103.41

	AVERAGE HOUSEHOLD SPENDING	BEST CUSTOMERS (index)	BIGGEST CUSTOMERS (market share)
AGE OF HOUSEHOLDER			
Average household	**$103.41**	**100**	**100.0%**
Under age 25	62.11	60	4.0
Aged 25 to 34	85.99	83	13.8
Aged 35 to 44	112.95	109	19.8
Aged 45 to 54	114.07	110	22.8
Aged 55 to 64	115.58	112	19.7
Aged 65 to 74	104.32	101	10.9
Aged 75 or older	97.56	94	9.0

	AVERAGE HOUSEHOLD SPENDING	BEST CUSTOMERS (index)	BIGGEST CUSTOMERS (market share)
HOUSEHOLD INCOME			
Average household	**$103.41**	**100**	**100.0%**
Under $20,000	74.68	72	15.8
$20,000 to $39,999	84.75	82	18.8
$40,000 to $49,999	108.00	104	9.9
$50,000 to $69,999	98.43	95	13.7
$70,000 to $79,999	109.55	106	6.3
$80,000 to $99,999	124.61	121	10.0
$100,000 or more	154.83	150	25.7
HOUSEHOLD TYPE			
Average household	**103.41**	**100**	**100.0**
Married couples	127.65	123	60.9
Married couples, no children	106.13	103	21.8
Married couples, with children	140.36	136	31.6
Oldest child under age 6	104.52	101	4.3
Oldest child aged 6 to 17	145.72	141	16.6
Oldest child aged 18 or older	150.71	146	10.5
Single parent with child under age 18	102.51	99	5.8
Single person	59.53	58	16.9
RACE AND HISPANIC ORIGIN			
Average household	**103.41**	**100**	**100.0**
Asian	102.72	99	4.2
Black	91.30	88	10.8
Hispanic	130.21	126	15.3
Non-Hispanic white and other	101.28	98	74.3
REGION			
Average household	**103.41**	**100**	**100.0**
Northeast	109.52	106	19.4
Midwest	100.12	97	21.6
South	104.17	101	37.0
West	100.48	97	22.0
EDUCATION			
Average household	**103.41**	**100**	**100.0**
Less than high school graduate	111.74	108	15.4
High school graduate	98.06	95	24.2
Some college	97.41	94	19.8
Associate's degree	100.97	98	9.2
Bachelor's degree or more	109.60	106	31.5
Bachelor's degree	105.68	102	19.3
Master's, professional, doctoral degree	117.32	113	12.3

Note: Market shares may not sum to 100.0 because of rounding and missing categories by household type. "Asian" and "black" include Hispanics and non-Hispanics who identify themselves as being of the respective race alone. "Hispanic" includes people of any race who identify themselves as Hispanic. "Other" includes people who identify themselves as non-Hispanic and as Alaska Native, American Indian, Asian (who are also included in the "Asian" row), or Native Hawaiian or other Pacific Islander as well as non-Hispanics reporting more than one race.

Source: Calculations by New Strategist based on the Bureau of Labor Statistics' 2010 Consumer Expenditure Survey

Laundry and Cleaning Supplies

Best customers: **Householders aged 35 to 54**
                         Married couples with school-aged or older children at home
                         Single parents
                         Hispanics

Customer trends: **Average household spending on laundry and cleaning supplies may stabilize when the large millennial generation begins to move into the best-customer lifestage.**

Households with children spend the most on laundry and cleaning supplies. Householders aged 35 to 54, most with children at home, spend 10 to 22 percent more than average on laundry and cleaning supplies. Married couples with school-aged or older children at home spend 42 to 62 percent more than average on this item. Single parents, whose spending on most categories is well below average, spend 4 percent more than average on cleaning supplies. Hispanics, who have the largest families, spend 30 percent more than average on laundry and cleaning supplies.

Average household spending on laundry and cleaning supplies fell by 9 percent between 2000 and 2010, after adjusting for inflation. Behind the decline was the baby-boom generation's exit from the crowded-nest lifestage. Average household spending on this item may stabilize when the large millennial generation begins to move into the best-customer lifestage.

Table 12.3 Laundry and cleaning supplies

Total household spending $18,197,537,820.00
Average household spends   150.26

	AVERAGE HOUSEHOLD SPENDING	BEST CUSTOMERS (index)	BIGGEST CUSTOMERS (market share)
AGE OF HOUSEHOLDER			
Average household	**$150.26**	**100**	**100.0%**
Under age 25	90.21	60	4.0
Aged 25 to 34	125.89	84	14.0
Aged 35 to 44	183.66	122	22.1
Aged 45 to 54	165.29	110	22.8
Aged 55 to 64	157.18	105	18.4
Aged 65 to 74	146.76	98	10.5
Aged 75 or older	130.00	87	8.3

	AVERAGE HOUSEHOLD SPENDING	BEST CUSTOMERS (index)	BIGGEST CUSTOMERS (market share)
HOUSEHOLD INCOME			
Average household	**$150.26**	**100**	**100.0%**
Under $20,000	103.39	69	15.0
$20,000 to $39,999	118.95	79	18.1
$40,000 to $49,999	144.76	96	9.1
$50,000 to $69,999	150.56	100	14.4
$70,000 to $79,999	184.85	123	7.4
$80,000 to $99,999	187.74	125	10.4
$100,000 or more	227.38	151	25.9
HOUSEHOLD TYPE			
Average household	**150.26**	**100**	**100.0**
Married couples	190.71	127	62.6
Married couples, no children	153.98	102	21.8
Married couples, with children	218.92	146	33.9
Oldest child under age 6	159.22	106	4.5
Oldest child aged 6 to 17	243.42	162	19.1
Oldest child aged 18 or older	212.95	142	10.2
Single parent with child under age 18	156.96	104	6.2
Single person	84.72	56	16.5
RACE AND HISPANIC ORIGIN			
Average household	**150.26**	**100**	**100.0**
Asian	97.19	65	2.8
Black	156.89	104	12.8
Hispanic	195.47	130	15.8
Non-Hispanic white and other	142.39	95	71.8
REGION			
Average household	**150.26**	**100**	**100.0**
Northeast	138.53	92	16.9
Midwest	161.71	108	24.0
South	150.41	100	36.7
West	148.04	99	22.3
EDUCATION			
Average household	**150.26**	**100**	**100.0**
Less than high school graduate	160.04	107	15.2
High school graduate	140.21	93	23.8
Some college	137.09	91	19.2
Associate's degree	157.07	105	9.9
Bachelor's degree or more	162.04	108	32.0
Bachelor's degree	153.13	102	19.3
Master's, professional, doctoral degree	179.58	120	12.9

Note: Market shares may not sum to 100.0 because of rounding and missing categories by household type. "Asian" and "black" include Hispanics and non-Hispanics who identify themselves as being of the respective race alone. "Hispanic" includes people of any race who identify themselves as Hispanic. "Other" includes people who identify themselves as non-Hispanic and as Alaska Native, American Indian, Asian (who are also included in the "Asian" row), or Native Hawaiian or other Pacific Islander as well as non-Hispanics reporting more than one race.

Source: Calculations by New Strategist based on the Bureau of Labor Statistics' 2010 Consumer Expenditure Survey

Lawn and Garden Supplies

Best customers: **Householders aged 55 to 74**
Married couples without children at home
Non-Hispanic whites
Households in the West

Customer trends: **Average household spending on lawn and garden supplies should rise as boomers**
continue to fill the best-customer age groups.

The best customers of lawn and garden supplies are older married couples, most of whom are homeowners with lawns and gardens to tend. Householders aged 55 to 64 spend 49 percent more than average on lawn and garden supplies, while those aged 65 to 74 spend well over twice the average on this item. Together the two age groups control just over half the market. Married couples without children at home (most of them older) spend 86 percent more than average on garden supplies. Non-Hispanic whites account for 91 percent of the market for lawn and garden supplies. Spending on this item by households in the West is 22 percent higher than average.

Average household spending on lawn and garden supplies increased by 24 percent between 2000 and 2006, after adjusting for inflation, but declined 8 percent over the rest of the decade in part because of the Great Recession. Spending on lawn and garden supplies should rise again as the baby-boom generation continues to fill the best-customer age groups.

Table 12.4 Lawn and garden supplies

Total household spending $11,637,171,630.00
Average household spends   96.09

	AVERAGE HOUSEHOLD SPENDING	BEST CUSTOMERS (index)	BIGGEST CUSTOMERS (market share)
AGE OF HOUSEHOLDER			
Average household	**$96.09**	**100**	**100.0%**
Under age 25	9.25	10	0.6
Aged 25 to 34	45.26	47	7.8
Aged 35 to 44	65.02	68	12.2
Aged 45 to 54	82.29	86	17.7
Aged 55 to 64	143.51	149	26.3
Aged 65 to 74	219.51	228	24.6
Aged 75 or older	104.74	109	10.4

	AVERAGE HOUSEHOLD SPENDING	BEST CUSTOMERS (index)	BIGGEST CUSTOMERS (market share)
HOUSEHOLD INCOME			
Average household	**$96.09**	**100**	**100.0%**
Under $20,000	30.40	32	6.9
$20,000 to $39,999	52.45	55	12.5
$40,000 to $49,999	74.28	77	7.3
$50,000 to $69,999	101.82	106	15.2
$70,000 to $79,999	169.33	176	10.5
$80,000 to $99,999	107.98	112	9.4
$100,000 or more	217.64	226	38.8
HOUSEHOLD TYPE			
Average household	**96.09**	**100**	**100.0**
Married couples	124.90	130	64.1
Married couples, no children	179.08	186	39.6
Married couples, with children	89.46	93	21.7
Oldest child under age 6	78.23	81	3.5
Oldest child aged 6 to 17	89.46	93	10.9
Oldest child aged 18 or older	95.21	99	7.2
Single parent with child under age 18	21.10	22	1.3
Single person	65.13	68	19.9
RACE AND HISPANIC ORIGIN			
Average household	**96.09**	**100**	**100.0**
Asian	97.30	101	4.3
Black	36.84	38	4.7
Hispanic	36.22	38	4.6
Non-Hispanic white and other	114.80	119	90.6
REGION			
Average household	**96.09**	**100**	**100.0**
Northeast	99.79	104	19.1
Midwest	87.37	91	20.3
South	86.55	90	33.1
West	117.61	122	27.7
EDUCATION			
Average household	**96.09**	**100**	**100.0**
Less than high school graduate	29.40	31	4.4
High school graduate	59.77	62	15.9
Some college	98.51	103	21.6
Associate's degree	130.81	136	12.9
Bachelor's degree or more	144.11	150	44.6
Bachelor's degree	154.97	161	30.5
Master's, professional, doctoral degree	122.73	128	13.8

Note: Market shares may not sum to 100.0 because of rounding and missing categories by household type. "Asian" and "black" include Hispanics and non-Hispanics who identify themselves as being of the respective race alone. "Hispanic" includes people of any race who identify themselves as Hispanic. "Other" includes people who identify themselves as non-Hispanic and as Alaska Native, American Indian, Asian (who are also included in the "Asian" row), or Native Hawaiian or other Pacific Islander as well as non-Hispanics reporting more than one race.

Source: Calculations by New Strategist based on the Bureau of Labor Statistics' 2010 Consumer Expenditure Survey

Postage

Best customers: **Householders aged 55 or older**
                            Married couples without children at home

Customer trends: **Average household spending on postage will decline as younger, online Americans**
                            replace older, off-line generations.

Older Americans are the biggest spenders on postage. Householders aged 55 or older spend 29 to 57 percent more than average on this item. Married couples without children at home (most of them older) spend 52 percent more than average on postage.

Average household spending on postage declined 27 percent between 2000 and 2010, after adjusting for inflation. Postage spending would have fallen more precipitously, but was shored up by repeated hikes in the cost of postage as well as the popularity of the U.S. Postal Service's priority mail options. Average household spending on postage is likely to decline sharply in the years ahead as online generations move into the older age groups.

Table 12.5 Postage

Total household spending $6,789,258,420.00
Average household spends   56.06

	AVERAGE HOUSEHOLD SPENDING	BEST CUSTOMERS (index)	BIGGEST CUSTOMERS (market share)
AGE OF HOUSEHOLDER			
Average household	**$56.06**	**100**	**100.0%**
Under age 25	8.39	15	1.0
Aged 25 to 34	24.04	43	7.1
Aged 35 to 44	56.41	101	18.2
Aged 45 to 54	56.75	101	20.9
Aged 55 to 64	74.65	133	23.5
Aged 65 to 74	88.12	157	16.9
Aged 75 or older	72.10	129	12.3

	AVERAGE HOUSEHOLD SPENDING	BEST CUSTOMERS (index)	BIGGEST CUSTOMERS (market share)
HOUSEHOLD INCOME			
Average household	**$56.06**	**100**	**100.0%**
Under $20,000	34.64	62	13.5
$20,000 to $39,999	38.38	68	15.7
$40,000 to $49,999	55.82	100	9.4
$50,000 to $69,999	52.79	94	13.5
$70,000 to $79,999	63.17	113	6.7
$80,000 to $99,999	80.29	143	11.9
$100,000 or more	96.70	172	29.6
HOUSEHOLD TYPE			
Average household	**56.06**	**100**	**100.0**
Married couples	70.30	125	61.9
Married couples, no children	85.16	152	32.3
Married couples, with children	59.30	106	24.6
Oldest child under age 6	32.53	58	2.5
Oldest child aged 6 to 17	63.14	113	13.2
Oldest child aged 18 or older	67.27	120	8.7
Single parent with child under age 18	29.18	52	3.1
Single person	38.85	69	20.3
RACE AND HISPANIC ORIGIN			
Average household	**56.06**	**100**	**100.0**
Asian	46.58	83	3.5
Black	34.73	62	7.6
Hispanic	30.30	54	6.6
Non-Hispanic white and other	63.52	113	85.9
REGION			
Average household	**56.06**	**100**	**100.0**
Northeast	59.67	106	19.5
Midwest	58.95	105	23.4
South	49.05	87	32.1
West	61.71	110	24.9
EDUCATION			
Average household	**56.06**	**100**	**100.0**
Less than high school graduate	29.19	52	7.4
High school graduate	45.49	81	20.7
Some college	48.74	87	18.3
Associate's degree	50.17	89	8.5
Bachelor's degree or more	84.54	151	44.8
Bachelor's degree	68.23	122	23.0
Master's, professional, doctoral degree	116.65	208	22.5

Note: Market shares may not sum to 100.0 because of rounding and missing categories by household type. "Asian" and "black" include Hispanics and non-Hispanics who identify themselves as being of the respective race alone. "Hispanic" includes people of any race who identify themselves as Hispanic. "Other" includes people who identify themselves as non-Hispanic and as Alaska Native, American Indian, Asian (who are also included in the "Asian" row), or Native Hawaiian or other Pacific Islander as well as non-Hispanics reporting more than one race.

Source: Calculations by New Strategist based on the Bureau of Labor Statistics' 2010 Consumer Expenditure Survey

Stationery, Stationery Supplies, and Giftwrap

Best customers:
Householders aged 35 to 74
Married couples without children at home
Married couples with school-aged or older children at home
Asians

Customer trends:
Average household spending on stationery, stationery supplies, and giftwrap
may continue to fall in the years ahead as households slash their discretionary
spending.

The biggest spenders on the discretionary category of stationery, stationery supplies, and giftwrap are married couples. They are best customers because of their extended families and large network of friends. Householders ranging in age from 35 to 74 control three-quarters of the market and spend 5 to 18 percent more than average on this item as they wrap gifts for their own and other children. Married couples without children at home spend 25 percent more than average on this item, while those with school-aged or older children at home spend 45 to 56 percent more. Asians, who have the highest incomes, spend 35 percent more than average on this item.

After growing by 15 percent from 2000 to 2006 (the year overall household spending peaked), average household spending on stationery, stationery supplies, and giftwrap shrank 21 percent during the remainder of the decade, after adjusting for inflation. Behind the earlier increase was the baby-boom generation's entry into the grandparent lifestage, while the later decline owes to the Great Recession. Spending on stationery and giftwrap may continue to fall in the years ahead as households slash their discretionary spending.

Table 12.6 Stationery, stationery supplies, giftwrap

Total household spending	$8,873,509,890.00
Average household spends	73.27

	AVERAGE HOUSEHOLD SPENDING	BEST CUSTOMERS (index)	BIGGEST CUSTOMERS (market share)
AGE OF HOUSEHOLDER			
Average household	**$73.27**	**100**	**100.0%**
Under age 25	25.78	35	2.3
Aged 25 to 34	68.20	93	15.5
Aged 35 to 44	86.59	118	21.4
Aged 45 to 54	78.99	108	22.3
Aged 55 to 64	77.01	105	18.5
Aged 65 to 74	84.84	116	12.5
Aged 75 or older	57.49	78	7.5

	AVERAGE HOUSEHOLD SPENDING	BEST CUSTOMERS (index)	BIGGEST CUSTOMERS (market share)
HOUSEHOLD INCOME			
Average household	**$73.27**	**100**	**100.0%**
Under $20,000	36.06	49	10.7
$20,000 to $39,999	44.81	61	14.0
$40,000 to $49,999	52.93	72	6.8
$50,000 to $69,999	66.56	91	13.0
$70,000 to $79,999	91.18	124	7.4
$80,000 to $99,999	109.16	149	12.4
$100,000 or more	155.33	212	36.4
HOUSEHOLD TYPE			
Average household	**73.27**	**100**	**100.0**
Married couples	96.53	132	65.0
Married couples, no children	91.58	125	26.5
Married couples, with children	103.95	142	33.0
Oldest child under age 6	76.19	104	4.5
Oldest child aged 6 to 17	106.48	145	17.1
Oldest child aged 18 or older	114.37	156	11.3
Single parent with child under age 18	42.13	57	3.4
Single person	40.87	56	16.3
RACE AND HISPANIC ORIGIN			
Average household	**73.27**	**100**	**100.0**
Asian	99.24	135	5.8
Black	33.56	46	5.6
Hispanic	46.86	64	7.8
Non-Hispanic white and other	83.64	114	86.5
REGION			
Average household	**73.27**	**100**	**100.0**
Northeast	80.49	110	20.2
Midwest	72.16	98	22.0
South	73.55	100	36.8
West	68.02	93	21.0
EDUCATION			
Average household	**73.27**	**100**	**100.0**
Less than high school graduate	34.74	47	6.8
High school graduate	54.17	74	18.9
Some college	64.23	88	18.4
Associate's degree	94.33	129	12.2
Bachelor's degree or more	106.62	146	43.2
Bachelor's degree	102.21	139	26.4
Master's, professional, doctoral degree	115.32	157	17.0

Note: Market shares may not sum to 100.0 because of rounding and missing categories by household type. "Asian" and "black" include Hispanics and non-Hispanics who identify themselves as being of the respective race alone. "Hispanic" includes people of any race who identify themselves as Hispanic. "Other" includes people who identify themselves as non-Hispanic and as Alaska Native, American Indian, Asian (who are also included in the "Asian" row), or Native Hawaiian or other Pacific Islander as well as non-Hispanics reporting more than one race.

Source: Calculations by New Strategist based on the Bureau of Labor Statistics' 2010 Consumer Expenditure Survey

Chapter 13.

Personal Care

Household Spending on Personal Care Products and Services, 2010

The average household spent $582 on personal care products and services in 2010. This category includes everything from haircuts, facials, and manicures to cosmetics, shampoo, and toothpaste. Spending on personal care products and services fell 18 percent between 2000 and 2010, after adjusting for inflation.

Personal care services (haircuts, manicures, etc.) account for the largest share of spending in the personal care category. Forty-eight percent of personal care spending was devoted to services in 2010. But spending on services fell by a substantial 29 percent between 2000 and 2010, after adjusting for inflation. Most of the decline occurred before the overall peak spending year of 2006, and average household spending on personal care services has remained relatively stable since then. Spending on the second-largest personal care category—cosmetics, perfume, and bath products—also fell between 2000 and 2010 (down 12 percent), but in this case a 9 percent rise between 2000 and 2006 was eclipsed by a 19 percent decline in spending between 2006 and 2010.

The only personal care categories to show a spending increase between 2000 and 2010 are oral hygiene products and shaving products, the smallest personal care categories in dollar terms. Average household spending on these items grew 4 and 7 percent, respectively, from 2000 to 2010.

Behind the decline in spending on personal care products and services was price discounting, which enabled consumers to buy more for less. Household belt-tightening was another reason, as house-poor consumers stretched out their hair-care and manicure appointments. Because older householders are among the biggest spenders on personal care products and services, average household spending on these items should rise along with the aging of the population.

Spending on personal care products and services

(average annual spending by households on personal care products and services, 2000, 2006, and 2010; in 2010 dollars)

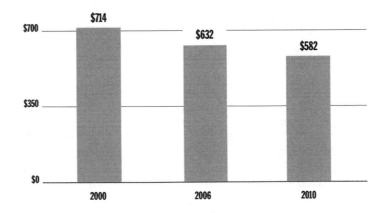

Table 13.1 Personal care spending, 2000 to 2010

(average annual household spending on personal care products and services by category, 2000, 2006, and 2010; percent change in spending, 2000–06, 2000–10, and 2006–10; in 2010 dollars; ranked by amount spent)

	2010 average household spending	2006 average household spending (in 2010$)	2000 average household spending (in 2010$)	percent change		
				2006–10	2000–06	2000–10
Average household spending on personal care products and services	**$582.04**	**$632.49**	**$713.71**	**–8.0%**	**–11.4%**	**–18.4%**
Personal care services	277.26	296.41	389.15	–6.5	–23.8	–28.8
Cosmetics, perfume, and bath products	134.20	164.96	151.84	–18.6	8.6	–11.6
Hair care products	62.00	60.63	65.16	2.3	–7.0	–4.9
Deodorants, feminine hygiene, miscellaneous products	35.24	37.94	36.99	–7.1	2.6	–4.7
Oral hygiene products	33.98	30.49	32.65	11.4	–6.6	4.1
Shaving products	17.95	18.21	16.70	–1.5	9.1	7.5

	2006–10	2000–06	2000–10	percentage point change		
				2006–10	2000–06	2000–10
PERCENT DISTRIBUTION OF SPENDING						
Average household spending on personal care products and services	**100.0%**	**100.0%**	**100.0%**	**–**	**–**	**–**
Personal care services	47.6	46.9	54.5	0.8	–7.7	–6.9
Cosmetics, perfume, and bath products	23.1	26.1	21.3	–3.0	4.8	1.8
Hair care products	10.7	9.6	9.1	1.1	0.5	1.5
Deodorants, feminine hygiene, miscellaneous products	6.1	6.0	5.2	0.1	0.8	0.9
Oral hygiene products	5.8	4.8	4.6	1.0	0.2	1.3
Shaving products	3.1	2.9	2.3	0.2	0.5	0.7

Note: Numbers do not add to total because not all categories are shown. "–" means not applicable.

Source: Bureau of Labor Statistics, 2000, 2006, and 2010 Consumer Expenditure Surveys; calculations by New Strategist

Cosmetics, Perfume, and Bath Products

Best customers:	Householders aged 35 to 54
	Married couples with school-aged or older children at home
	Asians and Hispanics
	Households in the West

| Customer trends: | Average household spending on cosmetics, perfume, and bath products may continue to decline now that generation X is in the best-customer lifestage. |

The best customers of cosmetics, perfume, and bath products are households with the most women. Married couples with school-aged or older children at home spend 29 to 49 percent more than average on cosmetics, perfume, and bath products. Householders aged 35 to 54, many with teenage girls, spend 12 to 20 percent more than average on such items. Asian households, the most affluent, spend 62 percent more than average on this item. Hispanics, who have the largest households, spend 25 percent more. Households in the West, where many Asians and Hispanics reside, spend 26 percent more.

Average household spending on cosmetics, perfume, and bath products rose 9 percent between 2000 and 2006, after adjusting for inflation, but declined 19 percent in the next four years for an overall 12 percent decline over the decade. The seesaw motion was the product of at least two factors—the expansion of the teenage population thanks to the large millennial generation and the counteracting belt-tightening of financially strapped households. Average household spending on cosmetics, perfume, and bath products may decline now that the small generation X is in the best-customer lifestage.

Table 13.2 Cosmetics, perfume, and bath products

Total household spending $16,252,559,400.00
Average household spends   134.20

	AVERAGE HOUSEHOLD SPENDING	BEST CUSTOMERS (index)	BIGGEST CUSTOMERS (market share)
AGE OF HOUSEHOLDER			
Average household	**$134.20**	**100**	**100.0%**
Under age 25	98.36	73	4.9
Aged 25 to 34	129.90	97	16.1
Aged 35 to 44	160.92	120	21.7
Aged 45 to 54	150.65	112	23.2
Aged 55 to 64	123.54	92	16.2
Aged 65 to 74	145.06	108	11.6
Aged 75 or older	87.00	65	6.2

	AVERAGE HOUSEHOLD SPENDING	BEST CUSTOMERS (index)	BIGGEST CUSTOMERS (market share)
HOUSEHOLD INCOME			
Average household	$134.20	100	100.0%
Under $20,000	72.71	54	11.8
$20,000 to $39,999	103.56	77	17.7
$40,000 to $49,999	123.90	92	8.7
$50,000 to $69,999	121.88	91	13.0
$70,000 to $79,999	120.06	89	5.4
$80,000 to $99,999	169.53	126	10.5
$100,000 or more	261.36	195	33.4
HOUSEHOLD TYPE			
Average household	134.20	100	100.0
Married couples	158.86	118	58.4
Married couples, no children	134.48	100	21.3
Married couples, with children	181.16	135	31.4
Oldest child under age 6	141.34	105	4.5
Oldest child aged 6 to 17	200.07	149	17.5
Oldest child aged 18 or older	173.34	129	9.3
Single parent with child under age 18	128.92	96	5.7
Single person	81.05	60	17.7
RACE AND HISPANIC ORIGIN			
Average household	134.20	100	100.0
Asian	217.77	162	6.9
Black	92.56	69	8.4
Hispanic	167.55	125	15.2
Non-Hispanic white and other	135.51	101	76.6
REGION			
Average household	134.20	100	100.0
Northeast	129.05	96	17.6
Midwest	109.03	81	18.1
South	130.91	98	35.8
West	169.31	126	28.6
EDUCATION			
Average household	134.20	100	100.0
Less than high school graduate	87.82	65	9.3
High school graduate	93.95	70	17.9
Some college	118.45	88	18.6
Associate's degree	187.11	139	13.2
Bachelor's degree or more	183.79	137	40.7
Bachelor's degree	174.40	130	24.5
Master's, professional, doctoral degree	202.30	151	16.3

Note: Market shares may not sum to 100.0 because of rounding and missing categories by household type. "Asian" and "black" include Hispanics and non-Hispanics who identify themselves as being of the respective race alone. "Hispanic" includes people of any race who identify themselves as Hispanic. "Other" includes people who identify themselves as non-Hispanic and as Alaska Native, American Indian, Asian (who are also included in the "Asian" row), or Native Hawaiian or other Pacific Islander as well as non-Hispanics reporting more than one race.

Source: Calculations by New Strategist based on the Bureau of Labor Statistics' 2010 Consumer Expenditure Survey

Deodorants, Feminine Hygiene, and Miscellaneous Personal Care Products

Best customers: **Householders aged 35 to 54**
Married couples with school-aged or older children at home
Single parents
Households in the West

Customer trends: **Average household spending on deodorants, feminine hygiene, and miscellaneous**
personal care products may continue to fall because the small generation X is in
the best-customer lifestage.

The best customers of deodorants, feminine hygiene, and miscellaneous personal care products are households with the most women of childbearing age. Married couples with school-aged or older children at home spend 25 to 29 percent more than average on this item. Householders aged 35 to 54, many with teenage girls at home, spend 10 to 39 percent more than average on deodorants, feminine hygiene, and miscellaneous products. Single parents, most of whom are female, spend 31 percent more than average on this item. Households in the West outspend the average by 24 percent.

Average household spending on deodorants, feminine hygiene, and miscellaneous personal care products declined 5 percent between 2000 and 2010, after adjusting for inflation. Behind the decline was price discounting, allowing consumers to buy more for less. Average household spending on this item may continue to fall because the small generation X is in the best-customer lifestage.

Table 13.3 Deodorants, feminine hygiene, and miscellaneous personal care products

| Total household spending | $4,267,810,680.00 |
| Average household spends | 35.24 |

	AVERAGE HOUSEHOLD SPENDING	BEST CUSTOMERS (index)	BIGGEST CUSTOMERS (market share)
AGE OF HOUSEHOLDER			
Average household	**$35.24**	**100**	**100.0%**
Under age 25	18.87	54	3.6
Aged 25 to 34	29.33	83	13.9
Aged 35 to 44	48.81	139	25.1
Aged 45 to 54	38.85	110	22.8
Aged 55 to 64	35.13	100	17.6
Aged 65 to 74	24.38	69	7.4
Aged 75 or older	36.41	103	9.9

	AVERAGE HOUSEHOLD SPENDING	BEST CUSTOMERS (index)	BIGGEST CUSTOMERS (market share)
HOUSEHOLD INCOME			
Average household	**$35.24**	**100**	**100.0%**
Under $20,000	22.28	63	13.8
$20,000 to $39,999	28.78	82	18.7
$40,000 to $49,999	37.72	107	10.1
$50,000 to $69,999	33.48	95	13.6
$70,000 to $79,999	37.82	107	6.4
$80,000 to $99,999	40.51	115	9.6
$100,000 or more	57.48	163	28.0
HOUSEHOLD TYPE			
Average household	**35.24**	**100**	**100.0**
Married couples	40.83	116	57.2
Married couples, no children	31.98	91	19.3
Married couples, with children	42.97	122	28.4
Oldest child under age 6	34.63	98	4.2
Oldest child aged 6 to 17	44.05	125	14.7
Oldest child aged 18 or older	45.62	129	9.3
Single parent with child under age 18	46.25	131	7.7
Single person	21.80	62	18.1
RACE AND HISPANIC ORIGIN			
Average household	**35.24**	**100**	**100.0**
Asian	29.75	84	3.6
Black	36.23	103	12.6
Hispanic	34.86	99	12.1
Non-Hispanic white and other	35.15	100	75.6
REGION			
Average household	**35.24**	**100**	**100.0**
Northeast	36.57	104	19.0
Midwest	31.90	91	20.2
South	31.45	89	32.8
West	43.77	124	28.1
EDUCATION			
Average household	**35.24**	**100**	**100.0**
Less than high school graduate	27.44	78	11.1
High school graduate	29.69	84	21.5
Some college	35.74	101	21.3
Associate's degree	42.12	120	11.3
Bachelor's degree or more	40.90	116	34.5
Bachelor's degree	41.23	117	22.1
Master's, professional, doctoral degree	40.23	114	12.4

Note: Market shares may not sum to 100.0 because of rounding and missing categories by household type. "Asian" and "black" include Hispanics and non-Hispanics who identify themselves as being of the respective race alone. "Hispanic" includes people of any race who identify themselves as Hispanic. "Other" includes people who identify themselves as non-Hispanic and as Alaska Native, American Indian, Asian (who are also included in the "Asian" row), or Native Hawaiian or other Pacific Islander as well as non-Hispanics reporting more than one race.

Source: Calculations by New Strategist based on the Bureau of Labor Statistics' 2010 Consumer Expenditure Survey

Hair Care Products

Best customers: **Householders aged 35 to 54**
                                Married couples with children at home

Customer trends: **Average household spending on hair care products may decline as boomers exit
the best-customer lifestage.**

The best customers of hair care products are the largest households and households with the most women. Married couples with children at home spend 64 percent more than average on this item, the figure peaking at twice the average among couples with adult children at home. Householders aged 35 to 54, many with children at home, spend 25 to 36 percent more than average on hair care products and control half the market.

Average household spending on hair care products declined 7 percent between 2000 and 2006, after adjusting for inflation, then grew 2 percent between 2006 and 2010. Average household spending on hair care products may decline in the years ahead as boomers age out of the best-customer lifestage.

Table 13.4 Hair care products

Total household spending $7,508,634,000.00
Average household spends   62.00

	AVERAGE HOUSEHOLD SPENDING	BEST CUSTOMERS (index)	BIGGEST CUSTOMERS (market share)
AGE OF HOUSEHOLDER			
Average household	**$62.00**	**100**	**100.0%**
Under age 25	43.09	70	4.6
Aged 25 to 34	54.24	87	14.6
Aged 35 to 44	77.56	125	22.6
Aged 45 to 54	84.28	136	28.1
Aged 55 to 64	65.62	106	18.7
Aged 65 to 74	34.88	56	6.1
Aged 75 or older	34.13	55	5.3

	AVERAGE HOUSEHOLD SPENDING	BEST CUSTOMERS (index)	BIGGEST CUSTOMERS (market share)
HOUSEHOLD INCOME			
Average household	**$62.00**	**100**	**100.0%**
Under $20,000	33.28	54	11.7
$20,000 to $39,999	36.98	60	13.7
$40,000 to $49,999	48.12	78	7.3
$50,000 to $69,999	68.72	111	15.9
$70,000 to $79,999	62.98	102	6.1
$80,000 to $99,999	78.82	127	10.6
$100,000 or more	128.06	207	35.4
HOUSEHOLD TYPE			
Average household	**62.00**	**100**	**100.0**
Married couples	82.40	133	65.6
Married couples, no children	61.48	99	21.1
Married couples, with children	101.70	164	38.2
Oldest child under age 6	80.53	130	5.6
Oldest child aged 6 to 17	93.62	151	17.8
Oldest child aged 18 or older	124.58	201	14.5
Single parent with child under age 18	50.53	82	4.8
Single person	35.03	57	16.6
RACE AND HISPANIC ORIGIN			
Average household	**62.00**	**100**	**100.0**
Asian	45.39	73	3.1
Black	40.87	66	8.1
Hispanic	66.15	107	13.0
Non-Hispanic white and other	64.74	104	79.2
REGION			
Average household	**62.00**	**100**	**100.0**
Northeast	53.25	86	15.8
Midwest	58.49	94	21.0
South	64.81	105	38.4
West	68.09	110	24.9
EDUCATION			
Average household	**62.00**	**100**	**100.0**
Less than high school graduate	44.16	71	10.2
High school graduate	50.11	81	20.6
Some college	57.69	93	19.6
Associate's degree	65.55	106	10.0
Bachelor's degree or more	82.27	133	39.4
Bachelor's degree	84.77	137	25.8
Master's, professional, doctoral degree	77.34	125	13.5

Note: Market shares may not sum to 100.0 because of rounding and missing categories by household type. "Asian" and "black" include Hispanics and non-Hispanics who identify themselves as being of the respective race alone. "Hispanic" includes people of any race who identify themselves as Hispanic. "Other" includes people who identify themselves as non-Hispanic and as Alaska Native, American Indian, Asian (who are also included in the "Asian" row), or Native Hawaiian or other Pacific Islander as well as non-Hispanics reporting more than one race.

Source: Calculations by New Strategist based on the Bureau of Labor Statistics' 2010 Consumer Expenditure Survey

Oral Hygiene Products

Best customers: **Householders aged 35 to 64**
Married couples with school-aged or older children at home
Asians and Hispanics

Customer trends: **Average household spending on oral hygiene products should rise as aging boomers try to maintain their teeth.**

Middle-aged to older married couples with children at home are the best customers of oral hygiene products because they have the largest families. Householders ranging in age from 35 to 64 spend 8 to 16 percent more than average on oral hygiene products. Married couples with school-aged or older children at home spend 35 to 57 percent more than average on this item. Asians outspend the average on this item by 28 percent and Hispanics do so by 24 percent.

Average household spending on oral hygiene products grew 4 percent between 2000 and 2010, after adjusting for inflation. Average household spending on oral hygiene products should continue to grow as boomers age and try to maintain the health of their teeth.

Table 13.5 **Oral hygiene products**

Total household spending $4,115,215,860.00
Average household spends   33.98

	AVERAGE HOUSEHOLD SPENDING	BEST CUSTOMERS (index)	BIGGEST CUSTOMERS (market share)
AGE OF HOUSEHOLDER			
Average household	**$33.98**	**100**	**100.0%**
Under age 25	18.29	54	3.6
Aged 25 to 34	31.99	94	15.7
Aged 35 to 44	37.14	109	19.8
Aged 45 to 54	36.65	108	22.3
Aged 55 to 64	39.25	116	20.4
Aged 65 to 74	31.20	92	9.9
Aged 75 or older	29.94	88	8.4

	AVERAGE HOUSEHOLD SPENDING	BEST CUSTOMERS (index)	BIGGEST CUSTOMERS (market share)
HOUSEHOLD INCOME			
Average household	**$33.98**	**100**	**100.0%**
Under $20,000	15.97	47	10.3
$20,000 to $39,999	33.18	98	22.4
$40,000 to $49,999	31.24	92	8.7
$50,000 to $69,999	30.97	91	13.1
$70,000 to $79,999	40.57	119	7.1
$80,000 to $99,999	39.78	117	9.8
$100,000 or more	57.13	168	28.8
HOUSEHOLD TYPE			
Average household	**33.98**	**100**	**100.0**
Married couples	43.00	127	62.4
Married couples, no children	37.58	111	23.5
Married couples, with children	47.40	139	32.4
Oldest child under age 6	32.79	96	4.1
Oldest child aged 6 to 17	53.45	157	18.5
Oldest child aged 18 or older	45.86	135	9.7
Single parent with child under age 18	25.29	74	4.4
Single person	22.06	65	19.0
RACE AND HISPANIC ORIGIN			
Average household	**33.98**	**100**	**100.0**
Asian	43.55	128	5.5
Black	22.67	67	8.2
Hispanic	42.19	124	15.1
Non-Hispanic white and other	34.49	102	77.0
REGION			
Average household	**33.98**	**100**	**100.0**
Northeast	33.44	98	18.1
Midwest	35.93	106	23.6
South	32.59	96	35.2
West	34.73	102	23.2
EDUCATION			
Average household	**33.98**	**100**	**100.0**
Less than high school graduate	31.23	92	13.1
High school graduate	26.90	79	20.2
Some college	28.24	83	17.5
Associate's degree	40.44	119	11.2
Bachelor's degree or more	43.41	128	38.0
Bachelor's degree	41.42	122	23.0
Master's, professional, doctoral degree	47.34	139	15.1

Note: Market shares may not sum to 100.0 because of rounding and missing categories by household type. "Asian" and "black" include Hispanics and non-Hispanics who identify themselves as being of the respective race alone. "Hispanic" includes people of any race who identify themselves as Hispanic. "Other" includes people who identify themselves as non-Hispanic and as Alaska Native, American Indian, Asian (who are also included in the "Asian" row), or Native Hawaiian or other Pacific Islander as well as non-Hispanics reporting more than one race.

Source: Calculations by New Strategist based on the Bureau of Labor Statistics' 2010 Consumer Expenditure Survey

Personal Care Services

Best customers: **Householders aged 35 to 74**
                                          Married couples

Customer trends: **Average household spending on personal care services will grow in the years ahead as aging boomers attempt to look their best, but only if discretionary income rebounds.**

The largest households and older householders are the best customers of personal care services such as haircuts, massages, manicures, and facials. Householders ranging in age from 35 to 74 spend more than average on this item. Married couples without children at home (most of them empty-nesters) spend 29 percent more than average on personal care services, while those with school-aged or older children at home (the largest households) spend 31 to 32 percent more than average.

Average household spending on personal care services fell by a substantial 29 percent between 2000 and 2010, after adjusting for inflation. Price discounting was one factor behind the decline, with low-cost hair and nail salons becoming common throughout the country. Another factor was household belt tightening. Average household spending on personal care services may grow in the years ahead as aging boomers attempt to look their best, but only if discretionary income rebounds.

Table 13.6 Personal care services

Total household spending $33,578,126,820.00
Average household spends   277.26

	AVERAGE HOUSEHOLD SPENDING	BEST CUSTOMERS (index)	BIGGEST CUSTOMERS (market share)
AGE OF HOUSEHOLDER			
Average household	**$277.26**	**100**	**100.0%**
Under age 25	137.33	50	3.3
Aged 25 to 34	232.52	84	14.0
Aged 35 to 44	304.18	110	19.8
Aged 45 to 54	316.70	114	23.6
Aged 55 to 64	297.54	107	18.9
Aged 65 to 74	304.84	110	11.8
Aged 75 or older	247.44	89	8.5

	AVERAGE HOUSEHOLD SPENDING	BEST CUSTOMERS (index)	BIGGEST CUSTOMERS (market share)
HOUSEHOLD INCOME			
Average household	**$277.26**	**100**	**100.0%**
Under $20,000	114.02	41	9.0
$20,000 to $39,999	174.63	63	14.4
$40,000 to $49,999	219.55	79	7.5
$50,000 to $69,999	269.15	97	13.9
$70,000 to $79,999	320.48	116	6.9
$80,000 to $99,999	397.55	143	12.0
$100,000 or more	587.17	212	36.3
HOUSEHOLD TYPE			
Average household	**277.26**	**100**	**100.0**
Married couples	349.25	126	62.1
Married couples, no children	356.85	129	27.3
Married couples, with children	352.74	127	29.6
Oldest child under age 6	295.15	106	4.6
Oldest child aged 6 to 17	366.69	132	15.6
Oldest child aged 18 or older	364.16	131	9.5
Single parent with child under age 18	232.22	84	4.9
Single person	181.91	66	19.2
RACE AND HISPANIC ORIGIN			
Average household	**277.26**	**100**	**100.0**
Asian	226.39	82	3.5
Black	294.86	106	13.0
Hispanic	225.07	81	9.9
Non-Hispanic white and other	283.48	102	77.5
REGION			
Average household	**277.26**	**100**	**100.0**
Northeast	313.97	113	20.8
Midwest	243.28	88	19.6
South	270.72	98	35.8
West	291.54	105	23.8
EDUCATION			
Average household	**277.26**	**100**	**100.0**
Less than high school graduate	139.50	50	7.2
High school graduate	207.91	75	19.1
Some college	236.48	85	17.9
Associate's degree	289.97	105	9.9
Bachelor's degree or more	427.92	154	45.9
Bachelor's degree	395.76	143	27.0
Master's, professional, doctoral degree	484.07	175	18.9

Note: Market shares may not sum to 100.0 because of rounding and missing categories by household type. "Asian" and "black" include Hispanics and non-Hispanics who identify themselves as being of the respective race alone. "Hispanic" includes people of any race who identify themselves as Hispanic. "Other" includes people who identify themselves as non-Hispanic and as Alaska Native, American Indian, Asian (who are also included in the "Asian" row), or Native Hawaiian or other Pacific Islander as well as non-Hispanics reporting more than one race.

Source: Calculations by New Strategist based on the Bureau of Labor Statistics' 2010 Consumer Expenditure Survey

Shaving Products

Best customers: Householders aged 35 to 44
Married couples with children at home
Households in the West

Customer trends: Average household spending on shaving products should decline as the small generation X fills the best-customer lifestage.

The best customers of shaving products are households with the most men. Householders aged 35 to 44 spend 46 percent more than average on this item. Married couples with children at home (who have the largest households) spend 71 percent more than average on shaving products. Households in the West spend 32 percent more than average on shaving products.

Average household spending on shaving products grew 9 percent between 2000 and the overall peak-spending year of 2006, after adjusting for inflation, then declined by 1 percent over the ensuing four years. Spending on shaving products should decline further in the years ahead as the small generation X fills the best-customer lifestage.

Table 13.7 Shaving products

Total household spending $2,173,870,650.00
Average household spends 17.95

	AVERAGE HOUSEHOLD SPENDING	BEST CUSTOMERS (index)	BIGGEST CUSTOMERS (market share)
AGE OF HOUSEHOLDER			
Average household	**$17.95**	**100**	**100.0%**
Under age 25	5.43	30	2.0
Aged 25 to 34	15.73	88	14.6
Aged 35 to 44	26.25	146	26.5
Aged 45 to 54	20.56	115	23.7
Aged 55 to 64	18.17	101	17.9
Aged 65 to 74	12.28	68	7.4
Aged 75 or older	15.39	86	8.2

	AVERAGE HOUSEHOLD SPENDING	BEST CUSTOMERS (index)	BIGGEST CUSTOMERS (market share)
HOUSEHOLD INCOME			
Average household	**$17.95**	**100**	**100.0%**
Under $20,000	7.67	43	9.3
$20,000 to $39,999	12.16	68	15.5
$40,000 to $49,999	10.71	60	5.6
$50,000 to $69,999	16.83	94	13.4
$70,000 to $79,999	18.80	105	6.3
$80,000 to $99,999	25.04	139	11.6
$100,000 or more	40.67	227	38.9
HOUSEHOLD TYPE			
Average household	**17.95**	**100**	**100.0**
Married couples	25.03	139	68.8
Married couples, no children	18.98	106	22.5
Married couples, with children	30.75	171	39.9
Oldest child under age 6	30.55	170	7.3
Oldest child aged 6 to 17	32.12	179	21.0
Oldest child aged 18 or older	28.82	161	11.6
Single parent with child under age 18	12.63	70	4.1
Single person	8.84	49	14.4
RACE AND HISPANIC ORIGIN			
Average household	**17.95**	**100**	**100.0**
Asian	13.99	78	3.3
Black	9.19	51	6.3
Hispanic	18.00	100	12.2
Non-Hispanic white and other	19.40	108	81.9
REGION			
Average household	**17.95**	**100**	**100.0**
Northeast	19.99	111	20.4
Midwest	14.72	82	18.3
South	15.40	86	31.5
West	23.76	132	30.0
EDUCATION			
Average household	**17.95**	**100**	**100.0**
Less than high school graduate	9.44	53	7.5
High school graduate	11.56	64	16.4
Some college	18.47	103	21.6
Associate's degree	19.75	110	10.4
Bachelor's degree or more	26.35	147	43.6
Bachelor's degree	25.82	144	27.2
Master's, professional, doctoral degree	27.39	153	16.5

Note: Market shares may not sum to 100.0 because of rounding and missing categories by household type. "Asian" and "black" include Hispanics and non-Hispanics who identify themselves as being of the respective race alone. "Hispanic" includes people of any race who identify themselves as Hispanic. "Other" includes people who identify themselves as non-Hispanic and as Alaska Native, American Indian, Asian (who are also included in the "Asian" row), or Native Hawaiian or other Pacific Islander as well as non-Hispanics reporting more than one race.

Source: Calculations by New Strategist based on the Bureau of Labor Statistics' 2010 Consumer Expenditure Survey

Chapter 14.

Reading Material

Household Spending on Reading Material, 2010

The average American household spent just $100 on books, newspapers, and magazines in 2010. Spending on reading material fell by a precipitous 46 percent between 2000 and 2010, after adjusting for inflation. Behind the decline is the rise of the Internet, with online news and features substituting for print magazines and newspapers among boomers and younger generations.

The best customers of periodicals are older Americans. Householders aged 55 or older are the biggest spenders on newspaper and magazine subscriptions. Books skew a bit younger, and average household spending on books fell by a smaller percentage than spending on newspapers and magazines—which suggests that printed books have a more stable future than printed newspapers and magazines. Paper-and-ink versions of newspapers and magazines face uncertainty in the years ahead as computer-savvy younger generations—who get their news and information online—replace older customers. These trends suggest that average household spending on reading material will continue to decline.

Spending on reading material

(average annual spending by households on reading material, 2000, 2006, and 2010; in 2010 dollars)

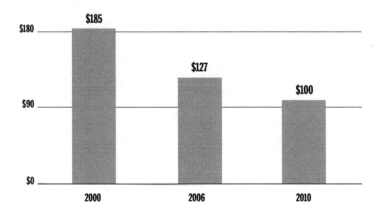

Table 14.1 Reading material spending, 2000 to 2010

(average annual household spending on reading material by category, 2000, 2006, and 2010; percent change in spending, 2000–06, 2000–10, and 2006–10; in 2010 dollars; ranked by amount spent)

	2010 average household spending	2006 average household spending (in 2010$)	2000 average household spending (in 2010$)	percent change		
				2006–10	2000–06	2000–10
AVERAGE ANNUAL SPENDING						
Average household spending on reading material	**$99.63**	**$126.54**	**$185.47**	**−21.3%**	**−31.8%**	**−46.3%**
Books	46.09	57.92	73.52	−20.4	−21.2	−37.3
Magazine and newspaper subscriptions	39.90	52.63	84.25	−24.2	−37.5	−52.6
Magazines and newspapers, nonsubscription	12.63	15.74	27.55	−19.7	−42.9	−54.2

				percentage point change		
	2006–10	2000–06	2000–10	2006–10	2000–06	2000–10
PERCENT DISTRIBUTION OF SPENDING						
Average household spending on reading material	**100.0%**	**100.0%**	**100.0%**	–	–	–
Books	46.3	45.8	39.6	0.5	6.1	6.6
Magazine and newspaper subscriptions	40.0	41.6	45.4	−1.5	−3.8	−5.4
Magazines and newspapers, nonsubscription	12.7	12.4	14.9	0.2	−2.4	−2.2

Note: Numbers do not add to total because not all categories are shown. "–" means not applicable.

Source: Bureau of Labor Statistics, 2000, 2006, and 2010 Consumer Expenditure Surveys; calculations by New Strategist

Books

Best customers:	**Householders aged 45 to 74**
	Married couples without children at home
	Married couples with school-aged or older children at home
	Asians and Non-Hispanic whites
	Households in the West
	College graduates
Customer trends:	**Average household spending on books may rise as a growing proportion of boomers become empty-nesters with more free time.**

Older householders are the best customers of books. Householders ranging in age from 45 to 74 spend 14 to 19 percent more than average on books. Most are empty-nesters with time to read. Married couples without children at home spend 30 percent more than average on books, while couples with school-aged or older children at home spend 26 to 50 percent more than average on this item—buying books not only for themselves but also for their children. Asians spend 21 percent more than average on books, but non-Hispanic whites, who spend 20 percent more than average, control 91 percent of the market for books. The spending on books by households in the West is 26 percent above average. College graduates spend nearly twice the average on books.

Average household spending on books fell 37 percent between 2000 and 2010, after adjusting for inflation. This decline was smaller than the one experienced by newspapers and magazines, which may be good news for the book industry. Books are likely to weather the Internet revolution better than other print media because there are no freely available electronic alternatives. Much of the decline in spending on books is due to price competition from discounters, used book sales, and the substitution of less expensive e-books for hardbacks. Average household spending on books may rise as a growing proportion of boomers become empty-nesters with more time to read.

Table 14.2 Books

Total household spending $5,581,821,630.00
Average household spends 46.09

	AVERAGE HOUSEHOLD SPENDING	BEST CUSTOMERS (index)	BIGGEST CUSTOMERS (market share)
AGE OF HOUSEHOLDER			
Average household	**$46.09**	**100**	**100.0%**
Under age 25	29.14	63	4.2
Aged 25 to 34	40.41	88	14.6
Aged 35 to 44	46.56	101	18.3
Aged 45 to 54	52.59	114	23.6
Aged 55 to 64	54.85	119	21.0
Aged 65 to 74	53.51	116	12.5
Aged 75 or older	28.23	61	5.8

	AVERAGE HOUSEHOLD SPENDING	BEST CUSTOMERS (index)	BIGGEST CUSTOMERS (market share)
HOUSEHOLD INCOME			
Average household	**$46.09**	**100**	**100.0%**
Under $20,000	16.35	35	7.7
$20,000 to $39,999	26.23	57	13.0
$40,000 to $49,999	33.23	72	6.8
$50,000 to $69,999	40.32	87	12.5
$70,000 to $79,999	48.61	105	6.3
$80,000 to $99,999	64.13	139	11.6
$100,000 or more	112.75	245	41.9
HOUSEHOLD TYPE			
Average household	**46.09**	**100**	**100.0**
Married couples	58.63	127	62.7
Married couples, no children	59.97	130	27.6
Married couples, with children	62.37	135	31.5
Oldest child under age 6	50.53	110	4.7
Oldest child aged 6 to 17	69.28	150	17.7
Oldest child aged 18 or older	58.14	126	9.1
Single parent with child under age 18	26.60	58	3.4
Single person	33.80	73	21.5
RACE AND HISPANIC ORIGIN			
Average household	**46.09**	**100**	**100.0**
Asian	55.68	121	5.1
Black	17.59	38	4.7
Hispanic	18.14	39	4.8
Non-Hispanic white and other	55.27	120	90.9
REGION			
Average household	**46.09**	**100**	**100.0**
Northeast	50.07	109	19.9
Midwest	44.10	96	21.3
South	37.80	82	30.1
West	58.27	126	28.6
EDUCATION			
Average household	**46.09**	**100**	**100.0**
Less than high school graduate	11.55	25	3.6
High school graduate	21.37	46	11.8
Some college	40.80	89	18.6
Associate's degree	39.56	86	8.1
Bachelor's degree or more	89.76	195	57.9
Bachelor's degree	74.91	163	30.7
Master's, professional, doctoral degree	115.70	251	27.2

Note: Market shares may not sum to 100.0 because of rounding and missing categories by household type. "Asian" and "black" include Hispanics and non-Hispanics who identify themselves as being of the respective race alone. "Hispanic" includes people of any race who identify themselves as Hispanic. "Other" includes people who identify themselves as non-Hispanic and as Alaska Native, American Indian, Asian (who are also included in the "Asian" row), or Native Hawaiian or other Pacific Islander as well as non-Hispanics reporting more than one race.

Source: Calculations by New Strategist based on the Bureau of Labor Statistics' 2010 Consumer Expenditure Survey

Magazines and Newspapers, Nonsubscription

Best customers: **Householders aged 55 to 74**
Married couples without children at home
Married couples with adult children at home
Households in the Northeast

Customer trends: **Average household spending on nonsubscription magazines and newspapers will continue to decline as the availability of online news dampens impulse purchasing.**

The best customers of nonsubscription magazines and newspapers are the mass-transit-riding residents of the Northeast's commuter-friendly cities. Households in the Northeast spend 59 percent more than average on this item, many buying from newsstands or vending machines. Householders aged 55 to 74 spend 28 to 43 percent more than average on this item. Married couples with adult children at home spend 22 percent more than average on nonsubscription magazines and newspapers, while those without children at home (most of them empty-nesters) spend 40 percent more than average.

Average household spending on nonsubscription magazines and newspapers declined prodigiously between 2000 and 2010, falling an enormous 54 percent after adjusting for inflation. The downward spiral is due in part to easy (and free) access to newspapers online, which dampens impulse purchasing. This trend is likely to intensify as wireless Internet access becomes more widely available to commuters and long-distance travelers.

Table 14.3   **Magazines and newspapers, nonsubscription**

Total household spending $1,529,581,410.00
Average household spends   12.63

	AVERAGE HOUSEHOLD SPENDING	BEST CUSTOMERS (index)	BIGGEST CUSTOMERS (market share)
AGE OF HOUSEHOLDER			
Average household	**$12.63**	**100**	**100.0%**
Under age 25	4.97	39	2.6
Aged 25 to 34	9.92	79	13.1
Aged 35 to 44	10.81	86	15.5
Aged 45 to 54	13.33	106	21.8
Aged 55 to 64	16.18	128	22.6
Aged 65 to 74	18.07	143	15.4
Aged 75 or older	11.93	94	9.0

	AVERAGE HOUSEHOLD SPENDING	BEST CUSTOMERS (index)	BIGGEST CUSTOMERS (market share)
HOUSEHOLD INCOME			
Average household	**$12.63**	**100**	**100.0%**
Under $20,000	6.57	52	11.4
$20,000 to $39,999	9.57	76	17.4
$40,000 to $49,999	12.77	101	9.6
$50,000 to $69,999	13.26	105	15.1
$70,000 to $79,999	14.00	111	6.6
$80,000 to $99,999	17.18	136	11.3
$100,000 or more	21.14	167	28.7
HOUSEHOLD TYPE			
Average household	**12.63**	**100**	**100.0**
Married couples	14.76	117	57.6
Married couples, no children	17.64	140	29.7
Married couples, with children	12.82	102	23.6
Oldest child under age 6	10.96	87	3.7
Oldest child aged 6 to 17	11.93	94	11.1
Oldest child aged 18 or older	15.36	122	8.8
Single parent with child under age 18	7.09	56	3.3
Single person	10.59	84	24.6
RACE AND HISPANIC ORIGIN			
Average household	**12.63**	**100**	**100.0**
Asian	6.95	55	2.3
Black	10.64	84	10.3
Hispanic	7.95	63	7.7
Non-Hispanic white and other	13.73	109	82.4
REGION			
Average household	**12.63**	**100**	**100.0**
Northeast	20.02	159	29.1
Midwest	11.31	90	20.0
South	10.75	85	31.2
West	11.00	87	19.7
EDUCATION			
Average household	**12.63**	**100**	**100.0**
Less than high school graduate	6.83	54	7.7
High school graduate	10.76	85	21.8
Some college	13.15	104	21.9
Associate's degree	14.81	117	11.1
Bachelor's degree or more	15.97	126	37.6
Bachelor's degree	15.39	122	23.0
Master's, professional, doctoral degree	16.97	134	14.5

Note: Market shares may not sum to 100.0 because of rounding and missing categories by household type. "Asian" and "black" include Hispanics and non-Hispanics who identify themselves as being of the respective race alone. "Hispanic" includes people of any race who identify themselves as Hispanic. "Other" includes people who identify themselves as non-Hispanic and as Alaska Native, American Indian, Asian (who are also included in the "Asian" row), or Native Hawaiian or other Pacific Islander as well as non-Hispanics reporting more than one race.

Source: Calculations by New Strategist based on the Bureau of Labor Statistics' 2010 Consumer Expenditure Survey

Magazine and Newspaper Subscriptions

Best customers:	**Householders aged 55 or older** **Married couples without children at home** **Married couples with adult children at home** **Non-Hispanic whites** **Households in the Northeast**
Customer trends:	**Average household spending on newspaper and magazine subscriptions will continue to decline as Internet-savvy younger generations flock to electronic alternatives.**

Older householders are by far the best customers of newspaper and magazine subscriptions. Householders aged 55 or older spend 37 to 124 percent more than average on this item and control 66 percent of the market. Married couples without children at home (most of them older) spend 88 percent more than average on newspaper and magazine subscriptions. Couples with adult children at home spend 25 percent above average on this item. Non-Hispanic white households spend 23 percent more than average on subscriptions and account for 93 percent of the market. Households in the Northeast outspend the average by 28 percent.

Average household spending on subscriptions fell by a precipitous 53 percent between 2000 and 2010, after adjusting for inflation. The downward trend is likely to continue as Internet-savvy younger generations flock to electronic alternatives. This trend will make magazine and newspaper publishers increasingly dependent on advertisers, rather than subscribers, for revenues.

Table 14.4 Magazine and newspaper subscriptions

Total household spending	$4,832,169,300.00
Average household spends	39.90

	AVERAGE HOUSEHOLD SPENDING	BEST CUSTOMERS (index)	BIGGEST CUSTOMERS (market share)
AGE OF HOUSEHOLDER			
Average household	**$39.90**	**100**	**100.0%**
Under age 25	5.10	13	0.8
Aged 25 to 34	10.93	27	4.6
Aged 35 to 44	22.43	56	10.2
Aged 45 to 54	35.91	90	18.6
Aged 55 to 64	54.51	137	24.1
Aged 65 to 74	75.56	189	20.4
Aged 75 or older	89.26	224	21.3

	AVERAGE HOUSEHOLD SPENDING	BEST CUSTOMERS (index)	BIGGEST CUSTOMERS (market share)
HOUSEHOLD INCOME			
Average household	**$39.90**	**100**	**100.0%**
Under $20,000	20.30	51	11.1
$20,000 to $39,999	33.85	85	19.4
$40,000 to $49,999	31.51	79	7.5
$50,000 to $69,999	39.99	100	14.4
$70,000 to $79,999	44.31	111	6.6
$80,000 to $99,999	39.21	98	8.2
$100,000 or more	76.29	191	32.8
HOUSEHOLD TYPE			
Average household	**39.90**	**100**	**100.0**
Married couples	52.20	131	64.5
Married couples, no children	75.03	188	39.9
Married couples, with children	36.61	92	21.3
Oldest child under age 6	16.69	42	1.8
Oldest child aged 6 to 17	35.72	90	10.5
Oldest child aged 18 or older	49.86	125	9.0
Single parent with child under age 18	8.36	21	1.2
Single person	32.63	82	24.0
RACE AND HISPANIC ORIGIN			
Average household	**39.90**	**100**	**100.0**
Asian	26.68	67	2.8
Black	12.87	32	3.9
Hispanic	10.67	27	3.3
Non-Hispanic white and other	48.91	123	92.9
REGION			
Average household	**39.90**	**100**	**100.0**
Northeast	51.23	128	23.6
Midwest	45.36	114	25.3
South	29.68	74	27.3
West	41.92	105	23.8
EDUCATION			
Average household	**39.90**	**100**	**100.0**
Less than high school graduate	16.26	41	5.8
High school graduate	32.71	82	20.9
Some college	33.61	84	17.7
Associate's degree	35.80	90	8.5
Bachelor's degree or more	63.21	158	47.1
Bachelor's degree	53.13	133	25.2
Master's, professional, doctoral degree	80.81	203	21.9

Note: Market shares may not sum to 100.0 because of rounding and missing categories by household type. "Asian" and "black" include Hispanics and non-Hispanics who identify themselves as being of the respective race alone. "Hispanic" includes people of any race who identify themselves as Hispanic. "Other" includes people who identify themselves as non-Hispanic and as Alaska Native, American Indian, Asian (who are also included in the "Asian" row), or Native Hawaiian or other Pacific Islander as well as non-Hispanics reporting more than one race.

Source: Calculations by New Strategist based on the Bureau of Labor Statistics' 2010 Consumer Expenditure Survey

Chapter 15.

Restaurants and Carry-Outs

Household Spending at Restaurants and Carry-outs, 2010

In 2010, the average household spent a considerable $2,304 at restaurants and carry-outs—a figure that does not include alcoholic beverage spending (see Alcohol chapter for those figures). What once was a special occasion—eating out—has become a necessity as busy two-earner families try to save time. The Bureau of Labor Statistics reports that during the average week of 2010, 69 percent of households purchased food from restaurants and carry-outs, spending an average of $58. Average household spending at restaurants and carry-outs fell 15 percent from 2006 to 2010, after adjusting for inflation. (Comparisons with 2000 figures are invalid because of changes in methodology.) Behind the decline is price discounting, as well as belt tightening as the economic downturn took hold.

Households devote more of their restaurant dollars to dinners (43 percent) than to lunches (32 percent). Breakfasts account for another 9 percent of restaurant spending, snacks for 7 percent, and restaurant meals on trips (which are not broken down by type of restaurant) account for 10 percent.

The average household devotes less of the eating-out dollar to fast food than to full-service restaurants. Of the $2,304 the average household spent on eating out in 2010, fast-food restaurants captured a 39 percent share, and full-service restaurants took a larger 45 percent. The remainder is spent at employer and school cafeterias, vending machines, mobile vendors, and on trips.

Older Americans, particularly empty-nesters, are far more likely to choose full-service over fast-food restaurants. Consequently, as the population ages, expect to see faster growth in spending on the full-service category—but only if discretionary income grows.

Restaurant Spending

(average annual spending by households on restaurants by type of establishment, 2010)

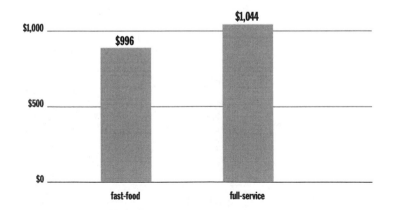

Table 15.1 Restaurant and carry-out spending, 2006 and 2010

(average annual and percent distribution of household spending at restaurants and carry-outs by category, 2006 and 2010; percent and percentage point change in spending, 2006–10, in 2010 dollars; ranked by amount spent)

	2010 average household spending	2006 average household spending (in 2010$)	percent change 2006–10
AVERAGE ANNUAL SPENDING			
AVERAGE HOUSEHOLD SPENDING AT RESTAURANTS BY TYPE OF MEAL			
Total restaurant spending	**$2,304.03**	**$2,695.75**	**–14.5%**
Dinner	986.99	1,160.26	–14.9
Lunch	726.61	831.36	–12.6
Restaurant meals on trips	223.08	262.76	–15.1
Breakfast and brunch	212.05	252.48	–16.0
Snacks and nonalcoholic beverages	155.29	188.88	–17.8
AVERAGE HOUSEHOLD SPENDING BY TYPE OF MEAL AND RESTAURANT			
Total restaurant spending	**$2,304.03**	**$2,695.75**	**–14.5%**
Dinner	986.99	1,160.26	–14.9
At full-service restaurants	645.44	783.71	–17.6
At fast-food restaurants*	331.42	365.48	–9.3
Lunch	726.61	831.36	–12.6
At fast-food restaurants*	351.38	400.27	–12.2
At full-service restaurants	285.15	325.67	–12.4
At employer and school cafeterias	82.14	93.18	–11.9
Restaurant meals on trips	223.08	262.76	–15.1
Breakfast and brunch	212.05	252.48	–16.0
At fast-food restaurants*	110.61	117.02	–5.5
At full-service restaurants	84.81	118.95	–28.7
Snacks and nonalcoholic beverages	155.29	188.88	–17.8
At fast-food restaurants*	102.25	116.22	–12.0
At full-service restaurants	28.53	32.23	–11.5
At vending machines, mobile vendors	18.59	33.05	–43.8
At employer and school cafeterias	5.93	7.38	–19.6

	2010	2006	percentage point change 2006–10
PERCENT DISTRIBUTION OF SPENDING			
AVERAGE HOUSEHOLD SPENDING AT RESTAURANTS BY TYPE OF MEAL			
Total restaurant spending	**100.0%**	**100.0%**	–
Dinner	42.8	43.0	–0.2
Lunch	31.5	30.8	0.7
Restaurant meals on trips	9.7	9.7	–0.1
Breakfast and brunch	9.2	9.4	–0.2
Snacks and nonalcoholic beverages	6.7	7.0	–0.3
AVERAGE HOUSEHOLD SPENDING BY TYPE OF MEAL AND RESTAURANT			
Total restaurant spending	**100.0%**	**100.0%**	–
Dinner	42.8	43.0	–0.2
At full-service restaurants	28.0	29.1	–1.1
At fast-food restaurants*	14.4	13.6	0.8
Lunch	31.5	30.8	0.7
At fast-food restaurants*	15.3	14.8	0.4
At full-service restaurants	12.4	12.1	0.3
At employer and school cafeterias	3.6	3.5	0.1
Restaurant meals on trips	9.7	9.7	–0.1
Breakfast and brunch	9.2	9.4	–0.2
At fast-food restaurants*	4.8	4.3	0.5
At full-service restaurants	3.7	4.4	–0.7
Snacks and nonalcoholic beverages	6.7	7.0	–0.3
At fast-food restaurants*	4.4	4.3	0.1
At full-service restaurants	1.2	1.2	0.0
At vending machines, mobile vendors	0.8	1.2	–0.4
At employer and school cafeterias	0.3	0.3	0.0

* The category fast-food restaurants also includes take-out, delivery, concession stands, buffets, and cafeterias other than employer and school.

Note: Subcategories do not add to total because not all types of restaurants or meals are shown. "–" means not applicable.

Source: Bureau of Labor Statistics, 2006 and 2010 Consumer Expenditure Surveys; calculations by New Strategist

Breakfast and Brunch at Fast-Food Restaurants, Including Take-Outs, Deliveries, Concession Stands, Buffets, and Cafeterias (except Employer and School)

Best customers: **Householders aged 25 to 44**
Married couples with school-aged or older children at home
Hispanics, Asians, and blacks
Households in the Northeast

Customer trends: **Average household spending on breakfast at fast-food restaurants is likely to stabilize as the large millennial generation fills the best-customer age group.**

The busiest people are the biggest spenders on breakfast at fast-food restaurants—workers and parents. Householders of prime working age, 25 to 44, spend 23 to 33 percent more than average on this item. Married couples with school-aged or older children at home spend 23 to 33 percent more than average on breakfast at fast-food restaurants as they try to fit meals into their busy schedules. Hispanics spend 28 percent more than average on breakfast at fast-food restaurants, and Asians and blacks spend 8 percent more. Together the three minority groups control one-third of the market. Households in the Northeast outspend the average by 29 percent.

Breakfast at fast-food restaurants is the category in this report that suffered the smallest decline in spending between 2006 and 2010, a 5 percent drop after adjusting for inflation. Spending on this item is likely to stabilize as the large millennial generation fills the best-customer age group.

Table 15.2 Breakfast and brunch at fast-food restaurants, including take-outs, deliveries, concession stands, buffets, and cafeterias (except employer and school)

Total household spending $13,395,645,270.00
Average household spends   110.61

	AVERAGE HOUSEHOLD SPENDING	BEST CUSTOMERS (index)	BIGGEST CUSTOMERS (market share)
AGE OF HOUSEHOLDER			
Average household	**$110.61**	**100**	**100.0%**
Under age 25	78.54	71	4.7
Aged 25 to 34	147.30	133	22.2
Aged 35 to 44	135.76	123	22.2
Aged 45 to 54	125.16	113	23.4
Aged 55 to 64	94.42	85	15.1
Aged 65 to 74	90.36	82	8.8
Aged 75 or older	42.16	38	3.6

	AVERAGE HOUSEHOLD SPENDING	BEST CUSTOMERS (index)	BIGGEST CUSTOMERS (market share)
HOUSEHOLD INCOME			
Average household	**$110.61**	**100**	**100.0%**
Under $20,000	61.97	56	12.2
$20,000 to $39,999	85.62	77	17.7
$40,000 to $49,999	112.10	101	9.6
$50,000 to $69,999	114.92	104	14.9
$70,000 to $79,999	133.19	120	7.2
$80,000 to $99,999	146.39	132	11.0
$100,000 or more	177.29	160	27.5
HOUSEHOLD TYPE			
Average household	**110.61**	**100**	**100.0**
Married couples	121.92	110	54.4
Married couples, no children	99.91	90	19.2
Married couples, with children	138.08	125	29.0
Oldest child under age 6	116.48	105	4.5
Oldest child aged 6 to 17	147.02	133	15.6
Oldest child aged 18 or older	135.80	123	8.9
Single parent with child under age 18	96.76	87	5.2
Single person	84.15	76	22.3
RACE AND HISPANIC ORIGIN			
Average household	**110.61**	**100**	**100.0**
Asian	119.81	108	4.6
Black	119.19	108	13.2
Hispanic	141.42	128	15.6
Non-Hispanic white and other	104.77	95	71.8
REGION			
Average household	**110.61**	**100**	**100.0**
Northeast	143.05	129	23.7
Midwest	86.71	78	17.5
South	100.11	91	33.2
West	125.50	113	25.7
EDUCATION			
Average household	**110.61**	**100**	**100.0**
Less than high school graduate	98.68	89	12.7
High school graduate	95.09	86	21.9
Some college	116.43	105	22.1
Associate's degree	140.46	127	12.0
Bachelor's degree or more	115.28	104	31.0
Bachelor's degree	115.07	104	19.7
Master's, professional, doctoral degree	115.70	105	11.3

Note: Market shares may not sum to 100.0 because of rounding and missing categories by household type. "Asian" and "black" include Hispanics and non-Hispanics who identify themselves as being of the respective race alone. "Hispanic" includes people of any race who identify themselves as Hispanic. "Other" includes people who identify themselves as non-Hispanic and as Alaska Native, American Indian, Asian (who are also included in the "Asian" row), or Native Hawaiian or other Pacific Islander as well as non-Hispanics reporting more than one race.

Source: Calculations by New Strategist based on the Bureau of Labor Statistics' 2010 Consumer Expenditure Survey

Breakfast and Brunch at Full-Service Restaurants

Best customers:
Householders aged 65 to 74
Married couples without children at home
Households in the Northeast and West

Customer trends:
Average household spending on breakfast at full-service restaurants may rise as baby boomers fill the best-customer age group—but only if discretionary income grows.

The biggest spenders on breakfast and brunch at full-service restaurants are older married couples enjoying a leisurely meal. Householders aged 65 to 74 spend 18 percent more than average on this item. Married couples without children at home (many of them empty-nesters) spend 32 percent more than average on breakfast and brunch at full-service restaurants. Households in the Northeast and West spend, respectively, 20 and 25 percent more than average on breakfast and brunch at full-service restaurants.

Average household spending on breakfast at full-service restaurants declined by a substantial 29 percent between 2006 and 2010, after adjusting for inflation. Behind the decline was the Great Recession and a reduction in spending on all types of restaurant meals. In the years ahead, spending on full-service breakfasts should rise as boomers fill the best-customer age group—but only if discretionary income grows.

Table 15.3 Breakfast and brunch at full-service restaurants

Total household spending $10,271,084,670.00
Average household spends 84.81

	AVERAGE HOUSEHOLD SPENDING	BEST CUSTOMERS (index)	BIGGEST CUSTOMERS (market share)
AGE OF HOUSEHOLDER			
Average household	$84.81	100	100.0%
Under age 25	57.30	68	4.5
Aged 25 to 34	79.52	94	15.6
Aged 35 to 44	86.66	102	18.5
Aged 45 to 54	87.42	103	21.3
Aged 55 to 64	85.26	101	17.7
Aged 65 to 74	100.00	118	12.7
Aged 75 or older	85.96	101	9.7

	AVERAGE HOUSEHOLD SPENDING	BEST CUSTOMERS (index)	BIGGEST CUSTOMERS (market share)
HOUSEHOLD INCOME			
Average household	**$84.81**	**100**	**100.0%**
Under $20,000	35.14	41	9.0
$20,000 to $39,999	56.83	67	15.4
$40,000 to $49,999	81.96	97	9.1
$50,000 to $69,999	105.51	124	17.8
$70,000 to $79,999	104.12	123	7.3
$80,000 to $99,999	116.98	138	11.5
$100,000 or more	147.81	174	29.9
HOUSEHOLD TYPE			
Average household	**84.81**	**100**	**100.0**
Married couples	101.26	119	58.9
Married couples, no children	111.80	132	28.0
Married couples, with children	84.69	100	23.2
Oldest child under age 6	46.29	55	2.3
Oldest child aged 6 to 17	99.03	117	13.7
Oldest child aged 18 or older	82.95	98	7.1
Single parent with child under age 18	38.49	45	2.7
Single person	65.99	78	22.8
RACE AND HISPANIC ORIGIN			
Average household	**84.81**	**100**	**100.0**
Asian	78.18	92	3.9
Black	46.06	54	6.6
Hispanic	91.00	107	13.1
Non-Hispanic white and other	90.18	106	80.6
REGION			
Average household	**84.81**	**100**	**100.0**
Northeast	101.57	120	22.0
Midwest	80.56	95	21.2
South	66.01	78	28.6
West	106.37	125	28.4
EDUCATION			
Average household	**84.81**	**100**	**100.0**
Less than high school graduate	58.28	69	9.8
High school graduate	65.96	78	19.9
Some college	85.05	100	21.1
Associate's degree	76.78	91	8.6
Bachelor's degree or more	115.63	136	40.5
Bachelor's degree	118.51	140	26.4
Master's, professional, doctoral degree	109.95	130	14.0

Note: Market shares may not sum to 100.0 because of rounding and missing categories by household type. "Asian" and "black" include Hispanics and non-Hispanics who identify themselves as being of the respective race alone. "Hispanic" includes people of any race who identify themselves as Hispanic. "Other" includes people who identify themselves as non-Hispanic and as Alaska Native, American Indian, Asian (who are also included in the "Asian" row), or Native Hawaiian or other Pacific Islander as well as non-Hispanics reporting more than one race.

Source: Calculations by New Strategist based on the Bureau of Labor Statistics' 2010 Consumer Expenditure Survey

Dinner at Fast-Food Restaurants, Including Take-Outs, Deliveries, Concession Stands, Buffets, and Cafeterias (except Employer and School)

Best customers:

Householders aged 25 to 44
Married couples with children at home
Single parents
Hispanics, Asians, and blacks

Customer trends:

Average household spending on dinner at fast-food restaurants may grow because the large millennial generation is moving into the best-customer lifestage.

Families with children are the biggest spenders on dinners at fast-food restaurants. Householders ranging in age from 25 to 44 spend 27 to 51 percent more than average on this item and account for 48 percent of the market. Married couples with children at home spend 54 percent more than average on dinner at fast-food restaurants as they try to fit meals into their busy schedules. Single parents, whose spending approaches average on only a few items, spend 15 percent more than average on fast-food dinners. Blacks, Asians, and Hispanics spend between 9 and 20 percent more than average on fast-food dinners and together account for nearly one-third of the market.

Average household spending on dinner at fast-food restaurants fell 9 percent between 2006 and 2010 as households cut their spending during the economic downturn. Because the large millennial generation is moving into the best-customer lifestage, average household spending on fast-food restaurant dinners may grow in the years ahead.

Table 15.4 **Dinner at fast-food restaurants, including take-outs, deliveries, concession stands, buffets, and cafeterias (except employer and school)**

Total household spending $40,137,281,940.00
Average household spends 331.42

	AVERAGE HOUSEHOLD SPENDING	BEST CUSTOMERS (index)	BIGGEST CUSTOMERS (market share)
AGE OF HOUSEHOLDER			
Average household	$331.42	100	100.0%
Under age 25	332.68	100	6.7
Aged 25 to 34	421.32	127	21.2
Aged 35 to 44	499.01	151	27.2
Aged 45 to 54	368.08	111	23.0
Aged 55 to 64	263.55	80	14.0
Aged 65 to 74	158.40	48	5.1
Aged 75 or older	100.14	30	2.9

	AVERAGE HOUSEHOLD SPENDING	BEST CUSTOMERS (index)	BIGGEST CUSTOMERS (market share)
HOUSEHOLD INCOME			
Average household	**$331.42**	**100**	**100.0%**
Under $20,000	175.02	53	11.5
$20,000 to $39,999	231.57	70	16.0
$40,000 to $49,999	344.92	104	9.8
$50,000 to $69,999	372.31	112	16.1
$70,000 to $79,999	412.55	124	7.5
$80,000 to $99,999	429.80	130	10.8
$100,000 or more	550.08	166	28.5
HOUSEHOLD TYPE			
Average household	**331.42**	**100**	**100.0**
Married couples	403.38	122	60.0
Married couples, no children	269.44	81	17.3
Married couples, with children	509.83	154	35.8
Oldest child under age 6	450.83	136	5.8
Oldest child aged 6 to 17	541.20	163	19.2
Oldest child aged 18 or older	493.24	149	10.7
Single parent with child under age 18	382.03	115	6.8
Single person	180.10	54	15.9
RACE AND HISPANIC ORIGIN			
Average household	**331.42**	**100**	**100.0**
Asian	373.80	113	4.8
Black	361.28	109	13.3
Hispanic	399.30	120	14.7
Non-Hispanic white and other	316.34	95	72.4
REGION			
Average household	**331.42**	**100**	**100.0**
Northeast	323.86	98	17.9
Midwest	316.27	95	21.3
South	329.72	99	36.5
West	355.77	107	24.3
EDUCATION			
Average household	**331.42**	**100**	**100.0**
Less than high school graduate	273.66	83	11.8
High school graduate	280.14	85	21.6
Some college	329.46	99	20.9
Associate's degree	401.96	121	11.5
Bachelor's degree or more	379.81	115	34.0
Bachelor's degree	392.97	119	22.4
Master's, professional, doctoral degree	353.91	107	11.6

Note: Market shares may not sum to 100.0 because of rounding and missing categories by household type. "Asian" and "black" include Hispanics and non-Hispanics who identify themselves as being of the respective race alone. "Hispanic" includes people of any race who identify themselves as Hispanic. "Other" includes people who identify themselves as non-Hispanic and as Alaska Native, American Indian, Asian (who are also included in the "Asian" row), or Native Hawaiian or other Pacific Islander as well as non-Hispanics reporting more than one race.

Source: Calculations by New Strategist based on the Bureau of Labor Statistics' 2010 Consumer Expenditure Survey

Dinner at Full-Service Restaurants

Best customers:
Householders aged 25 to 54
Married couples without children at home
Married couples with school-aged or older children at home
Asians
Households in the Northeast and West

Customer trends:
Average household spending on dinner at full-service restaurants should rise in the years ahead as growing numbers of baby boomers retire and gain more free time—but only if discretionary income grows.

The biggest spenders on dinners at full-service restaurants are married couples with children as well as empty-nesters. Householders ranging in age from 25 to 54 spend 8 to 26 percent more than average on this item. Married couples with school-aged children spend 40 percent, and those with adult children at home, 27 percent more than average on this item. Married couples without children at home (many of them empty-nesters) spend 23 percent more than average on full-service restaurant dinners. Asians spend 58 percent more than average on full-service dinners. Households in the Northeast lead those in other regions in full-service dinner spending—their bill is 27 percent higher than average. In the West, households spend 20 percent more.

Average household spending on dinners in full-service restaurants fell by 18 percent between 2006 and 2010, after adjusting for inflation, as households cut their budgets in the midst of the economic downturn. Spending in the category should rise in the years ahead as baby boomers retire and gain more free time—but only if discretionary income grows.

Table 15.5 Dinner at full-service restaurants

Total household spending $78,167,302,080.00
Average household spends 645.44

	AVERAGE HOUSEHOLD SPENDING	BEST CUSTOMERS (index)	BIGGEST CUSTOMERS (market share)
AGE OF HOUSEHOLDER			
Average household	**$645.44**	**100**	**100.0%**
Under age 25	372.23	58	3.8
Aged 25 to 34	698.48	108	18.0
Aged 35 to 44	811.09	126	22.7
Aged 45 to 54	713.77	111	22.9
Aged 55 to 64	648.73	101	17.7
Aged 65 to 74	573.81	89	9.6
Aged 75 or older	355.07	55	5.2

	AVERAGE HOUSEHOLD SPENDING	BEST CUSTOMERS (index)	BIGGEST CUSTOMERS (market share)
HOUSEHOLD INCOME			
Average household	**$645.44**	**100**	**100.0%**
Under $20,000	208.42	32	7.0
$20,000 to $39,999	349.73	54	12.4
$40,000 to $49,999	514.37	80	7.5
$50,000 to $69,999	653.92	101	14.5
$70,000 to $79,999	835.13	129	7.7
$80,000 to $99,999	859.48	133	11.1
$100,000 or more	1,525.93	236	40.5
HOUSEHOLD TYPE			
Average household	**645.44**	**100**	**100.0**
Married couples	809.63	125	61.9
Married couples, no children	792.26	123	26.1
Married couples, with children	854.08	132	30.8
Oldest child under age 6	764.46	118	5.1
Oldest child aged 6 to 17	906.44	140	16.5
Oldest child aged 18 or older	821.89	127	9.2
Single parent with child under age 18	323.55	50	3.0
Single person	452.71	70	20.5
RACE AND HISPANIC ORIGIN			
Average household	**645.44**	**100**	**100.0**
Asian	1,022.51	158	6.7
Black	301.50	47	5.7
Hispanic	498.66	77	9.4
Non-Hispanic white and other	723.02	112	84.9
REGION			
Average household	**645.44**	**100**	**100.0**
Northeast	822.18	127	23.4
Midwest	504.36	78	17.4
South	565.36	88	32.1
West	775.19	120	27.2
EDUCATION			
Average household	**645.44**	**100**	**100.0**
Less than high school graduate	291.56	45	6.5
High school graduate	434.37	67	17.2
Some college	571.59	89	18.6
Associate's degree	619.73	96	9.1
Bachelor's degree or more	1,049.74	163	48.3
Bachelor's degree	1,020.62	158	29.9
Master's, professional, doctoral degree	1,107.10	172	18.6

Note: Market shares may not sum to 100.0 because of rounding and missing categories by household type. "Asian" and "black" include Hispanics and non-Hispanics who identify themselves as being of the respective race alone. "Hispanic" includes people of any race who identify themselves as Hispanic. "Other" includes people who identify themselves as non-Hispanic and as Alaska Native, American Indian, Asian (who are also included in the "Asian" row), or Native Hawaiian or other Pacific Islander as well as non-Hispanics reporting more than one race.

Source: Calculations by New Strategist based on the Bureau of Labor Statistics' 2010 Consumer Expenditure Survey

Lunch at Employer and School Cafeterias

Best customers:

Householders aged 35 to 54
Married couples with school-aged or older children at home
Single parents
Asians
Households in the Northeast

Customer trends:

Average household spending on lunch at employer and school cafeterias may continue to decline as more children qualify for subsidized lunches and fewer employers offer cafeteria meals in an attempt to cut costs.

Not surprisingly, parents and workers are the biggest spenders on lunch at employer and school cafeterias. Householders aged 35 to 54, most of them in the workforce, spend 44 to 101 percent more than average on this item and account for two-thirds of the market. Married couples with school-aged children, many of them dual-income couples, spend two-and-one-half times the average on this item. Couples with adult children at home spend nearly twice the average on employer and school cafeteria lunches, while single parents spend over twice the average. Asians also spend nearly double the average on this item. The spending on lunch at employer and school cafeterias of Northeastern householders is one-quarter higher than average.

Average household spending on lunch at employer and school cafeterias fell 12 percent between 2006 and 2010, after adjusting for inflation. Behind the decline was household budget cutting in the midst of the economic downturn. This category may continue to decline as a growing percentage of children qualify for subsidized lunches and fewer employers offer cafeteria meals in an attempt to cut costs.

Table 15.6 Lunch at employer and school cafeterias

Total household spending $9,947,728,980.00
Average household spends 82.14

	AVERAGE HOUSEHOLD SPENDING	BEST CUSTOMERS (index)	BIGGEST CUSTOMERS (market share)
AGE OF HOUSEHOLDER			
Average household	**$82.14**	**100**	**100.0%**
Under age 25	86.47	105	7.0
Aged 25 to 34	73.29	89	14.9
Aged 35 to 44	165.44	201	36.4
Aged 45 to 54	118.12	144	29.7
Aged 55 to 64	38.13	46	8.2
Aged 65 to 74	19.83	24	2.6
Aged 75 or older	11.16	14	1.3

	AVERAGE HOUSEHOLD SPENDING	BEST CUSTOMERS (index)	BIGGEST CUSTOMERS (market share)
HOUSEHOLD INCOME			
Average household	**$82.14**	**100**	**100.0%**
Under $20,000	30.65	37	8.1
$20,000 to $39,999	51.47	63	14.4
$40,000 to $49,999	58.14	71	6.7
$50,000 to $69,999	106.73	130	18.6
$70,000 to $79,999	61.21	75	4.5
$80,000 to $99,999	122.00	149	12.4
$100,000 or more	172.79	210	36.1
HOUSEHOLD TYPE			
Average household	**82.14**	**100**	**100.0**
Married couples	102.94	125	61.8
Married couples, no children	30.87	38	8.0
Married couples, with children	166.18	202	47.1
Oldest child under age 6	55.57	68	2.9
Oldest child aged 6 to 17	208.71	254	29.9
Oldest child aged 18 or older	159.38	194	14.0
Single parent with child under age 18	171.11	208	12.3
Single person	31.99	39	11.4
RACE AND HISPANIC ORIGIN			
Average household	**82.14**	**100**	**100.0**
Asian	150.87	184	7.8
Black	79.88	97	11.9
Hispanic	89.89	109	13.3
Non-Hispanic white and other	81.24	99	75.0
REGION			
Average household	**82.14**	**100**	**100.0**
Northeast	102.45	125	22.9
Midwest	75.63	92	20.5
South	82.19	100	36.7
West	71.99	88	19.9
EDUCATION			
Average household	**82.14**	**100**	**100.0**
Less than high school graduate	35.45	43	6.2
High school graduate	66.64	81	20.7
Some college	75.55	92	19.3
Associate's degree	102.85	125	11.8
Bachelor's degree or more	114.29	139	41.3
Bachelor's degree	125.36	153	28.8
Master's, professional, doctoral degree	92.50	113	12.2

Note: Market shares may not sum to 100.0 because of rounding and missing categories by household type. "Asian" and "black" include Hispanics and non-Hispanics who identify themselves as being of the respective race alone. "Hispanic" includes people of any race who identify themselves as Hispanic. "Other" includes people who identify themselves as non-Hispanic and as Alaska Native, American Indian, Asian (who are also included in the "Asian" row), or Native Hawaiian or other Pacific Islander as well as non-Hispanics reporting more than one race.

Source: Calculations by New Strategist based on the Bureau of Labor Statistics' 2010 Consumer Expenditure Survey

Lunch at Fast-Food Restaurants, Including Take-Outs, Deliveries, Concession Stands, Buffets, and Cafeterias (except Employer and School)

Best customers:	**Householders aged 25 to 44** **Married couples with children at home** **Asians and Hispanics**
Customer trends:	**Average household spending on lunch at fast-food restaurants may continue to decline as boomers begin to retire and have time for more leisurely lunches at full-service restaurants.**

Workers and parents are the best customers of fast-food lunches. Householders of prime working age, 25 to 44, spend 27 to 34 percent more than average on this item and account for 45 percent of the market. Married couples with children at home spend 41 percent more than average on lunches at fast-food restaurants as they try to fit meals into their busy schedules. Asians spend 62 percent more than average on this item, and Hispanics, 28 percent.

Average household spending on fast-food lunches fell by 12 percent between 2006 and 2010, after adjusting for inflation. Behind the decline was belt-tightening as households cut their budget in the midst of the economic downturn. Spending on this item may continue to decline in the years ahead as boomers begin to retire.

Table 15.7 Lunch at fast-food restaurants, including take-outs, deliveries, concession stands, buffets, and cafeterias (except employer and school)

Total household spending	$42,554,577,660.00
Average household spends	351.38

	AVERAGE HOUSEHOLD SPENDING	BEST CUSTOMERS (index)	BIGGEST CUSTOMERS (market share)
AGE OF HOUSEHOLDER			
Average household	**$351.38**	**100**	**100.0%**
Under age 25	309.91	88	5.9
Aged 25 to 34	445.15	127	21.1
Aged 35 to 44	470.00	134	24.2
Aged 45 to 54	379.18	108	22.3
Aged 55 to 64	324.47	92	16.3
Aged 65 to 74	219.81	63	6.7
Aged 75 or older	130.90	37	3.6

	AVERAGE HOUSEHOLD SPENDING	BEST CUSTOMERS (index)	BIGGEST CUSTOMERS (market share)
HOUSEHOLD INCOME			
Average household	$351.38	100	100.0%
Under $20,000	188.32	54	11.7
$20,000 to $39,999	246.94	70	16.1
$40,000 to $49,999	346.74	99	9.3
$50,000 to $69,999	377.68	107	15.4
$70,000 to $79,999	445.83	127	7.6
$80,000 to $99,999	469.75	134	11.1
$100,000 or more	592.26	169	28.9
HOUSEHOLD TYPE			
Average household	351.38	100	100.0
Married couples	412.42	117	57.9
Married couples, no children	298.52	85	18.0
Married couples, with children	495.50	141	32.8
Oldest child under age 6	436.52	124	5.3
Oldest child aged 6 to 17	495.48	141	16.6
Oldest child aged 18 or older	525.72	150	10.8
Single parent with child under age 18	326.54	93	5.5
Single person	224.42	64	18.7
RACE AND HISPANIC ORIGIN			
Average household	351.38	100	100.0
Asian	569.22	162	6.9
Black	315.08	90	11.0
Hispanic	449.39	128	15.6
Non-Hispanic white and other	341.56	97	73.7
REGION			
Average household	351.38	100	100.0
Northeast	340.26	97	17.8
Midwest	293.88	84	18.6
South	357.75	102	37.4
West	408.17	116	26.3
EDUCATION			
Average household	351.38	100	100.0
Less than high school graduate	279.89	80	11.4
High school graduate	297.29	85	21.6
Some college	361.07	103	21.6
Associate's degree	387.71	110	10.4
Bachelor's degree or more	411.27	117	34.8
Bachelor's degree	411.70	117	22.1
Master's, professional, doctoral degree	410.42	117	12.6

Note: Market shares may not sum to 100.0 because of rounding and missing categories by household type. "Asian" and "black" include Hispanics and non-Hispanics who identify themselves as being of the respective race alone. "Hispanic" includes people of any race who identify themselves as Hispanic. "Other" includes people who identify themselves as non-Hispanic and as Alaska Native, American Indian, Asian (who are also included in the "Asian" row), or Native Hawaiian or other Pacific Islander as well as non-Hispanics reporting more than one race.

Source: Calculations by New Strategist based on the Bureau of Labor Statistics' 2010 Consumer Expenditure Survey

Lunch at Full-Service Restaurants

Best customers: **Householders aged 65 to 74**
Married couples
Asians

Customer trends: **Average household spending on lunch at full-service restaurants should rise**
as growing numbers of baby boomers become empty-nesters with more free
time—but only if discretionary income grows.

The biggest spenders on lunch at full-service restaurants are older married couples enjoying a leisurely meal. Householders aged 65 to 74 spend 20 percent more than average on this item. Married couples without children at home (many of them empty-nesters) spend 37 percent more than average on lunch at full-service restaurants. Couples with children at home spend one-quarter more than average on full-service lunches, in part because their households are larger than average. Asians outspend the average on lunch at full-service restaurants by 38 percent.

Average household spending on full-service lunches declined by 12 percent between 2006 and 2010, after adjusting for inflation. Behind the decline in spending was belt-tightening during the Great Recession. Spending on full-service lunches may increase in the years ahead as more boomers become empty-nesters with free time to enjoy a leisurely meal—but only if discretionary income grows.

Table 15.8 Lunch at full-service restaurants

Total household spending	$34,533,661,050.00
Average household spends	285.15

	AVERAGE HOUSEHOLD SPENDING	BEST CUSTOMERS (index)	BIGGEST CUSTOMERS (market share)
AGE OF HOUSEHOLDER			
Average household	**$285.15**	**100**	**100.0%**
Under age 25	175.25	61	4.1
Aged 25 to 34	270.00	95	15.8
Aged 35 to 44	310.45	109	19.7
Aged 45 to 54	266.53	93	19.3
Aged 55 to 64	294.55	103	18.2
Aged 65 to 74	341.40	120	12.9
Aged 75 or older	301.38	106	10.1

	AVERAGE HOUSEHOLD SPENDING	BEST CUSTOMERS (index)	BIGGEST CUSTOMERS (market share)
HOUSEHOLD INCOME			
Average household	**$285.15**	**100**	**100.0%**
Under $20,000	128.68	45	9.8
$20,000 to $39,999	171.87	60	13.8
$40,000 to $49,999	238.32	84	7.9
$50,000 to $69,999	273.38	96	13.7
$70,000 to $79,999	429.54	151	9.0
$80,000 to $99,999	356.64	125	10.4
$100,000 or more	597.91	210	36.0
HOUSEHOLD TYPE			
Average household	**285.15**	**100**	**100.0**
Married couples	370.96	130	64.2
Married couples, no children	389.77	137	29.0
Married couples, with children	357.49	125	29.2
Oldest child under age 6	324.18	114	4.9
Oldest child aged 6 to 17	370.81	130	15.3
Oldest child aged 18 or older	354.67	124	9.0
Single parent with child under age 18	88.02	31	1.8
Single person	208.77	73	21.4
RACE AND HISPANIC ORIGIN			
Average household	**285.15**	**100**	**100.0**
Asian	394.72	138	5.9
Black	161.35	57	6.9
Hispanic	262.50	92	11.2
Non-Hispanic white and other	308.23	108	82.0
REGION			
Average household	**285.15**	**100**	**100.0**
Northeast	303.85	107	19.6
Midwest	205.27	72	16.0
South	305.71	107	39.3
West	316.77	111	25.2
EDUCATION			
Average household	**285.15**	**100**	**100.0**
Less than high school graduate	166.95	59	8.4
High school graduate	201.45	71	18.0
Some college	246.50	86	18.2
Associate's degree	283.67	99	9.4
Bachelor's degree or more	439.58	154	45.8
Bachelor's degree	421.24	148	27.9
Master's, professional, doctoral degree	475.69	167	18.0

Note: Market shares may not sum to 100.0 because of rounding and missing categories by household type. "Asian" and "black" include Hispanics and non-Hispanics who identify themselves as being of the respective race alone. "Hispanic" includes people of any race who identify themselves as Hispanic. "Other" includes people who identify themselves as non-Hispanic and as Alaska Native, American Indian, Asian (who are also included in the "Asian" row), or Native Hawaiian or other Pacific Islander as well as non-Hispanics reporting more than one race.

Source: Calculations by New Strategist based on the Bureau of Labor Statistics' 2010 Consumer Expenditure Survey

Restaurant and Carry-out Food on Trips

Best customers: **Householders aged 45 to 74**
                                  Married couples without children at home
                                  Married couples with school-aged or older children at home
                                  Asians

Customer trends: **Average household spending on restaurant and carry-out food on trips should grow as boomers retire, but only if discretionary income rises.**

The biggest spenders on restaurant and carry-out meals on trips are the most-avid travelers—older married couples. Householders ranging in age from 45 to 74 spend 21 to 22 percent more than average on this item. Married couples without children at home (most of them empty-nesters) spend 63 percent more than average on restaurant and carry-out meals on trips and control over one-third of the market. Those with school-aged or older children at home spend 28 to 58 percent more. Asians, the most-affluent racial and ethnic group, spend 41 percent more than average on eating out while traveling.

Average household spending on restaurant and carry-out meals on trips fell 15 percent between 2006 and 2010, after adjusting for inflation. Behind the decline was household budget cutting in the midst of the Great Recession. Spending on this item should grow in the years ahead as boomers retire, but only if discretionary income grows.

Table 15.9 Restaurant and carry-out food on trips

Total household spending $27,016,549,560.00
Average household spends   223.08

	AVERAGE HOUSEHOLD SPENDING	BEST CUSTOMERS (index)	BIGGEST CUSTOMERS (market share)
AGE OF HOUSEHOLDER			
Average household	**$223.08**	**100**	**100.0%**
Under age 25	82.60	37	2.5
Aged 25 to 34	171.66	77	12.8
Aged 35 to 44	240.46	108	19.5
Aged 45 to 54	271.80	122	25.2
Aged 55 to 64	269.45	121	21.3
Aged 65 to 74	272.54	122	13.1
Aged 75 or older	130.35	58	5.6

	AVERAGE HOUSEHOLD SPENDING	BEST CUSTOMERS (index)	BIGGEST CUSTOMERS (market share)
HOUSEHOLD INCOME			
Average household	**$223.08**	**100**	**100.0%**
Under $20,000	49.53	22	4.8
$20,000 to $39,999	98.01	44	10.1
$40,000 to $49,999	139.46	63	5.9
$50,000 to $69,999	222.87	100	14.3
$70,000 to $79,999	255.80	115	6.9
$80,000 to $99,999	293.88	132	11.0
$100,000 or more	611.50	274	47.0
HOUSEHOLD TYPE			
Average household	**223.08**	**100**	**100.0**
Married couples	322.33	144	71.3
Married couples, no children	364.26	163	34.7
Married couples, with children	305.34	137	31.8
Oldest child under age 6	208.67	94	4.0
Oldest child aged 6 to 17	352.16	158	18.6
Oldest child aged 18 or older	286.42	128	9.3
Single parent with child under age 18	116.19	52	3.1
Single person	120.46	54	15.8
RACE AND HISPANIC ORIGIN			
Average household	**223.08**	**100**	**100.0**
Asian	315.10	141	6.0
Black	92.11	41	5.1
Hispanic	136.54	61	7.5
Non-Hispanic white and other	258.53	116	87.9
REGION			
Average household	**223.08**	**100**	**100.0**
Northeast	242.63	109	20.0
Midwest	224.79	101	22.5
South	186.37	84	30.7
West	265.03	119	26.9
EDUCATION			
Average household	**223.08**	**100**	**100.0**
Less than high school graduate	70.89	32	4.5
High school graduate	117.18	53	13.4
Some college	185.98	83	17.5
Associate's degree	216.19	97	9.2
Bachelor's degree or more	415.72	186	55.4
Bachelor's degree	377.29	169	31.9
Master's, professional, doctoral degree	482.81	216	23.4

Note: Market shares may not sum to 100.0 because of rounding and missing categories by household type. "Asian" and "black" include Hispanics and non-Hispanics who identify themselves as being of the respective race alone. "Hispanic" includes people of any race who identify themselves as Hispanic. "Other" includes people who identify themselves as non-Hispanic and as Alaska Native, American Indian, Asian (who are also included in the "Asian" row), or Native Hawaiian or other Pacific Islander as well as non-Hispanics reporting more than one race.

Source: Calculations by New Strategist based on the Bureau of Labor Statistics' 2010 Consumer Expenditure Survey

Snacks at Employer and School Cafeterias

Best customers: Householders under age 45
Married couples with children under age 18
Single parents
Asians
Households in the Northeast

Customer trends: Average household spending on snacks at employer and school cafeterias may continue its decline as fewer employers provide cafeterias in an attempt to cut costs.

Not surprisingly, parents and workers are the biggest spenders on snacks at employer and school cafeterias. Householders under age 35, most of them at school or in the workforce, spend 39 to 41 percent more than average on this item, and those aged 35 to 44 spend twice the average. Together these age groups account for 69 percent of the market. Married couples with preschoolers spend 40 percent more than average on cafeteria snacks, and those with school-aged children spend nearly three times the average on this item. Single parents, whose spending approaches average on only a few items, spend 9 percent more than average on this item. Asian householders spend well over two-and-one-half times the average on snacks at employer and school cafeterias. Households in the Northeast outspend the average by 30 percent.

Average household spending on snacks at employer and school cafeterias fell a substantial 20 percent between 2006 and 2010, after adjusting for inflation. In the years ahead, average household spending on snacks at employer and school cafeterias may continue its decline as employers cut costs by eliminating cafeterias.

Table 15.10 Snacks at employer and school cafeterias

Total household spending	$718,164,510.00
Average household spends	5.93

	AVERAGE HOUSEHOLD SPENDING	BEST CUSTOMERS (index)	BIGGEST CUSTOMERS (market share)
AGE OF HOUSEHOLDER			
Average household	**$5.93**	**100**	**100.0%**
Under age 25	8.38	141	9.4
Aged 25 to 34	8.23	139	23.1
Aged 35 to 44	12.06	203	36.8
Aged 45 to 54	4.83	81	16.9
Aged 55 to 64	3.15	53	9.4
Aged 65 to 74	1.73	29	3.1
Aged 75 or older	1.06	18	1.7

	AVERAGE HOUSEHOLD SPENDING	BEST CUSTOMERS (index)	BIGGEST CUSTOMERS (market share)
HOUSEHOLD INCOME			
Average household	$5.93	100	100.0%
Under $20,000	3.01	51	11.1
$20,000 to $39,999	4.68	79	18.1
$40,000 to $49,999	4.89	82	7.8
$50,000 to $69,999	4.57	77	11.1
$70,000 to $79,999	15.70	265	15.8
$80,000 to $99,999	9.66	163	13.6
$100,000 or more	8.20	138	23.7
HOUSEHOLD TYPE			
Average household	5.93	100	100.0
Married couples	7.35	124	61.1
Married couples, no children	3.50	59	12.5
Married couples, with children	11.70	197	45.9
Oldest child under age 6	8.28	140	6.0
Oldest child aged 6 to 17	17.29	292	34.3
Oldest child aged 18 or older	5.11	86	6.2
Single parent with child under age 18	6.49	109	6.5
Single person	3.41	58	16.8
RACE AND HISPANIC ORIGIN			
Average household	5.93	100	100.0
Asian	16.23	274	11.6
Black	3.20	54	6.6
Hispanic	5.74	97	11.8
Non-Hispanic white and other	6.38	108	81.6
REGION			
Average household	5.93	100	100.0
Northeast	7.70	130	23.8
Midwest	4.37	74	16.4
South	6.12	103	37.9
West	5.75	97	22.0
EDUCATION			
Average household	5.93	100	100.0
Less than high school graduate	3.13	53	7.5
High school graduate	3.12	53	13.4
Some college	8.06	136	28.6
Associate's degree	3.46	58	5.5
Bachelor's degree or more	8.91	150	44.6
Bachelor's degree	8.26	139	26.3
Master's, professional, doctoral degree	10.18	172	18.6

Note: Market shares may not sum to 100.0 because of rounding and missing categories by household type. "Asian" and "black" include Hispanics and non-Hispanics who identify themselves as being of the respective race alone. "Hispanic" includes people of any race who identify themselves as Hispanic. "Other" includes people who identify themselves as non-Hispanic and as Alaska Native, American Indian, Asian (who are also included in the "Asian" row), or Native Hawaiian or other Pacific Islander as well as non-Hispanics reporting more than one race.

Source: Calculations by New Strategist based on the Bureau of Labor Statistics' 2010 Consumer Expenditure Survey

Snacks at Fast-Food Restaurants, Including Take-Outs, Deliveries, Concession Stands, Buffets, and Cafeterias (except Employer and School)

Best customers:	**Householders aged 25 to 44** **Married couples with children at home** **Asians** **Households in the West**
Customer trends:	**Average household spending on snacks at fast-food restaurants should stabilize or even increase in the years ahead as the large millennial generation moves into the best-customer lifestage.**

Parents are the best customers of snacks from fast-food restaurants. Householders aged 25 to 44, most with children, spend 20 to 51 percent more than the average household on fast-food snacks. Married couples with children at home spend 67 percent more than average on this item, the figure peaking at 85 percent above average among parents with school-aged children. The spending on fast-food snacks by Asian householders is one-quarter higher than average. Households in the West outspend the average on fast-food snacks by 28 percent.

Average household spending on snacks from fast-food restaurants fell 12 percent between 2006 and 2010, after adjusting for inflation. Behind the decline was belt-tightening due to the Great Recession. Spending on this item should stabilize or even increase in the years ahead as the large millennial generation moves into the best-customer lifestage.

Table 15.11 Snacks at fast-food restaurants, including take-outs, deliveries, concession stands, buffets, and cafeterias (except employer and school)

Total household spending		$12,383,190,750.00	
Average household spends		102.25	
	AVERAGE HOUSEHOLD SPENDING	BEST CUSTOMERS (index)	BIGGEST CUSTOMERS (market share)
AGE OF HOUSEHOLDER			
Average household	**$102.25**	**100**	**100.0%**
Under age 25	91.26	89	5.9
Aged 25 to 34	122.66	120	20.0
Aged 35 to 44	154.03	151	27.3
Aged 45 to 54	110.82	108	22.4
Aged 55 to 64	91.71	90	15.8
Aged 65 to 74	56.82	56	6.0
Aged 75 or older	29.06	28	2.7

	AVERAGE HOUSEHOLD SPENDING	BEST CUSTOMERS (index)	BIGGEST CUSTOMERS (market share)
HOUSEHOLD INCOME			
Average household	$102.25	100	100.0%
Under $20,000	44.56	44	9.5
$20,000 to $39,999	63.29	62	14.2
$40,000 to $49,999	83.63	82	7.7
$50,000 to $69,999	117.67	115	16.5
$70,000 to $79,999	135.44	132	7.9
$80,000 to $99,999	129.10	126	10.5
$100,000 or more	204.18	200	34.2
HOUSEHOLD TYPE			
Average household	102.25	100	100.0
Married couples	131.22	128	63.3
Married couples, no children	87.52	86	18.2
Married couples, with children	170.88	167	38.9
Oldest child under age 6	149.97	147	6.3
Oldest child aged 6 to 17	189.15	185	21.8
Oldest child aged 18 or older	154.34	151	10.9
Single parent with child under age 18	78.08	76	4.5
Single person	55.38	54	15.9
RACE AND HISPANIC ORIGIN			
Average household	102.25	100	100.0
Asian	127.59	125	5.3
Black	74.75	73	8.9
Hispanic	107.11	105	12.8
Non-Hispanic white and other	105.75	103	78.4
REGION			
Average household	102.25	100	100.0
Northeast	115.40	113	20.7
Midwest	90.86	89	19.8
South	85.56	84	30.7
West	130.47	128	28.9
EDUCATION			
Average household	102.25	100	100.0
Less than high school graduate	65.32	64	9.1
High school graduate	74.99	73	18.7
Some college	98.38	96	20.2
Associate's degree	125.60	123	11.6
Bachelor's degree or more	137.50	134	40.0
Bachelor's degree	139.89	137	25.8
Master's, professional, doctoral degree	132.80	130	14.1

Note: Market shares may not sum to 100.0 because of rounding and missing categories by household type. "Asian" and "black" include Hispanics and non-Hispanics who identify themselves as being of the respective race alone. "Hispanic" includes people of any race who identify themselves as Hispanic. "Other" includes people who identify themselves as non-Hispanic and as Alaska Native, American Indian, Asian (who are also included in the "Asian" row), or Native Hawaiian or other Pacific Islander as well as non-Hispanics reporting more than one race.

Source: Calculations by New Strategist based on the Bureau of Labor Statistics' 2010 Consumer Expenditure Survey

Snacks at Full-Service Restaurants

Best customers: Householders aged 25 to 34 and 45 to 64
Married couples with adult children at home
People who live alone
Households in the Northeast

Customer trends: Average household spending on snacks at full-service restaurants should rise in
the years ahead as casual sit-down restaurants compete with fast-food establishments for the dollars of snackers.

The biggest spenders on snacks at full-service restaurants are young adults and middle-aged married couples with children. Householders aged 25 to 34 spend 19 percent more than average on snacks at full-service restaurants, and those aged 45 to 64 spend 11 to 17 percent more. Married couples with adult children at home spend 54 percent more than average on this item. People who live alone, whose spending is well below average on most items, spend 6 percent more than average on snacks at full-service restaurants. Households in the Northeast outspend the average on this item by 53 percent.

Average household spending on snacks at full-service restaurants fell by 11 percent between 2006 and 2010, after adjusting for inflation. Behind the decline was belt-tightening during the Great Recession. Spending on this item should grow in the years ahead as casual sit-down restaurants compete with fast-food establishments for the dollars of snackers.

Table 15.12 Snacks at full-service restaurants

Total household spending $3,455,182,710.00
Average household spends   28.53

	AVERAGE HOUSEHOLD SPENDING	BEST CUSTOMERS (index)	BIGGEST CUSTOMERS (market share)
AGE OF HOUSEHOLDER			
Average household	**$28.53**	**100**	**100.0%**
Under age 25	31.02	109	7.2
Aged 25 to 34	33.85	119	19.8
Aged 35 to 44	26.10	91	16.6
Aged 45 to 54	33.37	117	24.2
Aged 55 to 64	31.81	111	19.7
Aged 65 to 74	21.85	77	8.2
Aged 75 or older	12.52	44	4.2

	AVERAGE HOUSEHOLD SPENDING	BEST CUSTOMERS (index)	BIGGEST CUSTOMERS (market share)
HOUSEHOLD INCOME			
Average household	**$28.53**	**100**	**100.0%**
Under $20,000	10.86	38	8.3
$20,000 to $39,999	21.68	76	17.4
$40,000 to $49,999	18.45	65	6.1
$50,000 to $69,999	30.91	108	15.5
$70,000 to $79,999	37.42	131	7.9
$80,000 to $99,999	32.54	114	9.5
$100,000 or more	59.97	210	36.0
HOUSEHOLD TYPE			
Average household	**28.53**	**100**	**100.0**
Married couples	29.84	105	51.6
Married couples, no children	29.89	105	22.3
Married couples, with children	31.94	112	26.0
Oldest child under age 6	17.18	60	2.6
Oldest child aged 6 to 17	28.99	102	11.9
Oldest child aged 18 or older	43.89	154	11.1
Single parent with child under age 18	10.02	35	2.1
Single person	30.11	106	30.9
RACE AND HISPANIC ORIGIN			
Average household	**28.53**	**100**	**100.0**
Asian	25.86	91	3.9
Black	18.56	65	8.0
Hispanic	29.06	102	12.4
Non-Hispanic white and other	30.04	105	79.8
REGION			
Average household	**28.53**	**100**	**100.0**
Northeast	43.79	153	28.2
Midwest	25.19	88	19.7
South	20.37	71	26.2
West	32.83	115	26.1
EDUCATION			
Average household	**28.53**	**100**	**100.0**
Less than high school graduate	11.20	39	5.6
High school graduate	29.08	102	26.0
Some college	23.52	82	17.3
Associate's degree	22.42	79	7.4
Bachelor's degree or more	41.41	145	43.1
Bachelor's degree	39.68	139	26.3
Master's, professional, doctoral degree	44.81	157	17.0

Note: Market shares may not sum to 100.0 because of rounding and missing categories by household type. "Asian" and "black" include Hispanics and non-Hispanics who identify themselves as being of the respective race alone. "Hispanic" includes people of any race who identify themselves as Hispanic. "Other" includes people who identify themselves as non-Hispanic and as Alaska Native, American Indian, Asian (who are also included in the "Asian" row), or Native Hawaiian or other Pacific Islander as well as non-Hispanics reporting more than one race.

Source: Calculations by New Strategist based on the Bureau of Labor Statistics' 2010 Consumer Expenditure Survey

Snacks at Vending Machines and Mobile Vendors

Best customers: **Householders under age 55**
Married couples with school-aged or older children at home
Single parents
Asians and Hispanics
Households in the Northeast

Customer trends: **Average household spending on snacks from vending machines and mobile vendors may continue to decline as restaurants and supermarkets compete for snack dollars.**

The biggest spenders on snacks from vending machines and mobile vendors are the youngest householders and parents with children. Householders under age 25 spend 75 percent more than average on this item. Householders ranging in age from 25 to 54, most of them parents, spend 15 to 31 percent more than average on snacks from vending machines and mobile vendors. Married couples with school-aged or older children at home spend 26 to 55 percent more than average on vending machine snacks, and single parents, whose spending approaches average on only a few items, spend 45 percent more than average on this item. Asians spend 52 percent more than average on snacks from machines and street vendors, and Hispanics spend 26 percent more. Households in the Northeast outspend the average by 17 percent.

Average household spending on snacks from vending machines and mobile vendors fell by a steep 44 percent between 2006 and 2010, after adjusting for inflation. Spending on this category may continue to decline in the years ahead as fast-food and full-service restaurants, as well as grocery stores, compete for the snack dollar.

Table 15.13 Snacks at vending machines and mobile vendors

| Total household spending | $2,251,379,130.00 |
| Average household spends | 18.59 |

	AVERAGE HOUSEHOLD SPENDING	BEST CUSTOMERS (index)	BIGGEST CUSTOMERS (market share)
AGE OF HOUSEHOLDER			
Average household	**$18.59**	**100**	**100.0%**
Under age 25	32.53	175	11.6
Aged 25 to 34	21.38	115	19.2
Aged 35 to 44	24.35	131	23.7
Aged 45 to 54	23.34	126	26.0
Aged 55 to 64	14.94	80	14.2
Aged 65 to 74	6.71	36	3.9
Aged 75 or older	2.78	15	1.4

	AVERAGE HOUSEHOLD SPENDING	BEST CUSTOMERS (index)	BIGGEST CUSTOMERS (market share)
HOUSEHOLD INCOME			
Average household	**$18.59**	**100**	**100.0%**
Under $20,000	13.70	74	16.1
$20,000 to $39,999	17.54	94	21.6
$40,000 to $49,999	22.16	119	11.3
$50,000 to $69,999	17.79	96	13.7
$70,000 to $79,999	19.81	107	6.4
$80,000 to $99,999	20.29	109	9.1
$100,000 or more	24.16	130	22.3
HOUSEHOLD TYPE			
Average household	**18.59**	**100**	**100.0**
Married couples	20.27	109	53.8
Married couples, no children	13.11	71	15.0
Married couples, with children	25.24	136	31.6
Oldest child under age 6	18.34	99	4.2
Oldest child aged 6 to 17	28.83	155	18.2
Oldest child aged 18 or older	23.43	126	9.1
Single parent with child under age 18	26.92	145	8.5
Single person	12.14	65	19.1
RACE AND HISPANIC ORIGIN			
Average household	**18.59**	**100**	**100.0**
Asian	28.30	152	6.5
Black	13.31	72	8.8
Hispanic	23.46	126	15.4
Non-Hispanic white and other	18.65	100	76.1
REGION			
Average household	**18.59**	**100**	**100.0**
Northeast	21.77	117	21.5
Midwest	18.44	99	22.1
South	18.77	101	37.1
West	15.85	85	19.3
EDUCATION			
Average household	**18.59**	**100**	**100.0**
Less than high school graduate	16.19	87	12.4
High school graduate	20.50	110	28.2
Some college	21.73	117	24.6
Associate's degree	17.10	92	8.7
Bachelor's degree or more	16.20	87	25.9
Bachelor's degree	16.31	88	16.6
Master's, professional, doctoral degree	16.00	86	9.3

Note: Market shares may not sum to 100.0 because of rounding and missing categories by household type. "Asian" and "black" include Hispanics and non-Hispanics who identify themselves as being of the respective race alone. "Hispanic" includes people of any race who identify themselves as Hispanic. "Other" includes people who identify themselves as non-Hispanic and as Alaska Native, American Indian, Asian (who are also included in the "Asian" row), or Native Hawaiian or other Pacific Islander as well as non-Hispanics reporting more than one race.

Source: Calculations by New Strategist based on the Bureau of Labor Statistics' 2010 Consumer Expenditure Survey

Chapter 16.

Shelter

Household Spending on Shelter, 2010

Americans spend more on shelter than on any other category, an average of $9,812 per household in 2010. Almost one-third of this total goes toward mortgage interest, while 18 percent is devoted to property taxes. The average household spent 9 percent more on shelter in 2010 than in 2000, after adjusting for inflation. Spending on mortgage interest was flat over the decade, first rising then falling, for a 2000-to-2010 net gain of 1 percent, whereas spending on property taxes increased 26 percent.

The biggest spenders on shelter are the most-affluent households, who tend to buy the most-expensive homes. But the biggest spenders on many items, such as homeowner's insurance and property taxes, are older householders because they have the highest homeownership rate. Older homeowners are also the biggest spenders on maintenance and repair services since they are more likely than younger homeowners to hire others to do the work rather than do it themselves. Average household spending on shelter should continue to rise as the population ages.

Spending on mortgage interest

(average annual spending by households on mortgage interest, 2000, 2006, and 2010; in 2010 dollars)

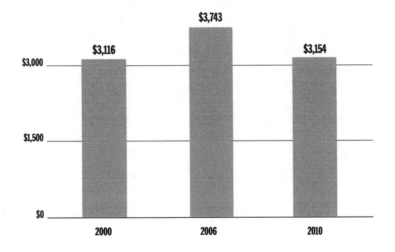

Table 16.1   Shelter spending, 2000 to 2010

(average annual household spending on shelter by category, 2000, 2006, and 2010; percent change in spending, 2000–06, 2000–10, and 2006–10; in 2010 dollars; ranked by amount spent)

	2010 average household spending	2006 average household spending (in 2010$)	2000 average household spending (in 2010$)	percent change		
				2006–10	2000–06	2000–10
AVERAGE ANNUAL SPENDING						
Average household spending on shelter	**$9,811.78**	**$10,462.96**	**$9,008.75**	**–6.2%**	**16.1%**	**8.9%**
Mortgage interest	3,154.47	3,743.47	3,115.69	–15.7	20.1	1.2
Rent	2,773.24	2,635.81	2,503.88	5.2	5.3	10.8
Property taxes	1,813.84	1,783.31	1,441.74	1.7	23.7	25.8
Maintenance and repair services, owned home	576.13	605.28	555.80	–4.8	8.9	3.7
Insurance, homeowner's	344.52	370.48	297.38	–7.0	24.6	15.9
Vacation homes, owned	278.94	199.70	187.30	39.7	6.6	48.9
Home equity loan/line of credit interest	196.74	315.50	225.38	–37.6	40.0	–12.7
Maintenance and repair materials, owned home	68.48	104.29	98.87	–34.3	5.5	–30.7
Property management and security, owned home	62.37	64.01	39.24	–2.6	63.1	58.9
Maintenance and repair services and materials, rented home	33.36	80.46	23.65	–58.5	240.2	41.0
Insurance, tenant's	12.28	10.30	11.22	19.3	–8.2	9.5

	2006–10	2000–06	2000–10	percentage point change		
				2006–10	2000–06	2000–10
PERCENT DISTRIBUTION OF SPENDING						
Average household spending on shelter	**100.0%**	**100.0%**	**100.0%**	–	–	–
Mortgage interest	32.1	35.8	34.6	–3.6	1.2	–2.4
Rent	28.3	25.2	27.8	3.1	–2.6	0.5
Property taxes	18.5	17.0	16.0	1.4	1.0	2.5
Maintenance and repair services, owned home	5.9	5.8	6.2	0.1	–0.4	–0.3
Insurance, homeowner's	3.5	3.5	3.3	0.0	0.2	0.2
Vacation homes, owned	2.8	1.9	2.1	0.9	–0.2	0.8
Home equity loan/line of credit interest	2.0	3.0	2.5	–1.0	0.5	–0.5
Maintenance and repair materials, owned home	0.7	1.0	1.1	–0.3	–0.1	–0.4
Property management and security, owned home	0.6	0.6	0.4	0.0	0.2	0.2
Maintenance and repair services and materials, rented home	0.3	0.8	0.3	–0.4	0.5	0.1
Insurance, tenant's	0.1	0.1	0.1	0.0	0.0	0.0

Note: Numbers do not add to total because not all categories are shown. "–" means not applicable.

Source: Bureau of Labor Statistics, 2000, 2006, and 2010 Consumer Expenditure Surveys; calculations by New Strategist

Home Equity Loan and Line of Credit Interest

Best customers: **Householders aged 45 to 64**
Married couples without children at home
Married couples with school-aged or older children at home
Non-Hispanic whites
Households in the West and Northeast

Customer trends: **Average household spending on home equity loan and line of credit interest is**
likely to continue to decline as home values fall, households pay down their debt,
and banks tighten lending standards.

Householders aged 45 to 64 spend 43 to 62 percent more than the average household on interest for home equity loans and lines of credit. Married couples with school-aged children spend 42 percent more than average, while couples with adult children at home spend over two-and-one-half times the average. Married couples without children at home outspend the average by 24 percent. Non-Hispanic whites spend 19 percent more than average on interest for home equity loans and lines of credit and control 90 percent of the market. Households in the West and Northeast spend, respectively, 58 and 22 percent above average on this item.

Average household spending on interest for home equity loans and lines of credit increased by an enormous 40 percent between 2000 and the overall peak-spending year of 2006, after adjusting for inflation. But when the housing bubble collapsed, so did spending on this item, plummeting 38 percent between 2006 and 2010 for an aggregate 13 percent decline over the decade. Spending on home equity interest is likely to continue to decline as home values fall, households pay down their debt, and banks tighten lending standards.

Table 16.2 Home equity loan and line of credit interest

Total household spending $23,826,591,180.00
Average household spends 196.74

	AVERAGE HOUSEHOLD SPENDING	BEST CUSTOMERS (index)	BIGGEST CUSTOMERS (market share)
AGE OF HOUSEHOLDER			
Average household	**$196.74**	**100**	**100.0%**
Under age 25	67.48	34	2.3
Aged 25 to 34	54.57	28	4.6
Aged 35 to 44	214.87	109	19.8
Aged 45 to 54	318.62	162	33.5
Aged 55 to 64	281.39	143	25.2
Aged 65 to 74	196.42	100	10.7
Aged 75 or older	79.94	41	3.9

	AVERAGE HOUSEHOLD SPENDING	BEST CUSTOMERS (index)	BIGGEST CUSTOMERS (market share)
HOUSEHOLD INCOME			
Average household	**$196.74**	**100**	**100.0%**
Under $20,000	50.45	26	5.6
$20,000 to $39,999	71.92	37	8.4
$40,000 to $49,999	109.58	56	5.3
$50,000 to $69,999	153.61	78	11.2
$70,000 to $79,999	189.65	96	5.8
$80,000 to $99,999	319.76	163	13.6
$100,000 or more	576.48	293	50.2
HOUSEHOLD TYPE			
Average household	**196.74**	**100**	**100.0**
Married couples	288.63	147	72.4
Married couples, no children	244.87	124	26.4
Married couples, with children	337.53	172	39.9
Oldest child under age 6	218.84	111	4.8
Oldest child aged 6 to 17	278.98	142	16.7
Oldest child aged 18 or older	503.26	256	18.5
Single parent with child under age 18	75.60	38	2.3
Single person	98.12	50	14.6
RACE AND HISPANIC ORIGIN			
Average household	**196.74**	**100**	**100.0**
Asian	190.05	97	4.1
Black	81.85	42	5.1
Hispanic	82.99	42	5.1
Non-Hispanic white and other	233.29	119	89.9
REGION			
Average household	**196.74**	**100**	**100.0**
Northeast	239.72	122	22.4
Midwest	160.40	82	18.2
South	127.04	65	23.7
West	310.60	158	35.8
EDUCATION			
Average household	**196.74**	**100**	**100.0**
Less than high school graduate	69.12	35	5.0
High school graduate	155.41	79	20.2
Some college	171.63	87	18.3
Associate's degree	177.00	90	8.5
Bachelor's degree or more	317.67	161	48.0
Bachelor's degree	286.92	146	27.5
Master's, professional, doctoral degree	371.35	189	20.4

Note: Market shares may not sum to 100.0 because of rounding and missing categories by household type. "Asian" and "black" include Hispanics and non-Hispanics who identify themselves as being of the respective race alone. "Hispanic" includes people of any race who identify themselves as Hispanic. "Other" includes people who identify themselves as non-Hispanic and as Alaska Native, American Indian, Asian (who are also included in the "Asian" row), or Native Hawaiian or other Pacific Islander as well as non-Hispanics reporting more than one race.

Source: Calculations by New Strategist based on the Bureau of Labor Statistics' 2010 Consumer Expenditure Survey

Insurance, Homeowner's

Best customers: Householders aged 55 or older
                                Married couples without children at home
                                Married couples with school-aged or older children at home

Customer trends: Average household spending on homeowner's insurance may rise along with
                                disaster-related insurance claims and the aging of the population.

Homeownership rises with age. This explains why householders aged 55 or older spend from 25 to 45 percent more than average on homeowner's insurance. Married couples without children at home (most of them empty-nesters) spend 41 percent more than average on this item. Those with school-aged or older children at home spend 25 to 44 percent more than average on homeowner's insurance.

Average household spending on homeowner's insurance rose 25 percent between 2000 and the overall peak-spending year of 2006, after adjusting for inflation, and then declined 7 percent in the ensuring four years as housing values and the homeownership rate declined. Average household spending on this item may increase as boomers age and disaster-related insurance claims boost rates.

Table 16.3   Insurance, homeowner's

Total household spending $41,723,783,640.00
Average household spends   344.52

	AVERAGE HOUSEHOLD SPENDING	BEST CUSTOMERS (index)	BIGGEST CUSTOMERS (market share)
AGE OF HOUSEHOLDER			
Average household	**$344.52**	**100**	**100.0%**
Under age 25	50.44	15	1.0
Aged 25 to 34	184.30	53	8.9
Aged 35 to 44	324.95	94	17.1
Aged 45 to 54	360.97	105	21.7
Aged 55 to 64	466.18	135	23.9
Aged 65 to 74	500.53	145	15.6
Aged 75 or older	429.22	125	11.9

	AVERAGE HOUSEHOLD SPENDING	BEST CUSTOMERS (index)	BIGGEST CUSTOMERS (market share)
HOUSEHOLD INCOME			
Average household	**$344.52**	**100**	**100.0%**
Under $20,000	160.92	47	10.2
$20,000 to $39,999	251.54	73	16.7
$40,000 to $49,999	305.20	89	8.4
$50,000 to $69,999	354.35	103	14.8
$70,000 to $79,999	377.92	110	6.6
$80,000 to $99,999	449.28	130	10.9
$100,000 or more	653.29	190	32.5
HOUSEHOLD TYPE			
Average household	**344.52**	**100**	**100.0**
Married couples	447.47	130	64.1
Married couples, no children	487.25	141	30.0
Married couples, with children	430.46	125	29.1
Oldest child under age 6	320.47	93	4.0
Oldest child aged 6 to 17	431.18	125	14.7
Oldest child aged 18 or older	494.51	144	10.4
Single parent with child under age 18	143.10	42	2.4
Single person	253.05	73	21.5
RACE AND HISPANIC ORIGIN			
Average household	**344.52**	**100**	**100.0**
Asian	302.35	88	3.7
Black	209.78	61	7.5
Hispanic	204.89	59	7.2
Non-Hispanic white and other	389.02	113	85.6
REGION			
Average household	**344.52**	**100**	**100.0**
Northeast	322.39	94	17.2
Midwest	349.43	101	22.6
South	389.21	113	41.5
West	285.19	83	18.8
EDUCATION			
Average household	**344.52**	**100**	**100.0**
Less than high school graduate	187.70	54	7.8
High school graduate	304.95	89	22.6
Some college	312.55	91	19.1
Associate's degree	336.21	98	9.2
Bachelor's degree or more	479.20	139	41.3
Bachelor's degree	429.83	125	23.6
Master's, professional, doctoral degree	565.40	164	17.8

Note: Market shares may not sum to 100.0 because of rounding and missing categories by household type. "Asian" and "black" include Hispanics and non-Hispanics who identify themselves as being of the respective race alone. "Hispanic" includes people of any race who identify themselves as Hispanic. "Other" includes people who identify themselves as non-Hispanic and as Alaska Native, American Indian, Asian (who are also included in the "Asian" row), or Native Hawaiian or other Pacific Islander as well as non-Hispanics reporting more than one race.

Source: Calculations by New Strategist based on the Bureau of Labor Statistics' 2010 Consumer Expenditure Survey

Insurance, Tenant's

Best customers: **Householders under age 45**
Single parents
People who live alone
Blacks and Asians
Households in the West

Customer trends: **Average household spending on tenant's insurance will continue to grow as the large millennial generation fills the best-customer age groups and renting becomes more common.**

Young families and people who live alone are the best customers of tenant's insurance because they are most likely to be renters. Householders under age 45 spend 15 to 36 percent more than the average household on renter's insurance. Single parents spend 30 percent more than average on tenant's insurance, and people who live alone spend 24 percent more. Blacks and Asians spend, respectively, 30 and 25 percent more than average on this item. Western householders spend 21 percent more than average on tenant's insurance.

Average household spending on tenant's insurance grew by a strong 19 percent between 2006 and 2010, after adjusting for inflation, after having fallen by 8 percent from 2000 and 2006. Behind the increase since 2006 is the rise in the number of renters following the collapse of the housing market. Spending on this item will continue to grow as the large millennial generation fills the best-customer age groups and renting becomes more common.

Table 16.4   Insurance, tenant's

Total household spending	$1,487,193,960.00
Average household spends	12.28

	AVERAGE HOUSEHOLD SPENDING	BEST CUSTOMERS (index)	BIGGEST CUSTOMERS (market share)
AGE OF HOUSEHOLDER			
Average household	**$12.28**	**100**	**100.0%**
Under age 25	14.08	115	7.6
Aged 25 to 34	16.68	136	22.6
Aged 35 to 44	15.83	129	23.3
Aged 45 to 54	10.06	82	16.9
Aged 55 to 64	9.07	74	13.0
Aged 65 to 74	12.11	99	10.6
Aged 75 or older	7.59	62	5.9

	AVERAGE HOUSEHOLD SPENDING	BEST CUSTOMERS (index)	BIGGEST CUSTOMERS (market share)
HOUSEHOLD INCOME			
Average household	**$12.28**	**100**	**100.0%**
Under $20,000	7.54	61	13.4
$20,000 to $39,999	13.62	111	25.4
$40,000 to $49,999	15.43	126	11.9
$50,000 to $69,999	15.28	124	17.8
$70,000 to $79,999	12.80	104	6.2
$80,000 to $99,999	12.50	102	8.5
$100,000 or more	12.01	98	16.8
HOUSEHOLD TYPE			
Average household	**12.28**	**100**	**100.0**
Married couples	9.29	76	37.3
Married couples, no children	9.24	75	16.0
Married couples, with children	10.30	84	19.5
Oldest child under age 6	13.98	114	4.9
Oldest child aged 6 to 17	11.83	96	11.3
Oldest child aged 18 or older	5.61	46	3.3
Single parent with child under age 18	15.97	130	7.7
Single person	15.23	124	36.3
RACE AND HISPANIC ORIGIN			
Average household	**12.28**	**100**	**100.0**
Asian	15.41	125	5.3
Black	16.02	130	16.0
Hispanic	9.84	80	9.8
Non-Hispanic white and other	12.07	98	74.5
REGION			
Average household	**12.28**	**100**	**100.0**
Northeast	10.00	81	14.9
Midwest	11.03	90	20.0
South	12.60	103	37.7
West	14.85	121	27.4
EDUCATION			
Average household	**12.28**	**100**	**100.0**
Less than high school graduate	7.14	58	8.3
High school graduate	7.94	65	16.5
Some college	13.91	113	23.8
Associate's degree	13.81	112	10.6
Bachelor's degree or more	16.86	137	40.8
Bachelor's degree	17.12	139	26.3
Master's, professional, doctoral degree	16.39	133	14.4

Note: Market shares may not sum to 100.0 because of rounding and missing categories by household type. "Asian" and "black" include Hispanics and non-Hispanics who identify themselves as being of the respective race alone. "Hispanic" includes people of any race who identify themselves as Hispanic. "Other" includes people who identify themselves as non-Hispanic and as Alaska Native, American Indian, Asian (who are also included in the "Asian" row), or Native Hawaiian or other Pacific Islander as well as non-Hispanics reporting more than one race.

Source: Calculations by New Strategist based on the Bureau of Labor Statistics' 2010 Consumer Expenditure Survey

Maintenance and Repair Materials, Owned Home

Best customers: **Householders aged 45 to 64**
Married couples
Households in the Midwest

Customer trends: **Average household spending on maintenance and repair materials for owned homes may rise as boomers fix up houses they cannot sell.**

Older married couples are the best customers of maintenance and repair materials for the owned home. These do-it-yourselfers are likely to be homeowners, and they are still able to tackle home improvement tasks themselves. Householders aged 45 to 64 spend 24 to 43 percent more than average on this item. Married couples without children at home (most of them empty-nesters) spend 45 percent more than average on maintenance and repair materials, and couples with children at home spend 49 percent more than average on this item. The Midwest is the only region in which householders spend more than average on maintenance and repair materials for owned homes—34 percent more.

Average household spending on maintenance and repair materials for owned homes, which had grown slowly between 2000 and the overall peak-spending year of 2006, fell by a significant 34 percent between 2006 and 2010, after adjusting for inflation. Behind the decline was the Great Recession and household belt tightening. Average household spending on maintenance and repair materials may begin to rise again as boomers fix up houses they cannot sell.

Table 16.5 Maintenance and repair materials, owned home

Total household spending $8,293,407,360.00
Average household spends   68.48

	AVERAGE HOUSEHOLD SPENDING	BEST CUSTOMERS (index)	BIGGEST CUSTOMERS (market share)
AGE OF HOUSEHOLDER			
Average household	**$68.48**	**100**	**100.0%**
Under age 25	40.21	59	3.9
Aged 25 to 34	50.94	74	12.4
Aged 35 to 44	71.47	104	18.9
Aged 45 to 54	98.10	143	29.6
Aged 55 to 64	84.63	124	21.8
Aged 65 to 74	58.58	86	9.2
Aged 75 or older	30.17	44	4.2

	AVERAGE HOUSEHOLD SPENDING	BEST CUSTOMERS (index)	BIGGEST CUSTOMERS (market share)
HOUSEHOLD INCOME			
Average household	**$68.48**	**100**	**100.0%**
Under $20,000	20.96	31	6.7
$20,000 to $39,999	41.07	60	13.7
$40,000 to $49,999	42.44	62	5.9
$50,000 to $69,999	95.49	139	20.0
$70,000 to $79,999	120.01	175	10.5
$80,000 to $99,999	144.01	210	17.5
$100,000 or more	102.64	150	25.7
HOUSEHOLD TYPE			
Average household	**68.48**	**100**	**100.0**
Married couples	100.84	147	72.6
Married couples, no children	99.23	145	30.8
Married couples, with children	101.82	149	34.6
Oldest child under age 6	91.81	134	5.7
Oldest child aged 6 to 17	106.63	156	18.3
Oldest child aged 18 or older	99.92	146	10.5
Single parent with child under age 18	19.30	28	1.7
Single person	28.45	42	12.2
RACE AND HISPANIC ORIGIN			
Average household	**68.48**	**100**	**100.0**
Asian	30.43	44	1.9
Black	23.01	34	4.1
Hispanic	43.56	64	7.7
Non-Hispanic white and other	79.67	116	88.2
REGION			
Average household	**68.48**	**100**	**100.0**
Northeast	58.37	85	15.6
Midwest	91.48	134	29.8
South	62.21	91	33.3
West	64.21	94	21.2
EDUCATION			
Average household	**68.48**	**100**	**100.0**
Less than high school graduate	37.13	54	7.7
High school graduate	74.39	109	27.7
Some college	49.42	72	15.2
Associate's degree	72.72	106	10.0
Bachelor's degree or more	90.63	132	39.3
Bachelor's degree	94.83	138	26.2
Master's, professional, doctoral degree	83.30	122	13.2

Note: Market shares may not sum to 100.0 because of rounding and missing categories by household type. "Asian" and "black" include Hispanics and non-Hispanics who identify themselves as being of the respective race alone. "Hispanic" includes people of any race who identify themselves as Hispanic. "Other" includes people who identify themselves as non-Hispanic and as Alaska Native, American Indian, Asian (who are also included in the "Asian" row), or Native Hawaiian or other Pacific Islander as well as non-Hispanics reporting more than one race.

Source: Calculations by New Strategist based on the Bureau of Labor Statistics' 2010 Consumer Expenditure Survey

Maintenance and Repair Services and Materials, Rented Home

Best customers: **Householders aged 35 to 64**
                          Married couples with school-aged children
                          People who live alone
                          Asians
                          Households in the Northeast

Customer trends: **Average household spending on maintenance and repair services and materials**
                          for rented homes may rise along with the number of renters.

Middle-aged householders are the best customers of maintenance and repair services and materials for rented homes. Householders ranging in age from 35 to 64 spend 10 to 25 percent more than average on this item. Married couples with school-aged children spend 33 percent more than average on maintenance and repair services and materials for rented homes, and people who live alone spend 37 percent more than average on this item. Asian householders outspend the average by two-and-one-half. Households in the Northeast spend 30 percent more than average on maintenance and repair services and materials for rented homes.

Average household spending on maintenance and repair services and materials for rented homes, which had exploded between 2000 and the overall peak-spending year of 2006, fell by a significant 59 percent between 2006 and 2010, after adjusting for inflation. Behind the decline was the Great Recession and household belt tightening. Average household spending on maintenance and repair services and materials for rented homes may begin to rise again as renters increase in number.

Table 16.6 Maintenance and repair services and materials, rented home

Total household spending $4,040,129,520.00
Average household spends   33.36

	AVERAGE HOUSEHOLD SPENDING	BEST CUSTOMERS (index)	BIGGEST CUSTOMERS (market share)
AGE OF HOUSEHOLDER			
Average household	**$33.36**	**100**	**100.0%**
Under age 25	23.48	70	4.7
Aged 25 to 34	35.34	106	17.6
Aged 35 to 44	40.04	120	21.7
Aged 45 to 54	36.60	110	22.7
Aged 55 to 64	41.74	125	22.1
Aged 65 to 74	14.90	45	4.8
Aged 75 or older	22.42	67	6.4

	AVERAGE HOUSEHOLD SPENDING	BEST CUSTOMERS (index)	BIGGEST CUSTOMERS (market share)
HOUSEHOLD INCOME			
Average household	**$33.36**	**100**	**100.0%**
Under $20,000	49.48	148	32.4
$20,000 to $39,999	16.58	50	11.4
$40,000 to $49,999	12.14	36	3.4
$50,000 to $69,999	21.06	63	9.1
$70,000 to $79,999	18.66	56	3.3
$80,000 to $99,999	51.49	154	12.9
$100,000 or more	53.59	161	27.5
HOUSEHOLD TYPE			
Average household	**33.36**	**100**	**100.0**
Married couples	29.42	88	43.5
Married couples, no children	24.97	75	15.9
Married couples, with children	28.88	87	20.1
Oldest child under age 6	23.23	70	3.0
Oldest child aged 6 to 17	44.22	133	15.6
Oldest child aged 18 or older	7.23	22	1.6
Single parent with child under age 18	15.13	45	2.7
Single person	45.79	137	40.2
RACE AND HISPANIC ORIGIN			
Average household	**33.36**	**100**	**100.0**
Asian	80.17	240	10.2
Black	18.62	56	6.8
Hispanic	17.63	53	6.4
Non-Hispanic white and other	38.28	115	87.0
REGION			
Average household	**33.36**	**100**	**100.0**
Northeast	43.29	130	23.8
Midwest	18.05	54	12.1
South	35.71	107	39.3
West	36.58	110	24.8
EDUCATION			
Average household	**33.36**	**100**	**100.0**
Less than high school graduate	15.55	47	6.7
High school graduate	23.14	69	17.7
Some college	29.33	88	18.5
Associate's degree	20.26	61	5.7
Bachelor's degree or more	57.74	173	51.4
Bachelor's degree	46.53	139	26.3
Master's, professional, doctoral degree	77.30	232	25.1

Note: Market shares may not sum to 100.0 because of rounding and missing categories by household type. "Asian" and "black" include Hispanics and non-Hispanics who identify themselves as being of the respective race alone. "Hispanic" includes people of any race who identify themselves as Hispanic. "Other" includes people who identify themselves as non-Hispanic and as Alaska Native, American Indian, Asian (who are also included in the "Asian" row), or Native Hawaiian or other Pacific Islander as well as non-Hispanics reporting more than one race.

Source: Calculations by New Strategist based on the Bureau of Labor Statistics' 2010 Consumer Expenditure Survey

Maintenance and Repair Services, Owned Home

Best customers: **Householders aged 55 or older**
                      Married couples without children at home
                      Non-Hispanic whites
                      Households in the Northeast

Customer trends: **Average household spending on maintenance and repair services for owned**
                      homes will continue to rise as aging boomers hire others to maintain and improve
                      their homes.

The best customers of maintenance and repair services for owned homes are householders aged 55 or older. Some are physically unable to do the work themselves, while others can better afford to hire help after the expenses of childrearing are over. Householders aged 55 or older spend 24 to 74 percent more than average on this item and control 53 percent of the market. Married couples without children at home (most of them empty-nesters) spend 66 percent more than average on maintenance and repair services for their homes. Non-Hispanic whites, because they are most likely to be homeowners, spend 20 percent more than average on this item and represent 91 percent of the market. Households in the Northeast outspend the average by 36 percent.

Average household spending on maintenance and repair services for owned homes rose 4 percent between 2000 and 2010, after adjusting for inflation. Behind the increase is the aging of the baby-boom generation into the best-customer lifestage, a trend that will continue to drive growth in this market.

Table 16.7 Maintenance and repair services, owned home

| Total household spending | $69,773,375,910.00 |
| Average household spends | 576.13 |

	AVERAGE HOUSEHOLD SPENDING	BEST CUSTOMERS (index)	BIGGEST CUSTOMERS (market share)
AGE OF HOUSEHOLDER			
Average household	**$576.13**	**100**	**100.0%**
Under age 25	70.07	12	0.8
Aged 25 to 34	278.95	48	8.1
Aged 35 to 44	490.59	85	15.4
Aged 45 to 54	624.98	108	22.4
Aged 55 to 64	712.18	124	21.8
Aged 65 to 74	1,003.45	174	18.7
Aged 75 or older	769.58	134	12.7

	AVERAGE HOUSEHOLD SPENDING	BEST CUSTOMERS (index)	BIGGEST CUSTOMERS (market share)
HOUSEHOLD INCOME			
Average household	**$576.13**	**100**	**100.0%**
Under $20,000	193.49	34	7.3
$20,000 to $39,999	375.29	65	14.9
$40,000 to $49,999	461.47	80	7.6
$50,000 to $69,999	597.55	104	14.9
$70,000 to $79,999	554.54	96	5.8
$80,000 to $99,999	593.92	103	8.6
$100,000 or more	1,375.67	239	40.9
HOUSEHOLD TYPE			
Average household	**576.13**	**100**	**100.0**
Married couples	770.88	134	66.0
Married couples, no children	955.66	166	35.2
Married couples, with children	676.27	117	27.3
Oldest child under age 6	727.51	126	5.4
Oldest child aged 6 to 17	592.56	103	12.1
Oldest child aged 18 or older	782.24	136	9.8
Single parent with child under age 18	166.59	29	1.7
Single person	418.90	73	21.3
RACE AND HISPANIC ORIGIN			
Average household	**576.13**	**100**	**100.0**
Asian	642.66	112	4.7
Black	228.43	40	4.9
Hispanic	202.97	35	4.3
Non-Hispanic white and other	691.01	120	90.9
REGION			
Average household	**576.13**	**100**	**100.0**
Northeast	785.36	136	25.0
Midwest	567.83	99	22.0
South	506.59	88	32.3
West	527.43	92	20.7
EDUCATION			
Average household	**576.13**	**100**	**100.0**
Less than high school graduate	170.21	30	4.2
High school graduate	397.94	69	17.6
Some college	417.25	72	15.2
Associate's degree	450.14	78	7.4
Bachelor's degree or more	1,076.96	187	55.5
Bachelor's degree	914.92	159	30.0
Master's, professional, doctoral degree	1,359.88	236	25.5

Note: Market shares may not sum to 100.0 because of rounding and missing categories by household type. "Asian" and "black" include Hispanics and non-Hispanics who identify themselves as being of the respective race alone. "Hispanic" includes people of any race who identify themselves as Hispanic. "Other" includes people who identify themselves as non-Hispanic and as Alaska Native, American Indian, Asian (who are also included in the "Asian" row), or Native Hawaiian or other Pacific Islander as well as non-Hispanics reporting more than one race.

Source: Calculations by New Strategist based on the Bureau of Labor Statistics' 2010 Consumer Expenditure Survey

Mortgage Interest

Best customers:	**Householders aged 35 to 54** **Married couples with children at home** **Asians** **Households in the West**
Customer trends:	**Average household spending on mortgage interest will continue to decline in the years ahead as a growing share of younger householders choose to rent rather than buy.**

The longer people have owned their home, the less they spend on mortgage interest. This explains why older householders spend less than younger ones, and why empty-nesters spend less than couples with children. Householders aged 35 to 44 spend the most on mortgage interest—58 percent more than the average household. Householders aged 45 to 54 rank second, spending 38 percent more than average. Married couples with children under age 18 spend close to twice the average on mortgage interest, while those with adult children at home spend 34 percent more than average. Higher home prices in the West explain why households there spend 40 percent more than average on mortgage interest. Because many Asians live in the West, their spending on mortgage interest is 39 percent above average.

Average household spending on mortgage interest rose 20 percent between 2000 and the overall peak-spending year of 2006, after adjusting for inflation, then dropped 16 percent over the four ensuing years as housing prices declined and the rate of homeownership fell. Average household spending on mortgage interest will continue to decline in the years ahead as a growing share of younger householders choose to rent rather than buy.

Table 16.8 Mortgage interest

Total household spending	$382,028,398,290.00
Average household spends	3,154.47

	AVERAGE HOUSEHOLD SPENDING	BEST CUSTOMERS (index)	BIGGEST CUSTOMERS (market share)
AGE OF HOUSEHOLDER			
Average household	**$3,154.47**	**100**	**100.0%**
Under age 25	618.08	20	1.3
Aged 25 to 34	3,360.47	107	17.7
Aged 35 to 44	4,981.07	158	28.6
Aged 45 to 54	4,348.67	138	28.5
Aged 55 to 64	2,917.09	92	16.3
Aged 65 to 74	1,691.56	54	5.8
Aged 75 or older	593.09	19	1.8

	AVERAGE HOUSEHOLD SPENDING	BEST CUSTOMERS (index)	BIGGEST CUSTOMERS (market share)
HOUSEHOLD INCOME			
Average household	**$3,154.47**	**100**	**100.0%**
Under $20,000	646.93	21	4.5
$20,000 to $39,999	1,312.83	42	9.5
$40,000 to $49,999	2,390.54	76	7.2
$50,000 to $69,999	3,315.23	105	15.1
$70,000 to $79,999	3,956.17	125	7.5
$80,000 to $99,999	5,172.14	164	13.7
$100,000 or more	7,832.62	248	42.6
HOUSEHOLD TYPE			
Average household	**3,154.47**	**100**	**100.0**
Married couples	4,509.21	143	70.5
Married couples, no children	3,415.12	108	23.0
Married couples, with children	5,502.32	174	40.6
Oldest child under age 6	6,305.40	200	8.6
Oldest child aged 6 to 17	5,996.50	190	22.4
Oldest child aged 18 or older	4,221.28	134	9.7
Single parent with child under age 18	2,228.51	71	4.2
Single person	1,452.84	46	13.5
RACE AND HISPANIC ORIGIN			
Average household	**3,154.47**	**100**	**100.0**
Asian	4,392.17	139	5.9
Black	2,159.78	68	8.4
Hispanic	2,827.51	90	10.9
Non-Hispanic white and other	3,368.21	107	81.0
REGION			
Average household	**3,154.47**	**100**	**100.0**
Northeast	3,000.75	95	17.5
Midwest	2,680.00	85	18.9
South	2,742.90	87	31.9
West	4,412.76	140	31.7
EDUCATION			
Average household	**3,154.47**	**100**	**100.0**
Less than high school graduate	1,372.81	44	6.2
High school graduate	2,093.10	66	16.9
Some college	2,625.69	83	17.5
Associate's degree	3,305.73	105	9.9
Bachelor's degree or more	5,249.52	166	49.4
Bachelor's degree	4,862.55	154	29.1
Master's, professional, doctoral degree	5,925.18	188	20.3

Note: Market shares may not sum to 100.0 because of rounding and missing categories by household type. "Asian" and "black" include Hispanics and non-Hispanics who identify themselves as being of the respective race alone. "Hispanic" includes people of any race who identify themselves as Hispanic. "Other" includes people who identify themselves as non-Hispanic and as Alaska Native, American Indian, Asian (who are also included in the "Asian" row), or Native Hawaiian or other Pacific Islander as well as non-Hispanics reporting more than one race.

Source: Calculations by New Strategist based on the Bureau of Labor Statistics' 2010 Consumer Expenditure Survey

Property Management and Security, Owned Home

Best customers:
Householders aged 65 or older
Married couples without children at home
Married couples with preschoolers
People who live alone
Asians and non-Hispanic whites
Households in the Northeast

Customer trends:
Average household spending on property management and security will rise along with the aging of the population.

Older householders are the best customers of property management and security for owned homes. Householders aged 65 or older spend 53 to 65 percent more than average on this item. Married couples without children at home (most of them empty-nesters) spend 53 percent more than average on property management and security. Single-person households (many of them older) spend 17 percent more. Married couples with preschoolers spend two-thirds more than average on property management and security. Asians spend twice the average on these property services, but non-Hispanic whites, who spend one-fifth more than average, account for 91 percent of the market. Northeastern householders spend twice the average on property management and security.

Average household spending on property management and security for owned homes increased by a massive 63 percent between 2000 and the overall peak-spending year of 2006, after adjusting for inflation, and then declined slightly over the next four years. Average household spending on this item may rise again along with the aging of the population.

Table 16.9 Property management and security, owned home

Total household spending $7,553,443,590.00
Average household spends   62.37

	AVERAGE HOUSEHOLD SPENDING	BEST CUSTOMERS (index)	BIGGEST CUSTOMERS (market share)
AGE OF HOUSEHOLDER			
Average household	**$62.37**	**100**	**100.0%**
Under age 25	6.90	11	0.7
Aged 25 to 34	49.79	80	13.3
Aged 35 to 44	52.34	84	15.2
Aged 45 to 54	69.40	111	23.0
Aged 55 to 64	55.08	88	15.6
Aged 65 to 74	95.23	153	16.4
Aged 75 or older	103.07	165	15.8

	AVERAGE HOUSEHOLD SPENDING	BEST CUSTOMERS (index)	BIGGEST CUSTOMERS (market share)
HOUSEHOLD INCOME			
Average household	**$62.37**	**100**	**100.0%**
Under $20,000	30.35	49	10.6
$20,000 to $39,999	41.00	66	15.1
$40,000 to $49,999	53.11	85	8.0
$50,000 to $69,999	67.05	108	15.4
$70,000 to $79,999	51.24	82	4.9
$80,000 to $99,999	47.33	76	6.3
$100,000 or more	144.05	231	39.6
HOUSEHOLD TYPE			
Average household	**62.37**	**100**	**100.0**
Married couples	70.20	113	55.5
Married couples, no children	95.42	153	32.5
Married couples, with children	59.46	95	22.2
Oldest child under age 6	103.66	166	7.1
Oldest child aged 6 to 17	60.24	97	11.4
Oldest child aged 18 or older	31.98	51	3.7
Single parent with child under age 18	23.93	38	2.3
Single person	73.19	117	34.4
RACE AND HISPANIC ORIGIN			
Average household	**62.37**	**100**	**100.0**
Asian	125.52	201	8.6
Black	23.77	38	4.7
Hispanic	22.07	35	4.3
Non-Hispanic white and other	75.03	120	91.2
REGION			
Average household	**62.37**	**100**	**100.0**
Northeast	126.25	202	37.2
Midwest	28.83	46	10.3
South	45.69	73	26.9
West	70.63	113	25.7
EDUCATION			
Average household	**62.37**	**100**	**100.0**
Less than high school graduate	13.11	21	3.0
High school graduate	38.93	62	15.9
Some college	43.25	69	14.6
Associate's degree	48.04	77	7.3
Bachelor's degree or more	124.28	199	59.2
Bachelor's degree	103.54	166	31.4
Master's, professional, doctoral degree	160.50	257	27.8

Note: Market shares may not sum to 100.0 because of rounding and missing categories by household type. "Asian" and "black" include Hispanics and non-Hispanics who identify themselves as being of the respective race alone. "Hispanic" includes people of any race who identify themselves as Hispanic. "Other" includes people who identify themselves as non-Hispanic and as Alaska Native, American Indian, Asian (who are also included in the "Asian" row), or Native Hawaiian or other Pacific Islander as well as non-Hispanics reporting more than one race.

Source: Calculations by New Strategist based on the Bureau of Labor Statistics' 2010 Consumer Expenditure Survey

Property Taxes

Best customers: **Householders aged 45 to 74**
                                   Married couples
                                   Asians
                                   Households in the Northeast

Customer trends: **Average household spending on property taxes is likely to continue to rise as local governments raise taxes to pay for services.**

Households in the Northeast spend 57 percent more than average on property taxes, while households in the South spend 27 percent less than average. Variations in state property tax law and rates are behind these regional differences. Married couples spend 39 percent more than average on property taxes because they are likely to be homeowners. This also explains the 17 to 27 percent greater spending of householders aged 45 to 74. Asian households, a relatively well-off demographic, spend 31 percent more on property taxes than the average household.

Average household spending on property taxes rose 26 percent between 2000 and 2010, after adjusting for inflation. Behind the increase were the rise in homeownership earlier in the decade and tax hikes. Spending on property taxes is likely to continue to rise as local governments raise taxes to pay for services.

Table 16.10 Property taxes

Total household spending   **$219,668,720,880.00**
Average household spends   **1,813.84**

	AVERAGE HOUSEHOLD SPENDING	BEST CUSTOMERS (index)	BIGGEST CUSTOMERS (market share)
AGE OF HOUSEHOLDER			
Average household	**$1,813.84**	**100**	**100.0%**
Under age 25	251.96	14	0.9
Aged 25 to 34	1,108.31	61	10.2
Aged 35 to 44	1,975.05	109	19.7
Aged 45 to 54	2,295.30	127	26.2
Aged 55 to 64	2,216.18	122	21.5
Aged 65 to 74	2,124.67	117	12.6
Aged 75 or older	1,687.24	93	8.9

	AVERAGE HOUSEHOLD SPENDING	BEST CUSTOMERS (index)	BIGGEST CUSTOMERS (market share)
HOUSEHOLD INCOME			
Average household	**$1,813.84**	**100**	**100.0%**
Under $20,000	608.90	34	7.3
$20,000 to $39,999	1,083.74	60	13.7
$40,000 to $49,999	1,399.59	77	7.3
$50,000 to $69,999	1,768.68	98	14.0
$70,000 to $79,999	2,099.60	116	6.9
$80,000 to $99,999	2,609.22	144	12.0
$100,000 or more	4,102.66	226	38.8
HOUSEHOLD TYPE			
Average household	**1,813.84**	**100**	**100.0**
Married couples	2,521.11	139	68.6
Married couples, no children	2,488.39	137	29.1
Married couples, with children	2,652.28	146	34.0
Oldest child under age 6	2,205.52	122	5.2
Oldest child aged 6 to 17	2,725.22	150	17.7
Oldest child aged 18 or older	2,798.41	154	11.1
Single parent with child under age 18	956.52	53	3.1
Single person	1,063.03	59	17.2
RACE AND HISPANIC ORIGIN			
Average household	**1,813.84**	**100**	**100.0**
Asian	2,385.06	131	5.6
Black	894.11	49	6.0
Hispanic	1,218.09	67	8.2
Non-Hispanic white and other	2,056.51	113	86.0
REGION			
Average household	**1,813.84**	**100**	**100.0**
Northeast	2,839.43	157	28.7
Midwest	1,960.73	108	24.1
South	1,315.44	73	26.6
West	1,645.88	91	20.6
EDUCATION			
Average household	**1,813.84**	**100**	**100.0**
Less than high school graduate	874.47	48	6.9
High school graduate	1,403.58	77	19.8
Some college	1,444.46	80	16.7
Associate's degree	1,808.89	100	9.4
Bachelor's degree or more	2,881.14	159	47.2
Bachelor's degree	2,617.29	144	27.3
Master's, professional, doctoral degree	3,341.83	184	19.9

Note: Market shares may not sum to 100.0 because of rounding and missing categories by household type. "Asian" and "black" include Hispanics and non-Hispanics who identify themselves as being of the respective race alone. "Hispanic" includes people of any race who identify themselves as Hispanic. "Other" includes people who identify themselves as non-Hispanic and as Alaska Native, American Indian, Asian (who are also included in the "Asian" row), or Native Hawaiian or other Pacific Islander as well as non-Hispanics reporting more than one race.

Source: Calculations by New Strategist based on the Bureau of Labor Statistics' 2010 Consumer Expenditure Survey

Rent

Best customers:	**Householders under age 35** **Married couples with preschoolers** **Single parents** **People who live alone** **Asians, Hispanics, and blacks** **Households in the West and Northeast**
Customer trends:	**Average household spending on rent will continue to rise as renting becomes more common and the large millennial generation fills the best-customer age groups.**

Young adults are the best customers of rental housing. Householders under age 35 spend 68 to 74 percent more than average on this item. Married couples with preschoolers spend 21 percent more on rent than the average household. Single parents spend 46 percent more than average on rent, and single-person households (many of them young adults) spend 17 percent more. Asians, Hispanics, and blacks spend 44 to 73 percent more than average on this item and account for 44 percent of the market. Households in the West, where many Asians and Hispanics reside, spend 45 percent more than average on rent. Households in the Northeast spend 25 percent more.

Average household spending on rent climbed 11 percent between 2000 and 2010, after adjusting for inflation. As renting becomes more common and the large millennial generation fills the best-customer age groups, average household spending on rent will continue to rise.

Table 16.11 Rent

Total household spending	$335,858,776,680.00
Average household spends	2,773.24

	AVERAGE HOUSEHOLD SPENDING	BEST CUSTOMERS (index)	BIGGEST CUSTOMERS (market share)
AGE OF HOUSEHOLDER			
Average household	**$2,773.24**	**100**	**100.0%**
Under age 25	4,656.47	168	11.1
Aged 25 to 34	4,823.38	174	29.0
Aged 35 to 44	3,338.24	120	21.8
Aged 45 to 54	2,377.05	86	17.7
Aged 55 to 64	1,574.48	57	10.0
Aged 65 to 74	1,187.65	43	4.6
Aged 75 or older	1,677.15	60	5.8

	AVERAGE HOUSEHOLD SPENDING	BEST CUSTOMERS (index)	BIGGEST CUSTOMERS (market share)
HOUSEHOLD INCOME			
Average household	**$2,773.24**	**100**	**100.0%**
Under $20,000	2,985.61	108	23.5
$20,000 to $39,999	3,203.56	116	26.5
$40,000 to $49,999	3,264.81	118	11.1
$50,000 to $69,999	2,890.67	104	14.9
$70,000 to $79,999	2,638.86	95	5.7
$80,000 to $99,999	2,214.20	80	6.7
$100,000 or more	1,877.49	68	11.6
HOUSEHOLD TYPE			
Average household	**2,773.24**	**100**	**100.0**
Married couples	1,956.03	71	34.8
Married couples, no children	1,360.67	49	10.4
Married couples, with children	2,302.09	83	19.3
Oldest child under age 6	3,366.83	121	5.2
Oldest child aged 6 to 17	2,362.48	85	10.0
Oldest child aged 18 or older	1,572.39	57	4.1
Single parent with child under age 18	4,044.19	146	8.6
Single person	3,252.89	117	34.4
RACE AND HISPANIC ORIGIN			
Average household	**2,773.24**	**100**	**100.0**
Asian	4,806.69	173	7.4
Black	4,001.61	144	17.7
Hispanic	4,392.64	158	19.3
Non-Hispanic white and other	2,324.95	84	63.6
REGION			
Average household	**2,773.24**	**100**	**100.0**
Northeast	3,457.51	125	22.9
Midwest	1,844.05	66	14.8
South	2,228.90	80	29.5
West	4,015.19	145	32.8
EDUCATION			
Average household	**2,773.24**	**100**	**100.0**
Less than high school graduate	2,931.08	106	15.1
High school graduate	2,614.46	94	24.1
Some college	2,836.57	102	21.5
Associate's degree	2,744.20	99	9.3
Bachelor's degree or more	2,798.22	101	30.0
Bachelor's degree	3,009.36	109	20.5
Master's, professional, doctoral degree	2,429.58	88	9.5

Note: Market shares may not sum to 100.0 because of rounding and missing categories by household type. "Asian" and "black" include Hispanics and non-Hispanics who identify themselves as being of the respective race alone. "Hispanic" includes people of any race who identify themselves as Hispanic. "Other" includes people who identify themselves as non-Hispanic and as Alaska Native, American Indian, Asian (who are also included in the "Asian" row), or Native Hawaiian or other Pacific Islander as well as non-Hispanics reporting more than one race.

Source: Calculations by New Strategist based on the Bureau of Labor Statistics' 2010 Consumer Expenditure Survey

Vacation Homes, Owned

Best customers: **Householders aged 45 to 74**
High-income households
Married couples without children at home
Asians
College graduates

Customer trends: **Average household spending on owned vacation homes may begin to fall because aging boomers have almost completely filled the best-customer lifestage and discretionary income is dwindling.**

Not surprisingly, the affluent are the best customers of owned vacation homes. Households with incomes of $100,000 or more spend over three times the average on vacation home ownership and control 56 percent of the market. Householders ranging in age from 45 to 74 spend 23 to 67 percent more than average on owned vacation homes. Married couples without children at home (most of them empty-nesters) spend nearly twice the average on this item. Asian householders outspend the average for vacation homes by 41 percent. College graduates, who dominate the affluent, spend over twice the average.

Average household spending on owned vacation homes grew by a small 7 percent between 2000 and the overall peak-spending year of 2006, then rose by an enormous 40 percent between 2006 and 2010, after adjusting for inflation. Behind the increase was the baby-boom generation in the best-customer age groups. Average household spending on owned vacation homes is likely to fall now that boomers have almost completely filled the best-customer age groups and the economic downturn diminishes discretionary income.

Table 16.12   Vacation homes, owned

Total household spending $33,781,586,580.00
Average household spends   278.94

	AVERAGE HOUSEHOLD SPENDING	BEST CUSTOMERS (index)	BIGGEST CUSTOMERS (market share)
AGE OF HOUSEHOLDER			
Average household	**$278.94**	**100**	**100.0%**
Under age 25	14.49	5	0.3
Aged 25 to 34	134.05	48	8.0
Aged 35 to 44	208.20	75	13.5
Aged 45 to 54	343.30	123	25.5
Aged 55 to 64	465.29	167	29.4
Aged 65 to 74	376.84	135	14.5
Aged 75 or older	255.44	92	8.7

	AVERAGE HOUSEHOLD SPENDING	BEST CUSTOMERS (index)	BIGGEST CUSTOMERS (market share)
HOUSEHOLD INCOME			
Average household	**$278.94**	**100**	**100.0%**
Under $20,000	66.60	24	5.2
$20,000 to $39,999	108.19	39	8.9
$40,000 to $49,999	90.25	32	3.1
$50,000 to $69,999	223.92	80	11.5
$70,000 to $79,999	191.62	69	4.1
$80,000 to $99,999	390.36	140	11.7
$100,000 or more	903.73	324	55.6
HOUSEHOLD TYPE			
Average household	**278.94**	**100**	**100.0**
Married couples	410.70	147	72.6
Married couples, no children	535.02	192	40.7
Married couples, with children	349.81	125	29.2
Oldest child under age 6	417.30	150	6.4
Oldest child aged 6 to 17	337.02	121	14.2
Oldest child aged 18 or older	330.64	119	8.6
Single parent with child under age 18	42.40	15	0.9
Single person	169.93	61	17.8
RACE AND HISPANIC ORIGIN			
Average household	**278.94**	**100**	**100.0**
Asian	392.33	141	6.0
Black	167.30	60	7.3
Hispanic	161.70	58	7.1
Non-Hispanic white and other	323.02	116	87.8
REGION			
Average household	**278.94**	**100**	**100.0**
Northeast	273.71	98	18.0
Midwest	281.72	101	22.5
South	254.80	91	33.5
West	319.56	115	26.0
EDUCATION			
Average household	**278.94**	**100**	**100.0**
Less than high school graduate	79.75	29	4.1
High school graduate	132.24	47	12.1
Some college	207.19	74	15.6
Associate's degree	167.71	60	5.7
Bachelor's degree or more	586.97	210	62.5
Bachelor's degree	554.84	199	37.6
Master's, professional, doctoral degree	643.05	231	24.9

Note: Market shares may not sum to 100.0 because of rounding and missing categories by household type. "Asian" and "black" include Hispanics and non-Hispanics who identify themselves as being of the respective race alone. "Hispanic" includes people of any race who identify themselves as Hispanic. "Other" includes people who identify themselves as non-Hispanic and as Alaska Native, American Indian, Asian (who are also included in the "Asian" row), or Native Hawaiian or other Pacific Islander as well as non-Hispanics reporting more than one race.

Source: Calculations by New Strategist based on the Bureau of Labor Statistics' 2010 Consumer Expenditure Survey

Chapter 17.

Telephone

Household Spending on Telephone Service and Equipment, 2010

American households spent an average of $1,202 on telephone service, equipment, and accessories in 2010, making the category one of the larger household expenses. Spending on this category rose by 5 percent between 2000 and 2010, after adjusting for inflation.

Spending on residential phone service (a category that includes the miniscule amount of money households spend on pay phones) fell 58 percent between 2000 and 2010 as prices for long-distance service plummeted and a growing number of households abandoned landline service altogether. Not surprisingly, average household spending on cellular phone service surged, quintupling between 2000 and 2010 as cell phones became the norm. The average household now spends nearly twice as much on cell phone service as on landline service, but the sum of spending on these two services remained nearly identical over those years.

Spending on cell versus landline phone service

(average annual spending by households on cell and landline phone service, 2000, 2006, and 2010; in 2010 dollars)

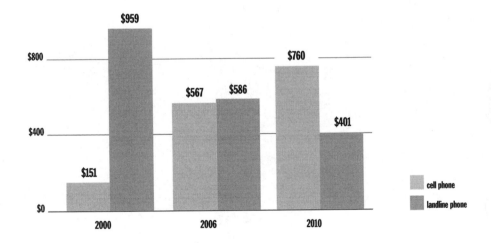

Table 17.1 Telephone spending, 2000 to 2010

(average annual household spending on telephone service and equipment by category, 2000, 2006, and 2010; percent change in spending, 2000–06, 2000–10, and 2006–10; in 2010 dollars; ranked by amount spent)

	2010 average household spending	2006 average household spending (in 2010$)	2000 average household spending (in 2010$)	percent change		
				2006–10	2000–06	2000–10
AVERAGE ANNUAL SPENDING						
Average household spending on telephone service and equipment	**$1,202.07**	**$1,213.14**	**$1,149.68**	**–0.9%**	**5.5%**	**4.6%**
Cellular phone service	759.68	566.53	151.31	34.1	274.4	402.1
Residential telephone service and pay phones	401.31	586.19	958.91	–31.5	–38.9	–58.1
Telephones and answering machines	32.94	37.53	39.46	–12.2	–4.9	–16.5
Phone cards	8.14	22.89	–	–64.4	–	–

				percentage point change		
	2006–10	2000–06	2000–10	2006–10	2000–06	2000–10
PERCENT DISTRIBUTION OF SPENDING						
Average household spending on telephone service and equipment	**100.0%**	**100.0%**	**100.0%**	**–**	**–**	**–**
Cellular phone service	63.2	46.7	13.2	16.5	33.5	50.0
Residential telephone service and pay phones	33.4	48.3	83.4	–14.9	–35.1	–50.0
Telephones and answering machines	2.7	3.1	3.4	–0.4	–0.3	–0.7
Phone cards	0.7	1.9	–	–1.2	–	–

Note: "–" means not applicable or data are unavailable.

Source: Bureau of Labor Statistics, 2000, 2006, and 2010 Consumer Expenditure Surveys; calculations by New Strategist

Cellular Phone Service

Best customers:
    Householders aged 25 to 54
    Married couples with children at home
    Single parents
    Hispanics

Customer trends:
    Average household spending on cellular phone service should stabilize as cell phones become the norm and prices for cell phone service fall.

Parents are the biggest spenders on cell phone service. Couples with children at home spend 41 percent more than average on this item, the number peaking at 52 percent among those with adult children at home. Single parents, whose spending approaches average on only a few items, spend 12 percent more than average on cell phone service. Householders ranging in age from 25 to 54, most with children at home, spend 21 to 26 percent more than average on cell phone service and control 69 percent of the market. Hispanics spend 17 percent more than average on cellular phone service.

Average household spending on cell phone service soared between 2000 and 2010, quintupling after adjusting for inflation. Behind the enormous increase is the growing share of households that spend on cell service, tripling from 21 percent during the average quarter of 2000 to 65 percent in 2010. The rapid growth in spending on cell service may soon lead to market saturation. Already the average annual rate of increase in average household spending on cell phone service went from 46 percent before the peak-spending year of 2006 to 9 percent since then. Not only is cell service becoming the norm, but cutthroat competition is lowering service prices.

Table 17.2 Cellular phone service

Total household spending $92,002,565,760.00
Average household spends   759.68

	AVERAGE HOUSEHOLD SPENDING	BEST CUSTOMERS (index)	BIGGEST CUSTOMERS (market share)
AGE OF HOUSEHOLDER			
Average household	**$759.68**	**100**	**100.0%**
Under age 25	615.38	81	5.4
Aged 25 to 34	917.26	121	20.1
Aged 35 to 44	960.19	126	22.9
Aged 45 to 54	957.72	126	26.1
Aged 55 to 64	699.40	92	16.2
Aged 65 to 74	454.49	60	6.4
Aged 75 or older	230.76	30	2.9

	AVERAGE HOUSEHOLD SPENDING	BEST CUSTOMERS (index)	BIGGEST CUSTOMERS (market share)
HOUSEHOLD INCOME			
Average household	**$759.68**	**100**	**100.0%**
Under $20,000	369.29	49	10.6
$20,000 to $39,999	627.73	83	18.9
$40,000 to $49,999	761.12	100	9.5
$50,000 to $69,999	871.40	115	16.5
$70,000 to $79,999	916.99	121	7.2
$80,000 to $99,999	1,038.97	137	11.4
$100,000 or more	1,147.88	151	25.9
HOUSEHOLD TYPE			
Average household	**759.68**	**100**	**100.0**
Married couples	913.68	120	59.3
Married couples, no children	710.77	94	19.9
Married couples, with children	1,067.45	141	32.7
Oldest child under age 6	956.14	126	5.4
Oldest child aged 6 to 17	1,056.11	139	16.3
Oldest child aged 18 or older	1,151.91	152	10.9
Single parent with child under age 18	851.68	112	6.6
Single person	415.71	55	16.0
RACE AND HISPANIC ORIGIN			
Average household	**759.68**	**100**	**100.0**
Asian	789.06	104	4.4
Black	764.34	101	12.3
Hispanic	886.46	117	14.2
Non-Hispanic white and other	737.95	97	73.6
REGION			
Average household	**759.68**	**100**	**100.0**
Northeast	731.16	96	17.7
Midwest	715.95	94	21.0
South	799.22	105	38.6
West	761.74	100	22.7
EDUCATION			
Average household	**759.68**	**100**	**100.0**
Less than high school graduate	549.25	72	10.3
High school graduate	709.63	93	23.8
Some college	751.06	99	20.8
Associate's degree	893.28	118	11.1
Bachelor's degree or more	867.49	114	33.9
Bachelor's degree	875.07	115	21.8
Master's, professional, doctoral degree	854.27	112	12.2

Note: Market shares may not sum to 100.0 because of rounding and missing categories by household type. "Asian" and "black" include Hispanics and non-Hispanics who identify themselves as being of the respective race alone. "Hispanic" includes people of any race who identify themselves as Hispanic. "Other" includes people who identify themselves as non-Hispanic and as Alaska Native, American Indian, Asian (who are also included in the "Asian" row), or Native Hawaiian or other Pacific Islander as well as non-Hispanics reporting more than one race.

Source: Calculations by New Strategist based on the Bureau of Labor Statistics' 2010 Consumer Expenditure Survey

Phone Cards

Best customers:
Householders aged 25 to 54
Asians and Hispanics
Householders without a high school diploma

Customer trends:
Average household spending on phone cards is unlikely to grow despite the increase in the Asian and Hispanic populations, as international rate plans and Internet telephony eat into the phone card business.

The biggest spenders on phone cards are households making international calls, many of them immigrants to the United States. Because immigrants tend to be younger adults, householders ranging in age from 25 to 54 spend more than others on this item—from 19 to 33 percent more than the average household. Asian householders spend twice the average on phone cards, and Hispanics spend more than three times the average. Householders without a high school diploma (many of them recent Hispanic immigrants) spend twice the average on this item.

Phone cards were not included in the Consumer Expenditure Survey until recently, which limits the analysis of spending trends. Average household spending on phone cards declined 64 percent between 2006 and 2010, largely because international rate plans and Internet telephony are eating into the phone card business. Despite the growth of the Asian and Hispanic populations, average household spending on phone cards is unlikely to rise in the years ahead.

Table 17.3 **Phone cards**

Total household spending $985,810,980.00
Average household spends 8.14

	AVERAGE HOUSEHOLD SPENDING	BEST CUSTOMERS (index)	BIGGEST CUSTOMERS (market share)
AGE OF HOUSEHOLDER			
Average household	**$8.14**	**100**	**100.0%**
Under age 25	6.88	85	5.6
Aged 25 to 34	9.75	120	19.9
Aged 35 to 44	10.81	133	24.0
Aged 45 to 54	9.68	119	24.6
Aged 55 to 64	5.85	72	12.7
Aged 65 to 74	6.79	83	9.0
Aged 75 or older	3.58	44	4.2

	AVERAGE HOUSEHOLD SPENDING	BEST CUSTOMERS (index)	BIGGEST CUSTOMERS (market share)
HOUSEHOLD INCOME			
Average household	**$8.14**	**100**	**100.0%**
Under $20,000	7.79	96	20.9
$20,000 to $39,999	8.82	108	24.8
$40,000 to $49,999	8.26	101	9.6
$50,000 to $69,999	7.74	95	13.6
$70,000 to $79,999	9.88	121	7.3
$80,000 to $99,999	6.26	77	6.4
$100,000 or more	8.26	101	17.4
HOUSEHOLD TYPE			
Average household	**8.14**	**100**	**100.0**
Married couples	8.19	101	49.6
Married couples, no children	5.77	71	15.1
Married couples, with children	9.25	114	26.4
Oldest child under age 6	8.71	107	4.6
Oldest child aged 6 to 17	9.36	115	13.5
Oldest child aged 18 or older	9.37	115	8.3
Single parent with child under age 18	7.70	95	5.6
Single person	5.87	72	21.1
RACE AND HISPANIC ORIGIN			
Average household	**8.14**	**100**	**100.0**
Asian	16.68	205	8.7
Black	7.60	93	11.4
Hispanic	26.28	323	39.3
Non-Hispanic white and other	5.32	65	49.5
REGION			
Average household	**8.14**	**100**	**100.0**
Northeast	9.06	111	20.4
Midwest	5.94	73	16.3
South	8.76	108	39.5
West	8.56	105	23.8
EDUCATION			
Average household	**8.14**	**100**	**100.0**
Less than high school graduate	16.21	199	28.5
High school graduate	8.42	103	26.4
Some college	5.20	64	13.4
Associate's degree	7.73	95	9.0
Bachelor's degree or more	6.23	77	22.7
Bachelor's degree	5.73	70	13.3
Master's, professional, doctoral degree	7.10	87	9.4

Note: Market shares may not sum to 100.0 because of rounding and missing categories by household type. "Asian" and "black" include Hispanics and non-Hispanics who identify themselves as being of the respective race alone. "Hispanic" includes people of any race who identify themselves as Hispanic. "Other" includes people who identify themselves as non-Hispanic and as Alaska Native, American Indian, Asian (who are also included in the "Asian" row), or Native Hawaiian or other Pacific Islander as well as non-Hispanics reporting more than one race.

Source: Calculations by New Strategist based on the Bureau of Labor Statistics' 2010 Consumer Expenditure Survey

Residential Telephone Service

Best customers:
    Householders aged 45 or older
Married couples without children at home
Married couples with school-aged or older children at home
Blacks
Households in the Northeast

Customer trends:
    Average household spending on residential telephone service will continue to decline as cell phones replace residential phones, especially among the younger generations.

Because most households buy residential phone service, there is little variation in spending on this item by demographic characteristic—although householders under age 35 spend far less on residential telephone service than older householders because many of the younger householders use cell phones only. Householders aged 45 or older spend 13 to 32 percent more than average on residential phone service. Married couples without children at home, most of them older empty-nesters, spend 25 percent more than average on this item. Married couples with adult children at home are the biggest spenders on residential phone service because their households are larger than average. These households spend 41 percent more than average on this service. Black households spend 10 percent more than average on residential phone service, and households in the Northeast spend 18 percent more.

Average household spending on residential phone service fell 58 percent between 2000 and 2010, after adjusting for inflation. Substitution of cell phones for residential phones was one factor behind the decline. As a consequence of the spending decline, residential phone service relinquished its position in 2007 as the number-one expenditure in the information and consumer electronics category, tumbling to third place behind cellular phone service and cable and satellite television service. Average household spending on residential telephone service will continue to decline as cell phones replace residential phones, especially among the younger generations.

Table 17.4 Residential telephone service

Total household spending $48,601,450,170.00
Average household spends   401.31

	AVERAGE HOUSEHOLD SPENDING	BEST CUSTOMERS (index)	BIGGEST CUSTOMERS (market share)
AGE OF HOUSEHOLDER			
Average household	**$401.31**	**100**	**100.0%**
Under age 25	86.99	22	1.4
Aged 25 to 34	223.59	56	9.3
Aged 35 to 44	379.67	95	17.1
Aged 45 to 54	452.48	113	23.3
Aged 55 to 64	511.84	128	22.5
Aged 65 to 74	529.69	132	14.2
Aged 75 or older	511.08	127	12.1

	AVERAGE HOUSEHOLD SPENDING	BEST CUSTOMERS (index)	BIGGEST CUSTOMERS (market share)
HOUSEHOLD INCOME			
Average household	**$401.31**	**100**	**100.0%**
Under $20,000	291.26	73	15.8
$20,000 to $39,999	356.84	89	20.4
$40,000 to $49,999	395.73	99	9.3
$50,000 to $69,999	415.09	103	14.8
$70,000 to $79,999	442.74	110	6.6
$80,000 to $99,999	473.94	118	9.8
$100,000 or more	542.58	135	23.2
HOUSEHOLD TYPE			
Average household	**401.31**	**100**	**100.0**
Married couples	488.59	122	60.1
Married couples, no children	500.57	125	26.5
Married couples, with children	474.42	118	27.5
Oldest child under age 6	293.91	73	3.1
Oldest child aged 6 to 17	485.08	121	14.2
Oldest child aged 18 or older	564.08	141	10.1
Single parent with child under age 18	271.47	68	4.0
Single person	293.61	73	21.4
RACE AND HISPANIC ORIGIN			
Average household	**401.31**	**100**	**100.0**
Asian	319.92	80	3.4
Black	440.07	110	13.4
Hispanic	321.31	80	9.8
Non-Hispanic white and other	408.06	102	77.1
REGION			
Average household	**401.31**	**100**	**100.0**
Northeast	472.67	118	21.6
Midwest	377.24	94	21.0
South	406.97	101	37.2
West	358.01	89	20.2
EDUCATION			
Average household	**401.31**	**100**	**100.0**
Less than high school graduate	374.90	93	13.3
High school graduate	389.55	97	24.8
Some college	361.40	90	18.9
Associate's degree	414.97	103	9.8
Bachelor's degree or more	448.02	112	33.2
Bachelor's degree	418.23	104	19.7
Master's, professional, doctoral degree	500.05	125	13.5

Note: Market shares may not sum to 100.0 because of rounding and missing categories by household type. "Asian" and "black" include Hispanics and non-Hispanics who identify themselves as being of the respective race alone. "Hispanic" includes people of any race who identify themselves as Hispanic. "Other" includes people who identify themselves as non-Hispanic and as Alaska Native, American Indian, Asian (who are also included in the "Asian" row), or Native Hawaiian or other Pacific Islander as well as non-Hispanics reporting more than one race.

Source: Calculations by New Strategist based on the Bureau of Labor Statistics' 2010 Consumer Expenditure Survey

Telephones, Answering Machines, and Accessories

Best customers:
Householders aged 35 to 64
Married couples with adult children at home
Single parents
Asians and blacks

Customer trends:
Average household spending on telephones, answering machines, and accessories may rise as smartphones become must-have items, but free phones with the purchase of cell phone service may dampen spending on this item.

Married couples with adult children at home spend 53 percent more than average on telephones, answering machines, and accessories. Single parents outspend the average by 27 percent. Householders ranging in age from 35 to 64 spend 8 to 42 percent more than average on telephones, answering machines, and accessories. Asian households spend three times the average on this item, and blacks spend one-half more than average on phones and accessories.

Average household spending on telephones, answering machines, and accessories declined 17 percent between 2000 and 2010, after adjusting for inflation. Average household spending on telephones may rise as smartphones become must-have items, but free phones with the purchase of cell phone service may dampen spending on this item.

Table 17.5 Telephones, answering machines, and accessories

Total household spending $3,989,264,580.00
Average household spends   32.94

	AVERAGE HOUSEHOLD SPENDING	BEST CUSTOMERS (index)	BIGGEST CUSTOMERS (market share)
AGE OF HOUSEHOLDER			
Average household	**$32.94**	**100**	**100.0%**
Under age 25	6.82	21	1.4
Aged 25 to 34	32.12	98	16.2
Aged 35 to 44	46.69	142	25.6
Aged 45 to 54	35.48	108	22.3
Aged 55 to 64	41.63	126	22.3
Aged 65 to 74	30.46	92	9.9
Aged 75 or older	7.62	23	2.2

	AVERAGE HOUSEHOLD SPENDING	BEST CUSTOMERS (index)	BIGGEST CUSTOMERS (market share)
HOUSEHOLD INCOME			
Average household	**$32.94**	**100**	**100.0%**
Under $20,000	13.23	40	8.8
$20,000 to $39,999	12.50	38	8.7
$40,000 to $49,999	34.58	105	9.9
$50,000 to $69,999	37.35	113	16.3
$70,000 to $79,999	55.87	170	10.2
$80,000 to $99,999	31.31	95	7.9
$100,000 or more	75.67	230	39.4
HOUSEHOLD TYPE			
Average household	**32.94**	**100**	**100.0**
Married couples	37.50	114	56.2
Married couples, no children	39.00	118	25.1
Married couples, with children	28.99	88	20.5
Oldest child under age 6	8.46	26	1.1
Oldest child aged 6 to 17	21.70	66	7.7
Oldest child aged 18 or older	50.33	153	11.0
Single parent with child under age 18	41.89	127	7.5
Single person	18.79	57	16.7
RACE AND HISPANIC ORIGIN			
Average household	**32.94**	**100**	**100.0**
Asian	101.48	308	13.1
Black	49.93	152	18.5
Hispanic	26.67	81	9.9
Non-Hispanic white and other	31.13	95	71.6
REGION			
Average household	**32.94**	**100**	**100.0**
Northeast	31.87	97	17.8
Midwest	30.31	92	20.5
South	38.72	118	43.1
West	26.97	82	18.5
EDUCATION			
Average household	**32.94**	**100**	**100.0**
Less than high school graduate	28.41	86	12.3
High school graduate	20.30	62	15.7
Some college	23.63	72	15.1
Associate's degree	53.17	161	15.3
Bachelor's degree or more	46.04	140	41.5
Bachelor's degree	28.36	86	16.3
Master's, professional, doctoral degree	80.85	245	26.6

Note: Market shares may not sum to 100.0 because of rounding and missing categories by household type. "Asian" and "black" include Hispanics and non-Hispanics who identify themselves as being of the respective race alone. "Hispanic" includes people of any race who identify themselves as Hispanic. "Other" includes people who identify themselves as non-Hispanic and as Alaska Native, American Indian, Asian (who are also included in the "Asian" row), or Native Hawaiian or other Pacific Islander as well as non-Hispanics reporting more than one race.

Source: Calculations by New Strategist based on the Bureau of Labor Statistics' 2010 Consumer Expenditure Survey

Chapter 18.

Tobacco Products

Household Spending on Tobacco Products, 2010

The average American household spent $362 on cigarettes, other tobacco products, and smoking accessories in 2010. Spending on this category declined 12 percent between 2000 and the overall peak-spending year of 2006 as consumers cut back on their tobacco purchases, then grew 2 percent over the ensuing four years as prices climbed.

Average household spending on cigarettes fell 12 percent between 2000 and 2006, after adjusting for inflation, despite rising prices, then grew 2 percent between 2006 and 2010. Behind the earlier decline was the shrinking percentage of people who smoke cigarettes. Spending on other tobacco products (such as cigars and chewing tobacco) declined 15 percent between 2000 and the overall peak-spending year of 2006, then grew 9 percent over the next three years. Spending on smoking accessories increased substantially over the decade.

Spending on tobacco products

(average annual spending by households on tobacco products, 2000, 2006, and 2010; in 2010 dollars)

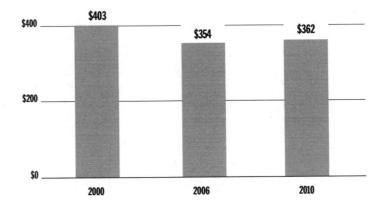

Table 18.1 Tobacco spending, 2000 to 2010

(average annual household spending on tobacco products by category, 2000, 2006, and 2010; percent change in spending, 2000–06, 2000–10, and 2006–10; in 2010 dollars; ranked by amount spent)

	2010 average household spending	2006 average household spending (in 2010$)	2000 average household spending (in 2010$)	percent change 2006–10	percent change 2000–06	percent change 2000–10
AVERAGE ANNUAL SPENDING						
Average annual household spending on tobacco products	**$362.05**	**$353.51**	**$403.47**	**2.4%**	**–12.4%**	**–10.3%**
Cigarettes	331.80	326.87	372.16	1.5	–12.2	–10.8
Tobacco products other than cigarettes	26.52	24.35	28.52	8.9	–14.6	–7.0
Smoking accessories	3.74	2.29	2.57	63.1	–10.8	45.5

	2006–10	2000–06	2000–10	percentage point change 2006–10	percentage point change 2000–06	percentage point change 2000–10
PERCENT DISTRIBUTION OF SPENDING						
Average annual household spending on tobacco products	**100.0%**	**100.0%**	**100.0%**	–	–	–
Cigarettes	91.6	92.5	92.2	–0.8	0.2	–0.6
Tobacco products other than cigarettes	7.3	6.9	7.1	0.4	–0.2	0.3
Smoking accessories	1.0	0.6	0.6	0.4	0.0	0.4

Note: Numbers may not add to total because not all categories are shown. "–" means not applicable.

Source: Bureau of Labor Statistics, 2000, 2006, and 2010 Consumer Expenditure Surveys; calculations by New Strategist

Cigarettes

Best customers: **Householders aged 45 to 64**
Married couples with adult children at home
Non-Hispanic whites
High school graduate or less education

Customer trends: **Average household spending on cigarettes should decline as smoking becomes less common.**

Cigarettes account for 92 percent of household spending on tobacco products and smoking accessories. Householders aged 45 to 64 spend one-quarter more than average on cigarettes and account for 48 percent of the market. Married couples with adult children at home spend 16 percent more than average on this item, in part because their households are the largest. Non-Hispanic whites spend 14 percent more than average. Householders with a high school diploma or less education spend 24 to 40 percent more than average on cigarettes.

Average household spending on cigarettes fell 12 percent between 2000 and the overall peak-spending year of 2006, after adjusting for inflation, then rose 2 percent in the four ensuing years for a net drop of 11 percent over the decade. Behind the decline is the smaller proportion of smokers in the population as health warnings and higher prices drive consumers away. Spending on cigarettes is likely to continue to decline as smoking becomes less common.

Table 18.2 Cigarettes

Total household spending $40,183,302,600.00
Average household spends   331.80

	AVERAGE HOUSEHOLD SPENDING	BEST CUSTOMERS (index)	BIGGEST CUSTOMERS (market share)
AGE OF HOUSEHOLDER			
Average household	**$331.80**	**100**	**100.0%**
Under age 25	253.20	76	5.1
Aged 25 to 34	327.49	99	16.4
Aged 35 to 44	327.72	99	17.9
Aged 45 to 54	412.62	124	25.7
Aged 55 to 64	415.49	125	22.1
Aged 65 to 74	275.12	83	8.9
Aged 75 or older	135.64	41	3.9

	AVERAGE HOUSEHOLD SPENDING	BEST CUSTOMERS (index)	BIGGEST CUSTOMERS (market share)
HOUSEHOLD INCOME			
Average household	**$331.80**	**100**	**100.0%**
Under $20,000	304.12	92	20.0
$20,000 to $39,999	368.10	111	25.4
$40,000 to $49,999	397.40	120	11.3
$50,000 to $69,999	373.93	113	16.2
$70,000 to $79,999	367.92	111	6.6
$80,000 to $99,999	353.90	107	8.9
$100,000 or more	223.76	67	11.6
HOUSEHOLD TYPE			
Average household	**331.80**	**100**	**100.0**
Married couples	316.38	95	47.0
Married couples, no children	280.69	85	18.0
Married couples, with children	289.07	87	20.3
Oldest child under age 6	214.48	65	2.8
Oldest child aged 6 to 17	257.01	77	9.1
Oldest child aged 18 or older	385.53	116	8.4
Single parent with child under age 18	290.64	88	5.2
Single person	248.02	75	21.9
RACE AND HISPANIC ORIGIN			
Average household	**331.80**	**100**	**100.0**
Asian	141.38	43	1.8
Black	217.99	66	8.0
Hispanic	159.88	48	5.9
Non-Hispanic white and other	376.90	114	86.1
REGION			
Average household	**331.80**	**100**	**100.0**
Northeast	353.97	107	19.6
Midwest	348.96	105	23.4
South	365.85	110	40.5
West	241.78	73	16.5
EDUCATION			
Average household	**331.80**	**100**	**100.0**
Less than high school graduate	411.36	124	17.7
High school graduate	464.43	140	35.7
Some college	348.48	105	22.1
Associate's degree	353.28	106	10.1
Bachelor's degree or more	160.92	48	14.4
Bachelor's degree	191.74	58	10.9
Master's, professional, doctoral degree	107.10	32	3.5

Note: Market shares may not sum to 100.0 because of rounding and missing categories by household type. "Asian" and "black" include Hispanics and non-Hispanics who identify themselves as being of the respective race alone. "Hispanic" includes people of any race who identify themselves as Hispanic. "Other" includes people who identify themselves as non-Hispanic and as Alaska Native, American Indian, Asian (who are also included in the "Asian" row), or Native Hawaiian or other Pacific Islander as well as non-Hispanics reporting more than one race.

Source: Calculations by New Strategist based on the Bureau of Labor Statistics' 2010 Consumer Expenditure Survey

Smoking Accessories

Best customers: **Householders aged 55 to 64**
                              Married couples with school-aged children
                              Single parents

Customer trends: **Average household spending on smoking accessories should decline as smoking becomes less common.**

Smoking accessories include cigarette papers, pipes, lighters, and so on. Householders aged 55 to 64 spend 32 percent more than average on smoking accessories. Married couples with school-aged children spend 48 percent more than average on smoking accessories. Single parents, whose spending approaches average on only a few items, spend 19 percent more than average on this item.

Average household spending on smoking accessories grew 45 percent between 2000 and 2010, after adjusting for inflation. Spending on this item should decline as smoking becomes less common.

Table 18.3 **Smoking accessories**

Total household spending $452,940,180.00
Average household spends   3.74

	AVERAGE HOUSEHOLD SPENDING	BEST CUSTOMERS (index)	BIGGEST CUSTOMERS (market share)
AGE OF HOUSEHOLDER			
Average household	**$3.74**	**100**	**100.0%**
Under age 25	4.27	114	7.6
Aged 25 to 34	4.02	107	17.9
Aged 35 to 44	4.04	108	19.5
Aged 45 to 54	3.75	100	20.7
Aged 55 to 64	4.95	132	23.3
Aged 65 to 74	1.71	46	4.9
Aged 75 or older	2.32	62	5.9

	AVERAGE HOUSEHOLD SPENDING	BEST CUSTOMERS (index)	BIGGEST CUSTOMERS (market share)
HOUSEHOLD INCOME			
Average household	**$3.74**	**100**	**100.0%**
Under $20,000	4.92	131	28.7
$20,000 to $39,999	2.28	61	14.0
$40,000 to $49,999	7.22	193	18.2
$50,000 to $69,999	4.23	113	16.2
$70,000 to $79,999	2.29	61	3.7
$80,000 to $99,999	4.11	110	9.2
$100,000 or more	2.33	62	10.7
HOUSEHOLD TYPE			
Average household	**3.74**	**100**	**100.0**
Married couples	4.21	113	55.5
Married couples, no children	3.91	105	22.2
Married couples, with children	4.65	124	28.9
Oldest child under age 6	3.43	92	3.9
Oldest child aged 6 to 17	5.53	148	17.4
Oldest child aged 18 or older	3.95	106	7.6
Single parent with child under age 18	4.44	119	7.0
Single person	2.08	56	16.3
RACE AND HISPANIC ORIGIN			
Average household	**3.74**	**100**	**100.0**
Asian	1.68	45	1.9
Black	4.02	107	13.2
Hispanic	1.50	40	4.9
Non-Hispanic white and other	4.03	108	81.7
REGION			
Average household	**3.74**	**100**	**100.0**
Northeast	3.69	99	18.1
Midwest	3.82	102	22.8
South	3.41	91	33.5
West	4.23	113	25.6
EDUCATION			
Average household	**3.74**	**100**	**100.0**
Less than high school graduate	3.19	85	12.2
High school graduate	4.04	108	27.6
Some college	3.35	90	18.8
Associate's degree	5.97	160	15.1
Bachelor's degree or more	3.25	87	25.8
Bachelor's degree	3.53	94	17.8
Master's, professional, doctoral degree	2.68	72	7.8

Note: Market shares may not sum to 100.0 because of rounding and missing categories by household type. "Asian" and "black" include Hispanics and non-Hispanics who identify themselves as being of the respective race alone. "Hispanic" includes people of any race who identify themselves as Hispanic. "Other" includes people who identify themselves as non-Hispanic and as Alaska Native, American Indian, Asian (who are also included in the "Asian" row), or Native Hawaiian or other Pacific Islander as well as non-Hispanics reporting more than one race.

Source: Calculations by New Strategist based on the Bureau of Labor Statistics' 2010 Consumer Expenditure Survey

Tobacco Products Other than Cigarettes

Best customers:	Householders aged 45 to 54
	Married couples with school-aged or older children at home
	Non-Hispanic whites
	Households in the South

Customer trends:	Average household spending on tobacco products other than cigarettes should decline as tobacco use becomes less common.

Cigars, chewing tobacco, and pipe tobacco are some of the products included in this category. Householders aged 45 to 54 spend 23 percent more than average on noncigarette tobacco products and account for one-quarter of the market. Married couples with adult children at home spend 48 percent more than average on this item, while married couples with school-aged children spend 69 percent more than average. Non-Hispanic whites spend 24 percent more than average on tobacco products other than cigarettes and control 94 percent of the market. Southern households spend 18 percent more than average on this item.

Average household spending on noncigarette tobacco products declined 7 percent between 2000 and 2010, after adjusting for inflation. Spending on this item is likely to continue to decline as tobacco use becomes less common.

Table 18.4 Tobacco products other than cigarettes

Total household spending	$3,211,757,640.00
Average household spends	26.52

	AVERAGE HOUSEHOLD SPENDING	BEST CUSTOMERS (index)	BIGGEST CUSTOMERS (market share)
AGE OF HOUSEHOLDER			
Average household	**$26.52**	**100**	**100.0%**
Under age 25	25.61	97	6.4
Aged 25 to 34	30.49	115	19.1
Aged 35 to 44	25.88	98	17.7
Aged 45 to 54	32.68	123	25.5
Aged 55 to 64	29.29	110	19.5
Aged 65 to 74	20.81	78	8.4
Aged 75 or older	9.38	35	3.4

	AVERAGE HOUSEHOLD SPENDING	BEST CUSTOMERS (index)	BIGGEST CUSTOMERS (market share)
HOUSEHOLD INCOME			
Average household	$26.52	100	100.0%
Under $20,000	19.10	72	15.7
$20,000 to $39,999	17.16	65	14.8
$40,000 to $49,999	27.73	105	9.9
$50,000 to $69,999	34.16	129	18.5
$70,000 to $79,999	36.25	137	8.2
$80,000 to $99,999	36.94	139	11.6
$100,000 or more	32.94	124	21.3
HOUSEHOLD TYPE			
Average household	26.52	100	100.0
Married couples	35.00	132	65.1
Married couples, no children	27.87	105	22.3
Married couples, with children	39.95	151	35.0
Oldest child under age 6	27.54	104	4.4
Oldest child aged 6 to 17	44.84	169	19.9
Oldest child aged 18 or older	39.33	148	10.7
Single parent with child under age 18	8.01	30	1.8
Single person	17.50	66	19.3
RACE AND HISPANIC ORIGIN			
Average household	26.52	100	100.0
Asian	2.93	11	0.5
Black	9.32	35	4.3
Hispanic	3.71	14	1.7
Non-Hispanic white and other	32.89	124	94.0
REGION			
Average household	26.52	100	100.0
Northeast	22.65	85	15.7
Midwest	28.71	108	24.1
South	31.29	118	43.3
West	19.75	74	16.9
EDUCATION			
Average household	26.52	100	100.0
Less than high school graduate	25.63	97	13.8
High school graduate	34.38	130	33.1
Some college	28.88	109	22.9
Associate's degree	26.60	100	9.5
Bachelor's degree or more	18.48	70	20.7
Bachelor's degree	23.69	89	16.9
Master's, professional, doctoral degree	9.40	35	3.8

Note: Market shares may not sum to 100.0 because of rounding and missing categories by household type. "Asian" and "black" include Hispanics and non-Hispanics who identify themselves as being of the respective race alone. "Hispanic" includes people of any race who identify themselves as Hispanic. "Other" includes people who identify themselves as non-Hispanic and as Alaska Native, American Indian, Asian (who are also included in the "Asian" row), or Native Hawaiian or other Pacific Islander as well as non-Hispanics reporting more than one race.

Source: Calculations by New Strategist based on the Bureau of Labor Statistics' 2010 Consumer Expenditure Survey

Chapter 19.

Transportation

Household Spending on Transportation, 2010

Transportation is one of the biggest expenses of American households, second only to spending on shelter. In 2010, the average household spent $7,677 on transportation, 17 percent less than in the overall peak-spending year of 2006, after adjusting for inflation, and 18 percent less than in 2000. More than one-quarter of transportation spending is devoted to gasoline, making it the largest transportation expense category.

Sharply reduced spending on new and used cars and trucks was behind the trend in spending on transportation. Even as car dealers pushed no-interest loans on new vehicles and as the price of used vehicles fell, spending on car purchases slipped substantially, down 47 percent for new cars and 50 percent for used cars between 2000 and 2010. Spending on new trucks, a category that includes sport utility vehicles, fell 31 percent during those years, and on used trucks, 29 percent. At the same time, spending on leased vehicles fell 59 to 68 percent as leasing became less popular. Spending on vehicle maintenance held essentially level over the decade, as an increase of 6 percent from 2006 to 2010 counteracted a decline of the same percentage over the preceding six years. Spending on vehicle insurance grew 3 percent between 2000 and 2010.

Spending on transportation may continue to decline during the next few years as households cut back on vehicle purchases.

Spending on transportation

(average annual spending by households on transportation, 2000, 2006, and 2010; in 2010 dollars)

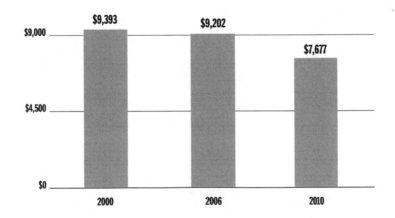

Table 19.1 Transportation spending, 2000 to 2010

(average annual household spending on transportation by category, 2000, 2006, and 2010; percent change in spending, 2000–06, 2000–10, and 2006–10; in 2010 dollars; ranked by amount spent)

	2010 average household spending	2006 average household spending (in 2010$)	2000 average household spending (in 2010$)	percent change		
				2006–10	2000–06	2000–10
AVERAGE ANNUAL SPENDING						
Average household spending on transportation	**7,677.32**	**9,202.37**	**9,392.57**	**–16.6%**	**–2.0%**	**–18.3%**
Gasoline and motor oil (including on trips)	2,132.31	2,409.28	1,635.10	–11.5	47.3	30.4
Vehicle insurance	1,010.42	958.79	985.34	5.4	–2.7	2.5
Vehicle maintenance and repair (including tires, oil changes)	787.28	744.64	789.86	5.7	–5.7	–0.3
Trucks, used	683.34	881.97	960.61	–22.5	–8.2	–28.9
Cars, used	634.64	814.40	1,280.54	–22.1	–36.4	–50.4
Cars, new	614.84	933.31	1,161.22	–34.1	–19.6	–47.1
Trucks, new	604.42	1,011.57	871.13	–40.2	16.1	–30.6
Airline fares	325.31	361.91	346.99	–10.1	4.3	–6.2
Vehicle finance charges	243.03	322.12	415.65	–24.6	–22.5	–41.5
Tires (purchased, replaced, installed)	139.40	111.76	110.46	24.7	1.2	26.2
Vehicle registration and inspection, driver's license	131.27	120.09	128.47	9.3	–6.5	2.2
Car lease payments	89.67	133.17	221.40	–32.7	–39.9	–59.5
Oil change, lube, and oil filters	72.88	72.33	74.39	0.8	–2.8	–2.0
Parking fees (excluding at residence) and tolls	66.91	58.32	55.45	14.7	5.2	20.7
Mass transit, intracity fares	66.87	55.26	60.04	21.0	–8.0	11.4
Truck lease payments	60.04	118.08	187.98	–49.2	–37.2	–68.1
Motorcycles (new and used)	51.15	58.80	45.37	–13.0	29.6	12.7
Ship fares	39.34	59.51	46.32	–33.9	28.5	–15.1
Rented vehicles (including rentals on trips)	36.78	40.55	56.92	–9.3	–28.8	–35.4
Automobile service clubs	18.63	17.62	10.57	5.7	66.6	76.2
Local transportation on trips	16.86	22.54	21.43	–25.2	5.2	–21.3
Taxi fares and limousine service in home town	16.43	15.00	15.39	9.5	–2.5	6.8
Train fares, intercity	15.67	17.62	26.74	–11.1	–34.1	–41.4
Bus fares, intercity	10.34	12.25	20.39	–15.6	–39.9	–49.3
Towing charges	3.99	5.53	5.93	–27.8	–6.7	–32.7

| | 2006–10 | 2000–06 | 2000–10 | percentage point change | | |
				2006–10	2000–06	2000–10
PERCENT DISTRIBUTION OF SPENDING						
Average household spending on transportation	**100.0%**	**100.0%**	**100.0%**	–	–	–
Gasoline and motor oil (including on trips)	27.8	26.2	17.4	1.6	8.8	10.4
Vehicle insurance	13.2	10.4	10.5	2.7	–0.1	2.7
Vehicle maintenance and repair (including tires, oil changes)	10.3	8.1	8.4	2.2	–0.3	1.8
Trucks, used	8.9	9.6	10.2	–0.7	–0.6	–1.3
Cars, used	8.3	8.8	13.6	–0.6	–4.8	–5.4
Cars, new	8.0	10.1	12.4	–2.1	–2.2	–4.4
Trucks, new	7.9	11.0	9.3	–3.1	1.7	–1.4
Airline fares	4.2	3.9	3.7	0.3	0.2	0.5
Vehicle finance charges	3.2	3.5	4.4	–0.3	–0.9	–1.3
Tires (purchased, replaced, installed)	1.8	1.2	1.2	0.6	0.0	0.6
Vehicle registration and inspection, driver's license	1.7	1.3	1.4	0.4	–0.1	0.3
Car lease payments	1.2	1.4	2.4	–0.3	–0.9	–1.2
Oil change, lube, and oil filters	0.9	0.8	0.8	0.2	0.0	0.2
Parking fees (excluding at residence) and tolls	0.9	0.6	0.6	0.2	0.0	0.3
Mass transit, intracity fares	0.9	0.6	0.6	0.3	0.0	0.2
Truck lease payments	0.8	1.3	2.0	–0.5	–0.7	–1.2
Motorcycles (new and used)	0.7	0.6	0.5	0.0	0.2	0.2
Ship fares	0.5	0.6	0.5	–0.1	0.2	0.0
Rented vehicles (including rentals on trips)	0.5	0.4	0.6	0.0	–0.2	–0.1
Automobile service clubs	0.2	0.2	0.1	0.1	0.1	0.1
Local transportation on trips	0.2	0.2	0.2	0.0	0.0	0.0
Taxi fares and limousine service in home town	0.2	0.2	0.2	0.1	0.0	0.1
Train fares, intercity	0.2	0.2	0.3	0.0	–0.1	–0.1
Bus fares, intercity	0.1	0.1	0.2	0.0	–0.1	–0.1
Towing charges	0.1	0.1	0.1	0.0	0.0	0.0

Note: Numbers do not add to total because spending on tires and oil changes is also included in vehicle maintenance and repairs and because some subcategories are not shown. "–" means not applicable.

Source: Bureau of Labor Statistics, 2000, 2006, and 2010 Consumer Expenditure Surveys; calculations by New Strategist

Automobile Service Clubs

Best customers: **Householders aged 55 or older**
Married couples without children at home
Married couples with adult children at home
Households in the Northeast and West

Customer trends: **Average household spending on automobile service clubs should rise again as the population ages.**

Older householders are the best customers of automobile service club memberships. Householders aged 55 or older spend 35 to 68 percent more than average on this item and control 57 percent of the market. Married couples without children at home (most of them empty-nesters) spend 66 percent more than average, while those with adult children at home spend 71 percent more. Households in the Northeast and West spend, respectively, 65 and 30 percent more than the average household on automobile service club fees.

Average household spending on automobile service club memberships rose sharply between 2000 and 2006, after adjusting for inflation, but has remained relatively flat since then. Spending on this item is likely to rise again along with the aging of the population.

Table 19.2 Automobile service clubs

Total household spending $2,256,223,410.00
Average household spends   18.63

	AVERAGE HOUSEHOLD SPENDING	BEST CUSTOMERS (index)	BIGGEST CUSTOMERS (market share)
AGE OF HOUSEHOLDER			
Average household	**$18.63**	**100**	**100.0%**
Under age 25	3.62	19	1.3
Aged 25 to 34	8.75	47	7.8
Aged 35 to 44	11.01	59	10.7
Aged 45 to 54	20.88	112	23.2
Aged 55 to 64	31.21	168	29.5
Aged 65 to 74	25.20	135	14.6
Aged 75 or older	25.24	135	12.9

	AVERAGE HOUSEHOLD SPENDING	BEST CUSTOMERS (index)	BIGGEST CUSTOMERS (market share)
HOUSEHOLD INCOME			
Average household	**$18.63**	**100**	**100.0%**
Under $20,000	7.70	41	9.0
$20,000 to $39,999	14.24	76	17.5
$40,000 to $49,999	17.08	92	8.7
$50,000 to $69,999	18.33	98	14.1
$70,000 to $79,999	23.77	128	7.6
$80,000 to $99,999	23.40	126	10.5
$100,000 or more	35.40	190	32.6
HOUSEHOLD TYPE			
Average household	**18.63**	**100**	**100.0**
Married couples	24.82	133	65.7
Married couples, no children	30.90	166	35.2
Married couples, with children	20.93	112	26.1
Oldest child under age 6	13.73	74	3.2
Oldest child aged 6 to 17	16.80	90	10.6
Oldest child aged 18 or older	31.91	171	12.4
Single parent with child under age 18	5.00	27	1.6
Single person	13.04	70	20.5
RACE AND HISPANIC ORIGIN			
Average household	**18.63**	**100**	**100.0**
Asian	20.94	112	4.8
Black	9.51	51	6.2
Hispanic	12.23	66	8.0
Non-Hispanic white and other	21.12	113	85.9
REGION			
Average household	**18.63**	**100**	**100.0**
Northeast	30.71	165	30.3
Midwest	13.75	74	16.5
South	12.15	65	23.9
West	24.14	130	29.4
EDUCATION			
Average household	**18.63**	**100**	**100.0**
Less than high school graduate	11.11	60	8.5
High school graduate	14.66	79	20.1
Some college	15.41	83	17.4
Associate's degree	19.59	105	9.9
Bachelor's degree or more	27.63	148	44.1
Bachelor's degree	24.12	129	24.5
Master's, professional, doctoral degree	33.75	181	19.6

Note: Market shares may not sum to 100.0 because of rounding and missing categories by household type. "Asian" and "black" include Hispanics and non-Hispanics who identify themselves as being of the respective race alone. "Hispanic" includes people of any race who identify themselves as Hispanic. "Other" includes people who identify themselves as non-Hispanic and as Alaska Native, American Indian, Asian (who are also included in the "Asian" row), or Native Hawaiian or other Pacific Islander as well as non-Hispanics reporting more than one race.

Source: Calculations by New Strategist based on the Bureau of Labor Statistics' 2010 Consumer Expenditure Survey

Car Lease Payments

Best customers:	**Householders aged 35 to 54**
	Married couples without children at home
	Married couples with adult children at home
	Asians
	Households in the Northeast
Customer trends:	**Average household spending on car lease payments will fluctuate depending on vehicle financing incentives.**

The best customers of car leasing are married couples with adult children at home. These consumer units spend twice the average on car lease payments. Married couples without children at home outspend the average on this item by 41 percent. Householders aged 35 to 54 spend 19 to 21 percent more than average on car lease payments. Asian householders spend 31 percent more than average on car lease payments. Spending on this item by households in the Northeast is 58 percent above average.

Average household spending on car lease payments fell 59 percent between 2000 and 2010, after adjusting for inflation. Behind the spending drop was the shift to buying rather than leasing as car dealers offered no-interest loans and other purchasing incentives. Spending on leasing will continue to fluctuate, depending on dealer incentives.

Table 19.3 Car lease payments

Total household spending $10,859,664,690.00
Average household spends   89.67

	AVERAGE HOUSEHOLD SPENDING	BEST CUSTOMERS (index)	BIGGEST CUSTOMERS (market share)
AGE OF HOUSEHOLDER			
Average household	**$89.67**	**100**	**100.0%**
Under age 25	69.92	78	5.2
Aged 25 to 34	100.30	112	18.6
Aged 35 to 44	108.24	121	21.8
Aged 45 to 54	106.42	119	24.6
Aged 55 to 64	64.97	72	12.8
Aged 65 to 74	85.78	96	10.3
Aged 75 or older	63.36	71	6.7

	AVERAGE HOUSEHOLD SPENDING	BEST CUSTOMERS (index)	BIGGEST CUSTOMERS (market share)
HOUSEHOLD INCOME			
Average household	**$89.67**	**100**	**100.0%**
Under $20,000	22.27	25	5.4
$20,000 to $39,999	37.71	42	9.6
$40,000 to $49,999	37.32	42	3.9
$50,000 to $69,999	92.56	103	14.8
$70,000 to $79,999	108.69	121	7.3
$80,000 to $99,999	124.91	139	11.6
$100,000 or more	247.56	276	47.3
HOUSEHOLD TYPE			
Average household	**89.67**	**100**	**100.0**
Married couples	116.82	130	64.3
Married couples, no children	126.07	141	29.9
Married couples, with children	110.16	123	28.6
Oldest child under age 6	97.71	109	4.7
Oldest child aged 6 to 17	70.71	79	9.3
Oldest child aged 18 or older	181.80	203	14.6
Single parent with child under age 18	70.18	78	4.6
Single person	53.13	59	17.4
RACE AND HISPANIC ORIGIN			
Average household	**89.67**	**100**	**100.0**
Asian	117.15	131	5.6
Black	57.41	64	7.8
Hispanic	70.64	79	9.6
Non-Hispanic white and other	97.66	109	82.6
REGION			
Average household	**89.67**	**100**	**100.0**
Northeast	141.92	158	29.0
Midwest	86.92	97	21.6
South	66.87	75	27.4
West	86.98	97	22.0
EDUCATION			
Average household	**89.67**	**100**	**100.0**
Less than high school graduate	26.73	30	4.3
High school graduate	56.83	63	16.2
Some college	95.94	107	22.5
Associate's degree	57.94	65	6.1
Bachelor's degree or more	153.83	172	51.0
Bachelor's degree	134.93	150	28.4
Master's, professional, doctoral degree	186.81	208	22.5

Note: Market shares may not sum to 100.0 because of rounding and missing categories by household type. "Asian" and "black" include Hispanics and non-Hispanics who identify themselves as being of the respective race alone. "Hispanic" includes people of any race who identify themselves as Hispanic. "Other" includes people who identify themselves as non-Hispanic and as Alaska Native, American Indian, Asian (who are also included in the "Asian" row), or Native Hawaiian or other Pacific Islander as well as non-Hispanics reporting more than one race.

Source: Calculations by New Strategist based on the Bureau of Labor Statistics' 2010 Consumer Expenditure Survey

Cars, New

Best customers:	**Householders aged 25 to 34 and 45 to 64** **Married couples without children at home** **Married couples with preschoolers or adult children at home** **Asians**
Customer trends:	**Average household spending on new cars should rise as downsizing boomers replace their gas-guzzling sport utility vehicles and minivans—but only if discretionary income grows.**

The best customers of new cars are middle-aged adults replacing large SUVs as their children leave home and young adults buying their first car. Householders aged 45 to 64 spend 21 to 29 percent more than average on new cars. Householders aged 25 to 34 spend 18 percent more. Married couples without children at home, most of them empty-nesters, spend 67 percent more than average. Couples with adult children at home, a demographic with more earners and drivers than average, spend 31 percent more than the average household on new cars. Couples with preschoolers outspend the average by 30 percent. Asians spend 77 percent more than average on new cars.

Average household spending on new cars fell 47 percent between 2000 and 2010, after adjusting for inflation. Behind the decline was the growing popularity of sport utility vehicles (considered trucks) during the earlier part of the time period and the Great Recession in the latter part. Spending on new cars should rise as empty-nest boomers downsize and search for greater fuel efficiency—but only if discretionary income grows.

Table 19.4 Cars, new

Total household spending $74,461,427,880.00
Average household spends 614.84

	AVERAGE HOUSEHOLD SPENDING	BEST CUSTOMERS (index)	BIGGEST CUSTOMERS (market share)
AGE OF HOUSEHOLDER			
Average household	**$614.84**	**100**	**100.0%**
Under age 25	349.63	57	3.8
Aged 25 to 34	724.62	118	19.6
Aged 35 to 44	482.79	79	14.2
Aged 45 to 54	795.00	129	26.7
Aged 55 to 64	741.47	121	21.3
Aged 65 to 74	418.09	68	7.3
Aged 75 or older	455.22	74	7.1

	AVERAGE HOUSEHOLD SPENDING	BEST CUSTOMERS (index)	BIGGEST CUSTOMERS (market share)
HOUSEHOLD INCOME			
Average household	**$614.84**	**100**	**100.0%**
Under $20,000	93.25	15	3.3
$20,000 to $39,999	431.20	70	16.1
$40,000 to $49,999	621.65	101	9.6
$50,000 to $69,999	565.24	92	13.2
$70,000 to $79,999	1,253.17	204	12.2
$80,000 to $99,999	833.73	136	11.3
$100,000 or more	1,256.26	204	35.0
HOUSEHOLD TYPE			
Average household	**614.84**	**100**	**100.0**
Married couples	820.78	133	65.8
Married couples, no children	1,029.43	167	35.6
Married couples, with children	690.81	112	26.1
Oldest child under age 6	796.79	130	5.5
Oldest child aged 6 to 17	580.45	94	11.1
Oldest child aged 18 or older	807.69	131	9.5
Single parent with child under age 18	479.91	78	4.6
Single person	335.68	55	16.0
RACE AND HISPANIC ORIGIN			
Average household	**614.84**	**100**	**100.0**
Asian	1,088.16	177	7.5
Black	391.79	64	7.8
Hispanic	399.58	65	7.9
Non-Hispanic white and other	683.54	111	84.3
REGION			
Average household	**614.84**	**100**	**100.0**
Northeast	760.15	124	22.7
Midwest	512.04	83	18.6
South	561.00	91	33.5
West	685.50	111	25.3
EDUCATION			
Average household	**614.84**	**100**	**100.0**
Less than high school graduate	106.88	17	2.5
High school graduate	465.44	76	19.3
Some college	522.24	85	17.9
Associate's degree	532.12	87	8.2
Bachelor's degree or more	1,079.36	176	52.2
Bachelor's degree	1,099.04	179	33.8
Master's, professional, doctoral degree	1,045.01	170	18.4

Note: Market shares may not sum to 100.0 because of rounding and missing categories by household type. "Asian" and "black" include Hispanics and non-Hispanics who identify themselves as being of the respective race alone. "Hispanic" includes people of any race who identify themselves as Hispanic. "Other" includes people who identify themselves as non-Hispanic and as Alaska Native, American Indian, Asian (who are also included in the "Asian" row), or Native Hawaiian or other Pacific Islander as well as non-Hispanics reporting more than one race.

Source: Calculations by New Strategist based on the Bureau of Labor Statistics' 2010 Consumer Expenditure Survey

Cars, Used

Best customers:	**Householders aged 25 to 34** **Married couples with adult children at home** **Households in the South**
Customer trends:	**Average household spending on used cars may climb as boomers downsize and the large millennial generation moves through the best-customer age group.**

The best customers of used cars are young adults and married couples with adult children at home. Householders aged 25 to 34 spend 52 percent more than average on used cars. Married couples with adult children at home spend nearly twice the average on this item. Households in the South spend 16 percent more than average on used cars.

Average household spending on used cars fell 50 percent between 2000 and 2010, after adjusting for inflation. Behind the decline was the growing popularity of sport utility vehicles (considered trucks), as well as dealer incentives to buy new rather than used vehicles. Average household spending on used cars may climb as boomers downsize and the large millennial generation moves through the best-customer age group.

Table 19.5 Cars, used

Total household spending $76,859,346,480.00
Average household spends 634.64

	AVERAGE HOUSEHOLD SPENDING	BEST CUSTOMERS (index)	BIGGEST CUSTOMERS (market share)
AGE OF HOUSEHOLDER			
Average household	**$634.64**	**100**	**100.0%**
Under age 25	403.04	64	4.2
Aged 25 to 34	962.20	152	25.2
Aged 35 to 44	631.17	99	18.0
Aged 45 to 54	744.25	117	24.3
Aged 55 to 64	576.08	91	16.0
Aged 65 to 74	453.08	71	7.7
Aged 75 or older	305.83	48	4.6

	AVERAGE HOUSEHOLD SPENDING	BEST CUSTOMERS (index)	BIGGEST CUSTOMERS (market share)
HOUSEHOLD INCOME			
Average household	**$634.64**	**100**	**100.0%**
Under $20,000	227.22	36	7.8
$20,000 to $39,999	721.50	114	26.1
$40,000 to $49,999	631.05	99	9.4
$50,000 to $69,999	636.32	100	14.4
$70,000 to $79,999	843.67	133	8.0
$80,000 to $99,999	820.98	129	10.8
$100,000 or more	874.09	138	23.6
HOUSEHOLD TYPE			
Average household	**634.64**	**100**	**100.0**
Married couples	753.96	119	58.6
Married couples, no children	720.92	114	24.1
Married couples, with children	819.85	129	30.1
Oldest child under age 6	705.75	111	4.8
Oldest child aged 6 to 17	617.16	97	11.4
Oldest child aged 18 or older	1,217.63	192	13.9
Single parent with child under age 18	633.32	100	5.9
Single person	309.77	49	14.3
RACE AND HISPANIC ORIGIN			
Average household	**634.64**	**100**	**100.0**
Asian	684.32	108	4.6
Black	624.12	98	12.0
Hispanic	617.87	97	11.9
Non-Hispanic white and other	641.40	101	76.6
REGION			
Average household	**634.64**	**100**	**100.0**
Northeast	458.90	72	13.3
Midwest	572.88	90	20.1
South	735.95	116	42.6
West	673.68	106	24.0
EDUCATION			
Average household	**634.64**	**100**	**100.0**
Less than high school graduate	570.84	90	12.9
High school graduate	552.40	87	22.2
Some college	605.47	95	20.1
Associate's degree	860.17	136	12.8
Bachelor's degree or more	684.92	108	32.1
Bachelor's degree	676.86	107	20.1
Master's, professional, doctoral degree	698.98	110	11.9

Note: Market shares may not sum to 100.0 because of rounding and missing categories by household type. "Asian" and "black" include Hispanics and non-Hispanics who identify themselves as being of the respective race alone. "Hispanic" includes people of any race who identify themselves as Hispanic. "Other" includes people who identify themselves as non-Hispanic and as Alaska Native, American Indian, Asian (who are also included in the "Asian" row), or Native Hawaiian or other Pacific Islander as well as non-Hispanics reporting more than one race.

Source: Calculations by New Strategist based on the Bureau of Labor Statistics' 2010 Consumer Expenditure Survey

Gasoline and Motor Oil (Including on Trips)

Best customers: **Householders aged 35 to 54**
                          Married couples with children at home

Customer trends: **Average household spending on gasoline will rise and fall along with the price of gas.**

Gasoline, the biggest transportation expense for the average household, accounts for 28 percent of transportation spending and is the fifth largest household expense overall. The biggest spenders on gasoline are middle-aged married couples because they have the largest households and the most vehicles. Householders aged 35 to 54 spend 19 to 21 percent more than average on gasoline and account for 47 percent of the market. Married couples with school-aged children at home spend 44 percent more than average on this item, while those with adult children at home spend 59 percent more than average on gasoline.

Average household spending on gasoline rose by a substantial 47 percent between 2000 and 2006, after adjusting for inflation, then declined 11 percent between 2006 and 2010. Behind the increase was the rise in the price of gasoline. The decline since 2006 is due to lower prices and household belt tightening in the face of the Great Recession. Average household spending on gasoline will fluctuate with gasoline prices.

Table 19.6 Gasoline and motor oil (including on trips)

Total household spending $258,237,667,170.00
Average household spends   2,132.31

	AVERAGE HOUSEHOLD SPENDING	BEST CUSTOMERS (index)	BIGGEST CUSTOMERS (market share)
AGE OF HOUSEHOLDER			
Average household	**$2,132.31**	**100**	**100.0%**
Under age 25	1,493.16	70	4.6
Aged 25 to 34	2,207.75	104	17.2
Aged 35 to 44	2,536.52	119	21.5
Aged 45 to 54	2,574.75	121	25.0
Aged 55 to 64	2,214.90	104	18.3
Aged 65 to 74	1,765.67	83	8.9
Aged 75 or older	979.64	46	4.4

	AVERAGE HOUSEHOLD SPENDING	BEST CUSTOMERS (index)	BIGGEST CUSTOMERS (market share)
HOUSEHOLD INCOME			
Average household	**$2,132.31**	**100**	**100.0%**
Under $20,000	1,028.86	48	10.5
$20,000 to $39,999	1,705.82	80	18.3
$40,000 to $49,999	2,151.60	101	9.5
$50,000 to $69,999	2,454.70	115	16.5
$70,000 to $79,999	2,685.97	126	7.5
$80,000 to $99,999	2,899.07	136	11.3
$100,000 or more	3,260.23	153	26.2
HOUSEHOLD TYPE			
Average household	**2,132.31**	**100**	**100.0**
Married couples	2,752.02	129	63.7
Married couples, no children	2,346.62	110	23.4
Married couples, with children	3,057.41	143	33.4
Oldest child under age 6	2,451.19	115	4.9
Oldest child aged 6 to 17	3,079.16	144	17.0
Oldest child aged 18 or older	3,381.46	159	11.5
Single parent with child under age 18	1,715.93	80	4.7
Single person	1,164.11	55	16.0
RACE AND HISPANIC ORIGIN			
Average household	**2,132.31**	**100**	**100.0**
Asian	2,098.12	98	4.2
Black	1,775.12	83	10.2
Hispanic	2,185.05	102	12.5
Non-Hispanic white and other	2,179.87	102	77.5
REGION			
Average household	**2,132.31**	**100**	**100.0**
Northeast	1,903.02	89	16.4
Midwest	2,107.68	99	22.0
South	2,228.57	105	38.4
West	2,186.35	103	23.2
EDUCATION			
Average household	**2,132.31**	**100**	**100.0**
Less than high school graduate	1,646.69	77	11.0
High school graduate	1,987.99	93	23.8
Some college	2,154.95	101	21.2
Associate's degree	2,526.26	118	11.2
Bachelor's degree or more	2,348.56	110	32.7
Bachelor's degree	2,357.64	111	20.9
Master's, professional, doctoral degree	2,332.72	109	11.8

Note: Market shares may not sum to 100.0 because of rounding and missing categories by household type. "Asian" and "black" include Hispanics and non-Hispanics who identify themselves as being of the respective race alone. "Hispanic" includes people of any race who identify themselves as Hispanic. "Other" includes people who identify themselves as non-Hispanic and as Alaska Native, American Indian, Asian (who are also included in the "Asian" row), or Native Hawaiian or other Pacific Islander as well as non-Hispanics reporting more than one race.

Source: Calculations by New Strategist based on the Bureau of Labor Statistics' 2010 Consumer Expenditure Survey

Mass Transit Fares, Intracity

Best customers:
Householders aged 25 to 54
Married couples with preschoolers
Married couples with adult children at home
Single parents
Asians, blacks, and Hispanics
Households in the Northeast

Customer trends:
Average household spending on mass transit may continue to increase as higher gas prices and the economic downturn encourage more workers to use mass transit for their daily commute.

Workers in the central cities of the Northeast are the best customers of mass transit. Households in the Northeast spend three times the average on intracity mass transit fares and account for 55 percent of the market. Householders aged 25 to 54, most in the workforce, spend 17 to 31 percent more than average on mass transit. Blacks and Hispanics spend two-thirds more than average on this item because many live in central cities, and Asians spend well over twice the average on mass transit. Together the three minority groups account for half the mass transit market. Married couples with adult children at home spend 20 percent more than average on this item because they have the most workers in their households. Married couples with preschoolers, many of whom have financial priorities other than car ownership, spend 45 percent more than average on mass transit fares. Single parents outspend the average by 7 percent.

Average household spending on intracity mass transit fares declined between 2000 and 2006, after adjusting for inflation, but increased by 21 percent between 2006 and 2010. Behind the increase was the rise in gasoline prices and the Great Recession, both of which encouraged greater mass transit use. Average household spending on mass transit may continue to increase as higher gas prices and the economic downturn encourage more workers to use mass transit.

Table 19.7 Mass transit fares, intracity

Total household spending $8,098,425,090.00
Average household spends   66.87

	AVERAGE HOUSEHOLD SPENDING	BEST CUSTOMERS (index)	BIGGEST CUSTOMERS (market share)
AGE OF HOUSEHOLDER			
Average household	**$66.87**	**100**	**100.0%**
Under age 25	69.83	104	6.9
Aged 25 to 34	85.10	127	21.2
Aged 35 to 44	87.30	131	23.6
Aged 45 to 54	78.27	117	24.2
Aged 55 to 64	64.56	97	17.0
Aged 65 to 74	25.46	38	4.1
Aged 75 or older	20.47	31	2.9

	AVERAGE HOUSEHOLD SPENDING	BEST CUSTOMERS (index)	BIGGEST CUSTOMERS (market share)
HOUSEHOLD INCOME			
Average household	**$66.87**	**100**	**100.0%**
Under $20,000	51.28	77	16.7
$20,000 to $39,999	52.46	78	18.0
$40,000 to $49,999	50.02	75	7.1
$50,000 to $69,999	54.44	81	11.7
$70,000 to $79,999	68.15	102	6.1
$80,000 to $99,999	74.10	111	9.2
$100,000 or more	121.68	182	31.2
HOUSEHOLD TYPE			
Average household	**66.87**	**100**	**100.0**
Married couples	65.16	97	48.1
Married couples, no children	47.89	72	15.2
Married couples, with children	76.22	114	26.5
Oldest child under age 6	97.14	145	6.2
Oldest child aged 6 to 17	66.22	99	11.6
Oldest child aged 18 or older	80.11	120	8.7
Single parent with child under age 18	71.36	107	6.3
Single person	52.33	78	22.9
RACE AND HISPANIC ORIGIN			
Average household	**66.87**	**100**	**100.0**
Asian	153.29	229	9.8
Black	110.24	165	20.2
Hispanic	111.48	167	20.3
Non-Hispanic white and other	52.99	79	60.1
REGION			
Average household	**66.87**	**100**	**100.0**
Northeast	200.45	300	55.0
Midwest	38.13	57	12.7
South	21.84	33	12.0
West	59.88	90	20.3
EDUCATION			
Average household	**66.87**	**100**	**100.0**
Less than high school graduate	69.34	104	14.8
High school graduate	46.37	69	17.7
Some college	49.05	73	15.4
Associate's degree	57.64	86	8.1
Bachelor's degree or more	98.84	148	43.9
Bachelor's degree	92.45	138	26.1
Master's, professional, doctoral degree	109.98	164	17.8

Note: Market shares may not sum to 100.0 because of rounding and missing categories by household type. "Asian" and "black" include Hispanics and non-Hispanics who identify themselves as being of the respective race alone. "Hispanic" includes people of any race who identify themselves as Hispanic. "Other" includes people who identify themselves as non-Hispanic and as Alaska Native, American Indian, Asian (who are also included in the "Asian" row), or Native Hawaiian or other Pacific Islander as well as non-Hispanics reporting more than one race.

Source: Calculations by New Strategist based on the Bureau of Labor Statistics' 2010 Consumer Expenditure Survey

Oil Change, Lube, and Oil Filters

Best customers:	**Householders aged 45 to 54** **Married couples**
Customer trends:	**Average household spending on oil changes, lubes, and oil filters may decline as more boomers become empty-nesters and downsize their fleets.**

Middle-aged married couples are the biggest spenders on oil changes. Householders aged 45 to 54 spend 18 percent more than average on this item. Married couples, particularly those with adult children at home, own more cars than average, which boosts spending on this item. Married couples with adult children (many with three cars) spend 43 percent more than average on oil changes, while couples with preschoolers spend 33 percent more than average on this item. Married couples without children at home, most empty-nesters, spend 24 percent more than average on oil changes.

Average household spending on oil changes, lubes, and oil filters fell 2 percent between 2000 and 2010, after adjusting for inflation. Average household spending on this item may continue to decline as more boomers become empty-nesters and downsize their fleets.

Table 19.8 Oil change, lube, and oil filters

Total household spending $8,826,278,160.00
Average household spends   72.88

	AVERAGE HOUSEHOLD SPENDING	BEST CUSTOMERS (index)	BIGGEST CUSTOMERS (market share)
AGE OF HOUSEHOLDER			
Average household	**$72.88**	**100**	**100.0%**
Under age 25	45.44	62	4.1
Aged 25 to 34	69.47	95	15.9
Aged 35 to 44	79.54	109	19.7
Aged 45 to 54	86.13	118	24.4
Aged 55 to 64	77.99	107	18.9
Aged 65 to 74	76.94	106	11.4
Aged 75 or older	42.49	58	5.6

	AVERAGE HOUSEHOLD SPENDING	BEST CUSTOMERS (index)	BIGGEST CUSTOMERS (market share)
HOUSEHOLD INCOME			
Average household	**$72.88**	**100**	**100.0%**
Under $20,000	31.97	44	9.6
$20,000 to $39,999	55.36	76	17.4
$40,000 to $49,999	70.58	97	9.2
$50,000 to $69,999	78.76	108	15.5
$70,000 to $79,999	94.63	130	7.8
$80,000 to $99,999	103.54	142	11.8
$100,000 or more	122.19	168	28.7
HOUSEHOLD TYPE			
Average household	**72.88**	**100**	**100.0**
Married couples	92.73	127	62.8
Married couples, no children	90.05	124	26.2
Married couples, with children	96.11	132	30.7
Oldest child under age 6	79.56	109	4.7
Oldest child aged 6 to 17	97.01	133	15.7
Oldest child aged 18 or older	104.45	143	10.3
Single parent with child under age 18	57.02	78	4.6
Single person	47.44	65	19.1
RACE AND HISPANIC ORIGIN			
Average household	**72.88**	**100**	**100.0**
Asian	73.06	100	4.3
Black	58.34	80	9.8
Hispanic	69.33	95	11.6
Non-Hispanic white and other	75.75	104	78.8
REGION			
Average household	**72.88**	**100**	**100.0**
Northeast	59.13	81	14.9
Midwest	75.12	103	23.0
South	75.40	103	38.0
West	77.72	107	24.2
EDUCATION			
Average household	**72.88**	**100**	**100.0**
Less than high school graduate	40.72	56	8.0
High school graduate	59.42	82	20.8
Some college	72.55	100	20.9
Associate's degree	83.82	115	10.9
Bachelor's degree or more	96.66	133	39.4
Bachelor's degree	93.03	128	24.1
Master's, professional, doctoral degree	102.99	141	15.3

Note: Market shares may not sum to 100.0 because of rounding and missing categories by household type. "Asian" and "black" include Hispanics and non-Hispanics who identify themselves as being of the respective race alone. "Hispanic" includes people of any race who identify themselves as Hispanic. "Other" includes people who identify themselves as non-Hispanic and as Alaska Native, American Indian, Asian (who are also included in the "Asian" row), or Native Hawaiian or other Pacific Islander as well as non-Hispanics reporting more than one race.

Source: Calculations by New Strategist based on the Bureau of Labor Statistics' 2010 Consumer Expenditure Survey

Parking Fees (Excluding at Residence) and Tolls

Best customers: **Householders aged 35 to 54**
Married couples with children at home
Asians
Households in the Northeast

Customer trends: **Average household spending on parking fees and tolls should continue to rise as localities recoup infrastructure costs by raising fees.**

The biggest spenders on parking fees (excluding residential parking) and tolls are the largest households with the most workers and children, paying for parking while they work or while out and about with their children. Married couples with children at home spend 48 percent more than average on this item. Householders aged 35 to 54 spend 18 to 38 percent more than average on parking and tolls. Asian householders spend more than twice the average on this item. Households in the Northeast spend double the national average on parking and tolls.

Average household spending on parking fees and tolls rose 21 percent between 2000 and 2010, after adjusting for inflation. Spending on this item should continue to rise as localities recover infrastructure costs by raising parking fees and tolls.

Table 19.9 **Parking fees (excluding at residence) and tolls**

Total household spending $8,103,269,370.00
Average household spends   66.91

	AVERAGE HOUSEHOLD SPENDING	BEST CUSTOMERS (index)	BIGGEST CUSTOMERS (market share)
AGE OF HOUSEHOLDER			
Average household	**$66.91**	**100**	**100.0%**
Under age 25	47.66	71	4.7
Aged 25 to 34	72.18	108	18.0
Aged 35 to 44	78.89	118	21.3
Aged 45 to 54	92.35	138	28.6
Aged 55 to 64	64.17	96	16.9
Aged 65 to 74	45.50	68	7.3
Aged 75 or older	22.46	34	3.2

	AVERAGE HOUSEHOLD SPENDING	BEST CUSTOMERS (index)	BIGGEST CUSTOMERS (market share)
HOUSEHOLD INCOME			
Average household	**$66.91**	**100**	**100.0%**
Under $20,000	18.24	27	6.0
$20,000 to $39,999	28.76	43	9.8
$40,000 to $49,999	34.94	52	4.9
$50,000 to $69,999	52.43	78	11.2
$70,000 to $79,999	77.20	115	6.9
$80,000 to $99,999	93.97	140	11.7
$100,000 or more	192.83	288	49.4
HOUSEHOLD TYPE			
Average household	**66.91**	**100**	**100.0**
Married couples	86.13	129	63.5
Married couples, no children	77.53	116	24.6
Married couples, with children	98.97	148	34.4
Oldest child under age 6	100.51	150	6.4
Oldest child aged 6 to 17	102.30	153	18.0
Oldest child aged 18 or older	92.64	138	10.0
Single parent with child under age 18	31.65	47	2.8
Single person	44.49	66	19.5
RACE AND HISPANIC ORIGIN			
Average household	**66.91**	**100**	**100.0**
Asian	139.06	208	8.8
Black	51.14	76	9.4
Hispanic	47.47	71	8.6
Non-Hispanic white and other	72.56	108	82.2
REGION			
Average household	**66.91**	**100**	**100.0**
Northeast	135.10	202	37.1
Midwest	52.14	78	17.4
South	45.70	68	25.1
West	60.58	91	20.5
EDUCATION			
Average household	**66.91**	**100**	**100.0**
Less than high school graduate	17.57	26	3.8
High school graduate	31.54	47	12.0
Some college	55.73	83	17.5
Associate's degree	62.85	94	8.9
Bachelor's degree or more	130.26	195	57.8
Bachelor's degree	115.98	173	32.7
Master's, professional, doctoral degree	155.15	232	25.1

Note: Market shares may not sum to 100.0 because of rounding and missing categories by household type. "Asian" and "black" include Hispanics and non-Hispanics who identify themselves as being of the respective race alone. "Hispanic" includes people of any race who identify themselves as Hispanic. "Other" includes people who identify themselves as non-Hispanic and as Alaska Native, American Indian, Asian (who are also included in the "Asian" row), or Native Hawaiian or other Pacific Islander as well as non-Hispanics reporting more than one race.

Source: Calculations by New Strategist based on the Bureau of Labor Statistics' 2010 Consumer Expenditure Survey

Taxi Fares and Limousine Service in Home Town

Best customers:	**Householders under age 25** **People who live alone** **Blacks** **Households in the Northeast**
Customer trends:	**Average household spending on taxi fares and limousine services may continue to rise as households cut costs by reducing vehicle ownership.**

Households in the highly urbanized Northeast are the best customers of taxi and limousine services. They spend three times the average on this item and account for 55 percent of the market. Much of this spending probably occurs in New York City, where many households do not own cars. Householders under age 25, many of them without a vehicle, spend twice the average on this item. People who live alone spend 60 percent more than average on cabs. Blacks, who are least likely to own a vehicle, spend 21 percent more than average on taxi and limousine fares.

Average household spending on taxi fares and limousine grew 7 percent between 2000 and 2010, after adjusting for inflation. One factor behind the increase was the use of taxis rather than cars among cash-strapped young adults. Average household spending on taxi fares and limousine services may continue to rise as households cut costs by reducing vehicle ownership.

Table 19.10 Taxi fares and limousine service in home town

Total household spending	$1,989,788,010.00
Average household spends	16.43

	AVERAGE HOUSEHOLD SPENDING	BEST CUSTOMERS (index)	BIGGEST CUSTOMERS (market share)
AGE OF HOUSEHOLDER			
Average household	**$16.43**	**100**	**100.0%**
Under age 25	34.03	207	13.7
Aged 25 to 34	18.94	115	19.2
Aged 35 to 44	19.90	121	21.9
Aged 45 to 54	13.70	83	17.3
Aged 55 to 64	16.07	98	17.3
Aged 65 to 74	3.15	19	2.1
Aged 75 or older	15.14	92	8.8

	AVERAGE HOUSEHOLD SPENDING	BEST CUSTOMERS (index)	BIGGEST CUSTOMERS (market share)
HOUSEHOLD INCOME			
Average household	**$16.43**	**100**	**100.0%**
Under $20,000	9.15	56	12.2
$20,000 to $39,999	12.96	79	18.1
$40,000 to $49,999	18.57	113	10.7
$50,000 to $69,999	8.27	50	7.2
$70,000 to $79,999	5.30	32	1.9
$80,000 to $99,999	14.38	88	7.3
$100,000 or more	41.93	255	43.8
HOUSEHOLD TYPE			
Average household	**16.43**	**100**	**100.0**
Married couples	12.88	78	38.7
Married couples, no children	12.20	74	15.8
Married couples, with children	14.29	87	20.2
Oldest child under age 6	10.45	64	2.7
Oldest child aged 6 to 17	18.90	115	13.5
Oldest child aged 18 or older	9.40	57	4.1
Single parent with child under age 18	7.61	46	2.7
Single person	26.34	160	47.0
RACE AND HISPANIC ORIGIN			
Average household	**16.43**	**100**	**100.0**
Asian	15.73	96	4.1
Black	19.95	121	14.9
Hispanic	7.71	47	5.7
Non-Hispanic white and other	17.23	105	79.5
REGION			
Average household	**16.43**	**100**	**100.0**
Northeast	49.21	300	55.0
Midwest	12.90	79	17.5
South	7.72	47	17.2
West	7.47	45	10.3
EDUCATION			
Average household	**16.43**	**100**	**100.0**
Less than high school graduate	22.06	134	19.2
High school graduate	7.10	43	11.0
Some college	9.53	58	12.2
Associate's degree	7.65	47	4.4
Bachelor's degree or more	30.09	183	54.4
Bachelor's degree	25.87	157	29.7
Master's, professional, doctoral degree	38.40	234	25.3

Note: Market shares may not sum to 100.0 because of rounding and missing categories by household type. "Asian" and "black" include Hispanics and non-Hispanics who identify themselves as being of the respective race alone. "Hispanic" includes people of any race who identify themselves as Hispanic. "Other" includes people who identify themselves as non-Hispanic and as Alaska Native, American Indian, Asian (who are also included in the "Asian" row), or Native Hawaiian or other Pacific Islander as well as non-Hispanics reporting more than one race.

Source: Calculations by New Strategist based on the Bureau of Labor Statistics' 2010 Consumer Expenditure Survey

Tires (Purchased, Replaced, Installed)

Best customers: **Householders aged 35 to 54**
Married couples

Customer trends: **Average household spending on tires is likely to decline as more boomers become empty-nesters and downsize their fleets.**

The best customers of tires are the households with the most cars—those headed by married couples, particularly households with teenage or adult children at home. Householders aged 35 to 54, many with teens and young adults at home, spend 18 to 25 percent more than the average household on tires and account for 47 percent of the market. Married couples with children at home spend 51 percent more than average on tires, and those without children at home spend 22 percent more.

Average household spending on tires held rather steady between 2000 and 2006, the year overall household spending peaked, but then rose a hefty 25 percent during the remainder of the decade, after adjusting for inflation. Behind the increase was the greater age of vehicles owned by the average household, boosting demand for replacement tires. Average household spending on tires is likely to decline in the years ahead as more boomers become empty-nesters and downsize their fleets.

Table 19.11 Tires (purchased, replaced, installed)

| Total household spending | $16,882,315,800.00 |
| Average household spends | 139.40 |

	AVERAGE HOUSEHOLD SPENDING	BEST CUSTOMERS (index)	BIGGEST CUSTOMERS (market share)
AGE OF HOUSEHOLDER			
Average household	**$139.40**	**100**	**100.0%**
Under age 25	101.55	73	4.8
Aged 25 to 34	122.70	88	14.7
Aged 35 to 44	164.91	118	21.4
Aged 45 to 54	174.45	125	25.9
Aged 55 to 64	151.43	109	19.2
Aged 65 to 74	124.22	89	9.6
Aged 75 or older	65.31	47	4.5

	AVERAGE HOUSEHOLD SPENDING	BEST CUSTOMERS (index)	BIGGEST CUSTOMERS (market share)
HOUSEHOLD INCOME			
Average household	**$139.40**	**100**	**100.0%**
Under $20,000	52.25	37	8.2
$20,000 to $39,999	96.04	69	15.8
$40,000 to $49,999	129.32	93	8.8
$50,000 to $69,999	151.19	108	15.6
$70,000 to $79,999	175.96	126	7.6
$80,000 to $99,999	179.65	129	10.7
$100,000 or more	271.60	195	33.4
HOUSEHOLD TYPE			
Average household	**139.40**	**100**	**100.0**
Married couples	190.55	137	67.4
Married couples, no children	170.54	122	26.0
Married couples, with children	210.49	151	35.1
Oldest child under age 6	183.12	131	5.6
Oldest child aged 6 to 17	210.33	151	17.7
Oldest child aged 18 or older	226.98	163	11.8
Single parent with child under age 18	89.46	64	3.8
Single person	76.58	55	16.1
RACE AND HISPANIC ORIGIN			
Average household	**139.40**	**100**	**100.0**
Asian	117.94	85	3.6
Black	83.65	60	7.3
Hispanic	106.70	77	9.3
Non-Hispanic white and other	153.34	110	83.4
REGION			
Average household	**139.40**	**100**	**100.0**
Northeast	129.31	93	17.0
Midwest	123.87	89	19.8
South	143.76	103	37.9
West	155.77	112	25.3
EDUCATION			
Average household	**139.40**	**100**	**100.0**
Less than high school graduate	82.10	59	8.4
High school graduate	115.18	83	21.1
Some college	143.74	103	21.7
Associate's degree	144.22	103	9.8
Bachelor's degree or more	183.16	131	39.0
Bachelor's degree	170.12	122	23.1
Master's, professional, doctoral degree	205.92	148	16.0

Note: Market shares may not sum to 100.0 because of rounding and missing categories by household type. "Asian" and "black" include Hispanics and non-Hispanics who identify themselves as being of the respective race alone. "Hispanic" includes people of any race who identify themselves as Hispanic. "Other" includes people who identify themselves as non-Hispanic and as Alaska Native, American Indian, Asian (who are also included in the "Asian" row), or Native Hawaiian or other Pacific Islander as well as non-Hispanics reporting more than one race.

Source: Calculations by New Strategist based on the Bureau of Labor Statistics' 2010 Consumer Expenditure Survey

Towing Charges

Best customers:
Householders under age 35
Married couples with preschoolers
Single parents
Asians and Hispanics
Households in the West

Customer trends:
Average household spending on towing charges may rise because the large millennial generation is in the best-customer age groups.

The biggest spenders on towing charges are households with unreliable vehicles who do not spend on automobile service clubs (which usually cover towing charges). They are also the heads of the largest households and most likely to own multiple and used vehicles, with frequent breakdowns. Householders under age 25 spend 61 percent more than average on towing charges, and those aged 25 to 34 spend 53 percent more. Married couples with preschoolers spend 13 percent more than average on towing charges. Single parents, whose spending is well below average on most items, spend 24 percent more than average on towing charges. Asians spend 66 percent more than average on towing charges and Hispanics, who tend to have the largest families, spend 31 percent more. Spending on towing charges by households in the West, where many Asians and Hispanics reside, is one-quarter above average.

Average household spending on towing charges declined by one-third between 2000 and 2010, after adjusting for inflation. Average household spending on this item may rise in the years ahead because the large millennial generation is in the best-customer age groups.

Table 19.12 Towing charges

Total household spending $483,216,930.00
Average household spends   3.99

	AVERAGE HOUSEHOLD SPENDING	BEST CUSTOMERS (index)	BIGGEST CUSTOMERS (market share)
AGE OF HOUSEHOLDER			
Average household	**$3.99**	**100**	**100.0%**
Under age 25	6.41	161	10.7
Aged 25 to 34	6.09	153	25.4
Aged 35 to 44	3.90	98	17.7
Aged 45 to 54	3.70	93	19.2
Aged 55 to 64	3.64	91	16.1
Aged 65 to 74	2.42	61	6.5
Aged 75 or older	1.82	46	4.4

	AVERAGE HOUSEHOLD SPENDING	BEST CUSTOMERS (index)	BIGGEST CUSTOMERS (market share)
HOUSEHOLD INCOME			
Average household	**$3.99**	**100**	**100.0%**
Under $20,000	3.01	75	16.4
$20,000 to $39,999	4.36	109	25.0
$40,000 to $49,999	5.37	135	12.7
$50,000 to $69,999	4.55	114	16.4
$70,000 to $79,999	3.99	100	6.0
$80,000 to $99,999	2.04	51	4.3
$100,000 or more	4.45	112	19.1
HOUSEHOLD TYPE			
Average household	**3.99**	**100**	**100.0**
Married couples	4.05	102	50.1
Married couples, no children	4.29	108	22.8
Married couples, with children	3.60	90	21.0
Oldest child under age 6	4.52	113	4.9
Oldest child aged 6 to 17	3.21	80	9.5
Oldest child aged 18 or older	3.69	92	6.7
Single parent with child under age 18	4.96	124	7.3
Single person	3.19	80	23.4
RACE AND HISPANIC ORIGIN			
Average household	**3.99**	**100**	**100.0**
Asian	6.63	166	7.1
Black	3.89	97	11.9
Hispanic	5.21	131	15.9
Non-Hispanic white and other	3.81	95	72.4
REGION			
Average household	**3.99**	**100**	**100.0**
Northeast	3.91	98	18.0
Midwest	3.65	91	20.4
South	3.61	90	33.2
West	4.99	125	28.3
EDUCATION			
Average household	**3.99**	**100**	**100.0**
Less than high school graduate	4.39	110	15.7
High school graduate	3.55	89	22.7
Some college	3.64	91	19.2
Associate's degree	4.54	114	10.8
Bachelor's degree or more	4.24	106	31.6
Bachelor's degree	4.33	109	20.5
Master's, professional, doctoral degree	4.09	103	11.1

Note: Market shares may not sum to 100.0 because of rounding and missing categories by household type. "Asian" and "black" include Hispanics and non-Hispanics who identify themselves as being of the respective race alone. "Hispanic" includes people of any race who identify themselves as Hispanic. "Other" includes people who identify themselves as non-Hispanic and as Alaska Native, American Indian, Asian (who are also included in the "Asian" row), or Native Hawaiian or other Pacific Islander as well as non-Hispanics reporting more than one race.

Source: Calculations by New Strategist based on the Bureau of Labor Statistics' 2010 Consumer Expenditure Survey

Truck Lease Payments

Best customers:
Householders aged 25 to 54
Married couples with children at home
Households in the Northeast

Customer trends:
Average household spending on truck lease payments is likely to continue to decline as the economic downturn drives consumers toward fuel-efficient cars.

The best customers of truck leasing are married couples with children at home, who lease a pickup, minivan, or sport utility vehicle (all are considered trucks). Householders aged 25 to 54 spend 20 to 49 percent more than average on truck lease payments and account for 73 percent of the market for this item. Married couples with children at home spend 84 percent more than average on truck lease payments, the number peaking among those with preschoolers at over two-and-one-half times the average. Households in the Northeast spend over twice the average on truck lease payments.

Average household spending on truck lease payments declined by a precipitous 68 percent between 2000 and 2010, after adjusting for inflation. Behind the spending decline was the shift to buying rather than leasing as automotive dealers offered no-interest loans and other purchasing incentives. Average household spending on truck leases is likely to continue to decline in the years ahead as the economic downturn drives consumers toward fuel-efficient cars.

Table 19.13 Truck lease payments

Total household spending $7,271,264,280.00
Average household spends 60.04

	AVERAGE HOUSEHOLD SPENDING	BEST CUSTOMERS (index)	BIGGEST CUSTOMERS (market share)
AGE OF HOUSEHOLDER			
Average household	**$60.04**	**100**	**100.0%**
Under age 25	12.07	20	1.3
Aged 25 to 34	75.10	125	20.8
Aged 35 to 44	89.67	149	27.0
Aged 45 to 54	72.25	120	24.9
Aged 55 to 64	58.26	97	17.1
Aged 65 to 74	36.80	61	6.6
Aged 75 or older	13.98	23	2.2

	AVERAGE HOUSEHOLD SPENDING	BEST CUSTOMERS (index)	BIGGEST CUSTOMERS (market share)
HOUSEHOLD INCOME			
Average household	**$60.04**	**100**	**100.0%**
Under $20,000	9.31	16	3.4
$20,000 to $39,999	28.10	47	10.7
$40,000 to $49,999	57.05	95	9.0
$50,000 to $69,999	37.06	62	8.9
$70,000 to $79,999	71.44	119	7.1
$80,000 to $99,999	89.03	148	12.4
$100,000 or more	170.10	283	48.6
HOUSEHOLD TYPE			
Average household	**60.04**	**100**	**100.0**
Married couples	84.75	141	69.6
Married couples, no children	60.91	101	21.5
Married couples, with children	110.77	184	42.9
Oldest child under age 6	155.31	259	11.1
Oldest child aged 6 to 17	95.86	160	18.8
Oldest child aged 18 or older	108.64	181	13.1
Single parent with child under age 18	54.51	91	5.4
Single person	25.75	43	12.6
RACE AND HISPANIC ORIGIN			
Average household	**60.04**	**100**	**100.0**
Asian	31.06	52	2.2
Black	55.75	93	11.4
Hispanic	46.12	77	9.4
Non-Hispanic white and other	62.79	105	79.3
REGION			
Average household	**60.04**	**100**	**100.0**
Northeast	129.42	216	39.6
Midwest	62.41	104	23.2
South	29.55	49	18.1
West	50.91	85	19.2
EDUCATION			
Average household	**60.04**	**100**	**100.0**
Less than high school graduate	13.54	23	3.2
High school graduate	34.22	57	14.6
Some college	58.76	98	20.6
Associate's degree	62.57	104	9.8
Bachelor's degree or more	104.70	174	51.8
Bachelor's degree	90.20	150	28.4
Master's, professional, doctoral degree	130.02	217	23.4

Note: Market shares may not sum to 100.0 because of rounding and missing categories by household type. "Asian" and "black" include Hispanics and non-Hispanics who identify themselves as being of the respective race alone. "Hispanic" includes people of any race who identify themselves as Hispanic. "Other" includes people who identify themselves as non-Hispanic and as Alaska Native, American Indian, Asian (who are also included in the "Asian" row), or Native Hawaiian or other Pacific Islander as well as non-Hispanics reporting more than one race.

Source: Calculations by New Strategist based on the Bureau of Labor Statistics' 2010 Consumer Expenditure Survey

Trucks, New

Best customers: **Householders aged 25 to 44**
Married couples with children under age 18
Non-Hispanic whites
Households in the South

Customer trends: **Average household spending on new trucks is likely to decline because of surging gas prices and aging boomers.**

The best customers of new trucks (a category that includes minivans, sport utility vehicles, and pickups) are younger married couples, most with children. Householders ranging in age from 25 to 44 spend 25 to 42 percent more than average on new trucks and control 47 percent of the market. Married couples with preschoolers spend 60 percent more, while couples with school-aged children spend two-and-one-half times more than the average on new trucks. Non-Hispanic whites outspend minorities by a wide margin and represent 89 percent of the market for new trucks. Spending on this item by households in the South is 27 percent above average.

Average household spending on new trucks grew 16 percent between 2000 and the overall peak-spending year of 2006, after adjusting for inflation. Then spending declined 40 percent over the next four years as vehicle purchases fell and trucks began to slip from the public's favor in the wake of the Great Recession. Spending on new trucks is likely to continue to decline in the years ahead because of higher gas prices. Also, as boomers become empty-nesters, they are likely to replace their SUVs and minivans with smaller, more fuel-efficient cars.

Table 19.14 Trucks, new

Total household spending $73,199,492,940.00
Average household spends   604.42

	AVERAGE HOUSEHOLD SPENDING	BEST CUSTOMERS (index)	BIGGEST CUSTOMERS (market share)
AGE OF HOUSEHOLDER			
Average household	**$604.42**	**100**	**100.0%**
Under age 25	43.53	7	0.5
Aged 25 to 34	758.34	125	20.9
Aged 35 to 44	858.67	142	25.7
Aged 45 to 54	685.41	113	23.5
Aged 55 to 64	710.26	118	20.7
Aged 65 to 74	300.98	50	5.4
Aged 75 or older	214.52	35	3.4

	AVERAGE HOUSEHOLD SPENDING	BEST CUSTOMERS (index)	BIGGEST CUSTOMERS (market share)
HOUSEHOLD INCOME			
Average household	**$604.42**	**100**	**100.0%**
Under $20,000	82.42	14	3.0
$20,000 to $39,999	235.67	39	8.9
$40,000 to $49,999	539.61	89	8.4
$50,000 to $69,999	435.91	72	10.3
$70,000 to $79,999	853.54	141	8.5
$80,000 to $99,999	842.63	139	11.6
$100,000 or more	1,756.41	291	49.8
HOUSEHOLD TYPE			
Average household	**604.42**	**100**	**100.0**
Married couples	932.21	154	76.1
Married couples, no children	717.96	119	25.2
Married couples, with children	1,133.18	187	43.6
Oldest child under age 6	966.88	160	6.8
Oldest child aged 6 to 17	1,562.92	259	30.4
Oldest child aged 18 or older	531.88	88	6.4
Single parent with child under age 18	454.79	75	4.4
Single person	145.03	24	7.0
RACE AND HISPANIC ORIGIN			
Average household	**604.42**	**100**	**100.0**
Asian	557.59	92	3.9
Black	372.05	62	7.5
Hispanic	237.04	39	4.8
Non-Hispanic white and other	709.02	117	88.9
REGION			
Average household	**604.42**	**100**	**100.0**
Northeast	564.67	93	17.1
Midwest	462.11	76	17.0
South	767.44	127	46.6
West	512.56	85	19.2
EDUCATION			
Average household	**604.42**	**100**	**100.0**
Less than high school graduate	210.84	35	5.0
High school graduate	414.65	69	17.5
Some college	563.60	93	19.6
Associate's degree	731.65	121	11.4
Bachelor's degree or more	945.22	156	46.5
Bachelor's degree	885.20	146	27.7
Master's, professional, doctoral degree	1,050.01	174	18.8

Note: Market shares may not sum to 100.0 because of rounding and missing categories by household type. "Asian" and "black" include Hispanics and non-Hispanics who identify themselves as being of the respective race alone. "Hispanic" includes people of any race who identify themselves as Hispanic. "Other" includes people who identify themselves as non-Hispanic and as Alaska Native, American Indian, Asian (who are also included in the "Asian" row), or Native Hawaiian or other Pacific Islander as well as non-Hispanics reporting more than one race.

Source: Calculations by New Strategist based on the Bureau of Labor Statistics' 2010 Consumer Expenditure Survey

Trucks, Used

Best customers:
    Householders aged 25 to 44
    Married couples with children at home
    Non-Hispanic whites
    Households in the Midwest and West

Customer trends:
    Average household spending on used trucks is likely to continue to fall as high gas prices and the economic downturn drive consumers toward fuel-efficient cars.

The best customers of used trucks (a category that includes minivans, sport utility vehicles, and pickups) are younger married couples with children. Householders aged 25 to 44, most with children, spend 24 to 36 percent more than average on used trucks and control 45 percent of the market. Married couples with children at home spend 86 percent more than the average on used trucks. Those with school-aged children spend over twice the average. Non-Hispanic whites outspend minorities by a wide margin on this item and control 86 percent of the market. Households in the Midwest and West spend, respectively, 18 and 22 percent more than average on used trucks.

Average household spending on used trucks fell 29 percent between 2000 and 2010, after adjusting for inflation. Most of the decline came since the overall peak-spending year of 2006. Behind the lower average household spending on used trucks were the generous incentives car dealers offered on new trucks as well as the Great Recession. Average household spending on used trucks is likely to continue to fall as higher gas prices and the economic downturn drive consumers toward fuel-efficient cars.

Table 19.15 Trucks, used

Total household spending $82,757,257,380.00
Average household spends   683.34

	AVERAGE HOUSEHOLD SPENDING	BEST CUSTOMERS (index)	BIGGEST CUSTOMERS (market share)
AGE OF HOUSEHOLDER			
Average household	**$683.34**	**100**	**100.0%**
Under age 25	703.95	103	6.8
Aged 25 to 34	931.51	136	22.7
Aged 35 to 44	846.34	124	22.4
Aged 45 to 54	777.75	114	23.5
Aged 55 to 64	476.49	70	12.3
Aged 65 to 74	457.42	67	7.2
Aged 75 or older	359.12	53	5.0

	AVERAGE HOUSEHOLD SPENDING	BEST CUSTOMERS (index)	BIGGEST CUSTOMERS (market share)
HOUSEHOLD INCOME			
Average household	**$683.34**	**100**	**100.0%**
Under $20,000	260.30	38	8.3
$20,000 to $39,999	411.98	60	13.8
$40,000 to $49,999	441.94	65	6.1
$50,000 to $69,999	685.90	100	14.4
$70,000 to $79,999	1,200.38	176	10.5
$80,000 to $99,999	1,037.58	152	12.7
$100,000 or more	1,362.54	199	34.2
HOUSEHOLD TYPE			
Average household	**683.34**	**100**	**100.0**
Married couples	1,001.51	147	72.3
Married couples, no children	686.51	100	21.3
Married couples, with children	1,270.75	186	43.3
Oldest child under age 6	1,273.74	186	8.0
Oldest child aged 6 to 17	1,436.27	210	24.7
Oldest child aged 18 or older	999.41	146	10.6
Single parent with child under age 18	663.46	97	5.7
Single person	206.18	30	8.8
RACE AND HISPANIC ORIGIN			
Average household	**683.34**	**100**	**100.0**
Asian	224.50	33	1.4
Black	202.83	30	3.6
Hispanic	594.80	87	10.6
Non-Hispanic white and other	773.02	113	85.8
REGION			
Average household	**683.34**	**100**	**100.0**
Northeast	524.14	77	14.1
Midwest	806.20	118	26.3
South	594.79	87	31.9
West	834.88	122	27.7
EDUCATION			
Average household	**683.34**	**100**	**100.0**
Less than high school graduate	451.94	66	9.4
High school graduate	711.27	104	26.6
Some college	695.87	102	21.4
Associate's degree	1,101.54	161	15.2
Bachelor's degree or more	628.75	92	27.3
Bachelor's degree	703.25	103	19.4
Master's, professional, doctoral degree	498.66	73	7.9

Note: Market shares may not sum to 100.0 because of rounding and missing categories by household type. "Asian" and "black" include Hispanics and non-Hispanics who identify themselves as being of the respective race alone. "Hispanic" includes people of any race who identify themselves as Hispanic. "Other" includes people who identify themselves as non-Hispanic and as Alaska Native, American Indian, Asian (who are also included in the "Asian" row), or Native Hawaiian or other Pacific Islander as well as non-Hispanics reporting more than one race.

Source: Calculations by New Strategist based on the Bureau of Labor Statistics' 2010 Consumer Expenditure Survey

Vehicle Finance Charges

Best customers: **Householders aged 25 to 54**
Married couples with children at home
Households in the South

Customer trends: **Average household spending on vehicle finance charges may continue to decline**
as boomers become empty-nesters and downsize their fleets.

The biggest spenders on vehicle finance charges are households with little savings and lots of vehicles—primarily young adults and couples with children. Householders ranging in age from 25 to 54 spend 23 to 27 percent more than average on vehicle finance charges and account for 69 percent of household spending on this item. Married couples with children at home spend 52 percent more than average on vehicle finance charges. Households in the South spend 14 percent more.

Average household spending on vehicle finance charges fell 42 percent between 2000 and 2010, after adjusting for inflation. Behind the decline were low-interest and no-interest loans on vehicles during the time period as well as diminished vehicle sales. Average household spending on vehicle finance charges may continue to decline as boomers become empty-nesters and downsize their fleets.

Table 19.16 Vehicle finance charges

Total household spending $29,432,634,210.00
Average household spends   243.03

	AVERAGE HOUSEHOLD SPENDING	BEST CUSTOMERS (index)	BIGGEST CUSTOMERS (market share)
AGE OF HOUSEHOLDER			
Average household	**$243.03**	**100**	**100.0%**
Under age 25	137.09	56	3.7
Aged 25 to 34	303.38	125	20.8
Aged 35 to 44	309.50	127	23.0
Aged 45 to 54	298.21	123	25.4
Aged 55 to 64	248.14	102	18.0
Aged 65 to 74	154.22	63	6.8
Aged 75 or older	56.27	23	2.2

	AVERAGE HOUSEHOLD SPENDING	BEST CUSTOMERS (index)	BIGGEST CUSTOMERS (market share)
HOUSEHOLD INCOME			
Average household	**$243.03**	**100**	**100.0%**
Under $20,000	49.06	20	4.4
$20,000 to $39,999	144.87	60	13.7
$40,000 to $49,999	236.06	97	9.2
$50,000 to $69,999	306.73	126	18.1
$70,000 to $79,999	382.53	157	9.4
$80,000 to $99,999	401.36	165	13.8
$100,000 or more	445.93	183	31.5
HOUSEHOLD TYPE			
Average household	**243.03**	**100**	**100.0**
Married couples	332.60	137	67.5
Married couples, no children	284.30	117	24.8
Married couples, with children	369.31	152	35.3
Oldest child under age 6	398.30	164	7.0
Oldest child aged 6 to 17	353.91	146	17.1
Oldest child aged 18 or older	377.20	155	11.2
Single parent with child under age 18	223.26	92	5.4
Single person	99.54	41	12.0
RACE AND HISPANIC ORIGIN			
Average household	243.03	100	100.0
Asian	188.70	78	3.3
Black	192.60	79	9.7
Hispanic	232.88	96	11.7
Non-Hispanic white and other	252.90	104	78.9
REGION			
Average household	**243.03**	**100**	**100.0**
Northeast	201.88	83	15.2
Midwest	223.73	92	20.5
South	275.86	114	41.7
West	242.15	100	22.6
EDUCATION			
Average household	**243.03**	**100**	**100.0**
Less than high school graduate	141.03	58	8.3
High school graduate	222.13	91	23.3
Some college	235.72	97	20.4
Associate's degree	346.05	142	13.5
Bachelor's degree or more	282.44	116	34.5
Bachelor's degree	288.91	119	22.5
Master's, professional, doctoral degree	271.15	112	12.1

Note: Market shares may not sum to 100.0 because of rounding and missing categories by household type. "Asian" and "black" include Hispanics and non-Hispanics who identify themselves as being of the respective race alone. "Hispanic" includes people of any race who identify themselves as Hispanic. "Other" includes people who identify themselves as non-Hispanic and as Alaska Native, American Indian, Asian (who are also included in the "Asian" row), or Native Hawaiian or other Pacific Islander as well as non-Hispanics reporting more than one race.

Source: Calculations by New Strategist based on the Bureau of Labor Statistics' 2010 Consumer Expenditure Survey

Vehicle Insurance

Best customers:
Householders aged 45 to 64
Married couples with adult children at home
Single parents
Asians

Customer trends:
Average household spending on vehicle insurance should fall as boomers become empty-nesters and downsize their fleets.

The biggest spenders on vehicle insurance are households with multiple cars and drivers—particularly teens and young adults. Householders aged 45 to 54 (the age group most likely to have teen or young-adult children in the home) spend 25 percent more than average on vehicle insurance, while those aged 55 to 64 spend 17 percent more. Together they account for 46 percent of the market for this item. Married couples with adult children at home spend 60 percent more than average on car insurance. Single parents, whose spending is well below average on most items, spend 3 percent more than average on vehicle insurance. Asians outspend the average by 32 percent.

Average household spending on vehicle insurance grew 3 percent between 2000 and 2010, after adjusting for inflation. Behind the growth was the baby-boom generation filling the best-customer age groups. Average household spending on this item may fall in the years ahead as boomers become empty-nesters and downsize their fleets.

Table 19.17 Vehicle insurance

Total household spending $122,368,934,940.00
Average household spends   1,010.42

	AVERAGE HOUSEHOLD SPENDING	BEST CUSTOMERS (index)	BIGGEST CUSTOMERS (market share)
AGE OF HOUSEHOLDER			
Average household	**$1,010.42**	**100**	**100.0%**
Under age 25	498.05	49	3.3
Aged 25 to 34	741.16	73	12.2
Aged 35 to 44	1,074.33	106	19.2
Aged 45 to 54	1,261.92	125	25.8
Aged 55 to 64	1,181.10	117	20.6
Aged 65 to 74	979.14	97	10.4
Aged 75 or older	878.03	87	8.3

	AVERAGE HOUSEHOLD SPENDING	BEST CUSTOMERS (index)	BIGGEST CUSTOMERS (market share)
HOUSEHOLD INCOME			
Average household	$1,010.42	100	100.0%
Under $20,000	537.95	53	11.6
$20,000 to $39,999	775.05	77	17.6
$40,000 to $49,999	1,060.89	105	9.9
$50,000 to $69,999	1,103.91	109	15.7
$70,000 to $79,999	1,358.13	134	8.0
$80,000 to $99,999	1,212.26	120	10.0
$100,000 or more	1,600.31	158	27.2
HOUSEHOLD TYPE			
Average household	1,010.42	100	100.0
Married couples	1,231.89	122	60.1
Married couples, no children	1,191.11	118	25.0
Married couples, with children	1,241.58	123	28.6
Oldest child under age 6	750.51	74	3.2
Oldest child aged 6 to 17	1,155.93	114	13.5
Oldest child aged 18 or older	1,620.57	160	11.6
Single parent with child under age 18	1,045.48	103	6.1
Single person	668.51	66	19.4
RACE AND HISPANIC ORIGIN			
Average household	1,010.42	100	100.0
Asian	1,336.06	132	5.6
Black	946.28	94	11.5
Hispanic	925.85	92	11.2
Non-Hispanic white and other	1,031.91	102	77.4
REGION			
Average household	1,010.42	100	100.0
Northeast	1,134.32	112	20.6
Midwest	875.20	87	19.3
South	1,032.43	102	37.5
West	1,009.33	100	22.6
EDUCATION			
Average household	1,010.42	100	100.0
Less than high school graduate	861.01	85	12.2
High school graduate	916.28	91	23.2
Some college	965.29	96	20.1
Associate's degree	1,161.49	115	10.9
Bachelor's degree or more	1,141.44	113	33.6
Bachelor's degree	1,029.59	102	19.2
Master's, professional, doctoral degree	1,361.73	135	14.6

Note: Market shares may not sum to 100.0 because of rounding and missing categories by household type. "Asian" and "black" include Hispanics and non-Hispanics who identify themselves as being of the respective race alone. "Hispanic" includes people of any race who identify themselves as Hispanic. "Other" includes people who identify themselves as non-Hispanic and as Alaska Native, American Indian, Asian (who are also included in the "Asian" row), or Native Hawaiian or other Pacific Islander as well as non-Hispanics reporting more than one race.

Source: Calculations by New Strategist based on the Bureau of Labor Statistics' 2010 Consumer Expenditure Survey

Vehicle Maintenance and Repair (Includes Oil Changes and Tires)

Best customers: **Householders aged 35 to 64**
                                   Married couples

Customer trends: **Average household spending on vehicle maintenance and repair is likely to rise as the economic downturn forces more Americans to drive aging cars.**

The biggest spenders on vehicle maintenance and repair are households with the most vehicles—married couples, particularly those with teenagers and young adults at home. Householders ranging in age from 35 to 64, many living with teens and young adults, spend 13 to 20 percent more than average on vehicle maintenance and repair. Married couples with school-aged or older children at home spend 38 to 56 percent more than average on this item. Couples without children at home spend 20 percent more.

Average household spending on vehicle maintenance and repair fell 6 percent between 2000 and 2006, after adjusting for inflation, then rose by the same percentage between 2006 and 2010. Behind the earlier decline in spending was the increased ownership of new vehicles as dealers offered low-interest loans and other incentives. Average household spending on vehicle maintenance and repair is likely to rise in the years ahead as the economic downturn forces more Americans to drive aging cars.

Table 19.18 Vehicle maintenance and repair (includes oil changes and tires)

Total household spending   **$95,345,118,960.00**
Average household spends   **787.28**

	AVERAGE HOUSEHOLD SPENDING	BEST CUSTOMERS (index)	BIGGEST CUSTOMERS (market share)
AGE OF HOUSEHOLDER			
Average household	**$787.28**	**100**	**100.0%**
Under age 25	480.16	61	4.0
Aged 25 to 34	705.48	90	14.9
Aged 35 to 44	889.37	113	20.4
Aged 45 to 54	947.17	120	24.9
Aged 55 to 64	894.27	114	20.0
Aged 65 to 74	700.87	89	9.6
Aged 75 or older	502.64	64	6.1

	AVERAGE HOUSEHOLD SPENDING	BEST CUSTOMERS (index)	BIGGEST CUSTOMERS (market share)
HOUSEHOLD INCOME			
Average household	**$787.28**	**100**	**100.0%**
Under $20,000	380.86	48	10.6
$20,000 to $39,999	568.39	72	16.5
$40,000 to $49,999	762.33	97	9.2
$50,000 to $69,999	750.12	95	13.7
$70,000 to $79,999	1,008.31	128	7.7
$80,000 to $99,999	1,044.29	133	11.1
$100,000 or more	1,445.94	184	31.5
HOUSEHOLD TYPE			
Average household	**787.28**	**100**	**100.0**
Married couples	1,018.31	129	63.8
Married couples, no children	944.05	120	25.5
Married couples, with children	1,095.32	139	32.4
Oldest child under age 6	897.14	114	4.9
Oldest child aged 6 to 17	1,084.76	138	16.2
Oldest child aged 18 or older	1,228.19	156	11.3
Single parent with child under age 18	593.73	75	4.4
Single person	482.83	61	18.0
RACE AND HISPANIC ORIGIN			
Average household	**787.28**	**100**	**100.0**
Asian	788.12	100	4.3
Black	602.00	76	9.4
Hispanic	620.99	79	9.6
Non-Hispanic white and other	842.13	107	81.1
REGION			
Average household	**787.28**	**100**	**100.0**
Northeast	825.68	105	19.2
Midwest	781.70	99	22.1
South	721.11	92	33.6
West	869.30	110	25.0
EDUCATION			
Average household	**787.28**	**100**	**100.0**
Less than high school graduate	489.53	62	8.9
High school graduate	604.74	77	19.6
Some college	794.78	101	21.2
Associate's degree	806.45	102	9.7
Bachelor's degree or more	1,076.80	137	40.6
Bachelor's degree	1,001.67	127	24.0
Master's, professional, doctoral degree	1,209.53	154	16.6

Note: Market shares may not sum to 100.0 because of rounding and missing categories by household type. "Asian" and "black" include Hispanics and non-Hispanics who identify themselves as being of the respective race alone. "Hispanic" includes people of any race who identify themselves as Hispanic. "Other" includes people who identify themselves as non-Hispanic and as Alaska Native, American Indian, Asian (who are also included in the "Asian" row), or Native Hawaiian or other Pacific Islander as well as non-Hispanics reporting more than one race.

Source: Calculations by New Strategist based on the Bureau of Labor Statistics' 2010 Consumer Expenditure Survey

Vehicle Rentals (Including Rentals on Trips)

Best customers:	**Householders aged 55 to 64** **Married couples** **Asians** **Households in the West**
Customer trends:	**Average household spending on vehicle rentals should rise as boomers age into the best-customer lifestage for travel, but only if discretionary income increases.**

The biggest spenders on rented vehicles are travelers, since three-quarters of spending on rented vehicles occurs on trips. Older married couples are the biggest travelers, which accounts for their above-average spending on rented vehicles. Householders aged 55 to 64 spend 34 percent more than average on rented vehicles. Married couples without children at home (most of them empty-nesters) spend 43 percent more than average on this item. Those with children at home spend 26 percent more than average on vehicle rentals. The figure peaks at 36 percent above average among those with adult children at home. Asian households outspend the average by 57 percent. Households in the West, where many Asians reside, spend 48 percent more than average on vehicle rentals.

Average household spending on rented vehicles fell 35 percent between 2000 and 2010, after adjusting for inflation. Behind the decline was the economic downturn, which reduced spending on travel, as well as price discounting. Average household spending on vehicle rentals should rise as boomers age into the best-customer lifestage, but only if discretionary income increases.

Table 19.19 Vehicle rentals (including rentals on trips)

Total household spending	$4,454,315,460.00
Average household spends	36.78

	AVERAGE HOUSEHOLD SPENDING	BEST CUSTOMERS (index)	BIGGEST CUSTOMERS (market share)
AGE OF HOUSEHOLDER			
Average household	**$36.78**	**100**	**100.0%**
Under age 25	8.10	22	1.5
Aged 25 to 34	31.59	86	14.3
Aged 35 to 44	34.85	95	17.1
Aged 45 to 54	40.06	109	22.5
Aged 55 to 64	49.17	134	23.6
Aged 65 to 74	39.01	106	11.4
Aged 75 or older	36.95	100	9.6

	AVERAGE HOUSEHOLD SPENDING	BEST CUSTOMERS (index)	BIGGEST CUSTOMERS (market share)
HOUSEHOLD INCOME			
Average household	**$36.78**	**100**	**100.0%**
Under $20,000	8.79	24	5.2
$20,000 to $39,999	14.10	38	8.8
$40,000 to $49,999	20.35	55	5.2
$50,000 to $69,999	27.37	74	10.7
$70,000 to $79,999	84.49	230	13.8
$80,000 to $99,999	41.97	114	9.5
$100,000 or more	100.48	273	46.8
HOUSEHOLD TYPE			
Average household	**36.78**	**100**	**100.0**
Married couples	47.89	130	64.2
Married couples, no children	52.61	143	30.4
Married couples, with children	46.16	126	29.2
Oldest child under age 6	47.57	129	5.5
Oldest child aged 6 to 17	43.38	118	13.9
Oldest child aged 18 or older	49.87	136	9.8
Single parent with child under age 18	20.05	55	3.2
Single person	24.71	67	19.7
RACE AND HISPANIC ORIGIN			
Average household	**36.78**	**100**	**100.0**
Asian	57.80	157	6.7
Black	31.21	85	10.4
Hispanic	27.62	75	9.1
Non-Hispanic white and other	39.17	106	80.7
REGION			
Average household	**36.78**	**100**	**100.0**
Northeast	40.82	111	20.4
Midwest	37.57	102	22.8
South	23.34	63	23.3
West	54.51	148	33.6
EDUCATION			
Average household	**36.78**	**100**	**100.0**
Less than high school graduate	13.82	38	5.4
High school graduate	20.32	55	14.1
Some college	29.65	81	16.9
Associate's degree	35.05	95	9.0
Bachelor's degree or more	67.58	184	54.6
Bachelor's degree	60.17	164	30.9
Master's, professional, doctoral degree	80.51	219	23.7

Note: Market shares may not sum to 100.0 because of rounding and missing categories by household type. "Asian" and "black" include Hispanics and non-Hispanics who identify themselves as being of the respective race alone. "Hispanic" includes people of any race who identify themselves as Hispanic. "Other" includes people who identify themselves as non-Hispanic and as Alaska Native, American Indian, Asian (who are also included in the "Asian" row), or Native Hawaiian or other Pacific Islander as well as non-Hispanics reporting more than one race.

Source: Calculations by New Strategist based on the Bureau of Labor Statistics' 2010 Consumer Expenditure Survey

Chapter 20.

Travel

Household Spending on Travel, 2010

Travel is one of the most-popular leisure-time activities of Americans. In 2010, the average household spent $1,306 on travel, including airfares, gasoline, lodging, luggage, food, and recreational expenses. Airline fares, lodging, and restaurant meals account for nearly two-thirds of travel spending. Ranking fourth are recreational expenses on trips, which account for 9 percent of the total although spending on this item declined 34 percent from 2000 to 2010.

After growing just 1 percent from 2000 to the overall peak-spending year of 2006, average household spending on travel declined 14 percent between 2006 and 2010, after adjusting for inflation. Behind the drop in spending on travel was household belt tightening as the Great Recession took hold. The only travel items that saw large increases in average household spending between 2000 and 2010 were luggage, up 20 percent, and parking fees and tolls on trips, up 17 percent. Spending on gasoline on trips increased 19 percent between 2000 and 2006 as prices rose, then dropped by 15 percent in the four ensuing years. Spending on intercity bus fares declined 49 percent between 2000 and 2010, and on intercity train fares, 41 percent. Spending on ship fares (mostly cruises), which had risen a strong 28 percent from 2000 to 2006, declined a sharp 34 percent over the next four years.

Because the best customers of travel are older Americans, average household spending on travel should rise in the future as the baby-boom generation ages—but only if discretionary income grows.

Spending on travel

(average annual spending by households on travel, 2000, 2006, and 2010; in 2010 dollars)

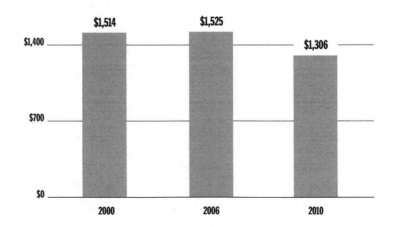

Table 20.1 Travel spending, 2000 to 2010

(average annual household spending on travel by category, 2000, 2006, and 2010; percent change in spending, 2000–06, 2000–10, and 2006–10; in 2010 dollars; ranked by amount spent)

	2010 average household spending	2006 average household spending (in 2010$)	2000 average household spending (in 2010$)	percent change		
				2006–10	2000–06	2000–10
AVERAGE ANNUAL SPENDING						
Average household spending on travel	**$1,306.10**	**$1,525.41**	**$1,513.83**	**–14.4%**	**0.8%**	**–13.7%**
Airline fares	325.31	361.91	346.99	–10.1	4.3	–6.2
Lodging on trips	299.03	346.81	318.63	–13.8	8.8	–6.1
Restaurant and carry-out food on trips	223.08	262.76	273.60	–15.1	–4.0	–18.5
Recreational expenses on trips	121.80	159.97	184.82	–23.9	–13.4	–34.1
Gasoline and motor oil on trips	119.18	139.43	117.41	–14.5	18.8	1.5
Groceries on trips	43.36	46.39	50.58	–6.5	–8.3	–14.3
Alcoholic beverages on trips	42.71	46.90	43.36	–8.9	8.2	–1.5
Ship fares	39.34	59.51	46.32	–33.9	28.5	–15.1
Vehicle rentals on trips	25.60	29.84	43.47	–14.2	–31.4	–41.1
Local transportation on trips	16.86	22.54	21.43	–25.2	5.2	–21.3
Train fares, intercity	15.67	17.62	26.74	–11.1	–34.1	–41.4
Luggage	12.64	8.47	10.54	49.2	–19.6	20.0
Parking fees and tolls on trips	11.18	10.99	9.57	-1.7	14.8	16.8
Bus fares, intercity	10.34	12.25	20.39	–15.6	–39.9	–49.3

				percentage point change		
	2006–10	2000–06	2000–10	2006–10	2000–06	2000–10
PERCENT DISTRIBUTION OF SPENDING						
Average household spending on travel	**100.0%**	**100.0%**	**100.0%**	–	–	–
Airline fares	24.9	23.7	22.9	1.2	0.8	2.0
Lodging on trips	22.9	22.7	21.0	0.2	1.7	1.8
Restaurant and carry-out food on trips	17.1	17.2	18.1	–0.1	–0.8	–1.0
Recreational expenses on trips	9.3	10.5	12.2	–1.2	–1.7	–2.9
Gasoline and motor oil on trips	9.1	9.1	7.8	0.0	1.4	1.4
Groceries on trips	3.3	3.0	3.3	0.3	–0.3	0.0
Alcoholic beverages on trips	3.3	3.1	2.9	0.2	0.2	0.4
Ship fares	3.0	3.9	3.1	–0.9	0.8	0.0
Vehicle rentals on trips	2.0	2.0	2.9	0.0	–0.9	–0.9
Local transportation on trips	1.3	1.5	1.4	–0.2	0.1	–0.1
Train fares, intercity	1.2	1.2	1.8	0.0	–0.6	–0.6
Luggage	1.0	0.6	0.7	0.4	–0.1	0.3
Parking fees and tolls on trips	0.9	0.7	0.6	0.1	0.1	0.2
Bus fares, intercity	0.8	0.8	1.3	0.0	–0.5	–0.6

Note: "–" means not applicable.

Source: Bureau of Labor Statistics, 2000, 2006, and 2010 Consumer Expenditure Surveys; calculations by New Strategist

Airline Fares

Best customers:

Householders aged 35 to 64
Married couples without children at home
Married couples with school-aged or older children at home
Asians
Households in the West
College graduates

Customer trends:

Average household spending on airline fares is likely to continue to decline because of the economic downturn, despite the presence of baby boomers in the peak-spending age groups.

The biggest spenders on airline fares are college-educated, middle-aged or older adults. Householders ranging in age from 35 to 64 spend 11 to 27 percent more than average on airfares and account for two-thirds of the market. College graduates spend over twice the average on airfares and account for 61 percent of the market. Married couples without children at home (most of them empty-nesters) spend 46 percent more than average on airfares, while those with school-aged or older children at home spend 29 to 64 percent more than average on this item. Asians spend two-and-one-half times the average on airfares. Spending on airline fares by households in the West is 46 percent above average.

Average household spending on airline fares showed a small increase early in the decade, but fell 10 percent between 2006 and 2010, after adjusting for inflation. Behind the decline was the Great Recession, which reduced spending on travel. Average household spending on airline fares is likely to continue to decline because of the economic downturn, despite the presence of baby boomers in the peak-spending age groups.

Table 20.2 Airline fares

Total household spending $39,397,318,170.00
Average household spends   325.31

	AVERAGE HOUSEHOLD SPENDING	BEST CUSTOMERS (index)	BIGGEST CUSTOMERS (market share)
AGE OF HOUSEHOLDER			
Average household	**$325.31**	**100**	**100.0%**
Under age 25	138.82	43	2.8
Aged 25 to 34	274.39	84	14.0
Aged 35 to 44	359.99	111	20.0
Aged 45 to 54	411.87	127	26.2
Aged 55 to 64	372.16	114	20.2
Aged 65 to 74	332.58	102	11.0
Aged 75 or older	195.54	60	5.7

	AVERAGE HOUSEHOLD SPENDING	BEST CUSTOMERS (index)	BIGGEST CUSTOMERS (market share)
HOUSEHOLD INCOME			
Average household	**$325.31**	**100**	**100.0%**
Under $20,000	75.13	23	5.0
$20,000 to $39,999	145.00	45	10.2
$40,000 to $49,999	186.76	57	5.4
$50,000 to $69,999	287.60	88	12.7
$70,000 to $79,999	352.54	108	6.5
$80,000 to $99,999	379.74	117	9.7
$100,000 or more	956.60	294	50.4
HOUSEHOLD TYPE			
Average household	**325.31**	**100**	**100.0**
Married couples	452.25	139	68.6
Married couples, no children	474.29	146	31.0
Married couples, with children	463.85	143	33.2
Oldest child under age 6	345.40	106	4.5
Oldest child aged 6 to 17	533.74	164	19.3
Oldest child aged 18 or older	420.26	129	9.3
Single parent with child under age 18	167.65	52	3.0
Single person	189.16	58	17.0
RACE AND HISPANIC ORIGIN			
Average household	**325.31**	**100**	**100.0**
Asian	821.09	252	10.7
Black	152.43	47	5.7
Hispanic	231.38	71	8.7
Non-Hispanic white and other	368.10	113	85.8
REGION			
Average household	**325.31**	**100**	**100.0**
Northeast	367.31	113	20.7
Midwest	291.13	89	19.9
South	231.89	71	26.2
West	476.28	146	33.2
EDUCATION			
Average household	**325.31**	**100**	**100.0**
Less than high school graduate	86.88	27	3.8
High school graduate	165.72	51	13.0
Some college	209.26	64	13.5
Associate's degree	295.13	91	8.6
Bachelor's degree or more	668.84	206	61.1
Bachelor's degree	570.13	175	33.1
Master's, professional, doctoral degree	841.19	259	28.0

Note: Market shares may not sum to 100.0 because of rounding and missing categories by household type. "Asian" and "black" include Hispanics and non-Hispanics who identify themselves as being of the respective race alone. "Hispanic" includes people of any race who identify themselves as Hispanic. "Other" includes people who identify themselves as non-Hispanic and as Alaska Native, American Indian, Asian (who are also included in the "Asian" row), or Native Hawaiian or other Pacific Islander as well as non-Hispanics reporting more than one race.

Source: Calculations by New Strategist based on the Bureau of Labor Statistics' 2010 Consumer Expenditure Survey

Alcoholic Beverages Purchased on Trips

Best customers: **Householders aged 45 to 54**
Married couples without children at home
Non-Hispanic whites and Asians
Households in the West

Customer trends: **Average household spending on alcoholic beverages while traveling should**
continue to grow as more boomers become empty-nesters, but only if
discretionary income grows.

The biggest spenders on alcoholic beverages purchased on trips are middle-aged, white, married travelers. Householders aged 45 to 54 spend 16 percent more than average on this item. Married couples without children at home (most of them older) spend 64 percent more than average on alcoholic beverages while on trips. These empty-nesters spend more than other household types on alcoholic beverages while traveling because they no longer need to devote their time and money to children's wants and needs. Non-Hispanic whites, who account for 90 percent of the market for alcoholic beverages purchased on trips, spend 19 percent more than average on this item, and Asians, 16 percent. Households in the West outspend the average by 22 percent.

Average household spending on alcoholic beverages purchased on trips fell 9 percent between 2006 and 2010, after adjusting for inflation, reversing the 8 percent gain accumulated from 2000 to 2006. Behind the decline was the economic downturn, which reduced spending on travel. In the years ahead, spending on this item should grow as more boomers become empty-nesters, but only if discretionary income grows.

Table 20.3 Alcoholic beverages purchased on trips

Total household spending $5,172,479,970.00
Average household spends   42.71

	AVERAGE HOUSEHOLD SPENDING	BEST CUSTOMERS (index)	BIGGEST CUSTOMERS (market share)
AGE OF HOUSEHOLDER			
Average household	**$42.71**	**100**	**100.0%**
Under age 25	29.73	70	4.6
Aged 25 to 34	45.24	106	17.6
Aged 35 to 44	46.40	109	19.7
Aged 45 to 54	49.52	116	24.0
Aged 55 to 64	46.14	108	19.1
Aged 65 to 74	42.48	99	10.7
Aged 75 or older	19.50	46	4.4

	AVERAGE HOUSEHOLD SPENDING	BEST CUSTOMERS (index)	BIGGEST CUSTOMERS (market share)
HOUSEHOLD INCOME			
Average household	**$42.71**	**100**	**100.0%**
Under $20,000	7.88	18	4.0
$20,000 to $39,999	16.85	39	9.0
$40,000 to $49,999	30.53	71	6.8
$50,000 to $69,999	44.39	104	14.9
$70,000 to $79,999	51.66	121	7.2
$80,000 to $99,999	50.20	118	9.8
$100,000 or more	120.15	281	48.2
HOUSEHOLD TYPE			
Average household	**42.71**	**100**	**100.0**
Married couples	56.35	132	65.1
Married couples, no children	69.94	164	34.8
Married couples, with children	49.69	116	27.1
Oldest child under age 6	43.35	101	4.3
Oldest child aged 6 to 17	52.26	122	14.4
Oldest child aged 18 or older	49.27	115	8.3
Single parent with child under age 18	22.89	54	3.2
Single person	30.35	71	20.8
RACE AND HISPANIC ORIGIN			
Average household	**42.71**	**100**	**100.0**
Asian	49.68	116	4.9
Black	16.42	38	4.7
Hispanic	20.80	49	5.9
Non-Hispanic white and other	50.74	119	90.1
REGION			
Average household	**42.71**	**100**	**100.0**
Northeast	49.70	116	21.4
Midwest	44.63	104	23.3
South	32.35	76	27.8
West	51.97	122	27.6
EDUCATION			
Average household	**42.71**	**100**	**100.0**
Less than high school graduate	7.90	18	2.6
High school graduate	20.82	49	12.4
Some college	35.96	84	17.7
Associate's degree	38.45	90	8.5
Bachelor's degree or more	84.41	198	58.7
Bachelor's degree	81.72	191	36.1
Master's, professional, doctoral degree	89.11	209	22.6

Note: Market shares may not sum to 100.0 because of rounding and missing categories by household type. "Asian" and "black" include Hispanics and non-Hispanics who identify themselves as being of the respective race alone. "Hispanic" includes people of any race who identify themselves as Hispanic. "Other" includes people who identify themselves as non-Hispanic and as Alaska Native, American Indian, Asian (who are also included in the "Asian" row), or Native Hawaiian or other Pacific Islander as well as non-Hispanics reporting more than one race.

Source: Calculations by New Strategist based on the Bureau of Labor Statistics' 2010 Consumer Expenditure Survey

Bus Fares, Intercity

Best customers: Householders aged 45 to 54
Married couples with school-aged or older children at home
Asians
Households in the Northeast and West

Customer trends: Average household spending on intercity bus fares should stabilize as travelers
look for less-expensive ways to get from point A to point B.

The best customers of intercity bus fares are the college-age children of middle-aged householders in the Northeast and West. Householders aged 45 to 54—many with adult children—spend 41 percent more than average on intercity bus fares. Married couples with school-aged or older children at home spend 46 to 72 percent more than average on this item, many of them paying for their college-age children to go to and from school. Asians spend 46 percent over average on intercity bus travel. Households in the Northeast spend 31 percent more and households in the West 28 percent more.

Average household spending on intercity bus fares fell by a substantial 49 percent between 2000 and 2010, after adjusting for inflation. Behind the decline was the Great Recession and the reduction in travel spending as well as discounters offering lower cost bus travel along well-traveled routes. Average household spending on intercity bus fares should stabilize as travelers look for less-expensive ways to get from point A to point B.

Table 20.4 Bus fares, intercity

Total household spending $1,252,246,380.00
Average household spends   10.34

	AVERAGE HOUSEHOLD SPENDING	BEST CUSTOMERS (index)	BIGGEST CUSTOMERS (market share)
AGE OF HOUSEHOLDER			
Average household	**$10.34**	**100**	**100.0%**
Under age 25	7.25	70	4.7
Aged 25 to 34	6.52	63	10.5
Aged 35 to 44	12.12	117	21.2
Aged 45 to 54	14.55	141	29.1
Aged 55 to 64	8.45	82	14.4
Aged 65 to 74	12.09	117	12.6
Aged 75 or older	8.18	79	7.5

	AVERAGE HOUSEHOLD SPENDING	BEST CUSTOMERS (index)	BIGGEST CUSTOMERS (market share)
HOUSEHOLD INCOME			
Average household	**$10.34**	**100**	**100.0%**
Under $20,000	3.70	36	7.8
$20,000 to $39,999	4.91	47	10.9
$40,000 to $49,999	9.80	95	9.0
$50,000 to $69,999	13.46	130	18.7
$70,000 to $79,999	6.42	62	3.7
$80,000 to $99,999	10.69	103	8.6
$100,000 or more	24.93	241	41.3
HOUSEHOLD TYPE			
Average household	**10.34**	**100**	**100.0**
Married couples	12.41	120	59.2
Married couples, no children	10.78	104	22.1
Married couples, with children	14.09	136	31.7
Oldest child under age 6	5.09	49	2.1
Oldest child aged 6 to 17	15.09	146	17.2
Oldest child aged 18 or older	17.79	172	12.4
Single parent with child under age 18	2.91	28	1.7
Single person	9.03	87	25.6
RACE AND HISPANIC ORIGIN			
Average household	**10.34**	**100**	**100.0**
Asian	15.14	146	6.2
Black	5.44	53	6.4
Hispanic	11.43	111	13.5
Non-Hispanic white and other	10.92	106	80.1
REGION			
Average household	**10.34**	**100**	**100.0**
Northeast	13.54	131	24.0
Midwest	10.50	102	22.6
South	6.88	67	24.4
West	13.20	128	28.9
EDUCATION			
Average household	**10.34**	**100**	**100.0**
Less than high school graduate	8.45	82	11.7
High school graduate	4.99	48	12.3
Some college	7.20	70	14.6
Associate's degree	8.96	87	8.2
Bachelor's degree or more	18.50	179	53.2
Bachelor's degree	16.84	163	30.8
Master's, professional, doctoral degree	21.41	207	22.4

Note: Market shares may not sum to 100.0 because of rounding and missing categories by household type. "Asian" and "black" include Hispanics and non-Hispanics who identify themselves as being of the respective race alone. "Hispanic" includes people of any race who identify themselves as Hispanic. "Other" includes people who identify themselves as non-Hispanic and as Alaska Native, American Indian, Asian (who are also included in the "Asian" row), or Native Hawaiian or other Pacific Islander as well as non-Hispanics reporting more than one race.

Source: Calculations by New Strategist based on the Bureau of Labor Statistics' 2010 Consumer Expenditure Survey

Gasoline and Motor Oil on Trips

Best customers: Householders aged 55 to 74
                        Married couples without children at home
                        Married couples with school-aged or older children at home
                        Households in the Midwest

Customer trends: Average household spending on gasoline and motor oil on trips should rise in the
                        next few years as more boomers fill the peak-traveling lifestage.

The biggest spenders on gasoline and motor oil purchased while traveling are the largest households as well as the most-avid travelers—empty-nesters. Householders aged 55 to 74 spend 25 to 37 percent more than average on this item. Married couples without children at home (most of them empty-nesters) spend 53 percent more than average on gasoline and motor oil while traveling and account for nearly one-third of the market. Couples with school-aged or older children at home spend 36 to 40 percent more than average on this item. Households in the Midwest outspend the average by one-third.

Average household spending on gasoline and motor oil on trips rose 19 percent between 2000 and the overall peak spending year of 2006, after adjusting for inflation, as gas prices increased. Spending then fell 15 percent between 2006 and 2010 as the Great Recession took hold and gas prices eased slightly. Average household spending on gasoline and motor oil while traveling should rise again in the next few years as more boomers fill the peak-traveling lifestage.

Table 20.5 Gasoline and motor oil on trips

Total household spending $14,433,532,260.00
Average household spends   119.18

	AVERAGE HOUSEHOLD SPENDING	BEST CUSTOMERS (index)	BIGGEST CUSTOMERS (market share)
AGE OF HOUSEHOLDER			
Average household	**$119.18**	**100**	**100.0%**
Under age 25	56.04	47	3.1
Aged 25 to 34	99.32	83	13.9
Aged 35 to 44	127.36	107	19.3
Aged 45 to 54	127.31	107	22.1
Aged 55 to 64	163.09	137	24.1
Aged 65 to 74	149.56	125	13.5
Aged 75 or older	49.13	41	3.9

	AVERAGE HOUSEHOLD SPENDING	BEST CUSTOMERS (index)	BIGGEST CUSTOMERS (market share)
HOUSEHOLD INCOME			
Average household	**$119.18**	**100**	**100.0%**
Under $20,000	37.59	32	6.9
$20,000 to $39,999	69.27	58	13.3
$40,000 to $49,999	97.79	82	7.8
$50,000 to $69,999	136.02	114	16.4
$70,000 to $79,999	154.74	130	7.8
$80,000 to $99,999	170.76	143	11.9
$100,000 or more	249.95	210	36.0
HOUSEHOLD TYPE			
Average household	**119.18**	**100**	**100.0**
Married couples	164.82	138	68.2
Married couples, no children	182.57	153	32.5
Married couples, with children	158.67	133	31.0
Oldest child under age 6	128.40	108	4.6
Oldest child aged 6 to 17	167.29	140	16.5
Oldest child aged 18 or older	162.57	136	9.8
Single parent with child under age 18	66.73	56	3.3
Single person	69.97	59	17.2
RACE AND HISPANIC ORIGIN			
Average household	**119.18**	**100**	**100.0**
Asian	97.29	82	3.5
Black	51.05	43	5.2
Hispanic	70.67	59	7.2
Non-Hispanic white and other	137.66	116	87.6
REGION			
Average household	**119.18**	**100**	**100.0**
Northeast	85.77	72	13.2
Midwest	157.18	132	29.4
South	101.88	85	31.4
West	136.88	115	26.0
EDUCATION			
Average household	**119.18**	**100**	**100.0**
Less than high school graduate	52.31	44	6.3
High school graduate	77.00	65	16.5
Some college	115.76	97	20.4
Associate's degree	175.87	148	13.9
Bachelor's degree or more	171.98	144	42.9
Bachelor's degree	167.34	140	26.5
Master's, professional, doctoral degree	180.06	151	16.3

Note: Market shares may not sum to 100.0 because of rounding and missing categories by household type. "Asian" and "black" include Hispanics and non-Hispanics who identify themselves as being of the respective race alone. "Hispanic" includes people of any race who identify themselves as Hispanic. "Other" includes people who identify themselves as non-Hispanic and as Alaska Native, American Indian, Asian (who are also included in the "Asian" row), or Native Hawaiian or other Pacific Islander as well as non-Hispanics reporting more than one race.

Source: Calculations by New Strategist based on the Bureau of Labor Statistics' 2010 Consumer Expenditure Survey

Groceries on Trips

Best customers: **Householders aged 35 to 74**
Married couples without children at home
Married couples with school-aged or older children at home
Households in the Northeast and West

Customer trends: **Average household spending on groceries while traveling should rise in the next few years as more boomers become empty-nesters.**

The biggest spenders on groceries purchased on trips are older married couples, the most-avid travelers. These couples are stocking up on food and drink for their hotel rooms or RVs. Householders ranging in age from 35 to 74 spend 10 to 46 percent more than average on this item. Married couples without children at home (most of them empty-nesters) spend 58 percent more than average on groceries while traveling and account for one-third of the market. Couples with school-aged or older children at home spend 36 to 60 percent more than average. Households in the Northeast and West spend, respectively, 18 and 23 percent more than average on groceries while traveling.

Average household spending on groceries while traveling fell 14 percent between 2000 and 2010, after adjusting for inflation. One factor behind the decline was the reduction in travel spending because of the Great Recession. Average household spending on groceries while traveling should rise in the next few years as more boomers become empty-nesters.

Table 20.6 Groceries on trips

Total household spending		$5,251,199,520.00	
Average household spends		43.36	
	AVERAGE HOUSEHOLD SPENDING	BEST CUSTOMERS (index)	BIGGEST CUSTOMERS (market share)
AGE OF HOUSEHOLDER			
Average household	**$43.36**	**100**	**100.0%**
Under age 25	12.75	29	2.0
Aged 25 to 34	25.22	58	9.7
Aged 35 to 44	52.99	122	22.1
Aged 45 to 54	47.74	110	22.8
Aged 55 to 64	55.90	129	22.7
Aged 65 to 74	63.44	146	15.7
Aged 75 or older	22.70	52	5.0

	AVERAGE HOUSEHOLD SPENDING	BEST CUSTOMERS (index)	BIGGEST CUSTOMERS (market share)
HOUSEHOLD INCOME			
Average household	**$43.36**	**100**	**100.0%**
Under $20,000	10.30	24	5.2
$20,000 to $39,999	22.15	51	11.7
$40,000 to $49,999	32.10	74	7.0
$50,000 to $69,999	45.17	104	14.9
$70,000 to $79,999	55.21	127	7.6
$80,000 to $99,999	69.60	161	13.4
$100,000 or more	101.58	234	40.2
HOUSEHOLD TYPE			
Average household	**43.36**	**100**	**100.0**
Married couples	63.04	145	71.7
Married couples, no children	68.63	158	33.6
Married couples, with children	61.13	141	32.8
Oldest child under age 6	42.60	98	4.2
Oldest child aged 6 to 17	69.19	160	18.8
Oldest child aged 18 or older	58.97	136	9.8
Single parent with child under age 18	21.91	51	3.0
Single person	23.00	53	15.5
RACE AND HISPANIC ORIGIN			
Average household	**43.36**	**100**	**100.0**
Asian	39.29	91	3.9
Black	16.43	38	4.6
Hispanic	30.33	70	8.5
Non-Hispanic white and other	49.76	115	87.0
REGION			
Average household	**43.36**	**100**	**100.0**
Northeast	51.18	118	21.7
Midwest	40.58	94	20.9
South	34.97	81	29.6
West	53.35	123	27.9
EDUCATION			
Average household	**43.36**	**100**	**100.0**
Less than high school graduate	18.73	43	6.2
High school graduate	28.58	66	16.8
Some college	37.58	87	18.2
Associate's degree	42.38	98	9.2
Bachelor's degree or more	72.31	167	49.5
Bachelor's degree	68.46	158	29.8
Master's, professional, doctoral degree	79.02	182	19.7

Note: Market shares may not sum to 100.0 because of rounding and missing categories by household type. "Asian" and "black" include Hispanics and non-Hispanics who identify themselves as being of the respective race alone. "Hispanic" includes people of any race who identify themselves as Hispanic. "Other" includes people who identify themselves as non-Hispanic and as Alaska Native, American Indian, Asian (who are also included in the "Asian" row), or Native Hawaiian or other Pacific Islander as well as non-Hispanics reporting more than one race.

Source: Calculations by New Strategist based on the Bureau of Labor Statistics' 2010 Consumer Expenditure Survey

Lodging on Trips

Best customers: **Householders aged 45 to 74**
Married couples without children at home
Married couples with school-aged or older children at home
Households in the Northeast
College graduates

Customer trends: **Average household spending on lodging should resume its growth as more**
boomers become empty-nesters, but only if discretionary income rises.

Lodging, the second-biggest travel expense after airline fares, accounts for 23 percent of all household travel spending. The biggest spenders on lodging are the most-avid travelers—middle-aged and older empty-nesters. Householders ranging in age from 45 to 74 spend 24 to 34 percent more than average on this item and account for 64 percent of the market. Married couples without children at home (most of them empty-nesters) spend 60 percent more than average on lodging. Couples with school-aged or older children at home spend 49 to 63 percent more than the average household on lodging on trips. Spending on this item by households in the Northeast is 21 percent above average. College graduates spend twice the average amount on accommodations while traveling.

Average household spending on lodging rose 9 percent between 2000 and the overall peak-spending year of 2006, after adjusting for inflation. Spending on this item then declined 14 percent between 2006 and 2010 as the Great Recession took hold. The earlier rise in spending occurred as the baby-boom generation aged into the peak-spending lifestage. Average household spending on lodging should resume its growth as more boomers become empty-nesters, but only if discretionary income rises.

Table 20.7 Lodging on trips

Total household spending $36,214,626,210.00
Average household spends   299.03

	AVERAGE HOUSEHOLD SPENDING	BEST CUSTOMERS (index)	BIGGEST CUSTOMERS (market share)
AGE OF HOUSEHOLDER			
Average household	**$299.03**	**100**	**100.0%**
Under age 25	87.67	29	1.9
Aged 25 to 34	179.01	60	10.0
Aged 35 to 44	291.06	97	17.6
Aged 45 to 54	401.67	134	27.8
Aged 55 to 64	379.67	127	22.4
Aged 65 to 74	370.97	124	13.3
Aged 75 or older	217.75	73	6.9

	AVERAGE HOUSEHOLD SPENDING	BEST CUSTOMERS (index)	BIGGEST CUSTOMERS (market share)
HOUSEHOLD INCOME			
Average household	**$299.03**	**100**	**100.0%**
Under $20,000	59.13	20	4.3
$20,000 to $39,999	133.54	45	10.2
$40,000 to $49,999	178.03	60	5.6
$50,000 to $69,999	273.60	91	13.1
$70,000 to $79,999	287.41	96	5.8
$80,000 to $99,999	378.29	127	10.5
$100,000 or more	878.98	294	50.4
HOUSEHOLD TYPE			
Average household	**299.03**	**100**	**100.0**
Married couples	439.84	147	72.6
Married couples, no children	478.86	160	34.0
Married couples, with children	430.56	144	33.5
Oldest child under age 6	252.43	84	3.6
Oldest child aged 6 to 17	487.08	163	19.2
Oldest child aged 18 or older	444.13	149	10.7
Single parent with child under age 18	149.65	50	3.0
Single person	152.80	51	15.0
RACE AND HISPANIC ORIGIN			
Average household	**299.03**	**100**	**100.0**
Asian	318.28	106	4.5
Black	105.21	35	4.3
Hispanic	129.77	43	5.3
Non-Hispanic white and other	357.16	119	90.6
REGION			
Average household	**299.03**	**100**	**100.0**
Northeast	360.95	121	22.2
Midwest	311.93	104	23.3
South	245.39	82	30.1
West	323.06	108	24.5
EDUCATION			
Average household	**299.03**	**100**	**100.0**
Less than high school graduate	54.86	18	2.6
High school graduate	162.83	54	13.9
Some college	218.21	73	15.3
Associate's degree	257.56	86	8.1
Bachelor's degree or more	603.87	202	60.0
Bachelor's degree	541.29	181	34.2
Master's, professional, doctoral degree	713.13	238	25.8

Note: Market shares may not sum to 100.0 because of rounding and missing categories by household type. "Asian" and "black" include Hispanics and non-Hispanics who identify themselves as being of the respective race alone. "Hispanic" includes people of any race who identify themselves as Hispanic. "Other" includes people who identify themselves as non-Hispanic and as Alaska Native, American Indian, Asian (who are also included in the Asian column), or Native Hawaiian or other Pacific Islander as well as non-Hispanics reporting more than one race. "–" means sample is too small to make a reliable estimate.

Source: Calculations by New Strategist based on the Bureau of Labor Statistics' 2010 Consumer Expenditure Survey

Luggage

Best customers: **Householders aged 25 to 44**
                                          High-income households
                                          Married couples with adult children at home
                                          Asians
                                          Households in the Northeast

Customer trends: **Average household spending on luggage is likely to decline until discretionary income grows.**

The biggest spenders on luggage are young adults and the well-to-do. Householders aged 25 to 44 spend 53 to 77 percent more than average on this item and control 58 percent of the market. Married couples with adult children at home spend more than three times the average on this item. Households with incomes of $100,000 or more outspend the average threefold, while Asians, who have the highest incomes among racial and ethnic groups, spend seven times the average on luggage. Households in the Northeast spend 84 percent more than average on luggage.

Average household spending on luggage declined 20 percent between 2000 and the overall peak-spending year of 2006, after adjusting for inflation. Then spending rose a whopping 49 percent between 2006 and 2010. This steep rise in spending on luggage may be a fluke in the 2010 data. Average household spending on luggage is likely to decline until discretionary income grows.

Table 20.8 Luggage

Total household spending $1,530,792,480.00
Average household spends   12.64

	AVERAGE HOUSEHOLD SPENDING	BEST CUSTOMERS (index)	BIGGEST CUSTOMERS (market share)
AGE OF HOUSEHOLDER			
Average household	**$12.64**	**100**	**100.0%**
Under age 25	—	—	—
Aged 25 to 34	19.37	153	25.5
Aged 35 to 44	22.37	177	32.0
Aged 45 to 54	11.14	88	18.2
Aged 55 to 64	9.64	76	13.5
Aged 65 to 74	12.31	97	10.5
Aged 75 or older	0.79	6	0.6

	AVERAGE HOUSEHOLD SPENDING	BEST CUSTOMERS (index)	BIGGEST CUSTOMERS (market share)
HOUSEHOLD INCOME			
Average household	$12.64	100	100.0%
Under $20,000	7.12	56	12.3
$20,000 to $39,999	2.35	19	4.3
$40,000 to $49,999	10.69	85	8.0
$50,000 to $69,999	4.27	34	4.8
$70,000 to $79,999	4.38	35	2.1
$80,000 to $99,999	26.98	213	17.8
$100,000 or more	39.01	309	52.9
HOUSEHOLD TYPE			
Average household	12.64	100	100.0
Married couples	14.77	117	57.6
Married couples, no children	11.34	90	19.1
Married couples, with children	19.62	155	36.1
Oldest child under age 6	2.61	21	0.9
Oldest child aged 6 to 17	12.04	95	11.2
Oldest child aged 18 or older	39.62	313	22.6
Single parent with child under age 18	8.67	69	4.0
Single person	4.23	33	9.8
RACE AND HISPANIC ORIGIN			
Average household	12.64	100	100.0
Asian	87.79	695	29.5
Black	8.02	63	7.8
Hispanic	2.97	23	2.9
Non-Hispanic white and other	14.88	118	89.2
REGION			
Average household	12.64	100	100.0
Northeast	23.22	184	33.7
Midwest	7.88	62	13.9
South	10.68	84	31.0
West	12.03	95	21.6
EDUCATION			
Average household	12.64	100	100.0
Less than high school graduate	0.65	5	0.7
High school graduate	2.36	19	4.8
Some college	8.69	69	14.5
Associate's degree	37.39	296	27.9
Bachelor's degree or more	21.57	171	50.7
Bachelor's degree	21.51	170	32.1
Master's, professional, doctoral degree	21.69	172	18.6

Note: Market shares may not sum to 100.0 because of rounding and missing categories by household type. "Asian" and "black" include Hispanics and non-Hispanics who identify themselves as being of the respective race alone. "Hispanic" includes people of any race who identify themselves as Hispanic. "Other" includes people who identify themselves as non-Hispanic and as Alaska Native, American Indian, Asian (who are also included in the "Asian" row), or Native Hawaiian or other Pacific Islander as well as non-Hispanics reporting more than one race.

Source: Calculations by New Strategist based on the Bureau of Labor Statistics' 2010 Consumer Expenditure Survey

Parking Fees and Tolls on Trips

Best customers:	**Householders aged 45 to 64** **Married couples without children at home** **Married couples with school-aged or older children at home** **Asians** **Households in the Northeast**
Customer trends:	**Average household spending on parking fees and tolls on trips should continue to rise as more boomers become empty-nesters and avid travelers—but only if discretionary income increases.**

The most-avid travelers spend the most on parking fees and tolls on trips. Householders aged 45 to 64 spend 21 to 28 percent more than average on this item. Married couples without children at home, most of them empty-nesters, spend 53 percent more than average on parking fees and tolls on trips, and couples with school-aged children spend 65 percent more. The spending on this item by Asian householders is 75 percent higher than average. Households in the Northeast spend 61 percent more than average on parking and tolls on trips because of the many toll roads in the region and the relatively high parking fees in congested Northeastern cities.

Average household spending on parking fees and tolls on trips rose 17 percent between 2000 and 2010, after adjusting for inflation. Average household spending on parking fees and tolls on trips should continue to rise as more boomers become empty-nesters and avid travelers—but only if discretionary income increases.

Table 20.9 Parking fees and tolls on trips

Total household spending $1,353,976,260.00
Average household spends   11.18

	AVERAGE HOUSEHOLD SPENDING	BEST CUSTOMERS (index)	BIGGEST CUSTOMERS (market share)
AGE OF HOUSEHOLDER			
Average household	**$11.18**	**100**	**100.0%**
Under age 25	2.75	25	1.6
Aged 25 to 34	9.18	82	13.7
Aged 35 to 44	11.81	106	19.1
Aged 45 to 54	13.57	121	25.1
Aged 55 to 64	14.36	128	22.7
Aged 65 to 74	12.55	112	12.1
Aged 75 or older	6.67	60	5.7

	AVERAGE HOUSEHOLD SPENDING	BEST CUSTOMERS (index)	BIGGEST CUSTOMERS (market share)
HOUSEHOLD INCOME			
Average household	**$11.18**	**100**	**100.0%**
Under $20,000	2.10	19	4.1
$20,000 to $39,999	4.78	43	9.8
$40,000 to $49,999	6.74	60	5.7
$50,000 to $69,999	12.32	110	15.8
$70,000 to $79,999	9.80	88	5.2
$80,000 to $99,999	12.80	114	9.5
$100,000 or more	32.44	290	49.8
HOUSEHOLD TYPE			
Average household	**11.18**	**100**	**100.0**
Married couples	15.81	141	69.8
Married couples, no children	17.11	153	32.5
Married couples, with children	16.26	145	33.8
Oldest child under age 6	11.80	106	4.5
Oldest child aged 6 to 17	18.46	165	19.4
Oldest child aged 18 or older	15.32	137	9.9
Single parent with child under age 18	3.91	35	2.1
Single person	7.13	64	18.7
RACE AND HISPANIC ORIGIN			
Average household	**11.18**	**100**	**100.0**
Asian	19.61	175	7.5
Black	4.43	40	4.8
Hispanic	7.43	66	8.1
Non-Hispanic white and other	12.83	115	87.0
REGION			
Average household	**11.18**	**100**	**100.0**
Northeast	17.98	161	29.5
Midwest	9.66	86	19.3
South	9.38	84	30.8
West	10.05	90	20.4
EDUCATION			
Average household	**11.18**	**100**	**100.0**
Less than high school graduate	2.85	25	3.6
High school graduate	5.99	54	13.7
Some college	7.82	70	14.7
Associate's degree	12.13	108	10.3
Bachelor's degree or more	21.70	194	57.7
Bachelor's degree	18.76	168	31.7
Master's, professional, doctoral degree	26.82	240	26.0

Note: Market shares may not sum to 100.0 because of rounding and missing categories by household type. "Asian" and "black" include Hispanics and non-Hispanics who identify themselves as being of the respective race alone. "Hispanic" includes people of any race who identify themselves as Hispanic. "Other" includes people who identify themselves as non-Hispanic and as Alaska Native, American Indian, Asian (who are also included in the "Asian" row), or Native Hawaiian or other Pacific Islander as well as non-Hispanics reporting more than one race.

Source: Calculations by New Strategist based on the Bureau of Labor Statistics' 2010 Consumer Expenditure Survey

Recreational Expenses on Trips

Best customers:

Householders aged 45 to 64
Married couples without children at home
Married couples with school-aged or older children at home
Asians
College graduates

Customer trends:

Average household spending on recreational expenses on trips should grow as more boomers become empty-nesters and avid travelers, but only if discretionary income rises.

Recreational expenses on trips, the fourth-largest travel expense, account for 9 percent of the average household's travel budget. The biggest spenders on recreational expenses on trips are older married couples. Householders ranging in age from 45 to 64 spend 33 percent more than average on this item. Married couples without children at home (most of them empty-nesters) spend 55 percent more than average on recreational expenses on trips, while those with school-aged children spend 85 percent more than average. Asians, who have the highest incomes among racial and ethnic groups, spend 30 percent more than average on recreational expenses on trips. College graduates spend twice the average amount on this item.

Average household spending on recreational expenses on trips fell by a steep 34 percent between 2000 and 2010, after adjusting for inflation. Behind the decline was the economic downturn, which reduced spending on travel. Average household spending on recreational expenses while traveling should grow as more boomers become empty-nesters and avid travelers, but only if discretionary income rises.

Table 20.10 Recreational expenses on trips

Total household spending $14,750,832,600.00
Average household spends   121.80

	AVERAGE HOUSEHOLD SPENDING	BEST CUSTOMERS (index)	BIGGEST CUSTOMERS (market share)
AGE OF HOUSEHOLDER			
Average household	**$121.80**	**100**	**100.0%**
Under age 25	35.08	29	1.9
Aged 25 to 34	75.80	62	10.4
Aged 35 to 44	142.56	117	21.2
Aged 45 to 54	161.82	133	27.5
Aged 55 to 64	161.75	133	23.4
Aged 65 to 74	129.51	106	11.4
Aged 75 or older	53.59	44	4.2

	AVERAGE HOUSEHOLD SPENDING	BEST CUSTOMERS (index)	BIGGEST CUSTOMERS (market share)
HOUSEHOLD INCOME			
Average household	**$121.80**	**100**	**100.0%**
Under $20,000	21.33	18	3.8
$20,000 to $39,999	51.19	42	9.6
$40,000 to $49,999	60.58	50	4.7
$50,000 to $69,999	122.69	101	14.4
$70,000 to $79,999	124.24	102	6.1
$80,000 to $99,999	172.72	142	11.8
$100,000 or more	351.40	289	49.5
HOUSEHOLD TYPE			
Average household	**121.80**	**100**	**100.0**
Married couples	177.52	146	71.9
Married couples, no children	188.60	155	32.9
Married couples, with children	178.74	147	34.1
Oldest child under age 6	93.51	77	3.3
Oldest child aged 6 to 17	225.36	185	21.8
Oldest child aged 18 or older	153.36	126	9.1
Single parent with child under age 18	69.88	57	3.4
Single person	57.38	47	13.8
RACE AND HISPANIC ORIGIN			
Average household	**121.80**	**100**	**100.0**
Asian	158.33	130	5.5
Black	36.92	30	3.7
Hispanic	75.96	62	7.6
Non-Hispanic white and other	142.81	117	88.9
REGION			
Average household	**121.80**	**100**	**100.0**
Northeast	128.82	106	19.4
Midwest	141.44	116	25.9
South	94.28	77	28.4
West	141.34	116	26.3
EDUCATION			
Average household	**121.80**	**100**	**100.0**
Less than high school graduate	18.93	16	2.2
High school graduate	63.76	52	13.4
Some college	98.78	81	17.0
Associate's degree	104.24	86	8.1
Bachelor's degree or more	243.01	200	59.3
Bachelor's degree	216.64	178	33.6
Master's, professional, doctoral degree	289.06	237	25.7

Note: Market shares may not sum to 100.0 because of rounding and missing categories by household type. "Asian" and "black" include Hispanics and non-Hispanics who identify themselves as being of the respective race alone. "Hispanic" includes people of any race who identify themselves as Hispanic. "Other" includes people who identify themselves as non-Hispanic and as Alaska Native, American Indian, Asian (who are also included in the "Asian" row), or Native Hawaiian or other Pacific Islander as well as non-Hispanics reporting more than one race.

Source: Calculations by New Strategist based on the Bureau of Labor Statistics' 2010 Consumer Expenditure Survey

Restaurant and Carry-out Food on Trips

Best customers: Householders aged 45 to 74
Married couples without children at home
Married couples with school-aged or older children at home
Asians

Customer trends: Average household spending on restaurant and carry-out food on trips should grow as boomers retire, but only if discretionary income rises.

The biggest spenders on restaurant and carry-out meals on trips are the most-avid travelers—older married couples. Householders ranging in age from 45 to 74 spend 21 to 22 percent more than average on this item. Married couples without children at home (most of them empty-nesters) spend 63 percent more than average on restaurant and carry-out meals on trips and control 35 percent of the market. Those with school-aged children spend 58 percent more. Asians, the most-affluent racial and ethnic group, spend 41 percent more than average on eating out while traveling.

Average household spending on restaurant and carry-out food on trips, the third-largest travel spending category, fell 15 percent between 2006 and 2010, after adjusting for inflation. Behind the decline was household budget cutting in the midst of the Great Recession. Spending on this item should grow in the years ahead as boomers retire, but only if discretionary income grows.

Table 20.11 Restaurant and carry-out food on trips

Total household spending $27,016,549,560.00
Average household spends 223.08

	AVERAGE HOUSEHOLD SPENDING	BEST CUSTOMERS (index)	BIGGEST CUSTOMERS (market share)
AGE OF HOUSEHOLDER			
Average household	**$223.08**	**100**	**100.0%**
Under age 25	82.60	37	2.5
Aged 25 to 34	171.66	77	12.8
Aged 35 to 44	240.46	108	19.5
Aged 45 to 54	271.80	122	25.2
Aged 55 to 64	269.45	121	21.3
Aged 65 to 74	272.54	122	13.1
Aged 75 or older	130.35	58	5.6

	AVERAGE HOUSEHOLD SPENDING	BEST CUSTOMERS (index)	BIGGEST CUSTOMERS (market share)
HOUSEHOLD INCOME			
Average household	**$223.08**	**100**	**100.0%**
Under $20,000	49.53	22	4.8
$20,000 to $39,999	98.01	44	10.1
$40,000 to $49,999	139.46	63	5.9
$50,000 to $69,999	222.87	100	14.3
$70,000 to $79,999	255.80	115	6.9
$80,000 to $99,999	293.88	132	11.0
$100,000 or more	611.50	274	47.0
HOUSEHOLD TYPE			
Average household	**223.08**	**100**	**100.0**
Married couples	322.33	144	71.3
Married couples, no children	364.26	163	34.7
Married couples, with children	305.34	137	31.8
Oldest child under age 6	208.67	94	4.0
Oldest child aged 6 to 17	352.16	158	18.6
Oldest child aged 18 or older	286.42	128	9.3
Single parent with child under age 18	116.19	52	3.1
Single person	120.46	54	15.8
RACE AND HISPANIC ORIGIN			
Average household	**223.08**	**100**	**100.0**
Asian	315.10	141	6.0
Black	92.11	41	5.1
Hispanic	136.54	61	7.5
Non-Hispanic white and other	258.53	116	87.9
REGION			
Average household	**223.08**	**100**	**100.0**
Northeast	242.63	109	20.0
Midwest	224.79	101	22.5
South	186.37	84	30.7
West	265.03	119	26.9
EDUCATION			
Average household	**223.08**	**100**	**100.0**
Less than high school graduate	70.89	32	4.5
High school graduate	117.18	53	13.4
Some college	185.98	83	17.5
Associate's degree	216.19	97	9.2
Bachelor's degree or more	415.72	186	55.4
Bachelor's degree	377.29	169	31.9
Master's, professional, doctoral degree	482.81	216	23.4

Note: Market shares may not sum to 100.0 because of rounding and missing categories by household type. "Asian" and "black" include Hispanics and non-Hispanics who identify themselves as being of the respective race alone. "Hispanic" includes people of any race who identify themselves as Hispanic. "Other" includes people who identify themselves as non-Hispanic and as Alaska Native, American Indian, Asian (who are also included in the "Asian" row), or Native Hawaiian or other Pacific Islander as well as non-Hispanics reporting more than one race.

Source: Calculations by New Strategist based on the Bureau of Labor Statistics' 2010 Consumer Expenditure Survey

Ship Fares

Best customers: Householders aged 45 to 74
High-income households
Married couples without children at home
Married couples with school-aged or older children at home
Non-Hispanic whites
Households in the West
College graduates

Customer trends: Average household spending on ship fares should increase in the years ahead as boomers fill the older age groups, but only if discretionary income grows.

The biggest spenders on ship fares are well-to-do older Americans. Householders aged 45 to 64 spend 29 percent more than average on this item, and those aged 65 to 74 spend 68 percent more than average. Together these age groups account for just over two-thirds of the market. Households with incomes of $100,000 or more spend nearly four-and-one-half times the average on ship fares and account for 76 percent of household spending on this item. Married couples without children at home (most of them empty-nesters) spend more than twice the average on cruises. Married couples with school-aged or older children at home spend 38 to 39 percent more than the average household on ship fares. Non-Hispanic whites dominate spending on this item and account for 87 percent of the market. Households in the West outspend the average by 31 percent. College graduates, an affluent demographic group, spend twice the average on this item.

Average household spending on ship fares, which had increased 28 percent from 2000 to 2006, declined 34 percent between 2006 and 2010, after adjusting for inflation. Behind the decline was the economic downturn, which reduced spending on travel. Average household spending on ship fares should increase in the years ahead as boomers fill the older age groups, but only if discretionary income grows.

Table 20.12 Ship fares

Total household spending $4,764,349,380.00
Average household spends   39.34

	AVERAGE HOUSEHOLD SPENDING	BEST CUSTOMERS (index)	BIGGEST CUSTOMERS (market share)
AGE OF HOUSEHOLDER			
Average household	**$39.34**	**100**	**100.0%**
Under age 25	6.36	16	1.1
Aged 25 to 34	26.88	68	11.4
Aged 35 to 44	32.57	83	15.0
Aged 45 to 54	50.59	129	26.6
Aged 55 to 64	50.61	129	22.7
Aged 65 to 74	65.97	168	18.0
Aged 75 or older	21.63	55	5.2

	AVERAGE HOUSEHOLD SPENDING	BEST CUSTOMERS (index)	BIGGEST CUSTOMERS (market share)
HOUSEHOLD INCOME			
Average household	**$39.34**	**100**	**100.0%**
Under $20,000	5.32	14	3.0
$20,000 to $39,999	8.35	21	4.9
$40,000 to $49,999	5.89	15	1.4
$50,000 to $69,999	10.90	28	4.0
$70,000 to $79,999	23.25	59	3.5
$80,000 to $99,999	33.28	85	7.1
$100,000 or more	174.87	445	76.2
HOUSEHOLD TYPE			
Average household	**39.34**	**100**	**100.0**
Married couples	62.20	158	78.0
Married couples, no children	84.27	214	45.5
Married couples, with children	48.51	123	28.7
Oldest child under age 6	22.06	56	2.4
Oldest child aged 6 to 17	54.61	139	16.3
Oldest child aged 18 or older	54.25	138	10.0
Single parent with child under age 18	2.59	7	0.4
Single person	13.89	35	10.3
RACE AND HISPANIC ORIGIN			
Average household	**39.34**	**100**	**100.0**
Asian	32.31	82	3.5
Black	25.11	64	7.8
Hispanic	17.28	44	5.4
Non-Hispanic white and other	45.15	115	87.0
REGION			
Average household	**39.34**	**100**	**100.0**
Northeast	39.25	100	18.3
Midwest	39.95	102	22.6
South	31.41	80	29.3
West	51.68	131	29.8
EDUCATION			
Average household	**39.34**	**100**	**100.0**
Less than high school graduate	7.05	18	2.6
High school graduate	12.22	31	7.9
Some college	30.76	78	16.4
Associate's degree	45.77	116	11.0
Bachelor's degree or more	82.21	209	62.1
Bachelor's degree	65.21	166	31.3
Master's, professional, doctoral degree	111.90	284	30.8

Note: Market shares may not sum to 100.0 because of rounding and missing categories by household type. "Asian" and "black" include Hispanics and non-Hispanics who identify themselves as being of the respective race alone. "Hispanic" includes people of any race who identify themselves as Hispanic. "Other" includes people who identify themselves as non-Hispanic and as Alaska Native, American Indian, Asian (who are also included in the "Asian" row), or Native Hawaiian or other Pacific Islander as well as non-Hispanics reporting more than one race.

Source: Calculations by New Strategist based on the Bureau of Labor Statistics' 2010 Consumer Expenditure Survey

Taxi Fares, Limousine Service, and Local Transportation on Trips

Best customers: **Householders aged 45 to 74**
Married couples without children at home
Asians
Households in the Northeast and West
College graduates

Customer trends: **Average household spending on taxi fares, limousine service, and local transportation on trips should rise as more boomers become empty-nesters and avid travelers, but only if discretionary income increases.**

Older married couples spend the most on local transportation on trips. Householders ranging in age from 45 to 74 spend 21 to 33 percent more than average on this item. Married couples without children at home (most of them empty-nesters) spend 80 percent more than average on taxi fares and local transportation on trips. College graduates spend twice the average. Asians spend nearly three-quarters more than average on this item. Households in the Northeast and West spend, respectively, 29 and 27 percent more than average on local transportation on trips.

Average household spending on taxi fares, limousine service, and local transportation on trips rose slowly in the first part of the decade, then declined 25 percent between 2006 and 2010, after adjusting for inflation. Average household spending on local transportation on trips should rise as more boomers become empty-nesters and avid travelers, but only if discretionary income increases.

Table 20.13 Taxi fares, limousine service, and local transportation on trips

Total household spending $2,041,864,020.00
Average household spends   16.86

	AVERAGE HOUSEHOLD SPENDING	BEST CUSTOMERS (index)	BIGGEST CUSTOMERS (market share)
AGE OF HOUSEHOLDER			
Average household	**$16.86**	**100**	**100.0%**
Under age 25	8.65	51	3.4
Aged 25 to 34	12.32	73	12.2
Aged 35 to 44	13.60	81	14.6
Aged 45 to 54	22.40	133	27.5
Aged 55 to 64	20.43	121	21.4
Aged 65 to 74	21.46	127	13.7
Aged 75 or older	12.84	76	7.3

	AVERAGE HOUSEHOLD SPENDING	BEST CUSTOMERS (index)	BIGGEST CUSTOMERS (market share)
HOUSEHOLD INCOME			
Average household	**$16.86**	**100**	**100.0%**
Under $20,000	3.86	23	5.0
$20,000 to $39,999	9.50	56	12.9
$40,000 to $49,999	8.16	48	4.6
$50,000 to $69,999	15.11	90	12.9
$70,000 to $79,999	12.91	77	4.6
$80,000 to $99,999	17.90	106	8.9
$100,000 or more	50.36	299	51.2
HOUSEHOLD TYPE			
Average household	**16.86**	**100**	**100.0**
Married couples	22.19	132	64.9
Married couples, no children	30.30	180	38.2
Married couples, with children	17.30	103	23.9
Oldest child under age 6	10.22	61	2.6
Oldest child aged 6 to 17	18.11	107	12.6
Oldest child aged 18 or older	20.19	120	8.6
Single parent with child under age 18	4.20	25	1.5
Single person	12.86	76	22.3
RACE AND HISPANIC ORIGIN			
Average household	**16.86**	**100**	**100.0**
Asian	29.24	173	7.4
Black	7.21	43	5.2
Hispanic	12.35	73	8.9
Non-Hispanic white and other	19.09	113	85.8
REGION			
Average household	**16.86**	**100**	**100.0**
Northeast	21.68	129	23.6
Midwest	15.32	91	20.3
South	12.54	74	27.3
West	21.46	127	28.8
EDUCATION			
Average household	**16.86**	**100**	**100.0**
Less than high school graduate	5.57	33	4.7
High school graduate	7.11	42	10.8
Some college	12.52	74	15.6
Associate's degree	11.87	70	6.7
Bachelor's degree or more	35.32	209	62.2
Bachelor's degree	34.32	204	38.5
Master's, professional, doctoral degree	37.08	220	23.8

Note: Market shares may not sum to 100.0 because of rounding and missing categories by household type. "Asian" and "black" include Hispanics and non-Hispanics who identify themselves as being of the respective race alone. "Hispanic" includes people of any race who identify themselves as Hispanic. "Other" includes people who identify themselves as non-Hispanic and as Alaska Native, American Indian, Asian (who are also included in the "Asian" row), or Native Hawaiian or other Pacific Islander as well as non-Hispanics reporting more than one race.

Source: Calculations by New Strategist based on the Bureau of Labor Statistics' 2010 Consumer Expenditure Survey

Train Fares, Intercity

Best customers: Householders aged 45 to 54 and 65 to 74
Married couples without children at home
Married couples with school-aged or older children at home
Asians
Households in the Northeast

Customer trends: Average household spending on train fares will continue to decline unless train service improves.

Middle-aged and older Americans are the best customers of intercity train fares. Householders aged 45 to 64 spend 28 percent more than average on intercity train tickets, and those aged 65 to 74 spend 40 percent more. Married couples without children at home (most of them empty-nesters) spend 60 percent more than average on intercity train fares, while those with school-aged or older children at home spend 22 to 23 percent more. Asians outspend the average by one-half. Households in the Northeast spend 33 percent more than average on train fares.

Average household spending on intercity train fares has been in a decade-long decline. It fell 34 percent between 2000 and 2006, after adjusting for inflation, and another 11 percent between 2006 and 2010. Behind the decline is increasingly limited train service in the United States. Unless train service improves, average household spending on this item is likely to continue to decline.

Table 20.14 Train fares, intercity

Total household spending $1,897,746,690.00
Average household spends   15.67

	AVERAGE HOUSEHOLD SPENDING	BEST CUSTOMERS (index)	BIGGEST CUSTOMERS (market share)
AGE OF HOUSEHOLDER			
Average household	**$15.67**	**100**	**100.0%**
Under age 25	9.75	62	4.1
Aged 25 to 34	9.40	60	10.0
Aged 35 to 44	16.12	103	18.6
Aged 45 to 54	20.12	128	26.6
Aged 55 to 64	15.30	98	17.2
Aged 65 to 74	21.99	140	15.1
Aged 75 or older	13.76	88	8.4

	AVERAGE HOUSEHOLD SPENDING	BEST CUSTOMERS (index)	BIGGEST CUSTOMERS (market share)
HOUSEHOLD INCOME			
Average household	**$15.67**	**100**	**100.0%**
Under $20,000	4.05	26	5.6
$20,000 to $39,999	10.93	70	16.0
$40,000 to $49,999	8.03	51	4.8
$50,000 to $69,999	15.35	98	14.0
$70,000 to $79,999	20.41	130	7.8
$80,000 to $99,999	17.72	113	9.4
$100,000 or more	38.61	246	42.2
HOUSEHOLD TYPE			
Average household	**15.67**	**100**	**100.0**
Married couples	20.01	128	63.0
Married couples, no children	25.04	160	33.9
Married couples, with children	16.96	108	25.2
Oldest child under age 6	6.98	45	1.9
Oldest child aged 6 to 17	19.28	123	14.5
Oldest child aged 18 or older	19.10	122	8.8
Single parent with child under age 18	9.83	63	3.7
Single person	12.05	77	22.5
RACE AND HISPANIC ORIGIN			
Average household	**15.67**	**100**	**100.0**
Asian	23.56	150	6.4
Black	11.89	76	9.3
Hispanic	8.83	56	6.9
Non-Hispanic white and other	17.47	111	84.5
REGION			
Average household	**15.67**	**100**	**100.0**
Northeast	20.81	133	24.4
Midwest	16.76	107	23.8
South	11.52	74	27.0
West	17.15	109	24.8
EDUCATION			
Average household	**15.67**	**100**	**100.0**
Less than high school graduate	5.24	33	4.8
High school graduate	7.04	45	11.5
Some college	16.09	103	21.6
Associate's degree	9.28	59	5.6
Bachelor's degree or more	29.83	190	56.6
Bachelor's degree	26.66	170	32.1
Master's, professional, doctoral degree	35.36	226	24.4

Note: Market shares may not sum to 100.0 because of rounding and missing categories by household type. "Asian" and "black" include Hispanics and non-Hispanics who identify themselves as being of the respective race alone. "Hispanic" includes people of any race who identify themselves as Hispanic. "Other" includes people who identify themselves as non-Hispanic and as Alaska Native, American Indian, Asian (who are also included in the "Asian" row), or Native Hawaiian or other Pacific Islander as well as non-Hispanics reporting more than one race.

Source: Calculations by New Strategist based on the Bureau of Labor Statistics' 2010 Consumer Expenditure Survey

Vehicle Rentals on Trips

Best customers:	Householders aged 45 to 74
	High-income households
	Married couples
	Asians
	Households in the West
	College graduates

Customer trends:	Average household spending on vehicle rentals on trips should grow in the years ahead as more boomers become empty-nesters and avid travelers, but only if discretionary income increases.

The biggest spenders on rented vehicles while traveling are older married couples. Householders ranging in age from 45 to 74 spend 22 to 57 percent more than average on this item. Married couples without children at home (most of them empty-nesters) spend 77 percent more than average on vehicle rentals while traveling. Couples with children at home spend 37 percent more than average on this item, the figure peaking among those with preschoolers at 59 percent. High-income households spend three times the average on vehicle rentals on trips, and college graduates spend two times the average. Asians spend 47 percent more than average. Households in the West, where many Asians reside, spend 54 percent more than average on vehicle rentals while traveling.

Average household spending on vehicle rentals while traveling declined by a steep 41 percent between 2000 and 2010, after adjusting for inflation. Price discounting was one factor behind the decline, as was the economic downturn. Average household spending on vehicle rentals while traveling should grow in the years ahead as more boomers become empty-nesters and avid travelers, but only if discretionary income increases.

Table 20.15 Vehicle rentals on trips

Total household spending $3,100,339,200.00

Average household spends 25.60

	AVERAGE HOUSEHOLD SPENDING	BEST CUSTOMERS (index)	BIGGEST CUSTOMERS (market share)
AGE OF HOUSEHOLDER			
Average household	**$25.60**	**100**	**100.0%**
Under age 25	5.67	22	1.5
Aged 25 to 34	17.17	67	11.2
Aged 35 to 44	24.13	94	17.1
Aged 45 to 54	31.73	124	25.6
Aged 55 to 64	40.18	157	27.7
Aged 65 to 74	31.21	122	13.1
Aged 75 or older	10.37	41	3.9

	AVERAGE HOUSEHOLD SPENDING	BEST CUSTOMERS (index)	BIGGEST CUSTOMERS (market share)
HOUSEHOLD INCOME			
Average household	$25.60	100	100.0%
Under $20,000	7.19	28	6.1
$20,000 to $39,999	9.56	37	8.6
$40,000 to $49,999	17.02	66	6.3
$50,000 to $69,999	18.83	74	10.5
$70,000 to $79,999	25.76	101	6.0
$80,000 to $99,999	30.41	119	9.9
$100,000 or more	79.14	309	53.0
HOUSEHOLD TYPE			
Average household	25.60	100	100.0
Married couples	38.45	150	74.1
Married couples, no children	45.32	177	37.6
Married couples, with children	35.03	137	31.8
Oldest child under age 6	40.83	159	6.8
Oldest child aged 6 to 17	33.42	131	15.4
Oldest child aged 18 or older	34.22	134	9.7
Single parent with child under age 18	16.15	63	3.7
Single person	11.50	45	13.2
RACE AND HISPANIC ORIGIN			
Average household	25.60	100	100.0
Asian	37.59	147	6.2
Black	13.51	53	6.5
Hispanic	17.89	70	8.5
Non-Hispanic white and other	28.72	112	85.1
REGION			
Average household	25.60	100	100.0
Northeast	30.53	119	21.9
Midwest	22.29	87	19.4
South	16.61	65	23.8
West	39.43	154	34.9
EDUCATION			
Average household	25.60	100	100.0
Less than high school graduate	9.48	37	5.3
High school graduate	9.02	35	9.0
Some college	17.77	69	14.6
Associate's degree	24.86	97	9.2
Bachelor's degree or more	53.38	209	61.9
Bachelor's degree	46.49	182	34.3
Master's, professional, doctoral degree	65.38	255	27.6

Note: Market shares may not sum to 100.0 because of rounding and missing categories by household type. "Asian" and "black" include Hispanics and non-Hispanics who identify themselves as being of the respective race alone. "Hispanic" includes people of any race who identify themselves as Hispanic. "Other" includes people who identify themselves as non-Hispanic and as Alaska Native, American Indian, Asian (who are also included in the "Asian" row), or Native Hawaiian or other Pacific Islander as well as non-Hispanics reporting more than one race.

Source: Calculations by New Strategist based on the Bureau of Labor Statistics' 2010 Consumer Expenditure Survey

Chapter 21.

Utilities

Household Spending on Utilities, 2010

Utilities—such as electricity and water—are one of the larger expenditure categories for American households. Electricity, in fact, ranks ninth among household expenditures. Overall, the average household spent $2,479 on utilities in 2010, 22 percent more than the $2,039 spent in 2000, after adjusting for inflation.

Average household spending on utilities increased between 2000 and 2010 because energy prices climbed during the time period. Spending on fuel oil rose a relatively modest 11 percent during the decade. Spending on water and sewer rose more than any other category, up by 34 percent. Spending on bottled gas and on trash collection climbed 21 percent. Natural gas saw a 20 percent decline in average household spending between the overall peak-spending year of 2006 and 2010, after having increased by 41 percent in the earlier part of the decade.

Oil prices being volatile, it is likely that average household spending on utilities will increase substantially in the years ahead. Only if consumers switch to more-energy-efficient appliances and attempt to conserve resources will spending remain stable or decline.

Spending on utilities

(average annual spending by households on utilities, 2000, 2006 and 2010; in 2010 dollars)

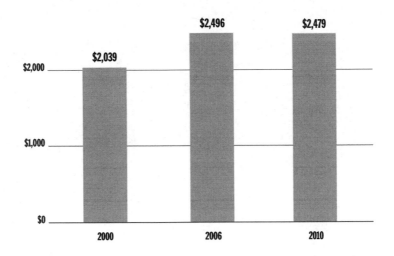

Table 21.1 Utilities spending, 2000 to 2010

(average annual household spending on utilities by category, 2000, 2006, and 2010; percent change in spending, 2000–06, 2000–10, and 2006–10; in 2010 dollars; ranked by amount spent)

	2010 average household spending	2006 average household spending (in 2010$)	2000 average household spending (in 2010$)	percent change		
				2006–10	2000–06	2000–10
AVERAGE ANNUAL SPENDING						
Average household spending on utlities	**$2,478.71**	**$2,495.99**	**$2,038.98**	**–0.7%**	**22.4%**	**21.6%**
Electricity	1,412.54	1,369.21	1,154.15	3.2	18.6	22.4
Natural gas	439.97	550.27	389.20	–20.0	41.4	13.0
Water and sewer	360.40	309.88	269.37	16.3	15.0	33.8
Trash collection	125.49	117.37	103.51	6.9	13.4	21.2
Fuel oil	77.47	89.40	69.75	–13.3	28.2	11.1
Bottled gas	53.88	53.27	44.65	1.1	19.3	20.7
Coal, wood, and other fuels	8.96	6.61	8.36	35.6	–20.9	7.2

				percentage point change		
	2006–10	2000–06	2000–10	2006–10	2000–06	2000–10
PERCENT DISTRIBUTION OF SPENDING						
Average household spending on utlities	**100.0%**	**100.0%**	**100.0%**	**–**	**–**	**–**
Electricity	57.0	54.9	56.6	2.1	–1.7	0.4
Natural gas	17.7	22.0	19.1	–4.3	3.0	–1.3
Water and sewer	14.5	12.4	13.2	2.1	–0.8	1.3
Trash collection	5.1	4.7	5.1	0.4	–0.4	0.0
Fuel oil	3.1	3.6	3.4	–0.5	0.2	–0.3
Bottled gas	2.2	2.1	2.2	0.0	–0.1	0.0
Coal, wood, and other fuels	0.4	0.3	0.4	0.1	–0.1	0.0

Note: "–" means not applicable.

Source: Bureau of Labor Statistics, 2000, 2006, and 2010 Consumer Expenditure Surveys; calculations by New Strategist

Bottled Gas

Best customers:
Householders aged 55 to 74
Married couples without children at home
Married couples with adult children at home
Non-Hispanic whites
Households in the Midwest

Customer trends:
Average household spending on bottled gas should decline as rural areas lose population.

Older, white householders in the Midwest are the best customers of bottled gas. The average household in the Midwest, where bottled gas is most popular, spends 38 percent more than the national average on this item. Householders aged 55 to 74 spend 47 to 67 percent more than average on bottled gas. Married couples without children at home, most of them empty-nesters, spend 63 percent more than average on bottled gas, while couples with adult children at home spend 27 percent more. Non-Hispanic white households spend 22 percent more than average on bottled gas and control 92 percent of the market.

Average household spending on bottled gas rose 21 percent between 2000 and 2010, after adjusting for inflation, despite the shift from bottled gas to other fuels during the time period. Average household spending on bottled gas should decline as rural areas lose population.

Table 21.2 Bottled gas

Total household spending $6,525,245,160.00
Average household spends 53.88

	AVERAGE HOUSEHOLD SPENDING	BEST CUSTOMERS (index)	BIGGEST CUSTOMERS (market share)
AGE OF HOUSEHOLDER			
Average household	$53.88	100	100.0%
Under age 25	8.19	15	1.0
Aged 25 to 34	31.37	58	9.7
Aged 35 to 44	36.92	69	12.4
Aged 45 to 54	54.94	102	21.1
Aged 55 to 64	89.90	167	29.4
Aged 65 to 74	78.99	147	15.8
Aged 75 or older	59.90	111	10.6

	AVERAGE HOUSEHOLD SPENDING	BEST CUSTOMERS (index)	BIGGEST CUSTOMERS (market share)
HOUSEHOLD INCOME			
Average household	**$53.88**	**100**	**100.0%**
Under $20,000	40.05	74	16.2
$20,000 to $39,999	40.57	75	17.3
$40,000 to $49,999	49.25	91	8.6
$50,000 to $69,999	66.84	124	17.8
$70,000 to $79,999	48.63	90	5.4
$80,000 to $99,999	55.38	103	8.6
$100,000 or more	82.09	152	26.1
HOUSEHOLD TYPE			
Average household	**53.88**	**100**	**100.0**
Married couples	68.34	127	62.6
Married couples, no children	87.79	163	34.6
Married couples, with children	55.67	103	24.0
Oldest child under age 6	26.65	49	2.1
Oldest child aged 6 to 17	58.47	109	12.8
Oldest child aged 18 or older	68.30	127	9.2
Single parent with child under age 18	28.46	53	3.1
Single person	41.16	76	22.4
RACE AND HISPANIC ORIGIN			
Average household	**53.88**	**100**	**100.0**
Asian	18.11	34	1.4
Black	19.34	36	4.4
Hispanic	14.98	28	3.4
Non-Hispanic white and other	65.59	122	92.3
REGION			
Average household	**53.88**	**100**	**100.0**
Northeast	47.42	88	16.2
Midwest	74.14	138	30.7
South	49.05	91	33.4
West	47.00	87	19.8
EDUCATION			
Average household	**53.88**	**100**	**100.0**
Less than high school graduate	46.54	86	12.3
High school graduate	43.25	80	20.5
Some college	43.54	81	17.0
Associate's degree	72.38	134	12.7
Bachelor's degree or more	67.98	126	37.5
Bachelor's degree	74.09	138	26.0
Master's, professional, doctoral degree	57.33	106	11.5

Note: Market shares may not sum to 100.0 because of rounding and missing categories by household type. "Asian" and "black" include Hispanics and non-Hispanics who identify themselves as being of the respective race alone. "Hispanic" includes people of any race who identify themselves as Hispanic. "Other" includes people who identify themselves as non-Hispanic and as Alaska Native, American Indian, Asian (who are also included in the "Asian" row), or Native Hawaiian or other Pacific Islander as well as non-Hispanics reporting more than one race.

Source: Calculations by New Strategist based on the Bureau of Labor Statistics' 2010 Consumer Expenditure Survey

Electricity

Best customers: **Householders aged 35 to 64**
Married couples with school-aged or older children at home
Households in the South

Customer trends: **Average household spending on electricity will increase as energy prices rise.**

Electricity is one of the biggest expenses for the average household, ranking ninth in 2010. Because almost every household buys electricity, there are few differences in spending by demographic characteristic. Household and dwelling sizes are the biggest factors in determining electricity consumption. Consequently, middle-aged married couples with children spend the most on this item. Householders aged 35 to 64 spend 9 to 12 percent more than average on electricity. Married couples with school-aged or older children at home spend 29 to 36 percent more than average. Households in the South spend 26 percent more than average on electricity because most homes in the region are cooled (and heated) by electricity.

Average household spending on electricity rose 22 percent between 2000 and 2010, after adjusting for inflation. Average household spending on electricity is certain to rise in the years ahead as energy prices climb.

Table 21.3 **Electricity**

| Total household spending | $171,068,481,780.00 |
| Average household spends | 1,412.54 |

	AVERAGE HOUSEHOLD SPENDING	BEST CUSTOMERS (index)	BIGGEST CUSTOMERS (market share)
AGE OF HOUSEHOLDER			
Average household	**$1,412.54**	**100**	**100.0%**
Under age 25	715.67	51	3.4
Aged 25 to 34	1,253.04	89	14.8
Aged 35 to 44	1,566.97	111	20.1
Aged 45 to 54	1,578.30	112	23.1
Aged 55 to 64	1,546.38	109	19.3
Aged 65 to 74	1,482.43	105	11.3
Aged 75 or older	1,196.86	85	8.1

	AVERAGE HOUSEHOLD SPENDING	BEST CUSTOMERS (index)	BIGGEST CUSTOMERS (market share)
HOUSEHOLD INCOME			
Average household	**$1,412.54**	**100**	**100.0%**
Under $20,000	972.23	69	15.0
$20,000 to $39,999	1,280.86	91	20.8
$40,000 to $49,999	1,373.42	97	9.2
$50,000 to $69,999	1,504.26	106	15.3
$70,000 to $79,999	1,586.33	112	6.7
$80,000 to $99,999	1,671.65	118	9.9
$100,000 or more	1,907.07	135	23.1
HOUSEHOLD TYPE			
Average household	**1,412.54**	**100**	**100.0**
Married couples	1,704.88	121	59.5
Married couples, no children	1,558.97	110	23.4
Married couples, with children	1,770.91	125	29.2
Oldest child under age 6	1,381.69	98	4.2
Oldest child aged 6 to 17	1,818.53	129	15.1
Oldest child aged 18 or older	1,924.15	136	9.8
Single parent with child under age 18	1,360.15	96	5.7
Single person	905.99	64	18.8
RACE AND HISPANIC ORIGIN			
Average household	**1,412.54**	**100**	**100.0**
Asian	1,108.21	78	3.3
Black	1,513.15	107	13.1
Hispanic	1,330.24	94	11.5
Non-Hispanic white and other	1,409.95	100	75.7
REGION			
Average household	**1,412.54**	**100**	**100.0**
Northeast	1,313.90	93	17.1
Midwest	1,174.76	83	18.5
South	1,784.67	126	46.4
West	1,123.49	80	18.0
EDUCATION			
Average household	**1,412.54**	**100**	**100.0**
Less than high school graduate	1,298.73	92	13.1
High school graduate	1,421.26	101	25.7
Some college	1,330.18	94	19.8
Associate's degree	1,477.52	105	9.9
Bachelor's degree or more	1,497.38	106	31.5
Bachelor's degree	1,461.26	103	19.5
Master's, professional, doctoral degree	1,560.44	110	12.0

Note: Market shares may not sum to 100.0 because of rounding and missing categories by household type. "Asian" and "black" include Hispanics and non-Hispanics who identify themselves as being of the respective race alone. "Hispanic" includes people of any race who identify themselves as Hispanic. "Other" includes people who identify themselves as non-Hispanic and as Alaska Native, American Indian, Asian (who are also included in the "Asian" row), or Native Hawaiian or other Pacific Islander as well as non-Hispanics reporting more than one race.

Source: Calculations by New Strategist based on the Bureau of Labor Statistics' 2010 Consumer Expenditure Survey

Fuel Oil

Best customers:	**Householders aged 55 or older** **Married couples** **Non-Hispanic whites** **Households in the Northeast**
Customer trends:	**Average household spending on fuel oil may decline as a growing proportion of households heat with natural gas or electricity.**

Older householders living in the Northeast are the biggest spenders on fuel oil. Households in the Northeast, where fuel oil heating systems are most common, spend more than four-and-one-half times the average on fuel oil and account for 84 percent of the market. Householders aged 55 to 74 spend 21 to 36 percent more than average on this item, in large part because they are most likely to live in older homes with fuel oil heating systems. For the same reason, householders aged 75 or older spend more than twice the average on fuel oil. Married couples spend 22 percent more than average on this item, the figure peaking at 39 percent among couples with adult children at home. Non-Hispanic whites spend 22 percent more than average on fuel oil and control 92 percent of the market.

Average household spending on fuel oil rose 28 percent between 2000 and 2006, after adjusting for inflation, then fell 13 percent in the ensuing four years. Average household spending on fuel oil may continue to decline as it is replaced by other energy sources.

Table 21.4 Fuel oil

Total household spending	$9,382,159,290.00
Average household spends	77.47

	AVERAGE HOUSEHOLD SPENDING	BEST CUSTOMERS (index)	BIGGEST CUSTOMERS (market share)
AGE OF HOUSEHOLDER			
Average household	**$77.47**	**100**	**100.0%**
Under age 25	9.46	12	0.8
Aged 25 to 34	34.72	45	7.5
Aged 35 to 44	56.94	73	13.3
Aged 45 to 54	81.50	105	21.8
Aged 55 to 64	93.82	121	21.4
Aged 65 to 74	105.58	136	14.7
Aged 75 or older	167.65	216	20.6

	AVERAGE HOUSEHOLD SPENDING	BEST CUSTOMERS (index)	BIGGEST CUSTOMERS (market share)
HOUSEHOLD INCOME			
Average household	**$77.47**	**100**	**100.0%**
Under $20,000	44.11	57	12.4
$20,000 to $39,999	69.68	90	20.6
$40,000 to $49,999	61.39	79	7.5
$50,000 to $69,999	69.35	90	12.8
$70,000 to $79,999	56.92	73	4.4
$80,000 to $99,999	124.05	160	13.4
$100,000 or more	130.52	168	28.9
HOUSEHOLD TYPE			
Average household	**77.47**	**100**	**100.0**
Married couples	94.90	122	60.4
Married couples, no children	94.65	122	26.0
Married couples, with children	92.65	120	27.8
Oldest child under age 6	88.28	114	4.9
Oldest child aged 6 to 17	84.92	110	12.9
Oldest child aged 18 or older	107.83	139	10.1
Single parent with child under age 18	26.14	34	2.0
Single person	61.15	79	23.1
RACE AND HISPANIC ORIGIN			
Average household	**77.47**	**100**	**100.0**
Asian	25.78	33	1.4
Black	26.94	35	4.3
Hispanic	22.73	29	3.6
Non-Hispanic white and other	94.18	122	92.2
REGION			
Average household	**77.47**	**100**	**100.0**
Northeast	355.98	460	84.3
Midwest	17.39	22	5.0
South	17.45	23	8.3
West	8.19	11	2.4
EDUCATION			
Average household	**77.47**	**100**	**100.0**
Less than high school graduate	50.89	66	9.4
High school graduate	87.11	112	28.7
Some college	53.64	69	14.6
Associate's degree	80.12	103	9.8
Bachelor's degree or more	98.00	127	37.6
Bachelor's degree	78.20	101	19.1
Master's, professional, doctoral degree	132.56	171	18.5

Note: Market shares may not sum to 100.0 because of rounding and missing categories by household type. "Asian" and "black" include Hispanics and non-Hispanics who identify themselves as being of the respective race alone. "Hispanic" includes people of any race who identify themselves as Hispanic. "Other" includes people who identify themselves as non-Hispanic and as Alaska Native, American Indian, Asian (who are also included in the "Asian" row), or Native Hawaiian or other Pacific Islander as well as non-Hispanics reporting more than one race.

Source: Calculations by New Strategist based on the Bureau of Labor Statistics' 2010 Consumer Expenditure Survey

Natural Gas

Best customers:	**Householders aged 35 to 54**
	Married couples with children at home
	Blacks
	Households in the Northeast and Midwest
Customer trends:	**Average household spending on natural gas will increase as energy prices rise.**

Because so many households heat with natural gas, there are few differences in spending on this item by demographic characteristic. Household and housing sizes are the biggest factors in determining natural gas consumption. Householders ranging in age from 35 to 54 spend 13 to 15 percent more than average on natural gas. Married couples with children at home spend 31 percent more than average on natural gas. Black householders outspend the average by 18 percent. Households in the Northeast and Midwest, the coldest parts of the country, spend 41 to 42 percent more than average on natural gas.

Average household spending on natural gas rose 41 percent between 2000 and 2006, after adjusting for inflation, then dropped 20 percent over the next four years. Average household spending on natural gas is likely to rise in the years ahead as energy prices increase.

Table 21.5 Natural gas

Total household spending	$53,283,446,790.00
Average household spends	439.97

	AVERAGE HOUSEHOLD SPENDING	BEST CUSTOMERS (index)	BIGGEST CUSTOMERS (market share)
AGE OF HOUSEHOLDER			
Average household	**$439.97**	**100**	**100.0%**
Under age 25	185.89	42	2.8
Aged 25 to 34	355.01	81	13.4
Aged 35 to 44	496.91	113	20.4
Aged 45 to 54	506.08	115	23.8
Aged 55 to 64	456.46	104	18.3
Aged 65 to 74	454.54	103	11.1
Aged 75 or older	466.64	106	10.1

	AVERAGE HOUSEHOLD SPENDING	BEST CUSTOMERS (index)	BIGGEST CUSTOMERS (market share)
HOUSEHOLD INCOME			
Average household	$439.97	100	100.0%
Under $20,000	249.21	57	12.4
$20,000 to $39,999	372.92	85	19.4
$40,000 to $49,999	417.38	95	9.0
$50,000 to $69,999	433.64	99	14.1
$70,000 to $79,999	498.06	113	6.8
$80,000 to $99,999	532.63	121	10.1
$100,000 or more	724.76	165	28.2
HOUSEHOLD TYPE			
Average household	439.97	100	100.0
Married couples	525.87	120	59.0
Married couples, no children	459.84	105	22.2
Married couples, with children	574.78	131	30.4
Oldest child under age 6	514.88	117	5.0
Oldest child aged 6 to 17	571.51	130	15.3
Oldest child aged 18 or older	615.63	140	10.1
Single parent with child under age 18	380.76	87	5.1
Single person	292.04	66	19.4
RACE AND HISPANIC ORIGIN			
Average household	439.97	100	100.0
Asian	446.97	102	4.3
Black	517.43	118	14.4
Hispanic	378.73	86	10.5
Non-Hispanic white and other	437.68	99	75.4
REGION			
Average household	439.97	100	100.0
Northeast	624.37	142	26.0
Midwest	618.76	141	31.4
South	260.25	59	21.7
West	405.80	92	20.9
EDUCATION			
Average household	439.97	100	100.0
Less than high school graduate	352.27	80	11.4
High school graduate	396.44	90	23.0
Some college	395.41	90	18.9
Associate's degree	446.66	102	9.6
Bachelor's degree or more	548.94	125	37.1
Bachelor's degree	511.24	116	21.9
Master's, professional, doctoral degree	614.78	140	15.1

Note: Market shares may not sum to 100.0 because of rounding and missing categories by household type. "Asian" and "black" include Hispanics and non-Hispanics who identify themselves as being of the respective race alone. "Hispanic" includes people of any race who identify themselves as Hispanic. "Other" includes people who identify themselves as non-Hispanic and as Alaska Native, American Indian, Asian (who are also included in the "Asian" row), or Native Hawaiian or other Pacific Islander as well as non-Hispanics reporting more than one race.

Source: Calculations by New Strategist based on the Bureau of Labor Statistics' 2010 Consumer Expenditure Survey

Trash Collection

Best customers:

Householders aged 55 or older
Married couples without children at home
Married couples with school-aged or older children at home
Asians
Households in the West

Customer trends:

Average household spending on trash collection should rise as local communities and private companies charge more for waste disposal.

The biggest spenders on trash collection are homeowners, who are most likely to be older householders and married couples. Householders aged 55 or older spend 12 to 20 percent more than average on trash collection. Married couples without children at home spend 21 percent more than average on trash collection. Those with school-aged or older children at home, the largest households, spend 25 to 27 percent more than average. Asians outspend the average by 16 percent. Households in the West spend 45 percent more than average on this category.

Average household spending on trash collection increased 21 percent between 2000 and 2010, after adjusting for inflation. Although governments strengthened recycling laws nationwide over the period, rising disposal fees counteracted the cost savings. Average household spending on trash collection should continue its long-term rise as it becomes more expensive to dispose of waste.

Table 21.6 Trash collection

Total household spending $15,197,717,430.00
Average household spends 125.49

	AVERAGE HOUSEHOLD SPENDING	BEST CUSTOMERS (index)	BIGGEST CUSTOMERS (market share)
AGE OF HOUSEHOLDER			
Average household	**$125.49**	**100**	**100.0%**
Under age 25	38.07	30	2.0
Aged 25 to 34	97.87	78	13.0
Aged 35 to 44	130.77	104	18.9
Aged 45 to 54	134.15	107	22.1
Aged 55 to 64	150.47	120	21.1
Aged 65 to 74	142.60	114	12.2
Aged 75 or older	140.23	112	10.7

	AVERAGE HOUSEHOLD SPENDING	BEST CUSTOMERS (index)	BIGGEST CUSTOMERS (market share)
HOUSEHOLD INCOME			
Average household	**$125.49**	**100**	**100.0%**
Under $20,000	69.10	55	12.0
$20,000 to $39,999	96.84	77	17.7
$40,000 to $49,999	114.20	91	8.6
$50,000 to $69,999	136.50	109	15.6
$70,000 to $79,999	149.63	119	7.1
$80,000 to $99,999	164.33	131	10.9
$100,000 or more	205.26	164	28.0
HOUSEHOLD TYPE			
Average household	**125.49**	**100**	**100.0**
Married couples	153.51	122	60.3
Married couples, no children	152.30	121	25.8
Married couples, with children	153.16	122	28.4
Oldest child under age 6	130.81	104	4.5
Oldest child aged 6 to 17	157.38	125	14.7
Oldest child aged 18 or older	159.55	127	9.2
Single parent with child under age 18	83.76	67	3.9
Single person	91.55	73	21.4
RACE AND HISPANIC ORIGIN			
Average household	**125.49**	**100**	**100.0**
Asian	146.09	116	5.0
Black	83.66	67	8.2
Hispanic	112.78	90	10.9
Non-Hispanic white and other	134.26	107	81.1
REGION			
Average household	**125.49**	**100**	**100.0**
Northeast	98.22	78	14.4
Midwest	117.97	94	21.0
South	109.17	87	31.9
West	181.42	145	32.7
EDUCATION			
Average household	**125.49**	**100**	**100.0**
Less than high school graduate	86.83	69	9.9
High school graduate	107.56	86	21.9
Some college	117.53	94	19.7
Associate's degree	129.01	103	9.7
Bachelor's degree or more	164.01	131	38.8
Bachelor's degree	151.72	121	22.8
Master's, professional, doctoral degree	185.46	148	16.0

Note: Market shares may not sum to 100.0 because of rounding and missing categories by household type. "Asian" and "black" include Hispanics and non-Hispanics who identify themselves as being of the respective race alone. "Hispanic" includes people of any race who identify themselves as Hispanic. "Other" includes people who identify themselves as non-Hispanic and as Alaska Native, American Indian, Asian (who are also included in the "Asian" row), or Native Hawaiian or other Pacific Islander as well as non-Hispanics reporting more than one race.

Source: Calculations by New Strategist based on the Bureau of Labor Statistics' 2010 Consumer Expenditure Survey

Water and Sewer

Best customers: Householders aged 35 to 64
                                    Married couples with school-aged or older children at home

Customer trends: Average household spending on water and sewer will rise as clean water becomes
                                    increasingly scarce and expensive.

Every household needs water and sewer service, but the category accounts for only 15 percent of household utility spending. Because most households consume water, there are few differences in spending on this item by demographic characteristic. Household and housing sizes are the biggest factors in determining spending on water and sewer. Householders ranging in age from 35 to 64, many with children, spend 11 to 14 percent more than average on this item. Married couples control 62 percent of spending on water and sewer. Married couples with school-aged or older children at home, who have the largest households, spend 38 to 40 percent more than average on this item. Households in the South and West, where water can be scarce, spend 10 to 18 percent more than average on water and sewer.

Average household spending on water and sewer rose 34 percent between 2000 and 2010, after adjusting for inflation. Higher fees charged by local communities were behind the increase. Average household spending on water and sewer is certain to rise in the years ahead as clean water becomes increasingly scarce and expensive.

Table 21.7 Water and sewer

Total household spending $43,646,962,800.00
Average household spends   360.40

	AVERAGE HOUSEHOLD SPENDING	BEST CUSTOMERS (index)	BIGGEST CUSTOMERS (market share)
AGE OF HOUSEHOLDER			
Average household	$360.40	100	100.0%
Under age 25	145.89	40	2.7
Aged 25 to 34	291.22	81	13.5
Aged 35 to 44	411.90	114	20.7
Aged 45 to 54	412.40	114	23.7
Aged 55 to 64	401.34	111	19.6
Aged 65 to 74	367.03	102	11.0
Aged 75 or older	336.77	93	8.9

	AVERAGE HOUSEHOLD SPENDING	BEST CUSTOMERS (index)	BIGGEST CUSTOMERS (market share)
HOUSEHOLD INCOME			
Average household	$360.40	100	100.0%
Under $20,000	210.43	58	12.7
$20,000 to $39,999	300.59	83	19.1
$40,000 to $49,999	327.93	91	8.6
$50,000 to $69,999	393.26	109	15.6
$70,000 to $79,999	432.75	120	7.2
$80,000 to $99,999	453.78	126	10.5
$100,000 or more	550.96	153	26.2
HOUSEHOLD TYPE			
Average household	360.40	100	100.0
Married couples	449.88	125	61.6
Married couples, no children	392.43	109	23.1
Married couples, with children	480.19	133	31.0
Oldest child under age 6	385.01	107	4.6
Oldest child aged 6 to 17	504.62	140	16.5
Oldest child aged 18 or older	496.83	138	10.0
Single parent with child under age 18	315.41	88	5.2
Single person	214.45	60	17.4
RACE AND HISPANIC ORIGIN			
Average household	360.40	100	100.0
Asian	395.64	110	4.7
Black	363.35	101	12.3
Hispanic	362.17	100	12.2
Non-Hispanic white and other	359.49	100	75.6
REGION			
Average household	360.40	100	100.0
Northeast	285.62	79	14.5
Midwest	295.00	82	18.2
South	397.11	110	40.4
West	425.88	118	26.8
EDUCATION			
Average household	360.40	100	100.0
Less than high school graduate	305.21	85	12.1
High school graduate	339.93	94	24.1
Some college	350.57	97	20.4
Associate's degree	375.67	104	9.8
Bachelor's degree or more	406.65	113	33.5
Bachelor's degree	395.48	110	20.7
Master's, professional, doctoral degree	426.14	118	12.8

Note: Market shares may not sum to 100.0 because of rounding and missing categories by household type. "Asian" and "black" include Hispanics and non-Hispanics who identify themselves as being of the respective race alone. "Hispanic" includes people of any race who identify themselves as Hispanic. "Other" includes people who identify themselves as non-Hispanic and as Alaska Native, American Indian, Asian (who are also included in the "Asian" row), or Native Hawaiian or other Pacific Islander as well as non-Hispanics reporting more than one race.

Source: Calculations by New Strategist based on the Bureau of Labor Statistics' 2010 Consumer Expenditure Survey

About the Consumer Expenditure Survey

History

The Consumer Expenditure Survey is an ongoing study of the day-to-day spending of American households. In taking the survey, government interviewers collect spending data on products and services as well as the amount and sources of household income, changes in saving and debt, and demographic and economic characteristics of household members. The Bureau of the Census collects data for the Consumer Expenditure Survey under contract with the Bureau of Labor Statistics, which is responsible for analysis and release of the survey data.

Since the late 19th century, the federal government has conducted expenditure surveys about every 10 years. Although the results have been used for a variety of purposes, their primary application is to track consumer prices. Beginning in 1980, the Consumer Expenditure Survey became a continuous survey with annual release of data. The survey is used to update prices for the market basket of products and services used in calculating the Consumer Price Index.

Description of the Consumer Expenditure Survey

The Consumer Expenditure Survey consists of two separate surveys: an interview survey and a diary survey. In the interview portion of the survey, respondents are asked each quarter for five consecutive quarters to report their expenditures for the previous three months. The interview survey records purchases of big-ticket items such as houses, cars, and major appliances as well as recurring expenses such as insurance premiums, utility payments, and rent. It covers about 95 percent of all expenditures.

The diary survey records expenditures on small, frequently purchased items during a two-week period. These detailed records include expenses for food and beverages purchased in grocery stores and at restaurants as well as other items such as tobacco, housekeeping supplies, nonprescription drugs, and personal care products and services. The diary survey is intended to capture expenditures respondents are likely to forget or recall incorrectly over longer periods of time.

The average spending figures shown in this report are the integrated data from both the diary and interview components of the survey. Integrated data provide a more complete accounting of consumer expenditures than either component of the survey is designed to do alone.

Data collection and processing

Two separate, nationally representative samples are used for the interview and diary surveys. For the interview survey, about 7,000 consumer units are interviewed on a rotating panel basis each quarter for five consecutive quarters. Another 7,000 consumer units keep weekly diaries of spending for two consecutive weeks. Data collection is carried out in 91 areas of the country.

The Bureau of Labor Statistics reviews, audits, and cleanses the data, then weights them to reflect the number and characteristics of all U.S. consumer units. Like any sample survey, the

Consumer Expenditure Survey is subject to two major types of error. Nonsampling error occurs when respondents misinterpret questions or interviewers are inconsistent in the way they ask questions or record answers. Respondents may forget items, recall expenses incorrectly, or deliberately give wrong answers. A respondent may remember how much he or she spent at the grocery store but forget the items picked up at a local convenience store. Most surveys of alcohol consumption or spending on alcohol, for example, suffer from underreporting. Mistakes during the various stages of data processing and refinement can also cause nonsampling error.

Sampling error occurs when a sample does not accurately represent the population it is supposed to represent. This kind of error is present in every sample-based survey and is minimized by using a proper sampling procedure. Standard error tables documenting the extent of sampling error in the Consumer Expenditure Survey are available from the Bureau of Labor Statistics at http://www.bls.gov/cex/csxstnderror.htm.

Although the Consumer Expenditure Survey is the best source of information about the spending behavior of American households, it should be treated with caution because of the above problems. Comparisons with consumption data from other sources show that Consumer Expenditure Survey data tend to underestimate expenditures except for rent, fuel, telephone service, furniture, transportation, and personal care services. Despite these problems, the data reveal important spending patterns by demographic segment that can be used to better understand consumer behavior.

Definition of consumer unit

The Consumer Expenditure Survey uses the consumer unit as the sampling unit rather than the household, which is the sampling unit used by the Census Bureau. The term "household" is used interchangeably with the term "consumer unit" in this book for convenience, although they are not exactly the same. Some households contain more than one consumer unit.

The Bureau of Labor Statistics defines consumer unit as (1) members of a household who are related by blood, marriage, adoption, or other legal arrangements; (2) a person living alone or sharing a household with others or living as a roomer in a private home or lodging house or in permanent living quarters in a hotel or motel, but who is financially independent; or (3) two or more persons living together who pool their income to make joint expenditure decisions. The bureau defines financial independence in terms of "the three major expenses categories: housing, food, and other living expenses. To be considered financially independent, at least two of the three major expense categories have to be provided by the respondent."

The Census Bureau uses the household as its sampling unit in the decennial census and in the monthly Current Population Survey. The Census Bureau's household "consists of all persons who occupy a housing unit. A house, an apartment or other group of rooms, or a single room is regarded as a housing unit when it is occupied or intended for occupancy as separate living quarters; that is, when the occupants do not live and eat with any other persons in the structure and there is direct access from the outside or through a common hall."

The definition goes on to specify that "a household includes the related family members and all the unrelated persons, if any, such as lodgers, foster children, wards, or employees who share the housing unit. A person living alone in a housing unit or a group of unrelated persons sharing a housing unit as partners is also counted as a household. The count of households excludes group quarters."

Because there can be more than one consumer unit in a household, consumer units outnumber households by several million. Young adults under age 25 head most of the additional consumer units.

For more information

To find out more about the Consumer Expenditure Survey, contact the specialists at the Bureau of Labor Statistics at (202) 691-6900, or visit the Consumer Expenditure Survey home page at http://www.bls.gov/cex/. The web site includes news releases, technical documentation, and current and historical summary-level data.

Percent Reporting Expenditure and Amount Spent, Average Quarter 2010

(percent of consumer units reporting expenditure and amount spent by purchasers during the average quarter, 2010)

	percent reporting expenditure during quarter	average amount spent by purchasers per quarter
ALCOHOLIC BEVERAGES	**37.7%**	**$225.39**
At home	**32.6**	**148.50**
Away from home	**23.6**	**154.79**
Alcoholic beverages at restaurants, taverns	17.1	150.91
Alcoholic beverages purchased on trips	12.1	88.39
APPAREL AND SERVICES	**75.1**	**369.59**
Men's apparel	**30.7**	**160.65**
Suits	1.2	442.94
Sportcoats and tailored jackets	0.9	194.72
Coats and jackets	4.1	115.95
Underwear	5.4	31.90
Hosiery	4.6	19.67
Nightwear	1.1	37.84
Accessories	3.4	45.70
Sweaters and vests	3.1	74.51
Active sportswear	1.4	45.14
Shirts	17.7	75.51
Pants and shorts	18.7	84.03
Uniforms	0.4	103.98
Costumes	0.4	98.72
Boys' (aged 2 to 15) apparel	**11.9**	**133.48**
Coats and jackets	2.0	64.09
Sweaters	0.9	76.42
Shirts	6.9	66.09
Underwear	2.3	35.11
Nightwear	1.1	32.55
Hosiery	1.5	19.00
Accessories	0.7	29.86
Suits, sportcoats, and vests	0.3	76.79
Pants and shorts	8.5	72.47
Uniforms	0.6	123.36
Active sportswear	1.0	32.18
Costumes	0.6	33.90
Women's apparel	**41.5**	**201.84**
Coats and jackets	6.0	108.93
Dresses	8.0	150.34
Sportcoats and tailored jackets	0.8	109.21
Sweaters and vests	7.6	75.66
Shirts, blouses, and tops	24.6	78.39
Skirts	3.2	70.82
Pants and shorts	23.2	85.61
Active sportswear	3.3	64.92
Nightwear	4.0	43.16
Undergarments	8.9	51.10

	percent reporting expenditure during quarter	average amount spent by purchasers per quarter
Hosiery	5.7%	$21.32
Suits	1.0	207.60
Accessories	5.8	67.26
Uniforms	1.0	119.01
Costumes	0.5	77.45
Girls' (aged 2 to 15) apparel	**12.8**	**147.80**
Coats and jackets	2.1	65.41
Dresses and suits	2.6	80.43
Shirts, blouses, and sweaters	8.0	67.88
Skirts, pants, and shorts	8.5	73.79
Active sportswear	1.5	34.59
Underwear and nightwear	3.4	40.40
Hosiery	1.7	17.05
Accessories	1.2	34.79
Uniforms	0.7	133.21
Costumes	0.7	53.41
Children's (under age 2) apparel	**13.4**	**122.20**
Coats, jackets, and snowsuits	1.2	58.06
Outerwear including dresses	7.1	66.22
Underwear	6.9	116.28
Nightwear and loungewear	2.7	38.53
Accessories	3.6	51.24
Footwear	**32.5**	**113.53**
Men's	12.5	91.29
Boys'	6.3	69.04
Women's	19.4	88.23
Girls'	6.6	61.83
Other apparel products and services	**36.4**	**155.17**
Material for making clothes	1.3	68.27
Sewing patterns and notions	1.9	28.49
Watches	3.2	167.90
Jewelry	8.1	299.26
Shoe repair and other shoe services	1.0	39.29
Coin-operated apparel laundry and dry cleaning	12.9	75.89
Apparel alteration, repair, and tailoring services	3.0	52.01
Clothing rental	0.3	137.50
Watch and jewelry repair	1.8	44.23
Professional laundry, dry cleaning	14.2	87.45
Clothing storage	0.1	115.63
COMPUTERS		
Computer information services	59.9	119.09
Computers and computer hardware, nonbusiness use	6.7	542.72
Computer software and accessories, nonbusiness use	4.3	99.35
Portable memory	4.4	40.48
Repair of computer systems for nonbusiness use	1.0	180.45
EDUCATION	**14.6**	**1,734.59**
College tuition	5.2	3,353.82
Elementary and high school tuition	1.4	2,708.68
Vocational and technical school tuition	0.3	883.65
Test preparation, tutoring services	0.7	375.00
Other school tuition	0.4	1,357.64
Other school expenses including rentals	3.7	233.60
Books and supplies for college	4.3	370.87
Books and supplies for elementary and high school	2.8	116.49

	percent reporting expenditure during quarter	average amount spent by purchasers per quarter
Books and supplies for vocational and technical schools	0.2%	$163.33
Books and supplies for day care and nursery	0.1	136.11
Books and supplies for other schools	0.2	165.28
ENTERTAINMENT	**90.8**	**623.61**
Fees and admissions	**46.1**	**314.00**
Recreation expenses on trips	7.7	70.34
Social, recreation, civic club memberships	12.9	233.41
Fees for participant sports	11.7	179.05
Participant sports on trips	3.4	162.94
Movie, theater, opera, ballet admissions	29.6	95.08
Movie, other admissions on trips	7.9	134.20
Admission to sports events	6.3	180.15
Admission to sports events on trips	7.9	44.72
Fees for recreational lessons	5.9	400.72
Other entertainment services on trips	7.7	70.34
Audio and visual equipment and services	**83.6**	**277.04**
Television sets	4.3	687.09
Cable and satellite television services	73.7	210.76
Satellite radio service	2.9	126.48
Online gaming services	1.3	50.20
Video cassette recorders and video disc players	2.0	125.62
Video cassettes, tapes, and discs	13.3	51.50
Video game hardware and software	6.3	149.44
Streamed, downloaded video	1.4	34.64
Repair of TV, radio, and sound equipment	0.5	146.20
Rental of television sets	0.1	215.00
Radios	0.5	79.25
Tape recorders and players	0.1	63.46
Personal digital audio players	1.6	174.09
Sound components and component systems	0.8	298.80
Compact discs, records, audio tapes	8.5	40.37
Streamed, downloaded audio	4.4	38.24
Rental of VCR, radio, sound equipment	0.0	50.00
Musical instruments and accessories	1.4	280.51
Rental and repair of musical instruments	0.3	122.41
Rental of video cassettes, tapes, discs, films	19.8	27.15
Rental of computer and video game hardware and software	0.0	93.75
Sound equipment accessories	1.0	134.18
Satellite dishes	0.2	145.24
Installation of Television sets	0.1	102.78
Pets, toys, hobbies, and playground equipment	**44.8**	**232.18**
Pets	33.6	227.75
Pet purchase, supplies, and medicines	27.9	145.57
Pet services	6.2	156.73
Veterinary services	9.9	263.90
Toys, games, arts and crafts, and tricycles	18.5	137.88
Stamp and coin collecting	0.6	123.66
Playground equipment	0.3	383.59
Other entertainment supplies, equipment, services	**22.0**	**389.30**
Unmotored recreational vehicles	0.2	9,672.06
Boat without motor and boat trailers	0.1	7,922.50
Trailer and other attachable campers	0.1	12,171.43
Motorized recreational vehicles	0.2	10,378.13
Purchase of motorized camper	0.1	4,646.88
Purchase of other vehicle	0.1	16,410.71

	percent reporting expenditure during quarter	average amount spent by purchasers per quarter
Purchase of boat with motor	0.6%	$302.12
Rental of recreational vehicles	0.6	302.12
Outboard motors	0.0	241.67
Docking and landing fees	0.4	614.53
Sports, recreation, and exercise equipment	12.6	219.85
Athletic gear, game tables, exercise equipment	7.2	168.98
Bicycles	1.8	219.18
Camping equipment	1.0	209.00
Hunting and fishing equipment	2.4	201.04
Winter sports equipment	0.5	281.50
Water sports equipment	0.6	190.52
Other sports equipment	1.0	159.02
Rental and repair of miscellaneous sports equipment	0.4	181.25
Photographic equipment and supplies	11.2	129.62
Film	1.2	25.20
Photo processing	6.9	41.20
Repair and rental of photographic equipment	0.1	109.38
Photographic equipment	2.4	257.98
Photographer fees	2.3	226.74
Live entertainment for catered affairs	0.3	861.67
Rental of party supplies for catered affairs	0.7	475.00
FINANCIAL PRODUCTS AND SERVICES		
Miscellaneous financial products and services	**38.2**	**475.59**
Lotteries and parimutuel losses	10.2	126.76
Legal fees	2.6	1,223.67
Funeral expenses	0.9	2,156.52
Safe deposit box rental	2.1	42.64
Checking accounts, other bank service charges	10.0	55.93
Cemetery lots, vaults, and maintenance fees	0.5	771.43
Accounting fees	5.6	291.46
Finance charges, except mortgage and vehicles	5.8	801.64
Dating services	0.1	66.67
Vacation clubs	0.2	473.61
Expenses for other properties	4.8	554.13
Occupational expenses	6.1	211.99
Credit card memberships	0.7	66.15
Shopping club membership fees	3.8	55.34
Cash contributions	**51.0**	**800.13**
Support for college students	3.0	812.13
Alimony expenditures	0.2	4,690.00
Child support expenditures	3.4	1,618.31
Gifts of stocks, bonds, and mutual funds to people in other households	0.2	1,470.83
Cash contributions to charities	18.6	213.94
Cash contributions to religious organizations	27.0	611.84
Cash contributions to educational organizations	2.2	400.22
Cash contributions to political organizations	1.5	220.69
Other cash gifts to people in other households	18.5	538.79
Personal insurance and pensions	**82.4**	**1,630.61**
Life and other personal insurance	27.3	291.85
Life, endowment, annuity, other personal insurance	26.2	288.34
Other nonhealth insurance	2.5	154.05
Pensions and Social Security	78.1	1,617.10
Deductions for government retirement	2.7	846.44

	percent reporting expenditure during quarter	average amount spent by purchasers per quarter
Deductions for railroad retirement	0.1%	$1,810.00
Deductions for private pensions	10.4	1,419.38
Nonpayroll deposit to retirement plans	7.0	1,670.55
Deductions for Social Security	77.9	1,252.10
Personal taxes	**55.9**	**791.09**
Federal income taxes	49.2	577.19
Federal income tax deducted	22.8	2,063.98
Additional federal income tax paid	7.8	1,174.52
Federal income tax refunds	37.0	−749.41
State and local income taxes	34.0	355.27
State and local income tax deducted	17.2	794.88
Additional state and local income tax paid	6.4	290.46
State and local income tax refunds	22.7	−153.89
Other taxes	16.1	234.29
FURNISHINGS AND EQUIPMENT FOR THE HOME	**56.6**	**513.80**
Household textiles	**20.6**	**100.35**
Bathroom linens	6.9	42.33
Bedroom linens	11.0	85.46
Kitchen and dining room linens	1.6	25.31
Curtains and draperies	2.7	165.02
Slipcovers and decorative pillows	1.6	57.25
Sewing materials for household items	3.5	68.46
Other linens	0.5	49.48
Furniture	**10.9**	**784.85**
Mattresses and springs	1.8	682.87
Other bedroom furniture	2.3	688.99
Sofas	2.3	936.33
Living room chairs	1.8	518.04
Living room tables	1.4	284.51
Kitchen and dining room furniture	1.5	540.65
Infants' furniture	0.7	272.64
Outdoor furniture	1.3	273.12
Wall units, cabinets, and other furniture	2.6	397.00
Floor coverings	**2.9**	**306.80**
Wall-to-wall carpeting, replacement (owner)	0.2	2,084.09
Floor coverings, nonpermanent	2.7	161.52
Major appliances	**8.8**	**567.51**
Dishwashers (built-in), garbage disposals, range hoods (renter)	0.0	193.75
Dishwashers (built-in), garbage disposals, range hoods (owner)	0.8	535.63
Refrigerators and freezers (renter)	0.3	369.12
Refrigerators and freezers (owner)	1.4	941.84
Washing machines (renter)	0.5	369.02
Washing machines (owner)	1.1	608.26
Clothes dryers (renter)	0.4	329.27
Clothes dryers (owner)	1.0	568.69
Cooking stoves, ovens (renter)	0.1	287.50
Cooking stoves, ovens (owner)	0.7	952.43
Microwave ovens (renter)	0.7	73.97
Microwave ovens (owner)	1.0	207.43
Window air conditioners (renter)	0.2	192.50
Window air conditioners (owner)	0.3	358.00
Electric floor-cleaning equipment	2.5	157.22

	percent reporting expenditure during quarter	average amount spent by purchasers per quarter
Sewing machines	0.3%	$235.00
Small appliances and miscellaneous housewares	**17.7**	**84.62**
Housewares	10.5	67.14
Plastic dinnerware	2.6	22.91
China and other dinnerware	2.4	77.19
Flatware	1.5	68.83
Glassware	2.0	32.48
Silver serving pieces	0.1	63.46
Other serving pieces	0.7	43.93
Nonelectric cookware	3.6	68.89
Small appliances	9.4	85.00
Small electric kitchen appliances	8.0	68.11
Portable heating and cooling equipment	1.6	155.31
Miscellaneous household equipment	**39.8**	**276.66**
Window coverings	1.5	375.16
Infants' equipment	0.8	181.49
Outdoor equipment	1.0	188.38
Lamps and lighting fixtures	3.7	110.76
Clocks and household decorative items	6.1	159.08
Telephones and accessories	6.5	130.13
Lawn and garden equipment	2.5	399.70
Power tools	2.1	167.45
Office furniture for home use	0.7	204.73
Hand tools	1.8	73.00
Indoor plants and fresh flowers	16.1	74.92
Closet and storage items	1.3	58.66
Rental of furniture	0.2	497.62
Luggage	1.7	94.85
Computers and computer hardware, nonbusiness use	6.7	542.72
Portable memory	4.4	40.48
Computer software and accessories, nonbusiness use	4.3	99.35
Personal digital assistants	0.3	365.63
Internet services away from home	0.5	89.42
Telephone answering devices	0.2	50.00
Business equipment for home use	0.8	118.44
Smoke alarms (owner)	0.6	55.70
Smoke alarms (renter)	0.1	45.45
Other household appliances (owner)	1.2	148.26
Other household appliances (renter)	0.5	70.56
GIFTS	**28.9**	**660.90**
Food	**1.3**	**797.18**
Housing	**10.4**	**333.30**
Household textiles	2.3	73.50
Appliances and miscellaneous housewares	1.9	139.52
Major appliances	0.4	315.00
Small appliances and miscellaneous housewares	1.6	95.06
Miscellaneous household equipment	4.7	131.71
Other housing	3.3	730.15
Apparel and services	**16.5**	**174.98**
Males aged 2 or older	4.4	135.56
Females aged 2 or older	5.8	158.46
Children under age 2	8.8	84.02
Other apparel products and services	4.2	150.77

	percent reporting expenditure during quarter	average amount spent by purchasers per quarter
Jewelry and watches	1.9%	$215.26
All other apparel products and services	2.6	88.53
Transportation	**4.3**	**482.28**
Health care	**0.8**	**567.50**
Entertainment	**9.2**	**201.89**
Toys, games, hobbies, and tricycles	6.1	119.21
Other entertainment	4.3	268.12
Education	**1.7**	**3,122.25**
All other gifts	**4.4**	**422.97**
GROCERIES	**98.8**	**1,197.76**
Purchased on trips	10.1	107.65
HEALTH CARE	**77.7**	**961.04**
Health insurance	**63.7**	**718.76**
Commercial health insurance	13.9	613.64
Traditional fee-for-service health plan (not BCBS)	4.2	574.70
Preferred-provider health plan (not BCBS)	9.9	617.71
Blue Cross, Blue Shield	22.6	614.56
Traditional fee-for-service health plan	3.6	649.72
Preferred-provider health plan	9.1	636.25
Health maintenance organization	7.8	567.17
Commercial Medicare supplement	2.2	557.29
Other BCBS health insurance	0.9	184.07
Health maintenance plans (HMOs)	13.0	552.23
Medicare payments	23.1	382.08
Medicare prescription drug premium	7.7	198.76
Commercial Medicare supplements/other health insurance	12.6	318.89
Commercial Medicare supplement (not BCBS)	5.3	500.28
Other health insurance (not BCBS)	7.8	174.17
Long-term care insurance	3.3	535.38
Medical Services	**42.2**	**427.29**
Physician's services	27.3	168.05
Dental services	14.5	454.36
Eye care services	6.8	126.83
Service by professionals other than physician	4.4	308.92
Lab tests, X-rays	5.6	198.45
Hospital room and services	4.6	634.51
Care in convalescent or nursing home	0.1	1,622.73
Other medical services	1.5	327.76
Prescription drugs	**42.1**	**207.93**
Medical supplies	**8.4**	**247.11**
Eyeglasses and contact lenses	6.8	224.59
Hearing aids	0.3	1,067.24
Medical equipment for general use	0.8	85.58
Supportive or convalescent medical equipment	0.6	166.53
Rental of medical equipment	0.4	123.78
Rental of supportive, convalescent medical equipment	0.3	98.33
HOUSEHOLD SERVICES	**70.2**	**356.96**
Personal services	**7.0**	**1,215.41**
Babysitting and child care in own home	1.8	758.43
Babysitting and child care in someone else's home	1.0	673.98
Care for elderly, invalids, handicapped, etc.	0.3	1,793.10

	percent reporting expenditure during quarter	average amount spent by purchasers per quarter
Adult day care centers	0.1%	$475.00
Day care centers, nurseries, and preschools	4.7	1,258.28
Other household services	**69.0**	**239.91**
Housekeeping services	5.7	488.20
Gardening and lawn care service	14.2	189.14
Water softening service	1.2	75.00
Nonclothing laundry and dry cleaning, sent out	0.6	42.74
Nonclothing laundry and dry cleaning, coin-operated	3.6	25.14
Termite and pest control services	3.7	123.56
Home security system service fee	4.8	123.28
Other home services	2.2	207.29
Termite and pest control products	2.6	28.07
Moving, storage, and freight express	2.2	503.83
Appliance repair, including at service center	2.7	176.11
Reupholstering and furniture repair	0.5	304.41
Repairs/rentals of lawn/garden equipment, hand/power tools, etc.	1.3	141.60
Appliance rental	0.3	118.00
Rental of office equipment for nonbusiness use	0.1	180.00
Repair of computer systems for nonbusiness use	1.0	180.45
Computer information services	59.9	119.09
Installation of computer	0.1	86.11
PERSONAL CARE PRODUCTS AND SERVICES	**60.4**	**118.61**
Wigs and hairpieces	0.9	92.73
Electric personal care appliances	3.3	45.47
Personal care services	59.3	116.83
READING	**36.9**	**66.85**
Newspaper and magazine subscriptions	17.2	57.96
Newspapers and magazines, nonsubscription	13.1	24.18
Books purchased through book clubs	1.1	64.82
Books not purchased through book clubs	17.6	61.04
RESTAURANTS AND CARRY-OUTS	**76.6**	**581.09**
Restaurant food on trips	23.7	235.02
SHELTER	**97.5**	**2,515.58**
Owned dwellings	**65.9**	**2,382.05**
Mortgage interest and charges	41.9	1,997.62
Mortgage interest	39.1	2,015.89
Interest paid, home equity loan	2.9	669.16
Interest paid, home equity line of credit	5.3	558.51
Property taxes	64.9	699.24
Maintenance, repairs, insurance, other expenses	36.1	769.32
Homeowner's insurance	23.9	360.38
Ground rent	1.6	889.57
Maintenance and repair services	13.3	1,081.33
Painting and papering	1.2	1,319.02
Plumbing and water heating	3.8	413.43
Heat, air conditioning, electrical work	5.0	614.83
Roofing and gutters	1.1	2,016.89
Other repair and maintenance services	4.6	1,089.95
Repair/replacement of hard-surface flooring	0.5	1,976.56
Repair of built-in appliances	0.4	135.53
Maintenance and repair materials	5.3	323.63
Paints, wallpaper, and supplies	1.9	147.88
Tools/equipment for painting, wallpapering	1.9	15.87
Plumbing supplies and equipment	0.7	188.73
Electrical supplies, heating/cooling equipment	0.3	235.19

	percent reporting expenditure during quarter	average amount spent by purchasers per quarter
Hard-surface flooring repair and replacement	0.4%	$666.03
Roofing and gutters	0.3	548.00
Plaster, paneling, siding, windows, doors, screens, awnings	0.7	517.03
Patio, walk, fence, driveway, masonry, brick, and stucco work	0.3	118.33
Miscellaneous supplies and equipment	1.8	232.40
Insulation, other maintenance/repair	1.8	231.01
Property management and security	6.0	259.88
Property management	5.8	230.59
Management and upkeep services for security	1.2	187.39
Parking	0.7	94.29
Rented dwellings	**32.8**	**2,213.37**
Rent	31.6	2,194.02
Rent as pay	1.4	1,450.18
Maintenance, insurance, and other expenses	5.1	225.10
Tenant's insurance	3.8	79.95
Maintenance and repair services	0.7	889.08
Maintenance and repair materials	0.8	250.31
Other lodging	**18.6**	**851.77**
Owned vacation homes	5.3	1,310.81
Mortgage interest and charges	1.5	1,781.91
Property taxes	5.2	563.86
Maintenance, insurance, and other expenses	1.9	728.76
Housing while attending school	0.9	1,660.17
Lodging on trips	14.3	522.05
TELEPHONE	**91.9**	**320.35**
Residential phone service and pay phones	62.5	160.52
Cellular phone service	64.8	293.13
Telephone answering devices	0.2	50.00
Phone cards	4.0	51.52
Voice over IP service	1.7	126.76
TOBACCO PRODUCTS AND SMOKING SUPPLIES	**20.9**	**428.61**
Cigarettes	18.3	453.28
Other tobacco products	3.5	188.89
TRANSPORTATION	**94.7**	**1,968.02**
Vehicle purchases	**5.0**	**12,864.81**
Cars and trucks, new	1.2	25,191.32
New cars	0.7	21,958.57
New trucks	0.5	27,982.41
Cars and trucks, used	3.6	9,077.00
Used cars	2.0	8,094.90
Used trucks	1.7	9,874.86
Other vehicles	0.2	5,328.13
Gasoline and motor oil	**90.1**	**591.52**
Gasoline	89.3	550.26
Diesel fuel	2.0	464.05
Gasoline on trips	19.9	148.23
Motor oil	8.4	29.42
Motor oil on trips	19.9	1.49
Other vehicle expenses	**81.8**	**684.73**
Vehicle finance charges	28.9	210.16
Automobile finance charges	15.5	168.16
Truck finance charges	15.0	189.88
Motorcycle and plane finance charges	0.8	120.54
Other vehicle finance charges	1.3	392.11

	percent reporting expenditure during quarter	average amount spent by purchasers per quarter
Maintenance and repairs	54.6%	$322.49
Coolant, additives, brake and transmission fluids	5.6	18.26
Tires	8.7	401.04
Vehicle products and cleaning services	4.1	39.29
Parts, equipment, and accessories	9.0	123.95
Vechicle audio equipment	0.2	253.57
Vehicle video equipment	0.2	217.65
Body work and painting	1.1	637.62
Clutch, transmission repair	1.3	697.05
Drive shaft and rear-end repair	0.4	359.29
Brake work	5.2	309.64
Repair to steering or front-end	1.3	378.52
Repair to engine cooling system	1.9	309.28
Motor tune-up	4.4	255.37
Lube, oil change, and oil filters	34.7	52.51
Front-end alignment, wheel balance, rotation	2.8	141.64
Shock absorber replacement	0.3	428.03
Repair tires and other repair work	6.2	207.68
Exhaust system repair	0.9	301.18
Electrical system repair	2.4	305.79
Motor repair, replacement	2.5	684.27
Auto repair service policy	0.5	777.88
Vehicle accessories, including labor	0.5	165.31
Vehicle air conditioning repair	1.0	336.62
Vehicle insurance	54.6	397.63
Vehicle rental, leases, licenses, other charges	45.1	234.65
Leased and rented vehicles	5.6	893.64
Rented vehicles	2.8	324.91
Auto rental	0.6	315.68
Auto rental on trips	2.0	293.31
Truck rental	0.2	136.25
Truck rental on trips	0.1	493.75
Leased vehicles	3.0	1,390.76
Car lease payments	1.9	1,167.58
Truck lease payments	1.2	1,261.34
Vehicle registration, state	18.8	136.20
Vehicle registration, local	1.9	107.86
Driver's license	5.5	41.06
Vehicle inspection	6.9	41.50
Parking fees	12.7	75.06
Parking fees in home city, excluding residence	10.3	76.24
Parking fees on trips	3.4	50.36
Tolls or electronic toll passes	9.5	64.55
Tolls on trips	6.3	16.94
Towing charges	1.0	103.91
Global positioning services	0.5	79.41
Automobile service clubs	5.2	89.22
Public transportation	**19.3**	**635.51**
Airline fares	10.6	770.15
Intercity bus fares	4.3	60.40
Intracity mass transit fares	7.8	214.33
Local transportation on trips	5.0	52.89
Taxi fares and limousine service on trips	5.0	31.08
Taxi fares and limousine service	3.5	102.05
Intercity train fares	4.3	91.74

	percent reporting expenditure during quarter	average amount spent by purchasers per quarter
Ship fares	2.5%	$396.57
School bus	0.1	491.67
TRAVEL		
Admission to sports events on trips	7.9	44.72
Airline fares	10.6	770.15
Alcoholic beverages purchased on trips	12.1	88.39
Auto rental on trips	2.0	293.31
Bus fares, intercity	4.3	60.40
Gasoline on trips	19.9	148.23
Groceries purchased on trips	10.1	107.65
Local transportation on trips	5.0	52.89
Lodging on trips	14.3	522.05
Luggage	1.7	94.85
Motor oil on trips	19.9	1.49
Movie, other admissions on trips	7.9	134.20
Parking fees on trips	3.4	50.36
Participant sports on trips	3.4	162.94
Recreation expenses on trips	7.7	70.34
Restaurant food on trips	23.7	235.02
Ship fares	2.5	396.57
Taxi fares and limousine service on trips	5.0	31.08
Tolls on trips	6.3	16.94
Train fares, intercity	4.3	91.74
Truck rental on trips	0.1	493.75
UTILITIES	**97.7**	**936.22**
Natural gas	49.6	221.58
Electricity	92.2	383.13
Fuel oil and other fuels	8.1	431.46
Fuel oil	3.0	643.44
Coal, wood, and other fuels	0.6	350.00
Bottled gas	4.9	273.78
Water and other public services	64.5	189.62
Water and sewerage maintenance	58.2	154.76
Trash and garbage collection	39.6	79.30
Septic tank cleaning	0.4	223.68

Note: The categories shown here may be different from those analyzed in the book because these are from only the interview portion of the Consumer Expenditure Survey. Some categories shown here are not analyzed in the book because the sample size was too small to make reliable estimates.

Source: Calculations by New Strategist based on the 2010 Consumer Expenditure Survey

Appendix C

Spending by Product and Service, Ranked by Amount Spent, 2010

(average annual spending of consumer units on products and services, ranked by amount spent, 2010)

1.	Deductions for Social Security	$3,902.53
2.	Groceries (also shown by individual category)	3,624.04
3.	Mortgage interest (or rent, $2,773.24)	3,154.47
4.	Vehicle purchases (net outlay)	2,588.40
5.	Gasoline and motor oil	2,132.31
6.	Restaurants (also shown by meal category)	2,080.95
7.	Health insurance	1,830.53
8.	Property taxes	1,813.84
9.	Electricity	1,412.54
10.	Federal income taxes	1,135.67
11.	Vehicle insurance	1,010.42
12.	Dinner at restaurants	986.99
13.	Vehicle maintenance and repairs	787.28
14.	Cellular phone service	759.68
15.	Lunch at restaurants	726.61
16.	College tuition	701.62
17.	Cash contributions to church, religious organizations	661.03
18.	Cable and satellite television services	621.49
19.	Deductions for private pensions	588.76
20.	Maintenance and repair services, owner	576.13
21.	Women's apparel	561.50
22.	State and local income taxes	482.45
23.	Nonpayroll deposit to retirement plans	469.09
24.	Natural gas	439.97
25.	Alcoholic beverages	411.97
26.	Residential telephone service and pay phones	401.31
27.	Cash gifts to members of other households	398.06
28.	Water and sewerage maintenance	360.40
29.	Prescription drugs	350.07
30.	Homeowner's insurance	344.52
31.	Cigarettes	331.80
32.	Airline fares	325.31
33.	Life and other personal insurance	318.12
34.	Men's apparel	304.05
35.	Lodging on trips	299.03
36.	Computer information services	285.14
37.	Owned vacation homes	278.94
38.	Personal care services	277.26
39.	Dental services	262.62
40.	Vehicle finance charges	243.03
41.	Day care centers, nurseries, and preschools	238.57
42.	Fresh fruits	232.24
43.	Restaurant meals on trips	223.08
44.	Child support expenditures	220.09
45.	Beef	216.70
46.	Breakfast at restaurants	212.05
47.	Fresh vegetables	210.47
48.	Interest paid, home equity loan/line of credit	196.74

49.	Finance charges, except mortgage and vehicles	$185.98
50.	Physician's services	183.17
51.	Pet food	165.20
52.	Leased vehicles	164.11
53.	Pet purchase, supplies, and medicines	162.51
54.	Cash contributions to charities	159.51
55.	Elementary and high school tuition	156.02
56.	Snacks at restaurants	155.29
57.	Movie, theater, amusement park, and other admissions	155.00
58.	Other taxes	151.07
59.	Laundry and cleaning supplies	150.26
60.	Pork	148.99
61.	Prepared foods except frozen, salads, and desserts	146.76
62.	Women's footwear	146.30
63.	Computers and computer hardware for nonbusiness use	144.58
64.	Poultry	138.12
65.	Cosmetics, perfume, and bath products	134.20
66.	Carbonated drinks	132.65
67.	Miscellaneous household products	129.52
68.	Legal fees	128.73
69.	Trash and garbage collection	125.49
70.	Fresh milk, all types	121.03
71.	Social, recreation, civic club membership	120.72
72.	Television sets	118.73
73.	Toys, games, hobbies, and tricycles	117.78
74.	Fish and seafood	117.08
75.	Hospital room and services	115.48
76.	Cheese	115.43
77.	Veterinarian services	113.52
78.	Housekeeping services	111.70
79.	Vehicle registration	110.90
80.	Fees for participant sports	108.25
81.	Gardening, lawn care service	107.66
82.	Expenses for other properties	107.28
83.	Cleansing and toilet tissue, paper towels, and napkins	103.41
84.	Beer and ale at home	102.83
85.	Household decorative items	101.37
86.	Men's footwear	101.14
87.	Girls' (aged 2 to 15) apparel	101.10
88.	Potato chips and other snacks	99.32
89.	Support for college students	97.78
90.	Jewelry	96.48
91.	Lawn and garden supplies	96.09
92.	Fees for recreational lessons	94.41
93.	Miscellaneous personal services	92.06
94.	Children's (under age 2) apparel	90.58
95.	Deductions for government retirement	90.40
96.	Nonprescription drugs	89.56
97.	Wine at home	87.69
98.	Sofas	84.27
99.	Ready-to-eat and cooked cereals	82.83
100.	Lunch meats (cold cuts)	81.80
101.	Rent as pay	80.63
102.	Babysitting and child care	79.51
103.	Funeral expenses	79.36
104.	Lottery and gambling losses	78.72
105.	Boys' (aged 2 to 15) apparel	77.77
106.	Fuel oil	77.47

107.	Candy and chewing gum	$77.34
108.	Stationery, stationery supplies, giftwrap	73.27
109.	Frozen prepared foods, except meals	71.17
110.	Catered affairs	70.71
111.	Maintenance and repair materials, owner	68.48
112.	Intracity mass transit fares	66.87
113.	Motorized recreational vehicles	66.42
114.	Unmotored recreational vehicles	65.77
115.	Accounting fees	65.52
116.	Books and supplies for college	63.79
117.	School lunches	63.40
118.	Beer and ale at bars, restaurants	62.96
119.	Bedroom furniture except mattresses and springs	62.56
120.	Hair care products	62.00
121.	Frozen meals	60.95
122.	Eyeglasses and contact lenses	60.64
123.	Coffee	60.25
124.	Bread, other than white	59.72
125.	Admission to sports events	59.62
126.	Refrigerators and freezers	58.14
127.	Ground rent	58.00
128.	Housing while attending school	57.11
129.	Postage	56.06
130.	Ice cream and related products	54.26
131.	Service by professionals other than physician	54.00
132.	Bottled gas	53.88
133.	Property management, owner	53.59
134.	Watches	53.09
135.	Canned vegetables	52.51
136.	Sauces and gravies	52.44
137.	Bottled water	52.04
138.	Canned and bottled fruit juice	51.97
139.	Occupational expenses	51.64
140.	Other alcoholic beverages at bars, restaurants	51.31
141.	Video game hardware and software	50.80
142.	Professional laundry, dry cleaning	49.53
143.	Biscuits and rolls	48.84
144.	Mattresses and springs	48.62
145.	Athletic gear, game tables, exercise equipment	47.28
146.	Other dairy (yogurt, etc.)	46.80
147.	Eggs	46.29
148.	Books	46.09
149.	Bedroom linens	45.95
150.	Cookies	45.90
151.	Nonprescription vitamins	45.54
152.	Moving, storage, and freight express	44.74
153.	Lab tests, X-rays	44.69
154.	Food prepared by consumer unit on trips	43.36
155.	Alcoholic beverages purchased on trips	42.71
156.	Indoor plants and fresh flowers	42.60
157.	Canned and packaged soups	42.30
158.	Wall units, cabinets, and other furniture	40.97
159.	Newspaper and magazine subscriptions	39.90
160.	White bread	39.83
161.	Ship fares	39.34
162.	Power tools	39.23
163.	Coin-operated apparel laundry and dry cleaning	39.07
164.	Board (including at school)	38.94

165.	Pet services	$38.87
166.	Parking fees	38.19
167.	Alimony expenditures	37.52
168.	Lawn and garden equipment	37.06
169.	Rented vehicles	36.78
170.	Living room chairs	36.47
171.	Crackers	36.26
172.	Topicals and dressings	36.17
173.	Frozen vegetables	36.16
174.	Cash contributions to educational institutions	35.86
175.	Prepared salads	35.43
176.	Cakes and cupcakes	35.30
177.	Deodorants, feminine hygiene, miscellaneous products	35.24
178.	Outdoor equipment	34.74
179.	Eye care services	34.65
180.	Washing machines	34.04
181.	Oral hygiene products	33.98
182.	Pasta, cornmeal, and other cereal products	33.92
183.	Nuts	33.65
184.	Wine at bars, restaurants	33.30
185.	Telephones and accessories	32.60
186.	Salt, spices, and other seasonings	32.49
187.	Baby food	32.48
188.	Kitchen and dining room furniture	31.79
189.	Fats and oils	31.49
190.	Tea	29.20
191.	Cooking stoves, ovens	28.81
192.	Salad dressings	28.77
193.	Tolls	28.72
194.	Girls' footwear	28.62
195.	Clothes dryers	27.92
196.	Sound components, equipment, and accessories	27.67
197.	Meals as pay	27.45
198.	Video cassettes, tapes, and discs	27.38
199.	Boys' footwear	27.32
200.	Tobacco products other than cigarettes	26.52
201.	Jams, preserves, other sweets	26.49
202.	Outdoor furniture	26.39
203.	Baking needs	26.18
204.	Hunting and fishing equipment	26.17
205.	Maintenance and repair services, renter	25.25
206.	Frozen and refrigerated bakery products	25.19
207.	Rice	24.72
208.	Frankfurters	24.51
209.	Noncarbonated fruit-flavored drinks	24.25
210.	Photographic equipment	24.25
211.	Home security system service fee	23.62
212.	Tableware, nonelectric kitchenware	23.57
213.	Butter	23.03
214.	Window coverings	22.96
215.	Sugar	22.76
216.	Checking accounts, other bank service charges	22.44
217.	Sweetrolls, coffee cakes, doughnuts	22.28
218.	Lamps and lighting fixtures	21.93
219.	Small electric kitchen appliances	21.85
220.	Recreation expenses on trips	21.58
221.	Rental of video cassettes, tapes, discs, films	21.51
222.	Termite and pest control products and services	20.97

223.	Care for elderly, invalids, handicapped, etc.	$20.80
224.	Canned fruits	20.53
225.	Cream	19.88
226.	School tuition other than college, vocational/technical, elementary, high school	19.55
227.	Fresh fruit juice	19.16
228.	Sports drinks	19.11
229.	Appliance repair, including at service center	19.02
230.	Other alcoholic beverages at home	18.98
231.	Portable heating and cooling equipment	18.73
232.	Wall-to-wall carpeting	18.69
233.	Bathroom linens	18.68
234.	Automobile service clubs	18.63
235.	Dried vegetables	18.25
236.	Shaving products	17.95
237.	Laundry and cleaning equipment	17.83
238.	Curtains and draperies	17.69
239.	Dishwashers (built-in), garbage disposals, range hoods	17.45
240.	Floor coverings, nonpermanent	17.38
241.	Nondairy cream and imitation milk	16.96
242.	Computer software and accessories for nonbusiness use	16.89
243.	Local transportation on trips	16.86
244.	Photographer fees	16.62
245.	Prepared desserts	16.53
246.	Infants' equipment	16.48
247.	Taxi fares and limousine service	16.43
248.	Pies, tarts, turnovers	16.30
249.	Living room tables	16.16
250.	Nonelectric cookware	16.07
251.	Closet and storage items	15.85
252.	Intercity train fares	15.67
253.	Electric floor-cleaning equipment	15.47
254.	Peanut butter	15.46
255.	Bicycles	15.43
256.	Musical instruments and accessories	15.26
257.	Prepared flour mixes	15.25
258.	Vegetable juices	15.14
259.	Nonalcoholic beverages (except carbonated, coffee, fruit-flavored drinks, and tea) and ice	15.12
260.	Cemetery lots, vaults, and maintenance fees	15.12
261.	Olives, pickles, relishes	14.86
262.	Satellite radio service	14.57
263.	Compact discs, records, and audio tapes	13.79
264.	Hand tools	13.76
265.	Camping equipment	13.41
266.	Books and supplies for elementary and high school	13.14
267.	Cash contributions to political organizations	12.80
268.	Rental of party supplies for catered affairs	12.73
269.	Luggage	12.64
270.	Newspapers and magazines, nonsubscription	12.63
271.	Hearing aids	12.38
272.	Tenant's insurance	12.28
273.	Whiskey at home	12.19
274.	Personal digital audio players	11.42
275.	Photo processing	11.42
276.	Vehicle inspection	11.37
277.	Electric personal care appliances	11.13
278.	Lamb, organ meats, and others	10.88
279.	Gifts of stocks, bonds, and mutual funds to members of other households	10.59
280.	Docking and landing fees	10.57

281.	Microwave ovens	$10.54
282.	Intercity bus fares	10.34
283.	Live entertainment for catered affairs	10.34
284.	Test preparation, tutoring services	10.20
285.	VCRs and video disc players	10.10
286.	Glassware	10.01
287.	Margarine	9.92
288.	Sewing materials for household items	9.53
289.	Vocational and technical school tuition	9.19
290.	Driver's license	9.00
291.	Coal, wood, and other fuels	8.96
292.	Security services, owner	8.77
293.	Voice over IP	8.62
294.	Shopping club membership fees	8.50
295.	Dried fruits	8.20
296.	Phone cards	8.14
297.	Maintenance and repair materials, renter	8.11
298.	Infants' furniture	8.07
299.	Flour	7.89
300.	China and other dinnerware	7.52
301.	Bread and cracker products	7.48
302.	Repair of computer systems for nonbusiness use	7.29
303.	Care in convalescent or nursing home	7.14
304.	Rental of recreational vehicles	7.13
305.	Hair accessories	7.11
306.	Repairs and rentals of lawn and garden equipment, hand and power tools, etc.	7.08
307.	Portable memory	7.06
308.	Frozen fruits	6.78
309.	Streamed and downloaded audio	6.70
310.	Reupholstering and furniture repair	6.21
311.	Apparel alteration, repair, and tailoring services	6.20
312.	Frozen fruit juices	6.11
313.	Office furniture for home use	6.06
314.	Kitchen and dining room linens	5.92
315.	Sewing patterns and notions	5.69
316.	Winter sports equipment	5.63
317.	Artificial sweeteners	5.40
318.	Global positioning system devices	5.20
319.	Window air conditioners	5.12
320.	Playground equipment	4.91
321.	Personal digital assistants	4.68
322.	Material for making clothes	4.46
323.	Water sports equipment	4.42
324.	Rental of furniture	4.18
325.	Flatware	4.13
326.	Towing charges	3.99
327.	Supportive and convalescent medical equipment	3.93
328.	Business equipment for home use	3.79
329.	Smoking accessories	3.74
330.	Slipcovers and decorative pillows	3.71
331.	Safe deposit box rental	3.65
332.	Deductions for railroad retirement	3.62
333.	Nonclothing laundry and dry cleaning, coin-operated	3.59
334.	Water-softening service	3.54
335.	Miscellaneous video equipment	3.51
336.	Vacation clubs	3.41
337.	Septic tank cleaning	3.40
338.	Watch and jewelry repair	3.22

339.	Wigs and hairpieces	$3.19
340.	Delivery services	2.97
341.	Rental and repair of miscellaneous sports equipment	2.90
342.	Sewing machines	2.82
343.	Stamp and coin collecting	2.77
344.	Repair of TV, radio, and sound equipment	2.69
345.	Medical equipment for general use	2.67
346.	Parking at owned home	2.64
347.	Online gaming services	2.55
348.	Plastic dinnerware	2.41
349.	Rental of medical equipment	2.03
350.	Streamed and downloaded video	1.94
351.	Internet services away from home	1.86
352.	Pinball, electronic video games	1.78
353.	School bus	1.77
354.	Clothing rental	1.76
355.	Credit card memberships	1.72
356.	Global positioning services	1.62
357.	Shoe repair and other shoe services	1.54
358.	Smoke alarms	1.47
359.	Rental and repair of musical instruments	1.42
360.	Fireworks	1.31
361.	Other serving pieces	1.23
362.	Film	1.23
363.	Satellite dishes	1.22
364.	Appliance rental	1.18
365.	Rental of supportive and convalescent medical equipment	1.18
366.	Nonclothing laundry and dry cleaning, sent out	1.06
367.	Books and supplies for vocational and technical schools	0.98
368.	Books and supplies for day care and nursery	0.49
369.	Rental of television sets	0.43
370.	Portable dishwashers	0.37
371.	Clothing storage	0.37
372.	Installation of television sets	0.37
373.	Rental of office equipment for nonbusiness use	0.36
374.	Repair and rental of photographic equipment	0.35
375.	Telephone answering devices	0.34
376.	Dating services	0.32
377.	Installation of computer	0.31
378.	Rental of computer and video game hardware and software	0.15
379.	Rental of VCR, radio, and sound equipment	0.04

Source: Calculations by New Strategist based on the 2010 Consumer Expenditure Survey

Household Spending Trends, 2000 to 2010

(average annual spending of consumer units, selected years, 2000 to 2010; percent change, 2006–10, 2000–06, and 2000–10; in 2010 dollars)

	2010	2009	2006	2000	percent change		
					2006–10	2000–06	2000–10
Number of consumer units (in 000s)	121,107	120,847	118,843	109,367	1.9%	8.7%	10.7%
Average before-tax income of consumer units	$62,481	$63,888	$65,474	$56,539	–4.6	15.8	10.5
Average annual spending of consumer units	48,109	49,872	52,349	48,176	–8.1	8.7	–0.1
FOOD	**6,129**	**6,477**	**6,610**	**6,532**	**–7.3**	**1.2**	**–6.2**
Food at home	3,624	3,815	3,696	3,825	–1.9	–3.4	–5.3
Cereals and bakery products	502	514	482	574	4.1	–15.9	–12.5
Cereals and cereal products	165	176	155	198	6.7	–21.7	–16.5
Bakery products	337	339	329	376	2.5	–12.6	–10.4
Meats, poultry, fish, and eggs	784	855	862	1,007	–9.1	–14.4	–22.1
Beef	217	230	255	301	–15.0	–15.3	–28.0
Pork	149	171	170	211	–12.3	–19.7	–29.5
Other meats	117	116	114	128	3.0	–11.2	–8.5
Poultry	138	157	153	184	–9.5	–16.9	–24.8
Fish and seafood	117	137	132	139	–11.3	–5.3	–16.0
Eggs	46	45	40	43	14.9	–7.0	6.8
Dairy products	380	413	398	412	–4.5	–3.3	–7.7
Fresh milk and cream	141	146	151	166	–6.9	–8.7	–15.0
Other dairy products	240	266	247	244	–2.7	0.9	–1.8
Fruits and vegetables	679	667	640	660	6.0	–2.9	2.9
Fresh fruits	232	224	211	206	10.0	2.2	12.4
Fresh vegetables	210	212	209	201	0.6	3.7	4.3
Processed fruits	113	120	118	146	–4.2	–19.0	–22.4
Processed vegetables	124	112	103	106	20.7	–3.4	16.6
Other food at home	1,278	1,365	1,311	1,174	–2.5	11.7	8.9
Sugar and other sweets	132	143	135	148	–2.4	–8.7	–10.9
Fats and oils	103	104	93	105	10.7	–11.5	–2.0
Miscellaneous foods	667	727	678	553	–1.6	22.6	20.5
Nonalcoholic beverages	333	343	359	317	–7.3	13.4	5.2
Food prepared by consumer unit on trips	43	50	47	51	–7.5	–8.2	–15.1
Food away from home	**2,505**	**2,662**	**2,914**	**2,706**	**–14.0**	**7.7**	**–7.4**
ALCOHOLIC BEVERAGES	**412**	**442**	**538**	**471**	**–23.4**	**14.1**	**–12.5**
HOUSING	**16,557**	**17,172**	**17,702**	**15,599**	**–6.5**	**13.5**	**6.1**
Shelter	**9,812**	**10,240**	**10,463**	**9,008**	**–6.2**	**16.1**	**8.9**
Owned dwellings	6,277	6,650	7,048	5,827	–10.9	20.9	7.7
Mortgage interest and charges	3,351	3,653	4,059	3,342	–17.4	21.5	0.3
Property taxes	1,814	1,841	1,784	1,442	1.7	23.7	25.8
Maintenance, repair, insurance, other expenses	1,112	1,157	1,206	1,045	–7.8	15.4	6.4
Rented dwellings	2,900	2,907	2,801	2,576	3.5	8.8	12.6
Other lodging	635	683	613	605	3.5	1.3	4.9

	2010	2009	2006	2000	percent change		
					2006–10	2000–06	2000–10
Utilities, fuels, and public services	$3,660	$3,705	$3,674	$3,152	–0.4%	16.6%	16.1%
Natural gas	440	491	551	389	–20.1	41.6	13.2
Electricity	1,413	1,400	1,369	1,154	3.2	18.7	22.5
Fuel oil and other fuels	140	143	149	123	–6.2	21.5	14.0
Telephone services	1,178	1,181	1,176	1,111	0.2	5.9	6.1
Water and other public services	489	489	429	375	13.9	14.6	30.5
Household services	1,007	1,028	1,025	866	–1.8	18.4	16.3
Personal services	340	395	425	413	–20.0	3.0	–17.6
Other household services	667	632	600	453	11.1	32.4	47.1
Housekeeping supplies	612	670	692	610	–11.6	13.4	0.3
Laundry and cleaning supplies	150	159	163	166	–8.2	–1.5	–9.6
Other household products	329	366	357	286	–7.8	24.7	15.0
Postage and stationery	132	145	172	160	–23.2	7.8	–17.3
Household furnishings and equipment	1,467	1,531	1,847	1,961	–20.6	–5.8	–25.2
Household textiles	102	126	167	134	–38.8	24.1	–24.0
Furniture	355	349	501	495	–29.1	1.1	–28.3
Floor coverings	36	30	52	56	–30.7	–6.8	–35.4
Major appliances	209	197	261	239	–19.8	8.9	–12.7
Small appliances and miscellaneous housewares	107	95	118	110	–9.2	7.0	–2.9
Miscellaneous household equipment	657	733	750	926	–12.3	–19.0	–29.0
APPAREL AND RELATED SERVICES	1,700	1,753	2,027	2,350	–16.1	–13.8	–27.7
Men and boys	382	389	480	557	–20.5	–13.8	–31.4
Men, aged 16 or older	304	309	382	436	–20.4	–12.3	–30.2
Boys, aged 2 to 15	78	80	98	122	–20.8	–19.0	–35.8
Women and girls	663	689	812	918	–18.4	–11.5	–27.8
Women, aged 16 or older	562	570	680	769	–17.4	–11.5	–26.9
Girls, aged 2 to 15	101	120	132	149	–23.5	–11.7	–32.4
Children under age 2	91	92	104	104	–12.4	0.0	–12.4
Footwear	303	328	329	434	–7.9	–24.3	–30.2
Other apparel products and services	261	253	303	337	–13.8	–10.1	–22.5
TRANSPORTATION	7,677	7,784	9,202	9,392	–16.6	–2.0	–18.3
Vehicle purchases	2,588	2,701	3,700	4,328	–30.1	–14.5	–40.2
Cars and trucks, new	1,219	1,318	1,945	2,032	–37.3	–4.3	–40.0
Cars and trucks, used	1,318	1,325	1,696	2,241	–22.3	–24.3	–41.2
Gasoline and motor oil	2,132	2,019	2,409	1,635	–11.5	47.3	30.4
Other vehicle expenses	2,464	2,578	2,547	2,888	–3.3	–11.8	–14.7
Vehicle finance charges	243	286	322	415	–24.6	–22.4	–41.5
Maintenance and repairs	787	745	744	790	5.8	–5.8	–0.4
Vehicle insurance	1,010	1,093	958	985	5.4	–2.7	2.5
Vehicle rentals, leases, licenses, other charges	423	454	521	698	–18.9	–25.3	–39.4
Public transportation	493	487	546	541	–9.7	1.0	–8.8
HEALTH CARE	3,157	3,177	2,992	2,616	5.5	14.4	20.7
Health insurance	1,831	1,814	1,585	1,245	15.6	27.3	47.1
Medical services	722	748	725	719	–0.4	0.8	0.4
Drugs	485	494	556	527	–12.8	5.5	–7.9
Medical supplies	119	121	127	125	–6.0	0.9	–5.1

	2010	2009	2006	2000	percent change 2006–10	percent change 2000–06	percent change 2000–10
ENTERTAINMENT	$2,504	$2,737	$2,570	$2,359	−2.6%	8.9%	6.1%
Fees and admissions	581	638	655	652	−11.4	0.5	−10.9
Audio and visual equipment and services	954	991	980	788	−2.6	24.4	21.1
Pets, toys, and playground equipment	$606	$701	$446	$423	36.0%	5.4%	43.3%
Other entertainment products and services	364	407	488	498	−25.4	−2.0	−26.9
PERSONAL CARE PRODUCTS AND SERVICES	582	606	633	714	−8.0	−11.4	−18.5
READING	100	112	127	185	−21.0	−31.5	−45.9
EDUCATION	1,074	1,086	960	800	11.8	20.0	34.2
TOBACCO PRODUCTS AND SMOKING SUPPLIES	362	386	354	404	2.3	−12.4	−10.4
MISCELLANEOUS	849	829	915	983	−7.2	−6.9	−13.6
CASH CONTRIBUTIONS	1,633	1,751	2,022	1,509	−19.2	33.9	8.2
PERSONAL INSURANCE AND PENSIONS	5,373	5,561	5,700	4,261	−5.7	33.8	26.1
Life and other personal insurance	318	314	348	505	−8.7	−31.1	−37.1
Pensions and Social Security*	5,054	5,247	5,352	3,756	−5.6	–	–
PERSONAL TAXES	1,769	2,139	2,631	3,947	−32.8	−33.4	−55.2
Federal income taxes	1,136	1,427	1,851	3,051	−38.6	−39.3	−62.8
State and local income taxes	482	533	561	712	−14.1	−21.1	−32.3
Other taxes	151	180	218	185	−30.9	18.2	−18.3
GIFTS FOR PEOPLE IN OTHER HOUSEHOLDS	1,029	1,085	1,248	1,371	−17.6	−9.0	−25.0

*Recent spending on pensions and Social Security is not comparable with 2000 because of changes in methodology.

Note: Spending by category does not add to total spending because gift spending is also included in the preceding product and service categories and personal taxes are not included in the total. "–" means data are not comparable.

Source: Bureau of Labor Statistics, 2000, 2006, 2009, and 2010 Consumer Expenditure Surveys, Internet site http://www.bls.gov/cex/; calculations by New Strategist

Glossary

age The age of the reference person.

alcoholic beverages Includes beer and ale, wine, whiskey, gin, vodka, rum, and other alcoholic beverages.

annual spending The annual amount spent per household. The Bureau of Labor Statistics calculates the annual average for all households in a segment, not just for those that purchased an item. The averages are calculated by integrating the results of the diary (weekly) and interview (quarterly) portions of the Consumer Expenditure Survey. For items purchased by most households—such as bread—average annual spending figures are a fairly accurate account of actual spending. For products and services purchased by few households during a year's time—such as cars—the average annual amount spent is much less than what purchasers spend.

apparel, accessories, and related services Includes the following:

• *men's and boys' apparel* Includes coats, jackets, sweaters, vests, sport coats, tailored jackets, slacks, shorts and short sets, sportswear, shirts, underwear, nightwear, hosiery, uniforms, and other accessories.

• *women's and girls' apparel* Includes coats, jackets, furs, sport coats, tailored jackets, sweaters, vests, blouses, shirts, dresses, dungarees, culottes, slacks, shorts, sportswear, underwear, nightwear, uniforms, hosiery, and other accessories.

• *infants' apparel* Includes coats, jackets, snowsuits, underwear, diapers, dresses, crawlers, sleeping garments, hosiery, footwear, and other accessories for children.

• *footwear* Includes articles such as shoes, slippers, boots, and other similar items. It excludes footwear for babies and footwear used for sports such as bowling or golf shoes.

• *other apparel products and services* Includes material for making clothes, shoe repair, alterations and sewing patterns and notions, clothing rental, clothing storage, dry cleaning, sent-out laundry, watches, jewelry, and repairs to watches and jewelry.

baby boom Americans born between 1946 and 1964.

cash contributions Includes cash contributed to persons or organizations outside the consumer unit including court-ordered alimony, child support payments, and support for college students, and contributions to religious, educational, charitable, or political organizations.

consumer unit (1) All members of a household who are related by blood, marriage, adoption, or other legal arrangements; (2) a person living alone or sharing a household with others or living as a roomer in a private home or lodging house or in permanent living quarters in a hotel or motel, but who is financially independent; or (3) two or more persons living together who pool their income to make joint expenditure decisions. Financial independence is determined by the three major expense categories: housing, food, and other living expenses. To be considered financially independent, at least two of the three major expense categories have to be provided by the respondent. For convenience, called household in the text of this report.

consumer unit, composition of The classification of interview households by type according to (1) relationship of other household members to the reference person; (2) age of the children of the reference person; and (3) combination of relationship to the reference person and age of the children. Stepchildren and adopted children are included with the reference person's own children.

earner A consumer unit member aged 14 or older who worked at least one week during the twelve months prior to the interview date.

education Includes tuition, fees, books, supplies, and equipment for public and private nursery schools, elementary and high schools, colleges and universities, and other schools.

entertainment Includes the following:

• *fees and admissions* Includes fees for participant sports; admissions to sporting events, movies, concerts, plays; health, swimming, tennis, and country club memberships, and other social recreational and fraternal organizations; recreational lessons or instructions; and recreational expenses on trips.

• *audio and visual equipment and services* Includes television sets; radios; cable TV; tape recorders and players; video cassettes, tapes, and discs; video cassette recorders and video disc players; video game hardware and software; personal digital audio players; streaming and downloading audio and video; sound components; CDs, records, and tapes; musical instruments; and rental and repair of TV and sound equipment.

• *pets, toys, hobbies, and playground equipment* Includes pet food, pet services, veterinary expenses, toys, games, hobbies, and playground equipment.

• *other entertainment equipment and services* Includes indoor exercise equipment, athletic shoes, bicycles, trailers, campers, camping equipment, rental of cameras and trailers, hunting and fishing equipment, sports equipment, winter sports equipment, water sports equipment, boats, boat motors and boat trailers, rental of boats, landing and docking fees, rental and repair of sports equipment, photographic equipment, film, photo processing, photographer fees, repair and rental of photo equipment, fireworks, pinball and electronic video games.

expenditure The transaction cost including excise and sales taxes of goods and services acquired during the survey period. The full cost of each purchase is recorded even though full payment may not have been made at the date of purchase. Expenditure estimates include gifts. Excluded from expenditures are purchases or portions of purchases directly assignable to business purposes and periodic credit or installment payments on goods and services already acquired.

federal income tax Includes federal income tax withheld in the survey year to pay for income earned in survey year plus additional tax paid in survey year to cover any underpayment or underwithholding of tax in the year prior to the survey.

financial products and services Includes accounting fees, legal fees, union dues, professional dues and fees, other occupational expenses, funerals, cemetery lots, dating services, shopping club memberships, and unclassified fees and personal services.

food Includes the following:

• *food at home* Refers to the total expenditures for food at grocery stores or other food stores during the interview period. It is calculated by multiplying the number of visits to a grocery or other food store by the average amount spent per visit. It excludes the purchase of nonfood items.

• *food away from home* Includes all meals (breakfast, lunch, brunch, and dinner) at restaurants, carry-outs, and vending machines, including tips, plus meals as pay, special catered affairs such as weddings, bar mitzvahs, and confirmations, and meals away from home on trips.

Generation X Americans born between 1965 and 1976, also known as the baby-bust generation.

gifts for people in other households Includes gift expenditures for people living in other consumer units. The amount spent on gifts is also included in individual product and service categories.

health care Includes the following:

• *health insurance* Includes health maintenance plans (HMOs), Blue Cross/Blue Shield, commercial health insurance, Medicare, Medicare supplemental insurance, long-term care insurance, and other health insurance.

• *medical services* Includes hospital room and services, physicians' services, services of a practitioner other than a physician, eye and dental care, lab tests, X-rays, nursing, therapy services, care in convalescent or nursing home, and other medical care.

• *drugs* Includes prescription and nonprescription drugs, internal and respiratory over-the-counter drugs.

• *medical supplies* Includes eyeglasses and contact lenses, topicals and dressings, antiseptics, bandages, cotton, first aid kits, contraceptives; medical equipment for general use such as syringes, ice bags, thermometers, vaporizers, heating pads; supportive or convalescent medical equipment such as hearing aids, braces, canes, crutches, and walkers.

Hispanic origin The self-identified Hispanic origin of the consumer unit reference person. All consumer units are included in one of two Hispanic origin groups based on the reference person's Hispanic origin: Hispanic or non-Hispanic. Hispanics may be of any race.

household According to the Census Bureau, all the people who occupy a household. A group of unrelated people who share a housing unit as roommates or unmarried partners is also counted as a household. Households do not include group quarters such as college dormitories, prisons, or nursing homes. A household may contain more than one consumer unit. The terms household and consumer unit are used interchangeably in this report.

household furnishings and equipment Includes the following:

• *household textiles* Includes bathroom, kitchen, dining room, and other linens, curtains and drapes, slipcovers and decorative pillows, and sewing materials.

• *furniture* Includes living room, dining room, kitchen, bedroom, nursery, porch, lawn, and other outdoor furniture.

• *carpet, rugs, and other floor coverings* Includes installation and replacement of wall-to-wall carpets, room-size rugs, and other soft floor coverings.

• *major appliances* Includes refrigerators, freezers, dishwashers, stoves, ovens, garbage disposals, vacuum cleaners, microwave ovens, air-conditioners, sewing machines, washing machines, clothes dryers, and floor-cleaning equipment.

• *small appliances and miscellaneous housewares* Includes small electrical kitchen appliances, portable heating and cooling equipment, china and other dinnerware, flatware, glassware, silver and other serving pieces, nonelectric cookware, and plastic dinnerware. Excludes personal care appliances.

• *miscellaneous household equipment* Includes computer hardware and software, luggage, lamps and other lighting fixtures, window coverings, clocks, lawn mowers and gardening equipment, hand and power tools, telephone answering devices, personal digital assistants, Internet services away from home, office equipment for home use, fresh flowers and house plants, rental of furniture, closet and storage items, household decorative items, infants' equipment, outdoor equipment, smoke alarms, other household appliances, and small miscellaneous furnishing.

household services Includes the following:

• *personal services* Includes baby sitting, day care, and care of elderly and handicapped persons.

• *other household services* Includes computer information services; housekeeping services; gardening and lawn care services; coin-operated laundry and dry-cleaning of household textiles; termite and pest control products; moving, storage, and freight expenses; repair of household appliances and other household equipment; reupholstering and furniture repair; rental and repair of lawn and gardening tools; and rental of other household equipment.

housekeeping supplies Includes soaps, detergents, other laundry cleaning products, cleansing and toilet tissue, paper towels, napkins, and miscellaneous household products; lawn and garden supplies, postage, stationery, stationery supplies, and gift wrap.

housing tenure Owner includes households living in their own homes, cooperatives, condominiums, or townhouses. Renter includes households paying rent as well as families living rent free in lieu of wages.

income before taxes The total money earnings and selected money receipts accruing to a consumer unit during the 12 months prior to the interview date. Income includes the following components:

• *wages and salaries* Includes total money earnings for all members of the consumer unit aged 14 or older from all jobs, including civilian wages and salaries, Armed Forces pay and allowances, piece-rate payments, commissions, tips, National Guard or Reserve pay (received for training periods), and cash bonuses before deductions for taxes, pensions, union dues, etc.

• *self-employment income* Includes net business and farm income, which consists of net income (gross receipts minus operating expenses) from a profession or unincorporated business or from the operation of a farm by an owner, tenant, or sharecropper. If the business or farm is a partnership, only an appropriate share of net income is recorded. Losses are also recorded.

• *Social Security, private and government retirement* Includes payments by the federal government made under retirement, survivor, and disability insurance programs to retired persons, dependents of deceased insured workers, or to disabled workers; and private pensions or retirement

benefits received by retired persons or their survivors, either directly or through an insurance company.

• *interest, dividends, rental income, and other property income* Includes interest income on savings or bonds; payments made by a corporation to its stockholders, periodic receipts from estates or trust funds; net income or loss from the rental of property, real estate, or farms, and net income or loss from roomers or boarders.

• *unemployment and workers' compensation and veterans' benefits* Includes income from unemployment compensation and workers' compensation, and veterans' payments including educational benefits, but excluding military retirement.

• *public assistance, supplemental security income, and food stamps* Includes public assistance or welfare, including money received from job training grants; supplemental security income paid by federal, state, and local welfare agencies to low-income persons who are aged 65 or older, blind, or disabled; and the value of food stamps obtained.

• *regular contributions for support* Includes alimony and child support as well as any regular contributions from persons outside the consumer unit.

• *other income* Includes money income from care of foster children, cash scholarships, fellowships, or stipends not based on working; and meals and rent as pay.

indexed spending Indexed spending figures compare the spending of particular demographic segments with that of the average household. To compute an index, the amount spent on an item by a demographic segment is divided by the amount spent on the item by the average household. That figure is then multiplied by 100. An index of 100 is the average for all households. An index of 132 means average spending by households in a segment is 32 percent above average (100 plus 32). An index of 75 means average spending by households in a segment is 25 percent below average (100 minus 25). Indexed spending figures identify the consumer units that spend the most on a product or service.

life and other personal insurance Includes premiums from whole life and term insurance; endowments; income and other life insurance; mortgage guarantee insurance; mortgage life insurance; premiums for personal life liability, accident and disability; and other non–health insurance other than homes and vehicles.

market share The market share is the percentage of total household spending on an item that is accounted for by a demographic segment. Market shares are calculated by dividing a demographic segment's total spending on an item by the total spending of all households on the item. Total spending on an item for all households is calculated by multiplying average spending by the total number of households. Total spending on an item for each demographic segment is calculated by multiplying the segment's average spending by the number of households in the segment. Market shares reveal the demographic segments that account for the largest share of spending on a product or service.

Millennial generation Americans born between 1977 and 1994.

occupation The occupation in which the reference person received the most earnings during the survey period. The occupational categories follow those of the Census of Population. Categories shown in the tables include the following:

• *self-employed* Includes all occupational categories; the reference person is self-employed in own business, professional practice, or farm.

• *wage and salary earners, managers and professionals* Includes executives, administrators, managers, and professional specialties such as architects, engineers, natural and social scientists, lawyers, teachers, writers, health diagnosis and treatment workers, entertainers, and athletes.

• *wage and salary earners, technical, sales, and clerical workers* Includes technicians and related support workers; sales representatives, sales workers, cashiers, and sales-related occupations; and administrative support, including clerical.

• *retired* People who did not work either full- or part-time during the survey period.

owner See housing tenure.

pensions and Social Security Includes all Social Security contributions paid by employees; employees' contributions to railroad retirement, government retirement and private pensions programs; retirement programs for self-employed.

personal care Includes products for the hair, oral hygiene products, shaving needs, cosmetics, bath products, suntan lotions, hand creams, electric personal care appliances, incontinence products, other personal care products, personal care services such as hair care services (haircuts, bleaching, tinting, coloring, conditioning treatments, permanents, press, and curls), styling and other services for wigs and hairpieces, body massages or slenderizing treatments, facials, manicures, pedicures, shaves, electrolysis.

quarterly spending Quarterly spending data are collected in the interview portion of the Consumer Expenditure Survey. The quarterly spending tables show the percentage of households that purchased an item during an average quarter, and the amount spent during the quarter on the item by purchasers. Not all items are included in the interview portion of the Consumer Expenditure Survey.

reading Includes subscriptions for newspapers, magazines, and books through book clubs; purchase of single-copy newspapers and magazines, books, and encyclopedias and other reference books.

reference person The first member mentioned by the respondent when asked to Start with the name of the person or one of the persons who owns or rents the home. It is with respect to this person that the relationship of other consumer unit members is determined. Also called the householder or head of household.

region Consumer units are classified according to their address at the time of their participation in the survey. The four major census regions of the United States are the following state groupings:

• *Northeast* Connecticut, Maine, Massachusetts, New Hampshire, New Jersey, New York, Pennsylvania, Rhode Island, and Vermont.

• *Midwest* Illinois, Indiana, Iowa, Kansas, Michigan, Minnesota, Mississippi, Nebraska, North Dakota, Ohio, South Dakota, and Wisconsin.

• *South* Alabama, Arkansas, Delaware, District of Columbia, Florida, Georgia, Kentucky, Louisiana, Maryland, Mississippi, North Carolina, Oklahoma, South Carolina, Tennessee, Texas, Virginia, and West Virginia.

• *West* Alaska, Arizona, California, Colorado, Hawaii, Idaho, Minnesota, Nevada, New Mexico, Oregon, Utah, Washington, and Wyoming.

renter *See* Housing tenure.

shelter Includes the following:

• *owned dwellings* Includes interest on mortgages, property taxes and insurance, refinancing and prepayment charges, ground rent, expenses for property management and security, homeowner's insurance, fire insurance and extended coverage, landscaping expenses for repairs and maintenance contracted out (including periodic maintenance and service contracts), and expenses of materials for owner-performed repairs and maintenance for dwellings used or maintained by the consumer unit, but not dwellings maintained for business or rent.

• *rented dwellings* Includes rent paid for dwellings, rent received as pay, parking fees, maintenance, and other expenses.

• *other lodging* Includes all expenses for vacation homes, school, college, hotels, motels, cottages, trailer camps, and other lodging while out of town.

• *utilities, fuels, and public services* Includes natural gas, electricity, fuel oil, coal, bottled gas, wood, other fuels; residential telephone service, cell phone service, phone cards; water, garbage, trash collection; sewerage maintenance, septic tank cleaning; and other public services.

size of consumer unit The number of people whose usual place of residence at the time of the interview is in the consumer unit.

state and local income taxes Includes state and local income taxes withheld in the survey year to pay for income earned in survey year plus additional taxes paid in the survey year to cover any underpayment or underwithholding of taxes in the year prior to the survey.

tobacco and smoking supplies Includes cigarettes, cigars, snuff, loose smoking tobacco, chewing tobacco, and smoking accessories such as cigarette or cigar holders, pipes, flints, lighters, pipe cleaners, and other smoking products and accessories.

transportation Includes the following:

• *vehicle purchases (net outlay)* Includes the net outlay (purchase price minus trade-in value) on new and used domestic and imported cars and trucks and other vehicles, including motorcycles and private planes.

• *gasoline and motor oil* Includes gasoline, diesel fuel, and motor oil.

• *other vehicle expenses* Includes vehicle finance charges, maintenance and repairs, vehicle insurance, and vehicle rental licenses and other charges.

• *vehicle finance charges* Includes the dollar amount of interest paid for a loan contracted for the purchase of vehicles described above.

• *maintenance and repairs* Includes tires, batteries, tubes, lubrication, filters, coolant, additives, brake and transmission fluids, oil change, brake adjustment and repair, front-end alignment, wheel balancing, steering repair, shock absorber replacement, clutch and transmission repair, electrical system repair, repair to cooling system, drive train repair, drive shaft and rear-end repair, tire repair, vehicle video equipment, other maintenance and services, and auto repair policies.

• *vehicle insurance* Includes the premium paid for insuring cars, trucks, and other vehicles.

• *vehicle rental, licenses, and other charges* Includes leased and rented cars, trucks, motorcycles, and aircraft, inspection fees, state and local registration, drivers' license fees, parking fees, towing charges, tolls on trips, and global positioning services.

• *public transportation* Includes fares for mass transit, buses, trains, airlines, taxis, private school buses, and fares paid on trips for trains, boats, taxis, buses, and trains.

weekly spending Weekly spending data are collected in the diary portion of the Consumer Expenditure Survey. The data show the percentage of households that purchased an item during the average week, and the amount spent per week on the item by purchasers. Not all items are included in the diary portion of the Consumer Expenditure Survey.

Index

accounting fees, 167-168, 170-171
admission
>   to movies, theater, amusement parks, 89-90, 116-117
>   to sports events, 89-90, 92-93
airline fares, 715-717
alcoholic beverages purchased on trips, 11–13, 715, 718-719
amusement park tickets, 89-90, 116-117
answering machines, 651, 658-659
apparel
>   boys', 29–31
>   footwear, 29, 32–33, 44–45, 54–55
>   gifts of, 287, 304-305, 308-309, 312-313
>   girls', 29, 36–37
>   infants', 29, 38–39
>   laundry and dry cleaning of, coin–operated, 29, 34–35
>   laundry and dry cleaning of, professional, 29, 46–47
>   men's, 29, 42–43
>   repair, 29, 50-51
>   women's, 29, 52–53
apples, 317-320, 322-323
appliances
>   gifts of, 287-289
>   kitchen, small electric, 223-224, 226-227
>   major, 223-224, 228-229
>   repair of, 531-533
artificial sweeteners, 317-320, 324-325
athletic gear, 89-90, 94-95
audio
>   equipment, 89-90, 142-143
>   personal digital players, 89-90, 120-121
>   streamed and downloaded, 89-90, 146-147
>   tapes, 89-90, 104-105
automobile service clubs, 673-674, 676-677
automobiles. See Cars; Trucks.

baby. See Infant.
baby food, 317-320, 326-327
babysitting, 531, 534-535
bacon, 317-320, 328-329
bakery products. See individual categories.
>   frozen and refrigerated, 317-320, 330-331
baking needs and miscellaneous products, 317-320, 332-333
bananas, 317-320, 334-335
bank service charges, 167-168, 172-173
bath products, 569-571
bathroom linens, 223-224, 230-231
bedroom
>   furniture, 223-224, 232-233
>   linens, 223-224, 234-235
beds. See Mattresses and springs.
beef
>   ground, 317-320, 336-337
>   roast, 317-320, 338-339
>   steak, 317-320, 340-341

beer and ale
>   at home, 11, 14–15
>   at restaurants and bars, 11, 16–17
beverages. See Drinks.
bicycles, 89-90, 96-97
biscuits and rolls, 317-320, 342-343
boats, 89-90, 134-135
books, 585-587
>   and supplies, college, 75-77
>   and supplies, elementary and high school, 75, 78-79
bottled gas, 747-749
boys'
>   apparel, 29–31
>   apparel, gifts of, 287, 308-309
bread
>   and cracker products, 317-320, 344-345
>   except white, 317-320, 346-347
>   makers. See Appliances, kitchen, small electric.
>   white, 317-320, 348-349
breakfast and brunch
>   at fast-food restaurants, 595-596, 598-599
>   at full-service restaurants, 595-596, 600-601
brunch. See Breakfast and brunch.
bus fares, intercity, 715, 720-721
butter, 317-320, 350-351

cabinets, 223-224, 280-281
cable and satellite television service, 89-90, 98-99
cafeterias, food from employer or school
>   lunch, 595-596, 606-607
>   snacks, 595-596, 614-615
cakes and cupcakes, 317-320, 352-353
campers, 89-90, 134-135
camping equipment, 89-90, 100-101
candy, 317-320, 354-355
canned
>   fish and seafood, 317-320, 382-383
>   fruit, 317-320, 394-395
>   fruit juice, 317-320, 404-405
>   soup, 317-320, 464-465
>   vegetable juice, 317-320, 476-477
>   vegetables, 317-320, 478-479
carbonated drinks, 317-320, 356-357
carpeting. See Floor coverings.
cars
>   lease payments, 673-674, 678-679
>   new, 673-674, 680-681
>   used, 673-674, 682-683
catered affairs
>   live entertainment for, 89-90, 114-115
>   rental of party supplies for, 89-90, 136-137
CDs, 89-90, 104-105
cellular phone service, 651-653
cemetery lots, 167-168, 184-185
cereal, ready-to-eat and cooked, 317-320, 358-359
chairs, living room, 223-224, 260-261

charities, cash contributions to, 167-168, 174-175
cheese, 317-320, 360-361
chewing gum, 317-320, 354-355
chewing tobacco. *See* Tobacco products other than cigarettes.
chicken, 317-320, 362-363
child
    care, 531, 534-535, 538-539
    support, 167-168, 186-187
children's shoes, 29, 32-33
churches, contributions to, 167-168, 180-181
cigarettes, 663-665
cigars. *See* Tobacco products other than cigarettes.
citrus fruit, 317-320, 364-365, 430-431
cleaning
    equipment, 223-224, 256-257
    supplies, 555, 558-559
cleansing and toilet tissue, 555-557
closet and storage items, 223-224, 236-237
clothes. *See* Apparel.
clubs
    automobile service, 673-674, 676-677
    shopping, 167-168, 212-213
    social, recreational, civic, 89-90, 102-103
coffee, 317-320, 366-367
coffee cakes, 317-320, 470-471
coin collecting, 89-90, 144-145
colas, 317-320, 356-357
cold cuts, 317-320, 418-419
college. See also Vocational and technical schools.
    books and supplies, 75-77
    students, support for, 167-168, 214-215
    tuition, 75, 80-81
compact discs, 89-90, 104-405
computer
    hardware, 59, 64-65
    information services, 59-61, 66-67
    memory, portable, 59, 68-69
    repair, 59, 70-71
    software and accessories, 59, 62-63
contact lenses, 491-492, 502-503
contributions of cash
    as gifts, 167-168, 182-183
    to charities, 167-168, 174-175
    to educational organizations, 167-168, 176-177
    to political organizations, 167-168, 178-179
    to religious organizations, 167-168, 180-181
    to retirement accounts (nonpayroll) , 167-168, 188-189
cookies, 317-320, 368-369
cookware, nonelectric. *See* Housewares.
cooling equipment, portable, 223-224, 270-271
cornmeal. *See* Pasta, cornmeal, and other cereal products.
cosmetics, 569-571
couches. *See* Sofas.
cracker products. *See* Bread and cracker products.
crackers, 317-320, 370-371
cream, 317-320, 372-373
    nondairy, 317-320, 424-425
credit card membership fees, 167-168, 190-191

cupcakes. *See* Cakes and cupcakes.
curtains, 223-224, 238-239

dairy products, other, 317-320, 374-375
day care centers, nurseries, preschools, 531, 538-539
decorative items for the home, 223-224, 240-241
deductions
    for government retirement, 167-168, 192-193
    for private pensions, 167-168, 194-195
    for Social Security, 167-168, 196-197
dental
    products, 569, 576-577
    services, 491-492, 494-495
deodorants, 569, 572-573
desserts, prepared, 317-320, 376-377
dining room
    furniture, 223-224, 250-251
    linens, 223-224, 252-253
dinner
    at fast-food restaurants, 595-596, 602-603
    at full-service restaurants, 595-596, 604-605
dishes. *See* Housewares.
doctors. *See* Physician services.
doughnuts, 317-320, 470-471
downloads
    audio, 89-90, 146-147
    video, 89-90, 148-149
draperies, 223-224, 238-239
dried
    fruit, 317-320, 396-397
    vegetables, 317-320, 480-481
drinks. *See also* Fruit juice.
    alcoholic, 11–25
    carbonated, 317-320, 356-357
    coffee, 317-320, 366-367
    fruit-flavored, noncarbonated, 317-320, 398-399
    milk, 317-320, 422-423
    sports, 317-320, 466-467
    tea, 317-320, 472-473
    vegetable juice, 317-320, 476-477
    water, bottled, 317-320, 486-487
drugs
    Medicare premiums, 491-492, 516-517
    nonprescription, 491-492, 496-497
    prescription, 491-492, 498-499, 516-517
dry cleaning. *See* Laundry and dry cleaning.
DVD
    players, 89-90, 154-155
    rental, 89-90, 162-163
DVDs, 89-90, 158-159

eating out, 595-621
education
    contributions to organizations, 167-168, 176-177
    expenses, gifts of, 287, 290-291
    tuition, 74, 80-85
eggs, 317-320, 378-379
elderly, care for, 531, 536-537
electricity, 747, 750-751
elementary school

books and supplies, 75, 78-79
tuition, 75, 82-83
entertainment,
    gifts of, 287, 292-293
    live, at catered affairs, 89-90, 114-115
equipment
    camping, 89-90, 100-101
    exercise, 89-90, 94-95
    fishing, 89-90, 112-113
    gifts of household, 287, 298-299
    heating and cooling, portable, 223-224, 270-271
    hunting, 89-90, 112-113
    infants', 223-224, 248-249
    lawn and garden, 223-224, 258-259
    laundry and cleaning, 223-224, 256-257
    outdoor, 223-224, 264-265
    photographic, 89-90, 130-131
    repair, 531-533
    sound, 89-90, 142-143
exercise equipment, 89-90, 94-95
eye care services, 491-492, 500-501
eyeglasses, 491-492, 502-503

fast-food. *See* Breakfast, Dinner, Lunch, and Snacks.
fats and oils, 317-320, 380-381
federal income tax, 167-168, 216-217
fees
    accounting, 167-168, 170-171
    credit card membership, 167-168, 190-191
    for participant sports, 89-90, 106-107
    for recreational lessons, 89-90, 108-109
    legal, 167-168, 204-205
    parking, 673-674, 715, 730-731
    photographer's, 89-90, 128-129
    security system service, 531, 546-547
    shopping club membership, 167-168, 212-213
feminine hygiene products, 569, 572-573
film, 89-90, 110-111
finance charges. *See also* Interest.
    except mortgage and vehicle, 167-168, 198-199
    vehicle, 673-674, 704-705
fish and seafood
    canned, 317-320, 382-383
    fresh, 317-320, 384-385
    frozen, 317-320, 386-387
fishing equipment, 89-90, 112-113
flatware. *See* Housewares.
floor coverings
    nonpermanent, 223-224, 242-243
    wall-to-wall, 223-224, 244-245
flour, 317-320, 388-389
    prepared mixes, 317-320, 390-391
flowers, fresh, 223-224, 268-269
food. *See also* Prepared food and individual grocery
categories.
    from restaurants and carry–outs, 595-621, 715, 734-
    735
    gifts of, 287, 294-295
    on trips, 715, 612-613, 724-725, 734-735
    processors. *See* Appliances, kitchen, small electric.

frankfurters, 317-320, 392-393
frozen
    bakery products, 317-320, 330-331
    fish and seafood, 317-320, 386-387
    fruit, 317-320, 402-403
    fruit juice, 317-320, 408-409
    prepared food, 317-320, 448-451
    vegetables, 317-320, 484-485
fruit. *See also* individual categories.
    canned, 317-320, 394-395
    citrus, 317-320, 364-365, 430-431
    dried, 317-320, 396-397
    fresh, 317-320, 322-323, 334-335, 364-365, 400-401,
    430-431
    frozen, 317-320, 402-403
fruit-flavored drinks, noncarbonated, 317-320, 398-399
fruit juice
    canned and bottled, 317-320, 404-405
    fresh, 317-320, 406-407
    frozen, 317-320, 408-409
fuel oil, 747, 752-753
funeral expenses, 167-168, 200-201
furniture
    bedroom, 223-224, 232-233, 262-263
    cabinets, 223-224, 280-281
    dining room, 223-224, 250-251
    infants', 223-224, 248-249
    kitchen, 223-224, 250-251
    living room, 223-224, 260-261
    outdoor, 223-224, 266-267
    sofas, 223-224, 278-279
    wall units, 223-224, 280-281

gambling losses, 167-168, 206-207
game
    tables, 89-90, 94-95
    video, 89-90, 160-161
games, 89-90 152-153
garbage collection, 747, 756-757
garden equipment, 223-224, 258-259
garden supplies, 555, 560-561
gardening, lawn care service, 531, 540-541
gas
    bottled, 747-749
    natural, 747, 754-755
gasoline, 673-674, 684-685
    on trips, 715, 722-723
gifts for people in other households, 287-313
    of cash, 167-168, 182-183
giftwrap, 555, 564-565
girls'
    apparel, 29, 36–37
    apparel, gifts of, 287, 312-313
glasses. See Eyeglasses.
glassware. *See* Housewares.
gravies. *See* Sauces and gravies.
grills, outdoor. *See* Outdoor equipment.
groceries. *See* individual categories.
    on trips, 715, 724-725
ground beef, 317-320, 336-337

hair care products, 569, 574-575
ham, 317-320, 410-411
hand tools, 223-224, 272-273
handicapped, care for, 531, 536-537
health care expenses, gifts of, 287, 296-297
health care services by nonphysicians, 491-492, 520-521
health insurance, 491-492, 504-505, 514-519
hearing aids, 491-492, 506-507
heating equipment, portable, 223-224, 270-271
high school
    books and supplies, 75, 78-79
    tuition, 75, 82-83
hobbies, 89-90, 152-153
home equity loan/line of credit interest, 625-627
homeowner's insurance, 625, 628-629
hospital room and services, 491-492, 508-509
hot dogs. See Frankfurters.
hotels. See Lodging on trips.
household equipment, gifts of, 287, 298-299
household textiles
    bathroom, 223-224, 230-231
    bedroom, 223-224, 234-235
    dining room, 223-224, 252-253
    kitchen, 223-224, 252-253
    curtains and draperies, 223-224, 238-239
    gifts of, 287, 298-299
housekeeping services, 531, 542-543
housekeeping supplies, gifts of, 287, 302-303
housewares, 223-224, 246-247
    gifts of, 287-289
hunting equipment, 89-90, 112-113

ice cream and related products, 317-320, 412-413
income tax. See Tax.
infant
    apparel, 29, 38-39
    apparel, gifts of, 287, 304-305
    equipment and furniture, 223-224, 248-249
insurance
    health, 491-492, 504-505, 514-519
    homeowner's, 625, 628-629
    life and other personal, 167-168, 202-203
    long-term care, 491-492, 512-513
    tenant's, 625, 630-631
    vehicle, 673-674, 706-707
interest. See also Finance charges.
    home equity loan/line of credit, 625-627
    mortgage, 625, 638-639
Internet service, 59-61, 66-67
invalids, care for, 531, 536-537

jams, preserves, other sweets, 317-320, 414-415
jewelry, 29, 40-41
    gifts of, 287, 306-307
juices
    fruit, 317-320, 404-409
    vegetable, 317-320, 476-477

kitchen
    appliances, major, 223-224, 228-229

appliances, small electric, 223-224, 226-227
    furniture, 223-224, 250-251
    linens, 223-224, 252-253

lab tests, 491-492, 510-511
lamps, 223-224, 254-255
landline phone, 651, 656-657
laundry and cleaning
    equipment, 223-224, 256-257
    supplies, 555, 558-559
laundry and dry cleaning
    apparel, coin-operated, 29, 34-35
    apparel, professional, 29, 46-47
lawn and garden
    equipment, 223-224, 258-259
    service, 531, 540-541
    supplies, 555, 560-561
leasing
    cars, 673-674, 678-679
    trucks, 673-674, 698-699
legal fees, 167-168, 204-205
lessons, fees for recreational, 89-90, 108-109
lettuce, 317-320, 416-417
life insurance. See Insurance.
lighting fixtures, 223-224, 254-255
limousine service. See Taxi fares and limousine service.
linens
    bathroom, 223-224, 230-231
    bedroom, 223-224, 234-235
    dining room, 223-224, 252-253
    kitchen, 223-224, 252-253
living room
    chairs, 223-224, 260-261
    sofas, 223-224, 278-279
    tables, 223-224, 260-261
lodging on trips, 715, 726-727
long term care insurance, 491-492, 512-513
lottery losses, 167-168, 206-207
luggage, 715, 728-729
lunch
    at employer and school cafeterias, 595-596, 606-607
    at fast-food restaurants, 595-596, 608-609
    at full-service restaurants, 595-596, 610-611
lunch meats, 317-320, 418-419

magazines, 585, 588-591
maintenance and repair
    materials for owned home, 625, 632-633
    services for owned home, 625, 636-637
    services and materials, rented home, 625, 634-635
    vehicle, 673-674, 688-689, 694-695, 708-709
manicures, 569, 578-579
margarine, 317-320, 420-421
mass transit fares, intracity, 673-674, 686-687
mattresses and springs, 223-224, 262-263
meat. See individual categories.
Medicare
    premiums, 491-492, 514-515
    prescription drug premiums, 491-492, 516-517
    supplements, commercial, 491-492, 518-519

memberships
  automobile service club, 673-674, 676-677
  credit card, 167-168, 190-191
  shopping, 167-168, 212-213
  social, recreational, civic, 89-90, 102-103
men's
  apparel, 29, 42–43
  apparel, gifts of, 287, 308-309
  shoes, 29, 44–45
milk
  fresh, 317-320, 422-423
  imitation, 317-320, 424-425
mobile vendors, food from. *See* Vending machines
            and mobile vendors.
mortgage interest, 625, 638-639
motels. *See* Lodging on trips.
motor oil, 673-674, 684-685, 722-723
motorboats. *See* Recreational vehicles.
movie tickets, 89-90, 116-117
moving, storage, freight express, 531, 544-545
musical instruments and accessories, 89-90, 118-119

napkins, 555-557
natural gas, 747, 754-755
newspapers, 585, 588-591
nondairy cream and imitation milk, 317-320, 424-425
nonphysician health care services, 491-492, 520-521
noodles. *See* Pasta.
nursery schools. *See* Day care centers, nurseries,
            preschools.
nuts, 317-320, 426-427

occupational expenses, 167-168, 208-209
oil change, lube, and oil filters, 673-674, 688-689
oils. *See* Fats and oils.
olives, pickles, relishes, 317-320, 428-429
oral hygiene products, 569, 576-577
oranges, 317-320, 430-431
outdoor
  equipment, 223-224, 264-265
  furniture, 223-224, 266-267

paper towels, 555-557
parking fees, 673-674, 690-691
  on trips, 715, 730-731
pasta, cornmeal, and other cereal products, 317-320, 432-433
peanut butter, 317-320, 434-435
pedicures, 569, 578-579
pensions, deductions for private, 167-168, 194-195
perfume, 569-571
personal care services, 569, 578-579
personal digital audio players, 89-90, 120-121
personal insurance. *See* Insurance.
pest control products and services, 531, 548-549
pet. *See also* Veterinary services.
  food, 89-90, 122-123
  purchase, supplies, medicine, 89-90, 124-125
  services, 89-90, 126-127

phone. *See* Telephone.
phone cards, 651, 654-655
photographer's fees, 89-90, 128-129
photographic equipment, 89-90, 130-131
photographic processing, 89-90, 132-133
physician services, 491-492, 522-523
pickles, 317-320, 428-429
pies, tarts, turnovers, 317-320, 436-437
pillows, decorative, 223-224, 276-277
pipe tobacco. *See* Tobacco products other than cigarettes.
plants and fresh flowers, indoor, 223-224, 268-269
political organizations, contributions to, 167-168, 178-179
pork chops, 317-320, 438-439
portable memory, 59, 68-69
postage, 555, 562-563
potato chips, 317-320, 440-441
potatoes, fresh, 317-320, 442-443
poultry
  chicken, 317-320, 362-363
  except chicken, 317-320, 444-445
power tools, 223-224, 272-273
prepared food
  desserts, 317-320, 376-377
  flour mixes, 317-320, 390-391
  fresh, 317-320, 446-447
  frozen, 317-320, 448-451
  salads, 317-320, 456-457
preschools. *See* Day care centers, nurseries, preschools.
prescription drugs, 491-492, 498-499, 516-517
preserves, 317-320, 414-415
property
  management and security for owned homes, 625, 640-641
  taxes, 625, 642-643

radio
  repair, 89-90, 138-139
  satellite, 89-90, 140-141
records, 89-90, 104-105
recreational
  club memberships, 89-90, 102-103
  expenses on trips, 89-90, 715, 732-733
  lessons, fees for, 89-90, 108-109
recreational vehicles, 89-90, 134-135
religious organizations, contributions to, 167-168, 180-181
relishes, 317-320, 428-429
rent, 625, 644-645
rental
  recreational vehicles, 89-90, 134-135
  party supplies for catered affairs, 89-90, 136-137
  safe deposit box, 167-168, 210-211
  vehicles, 673-674, 710-711
  vehicles on trips, 715, 742-743
  videotape, disc, and film, 89-90, 162-163
renter's insurance, 625, 630-631
repair
  apparel, 29, 50-51
  appliance, 531-533
  computer, 59, 70-71

materials for owned home, 625, 632-633
musical instruments, 89-90, 118-119
services for owned home, 625, 636-637
services and material for rented home, 625, 634-635
shoe, 29, 50-51
television, radio, sound equipment, 89-90, 138-139
vehicle, 673-674
restaurants and carryouts, 595-621
on trips, 715, 612-613, 734-735
retirement
accounts, contributions to (nonpayroll) , 167-168, 188-189
deductions for private pension, 167-168, 194-195
deductions for Social Security, 167-168, 196-197
government, deductions for, 167-168, 192-193
rice, 317-320, 452-453
roast beef, 317-320, 338-339
rolls. *See* Biscuits and rolls.
rugs. *See* Floor coverings.

safe deposit box rental, 167-168, 210-211
salad dressings, 317-320, 454-455
salads, prepared, 317-320, 456-457
salt, spices, other seasonings, 317-320, 458-459
satellite
radio service, 89-90, 140-141
television service, 89-90, 98-99
sauces and gravies, 317-320, 460-461
sausage, 317-320, 460-461
school. *See* Education.
seafood. *See* Fish and seafood.
seasonings, 317-320, 458-459
security system service fee for home, 531, 546-547
sewer. *See* Water and sewerage maintenance.
sewing materials
for apparel, 29, 48–49
for household items, 223-224, 274-275
shampoo, 569, 574-575
shaving products, 569, 580-581
sheets, bed. *See* Linens, bedroom.
shellfish. *See* Fish and seafood.
ship fares, 715, 736-737
shoes
children's, 29, 32–33
men's, 29, 44–45
repair, 29, 50-51
women's, 29, 54–55
shopping club memberships, 167-168, 212-213
slipcovers and decorative pillows, 223-224, 276-277
smoking, 663-669
smoking accessories, 663, 666-667
snacks
at employer and school cafeterias, 595-596, 614-615
at fast-food restaurants, 595-596, 616-617
at full-service restaurants, 595-596, 618-619
at vending machines and mobile vendors, 595-596, 620-621
potato chips and other, 317-320, 440-441
snuff. *See* Tobacco products other than cigarettes.
social, recreational, civic clubs, 89-90, 102-103
Social Security, deductions for, 167-168, 196-197

sofas, 223-224, 278-279
software. *See* Computers.
sound
components, equipment, accessories, 89-90, 142-143
equipment repair, 89-90, 138-139
soups, canned and packaged, 317-320, 464-465
spices, 317-320, 458-459
sports drinks, 317-320, 466-467
sports events
admission to, 89-90, 92-93
fees for participant, 89-90, 106-107
stamp and coin collecting, 89-90, 144-145
state income tax, 167-168, 218-219
stationery, 555, 564-565
steak, 317-320, 340-341
storage
items, 223-224, 236-237
service, 531, 544-545
streamed
audio, 89-90, 146-147
video, 89-90, 148-149
subscriptions, 585, 590-591
sugar, 317-320, 468-469
sweetrolls, 317-320, 470-471

tablecloths. *See* Linens.
tables, living room, 223-224, 260-261
taxes
federal income, 167-168, 216-217
property, 625, 642-643
state and local income, 167-168, 218-219
taxi fares and limousine service
in home city, 673-674, 692-693
on trips, 715, 738-739
tea, 317-320, 472-473
technical school tuition, 75, 84-85
telephone
answering machines and accessories, 651, 658-659
cards, 651, 654-655
cellular service, 651-653
residential service, 651, 656-657
telephones, 651, 658-659
television. *See also* Cable and satellite television service.
repair, 89-90, 138-139
service, 89-90, 98-99
sets, 89-90, 150-151
tenant's insurance, 625, 630-631
termite and pest control, 531, 548-549
textiles, household, gifts of, 287, 300-301
theater tickets, 89-90, 116-117
tires, 673-674, 694-695
tobacco products other than cigarettes, 663, 668-669
toilet tissue, 555-557
tolls , 673-674, 690-691
on trips, 715, 730-731
tomatoes, 317-320, 474-475
tools, power and hand, 223-224, 272-273
toothpaste, 569, 576-577
topicals and dressings, 491-492, 524-525
towels. *See* Linens.
towing charges, 673-674, 696-697

toys, 89-90, 152-153
trailers, 89-90, 134-135
train fares, intercity, 715, 740-741
transportation
    gifts of, 287, 310-311
    local, on trips, 715, 738-739
    public, 673-674, 686-687, 715-717, 720-721, 740-741
trash collection, 747, 756-757
tricycles, 89-90, 152-153
trucks
    lease payments, 673-674, 698-699
    new, 673-674, 700-701
    used, 673-674, 702-703
tuition
    college, 75, 80-81
    elementary and high school, 75, 82-83
    vocational and technical school, 75, 84-85
turkey. See Poultry other than chicken.
utilities. See individual categories.

vacation homes, owned, 625, 646-647
VCRs, 89-90, 154-155
vegetable juices, 317-320, 476-477
vegetables. See also individual categories.
    canned, 317-320, 478-479
    dried, 317-320, 480-481
    fresh, 317-320, 416-417, 442-443, 474-475, 482-483
    frozen, 317-320, 484-485
vehicle
    finance charges, 673-674, 704-705
    insurance, 673-674, 706-707
    leasing, 673-674, 678-679, 698-699
    maintenance and repair, 673-674, 688-689, 694-695,
    708-709
    recreational, 89-90, 134-135
    rentals, 673-674, 710-711
    rentals on trips, 715, 742-743
vending machines and mobile vendors, snacks from, 595-
596, 620-621
veterinary services, 89-90, 156-157
video
    cassettes, tapes, discs, 89-90, 158-159
    disc players, 89-90, 154-155
    game hardware and software, 89-90, 160-161
    rental, tape and disc, 89-90, 162-163
    streamed and downloaded, 89-90, 148-149
vitamins, nonprescription, 491-492, 526-527
vocational school tuition, 75, 84-85

wall units, 223-224, 280-281
washcloths. See Linens, bathroom.
watches, gifts of, 287, 306-307
water and sewerage maintenance, 747, 758-759
water, bottled, 317-320, 486-487
water softening services, 531, 550-551
whiskey
    at home, 11, 18–19
    at restaurants and bars, 11, 20–21
window coverings, 223-224, 282-283

wine
    at home, 11, 22–23
    at restaurants and bars, 11, 24–25
women's
    apparel, 29, 52–53
    apparel, gifts of, 287, 312-313
    shoes, 29, 54–55

X–rays, 491–492, 510-511